South Asian Perspectives in Mental Health and Psychology

Series Editors

S. M. Yasir Arafat, Bangladesh Specialized Hospital, Dhaka, Bangladesh

Sujita Kumar Kar, Department of Psychiatry, King George's Medical University, Lucknow, Uttar Pradesh, India

This series of books is an endeavor to gather and present a comprehensive understanding of the various aspects of mental health that are relevant to people living in South Asia. The books aim to provide in-depth guidance and practical solutions to the mental health challenges that are unique to these areas. The content covers a wide range of topics, including but not limited to, climate change and its impact, prison mental health, perinatal mental health, social psychiatry, mental health and disorder among the elderly population, psychiatry education and training, suicide, SDGs and mental health, trauma, addiction, and social isolation. The books also emphasize the importance of early intervention and provide resources for seeking help. The ultimate goal of this series is to empower individuals and communities to take proactive steps toward enhancing their mental wellbeing. The proposed books will fill the existing unmet need in the region with huge populations in low and middle-income country (LMIC) settings.

South Asia, home to about 2 billion people, is a region of diverse cultures, languages, and religions. It caters to about 25% of the global population. This densely populated region faces a myriad of challenges, both natural and man-made. The frequent occurrence of natural disasters, such as earthquakes, floods, and landslides, threaten the lives and livelihoods of millions of people. War, terrorism, and political instability have caused significant disruptions to the region's socio-political fabric. Poverty, migration, and tropical infectious diseases remain major challenges that hinder progress towards sustainable development. Climate change exacerbates these challenges, causing widespread environmental degradation, food insecurity, and water scarcity. Despite these obstacles, South Asian people have shown remarkable resilience and strength in the face of adversity.

Mental health issues in the South Asian region significantly contribute to the global burden of mental illnesses. However, the region faces plenty of challenges such as high stigma, low mental health literacy, poor budgetary allocation, high out-of-pocket expense for mental health services, lack of adequate infrastructure, and limited human resources are significant barriers in mental healthcare. The majority of research on mental health issues is produced by the western countries which may not fit all in the South Asian culture, albeit evidence is needed to test. There is a paucity of research and evidence-based strategies that are region-specific. This series of books is an attempt to compile the important dimensions of mental health that will benefit the regional people.

Sujita Kumar Kar · Russell Kabir ·
S. M. Yasir Arafat
Editors

Sustainable Development Goals and Mental Health in South Asia

Springer

Editors
Sujita Kumar Kar
Department of Psychiatry
King George's Medical University
Lucknow, Uttar Pradesh, India

Russell Kabir
School of Allied Health
Anglia Ruskin University
Chelmsford, UK

S. M. Yasir Arafat
Bangladesh Specialized Hospital
Dhaka, Bangladesh

ISSN 3059-3646 ISSN 3059-3522 (electronic)
South Asian Perspectives in Mental Health and Psychology
ISBN 978-981-95-2683-3 ISBN 978-981-95-2684-0 (eBook)
https://doi.org/10.1007/978-981-95-2684-0

This Springer imprint is published by the registered company Springer Nature Singapore Pte Ltd.
The registered company address is: 152 Beach Road, #21-01/04 Gateway East, Singapore 189721, Singapore

Preface

The World Health Organization (WHO) emphasizes that Sustainable Development Goal 3 (SDG 3) is centered on achieving "good health and well-being," which encompasses not only physical health but also mental health. Mental well-being is integral to overall individual flourishing, as it affects every aspect of a person's life. When individuals experience poor mental health, it can significantly hamper progress in other critical areas, such as poverty reduction (SDG 1) and education (SDG 4). Mental illnesses can severely impair one's capacity to maintain stable employment, succeed academically, or effectively carry out daily tasks. This, in turn, contributes to a cycle of poverty and limits access to opportunities for personal growth and development. Therefore, it becomes clear that mental health is a vital component of a sustainable future, with far-reaching implications for social and economic well-being. The advancement of the SDGs is a paramount priority on the global agenda. Yet, despite the recognized importance of mental health, there has been a conspicuous lack of comprehensive research exploring the connection between the SDGs and mental health specifically in South Asia, a region that supports nearly 2 billion people. South Asia has certain unique characteristics, which makes it different from other regions of the world. Heavily populated region with significant socio-cultural diversity, proneness for politico-religious conflicts, migration, natural disasters, and under privileged population makes the region struggle in achieving the SDGs. This book aims to fill that critical gap by providing an in-depth analysis of this relationship. It is designed for a diverse audience, including academics, policymakers, and NGO workers who are focused on mental health issues within South Asia and other low- and middle-income countries (LMICs).

This publication will mark the first systematic attempt to intertwine discussions of the SDGs with mental health challenges and opportunities in South Asia. It comprehensively evaluates the progress made in the region toward achieving mental health well-being, highlighting successful initiatives, ongoing challenges, and the role of various stakeholders. By doing so, the book serves as an essential resource for a wide range of professionals, including clinicians, researchers, health and social care authorities, government agencies, and NGO staff who are actively engaged with the SDGs and mental health projects. Moreover, this book identifies existing research gaps and provides insights into opportunities that can help realize the SDGs in resource-limited settings across South Asia. By presenting a nuanced understanding of mental health's intersection with sustainable development, this publication aims to catalyze further research and inform policy-making that prioritizes mental health as a cornerstone of achieving broader developmental goals.

Lucknow, Uttar Pradesh, India — Sujita Kumar Kar
Chelmsford, UK — Russell Kabir
Dhaka, Bangladesh — S. M. Yasir Arafat

Contents

1 **Overview of Sustainable Development Goals and Their Health Significance** 1
Ankita Saroj, Khirod Chandra Moharana, Sujita Kumar Kar, and Russell Kabir

2 **Relevance of Sustainable Development Goals in the Context of Mental Health** 21
Sujita Kumar Kar, Khirod Chandra Moharana, Ankita Saroj, and Russell Kabir

3 **Barriers to SDGs to Improve Mental Health in South Asia** 45
Adarsh Tripathi and Anupam Singh Yadav

4 **Poverty and Mental Health** 63
Ali Davod Parsa, Ganesh Bushi, Muhammed Shabil, Leila Dehghani, and Russell Kabir

5 **Gender Inequalities and Mental Health** 99
Ali Davod Parsa, Leila Dehghani, Divya Vinnakota, and Russell Kabir

6 **Unemployment and Mental Health** 117
Karthick Subramanian, Vigneshvar Chandrasekaran, Sabaresh Pandiyan, Kiruthika Asokan, and Vikas Menon

7 **Education, Mental Health, and Sustainable Development Goals in South Asia: An Intersectoral Analysis** 155
Darya Rostam Ahmed, Rania H. Al-Taie, and Jaafar O. Ahmed

8 **Sustainable Development Goals and Mental Health in Bangladesh** 173
Md. Abdullah Saeed Khan and S. M. Yasir Arafat

9 **Synergizing Sustainable Development Goals and Mental Health in India** 189
Ravi Philip Rajkumar

10 **Synergizing Sustainable Development Goals and Mental Health in Nepal** 239
Pawan Sharma, Pramita Sharma, and Gaurav Devkota

11 **Sustainable Development Goals and Mental Health in Pakistan** 255
Rizwana Amin

12 **Sustainable Development Goals and Mental Health in Sri Lanka** 283
Anuradha Baminiwatta, Aruni Hapangama, Nazneen Nazeer, and Miyuru Chandradasa

13 **Sustainable Development Goals and Mental Health in Afghanistan, Bhutan, and Maldives** 301
Deblina Roy, Anil Mavliya, Sneha Roy, and Debashish Banerjee

14 **Public Health Initiatives to Attain Sustainable Development Goals to Improve Mental Health in South Asia** 327
Apurvakumar Pandya

About the Editors

Sujita Kumar Kar is currently working as an Additional Professor of Psychiatry at King George's Medical University, Lucknow, Uttar Pradesh, India. He is the editor-in-chief of Indian Journal of Health, Sexuality and Culture. He is also an editorial board member and reviewer of various national and international journals. He had written 83 book chapters and more than 500 articles in various national and international journals and made 80 presentations at various national and international conferences. He has been included in the global 2% researcher list released by Stanford University in 2021, 2022, 2023, and 2024. His research interests include brain stimulation, neuropsychiatry, and suicide prevention.

Russell Kabir is an Associate Professor of Public Health & Biostatistics at Anglia Ruskin University, UK. He leads the MSc Public Health and Community Wellbeing program at Chelmsford, Essex. The author of over 150 peer-reviewed publications, his books include *Learning SPSS Without Pain* (2021), *Data Analysis with STATA* (2022) *Panic Buying and Environmental Disasters* (2022), and *Basic Principles of Epidemiology* (2023). He leads Epidemiology and Statistics module for the postgraduate Public Health students. He runs the Quantitative Methods sessions for the Doctoral School. He is currently serving as an Academic Editor for PLOS ONE, BMC Public Health and Peerj. Dr Kabir is interested to perform collaborative and interdisciplinary research in public health issues with a special focus on suicide and mental health, dental public health, reproductive health issues, violence against women, and aging-related research.

S. M. Yasir Arafat is currently working as an Associate Consultant of Psychiatry at Bangladesh Specialized Hospital, Dhaka, Bangladesh. He is affiliated with Dnet as an honorary Research Fellow and the Biomedical Research Foundation, Bangladesh, as Senior Research Fellow. He was affiliated with the University of Bristol, UK, as Visiting Senior Research Associate (August 2021–2023). He completed an MD in Psychiatry from Bangabandhu Sheikh Mujib Medical University, Dhaka, and an MBBS from the Dhaka Medical College, Dhaka, Bangladesh. He also did an MPH in Health Economics and an MBA in Marketing. Dr. Arafat has (co)authored more than 350 peer-reviewed articles and 50 book chapters, and (co)edited more than 10 books with Springer. He has been included in the global 2% researcher list in 2021, 2022, and 2023. He is acting as an editorial member in more than 10 leading journals in mental health published by Elsevier, Wiley, Springer, and Taylor and Francis. His research focused on mental health, suicidal behavior, psychometrics, panic buying, and psycho-sexual disorders.

List of Figures

Chapter 1

Fig. 1 Dynamic interplay of SDGs influencing health 15

Chapter 4

Fig. 1 Different types of poverty. *Source* Faculty of public health (FPH) 65
Fig. 2 Global trend of poverty (1990–2020). *Source* Development Initiatives 66
Fig. 3 Share of population living in extreme poverty (1990–2024). *Data sources* World Bank (2024) 67
Fig. 4 Share of South Asian countries' population living in extreme poverty (1977–2024). *Data sources* World Bank (2024) 68
Fig. 5 Multiple dimensions of poverty. *Source* Gweshengwe (2020) 69
Fig. 6 Bio-psycho-social model showing the associated factors between poverty and mental health 76

Chapter 6

Fig. 1 Dynamic relationship of SDG 8 with some of the other SDGs 122
Fig. 2 Relationship between unemployment and the health of an individual 123
Fig. 3 Unemployment trends in South Asia between 2000 and 2023 (data obtained from the International Labour Organisation) 128

Chapter 7

Fig. 1 Multidimensional poverty and income poverty in South Asian countries (%) (UN ESCAP, 2021) 158
Fig. 2 Growth of MH professionals in Sri Lanka (2005–2017) 166

Chapter 8

Fig. 1 Link diagram showing direct and indirect connections of different Sustainable Development Goals with mental health ... 176

List of Tables

Chapter 3

Table 1 South Asian performance towards SDGs (Asia and the Pacific SDG Progress Report 2024: Showcasing Transformative Actions|ESCAP, 2024; Sustainable Development Report, 2024) 47

Chapter 4

Table 1 Country-specific indicators of SDGs 77
Table 2 Poverty eradication strategies in South Asia 83

Chapter 6

Table 1 Types of unemployment and their characteristics 119
Table 2 Unemployment and mental health studies from South Asian countries 131

Chapter 7

Table 1 Progress in the SDGs in the health and education sectors in South Asia (UN ESCAP, 2017) 159
Table 2 Number and percentage from MH professionals of South Asian countries in 2020 (Grover, 2023) 162

Chapter 10

Table 1 Mental health-related targets of SDGs and data gaps (Nepal Health Research Council, 2019) 247

Chapter 13

Table 1 Comparative Demographic Indicators for Afghanistan, Bhutan, and Maldives 303

Table 2 Key SDG Performance Indicators–Afghanistan, Bhutan, and the Maldives 305
Table 3 Summary of SDG Impacts on Mental Health by Country and SDG Theme 306
Table 4 Key SDG and Mental Health Initiatives–Afghanistan, Bhutan, Maldives 317

Chapter 14

Table 1 Mental health scenario in LMIC and South Asia 331

Chapter 1
Overview of Sustainable Development Goals and Their Health Significance

Ankita Saroj, Khirod Chandra Moharana, Sujita Kumar Kar, and Russell Kabir

Abstract People across the globe struggle with poverty, hunger, unemployment, health issues, gender inequality, issues of sanitation and clean water, getting quality education, and access to clean energy. Economic growth, infrastructure development, effective community bonding, energy regulation, developing peace, providing justice, and collaborative efforts are other major challenges faced by a majority of countries across the world. Climate change is emerging as an important threat to mankind and also affecting life on land and underwater. To systematically deal with these issues effectively, the United Nations has developed 17 goals in 2015, which are targeted to be achieved by 2030. Several initiatives have been taken to achieve these goals at the national and regional levels over the past decade. This chapter gives an overview of Sustainable Development Goals (SDGs) to comprehensively understand these goals and their health implications.

Keywords Sustainable Development Goals · United Nations · Health · Global Development · Climate Change

1 Introduction

Countries worldwide have been experimenting with various development models since the inception of the United Nations Organization (UNO) in 1945. Till 1987, the major thrust of development was economic growth and industrialization. Increasing environmental pollution and climate change lead the UN member countries to rethink

A. Saroj · S. K. Kar (✉)
Department of Psychiatry, King George's Medical University, Uttar Pradesh, Lucknow, India
e-mail: sujitakumarkar@kgmcindia.edu

K. C. Moharana
Department of Anthropology, University of Allahabad, Uttar Pradesh, Prayagraj, India

R. Kabir
School of Allied Health, Faculty of Health, Education, Medicine and Social Care, Anglia Ruskin University, Essex, UK

S. K. Kar et al. (eds.), *Sustainable Development Goals and Mental Health in South Asia*,
South Asian Perspectives in Mental Health and Psychology ,
https://doi.org/10.1007/978-981-95-2684-0_1

the world's developmental practices. The concept of sustainable development was popularized by the Brundtland Commission's report, published in 1987, which aimed at development "that meets the needs of the present without compromising the ability of the future generations to meet their own needs" (Keeble, 1988; WCED, 1987). The Rio Earth Summit adopted Agenda 21 in 1992, which focused on global partnership for sustainable development comprising social, economic, and environmental goals. In 2000, the UN adopted the Millennium Declaration which led to 8 Millennium Development Goals (MDGs) focusing on poverty, education, and health. All these initiatives, however, could not address various nuances of integrating environmental sustainability with development. Thus, in 2015 the UN General Assembly adopted 2030 Agenda, which included 17 Sustainable Development Goals (SDGs) and 169 targets to end poverty and protect the planet (United Nations, 2024; United Nations & Development Programme (UNDP), 2023; World Health Organization, 2023).

2 Sustainable Development Goals

2.1 No Poverty (SDG 1)

SDG 1 was formulated to "end poverty in all its forms everywhere." To achieve this goal by 2030, seven targets and their indicators were identified. The key targets were to eradicate extreme poverty for all persons living on less than $1.25 a day, reduce at least by half the proportion of men, women, and children of all ages living in poverty, and ensure all men and women have equal rights to economic resources and basic services (DESA, 2016; United Nations, 2025a).

Around the world, government's total expenditure on essential services has increased from 47% in 2015 to 53% in 2021 (United Nations, 2023). The efforts made worldwide to eradicate extreme poverty met with significant challenges during the years 2020–22 as a consequence of the COVID-19 pandemic. The pandemic not only reversed the global progress made in 3 years but also led to an increase in extreme poverty in decades. It is projected that if the current trend continues, 575 million people will still be living in extreme poverty by 2030 (World Bank, 2022).

2.2 Zero Hunger (SDG 2)

SDG 2 aims to end hunger, achieve food security, improve nutrition, and promote sustainable agriculture. The key targets include ending hunger and malnutrition and ensuring everyone has access to nutritious and sufficient food throughout the year. The goal also aims to address the nutritional needs of adolescent girls, pregnant and lactating women, and older persons and reduce stunting and wasting in children under 5 years of age. Increasing agricultural productivity, sustainable food production systems, maintaining the genetic diversity of seeds, cultivated plants, farmed and domesticated animals, and their related wild species are other targets in this goal (United Nations, 2025b).

Since 2000, minimal progress has been made in reducing anemia worldwide, with the prevalence of anemia in women aged 15–49 stagnant at 30%. Despite following a decreasing trend in 2021, food prices continue to soar in many nations, posing a challenge to this goal. The aftermath of this situation led to the persistence of malnutrition worldwide, affecting children's well-being and future development (FAO et al., 2023).

The zero-hunger goal is at risk, as it is estimated that around 600 million people worldwide will face hunger in 2030. In 2022, nearly one in ten of the world's population faced hunger, and 2.4 billion people experienced moderate to severe food insecurity. This was added to by increasing food prices in 60% of countries globally due to conflicts and disrupted supply chains (United Nations, 2023).

2.3 Good Health and Well-Being (SDG 3)

SDG 3 aims to ensure healthy lives and promote well-being for all ages. One of the key targets is reducing maternal mortality to less than 70 per 100,000 live births globally, ending preventable deaths of newborns and children under 5 years of age, ending epidemics of AIDS, tuberculosis, malaria, and neglected tropical diseases, and combating hepatitis, waterborne diseases and other communicable diseases, strengthen the prevention and treatment of substance abuse, halve the number of global deaths and injuries from road traffic accidents, and ensure universal health coverage and access to sexual and reproductive healthcare to all (DESA, 2016; United Nations, 2025c).

Significant challenges were faced in achieving global health goals, as progress has slowed since 2015 in areas like maternal mortality, premature deaths from major non-communicable diseases, and access to essential healthcare (DESA, 2016). These were exacerbated by inequalities in healthcare services, especially to vulnerable populations, and the climate crisis.

The year 2020 saw the death of one woman every two minutes from preventable causes related to pregnancy and childbirth (Organization, 2023a). In 2021, 25 million children missed necessary routine immunizations, 6 million more than in 2019 (Jones, 2024). Malaria cases surged worldwide to nearly 247 million cases reported in 2021 (Organization, 2023c). 4.9% of the population was pushed into extreme poverty due to out-of-pocket payments for health-related expenditures (United Nations, 2023).

2.4 Quality Education (SDG 4)

SDG 4 was formulated to ensure inclusive and equitable quality education and promote lifelong learning opportunities for all. The key targets are to ensure that all girls and boys complete free, equitable, and quality primary and secondary education leading to relevant and effective learning outcomes, to ensure all girls and boys have access to quality early childhood development, care, and pre-primary education, substantially increase the number of youth and adults who have relevant skills, eliminate gender disparities in education, and ensure equal access to all levels of education and vocational training (United Nations, 2025d).

SDG 4 plays a crucial role in advancing many other Sustainable Development Goals. However, progress in global education has been too slow. The current trends suggest that the world is falling behind in achieving quality education. At the current rate, 84 million children and youth will be out of school, 300 million students will lack basic numeracy/literacy skills, and only 1 in 6 countries will achieve the universal secondary school completion target. According to reports, the COVID-19 pandemic caused learning losses in four out of five countries studied (Engzell et al., 2021). Although primary and secondary school completion rates are rising, the rate is slow and uneven. Low- and lower-middle-income countries currently face a nearly $100 billion annual financial gap to reach their education targets (Patil & Stipanovic, 2023; United Nations, 2023). Certain regions, such as sub-Saharan Africa, are experiencing teacher shortages, overcrowded classrooms, insufficient training, and limited professional development for educators (Schotgues, 2022). Prioritizing accelerated progress toward SDG 4 is essential, as it can drive broader success in achieving the entire 2030 Agenda.

2.5 Gender Equality (SDG 5)

SDG 5 aims to achieve gender equality and empower all women and girls. The key targets are to end all forms of discrimination against all women and girls everywhere, eliminate all forms of violence against all women and girls in the public and private sphere, and eliminate all harmful practices, including a child, early and forced marriages, and female genital mutilation. It also aims to ensure universal access to sexual and reproductive health and reproductive rights, to undertake reforms to give women equal rights to economic resources and access to ownership and control over land and other forms of property, financial services, inheritance, and natural resources (United Nations, 2025e).

The current trends do not indicate that gender equality will be achieved worldwide by 2030. Although harmful traditions like female genital mutilation and child marriage are declining, they are not doing enough to keep up with the population increase. Particularly regarding women's involvement in public life and administrative positions, gender equality is still considerably farther off (Albu, 2023). At the present rate, it will take more than 300 years to end child marriage, 286 years to close gaps in legal protection and remove discriminatory laws, and 140 years to achieve equal representation in leadership in the workplace. Nearly half of married women around the world lack decision-making power over their sexual and reproductive health and rights. 1 in 5 young women is married before her 18th birthday. Women's representation in parliament has increased to 30.9% due to legislated gender quotas, proving an effective measure to achieve political equality (Sarangi et al., 2023; United Nations, 2023). Immediate actions are required to confront biased social norms, eradicate harmful practices, and reform discriminatory laws. Enhancing women's leadership and boosting investments in gender equality are vital at national, regional, and global scales (Faugoo, 2024).

2.6 Clean Water and Sanitation (SDG 6)

SDG 6 aims to ensure the availability and sustainable management of water and sanitation for all. Its primary targets are to achieve universal and equitable access to safe and affordable drinking water for all, access to adequate and equitable sanitation and hygiene for all, and end open defecation, improve water quality by reducing pollution, eliminating dumping, and minimizing the release of hazardous chemicals and materials, to substantially increase water-use efficiency across all sectors, and to ensure sustainable withdrawals and supply of freshwater to address water scarcity. It also targets to implement integrated water resources management at all levels, including through transboundary cooperation (United Nations, 2025f).

Not a single target under SDG 6 is currently on track to be achieved. Safe drinking water, sanitation, and hygiene are still out of reach for billions of people worldwide, among whom 2.4 billion live in water-stressed countries (Organization, 2023b). Implementation of integrated water resources management needs acceleration. To meet 2030 targets, the pace of progress will have to accelerate sixfold for drinking water, fivefold for sanitation, and threefold for hygiene. Climate change exacerbates these challenges, threatening social stability. Around 40% of the global population lives in transboundary river and lake basins shared by 153 countries, yet fewer than 20% of these nations have effective cooperation agreements for all their shared water resources (United Nations, 2023; Water, 2021). Strengthening global coordination on integrated water management, addressing climate-related water impacts, and improving the governance of shared water bodies are essential to restoring progress on this goal (Fund & Organization, 2024).

2.7 Affordable and Clean Energy (SDG 7)

SDG 7 aims to ensure access to affordable, reliable, sustainable, and modern energy for all. The key targets are to ensure universal access to affordable, reliable, and modern energy services, substantially increase the share of renewable energy in the global energy mix, double the global rate of improvement in energy efficiency, and enhance international cooperation to facilitate access to clean energy research and technology, including renewable energy. It also aims to expand infrastructure and upgrade technology to supply modern and sustainable energy services for all in developing countries, per their respective programmers' support (United Nations, 2025g).

In 2022, global access to electricity dropped for the first time in ten years, mainly due to disruptions caused by COVID-19 and the conflict in Ukraine. While energy efficiency and renewable energy growth have improved, international financial support for clean energy in developing nations remains inadequate (Raimi et al., 2023). Around 675 million people in the world still live in the dark, of whom 4 out of 5 are from sub-Saharan Africa. The annual energy-intensity improvement rate needs to be doubled. International public financing for clean energy for developing countries continues to decline. Modern renewables power nearly 30% of electricity but remain low in heating and transport. As per current trends, 1 in 4 people will still use unsafe and inefficient cooking methods by 2030 (United Nations, 2023; Walesiak & Dehnel, 2024). Accelerated electrification, increased investments in renewable energy, improved energy efficiency, and the establishment of supportive laws and regulatory frameworks are all necessary to ensure universal access to electricity by 2030 (Initiative, 2019).

2.8 Decent Work and Economic Growth (SDG 8)

SDG 8 aims to promote sustained, inclusive, and sustainable economic growth, full and productive employment, and decent work for all. It mainly targets maintaining per capita economic growth in accordance with national circumstances, achieving higher levels of economic productivity through diversification, technological upgrading, and innovation, promoting development-oriented policies that support productive activities, decent job creation, and entrepreneurship, and substantially reducing the proportion of youth not in employment, education, or training (United Nations, 2025h).

The global economy is recovering on a slow trajectory. Global unemployment has fallen below pre-pandemic levels, but not in low-income countries. During the pandemic, around 4 in 10 adults in low- and middle-income countries opened their first bank account. One in four young people is not engaged in education, employment, or training, with young women being more than twice as likely as young men to face this situation. Two billion workers are engaged in unstable informal employment, often lacking access to social protection (Horne, 2024; United Nations, 2023).

The aftermath of COVID-19, trade tensions, growing debt in developing countries, conflicts, and geopolitical strains all pose threats to global economic development and hinder progress toward SDG 8. Policies that promote economic growth, emphasizing social justice and inclusive employment, are necessary to achieve SDG 8 (Prabhakar, 2025).

2.9 *Industry, Innovation, and Infrastructure (SDG 9)*

SDG 9 aims to build resilient infrastructure, promote inclusive and sustainable industrialization, and foster innovation. The key targets include the development of quality, reliable, sustainable, and resilient infrastructure, including regional and transborder infrastructure, to promote inclusive and sustainable industrialization and increase access of small-scale industrial and other enterprises to financial services. It also aims to upgrade infrastructure and retrofit industries to make them sustainable, with increased resource-use efficiency and greater adoption of clean and environmentally sound technologies and industrial processes (United Nations, 2025i).

Since 2022, the manufacturing sector has experienced stagnation due to factors such as geopolitical tensions, inflation, supply chain disruptions, increasing energy prices, and an overall global economic downturn. Worldwide, the proportion of employment in manufacturing has declined. Due to inflation, energy price shocks, supply disruptions, and global economic deceleration, global manufacturing growth slowed from 7.4% in 2021 to 3.3% in 2022. As of 2022, 95% of the world has mobile broadband access, but coverage is only 82% in sub-Saharan Africa and 68% in Oceania. Medium-high- and high-technology industries experienced strong growth in 2022, although regional variation was present. Energy-related CO2 emissions reached a record high of 36.8 billion metric tons in 2022 (Giroud, 2024; United Nations, 2023). Accelerating the green transition, strategically selecting sectors, and addressing inequality in the technology and innovation industries should be the top priorities in order to accelerate progress toward SDG 9 (Filipović et al., 2022).

2.9.1 Reduced Inequalities (SDG 10)

SDG 10 was formulated to reduce inequality within and among countries. The key targets include sustained income growth of the bottom 40% of the population at a rate higher than the national average, empowering social, economic, and political inclusion of all to ensure equal opportunity and reduce inequalities of outcome and improving the regulation and monitoring of global financial markets and institutions, and strengthening the implementation of such rules. It also ensures enhanced representation and voice for developing countries in global international economic and financial institutions' decision-making (United Nations, 2025j).

In many countries, the incomes of the poorest 40% have grown at a rate exceeding the national average, and financial support during the pandemic helped enhance shared prosperity. Nevertheless, the per capita income growth disparity between the wealthiest and poorest nations has increased in the past five years (Estes, 2019). The COVID-19 pandemic triggered the most significant increase in between-country inequality in three decades, with a pre-pandemic forecast of -0.8% to a post-pandemic projection of 4.4%. Among 34.6 million refugees recorded in 2022, 41% were children (Palattiyil et al., 2022; United Nations, 2023). The loss of thousands of lives along migratory routes in 2022 also needs immediate action to ensure safe migration. Also, women around the world are twice as likely to experience discrimination based on their sex (Bank, 2023). Tackling inequality within and between countries requires fair resource allocation, investment in education and skill-building, social protection policies, efforts to eliminate discrimination, support for marginalized communities, and international collaboration to promote equitable trade and financial systems (Saiz & Donald, 2018).

2.10 Sustainable Cities and Communities (SDG 11)

SDG 11 works to make cities and human settlements inclusive, safe, resilient, and sustainable. The key targets in this goal are to ensure access for all to adequate, safe, and affordable housing and basic services, upgrade slums, provide access to safe, affordable, accessible, and sustainable transport systems for all, and improve road safety. It also aims to strengthen efforts to protect and safeguard the world's cultural and natural heritage and provide universal access to safe, inclusive, and accessible green and public spaces (United Nations, 2025k).

Over half of the global population now lives in urban areas, yet cities face a range of complex challenges, further intensified by the rise in urban poverty following the COVID-19 pandemic (Martínez & Short, 2021). Despite steps being taken, slums are on the rise. As of 2020, around 1.1 billion urban residents lived in slums, and 2 billion more are expected in the next 30 years (Boanada-Fuchs et al., 2024). Air pollution is no longer an exclusively urban problem, as towns experience poorer air quality than cities in eastern and south-eastern Asia (Rezaei & Millard-Ball, 2023). In the developing world, a billion people lack access to all-weather roads, and globally, 3 in 4 cities have less than 20% of their area dedicated to public spaces and streets, which is much lower than the target of 45–50% (United Nations, 2023). With growing slum populations, inadequate public transport, urban expansion surpassing population growth, and increasing risks to vital infrastructure and basic services due to disasters, it is vital that cities are prepared to manage these challenges effectively. As urbanization accelerates—projected to reach nearly 70% of the global population by 2050—developing resilient and sustainable cities will require robust infrastructure, accessible housing, efficient transportation, and reliable social services for all (Anestis & Stathakis, 2024).

2.11 Responsible Consumption and Production (SDG 12)

SDG 12 ensures sustainable consumption and production patterns. The key targets are to achieve sustainable management and efficient use of natural resources, halve the global food waste at the retail and consumer levels, reduce food losses along production and supply chains, substantially reduce waste generation through prevention, reduction, recycling, and reuse, and achieve environmentally sound management of chemicals and all wastes throughout their life cycle, by agreed international frameworks. It also encourages substantial and transnational companies to adopt sustainable practices, integrate sustainability information into the reporting cycle, and promote sustainable public procurement practices, in accordance with national policies and priorities (United Nations, 2025l).

The global unsustainable consumption and production crisis drives the interconnected triple planetary climate change crisis, biodiversity loss, and pollution (Miao & Nduneseokwu, 2024). High-income countries have left a larger environmental footprint than low-income countries, with the maternal footprint being ten times larger in high-income countries than low-income countries (Khan & Yahong, 2022). The global crisis led to a return and doubling of fossil fuel subsidies in 2021. On average, each person wastes 120 kg of food per year. The company's sustainability reporting has tripled since 2016. Over 62 countries have introduced 485 policies for sustainable consumption and production shifts (McCulloch, 2023; United Nations, 2023). Although nations are meeting their environmental agreement commitments and adopting broad strategies to combat environmental degradation, public funding for fossil fuel production and consumption has tripled since 2015, hindering progress toward achieving net-zero emissions (Liu & Xu, 2022).

2.12 Climate Action (SDG 13)

SDG 13 aims to take urgent action to combat climate change and its impacts. The key targets include strengthening resilience and adaptive capacity to climate-related hazards and natural disasters and integrating climate change measures into national policies, strategies, and planning. It aims to improve education, awareness-raising, and human and institutional capacity for climate change mitigation, adaptation, impact reduction, and early warning. It also promotes mechanisms for raising capacity for effective climate change-related planning and management in least-developed countries and small island developing states (United Nations, 2025m).

In 2023, climate records were broken, making the unfolding climate crisis visible in real time. The destructive effects of extreme weather are being felt by communities all around the world, endangering lives and livelihoods on a daily basis. The world's temperature will exceed 1.5 °C by 2035 and reach 2.5 °C by 2100. Global warming has also doubled the rate of sea-level rise in the last decade (Lee et al., 2023). To combat this, deep, rapid, and sustained greenhouse gas emission reductions are required by 43% by 2030 and to reach net zero by 2050. Global climate finance flows reached an annual average of $803 billion in 2019–2020. However, developing countries require nearly $6 trillion by 2030 to achieve sustainable goals (United Nations, 2023). Due to climate change, highly vulnerable regions have experienced fifteen times higher mortality rates from disasters compared to very low vulnerability regions in the last decade (Initiative, 2021).

2.13 Life Below Water (SDG 14)

SDG 14 was formulated to conserve and sustainably use the oceans, seas, and marine resources for sustainable development. The key targets to achieve this goal were to prevent and significantly reduce marine pollution of all kinds, sustainably manage and protect marine and coastal ecosystems to avoid significant adverse impacts, minimize and address impacts of ocean acidification, and effectively regulate harvesting and end overfishing, illegal, unreported and unregulated fishing, and destructive fishing practices. It also aims to conserve at least 10% of coastal and marine areas, prohibit fisheries subsidies, and enhance the conservation and sustainable use of oceans and their resources by implementing international laws as classified in the United Nations Convention on the Law of the Sea (United Nations, 2025n).

Oceans span more than 70% of the Earth's surface. They are vital for supporting the livelihoods and food security of over 3 billion people and playing a key role in mitigating climate change impacts. Urgent measures are needed to safeguard the planet's largest ecosystem, as many ocean emergencies are emerging. There has been a rise in coastal eutrophication, causing algal blooms and dead zones and eventually leading to crustacean withdrawal from the ocean. Although the number of ocean acidification reporting stations has tripled worldwide, it remains 30% higher than in pre-industrial times. Due to climate change, ocean warming has emerged as a significant challenge, leading to sea-level rise and affecting marine ecosystems. Plastic pollution has not even spared the ocean, with around 17 million metric tons of plastic recovered from oceans in 2021, which is projected to increase two to three times by 2040 (McGlade et al., 2021; United Nations, 2023). Citizen beach clean-ups have shed light on the magnitude of ocean plastic pollution. Overfishing has also caused damage to the ocean ecosystem. More than a third of global fish stocks are overfished, with 1 in 5 fish caught originating from illegal, unreported, and unregulated fishing (Lichna et al., 2023). These issues need to be addressed to ensure the long-term health and sustainability of the oceans for future generations. To do so, we must encourage sustainable fishing, improve marine conservation, lower pollution, and foster international cooperation.

2.14 *Life on Land (SDG 15)*

SDG 15 aims to protect, restore, and promote sustainable use of terrestrial ecosystems, sustainably manage forests, combat desertification, and halt and reverse land degradation and biodiversity loss. SDG 15 emphasizes how vital biodiversity is to humanity's survival capacity. The key targets include conservation, restoration, and sustainable use of terrestrial and inland freshwater ecosystems, mountain ecosystems, implementing sustainable management of all types of forests, halting deforestation, combating deforestation, and restoring degraded forests, land, and soil. The goal also targets urgent and significant actions to reduce natural habitat degradation, halt biodiversity loss, and protect and prevent the extinction of threatened species. It also promotes fair and equitable sharing of benefits from using genetic resources and appropriate access to them (United Nations, 2025o).

Increasing forest losses, land degradation, and species extinction pose serious threats to people owing to an essential fundamental shift in humanity's relationship with nature. Equivalent to twice the size of Greenland, around 100 million hectares of healthy and productive land were degraded every year from 2015 to 2029. Since 2015, the protected area coverage of key biodiversity areas has also been stalled (United Nations, 2023). The Kunming-Montreal Global Biodiversity Framework was adopted to hasten the Sustainable Development Goal of conserving terrestrial ecosystems. It includes four outcome-oriented goals by 2050 and 23 targets by 2030 (Joly, 2022). To effectively confront the growing global environmental crises—including climate change, biodiversity loss, pollution, desertification, land and soil degradation, drought, and deforestation—it is essential to scale up efforts to honor and implement our international environmental and biodiversity commitments.

2.15 *Peace, Justice, and Strong Institutions (SDG 16)*

SDG 16 promotes peaceful and inclusive societies for sustainable development, provides access to justice for all, and builds effective, accountable, and inclusive institutions at all levels. Key targets mainly include a significant reduction in all forms of violence and related death rates, including strengthening of relevant national institutions, ending abuse, exploitation, trafficking, and all forms of violence against and torture of children, and a substantial reduction in corruption and bribery in all forms, along with promotion and enforcement of non-discriminatory laws and policies for sustainable development. SDG 16 also aims to provide legal identity for all, including birth registrations (United Nations, 2025p).

The intentional homicides were highest in 2021 in the last 20 years, involving the loss of 458,000 lives, of which 9 in 10 victims were male (Santos & Testa, 2024). There was a sharp rise in conflict-related civilian deaths, fueled by the Ukraine war, leading to a 50% surge in 2022. The path to global peace and security has become more complex than ever (Sokan-Adeaga et al., 2023). Around 108.4 million people worldwide had been forcibly displaced as of the end of 2022, which is two and a half times more than a decade ago. The reasons included fleeing from persecution, conflict, violence, and human rights violations (Henningsen, 2025). Although many remain undetected, nearly 200,000 trafficking victims were identified between 2017 and 2020 around the world. Also, there was an underrepresentation of youth in politics, with 30 years being the global median age, which hindered their participation in decision-making processes (United Nations, 2023). Persistent threats to human security around the world highlight how inclusive and peaceful societies have broken down, which is essential for sustainable development. It also highlights the need to rebuild trust and update and strengthen international peace and security frameworks to respond to the pleas for peace made by countless voices worldwide (Luckham, 2018).

2.16 Partnerships for the Goals (SDG 17)

SDG 17 aims to strengthen the means of implementation and revitalize the global partnership for sustainable development. These include key areas such as finance, technology, trade, and data. Key targets include strengthening domestic resource mobilization, additional financial resources for developing countries from multiple sources, adoption and implementation of investment promotion regimes for least-developed countries, enhancement of global partnership for sustainable development, complemented by multi-stakeholder partnerships that mobilize and share knowledge, expertise, technology, and financial resources, to support the achievement of the Sustainable Development Goals in all countries particularly in developing countries (United Nations, 2025q).

Many developing countries face a serious debt crisis. As of November 2022, 37 out of 69 of the world's poorest countries were in debt distress or at high risk of it (Wade, 2023). The share of exports from LDCs in the global merchandise trade has remained stagnant at around 1% since 2011. The trends regarding expanding internet access, improving statistics systems, and raising funds for development are not entirely uniform. Net ODA reached 0.37% of GNI, which was still below the target of 0.7% in 2022. Although ODA funding for data has been dropped by more than 20%, the number of internet users worldwide has seen a rise. In 2022, 2 in 3 people used the internet, with 259 million more male than female users (Son, 2025; United Nations, 2023). Nonetheless, a significant $4 trillion yearly investment gap for developing nations to meet the SDGs, as well as enduring and debilitating problems like historically high levels of external debt and restricted internet connectivity in low-income nations, highlights the necessity of continued cooperation and improved support in an environment of escalating geopolitical tensions and international cooperation (Stephenson et al., 2021).

3 Health Significance of the SDGs

SDGs recognize the inter-linkages between economic, social, and environmental development. It aims to reduce poverty and ensure the health of our planet by realizing various interrelated goals including goals and targets related to health. While SDG 3 is directly related to good health and well-being, other goals too have direct or indirect health impacts. SDG 3 ensures healthy lives and promotes well-being for all at all ages (DESA, 2016). The title of the goal indicates the inclusion of various targets which not only focus on the prevention and treatment of diseases but also promote strategies for good health and well-being. SDG 3 includes targets for reducing maternal and child mortality, ending epidemics such as HIV/AIDS, tuberculosis, malaria and other communicable diseases, reducing non-communicable diseases, promoting mental health, reducing road traffic accidents, providing universal access to sexual and reproductive healthcare services, providing universal health coverage, reducing pollution deaths, implementing WHO framework of tobacco control, and increasing health financing. All these health targets can be achieved only by working with other SDGs in a coordinated way. Many other SDGs have a direct or indirect impact on health. They are discussed below.

SDG 1 (No poverty) is directly associated with health. Poverty limits access to nutrition, drinking water, and clean-living conditions leading to various diseases. The goal explicitly states that ending extreme poverty is critical for improving global health (DESA, 2016). Poverty virtually worsens every health outcome. Poverty significantly impacts physical and mental health through social stress, stigma, unemployment, and broken relationships (Knifton & Inglis, 2020). Globally, health outcomes are determined by the socio-economic conditions of a community. There is a clear social gradient to health outcomes worldwide. Poverty adversely affects health during childhood and infancy. Study shows that in England each 1% rise in child poverty is associated with about 5.8% rise in infant deaths per 100,000 live births (Taylor-Robinson et al., 2019).

SDG 2 (Zero Hunger) is a proclamation of the direct relationship between food insecurity and health issues. Lack of nutrition and hunger is directly linked to stunted growth, deficiency diseases, and other immunity-related disorders. We essentially need safe and nutritious food during infancy, childhood, and pregnancy. The human immune system too is directly linked to the intake of nutritious and sufficient food. It is a well-known fact that a stronger immune system is required to fight off infections and diseases. Thus, the zero-hunger goal is intricately related to health in its various dimensions. Lack of health can also give rise to poverty and hunger. Chronic disease, increasing health costs, and poor health insurance services are linked to continuous poverty and hunger. Food insecurity was found associated with significantly more emergency department visits, hospitalizations, and days hospitalized (Berkowitz et al., 2018). Thus, poor health conditions can also lead to hunger. Moreover, SDG 2 states that the global issues of hunger and food insecurity are exacerbated by the pandemic, conflict, climate change, and deepening inequalities (American Psychological Association, 2023; Ansari & Kar, 2024; Martínez & Short, 2021). So, we can see how health is linked to many macro factors at the world level through hunger. Ending hunger demands greater efforts to reshape food systems to be more sustainable, resilient, and equitable. Moreover, to achieve the SDG target of halving the number of children suffering from chronic under-nutrition, the expansion of improvement in diets, nutrition, health, and hygiene is a very crucial step (Katoch, 2024).

SDG 4 (Quality Education) is another Sustainable Development Goal which has a direct impact on health outcomes. Education is responsible for bringing awareness, knowledge, and practices for a healthy lifestyle. It has been found that health education is directly linked to behavior, which is linked to disease prevention. A study in China shows that health education seemed to increase the knowledge related to respiratory infection diseases among students (Wang & Fang, 2020).

SDG 5 (Gender Equality) is a goal which can contribute substantially to eliminating gender disparity in health. Unequal access to food and health services is a structural issue that needs to be tackled by designing proper interventions at social and cultural level. Poor health status among women, maternal death, and poor menstrual health are direct consequences of gender equality. Thus, the SDG 5 can substantially contribute to ensuring women's health in various dimensions.

SDG 6 (Clean Water and Sanitation) is directly linked to communicable diseases and waterborne diseases. Though access to clean and safe water is a fundamental human right recognized by most countries, it is equally vital for maintaining a minimum standard of health everywhere. The goal explicitly states that access to safe water, sanitation, and hygiene is the most basic human need for health and well-being (DESA, 2016).

SDG 11 (Sustainable Cities) can't be fulfilled without significant attention to the urban health system. Increasing urban areas in the world, especially in South Asia, are a major concern today. The ever-increasing rate of urbanization necessitates corresponding strategies and interventions to respond to the challenges related to health and the environment. Air and water pollution, garbage management, concretization of land, industrial waste, etc., are major threat to human health and well-being. Thus, sustainable cities are possible only when inter-sectoral strategies are designed with factors related to urbanization and health.

SDG 13 (Climate Action) indicates a looming threat to the people who are least prepared for it. The ecosystem people who are not responsible for climate change are the ones who will be affected the most (Bathiany et al., 2018). The climate action goal states the increasing frequency of extreme weather events which have a direct impact on human health. Climate change is also linked to changing disease patterns and disruptions in food and water security. All these have a fundamental impact on human health.

SDG 16 (Peace, Justice, and Strong Institutions) talks about inclusive society, freedom from all forms of violence, and working toward justice for the victims of war and conflicts. Deaths, physical torture, mental trauma, and sexual violence are the consequences of war and conflicts. The health sector needs to work in association with national and international organizations to alleviate the suffering of the victims. SDG 16 can be fulfilled only when it works along with the health sector.

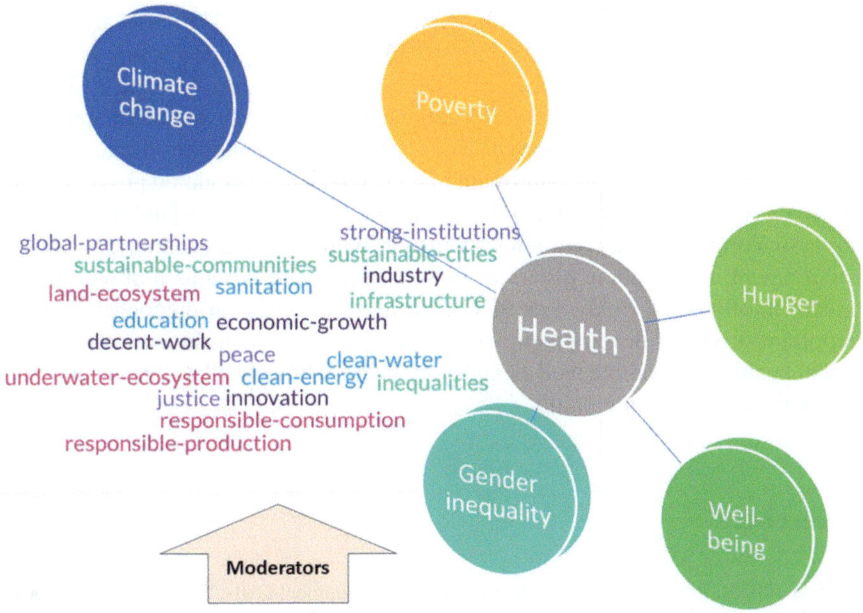

Fig. 1 Dynamic interplay of SDGs influencing health

SDG 17 (Partnerships for the Goals) focuses on enhancing collaboration, building meaningful partnerships between relevant stakeholders to achieve the Sustainable Development Goals. Attaining the all-other SDGs through attainment of SDG 17 can help in improving the health and well-being.

Figure 1 summarizes how the SDGs are directly or indirectly linked to health and well-being. Some of the SDGs (poverty, hunger, gender inequality, climate change, and well-being) have a direct influence on physical and mental health, while several other SDGs interact complexly as moderators to determine the state of health.

4 Conclusion

Sustainable Development Goals emerged as a coordinated and well-consulted effort to integrate economic development, social inclusion, and environmental sustainability. 193 UN member countries adopted the 2030 Agenda for Sustainable Development in 2015 at the UN Sustainable Development Summit. 17 SDGs and 169 targets were framed to bring positive changes in a wide range of issues such as poverty, education, economic growth, health, climate change, gender equality, peace, water, and sanitation. Health, as discussed above, is linked to most goals directly or indirectly. SDGs provide a broader and more integrative framework than the earlier goals, such as the Millennial Development Goals (MDGs). The goals are interconnected, universal, and measurable. Since 2015, SDGs have guided policy-making and partnerships for both national and international developments. Despite efforts at the international, regional, and national level, the progress has been uneven and insufficient. The 2023 United Nations SDG Report states that the ongoing climate crisis, the Russia-Ukraine war, and the aftermath of COVID-19 have hindered progress toward the goals (United Nations, 2023). Nevertheless, the SDGs are a landmark in global policy-making toward a common sustainable future. Though economy, society, and environment are the three pillars of these goals, health remains a universal determinant in almost all goals. For SDGs, health is not only an outcome but also an important driver of development. Achieving the SDGs will dramatically improve global health and promote well-being everywhere. Thus, the SDGs have very crucial implications for health globally.

References

Albu, D. (2023). Report progress on the sustainable development goals: The gender snapshot 2023 (UN Women, UN DESA, 2023). *Drepturile Omului, 94.*

American Psychological Association. (2023, May). *Climate change and mental health connections.* https://www.psychiatry.org:443/patients-families/climate-change-and-mental-health-connections

Anestis, G., & Stathakis, D. (2024). Urbanization trends from global to the local scale. In *Geographical information science* (pp. 357–375). Elsevier. https://www.sciencedirect.com/science/article/pii/B9780443136054000102

Ansari, E., & Kar, S. K. (2024). Mental health amid climate crisis: A narrative review. *Indian Journal of Psychiatry, 66*(11), 987. https://doi.org/10.4103/indianjpsychiatry.indianjpsychiatry_526_24

Bank, W. (2023). *World Development Report 2023.*

Bathiany, S., Dakos, V., Scheffer, M., & Lenton, T. M. (2018). Climate models predict increasing temperature variability in poor countries. *Science Advances, 4*(5), eaar5809. https://doi.org/10.1126/sciadv.aar5809

Berkowitz, S. A., Seligman, H. K., Meigs, J. B., & Basu, S. (2018). Food insecurity, healthcare utilization, and high cost: A longitudinal cohort study. *The American Journal of Managed Care, 24*(9), 399–404.

Boanada-Fuchs, A., Kuffer, M., & Samper, J. (2024). A global estimate of the size and location of informal settlements. *Urban Science, 8*(1), 18.

DESA, U. (2016). *Transforming our world: The 2030 Agenda for Sustainable Development.*

Engzell, P., Frey, A., & Verhagen, M. D. (2021). Learning loss due to school closures during the COVID-19 pandemic. *Proceedings of the National Academy of Sciences, 118*(17), Article e2022376118. https://doi.org/10.1073/pnas.2022376118

Estes, R. J. (2019). The 'Rich' and 'Poor': The widening income and development gap between rich and poor nations worldwide. In G. Brulé & C. Suter (Eds.), *Wealth(s) and subjective well-being* (Vol. 76, pp. 463–484). Springer International Publishing. https://doi.org/10.1007/978-3-030-05535-6_21

FAO, IFAD, UNICEF, WFP, & WHO. (2023). The state of food security and nutrition in the world 2023. Urbanization, agrifood systems transformation and healthy diets across the rural–urban continuum. In *The state of food security and nutrition in the world (SOFI).* FAO, IFAD, UNICEF, WFP, WHO Rome, Italy.

Faugoo, D. (2024). Women's leadership as an accelerator for gender equality and advancing SDGs for a sustainable future. *Asian Journal of Research in Business and Management, 6*(3), 25–39.
Filipović, S., Lior, N., & Radovanović, M. (2022). The green deal–just transition and sustainable development goals Nexus. *Renewable and Sustainable Energy Reviews, 168*, Article 112759.
Fund, U. N. C., & Organization, W. H. (2024). *Progress on household drinking water, sanitation and hygiene 2000–2022: Special focus on gender*. World Health Organization. https://books.google.com/books?hl=en&lr=&id=QCcUEQAAQBAJ&oi=fnd&pg=PR4&dq=Progress+on+household+drinking+water,+sanitation+and+hygiene+2000%E2%80%932022:+Special+focus+on+gender&ots=9BaO-WlH5z&sig=pUdgJc22aG6haoEPhnRHKXGNnQY
Giroud, A. (2024). World Investment Report 2023: Investing in sustainable energy for all: United Nations Conference on Trade and Development, Geneva and New York, 2023, 205 pp. *Journal of International Business Policy, 7*(1), 128–131. https://doi.org/10.1057/s42214-023-00178-9
Henningsen, G. (2025). Big data for the prediction of forced displacement. *International Migration Review, 59*(1), 141–164. https://doi.org/10.1177/01979183231195296
Horne, R. (2024). Employment and social trends by region. *World Employment and Social Outlook, 2024*(1), 37–60. https://doi.org/10.1002/wow3.204
Initiative, C. P. (2019). *Energizing finance: Understanding the landscape 2019*. Sustainable Energy for All.
Initiative, C. P. (2021). Global landscape of climate finance 2021. *Climate policy initiative*. Retrieved September 20, 2022, from https://www.Climatepolicyinitiative.Org/Wp-Content/Uploads/2021/10/Full-Report-Global-Landscape-of-Climate-Finance-2021.Pdf
Joly, C. A. (2022). The Kunming-Montréal global biodiversity framework. In *Biota Neotropica* (Vol. 22, Issue 04, p. e2022e001). SciELO Brasil. https://www.scielo.br/j/bn/a/wgQ5DTRfZrxhrrTs9n3JWYs/?lang=en
Jones, C. E. (2024). Routine Vaccination Coverage—Worldwide, 2023. *MMWR. Morbidity and Mortality Weekly Report, 73*. https://www.cdc.gov/mmwr/volumes/73/wr/mm7343a4.htm
Katoch, O. R. (2024). Tackling child malnutrition and food security: Assessing progress, challenges, and policies in achieving SDG 2 in India. *Nutrition & Food Science, 54*(2), 349–365. https://doi.org/10.1108/NFS-03-2023-0055
Keeble, B. R. (1988). The Brundtland report: 'Our common future.' *Medicine and War, 4*(1), 17–25. https://doi.org/10.1080/07488008808408783
Khan, S., & Yahong, W. (2022). Income inequality, ecological footprint, and carbon dioxide emissions in Asian developing economies: What effects what and how? *Environmental Science and Pollution Research, 29*(17), 24660–24671. https://doi.org/10.1007/s11356-021-17582-4
Knifton, L., & Inglis, G. (2020). Poverty and mental health: Policy, practice and research implications. *BJPsych Bulletin, 44*(5), 193–196. https://doi.org/10.1192/bjb.2020.78
Lee, H., Calvin, K., Dasgupta, D., Krinner, G., Mukherji, A., Thorne, P., Trisos, C., Romero, J., Aldunce, P., & Barret, K. (2023). *IPCC, 2023: Climate Change 2023: Synthesis Report, Summary for Policymakers. Contribution of Working Groups I, II and III to the Sixth Assessment Report of the Intergovernmental Panel on Climate Change [Core Writing Team, H. Lee and J. Romero (eds.)]. IPCC, Geneva, Switzerland*. https://mural.maynoothuniversity.ie/17886/
Lichna, A. I., Bezyk, KI, & Kudelina, O. Y. (2023). Analysis of FAO data on the global fisheries and aquaculture production volume. *Водні Біоресурси, 1*(13), 188–197.
Liu, C., & Xu, Y. (2022). Fossil fuel subsidy reform policy. In F. Taghizadeh-Hesary & D. Zhang (Eds.), *The handbook of energy policy* (pp. 1–25). Springer Nature Singapore. https://doi.org/10.1007/978-981-16-9680-0_12-1
Luckham, R. (2018). Building inclusive peace and security in times of unequal development and rising violence. *Peacebuilding, 6*(2), 87–110. https://doi.org/10.1080/21647259.2018.1449185
Martínez, L., & Short, J. R. (2021). The pandemic city: Urban issues in the time of COVID-19. *Sustainability, 13*(6), 3295.
McCulloch, N. (2023). *Ending fossil fuel subsidies: The politics of saving the planet*. Practical Action Publishing Rugby, Warwickshire. https://thepolicypractice.com/web/sites/default/files/2023-01/Ending%20Fossil%20Fuel%20Subsidies%20-%20final%20published%20book.pdf

McGlade, J., Samy Fahim, I., Green, D., Landrigan, P., Andrady, A., Costa, M., Geyer, R., Gomes, R., Tan Shau Hwai, A., & Jambeck, J. (2021). *From pollution to solution: A global assessment of marine litter and plastic pollution.* https://nottingham-repository.worktribe.com/output/8047115

Miao, Q., & Nduneseokwu, C. (2024). Global environmental leadership: Addressing the triple planetary crisis. In Q. Miao & C. Nduneseokwu (Eds.), *Environmental leadership in a VUCA era* (pp. 37–119). Springer Nature Singapore. https://doi.org/10.1007/978-981-96-0324-4_2

Organization, W. H. (2023a). *Trends in maternal mortality 2000 to 2020: Estimates by WHO, UNICEF, UNFPA, World Bank Group and UNDESA/Population Division.* World Health Organization. https://books.google.com/books?hl=en&lr=&id=6WnWEAAAQBAJ&oi=fnd&pg=PR17&dq=Trends+in+maternal+mortality+2000+to+2020:+Estimates+by+WHO,+UNICEF,+UNFPA,+World+Bank+Group+and+UNDESA/Population+Division.&ots=93VLgR0oZC&sig=AE2PCTDhON1T-pdqYnwiZDS4GGo

Organization, W. H. (2023b). *WHO Global water, sanitation and hygiene: Annual report 2022.* World Health Organization. https://books.google.com/books?hl=en&lr=&id=A6MOEQAAQBAJ&oi=fnd&pg=PR5&dq=.+2023+UN+World+Water+Development+Report:+Partnerships+and+cooperation+for+water&ots=iDlrcDlFkT&sig=zF_p8P6x9squnbSEQVLSjyUWUCE

Organization, W. H. (2023c). *World malaria report 2023.* World Health Organization. https://books.google.com/books?hl=en&lr=&id=u6UOEQAAQBAJ&oi=fnd&pg=PR6&dq=World+Health+Organization+(WHO).+(2022).+World+malaria+report+2022.&ots=cvpWg9Inhk&sig=BEu2wDm1bPQRGkW_G7yFTI4trb8

Palattiyil, G., Sidhva, D., Seraphia Derr, A., & Macgowan, M. (2022). Global trends in forced migration: Policy, practice and research imperatives for social work. *International Social Work, 65*(6), 1111–1129. https://doi.org/10.1177/00208728211022791

Patil, L., & Stipanovic, L. (2023). *2023 Global Education Monitoring Report on technology and education: Expert consultation convened by NORRAG.* https://repository.graduateinstitute.ch/record/319167/files/2023-global-education-monitoring-report-on-technology-and-education-expert-consultation-convened-by-norrag-english.pdf

Prabhakar, A. (2025). A sustainable and inclusive economic development: A global imperative. *Journal of Recycling Economy & Sustainability Policy, 4*(1), 1–16.

Raimi, D., Zhu, Y., Newell, R. G., Prest, B. C., & Bergman, A. (2023). Global energy outlook 2023: Sowing the seeds of an energy transition. *Resources for the Future, 1*(1), 1–44.

Rezaei, N., & Millard-Ball, A. (2023). Urban form and its impacts on air pollution and access to green space: A global analysis of 462 cities. *PloS One, 18*(1), Article e0278265.

Saiz, I., & Donald, K. (2018). Tackling inequality through the sustainable development goals: Human rights in practice. In *The sustainable development goals and human rights* (pp. 7–27). Routledge. https://www.taylorfrancis.com/chapters/edit/10.4324/9781351024303-2/tackling-inequality-sustainable-development-goals-human-rights-practice-ignacio-saiz-kate-donald

Santos, M. R., & Testa, A. (2024). Global trends in homicide: A comparison between the UNODC homicide data and the WHO mortality database. In *Routledge handbook of homicide studies* (pp. 7–40). Routledge. https://www.taylorfrancis.com/chapters/edit/10.4324/9781003399476-3/global-trends-homicide-mateus-renn%C3%B3-santos-alexander-testa

Sarangi, S., Singh, R. R., & Thakur, B. K. (2023). Interrelationship between share of women in parliament and gender and development: A critical analysis. *Administrative Sciences, 13*(4), 106.

Schotgues, B. (2022). Sub-Saharan teachers' conditions and circumstances: A review. *Journal of Applied Learning and Teaching*, *5*(Sp. Iss. 2), 10–22.

Sokan-Adeaga, A. A., Sokan-Adeaga, M. A., Esan, D. T., Sokan-adeaga, E. D., Oparaji, A. N., Aledeh, M., Balogun, F. A., & Oyeyemi, T. (2023). Review of the Russia-Ukraine war and its impact on public health. *Iranian Journal of War and Public Health, 15*(3), 295–303.

Son, Y. (2025). Are we there yet?: A feasibility analysis of ODA/GNI target of 0.7%. 사회적경제와 정책연구, *15*(1), 1–34.

Stephenson, M., Hamid, M. F. S., Peter, A., Sauvant, K. P., Seric, A., & Tajoli, L. (2021). More and better investment now! How unlocking sustainable and digital investment flows can help achieve the SDGs. *Journal of International Business Policy, 4*(1), 152.

Taylor-Robinson, D., Lai, E. T. C., Wickham, S., Rose, T., Norman, P., Bambra, C., Whitehead, M., & Barr, B. (2019). Assessing the impact of rising child poverty on the unprecedented rise in infant mortality in England, 2000–2017: Time trend analysis. *BMJ Open, 9*(10), Article e029424. https://doi.org/10.1136/bmjopen-2019-029424

United Nations. (2023). *The Sustainable Development Goals Report 2023: Special Edition.* United Nations Sustainable Development Goals. https://unstats.un.org/sdgs/report/2023/?_gl=1*fa1n04*_ga*MzQwNDAyNjg2LjE3NDQyMTMzMzg.*_ga_TK9BQL5X7Z*MTc0NDYwMzIwMy4xMC4xLjE3NDQ2MDM2NTAuMC4wLjA

United Nations. (2024, June). *The Sustainable Development Goals Report 2024.* United Nations Sustainable Development Goals. https://unstats.un.org/sdgs/report/2024/

United Nations. (2025a). *Goal 1 | End poverty in all its forms everywhere.* Department of Economic and Social Affairs Sustainable Development. https://sdgs.un.org/goals/goal1#overview

United Nations. (2025b). *Goal 2 | End hunger, achieve food security and improved nutrition and promote sustainable agriculture.* Department of Economic and Social Affairs Sustainable Development. https://sdgs.un.org/goals/goal2

United Nations. (2025c). *Goal 3 | Ensure healthy lives and promote well-being for all at all ages.* https://sdgs.un.org/goals/goal3

United Nations. (2025d). *Goal 4 | Ensure inclusive and equitable quality education and promote lifelong learning opportunities for all.* https://sdgs.un.org/goals/goal4

United Nations. (2025e). *Goal 5 | Achieve gender equality and empower all women and girls.* https://sdgs.un.org/goals/goal5

United Nations. (2025f). *Goal 6 | Ensure availability and sustainable management of water and sanitation for all.* https://sdgs.un.org/goals/goal6

United Nations. (2025g). *Goal 7 | Ensure access to affordable, reliable, sustainable and modern energy for all.* https://sdgs.un.org/goals/goal7

United Nations. (2025h). *Goal 8 | Promote sustained, inclusive and sustainable economic growth, full and productive employment and decent work for all.* https://sdgs.un.org/goals/goal8

United Nations. (2025i). *Goal 9 | Build resilient infrastructure, promote inclusive and sustainable industrialization and foster innovation.* https://sdgs.un.org/goals/goal9

United Nations. (2025j). *Goal 10 | Reduce inequality within and among countries.* https://sdgs.un.org/goals/goal10

United Nations. (2025k). *Goal 11 | Make cities and human settlements inclusive, safe, resilient and sustainable.* https://sdgs.un.org/goals/goal11

United Nations. (2025l). *Goal 12 | Ensure sustainable consumption and production patterns.* https://sdgs.un.org/goals/goal12

United Nations. (2025m). *Goal 13 | Take urgent action to combat climate change and its impacts.* https://sdgs.un.org/goals/goal13

United Nations. (2025n). *Goal 14 | Conserve and sustainably use the oceans, seas and marine resources for sustainable development.* https://sdgs.un.org/goals/goal14

United Nations. (2025o). *Goal 15 | Protect, restore and promote sustainable use of terrestrial ecosystems, sustainably manage forests, combat desertification, and halt and reverse land degradation and halt biodiversity loss.* https://sdgs.un.org/goals/goal15

United Nations. (2025p). *Goal 16 | Promote peaceful and inclusive societies for sustainable development, provide access to justice for all and build effective, accountable and inclusive institutions at all levels.* https://sdgs.un.org/goals/goal16

United Nations. (2025q). *Goal 17 | Strengthen the means of implementation and revitalize the Global Partnership for Sustainable Development.* https://sdgs.un.org/goals/goal17

United Nations & Development Programme (UNDP). (2023). *Sustainable Development Goals | United Nations Development Programme.* UNDP. https://www.undp.org/sustainable-development-goals

Wade, R. H. (2023). The world development report 2022: Finance for an equitable recovery in the context of the international debt crisis. *Development and Change, 54*(5), 1354–1373.

Walesiak, M., & Dehnel, G. (2024). Progress on SDG 7 achieved by EU countries in relation to the target year 2030: A multidimensional indicator analysis using dynamic relative taxonomy. *PLoS One, 19*(2), Article e0297856.

Wang, M., & Fang, H. (2020). The effect of health education on knowledge and behavior toward respiratory infectious diseases among students in Gansu, China: A quasi-natural experiment. *BMC Public Health, 20*(1), 681. https://doi.org/10.1186/s12889-020-08813-3

Water, U. N. (2021). *Progress on transboundary water cooperation.* UNESCO.

WCED, S. W. S. (1987). World commission on environment and development. *Our Common Future, 17*(1), 1–91.

World Bank. (2022). *Poverty and shared prosperity 2022.* World Bank. https://www.worldbank.org/en/publication/poverty-and-shared-prosperity

World Health Organization. (2023). *Sustainable development goals.* https://www.who.int/europe/about-us/our-work/sustainable-development-goals

Chapter 2
Relevance of Sustainable Development Goals in the Context of Mental Health

Sujita Kumar Kar, Khirod Chandra Moharana, Ankita Saroj, and Russell Kabir

Abstract The member states of the United Nations have collaboratively developed 17 goals to be met by the year 2030, all aimed at fostering sustainable global development. These goals have been thoughtfully crafted to take into account pressing global priorities, seeking to create a more equitable and sustainable world. Among the various dimensions of the Sustainable Development Goals (SDGs), the impact on health is particularly notable, especially concerning mental health. This chapter delves into the intricate relationship between each of the 17 SDGs and their implications for mental well-being, highlighting how progress in these areas can influence and enhance mental health outcomes across diverse populations.

Keywords Sustainable Development Goals · Mental Health · Health · Global Health · Environment · Planetary Health

1 Introduction

In 2016, member states of the United Nations set 17 goals to create a better future for a rapidly transforming world (Friedrich, 2016). The goals set are aimed at achieving the goals set by 2030. The Sustainable Development Goals (SDGs) include 8 of the Millennium Development Goals (MDGs) that aim to combat poverty (Friedrich, 2016). The Sustainable Development Goals are a global initiative designed to foster transformative change across nations. These goals promote a comprehensive framework for action, encouraging countries to implement well-organized and strategic

S. K. Kar (✉) · A. Saroj
Department of Psychiatry, King George's Medical University, Uttar Pradesh, Lucknow, India
e-mail: sujitakumarkar@kgmcindia.edu

K. C. Moharana
Department of Anthropology, University of Allahabad, Uttar Pradesh, Prayagraj, India

R. Kabir
School of Allied Health, Faculty of Health, Education, Medicine and Social Care, Anglia Ruskin University, Essex, UK

S. K. Kar et al. (eds.), *Sustainable Development Goals and Mental Health in South Asia*, South Asian Perspectives in Mental Health and Psychology ,
https://doi.org/10.1007/978-981-95-2684-0_2

plans that address pressing social, economic, and environmental challenges. By working collaboratively, nations can strive toward creating a more equitable and sustainable future for all (Lim et al., 2016; United Nations, 2025b). The 17 Sustainable Development Goals are (United Nations, 2024; United Nations & Development Programme (UNDP), 2023) summarized in the Box 1.

Box 1: Sustainable Development Goals

I. No poverty (SDG 1)
II. Zero hunger (SDG 2)
III. Good health and well-being (SDG 3)
IV. Quality education (SDG 4)
V. Gender equality (SDG 5)
VI. Clean water and sanitation (SDG 6)
VII. Affordable and clean energy (SDG 7)
VIII. Decent work and economic growth (SDG 8)
IX. Industry, innovation and infrastructure (SDG 9)
X. Reduced inequalities (SDG 10)
XI. Sustainable cities and communities (SDG 11)
XII. Responsible consumption and production (SDG 12)
XIII. Climate action (SDG 13)
XIV. Life below water (SDG 14)
XV. Life on land (SDG 15)
XVI. Peace, justice, and strong institutions (SDG 16)
XVII. Partnerships for the goals (SDG 17).

Countries are working toward achieving the SDGs. An interim analysis on the progress in achieving SDGs in Indian states revealed that many districts in the country are lagging behind because of improper planning and target setting (Subramanian et al., 2023). Hence, there is a need for a strategic approach to achieve the SDGs. The SDGs have significant health impacts, including relevance with respect to mental health. This chapter focuses on the mental health implications of each of the 17 SDGs.

2 Implication of SDGs in Mental Health

2.1 No Poverty (SDG 1): Mental Health Implications

Poverty is a global challenge. Even in the twenty-first century, a significant number of people globally struggle with poverty. People with poverty often struggle to meet their daily basic needs. People struggling with poverty encounter several health issues, which can be directly or indirectly related to poverty. The examples of direct health impact of poverty are: malnutrition, nutritional deficiency, poor immunization leading to frequent infectious diseases (Adeyeye et al., 2023; Prentice, 2023; Siddiqui et al., 2020). The indirect impacts of poverty on health include: non-adherence to medications, poor healthcare seeking, and lack of education resulting in unawareness about health (Hensley et al., 2018). Poverty may affect individuals at the microlevel to the whole nation at the macrolevel. When the whole nation struggles with poverty (examples—low-income countries and lower- and middle-income countries), health is significantly affected due to poor investment on health and inadequate healthcare infrastructures (Adeyeye et al., 2023; Arif, 2004; Deborah, 2014; Iyengar & Dholakia, 2012; Keane & Thakur, 2018; Singh & Kumar, 2017; Trani et al., 2010).

Poverty adversely affects the mental health at the individual level to the country level. It has been seen that the developing and underdeveloped countries struggle with mental health issues due to poor budgeting for mental health, lack of mental health infrastructure, lack of human resources to deliver mental healthcare, lack of facilities for training the manpower, poor salary of the trained manpower leading to migration of the trained manpower to other countries, and poor awareness campaign (Adeyeye et al., 2023; Das et al., 2007; Funk et al., 2012; Hensley et al., 2018). Poverty is a major factor responsible for the inequitable distribution of mental health facilities across the globe. Poverty is also responsible for the paucity of research. Due to a lack of infrastructure and funds, research in mental health is scarce in low-income and low- and middle-income countries (Marbin et al., 2022). Poverty is a significant cause of distress and it may adversely affect the recovery from mental illnesses in individuals who already suffer from mental illnesses (Sylvestre et al., 2018).

The relationship between poverty and mental illness is bidirectional (Marchi et al., 2024). Mental illnesses also affect the poverty adversely as the patients with mental illness are often unemployed, lose their job, become homeless, and have poor income, poor educational attainment, and higher rates of imprisonment (Funk et al., 2012). All these impairments significantly obstruct socioeconomic development (Funk et al., 2012). Stigma associated with mental illness significantly decreases the chances of being employed leading to more poverty. Individuals with mental illness often encounter stigma and discrimination regarding employment opportunities (Brouwers, 2020). This illustrates a fundamental link between poverty and mental health conditions. It has been seen that mental health interventions in people with mental illnesses improve their economic condition and help in combating poverty (Lund et al., 2011).

2.2 *Zero Hunger (SDG 2): Mental Health Implications*

Hunger is closely associated with poverty. Eliminating hunger is difficult without food security. Hunger may lead to malnutrition and nutritional deficiency-related hazards. Hunger may increase crime and social instability. Hunger may produce several intrafamilial issues like intimate partner violence, family malfunctioning (for example: lack of shared decision making, interpersonal conflicts, abuse), child neglect, and abuse (Jansen et al., 2020). Hunger-related issues are common in households with a larger number of children (Jansen et al., 2020) and significantly associated with parental anxiety and depression. A study on children reported that hunger increases the risk of homelessness, and stressful life events, in comparison with children with no hunger (Weinreb et al., 2002). Hunger is an important social determinant of mental health (Allen et al., 2014). Hunger in children is associated with high internalizing behavior and higher subjectively reported anxiety and depression (Weinreb et al., 2002). A study done on adolescents in Ecuador revealed that hunger increases the risk of suicidal behavior and depression among adolescents (Romo et al., 2016). A study conducted in 9 high-income, 31 middle-income, and 4 low-income countries on 179,771 school-going adolescents reports that severe food insecurity (hunger) is associated with higher odds for suicide attempts (Koyanagi et al., 2019). This phenomenon (association of suicidal behavior with food insecurity) is also being reported among adults (Kaggwa et al., 2023). Hunger increases the risk of non-adherence to essential medications for serious health conditions (Cordoba et al., 2021). Hunger and food insufficiency significantly affect the physical health and mental health of women in low-income countries as reported in an earlier study (Siefert et al., 2001). Nutritional deficiencies are associated with food insecurity and linked with mental illnesses (Ransing et al., 2022). Dealing with the hunger-related issues is expected to improve the mental well-being.

2.3 Good Health and Well-Being (SDG 3): Mental Health Implications

A healthy life gives a sense of subjective well-being (Fet, 2024). Diseases significantly affect the health and attribute to impairments and disabilities, compromising the subjective well-being (GBD 2019 Mental Disorders Collaborators, 2022; Vollset et al., 2024). Good health can be achieved by minimizing the mortality and morbidities due to infectious diseases, non-communicable diseases, accidents, and injuries (Fet, 2024). It is well known that all these health conditions have mental health consequences (Arafat et al., 2020; Chatterjee & Kar, 2022; Dubey et al., 2020; Howlett et al., 2022; Jain et al., 2017; Kar, 2016; Kar et al., 2015, 2020, 2025; Menon et al., 2020; Roy et al., 2020; Somani et al., 2016; Thakur et al., 2021; Tripathi et al., 2019). Good health is responsible for active and effective participation in the life events. It gives a sense of satisfaction. Good health gives a sense of security and subjective well-being. People with good health and better subjective well-being often lead a productive life. Hence, a positive mental health needs good physical health and better subjective well-being. Positive psychological interventions are known to improve psychiatric disorders (Jain et al., 2023; Stemmler et al., 2021). Governments allocate a health budget to facilitate healthcare. Schools incorporate components of good health in the educational curriculum. Societies facilitate a support system to promote health. Hospitals provide facilities to deal with ill-health. Religious and spiritual organizations work for social and spiritual harmony. All these efforts are organizational efforts toward good health and well-being. The successful delivery of these elements is expected to promote mental health as well.

2.4 Quality Education (SDG 4): Mental Health Implications

Education is a basic human right; still, a significant number of people are deprived of education. Education helps in enhancing awareness including general health as well as mental health awareness. It has been seen that education has beneficial effect on the overall mental health (Kondirolli & Sunder, 2022). Mental illnesses are closely associated with stigma. Education helps in reducing stigma associated with mental illnesses (Kondirolli & Sunder, 2022). Parent's education may also have positive effect on the mental health of children (Fakhrunnisak & Patria, 2022). Low levels of education lead to inadequate knowledge, which adversely affects the help-seeking behavior for mental health issues (Lanfredi et al., 2019). Low level of education is associated with poor mental health. People with low education often have less opportunities for employment and earning, which is expected to increase the psychological distress and mental health issues (Sperandei et al., 2023). Increasing employment opportunities for people with a low educational level significantly reduces the adverse mental health consequences (Milner et al., 2018). Maternal education also influences the mental health of children. Low level of education of the mother is associated with poor mental health of the children (Meyrose et al., 2018). Individuals with mental health issues often have poor educational attainment. Mental illnesses adversely affect the learning process. Early diagnosis and adequate treatment of mental illnesses may facilitate having educational attainment.

2.5 Gender Equality (SDG 5): Mental Health Implications

Gender discrimination is a significant social concern globally. Though healthcare needs are equally important for every individual, females are often deprived of their healthcare rights (Vigod & Rochon, 2020). They are also discriminated in the matter of schooling, employment, salary, socioeconomic opportunities, leadership positions, and participation in research and academia (Arafat et al., 2022, 2024; Bernardi et al., 2020; Vigod & Rochon, 2020). Women facing gender discrimination are at higher risk of developing depression (Stepanikova et al., 2020; Vigod & Rochon, 2020). Women and girls face significant health and safety risks throughout their lives. They are particularly vulnerable to unintended pregnancies, which can affect their education, health, and economic stability. They also have a higher risk of sexually transmitted infections, including HIV, and cervical cancer, often due to limited access to preventive care (WHO, 2025). Malnutrition is a critical issue, especially in marginalized communities, impacting overall health and development. Vision impairments can hinder educational and employment opportunities, while respiratory infections disproportionately affect them, exacerbated by environmental factors and inadequate healthcare. A study across 73 countries involving 566,829 adolescents reported that girls have more significant mental health issues than boys, and there is a significant gender gap in availing mental healthcare (Campbell et al., 2021).

Females have a higher risk of mental health issues in comparison with males due to several biological and psychosocial factors; however, they face more challenges in getting mental healthcare than their male counterparts (Burger & Scholz, 2018; Campbell et al., 2021; Getik & Meier, 2022; Liu et al., 2021; Stepanikova et al., 2020; Vigod & Rochon, 2020; Yu, 2018). The gender minority people (LGBTQ) have significant mental health issues; however, they also face significant challenges in getting healthcare because of discrimination (Lipson et al., 2019).

Elder abuse is a growing concern linked to ageism and insufficient support systems (WHO, 2025). Gender-based violence remains alarmingly high, stemming from long-standing gender inequality, and can manifest as domestic and sexual violence. Harmful cultural practices, such as female genital mutilation and child, early, and forced marriage, pose severe risks and disrupt education, leading to cycles of poverty (WHO, 2025). To address these challenges, comprehensive strategies are necessary to promote gender equality, empower women and girls, and ensure access to essential health services and protections (WHO, 2025). Gender equality is expected to bring a balance in healthcare delivery and expected to improve the mental healthcare support to females and gender minority groups (Newbigging, 2017). The convergence model of healthcare promotes gender equality and aims to facilitate healthcare equally for women and men, irrespective of gender (King et al., 2020).

2.6 Clean Water and Sanitation (SDG 6): Mental Health Implications

Clean water and sanitation are still major challenges globally, with the developing and underdeveloped countries being most affected. Nearly one-third of the global population lives without sanitation (The Global Goals, 2025a). Water scarcity is also significantly increasing in recent centuries; global warming and the rise in temperature further add to the crisis (United Nations, 2025d). As per a report, by 2022, about 2.2 billion people worldwide were deprived of safe drinking water, and 3.5 million people were deprived of sanitation (United Nations, 2025d). As per the Sustainable Development Goals Report 2023, there is a gross lack of data related to water security and sanitation from the majority of the South Asian countries (United Nations, 2023). However, as per the Sustainable Development Goals Report 2024, significant efforts are taken to integrate water management to deal with climate change-related issues effectively (United Nations, 2024).

Deprivation from clean water and lack of sanitation often lead to several health hazards. A study from Africa reported that the rural population in Africa are deprived of clean water and sanitation. It is associated with poor mental health and poor quality of life (Mngadi et al., 2023). Water scarcity can produce stress, anxiety, and frustration and may lead to violence. Similarly, open defecation due to a lack of sanitation increases the risk of sexual violence (Kimutai et al., 2023). It has also been reported that a lack of privacy in the sanitary facilities increases anxiety and distress and impairs subjective well-being (Sclar et al., 2018). Easy access to clean water and having sanitation facilities is associated with better mental well-being (O'Gorman, 2021). Unavailability of clean water and sanitation also affects the organizations at large. When these essential things are not available at school, hospitals, and several other public health facilities, it affects the health of the consumers adversely and may also impact their mental health (Chagan, 2025). Initiatives to facilitate clean water and sanitation facilities are expected to minimize the health hazards and improve the well-being of the people (Hutton & Chase, 2017).

2.7 Affordable and Clean Energy (SDG 7): Mental Health Implications

Affordable and sustainable energy is essential for attaining almost all the Sustainable Development Goals (Ferdous, 2021; Julia & Kassim, 2021). Sustainable, renewable affordable clean energy is essential from the individual household level to the industry and organization level at large (Rivera-Rodríguez et al., 2025). It has been seen that shifting from fossil fuel to a renewable energy source results in a reduction in climate change-related adverse consequences (Jaiswal et al., 2022). The clean energy transition focuses on moving toward low-carbon energy sources (Babayomi et al., 2022), which will reduce pollution and its associated environmental hazards. This is expected to have a positive impact on the general health, including mental health.

Evidences support that failure and instability in the availability of sustainable energy adversely affect the mental health of individuals, whereas access to renewable sources of energy (like solar energy) decreases the psychological distress (Rivera-Rodríguez et al., 2025). A study from China reports that cooking energy transition significantly improves the mental health (by reducing depression) both directly and indirectly (Liu et al., 2022). A study from Southwestern Uganda reported that improving access to lighting and illumination helped to improve social integration, self-esteem, sense of subjective well-being, and reduction of stress (Ponticiello et al., 2023).

2.8 Decent Work and Economic Growth (SDG 8): Mental Health Implications

Decent work and economic growth is an important Sustainable Development Goal, which emphasizes on productivity and income (Kreinin & Aigner, 2022). A decent work leads to good productivity and a sustained income leads to economic growth. Hence, this goal directly or indirectly deals with employment, financial growth, job opportunities, income, and poverty. Appropriate and optimal use of the resources also fosters sustained economic growth (Eisenmenger et al., 2020). Decent work implies quality work that is made available to people across the globe, who seek for it (Blustein et al., 2016). Making decent work available for the people is a form of social justice. Evidence supports that decent work determines satisfaction and it predicts survival and social contribution (Duffy et al., 2019). Decent work influences physical and mental health via several mediators (Duffy et al., 2019).

There is a bidirectional relationship between economic growth and mental health. If an individual has better mental health, it increases the possibility of effective learning, more chances of employment, a better job, and more income, which leads to economic growth. Economic growth, on the other hand, gives better satisfaction in life, availing mental health support, meeting the cost of care, more investment by the country on the development of infrastructure and building resources, which is expected to have a positive impact on mental health (Bhargava et al., 2001; Burns, 2015; Knapp & Wong, 2020).

2.9 Industry, Innovation, and Infrastructure (SDG 9): Mental Health Implications

In the recent century, industrialization, innovation, and development of infrastructure are at their peak (The Global Goals, 2025b). A resilient infrastructure adds to the success of a society (The Global Goals, 2025b). Industrialization and infrastructure development also contribute to the economic growth of the society and create employment opportunities for people, which is expected to improve the mental health indirectly (The Global Goals, 2025b). Innovations improve the help-seeking behavior (Du et al., 2023). In improving the help-seeking behavior, innovations in mental health are expected to improve treatment adherence and outcomes. Innovations in mental health are expected to bridge the treatment gap of mental illnesses (Du et al., 2023). Research innovations in the past several decades helped in the development of drugs for various mental health conditions, which is revolutionizing mental healthcare and the outcome (Insel et al., 2013). Innovations in technology development helped in reducing stigma associated with mental illnesses (Rodríguez-Rivas et al., 2022). Technology innovations led to the birth of artificial intelligence, which is revolutionizing healthcare, including the mental healthcare (Olawade et al., 2024). During the COVID-19 pandemic, innovations result in diversification of digital platforms to facilitate mental healthcare (Agarwal et al., 2023; Eyre et al., 2020). Technology innovations also helped the researchers to carryout research in mental health (Suh et al., 2024).

2.10 Reduced Inequalities (SDG 10): Mental Health Implications

Inequalities result in an imbalance in the social system. The SDGs focus on reducing inequalities. Inequality affects the health system, including the mental health system (Henderson et al., 1998; Pinto-Meza et al., 2013; Stansfield & Bell, 2019). Inequalities impact gender, access to education, healthcare facilities, employment opportunities, income, funding of various health sectors, and availability of resources and infrastructure for care. All these factors significantly affect public mental health. An European study reported that inequalities in employment, education, habitation, and abilities are associated with increased risk of mental illnesses (Pinto-Meza et al., 2013). This finding is fairly generalizable to other parts of the world. It is expected that socioeconomic inequalities to cause significant psychological distress and the development of mental illnesses. To minimize the inequalities due to challenges in in-person consultation for health issues, digital platform may be an effective solution by facilitating online consultation for the remotely located people, who need mental healthcare (Agarwal et al., 2023; Taiminen et al., 2019).

2.11 Sustainable Cities and Communities (SDG 11): Mental Health Implications

Urbanization is a global phenomenon. The urban population is rapidly increasing globally. However, in majority of the urban areas, the planning of the cities is not smart enough to accommodate the sustained needs of the public. To have a sustainable city and community, there should be intelligent urban planning, nature-friendly initiatives, a safe and secure environment, as well as affordable facilities (The Global Goals, 2025c). Sustainable cities and communities aim to deliver safe housing and transport, appropriate human settlement, minimizing the risk of natural disasters, preserving the green spaces, and regional development planning to integrate urban with semi-urban and rural areas (The Global Goals, 2025c).

Industrialization is in rapid progress globally. Industrialization results in depletion of biodiversity, pollution, and significant climate change, which have adverse public health consequences (Reyes Plata & Galindo Pérez, 2020). Industrialization is more evident in cities and it leads to the expansion of the cities. As per the global report, cities occupy 3% of the total land area on earth; however, they consume around 60 to 80% of the total energy and contribute to 70% of total global carbon emissions (UNDP, 2025a). Evidence suggests that mental health issues are more prevalent in urban areas and urban metros (Amudhan et al., 2020; Gautham et al., 2020; Gruebner et al., 2017).

Initiatives are taken in countries like China to have healthy and sustainable cities, which will promote health, enhance best practices for health, and will have local as well as global impact (Bai et al., 2022). Similarly, having more communication-friendly green and public spaces also facilitates to the development of sustainable cities (Wallis et al., 2023). As the city design and dynamics significantly affect the psychological well-being, it is important to work for restoring and rebuilding sustainable and healthy cities to promote psychological well-being (Roe & McCay, 2021).

2.12 Responsible Consumption and Production (SDG 12): Mental Health Implications

There should be a balance between production and consumption to ensure sustainability. Decreased production increases the consumer demand. Excessive production results in wastage. Increased demand produces scarcity and panic consumption (Adams, 2020; Arafat & Kar, 2021). Reduced demand results in a fall of price and wastage. As the demand or need is the driving force between consumption and production, there is an urgent need to understand the needs and demands. Also, it is important to keep a close watch on the changing dynamics of needs and demands to have responsible consumption and production. It has been reported that religious and cultural beliefs direct responsible consumption behavior (Nawaz et al., 2025). Responsible consumption may facilitate healthy development and harmony in the community. One of the classic examples of the consumption and production cycle is energy. The energy that is obtained from non-renewable sources is often exhausted because of irresponsible consumption (Arora & Mishra, 2023). Excessive consumption and limited production are expected to produce social chaos and stress, adversely affecting mental health. Responsible consumption is linked to awareness about the anticipated impact of consumption decisions (Giesler & Veresiu, 2014). Initiatives taken to enhance responsible consumption and production are expected to promote mental well-being in society.

2.13 Climate Action (SDG 13): Mental Health Implications

Climate change is a significant matter of concern globally. Climate changes include a range of alterations in the climate, like floods, cyclones, fire, pollution, temperature change, rise in sea level, and melting of glaciers (American Psychological Association, 2023; Brailovskaia & Teismann, 2024; Burke et al., 2018; Palinkas & Wong, 2020). The common mental health impacts of climate change are depression, anxiety, and post-traumatic stress (Palinkas & Wong, 2020). Children, the elderly, and people from low- and middle-income countries are worst affected by climatic adversities (Palinkas & Wong, 2020). Climate changes lead to unemployment, loss of jobs, migration, and collective violence and conflict (Ansari & Kar, 2024; Palinkas &

Wong, 2020). At the broader level, climate change causes disruption of the economy of a country, hampering the sustainable growth and development of a community (Ansari & Kar, 2024; Padhy et al., 2015). Several studies across the globe report that the perception of climate change evokes anxiety, depression, and suicidal behavior in public (Ansari & Kar, 2024; Burke et al., 2018; Gianfredi et al., 2024; Tito et al., 2024). As climate change is happening rapidly and the mental health issues associated with climate change are increasing exponentially, the actions aimed at minimizing climate change are expected to improve mental health.

2.14 Life Below Water (SDG 14): Mental Health Implications

Life below water significantly contributes to the biodiversity. At least 200,000 species have been identified underwater in the ocean life (UNDP, 2025b). About 40% of the ocean across the globe is heavily polluted, which is significantly affecting the life below water (UNDP, 2025b). About 3 billion people across the globe largely depend on the underwater biodiversity (UNDP, 2025b). However, recent decades witnessed a change in the temperature of marine water, increasing acidification of ocean water due to industrial wastes (UNDP, 2025b). Illegal and unauthorized overfishing also adversely affects the underwater ecosystem (UNDP, 2025b). Water pollution and disruption of the underwater ecosystem may result in scarcity of clean water, and it may adversely affect mental health by producing stress among people, particularly those who largely depend on it (Wutich et al., 2015).

2.15 Life on Land (SDG 15): Mental Health Implications

Life on land is not limited to human beings and animals; rather, it refers to all living organisms, including the plants. Uncontrolled, irresponsible, and irrational human activities damage the ecosystem and damage the lives of animals, birds, and plants (WHO, 2022, p. 15). Urbanization, cutting forests, industrialization, population growth, and poor waste management are the major contributing factors to the chaos in land life, which has resulted in climate change (WHO, 2022). All these changes adversely affect mental health directly and indirectly. Life on land is also affected by the unequal distribution of resources. It results in a scarcity of resources and facilities in several regions, which compels migration. Migration has its own mental health consequences (Alegría et al., 2017; Schouler-Ocak et al., 2020; Virupaksha et al., 2014). Climate change, natural calamities, war, terrorism, geo-political conflicts, and religious conflicts are major threats to life on land. These factors significantly impact mental well-being adversely. To enhance the mental health of individuals facing land-life challenges, specific interventions known as land-based interventions have been developed. These interventions aim to strengthen cultural identity, facilitate the transfer of inter-generational knowledge, and build relationships (Walsh et al., 2020). Deforestation is putting the life on land at risk (UNDP, 2025c). As per the report, about 1.6 billion people depend on forests for their daily living, and 80% of the terrestrial animals, plants, and insects live in forests (UNDP, 2025c). Evidences support that the presence of green space, wetland, shrub land, and bare land improves public mental health (Li & Managi, 2024). Similarly, an increase in urban areas negatively affects the mental health (Li & Managi, 2024).

2.16 Peace, Justice, and Strong Institutions (SDG 16): Mental Health Implications

Peace and justice are precious for the society. Justice is a human right. Violence, abuse, discrimination, injustice, and harassment are rampant in society and are major obstacles to peace and social harmony (The Global Goals, 2025d; United Nations, 2025c). Violent acts of terrorism in South Asia and the Middle East resulted in impairment of regional peace. War, religious violence, and geo-political conflicts also significantly affected the global peace adversely (United Nations, 2025c). The pursuit of peace, the longing for harmonious relationships, and the commitment to establishing equilibrium among individuals as well as between humanity and the natural environment are fundamental principles rooted in ancient Vedic philosophy. This philosophical framework emphasizes that conflicts, whether internal—originating in one's own mind—or external, arising between individuals or between people and nature, lead to the disruption of peace and overall well-being. In this context, peace is not merely the absence of conflict; rather, it is defined by the presence of harmony and understanding (Kapadia, 2024). When individuals cultivate a state of inner calm, engage in constructive dialogue, and respect the interconnectedness of all living beings, they contribute to a broader sense of tranquility (Mayseless et al., 2024). Therefore, achieving a state of peace involves both personal reflection and a collective effort to foster positive relationships, ensuring that harmony prevails not only within ourselves but also in our interactions with others and the environment around us (Kapadia, 2024). The Buddhist and Christian philosophies also emphasize peace and strategies to enhance peace and harmony within oneself and the society (Harris, 2018; Spencer, 2007).

Peace and justice can be attained in society in several ways, like (The Global Goals, 2025d):

- Reducing violence
- Preventing child abuse and human trafficking
- Developing the law and effective implementation of the law
- Controlling crime
- Preventing corruption.

The institutions that oversee critical functions, including the judiciary, constitutional matters, public administration, and government operations, must possess the strength and integrity necessary to implement effective and impartial measures that can lead to meaningful change. Building sustainable peace necessitates a comprehensive and integrated strategy, as it involves the collaboration of various sectors and communities. Furthermore, successful peacebuilding initiatives are anticipated to significantly enhance public mental health by fostering an environment where social harmony can flourish, ultimately allowing individuals and communities to restore their connections and rebuild trust (Marujo, 2023; Rich & Gonot-Schoupinsky, 2025; Tankink & Bubenzer, 2017). Thus, mental health is both a cause and an effect of strong institutions associated with creating a peaceful and just society.

2.17 Partnerships for the Goals (SDG 17): Mental Health Implications

The successful attainment of the SDGs largely depends on a collective effort that brings together various stakeholders, including governments, organizations, and communities. This compelling collaboration can be effectively realized through strategic partnerships that leverage diverse expertise and resources (The Global Goals, 2025e; United Nations, 2025a). Funding to attain these goals and particularly targeting countries with scarce resources will facilitate to achieve these goals (The Global Goals, 2025e).

Mental health, being intricately linked to every aspect of the Sustainable Development Goals—ranging from poverty alleviation to gender equality—plays a crucial role in achieving these objectives. By fostering strong, meaningful partnerships, we can create a more supportive environment that not only addresses various SDGs but also significantly enhances mental health outcomes across populations.

3 Future Direction

The impact of the SDGs on the mental health are enormous. The SDGs impact mental health both directly and indirectly. As mental health is one of the health priorities, globally working toward attaining the SDGs will help in improving the public mental health. SDGs facilitate funding, intersectoral collaboration, and global participation to achieve the targets within a stimulated time. It also encourages research to estimate the impact of the SDGs-related initiatives on different health domains, including mental health (Patel et al., 2018). Prioritizing of achieving the SDGs is expected to promote mental health globally. There is a vital opportunity to reshape and reframe the global mental health agenda, aligning it with the comprehensive understanding of mental health and mental disorders as envisioned in the SDGs. This new perspective emphasizes the importance of recognizing mental health not only as the absence of mental illness but also as a state of well-being that encompasses emotional, psychological, and social health. By integrating this broader conceptualization into policies and programs, we can address the multiple determinants of mental health, promote holistic approaches to care, and ultimately improve mental health outcomes for individuals and communities worldwide (Lund et al., 2018; Patel et al., 2018). This alignment with the SDGs can facilitate a more inclusive and effective response to the global mental health crisis, fostering collaboration across sectors and encouraging investments in mental health initiatives.

On the other hand, attainment of several SDGs requires promotion of mental health and prevention of mental illnesses. For example, a positive mental health will help in combating poverty, ensure gender equality, and help in restoring peace, harmony, and justice as well as most of the other SDGs either directly or indirectly (Takashita et al., 2022).

4 Conclusion

A bidirectional association exists between the SDGs and mental health. SDGs aim at achieving specific, achievable, and realistic targets in a time-bound manner. The progress in achieving the goals is not uniform across countries due to the differences in socioeconomic-geo-political scenarios. However, through the joint efforts of countries this goal can be achieved, which is expected to improve the global mental health.

References

Adams S. (2020, March 5). *The economics of panic buying*. https://www.forbes.com/sites/susanadams/2020/03/05/the-economics-of-panic-buying/#5eb37fe15e27

Adeyeye, S. A. O., Ashaolu, T. J., Bolaji, O. T., Abegunde, T. A., & Omoyajowo, A. O. (2023). Africa and the Nexus of poverty, malnutrition and diseases. *Critical Reviews in Food Science and Nutrition, 63*(5), 641–656. https://doi.org/10.1080/10408398.2021.1952160

Agarwal, A., Gupta, P. K., Singh, A., & Kar, S. K. (2023). Conceptual model of Remotely Accessed Mobile Application for Psychiatric disorder Screening (RoAdMAPS): A self-screening and referral aid for mental health in India. *The Lancet Regional Health - Southeast Asia, 8*. https://doi.org/10.1016/j.lansea.2022.100100

Alegría, M., Álvarez, K., & DiMarzio, K. (2017). Immigration and mental health. *Current Epidemiology Reports, 4*(2), 145–155. https://doi.org/10.1007/s40471-017-0111-2

Allen, J., Balfour, R., Bell, R., & Marmot, M. (2014). Social determinants of mental health. *International Review of Psychiatry, 26*(4), 392–407. https://doi.org/10.3109/09540261.2014.928270

American Psychological Association. (2023, May). *Climate Change and mental health connections*. https://www.psychiatry.org:443/patients-families/climate-change-and-mental-health-connections

Amudhan, S., Gururaj, G., Varghese, M., Benegal, V., Rao, G. N., Sheehan, D. V., Kokane, A. M., Chavan, B. S., Dalal, P. K., Ram, D., Pathak, K., Lenin Singh, R. K., Singh, L. K., Sharma, P., Saha, P. K., Ramasubramanian, C., Mehta, R. Y., & Shibukumar, T. M. (2020). A population-based analysis of suicidality and its correlates: Findings from the National Mental Health Survey of India, 2015–16. *The Lancet. Psychiatry, 7*(1), 41–51. https://doi.org/10.1016/S2215-0366(19)30404-3

Ansari, E., & Kar, S. K. (2024). Mental health amid climate crisis: A narrative review. *Indian Journal of Psychiatry, 66*(11), 987. https://doi.org/10.4103/indianjpsychiatry.indianjpsychiatry_526_24

Arafat, S. M. Y., Amin, R., Baminiwatta, A., Hussain, F., Singh, R., Kar, S. K., & Mubashir, A. S. (2022). Gender distribution of editors in psychiatry journals of South Asia. *Psychiatry Research, 317*, Article 114819. https://doi.org/10.1016/j.psychres.2022.114819

Arafat, S. M. Y., & Kar, S. K. (2021). Prevention of panic buying during public health emergency. *Asia Pacific Journal of Public Health*. https://doi.org/10.1177/10105395211014699

Arafat, S. M. Y., Kar, S. K., & Amin, R. (2024). Gender and geographical distribution of editorial board members of three leading suicide journals. *Crisis: The Journal of Crisis Intervention and Suicide Prevention, 45*(2), 159–163. https://doi.org/10.1027/0227-5910/a000919

Arafat, S. M. Y., Kar, S. K., Menon, V., Kaliamoorthy, C., Mukherjee, S., Alradie-Mohamed, A., Sharma, P., Marthoenis, M., & Kabir, R. (2020). Panic buying: An insight from the content analysis of media reports during COVID-19 pandemic. *Neurology, Psychiatry and Brain Research, 37*, 100–103. https://doi.org/10.1016/j.npbr.2020.07.002

Arif, G. M. (2004). Child health and poverty in Pakistan. *The Pakistan Development Review*, 211–238.

Arora, N. K., & Mishra, I. (2023). Responsible consumption and production: A roadmap to sustainable development. *Environmental Sustainability, 6*(1), 1–6. https://doi.org/10.1007/s42398-023-00266-9

Babayomi, O. O., Dahoro, D. A., & Zhang, Z. (2022). Affordable clean energy transition in developing countries: Pathways and technologies. *iScience, 25*(5), 104178. https://doi.org/10.1016/j.isci.2022.104178

Bai, Y., Zhang, Y., Zotova, O., Pineo, H., Siri, J., Liang, L., Luo, X., Kwan, M.-P., Ji, J., Jiang, X., Chu, C., Cong, N., Lin, V., Summerskill, W., Luo, Y., Yu, H., Wu, T., Yang, C., Li, J., … Gong, P. (2022). Healthy cities initiative in China: Progress, challenges, and the way forward. *The Lancet Regional Health – Western Pacific, 27*. https://doi.org/10.1016/j.lanwpc.2022.100539

Bernardi, K., Lyons, N. B., Huang, L., Holihan, J. L., Olavarria, O. A., Loor, M. M., Ko, T. C., & Liang, M. K. (2020). Gender disparity among surgical peer-reviewed literature. *The Journal of Surgical Research, 248*, 117–122. https://doi.org/10.1016/j.jss.2019.11.007

Bhargava, A., Jamison, D. T., Lau, L. J., & Murray, C. J. L. (2001). Modeling the effects of health on economic growth. *Journal of Health Economics, 20*(3), 423–440. https://doi.org/10.1016/S0167-6296(01)00073-X

Blustein, D. L., Olle, C., Connors-Kellgren, A., & Diamonti, A. J. (2016). Decent work: A psychological perspective. *Frontiers in Psychology, 7*. https://doi.org/10.3389/fpsyg.2016.00407

Brailovskaia, J., & Teismann, T. (2024). Climate change distress, entrapment, and suicidal ideation. *Climatic Change, 177*(8), 127. https://doi.org/10.1007/s10584-024-03784-5

Brouwers, E. P. (2020). Social stigma is an underestimated contributing factor to unemployment in people with mental illness or mental health issues: Position paper and future directions. *BMC Psychology, 8*, 1–7.

Burger, P. H. M., & Scholz, M. (2018). Gender as an underestimated factor in mental health of medical students. *Annals of Anatomy - Anatomischer Anzeiger, 218*, 1–6. https://doi.org/10.1016/j.aanat.2018.02.005

Burke, S. E. L., Sanson, A. V., & Van Hoorn, J. (2018). The psychological effects of climate change on children. *Current Psychiatry Reports, 20*(5), 35. https://doi.org/10.1007/s11920-018-0896-9

Burns, J. K. (2015). Poverty, inequality and a political economy of mental health. *Epidemiology and Psychiatric Sciences, 24*(2), 107–113. https://doi.org/10.1017/S2045796015000086

Campbell, O. L. K., Bann, D., & Patalay, P. (2021). The gender gap in adolescent mental health: A cross-national investigation of 566,829 adolescents across 73 countries. *SSM - Population Health, 13*, Article 100742. https://doi.org/10.1016/j.ssmph.2021.100742

Chagan RS. (2025). *Clean water for health and wellbeing*. Economist Impact - Perspectives. https://impact.economist.com/perspectives/health/clean-water-health-and-wellbeing

Chatterjee, S., & Kar, S. K. (2022). COVID 19 in pregnancy and neurodevelopmental disorder: The four-fold levels of prevention. *Asian Journal of Psychiatry, 70*, Article 103046. https://doi.org/10.1016/j.ajp.2022.103046

Cordoba, E., Parcesepe, A. M., Gallis, J. A., Headley, J., Soffo, C., Tchatchou, B., Hembling, J., & Baumgartner, J. N. (2021). The syndemic effects of mental ill health, household hunger, and intimate partner violence on adherence to antiretroviral therapy among pregnant women living with HIV in Yaoundé, Cameroon. *Plos One, 16*(2), Article e0246467. https://doi.org/10.1371/journal.pone.0246467

Das, J., Do, Q.-T., Friedman, J., McKenzie, D., & Scott, K. (2007). Mental health and poverty in developing countries: Revisiting the relationship. *Social Science & Medicine, 65*(3), 467–480. https://doi.org/10.1016/j.socscimed.2007.02.037

Deborah, M. (2014). Poor healthcare in Pakistan. *Harvard International Review, 35*(4), 52–57.

Du, Y., Shahiri, H., & Wei, X. (2023). "I'm stressed!": The work effect of process innovation on mental health. *SSM - Population Health, 21*, Article 101347. https://doi.org/10.1016/j.ssmph.2023.101347

Dubey, S., Biswas, P., Ghosh, R., Chatterjee, S., Dubey, M. J., Chatterjee, S., Lahiri, D., & Lavie, C. J. (2020). Psychosocial impact of COVID-19. *Diabetes & Metabolic Syndrome, 14*(5), 779–788. https://doi.org/10.1016/j.dsx.2020.05.035

Duffy, R. D., Kim, H. J., Gensmer, N. P., Raque-Bogdan, T. L., Douglass, R. P., England, J. W., & Buyukgoze-Kavas, A. (2019). Linking decent work with physical and mental health: A psychology of working perspective. *Journal of Vocational Behavior, 112*, 384–395. https://doi.org/10.1016/j.jvb.2019.05.002

Eisenmenger, N., Pichler, M., Krenmayr, N., Noll, D., Plank, B., Schalmann, E., Wandl, M.-T., & Gingrich, S. (2020). The sustainable development goals prioritize economic growth over sustainable resource use: A critical reflection on the SDGs from a socio-ecological perspective. *Sustainability Science, 15*(4), 1101–1110. https://doi.org/10.1007/s11625-020-00813-x

Eyre, H. A., Ellsworth, W., Fu, E., Manji, H. K., & Berk, M. (2020). Responsible innovation in technology for mental health care. *The Lancet Psychiatry, 7*(9), 728–730. https://doi.org/10.1016/S2215-0366(20)30192-9

Fakhrunnisak, D., & Patria, B. (2022). The positive effects of parents' education level on children's mental health in Indonesia: A result of longitudinal survey. *BMC Public Health, 22*(1), 949. https://doi.org/10.1186/s12889-022-13380-w

Ferdous, J. (2021). Access to energy at the household level. In W. Leal Filho, A. Marisa Azul, L. Brandli, A. Lange Salvia, & T. Wall (Eds.), *Affordable and clean energy* (pp. 1–11). Springer International Publishing. https://doi.org/10.1007/978-3-319-95864-4_134

Fet, A. M. (2024). Linking sustainable good health and well-being to the sustainable development goals: An historical perspective. In *Towards sustainable good health and well-being: The role of health literacy* (pp. 3–20). Springer Nature Switzerland Cham. https://library.oapen.org/bitstream/handle/20.500.12657/93840/1/978-3-031-61810-9.pdf#page=21

Friedrich, M. J. (2016). Sustainable development goals launched. *JAMA, 315*(7), 647. https://doi.org/10.1001/jama.2016.0608

Funk, M., Drew, N., & Knapp, M. (2012). Mental health, poverty and development. *Journal of Public Mental Health, 11*(4), 166–185. https://doi.org/10.1108/17465721211289356

Gautham, M. S., Gururaj, G., Varghese, M., Benegal, V., Rao, G. N., Kokane, A., Chavan, B. S., Dalal, P. K., Ram, D., Pathak, K., Lenin Singh, R. K., Singh, L. K., Sharma, P., Saha, P. K., Ramasubramanian, C., Mehta, R. Y., Shibukumar, T. M., Deuri, S. P., Krishnatreya, M., … Majhi, G. (2020). The National Mental Health Survey of India (2016): Prevalence, socio-demographic correlates and treatment gap of mental morbidity. *International Journal of Social Psychiatry, 66*(4), 361–372. https://doi.org/10.1177/0020764020907941

GBD 2019 Mental Disorders Collaborators. (2022). Global, regional, and national burden of 12 mental disorders in 204 countries and territories, 1990–2019: A systematic analysis for the Global Burden of Disease Study 2019. *The Lancet. Psychiatry, 9*(2), 137–150. https://doi.org/10.1016/S2215-0366(21)00395-3

Getik, D., & Meier, A. N. (2022). Peer gender and mental health*. *Journal of Economic Behavior & Organization, 197*, 643–659. https://doi.org/10.1016/j.jebo.2022.03.014

Gianfredi, V., Mazziotta, F., Clerici, G., Astorri, E., Oliani, F., Cappellina, M., Catalini, A., Dell'Osso, B. M., Pregliasco, F. E., Castaldi, S., & Benatti, B. (2024). Climate change perception and mental health. Results from a systematic review of the literature. *European Journal of Investigation in Health, Psychology and Education, 14*(1), 215–229. https://doi.org/10.3390/ejihpe14010014

Giesler, M., & Veresiu, E. (2014). Creating the responsible consumer: Moralistic governance regimes and consumer subjectivity. *Journal of Consumer Research, 41*(3), 840–857. https://doi.org/10.1086/677842

Gruebner, O., Rapp, M. A., Adli, M., Kluge, U., Galea, S., & Heinz, A. (2017). Cities and mental health. *Deutsches Ärzteblatt International, 114*(8), 121–127. https://doi.org/10.3238/arztebl.2017.0121

Harris, S. E. (2018). A Nirvana that is burning in hell: Pain and flourishing in Mahayana Buddhist moral thought. *Sophia, 57*(2), 337–347. https://doi.org/10.1007/s11841-017-0619-4

Henderson, C., Thornicroft, G., & Glover, G. (1998). Inequalities in mental health. *The British Journal of Psychiatry, 173*(2), 105–109. https://doi.org/10.1192/bjp.173.2.105

Hensley, C., Heaton, P. C., Kahn, R. S., Luder, H. R., Frede, S. M., & Beck, A. F. (2018). Poverty, transportation access, and medication nonadherence. *Pediatrics, 141*(4), Article e20173402. https://doi.org/10.1542/peds.2017-3402

Howlett, J. R., Nelson, L. D., & Stein, M. B. (2022). Mental health consequences of traumatic brain injury. *Biological Psychiatry, 91*(5), 413–420.

Hutton, G., & Chase, C. (2017). Water supply, sanitation, and hygiene. In C. N. Mock, R. Nugent, O. Kobusingye, & K. R. Smith (Eds.), *Injury prevention and environmental health* (3rd ed.). The International Bank for Reconstruction and Development / The World Bank. http://www.ncbi.nlm.nih.gov/books/NBK525207/

Insel, T. R., Voon, V., Nye, J. S., Brown, V. J., Altevogt, B. M., Bullmore, E. T., Goodwin, G. M., Howard, R. J., Kupfer, D. J., Malloch, G., Marston, H. M., Nutt, D. J., Robbins, T. W., Stahl, S. M., Tricklebank, M. D., Williams, J. H., & Sahakian, B. J. (2013). Innovative solutions to novel drug development in mental health. *Neuroscience & Biobehavioral Reviews, 37*(10, Part 1), 2438–2444. https://doi.org/10.1016/j.neubiorev.2013.03.022

Iyengar, S., & Dholakia, R. H. (2012). Access of the rural poor to primary healthcare in India. *Review of Market Integration, 4*(1), 71–109. https://doi.org/10.1177/097492921200400103

Jain, M., Kar, S. K., & Yadav, M. (2017). A questionnaire survey of stigma related to human immunodeficiency virus infection/acquired immunodeficiency syndrome among healthy population. *Community Acquired Infection, 4*. https://www.hksmp.com/journals/cai/article/view/196

Jain, M., Pradhan, M., Kar, S. K., & Kumar, P. (2023). Positive psychology interventions in patients with depression: A review. *Mind and Society, 12*(02), Article 02. https://doi.org/10.56011/mind-mri-122-20236

Jaiswal, K. K., Chowdhury, C. R., Yadav, D., Verma, R., Dutta, S., Jaiswal, K. S., SangmeshB, & Karuppasamy, K. S. K. (2022). Renewable and sustainable clean energy development and impact on social, economic, and environmental health. *Energy Nexus, 7*, 100118. https://doi.org/10.1016/j.nexus.2022.100118

Jansen, E., Lachman, J. M., Heinrichs, N., Hutchings, J., Baban, A., & Foran, H. M. (2020). Hunger in vulnerable families in Southeastern Europe: Associations with mental health and violence. *Frontiers in Public Health, 8*, 115. https://doi.org/10.3389/fpubh.2020.00115

Julia, T., & Kassim, S. (2021). Affordable and clean renewable and nonrenewable energy. In W. Leal Filho, A. Marisa Azul, L. Brandli, A. Lange Salvia, & T. Wall (Eds.), *Affordable and clean energy* (pp. 32–40). Springer International Publishing. https://doi.org/10.1007/978-3-319-95864-4_39

Kaggwa, M. M., Akatussasira, R., Al-Mamun, F., Prat, S., Mamun, M. A., Combey, I., Bongomin, F., Harms, S., Chaimowitz, G., Griffiths, M. D., & Olagunju, A. T. (2023). The global burden of suicidal behavior among people experiencing food insecurity: A systematic review and meta-analysis. *Journal of Affective Disorders, 342*, 91–120. https://doi.org/10.1016/j.jad.2023.09.012

Kapadia, M. (2024). Toward a new dharma of peace, health, and global well-being. In A. K. Giri & S. Varghese (Eds.), *Towards a new dharma of peace building: Conflict transformations and alternative planetary futures* (pp. 109–123). Springer Nature. https://doi.org/10.1007/978-981-99-6066-8_9

Kar, S. K. (2016). Lost online, then lust online. *Journal of Psychiatric Nursing, 5*(3), 117–119. https://doi.org/10.21088/jpn.2277.9035.5316.4

Kar, S. K., Arafat, S. M. Y., Sharma, P., Dixit, A., Marthoenis, M., & Kabir, R. (2020). COVID-19 pandemic and addiction: Current problems and future concerns. *Asian Journal of Psychiatry, 51*, Article 102064. https://doi.org/10.1016/j.ajp.2020.102064

Kar, S. K., Kumar, D., Singh, P., & Upadhyay, P. K. (2015). Psychiatric manifestation of chronic subdural hematoma: The unfolding of mystery in a homeless patient. *Indian Journal of Psychological Medicine, 37*(2), 239–242. https://doi.org/10.4103/0253-7176.155656

Kar, S. K., Shankar, A., Kabir, R., Sharma, P. K., Kumar, S., & Saxena, S. K. (2025). Survivors of Japanese encephalitis and associated neuropsychiatric complications. In S. K. Saxena (Ed.), *Japanese encephalitis: Epidemiology, pathogenesis, diagnosis, and therapeutics* (pp. 159–172). Springer Nature. https://doi.org/10.1007/978-981-97-5433-5_13

Keane, M., & Thakur, R. (2018). Health care spending and hidden poverty in India. *Research in Economics, 72*(4), 435–451.

Kimutai, J. J., Lund, C., Moturi, W. N., Shewangizaw, S., Feyasa, M., & Hanlon, C. (2023). Evidence on the links between water insecurity, inadequate sanitation and mental health: A systematic review and meta-analysis. *PLoS ONE, 18*(5), Article e0286146. https://doi.org/10.1371/journal.pone.0286146

King, T. L., Kavanagh, A., Scovelle, A. J., & Milner, A. (2020). Associations between gender equality and health: A systematic review. *Health Promotion International, 35*(1), 27–41. https://doi.org/10.1093/heapro/day093

Knapp, M., & Wong, G. (2020). Economics and mental health: The current scenario. *World Psychiatry, 19*(1), 3–14. https://doi.org/10.1002/wps.20692

Kondirolli, F., & Sunder, N. (2022). Mental health effects of education. *Health Economics, 31*(S2), 22–39. https://doi.org/10.1002/hec.4565

Koyanagi, A., Stubbs, B., Oh, H., Veronese, N., Smith, L., Haro, J. M., & Vancampfort, D. (2019). Food insecurity (hunger) and suicide attempts among 179,771 adolescents attending school from 9 high-income, 31 middle-income, and 4 low-income countries: A cross-sectional study. *Journal of Affective Disorders, 248*, 91–98. https://doi.org/10.1016/j.jad.2019.01.033

Kreinin, H., & Aigner, E. (2022). From "Decent work and economic growth" to "Sustainable work and economic degrowth": A new framework for SDG 8. *Empirica, 49*(2), 281–311. https://doi.org/10.1007/s10663-021-09526-5

Lanfredi, M., Macis, A., Ferrari, C., Rillosi, L., Ughi, E. C., Fanetti, A., Younis, N., Cadei, L., Gallizioli, C., Uggeri, G., & Rossi, R. (2019). Effects of education and social contact on mental health-related stigma among high-school students. *Psychiatry Research, 281*, Article 112581. https://doi.org/10.1016/j.psychres.2019.112581

Li, C., & Managi, S. (2024). Mental health and natural land cover: A global analysis based on random forest with geographical consideration. *Scientific Reports, 14*(1), 2894. https://doi.org/10.1038/s41598-024-53279-7

Lim, S. S., Allen, K., Bhutta, Z. A., Dandona, L., Forouzanfar, M. H., Fullman, N., Gething, P. W., Goldberg, E. M., Hay, S. I., Holmberg, M., Kinfu, Y., Kutz, M. J., Larson, H. J., Liang, X., Lopez, A. D., Lozano, R., McNellan, C. R., Mokdad, A. H., Mooney, M. D., … Murray,

C. J. L. (2016). Measuring the health-related sustainable development goals in 188 countries: A baseline analysis from the Global Burden of Disease Study 2015. *The Lancet*, *388*(10053), 1813–1850. https://doi.org/10.1016/S0140-6736(16)31467-2

Lipson, S. K., Raifman, J., Abelson, S., & Reisner, S. L. (2019). Gender minority mental health in the U.S.: Results of a national survey on college campuses. *American Journal of Preventive Medicine, 57*(3), 293–301. https://doi.org/10.1016/j.amepre.2019.04.025

Liu, P., Han, C., & Teng, M. (2022). Does clean cooking energy improve mental health? Evidence from China. *Energy Policy, 166*, Article 113011. https://doi.org/10.1016/j.enpol.2022.113011

Liu, S., Yang, L., Zhang, C., Xu, Y., Cai, L., Ma, S., Wang, Y., Cai, Z., Du, H., Li, R., Kang, L., Zheng, H., Liu, Z., & Zhang, B. (2021). Gender differences in mental health problems of healthcare workers during the coronavirus disease 2019 outbreak. *Journal of Psychiatric Research, 137*, 393–400. https://doi.org/10.1016/j.jpsychires.2021.03.014

Lund, C., Brooke-Sumner, C., Baingana, F., Baron, E. C., Breuer, E., Chandra, P., Haushofer, J., Herrman, H., Jordans, M., Kieling, C., Medina-Mora, M. E., Morgan, E., Omigbodun, O., Tol, W., Patel, V., & Saxena, S. (2018). Social determinants of mental disorders and the sustainable development goals: A systematic review of reviews. *The Lancet Psychiatry, 5*(4), 357–369. https://doi.org/10.1016/S2215-0366(18)30060-9

Lund, C., Silva, M. D., Plagerson, S., Cooper, S., Chisholm, D., Das, J., Knapp, M., & Patel, V. (2011). Poverty and mental disorders: Breaking the cycle in low-income and middle-income countries. *The Lancet, 378*(9801), 1502–1514. https://doi.org/10.1016/S0140-6736(11)60754-X

Marbin, D., Gutwinski, S., Schreiter, S., & Heinz, A. (2022). Perspectives in poverty and mental health. *Frontiers in Public Health, 10*. https://doi.org/10.3389/fpubh.2022.975482

Marchi, M., Alkema, A., Xia, C., Thio, C. H. L., Chen, L.-Y., Schalkwijk, W., Galeazzi, G. M., Ferrari, S., Pingani, L., Kweon, H., Evans-Lacko, S., David Hill, W., & Boks, M. P. (2024). Investigating the impact of poverty on mental illness in the UK biobank using Mendelian randomization. *Nature Human Behaviour, 8*(9), 1771–1783. https://doi.org/10.1038/s41562-024-01919-3

Marujo, H. Á. (2023). The nexus between peace and mental well-being: Contributions for public happiness. *Mental Health and Social Inclusion, 27*(4), 355–379. https://doi.org/10.1108/MHSI-07-2023-0077

Mayseless, O., Russo-Netzer, P., & Barr, S. (2024). Spirituality for peace. In R. M. Niemiec (Ed.), *Peace psychology and character strengths: Integrating science and practice* (pp. 345–365). Springer Nature Switzerland. https://doi.org/10.1007/978-3-031-66928-6_15

Menon, V., Kar, S. K., Suthar, N., & Nebhinani, N. (2020). Vitamin D and depression: A critical appraisal of the evidence and future directions. *Indian Journal of Psychological Medicine, 42*(1), 11–21. https://doi.org/10.4103/IJPSYM.IJPSYM_160_19

Meyrose, A.-K., Klasen, F., Otto, C., Gniewosz, G., Lampert, T., & Ravens-Sieberer, U. (2018). Benefits of maternal education for mental health trajectories across childhood and adolescence. *Social Science & Medicine, 1982*(202), 170–178. https://doi.org/10.1016/j.socscimed.2018.02.026

Milner, A., LaMontagne, A. D., Spittal, M. J., Pirkis, J., & Currier, D. (2018). Job stressors and employment precarity as risks for thoughts about suicide: An Australian study using the ten to men cohort. *Annals of Work Exposures and Health, 62*(5), 583–590. https://doi.org/10.1093/annweh/wxy024

Mngadi, L. C., Cuadros, D. F., Tanser, F., Burns, J. K., Slotow, R., & Tomita, A. (2023). Water, sanitation and depression in rural communities: Evidence from nationally representative study data in South Africa. *Psychology, Health & Medicine, 28*(9), 2441–2449. https://doi.org/10.1080/13548506.2023.2179643

Nawaz, M., Zhang, L., & Hanif, M. W. (2025). Motivators of sustainable responsible consumption behaviour: A sequential mediation. *Journal of Islamic Marketing*, *ahead-of-print*(ahead-of-print). https://doi.org/10.1108/JIMA-12-2023-0406

Newbigging, K. (2017). Chapter 12—Mainstreaming gender equality to improve women's mental health in England. In M. P. Sánchez-López & R. M. Limiñana-Gras (Eds.), *The psychology of gender and health* (pp. 343–361). Academic Press. https://doi.org/10.1016/B978-0-12-803864-2.00012-2

O'Gorman, M. (2021). Mental and physical health impacts of water/sanitation infrastructure in first nations communities in Canada: An analysis of the regional health survey. *World Development, 145*, Article 105517. https://doi.org/10.1016/j.worlddev.2021.105517

Olawade, D. B., Wada, O. Z., Odetayo, A., David-Olawade, A. C., Asaolu, F., & Eberhardt, J. (2024). Enhancing mental health with artificial intelligence: Current trends and future prospects. *Journal of Medicine, Surgery, and Public Health, 3*, Article 100099. https://doi.org/10.1016/j.glmedi.2024.100099

Padhy, S. K., Sarkar, S., Panigrahi, M., & Paul, S. (2015). Mental health effects of climate change. *Indian Journal of Occupational and Environmental Medicine, 19*(1), 3. https://doi.org/10.4103/0019-5278.156997

Palinkas, L. A., & Wong, M. (2020). Global climate change and mental health. *Current Opinion in Psychology, 32*, 12–16. https://doi.org/10.1016/j.copsyc.2019.06.023

Patel, V., Saxena, S., Lund, C., Thornicroft, G., Baingana, F., Bolton, P., Chisholm, D., Collins, P. Y., Cooper, J. L., Eaton, J., Herrman, H., Herzallah, M. M., Huang, Y., Jordans, M. J. D., Kleinman, A., Medina-Mora, M. E., Morgan, E., Niaz, U., Omigbodun, O., … UnÜtzer, Jü. (2018). The lancet commission on global mental health and sustainable development. *The Lancet, 392*(10157), 1553–1598. https://doi.org/10.1016/S0140-6736(18)31612-X

Pinto-Meza, A., Moneta, M. V., Alonso, J., Angermeyer, M. C., Bruffaerts, R., Caldas de Almeida, J. M., de Girolamo, G., de Graaf, R., Florescu, S., Kovess Masfety, V., O'Neill, S., Vassilev, S., & Haro, J. M. (2013). Social inequalities in mental health: Results from the EU contribution to the world mental health surveys initiative. *Social Psychiatry and Psychiatric Epidemiology, 48*(2), 173–181. https://doi.org/10.1007/s00127-012-0536-3

Ponticiello, M., Nuwagira, E., Tayebwa, M., Mugerwa, J., Nahabwe, H., Nakasita, C., Tumuhimbise, J. B., Lam, N. L., Wiens, M. O., Vallarino, J., Allen, J. G., Muyanja, D., Tsai, A. C., Sundararajan, R., & Lai, P. S. (2023). "If you have light, your heart will be at peace": A qualitative study of household lighting and social integration in southwestern Uganda. *Journal of Global Health, 13*, 04026. https://doi.org/10.7189/jogh.13.04026

Prentice, A. M. (2023). The triple burden of malnutrition in the era of globalization. *Nestle Nutrition Institute Workshop Series, 97*, 51–61. https://doi.org/10.1159/000529005

Ransing, R., Menon, V., Kar, S. K., de Filippis, R., & Mohamed, W. (2022). Nutrition and depression. In W. Mohamed & F. Kobeissy (Eds.), *Nutrition and psychiatric disorders* (pp. 139–169). Springer Nature. https://doi.org/10.1007/978-981-19-5021-6_8

Reyes Plata, J. A., & Galindo Pérez, M. C. (2020). Access to basic services: From public benefit practice to a sustainable development approach. In W. Leal Filho, A. Marisa Azul, L. Brandli, P. Gökçin Özuyar, & T. Wall (Eds.), *Sustainable cities and communities* (pp. 1–10). Springer International Publishing. https://doi.org/10.1007/978-3-319-95717-3_80

Rich, G. J., & Gonot-Schoupinsky, F. (2025). Mental health and peace: A positive autoethnographic case study of grant rich. *Mental Health and Social Inclusion, ahead-of-print*(ahead-of-print). https://doi.org/10.1108/MHSI-12-2024-0226

Rivera-Rodríguez, S., Varas-Díaz, N., Rodríguez-Madera, S., Padilla, M., Rivera-Bustelo, K., Reid, G., Santiago-Santiago, A., Mercado-Rios, C., Grove, K., Massol-Deyá, A., Rodríguez-Banch, R., Vertovec, J., & Ramos, J. (2025). Powering well-being: Energy independence and mental health in a zone of ongoing disasters. *Health & Place, 91*, Article 103418. https://doi.org/10.1016/j.healthplace.2025.103418

Rodríguez-Rivas, M. E., Cangas, A. J., Cariola, L. A., Varela, J. J., & Valdebenito, S. (2022). Innovative technology-based interventions to reduce stigma toward people with mental illness: Systematic review and meta-analysis. *JMIR Serious Games, 10*(2), Article e35099. https://doi.org/10.2196/35099

Roe, J., & McCay, L. (2021). *Restorative cities: Urban design for mental health and wellbeing*. Bloomsbury Publishing. https://books.google.com/books?hl=en&lr=&id=_NIxEAAAQBAJ&oi=fnd&pg=PP1&dq=Restorative+Cities:+urban+design+for+mental+health+and+wellbeing+By+Jenny+Roe,+Layla+McCay&ots=_6Pkv1qj8M&sig=bJQNK4Ek_1u5jSz3wusNYOjtyAI

Romo, M. L., Abril-Ulloa, V., & Kelvin, E. A. (2016). The relationship between hunger and mental health outcomes among school-going Ecuadorian adolescents. *Social Psychiatry and Psychiatric Epidemiology, 51*(6), 827–837. https://doi.org/10.1007/s00127-016-1204-9

Roy, D., Tripathy, S., Kar, S. K., Sharma, N., Verma, S. K., & Kaushal, V. (2020). Study of knowledge, attitude, anxiety & perceived mental healthcare need in Indian population during COVID-19 pandemic. *Asian Journal of Psychiatry, 51*, Article 102083. https://doi.org/10.1016/j.ajp.2020.102083

Schouler-Ocak, M., Kastrup, M. C., Vaishnav, M., & Javed, A. (2020). Mental health of migrants. *Indian Journal of Psychiatry, 62*(3), 242. https://doi.org/10.4103/psychiatry.IndianJPsychiatry_358_20

Sclar, G. D., Penakalapati, G., Caruso, B. A., Rehfuess, E. A., Garn, J. V., Alexander, K. T., Freeman, M. C., Boisson, S., Medlicott, K., & Clasen, T. (2018). Exploring the relationship between sanitation and mental and social well-being: A systematic review and qualitative synthesis. *Social Science & Medicine, 217*, 121–134. https://doi.org/10.1016/j.socscimed.2018.09.016

Siddiqui, F., Salam, R. A., Lassi, Z. S., & Das, J. K. (2020). The intertwined relationship between malnutrition and poverty. *Frontiers in Public Health, 8*, 453. https://doi.org/10.3389/fpubh.2020.00453

Siefert, K., Heflin, C. M., Corcoran, M. E., & Williams, D. R. (2001). Food insufficiency and the physical and mental health of low-income women. *Women & Health, 32*(1–2), 159–177. https://doi.org/10.1300/J013v32n01_08

Singh, P., & Kumar, V. (2017). The rising burden of healthcare expenditure in India: A poverty nexus. *Social Indicators Research, 133*, 741–762.

Somani, A., Kar, S. K., & Parida, J. R. (2016). Depression in systemic sclerosis: Review of the neuro-immunologic link and pharmacological management. In *Medical Journal of Dr. DY Patil ....* mjdrdypu.org. https://mjdrdypu.org/article.asp?issn=0975-2870;year=2016;volume=9;issue=3;spage=294;epage=299;aulast=Somani

Spencer, R. (2007). *Religion of peace?: Why Christianity is and Islam isn't*. Simon and Schuster. https://books.google.co.in/books?hl=en&lr=&id=V4gUQZhRGKUC&oi=fnd&pg=PP1&dq=global+peace+in+christianity&ots=P5yjHNLBVE&sig=lSGFJ2VUcmJrR3N7bCj3KdtIICI

Sperandei, S., Page, A., Spittal, M. J., & Pirkis, J. (2023). Low education and mental health among older adults: The mediating role of employment and income. *Social Psychiatry and Psychiatric Epidemiology, 58*(5), 823–831. https://doi.org/10.1007/s00127-021-02149-y

Stansfield, J., & Bell, R. (2019). Applying a psychosocial pathways model to improving mental health and reducing health inequalities: Practical approaches. *International Journal of Social Psychiatry, 65*(2), 107–113. https://doi.org/10.1177/0020764018823816

Stemmler, A., Staehle, R., Heinemann, T., Bender, M., & Hennig, J. (2021). Positive psychology interventions in in-patients with depression: Influences of comorbidity and subjective evaluation of the training programme. *Bjpsych Open, 7*(4), Article e109. https://doi.org/10.1192/bjo.2021.65

Stepanikova, I., Acharya, S., Abdalla, S., Baker, E., Klanova, J., & Darmstadt, G. L. (2020). Gender discrimination and depressive symptoms among child-bearing women: ELSPAC-CZ cohort study. *eClinicalMedicine, 20*. https://doi.org/10.1016/j.eclinm.2020.100297

Subramanian, S. V., Ambade, M., Kumar, A., Chi, H., Joe, W., Rajpal, S., & Kim, R. (2023). Progress on sustainable development goal indicators in 707 districts of India: A quantitative mid-line assessment using the National Family Health Surveys, 2016 and 2021. *The Lancet Regional Health - Southeast Asia, 13*. https://doi.org/10.1016/j.lansea.2023.100155

Suh, J., Pendse, S. R., Lewis, R., Howe, E., Saha, K., Okoli, E., Amores, J., Ramos, G., Shen, J., Borghouts, J., Sharma, A., Pedrelli, P., Friedman, L., Jackman, C., Benhalim, Y., Ong,

D. C., Segal, S., Althoff, T., & Czerwinski, M. (2024). Rethinking technology innovation for mental health: Framework for multi-sectoral collaboration. *Nature Mental Health, 2*(5), 478–488. https://doi.org/10.1038/s44220-024-00232-2

Sylvestre, J., Notten, G., Kerman, N., Polillo, A., & Czechowki, K. (2018). Poverty and serious mental illness: Toward action on a seemingly intractable problem. *American Journal of Community Psychology, 61*(1–2), 153–165. https://doi.org/10.1002/ajcp.12211

Taiminen, H. M., Saraniemi, S., Joffe, G., Stenberg, J.-H., & Parkinson, J. (2019). Reducing health inequalities trough digital options in mental health: A physician's perspective. *Health Marketing Quarterly, 36*(2), 93–106. https://doi.org/10.1080/07359683.2019.1575059

Takashita, E., Kinoshita, N., Yamayoshi, S., Sakai-Tagawa, Y., Fujisaki, S., Ito, M., Iwatsuki-Horimoto, K., Chiba, S., Halfmann, P., Nagai, H., Saito, M., Adachi, E., Sullivan, D., Pekosz, A., Watanabe, S., Maeda, K., Imai, M., Yotsuyanagi, H., Mitsuya, H., … Kawaoka, Y. (2022). Efficacy of antibodies and antiviral drugs against covid-19 omicron variant. *New England Journal of Medicine, 386*(10), 995–998. https://doi.org/10.1056/NEJMc2119407

Tankink, M., & Bubenzer, F. (2017). Building sustainable peace through an integrated approach to peacebuilding and mental health and psychosocial support: A literature review. *Intervention Journal of Mental Health and Psychosocial Support in Conflict Affected Areas, 15*(3), 199. https://doi.org/10.1097/WTF.0000000000000165

Thakur, M., Gupta, B., Kumar, R., Mishra, A. K., Gupta, S., & Kar, S. K. (2021). Depression among women diagnosed with breast cancer: A study from North India. *Indian Journal of Medical and Paediatric Oncology, 40*, 347–352. https://doi.org/10.4103/ijmpo.ijmpo_43_18

The Global Goals. (2025a). *Goal 6: Clean water and sanitation.* The Global Goals. https://globalgoals.org/goals/6-clean-water-and-sanitation/

The Global Goals. (2025b). *Goal 9: Industry, innovation and infrastructure.* The Global Goals. https://globalgoals.org/goals/9-industry-innovation-and-infrastructure/

The Global Goals. (2025c). *Goal 11: Sustainable cities and communities.* The Global Goals. https://globalgoals.org/goals/11-sustainable-cities-and-communities/

The Global Goals. (2025d). *Goal 16: Peace, justice and strong institutions.* The Global Goals. https://globalgoals.org/goals/16-peace-justice-and-strong-institutions/

The Global Goals. (2025e). *Goal 17: Partnerships for the goals.* The Global Goals. https://globalgoals.org/goals/17-partnerships-for-the-goals/

Tito, V. R., Kazem, H., Kadia, S.-O., & Paquito, B. (2024). A systematic review of mental health and climate change in the Philippines. *Asian Journal of Psychiatry, 101*, Article 104191. https://doi.org/10.1016/j.ajp.2024.104191

Trani, J.-F., Bakhshi, P., Noor, A. A., Lopez, D., & Mashkoor, A. (2010). Poverty, vulnerability, and provision of healthcare in Afghanistan. *Social Science & Medicine, 70*(11), 1745–1755. https://doi.org/10.1016/j.socscimed.2010.02.007

Tripathi, A., Das, A., & Kar, S. K. (2019). Biopsychosocial model in contemporary psychiatry: Current validity and future prospects. *Indian Journal of Psychological Medicine, 41*(6), 582–585. https://doi.org/10.4103/IJPSYM.IJPSYM_314_19

UNDP. (2025a). *Goal 11: Sustainable cities and communities | United Nations Development Programme.* UNDP. https://www.undp.org/sustainable-development-goals/sustainable-cities-and-communities

UNDP. (2025b). *Goal 14: Life Below Water | United Nations Development Programme.* UNDP. https://www.undp.org/sustainable-development-goals/below-water

UNDP. (2025c). *Goal 15: Life on land | United Nations Development Programme.* UNDP. https://www.undp.org/sustainable-development-goals/life-on-land

United Nations. (2023). *The Sustainable Development Goals Report 2023: Special Edition.* United Nations Sustainable Development Goals. https://unstats.un.org/sdgs/report/2023/?_gl=1*fa1n04*_ga*MzQwNDAyNjg2LjE3NDQyMTMzMzg.*_ga_TK9BQL5X7Z*MTc0NDYwMzIwMy4xMC4xLjE3NDQ2MDM2NTAuMC4wLjA

United Nations. (2024, June). *The Sustainable Development Goals Report 2024.* United Nations Sustainable Development Goals. https://unstats.un.org/sdgs/report/2024/

United Nations. (2025a). Global Partnerships. *United Nations Sustainable Development.* https://www.un.org/sustainabledevelopment/globalpartnerships/

United Nations. (2025b). *Home.* United Nations Sustainable Development. https://www.un.org/sustainabledevelopment/

United Nations. (2025c). Peace, justice and strong institutions. *United Nations Sustainable Development.* https://www.un.org/sustainabledevelopment/peace-justice/

United Nations. (2025d). Water and Sanitation. *United Nations Sustainable Development.* https://www.un.org/sustainabledevelopment/water-and-sanitation/

United Nations & Development Programme (UNDP). (2023). *Sustainable Development Goals | United Nations Development Programme.* UNDP. https://www.undp.org/sustainable-development-goals

Vigod, S. N., & Rochon, P. A. (2020). The impact of gender discrimination on a woman's mental health. *eClinicalMedicine, 20.* https://doi.org/10.1016/j.eclinm.2020.100311

Virupaksha, H. G., Kumar, A., & Nirmala, B. P. (2014). Migration and mental health: An interface. *Journal of Natural Science, Biology, and Medicine, 5*(2), 233–239. https://doi.org/10.4103/0976-9668.136141

Vollset, S. E., Ababneh, H. S., Abate, Y. H., Abbafati, C., Abbasgholizadeh, R., Abbasian, M., Abbastabar, H., Magied, A. H. A. A. A., ElHafeez, S. A., Abdelkader, A., Abdelmasseh, M., Abd-Elsalam, S., Abdi, P., Abdollahi, M., Abdoun, M., Abdullahi, A., Abebe, M., Abiodun, O., Aboagye, R. G., … Murray, C. J. L. (2024). Burden of disease scenarios for 204 countries and territories, 2022–2050: A forecasting analysis for the Global Burden of Disease Study 2021. *The Lancet, 403*(10440), 2204–2256. https://doi.org/10.1016/S0140-6736(24)00685-8

Wallis, A. K., Westerveld, M. F., & Burton, P. (2023). Ensuring communication-friendly green and public spaces for sustainable cities: Sustainable Development Goal 11. *International Journal of Speech-Language Pathology, 25*(1), 27–31. https://doi.org/10.1080/17549507.2022.2138544

Walsh, R., Danto, D., & Sommerfeld, J. (2020). Land-based intervention: A qualitative study of the knowledge and practices associated with one approach to mental health in a Cree community. *International Journal of Mental Health and Addiction, 18*(1), 207–221. https://doi.org/10.1007/s11469-018-9996-3

Weinreb, L., Wehler, C., Perloff, J., Scott, R., Hosmer, D., Sagor, L., & Gundersen, C. (2002). Hunger: Its impact on children's health and mental health. *Pediatrics, 110*(4), Article e41. https://doi.org/10.1542/peds.110.4.e41

WHO. (2022, September 30). *SDG 15 life on land.* https://www.who.int/tools/your-life-your-health/a-healthy-world/planet/SDG-15-Life-on-Land

WHO. (2025). *Gender and health.* https://www.who.int/health-topics/gender

Wutich, A., Brewis, A., Chavez, J. B. R., & Jaiswal, C. L. (2015). Water, worry, and Doña Paloma: Why water security is fundamental to global mental health. In *Global mental health.* Routledge. https://www.taylorfrancis.com/books/edit/10.4324/9781315428055/global-mental-health-emily-mendenhall-brandon-kohrt?refId=36f5c4f4-b720-4ff0-ae44-031feb057815&context=ubx

Yu, S. (2018). Uncovering the hidden impacts of inequality on mental health: A global study. *Translational Psychiatry, 8*, 98. https://doi.org/10.1038/s41398-018-0148-0

Chapter 3
Barriers to SDGs to Improve Mental Health in South Asia

Adarsh Tripathi and Anupam Singh Yadav

Abstract Home to one-fourth of the world population, the South Asian region is a bouquet of diversity. This region faces an uphill task to meet the Sustainable Development Goals (SDGs) in the presence of a large number of shared and diverse challenges. Each country has tried to devise programmes to address these challenges with varying degrees of success. All SDGs are interdependent and have an impact on mental well-being. This chapter examines the relationship between various SDGs and mental health. It also explores various barriers to the SDGs to improve mental health. There is a need to integrate mental wellness with these SDGs and devise programmes jointly with shared experiences.

Keywords Mental health · South Asia · SDG

1 Introduction

Nearly one-fourth of the world's population resides in South Asia, characterised by diverse culture, ethnicity and socio-economic conditions. Large youth population, rapid urbanisation and other development challenges are grossly shared by all the South Asian countries, including India, Pakistan, Bangladesh, Nepal, Sri Lanka, Bhutan and Maldives. There is a large diversity between countries as well as within the countries, from the most densely populated cities of Dhaka, Delhi, Mumbai and Karachi to sparsely populated northeastern states of India and the hills of Nepal. Similarly, large diversity is seen in the landscapes across the South Asia region. This variety presents both a challenge and an opportunity in many ways, including mental health needs (Arafat & Kar, 2024).

Aspirations of a healthier world cannot be fulfilled without taking into considerations the needs of South Asia. There is an urgent need to identify and address the specific needs of the population in this region. Socio-economic disparities, cultural

A. Tripathi (✉) · A. S. Yadav
Department of Psychiatry, King George's Medical University, Chowk, Lucknow, UP, India
e-mail: dradarshtripathi@gmail.com

S. K. Kar et al. (eds.), *Sustainable Development Goals and Mental Health in South Asia*,
South Asian Perspectives in Mental Health and Psychology ,
https://doi.org/10.1007/978-981-95-2684-0_3

stigmas and inadequate infrastructure are among the various factors for the lagging health indices of this region, including mental health. Sustainable Development Goals (SDGs), designed by the United Nations, are comprehensive measures of the different elements influencing the general health and mental well-being of the people in this area. These goals encompass a wide range of targets, including the eradication of poverty, promotion of health, gender equality, education and climate action, which ultimately contribute to mental well-being (Votruba et al., 2016).

Mental health is deeply interconnected with broader developmental factors such as poverty alleviation economic growth and the establishment of peaceful and just societies. It is the building block of a society where there is social inclusion, equity, universal health coverage, access to justice, respect for human rights and all this culminating into sustainable economic development (World Health Organization, 2011).

There exists a two-way relationship between poverty alleviation (SDG1) and mental health, as is evidenced in many studies that mental illness adds to financial stress and thus to poverty, and poverty leads to mental distress and adds to vulnerability to various psychiatric disorders. Similarly, a mentally healthy population is the prerequisite for sustainable economic growth (SDG8) and the creation of safe, inclusive and resilient cities (SDG11). Mental health has cross cross-cutting impact on various SDGs such as education (SDG4), gender equality (SDG5) and reducing inequalities (SDG10). This interdependence among SDGs and the self-evident relevance of mental health across the entire SDG framework highlight the need for integrated strategies that prioritise mental health (Votruba et al., 2016).

Significant improvement in literacy rates and access to basic healthcare are noted in this region, but still, achieving an appropriate pace of improvement to achieve the SDGs seems an uphill task. Multiple issues, such as immense poverty, malnutrition, gender inequality and technological challenges, act as roadblocks on the way to achieving these SDGs (Macroeconomic Policy & Financing for Development Division, 2017).

This chapter presents a comprehensive outlook of various factors affecting the efforts to realise various SDGs affecting mental health. While presenting an overall understanding of the general trends in the region, this chapter also delves deeper in to scenarios in a few major nations of the region.

2 Current State of SDGs and Their Impact on Mental Health in Countries of South Asia

The third Sustainable Development Goal of good health and well-being seems to be emphasising on ensuring good health, but it is very well evidenced that this SDG is deeply interdependent with various other SDGs. This is affected by various factors like poverty, hunger, education, gender inequality, access to clean water and sanitation, affordable energy, decent work and economic growth. Therefore, achieving good health is not possible without significant strides in all other SDGs. Addressing mental health requires a holistic approach across indicators of all SDGs (Nunes et al., 2016; Votruba et al., 2016).

In 2021, South Asia recorded an average SDG Index score of 63.58, reflecting 63.58% progress towards achieving optimal outcomes across the 17 SDGs and marking a 2.64% improvement since the 2015 baseline. Among South Asian nations, Bhutan (70.02), Maldives (69.27) and Sri Lanka (68.1) emerged as the top performers, while Afghanistan (53.56), Pakistan (57.62) and India (60.07) ranked the lowest (Table 1). On a global scale, as of 2024, only 16% of SDG targets are on track to be met by 2030, with 84% demonstrating either slow progress or regression (Asia and the Pacific SDG Progress Report 2024 : Showcasing Transformative Actions|ESCAP, 2024; Sustainable Development Report, 2024, 2024).

South Asia faces multiple barriers to achieving mental health, rooted in socio-economic inequalities and governance issues. Economic inequality based on region, caste and gender limiting access to basic services like education healthcare and economic opportunities is the most alarming challenge. World Bank data suggest that South Asia is home to nearly 40% of the world's poor, with India alone housing 228.9 million people living below the poverty line as of 2022. Marginalised groups, including Dalits and tribal populations, experience entrenched barriers to social mobility and economic participation, perpetuating cycles of poverty and exclusion.

Table 1 South Asian performance towards SDGs (Asia and the Pacific SDG Progress Report 2024: Showcasing Transformative Actions|ESCAP, 2024; Sustainable Development Report, 2024)

Country	2015 score	2015 rank	2023 score	2023 rank
Afghanistan	47.6	149	53.56	158
Bangladesh	56.2	120	64.22	104
Bhutan	59.1	102	70.02	81
India	55.3	125	60.07	112
Maldives	58.4	105	69.27	83
Nepal	54.1	129	66.22	98
Pakistan	51.1	136	57.62	128
Sri Lanka	61.3	97	68.1	85

The scores represent the percentage achievement towards the SDGs, with higher scores indicating better performance. Ranks are out of 193 countries

3 Barriers to Mental Health in South Asia

3.1 *Mental Health Literacy*

There is an evident lack of awareness about the nature and progression of psychiatric disorders in the majority of the population of the South Asian region. Many times these are believed to have occurred due to supernatural causes and people resort to faith healing. Also, at times, many psychiatric disorders are written off as the very nature of that person and no remedial action is taken. This lack of understanding about mental health is a significant barrier that stops people from seeking appropriate evidence-based care (Faizan et al., 2012).

3.2 *Stigma*

Stigma towards patients and families suffering from psychiatric disorders is deeply entrenched in South Asian societies. Individuals suffering from mental health issues face critical comments, shaming, social exclusion and discrimination, which results in them not seeking mental health care promptly (Vaishnav et al., 2023).

3.3 *Treatment Gap*

India has only 0.75 psychiatrists per lakh population, far below the WHO recommended 3 psychiatrists per lakh (Murthy, 2017). Almost similar condition is seen in the whole region. Although number of psychiatrists are quickly increasing in India, concerns like equal distribution across areas and rural and urban divide are still important.

3.4 *Inadequate Nonpharmacological Rehabilitation Services*

Nonpharmacological interventions like psychotherapy and counselling require more time to be spent with each individual, and thus, a lack of mental health professionals becomes a barrier. Due to the constraints related to finances and accessibility, there is a lack of rehabilitation services that focus on long-term recovery, including social reintegration and vocational support which are often unavailable (Arafat & Kar, 2024; Kim et al., 2017; Murthy, 2017).

3.5 Lack of Specialised Services for Vulnerable Groups

Mental health services require further specialisation to address the unique needs of vulnerable groups like children and adolescents, women, elderly and sexual minorities. There seems to be a lack of such services.

- **Children and adolescents**—Child-friendly environment and specialised tools of assessment by specially trained professionals are needed for optimal care.
- **Women**—Mental health issues in women are related to multiple factors such as domestic violence, postpartum depression and other gender specific challenges, and it requires a nuanced approach by qualified specialists.
- **Elderly**—The elderly population suffers from neglect of mental health issues like dementia, depression and loneliness.
- **Sexual minorities**—Sexual minorities face added stigma, lack of social support and legal trouble, leading to heightened psychological distress.

3.6 Challenges from Migration, Conflict and Climate-Induced Displacement

Internal migration—Internal migration occurs due to multiple causes, such as seeking better economic opportunities and better living conditions. This has led to rapid urbanisation, mostly unplanned, leading to strain on the existing resources and thus creating precarious living and working conditions.

Conflict and communal violence—Conflict and communal violence contribute to the psychological distress of society as a whole and further predispose already vulnerable individuals into worsened states of their illness.

Climate-Induced Displacement—In 2021 alone, nearly 5 million people were displaced in South Asia due to climate-related disasters, disrupting communities and increasing vulnerability to mental health issues (United Nations, 2022).

3.7 Governance and Systemic Challenges

Bureaucratic red tapes and siphoning of resources lead to ineffective implementation of programmes. Governance issues such as weak institutional framework, corruption and poor policy implementation hinder the delivery of mental health services.

An Indian survey revealed that 70% of individuals with mental health disorders do not seek help due to stigma, lack of awareness or inadequate access to care (Murthy, 2017).

These challenges also affect various other SDG targets related to poverty eradication (SDG 1), health (SDG 3), education (SDG 4), gender equality (SDG 5) and climate action (SDG 13).

To overcome these obstacles, a multi-pronged strategy that incorporates laws that promote equity, improve health care facilities, ensure access to marginalised communities and deal with the root causes of migration and violence is required. Also, community-based mental health initiatives and destigmatisation efforts need to be encouraged to help overcome the stigma. Although the challenges to every country are unique, Bangladesh, Sri Lanka, India and Pakistan have all taken several steps to improve mental health care through various programmes addressing the different challenges.

4 Country-Specific Scenario

4.1 SDGs: The India Story

India, the largest democracy in the world and the second most populous nation, has made great strides towards several SDGs despite several persistent developmental obstacles. Although there has been steady economic progress, a sizable portion of the population appears to be marginalised and subjected to poverty.

Despite several efforts for poverty alleviation, approximately 10% of the population still lives below the international poverty line of $2.15 per day (World Bank, 2024). 35.5% of children under five are stunted, and 19.3% are suffering from wasting (Parida et al., 2022). Non-communicable diseases, including mental health disorders, account for over 60% of India's disease burden, with suicide emerging as the leading cause of death among young adults aged 15–29 (Crime in India, 2023).

Literacy rate in India has reached 77.7% but there seems to be disparities among groups, with rural areas lagging. Female enrolment in higher education is alarmingly low at 27% (Ministry of Education, 2023).

Gender inequality is stark, with only 19% of women participating in the workforce and just 14% holding parliamentary seats (International Labour Organization, 2024). 11% of households in rural areas lack safe drinking water and only 87% of households consistently use sanitation facilities (Gurung et al., 2023). India has achieved universal electricity access, but it is mostly sourced from fossil fuels with renewable energy sources contributing just 30% of the energy mix (Dey et al., 2022).

Unemployment stands at 7.8%, with the informal sector dominating the labour market. While investments in innovation and infrastructure are growing, rural-urban disparities persist, and India ranks 40th globally in innovation (*Global Innovation Index 2024—GII 2024 Results*, 2024). Income inequality remains pronounced, with the top 10% of earners holding 57% of the national income, and states like Bihar and Uttar Pradesh lagging in human development indicators (*India: Extreme Inequality in Numbers | Oxfam International*, 2022). Urbanisation continues, with 35% of the population residing in cities, but challenges like inadequate housing persist for 13.9 million urban households (*India's Enduring Urban Housing Shortage: The Case for Upgrading Informal Settlements*, 2021).

India generates about 62 million tonnes of waste annually, and only 30% of this is processed, thus highlighting a significant lack in waste processing (International Trade Administration U.S. Department of Commerce, 2023). About 75% of the districts are affected by climate vulnerabilities (Mohanty, 2020). India ranks 19th among the world's largest contributors to marine plastic, thus endangering marine ecosystems (Sivadas et al., 2022). About 30% of India's land area is affected by deforestation or degradation, endangering biodiversity and agricultural productivity (Rashmi & Anand, 2024).

The National Crime rate in India is 39.2 per lakh population (*Crime in India*, 2023). India suffers from significant judicial backlogs. India ranks 85th on the corruption perception index, reflecting ongoing governance challenges (Transparency International, 2023).

Despite several challenges, India continues to demonstrate its commitment to global partnerships as evidenced to buy its G20 presidency in 2023 and initiatives like the International Solar Alliance. The next section sheds some light on similar ongoing initiatives.

4.2 *Ongoing Initiatives*

India has launched multiple programmes to address the critical areas of health, education, gender equality, poverty alleviation and environmental sustainability. Many of these programmes have started showing a significant effect on the various indicators. These initiatives collectively aim for holistic development and ensure physical as well as mental well-being. These initiatives as a whole underscore the government's commitment to a more inclusive and resilient society with a cascading effect on mental health.

Ayushman Bharat-Pradhan Mantri Jan Arogya Yojana (PM-JAY) has revolutionised healthcare access to millions of economically vulnerable families. Ayushman Bharat provides the beneficiaries a health insurance of 5,00,000 per annum, thus protecting the family from a lot of financial and emotional distress. Under its umbrella, it provides not only secondary and tertiary healthcare services but also mental health support through counselling and referrals for severe cases. By 2023, over 30,000 HWCs were operational, offering mental health interventions. This aligns with the SDGs of good health and well-being and reducing inequalities by ensuring equitable access to healthcare services (Garg et al., 2024; Sharma et al., 2024).

India introduced the National Mental Health Programme (NMHP) in 1982. This strengthened mental health infrastructure across the nation. The District Mental Health Programme provides mental health education, treatment and rehabilitation services reaching both urban and rural areas. By the year 2020, three NMHP services were integrated into 122 districts with an increased budget allocation of 500 crores. This programme reduces stigma by increasing awareness and access to mental health services, thus contributing significantly to the attainment of SDG-3 (Kirpekar et al., 2024).

India aims to target malnutrition among children, adolescent, and pregnant or lactating women through Poshan Abhiyan (National Nutrition Mission). Poor nutrition is linked to stunted growth, delayed developmental milestones, intellectual disability and several mental health challenges. Thus, countering malnutrition is pertinent for achieving SDG2 and SDG 3. This programme has reduced malnutrition by 2 to 3 per cent annually in several districts from 2020 to 2023, promoting holistic physical and mental well-being (Singh et al., 2023).

Gender equity is another critical area influencing mental health. The *Beti Bachao Beti Padhao* initiative, aimed at addressing gender discrimination and promoting girl child education, has shown promising results. By improving the female literacy rate to 70.3% in 2021 and enhancing the sex ratio at birth from 918 in 2014 to 934 in 2023, the programme contributes to SDG 5 (Gender Equality) and SDG 4 (Quality Education). It reduces gender-based violence and mental health stress among women, promoting psychological well-being and self-esteem.

The Mahatma Gandhi National Rural Employment Guarantee Act (MGNREGA) has been a cornerstone in poverty alleviation, guaranteeing 100 days of wage employment annually to rural households. By addressing financial insecurity, MGNREGA directly impacts mental health by alleviating stress and promoting dignity and self-worth among marginalised communities. With 6.36 crore households benefiting in FY 2022-23, this programme furthers SDG 1 (No Poverty) and SDG 8 (Decent Work and Economic Growth) (Kumari et al., 2024).

The National Education Policy, 2020 laid significant stress on holistic education and all-around development. It integrates mental health awareness and life skills in school curriculum. It also provides access to counsellors and psychologists for children who face difficulties, thus ensuring access to mental health to over 27.5 crore students covered under the school education system. This helps in inching closer to SDG 3 and SDG 4 by promoting well-being, resilience and prompt access to mental healthcare (Rani, 2024).

Access to clean water and sanitation is pertinent for optimal mental health as well as overall health indicators. *Swachh Bharat Mission* (SBM) and *Jal Jeevan Mission* (JJM) aim to achieve these objectives. By 2023, 12 crore households had received tap water connections under JJM (Ministry of Jal Shakti, 2024; Press Information Bureau, 2024). SBM has also positively impacted on overall health indicators of the country contributing to SDG 6 (Clean Water and Sanitation) and SDG 3 (Dandabathula et al., 2019; Singh et al., 2018). These two programmes have ensured an adequate supply of clean water and optimal sanitary conditions, leading to a reduction in psychological burden due to these scarcities, thus contributing to overall mental well-being.

India's agrarian economy and the well-being of its farmers are closely tied to mental health outcomes. The PM-Kisan Samman Nidhi, which provides direct financial support to farmers, has transferred over ₹2.2 lakh crores to more than 11 crore farmers between 2019 and 2023. This initiative alleviates economic stress, reducing anxiety and depression among farmers while promoting resilience. It supports SDG

1 (No Poverty) and SDG 2 (Zero Hunger) by ensuring a stable livelihood for agricultural communities.

Smart cities' mission has envisioned sustainable urban planning with mental health considerations. By creating green spaces, enhancing public transportation and ensuring community participation, the mission supports SDG 11 (Sustainable Cities and Communities). Better planning will lead to a reduction in traffic jams, walkable streets and access to recreational and social interaction, enhancing the quality of life of millions.

The application of information technology in the delivery of services has revolutionised accessibility. This initiative supports SDG 9 (Industry, Innovation and Infrastructure) by bridging the digital divide and enhancing access to healthcare services, including mental health care. The integration of telepsychiatry services into government programmes has further expanded the reach of mental health support.

As discussed earlier, climate change-induced disaster can exacerbate adversities for individuals thus predisposing to various psychiatric disorders. There is continued effort to ensure environmental sustainability through programmes like the National Action Plan on Climate Change (NAPCC). By focusing on renewable energy, water conservation and sustainable agriculture, NAPCC contributes to SDG 13 (Climate Action) and supports mental health indirectly by building community resilience and reducing climate-related stressors (Department Of Science & Technology, 2008).

Pradhan Mantri Ujjwala Yojana (PMUY) address household energy poverty by providing subsidised LPG connections to women from below-poverty-line families. Over 9 crore LPG connections were provided by 2023 under this programme. It has contributed to women's empowerment by improving their health and working condition getting rid of smoke due to firewood use. It has enhanced physical and mental health outcomes, thus contributing to SDG 5 and SDG 3 (Asharaf & Tol, 2024).

India's approach to skilling and employment, particularly through the Skill India Mission, supports mental health by enhancing economic opportunities and fostering self-reliance. By training over 1.25 crore youth annually in various trades and vocations, the initiative contributes to SDG 4 (Quality Education) and SDG 8, reducing unemployment-related stress and promoting mental well-being (Gholap, 2024).

Rashtriya Kishor Swasthya Karyakram (RKSK), focusing on adolescents, targets mental health, sexual and reproductive health, and nutrition. The programme integrates peer educators and community participation to address stigma and provide counselling services. Inculcating healthy behaviour lays the foundation for lifelong mental well-being, thus contributing to SDG 3.

Stand-Up India Scheme promotes entrepreneurship among Scheduled Castes, Scheduled Tribes and women. By supporting over 1 lakh new enterprises with financial and technical assistance by 2023, the initiative contributes to SDG 10 and SDG 5. It reduces socio-economic disparities and promotes self-confidence and mental health resilience among marginalised groups.

Additionally, the Integrated Child Development Services (ICDS) programme addresses early childhood development, focusing on nutrition, immunisation and pre-school education. With over 13.7 lakh Anganwadi centres operational by 2023, the ICDS contributes to SDG 2 and SDG 4, ensuring holistic physical and mental development in early childhood and reducing risks of mental health disorders later in life.

These initiatives collectively have catapulted India towards achieving the SDGs. While programmes like Ayushman Bharat and NMHP directly provide mental health services, others, such as Poshan Abhiyaan, Beti Bachao Beti Padhao and MGNREGA, address underlying factors influencing mental well-being. Despite the ongoing programmes, there remains a significant mental health burden. Therefore, more such programmes and better implementation of the programmes, ensuring greater reach and equitable sharing of benefits, are crucial for achieving the SDGs.

4.3 Pakistan: Striving for Holistic Development

Pakistan, with a population of over 240 million, faces significant challenges, including poverty, political instability and inadequate healthcare infrastructure. According to the Pakistan Economic Survey (2023), 21.9% of the population lives below the poverty line, and only 1% of GDP is allocated to healthcare. Mental health remains a neglected area, with only 0.4 psychiatrists per 100,000 people and limited awareness about mental health issues.

Sehat Sahulat Program (SSP) is aligned with SDG 3 (Good Health and Well-being), and it is a universal health coverage initiative providing free inpatient services to low-income families. The inclusion of psychiatric services under SSP is a step towards integrating mental health into primary healthcare. By 2023, the programme had enrolled over 8 million families, reducing financial stress and increasing access to mental healthcare (Hasan et al., 2022).

Pakistan's largest poverty alleviation initiative, Ehsaas, along with Kafalat (cash transfers) and Langar (free meals), addresses SDG 1 (No Poverty) and SDG 10 (Reduced Inequalities) (Dogar, 2023).

In 2021, Pakistan launched the National Mental Health Framework, aiming to integrate mental health services into existing healthcare systems. It was an initiative to promote awareness and address stigma. It included training programmes for healthcare providers and community outreach, aligning with SDG 3 and SDG 4 (Quality Education).

Clean Green Pakistan Movement improves urban and rural environments, mitigating stress linked to poor living conditions. Along with mental well-being promotion, it addresses SDG 6 (Clean Water and Sanitation) and SDG 13 (Climate Action), Vidya programmes mentioned that Pakistan seems to have made significant progress towards achieving the SDGs, but the pace of implementation seems to be slower. Implementation of programmes needs to be accelerated to meet the ever-changing challenges and promote mental well-being through the achievement of SDGs.

4.4 Bangladesh: Quest for Inclusive Growth

Bangladesh, with a population exceeding 170 million, is one of the most densely populated countries in the world. Despite commendable economic growth, poverty and environmental vulnerabilities persist. The prevalence of mental health disorders is high, with 16.8% of adults affected, according to a 2022 study by the National Institute of Mental Health (NIMH). The ratio of psychiatrists to the population remains critically low, at approximately 0.07 per 100,000 people (Arafat et al., 2024; Hasan et al., 2021).

Bangladesh implemented a national health policy in 2011 with the target of universal health coverage, including mental health services by 2023. Over 13,000 clinics were functioning as primary healthcare centres for rural populations. This initiative aims to achieve SDG 3.

Various social safety net programmes, such as vulnerable group feeding and employment generation for the poor, reduce economic hardship and ensure nutrition. By decreasing poverty and unemployment, these programmes indirectly improve mental health.

National strategy for adolescent health (2017–2030) addresses adolescent mental health through school-based counselling and awareness programmes. This programme aims to reduce stigma and ensure accessibility to mental health services.

The Mujeeb climate prosperity plan aligns with SDG13 (Climate Action). It aims to promote community resilience and sustainable livelihood in the face of challenges due to climate change. Under this programme, flood and cyclone shelters have been made, and a disaster management plan is in place. This preparedness helps in alleviating anxiety and trauma during the period of environmental crisis (Arfanuzzaman, 2024).

Bangladesh has made efforts to integrate mental health promotion in broader developmental initiatives. There is an urgent need to expand the existing health infrastructure and train more mental health professionals to meet the needs of its population.

4.5 Sri Lanka: Building a Resilient Healthcare System

Sri Lanka boasts impressive health indicators in comparison with its regional counterparts. However, the financial crisis of 2022 has pushed Sri Lanka into new set of challenges. These times of economic distress pose the threat to mental well-being of its citizens. Suicide rate in Sri Lanka is alarmingly high at 15 per lakh people (Bandara et al., 2024).

Sri Lanka launched national mental health policy in 2005 to integrate mental health services into primary health care. This programme aims to provide community-based mental health services and psychiatric units in district hospitals. By 2023, nearly 75% of the districts will have dedicated mental health units (Rajapakshe et al., 2023).

Sri Lanka plans to invest in education, employment and health care, under the Vision 2025 development framework, indirectly benefiting mental health. "Suraksha insurance scheme" provides free health insurance for school children including coverage for mental health services. It ensures early intervention and support for mental health needs of children (Kumar, 2019).

Sri Lanka, being an island nation, is vulnerable to natural disasters. The disaster preparedness programmes align with SDG 13 and include mental health components such as trauma counselling and community resilience building.

'Ekwa Gamna' (moving forward together), a gender equality programme, focuses on women's empowerment through education and employment opportunities. This programme also addresses gender-based violence and the economic dependence of females, thus alleviating the mental health of women.

Mental healthcare systems in Sri Lanka are robust, as evidenced by the mental health indicators in comparison with other countries of the region. However, recent economic crisis has put the healthcare system under stress. Ensuring adequate funding to mental health programmes and increasing community-based services will be critical in sustaining the growth towards achieving the SDGs.

South Asian countries share common challenges like limited funding, lack of mental health resources, stigma and socio-economic disparities. Each country in the region has devised its own strategy to achieve the SDGs and improve the mental health of its population. These programmes share commonalities like universal health coverage, health insurance, climate action plans, poverty alleviation programmes, nutrition programmes, etc. Increasing awareness, expanding mental health infrastructure and promoting regional collaboration for the exchange of ideas can further accelerate the process to achieve SDGs and improve mental health indices.

5 Future Directions and Recommendations

The inherent interdependence of various SDGs needs to be taken into account to develop integrated policies that address these goals. Programmes to address challenges in different sectors of health, education, social welfare and economic growth collectively culminate in the progress to achieve SDGs and tackling mental health challenges. Bhutan has integrated Gross National Happiness (GNH) into its developmental policies, putting forward an example of holistic strategies in action to achieve overall well-being (Tobgay et al., 2011).

The stigma associated with mental illnesses and their outcomes can be addressed by increasing awareness. Culturally sensitive awareness campaigns using mass media and social media platforms should be used to disseminate this information. Media reporting of mental illnesses and various outcomes, such as acts of suicide, should be done in a reasonable way.

Strengthening primary health care and capacity building can offer cost-effective and accessible solution. Training and sensitising the first caregivers about mental health disorders and their presentations can help in timely referral and adequate management of patients.

Developing speciality psychiatric services to provide care to the vulnerable groups, such as women, children elderly and marginalised communities, should be done. The ongoing refugee crisis and internal displacement of population due to multiple factors add to the challenge of ensuring mental well-being. Community outreach programmes can help in addressing this challenge. Awareness programmes for gender sensitisation can help in providing a comforting environment for sexual minorities.

The mental health impact of climate-related disasters in South Asia is profound, with a significant increase in anxiety, depression and PTSD cases. This region is particularly vulnerable to frequent cyclones, floods, droughts and earthquakes necessitating integration of mental health support into disaster management frameworks. Sri Lanka has incorporated psychosocial support into its disaster response protocols, providing a replicable model for other countries in the region.

Many of the programmes' outreach activities are limited by the financial constraints faced by the governments. Public-private partnership has the potential to overcome this barrier and scale mental health interventions to meet the needs of the large population in this area.

Systemic barriers such as economic disparity, rural-urban divide and unequal distribution of mental health resources pose a challenge to the efforts towards achieving SDGs.

Governments must prioritise mental health in national budgets, ensuring adequate funding for infrastructure, training and research. For instance, India's allocation to mental health was only 0.8% of its total health budget in 2023, far below the global average of 2%. Increasing this allocation is critical to addressing existing gaps. Additionally, innovative policy frameworks such as telepsychiatry programmes can bridge the urban-rural divide. During the COVID-19 pandemic, India's Tele-Mental Health Assistance and Networking Across States (Tele-MANAS) initiative demonstrated the potential of digital health solutions by providing remote consultations to thousands.

Integrating mental health within the broader SDG agenda can bring transformative change. Embedding provisions of providing mental health services in various programmes to achieve SDGs has been shown to bring change in mental well-being as well as various other indicators like educational performance, work output and better physical health.

Regional collaboration to share experiences and draw innovative policies jointly to address shared challenges can benefit all stakeholders. The SAARC Mental Health Strategy, though underutilised, offers a framework for such collaboration. Revitalising this strategy and aligning it with the SDG framework can enhance its impact.

6 Conclusion

Mental health is deeply intertwined with sustainable development. Mental health is itself a contributor to sustainable development as well as an outcome of sustainable development. By recognising this interdependence and inevitability of its effect, mental health should be integrated within the SDG agenda. Experience with various programmes in all countries of the regions provides an opportunity to share this with others and devise more robust frameworks.

References

Arafat, S. M. Y., Giasuddin, N. A., & Mazumder, A. H. (2024). Access to mental health care in Bangladesh—Current status, potential challenges, and ways out. In *Access to Mental Health Care in South Asia* (pp. 29–55). Springer Nature. https://doi.org/10.1007/978-981-99-9153-2_3

Arafat, S. M. Y., & Kar, S. K. (2024). Epidemiology of psychiatric disorders and overview of access to mental health care in South Asia. In *Access to Mental Health Care in South Asia* (pp. 1–15). Springer Nature. https://doi.org/10.1007/978-981-99-9153-2_1

Arfanuzzaman, M. (2024). Bangladesh's pathways to climate-resilient development: A methodical review. *World Development Sustainability, 4*, Article 100144. https://doi.org/10.1016/J.WDS.2024.100144

Asharaf, N., & Tol, R. S. J. (2024). The impact of Pradhan Mantri Ujjwala Yojana on Indian households. *Economic Analysis and Policy, 84*, 878–897. https://doi.org/10.1016/J.EAP.2024.09.026

Asia and the Pacific SDG progress report 2024 : showcasing transformative actions | ESCAP. (2024). https://unescap.org/kp/2024/asia-and-pacific-sdg-progress-report-2024?utm_source=chatgpt.com

Bandara, P., Wickrama, P., Sivayokan, S., Knipe, D., & Rajapakse, T. (2024). Reflections on the trends of suicide in Sri Lanka, 1997–2022: The need for continued vigilance. *PLOS Global Public Health, 4*(4), Article e0003054. https://doi.org/10.1371/journal.pgph.0003054

Dandabathula, G., Bhardwaj, P., Burra, M., Rao, PeddineniV. V. P., & Rao, S. (2019). Impact assessment of India's Swachh Bharat Mission—Clean India Campaign on acute diarrheal disease outbreaks: Yes, there is a positive change. *Journal of Family Medicine and Primary Care, 8*(3), 1202. https://doi.org/10.4103/JFMPC.JFMPC_144_19

Dey, S., Sreenivasulu, A., Veerendra, G. T. N., Rao, K. V., & Babu, P. S. S. A. (2022). Renewable energy present status and future potentials in India: An overview. *Innovation and Green Development, 1*(1), Article 100006. https://doi.org/10.1016/J.IGD.2022.100006

Dogar, A. H. (2023). Evaluating the effectiveness of social safety nets: A case study of Pakistan's Ehsaas program and poverty alleviation. *Journal of Development and Social Sciences, 4*(1), 760–770. https://doi.org/10.47205/JDSS.2023(4-I)68

Faizan, S., Raveesh, B., Ravindra, L., & Sharath, K. (2012). Pathways to psychiatric care in South India and their socio-demographic and attitudinal correlates. *BMC Proceedings, 6*(S4), P13. https://doi.org/10.1186/1753-6561-6-S4-P13

Garg, S., Bebarta, K. K., & Tripathi, N. (2024). The Ayushman Bharat Pradhan Mantri Jan Arogya Yojana (AB-PMJAY) after four years of implementation—Is it making an impact on quality of inpatient care and financial protection in India? *BMC Health Services Research, 24*(1), 1–10. https://doi.org/10.1186/S12913-024-11393-2/TABLES/7

Gholap, K. (2024). Role of skill india program in entrepreneurship development of India. *SSRN Electronic Journal*. https://doi.org/10.2139/SSRN.4702558

Global Innovation Index 2024 - GII 2024 results. (2024). https://www.wipo.int/web-publications/global-innovation-index-2024/en/gii-2024-results.html

Gurung, R., Tirkey, C., Takri, K. K., Diyali, N., Choubey, M., & Rai, R. (2023). Determinants of access to improved drinking water and sanitation in India: Evidence from India human development survey-II (IHDS). *Water Policy, 25*(10), 980–995. https://doi.org/10.2166/wp.2023.083

Hasan, M. T., Anwar, T., Christopher, E., Hossain, S., Hossain, M. M., Koly, K. N., Saif-Ur-Rahman, K. M., Ahmed, H. U., Arman, N., & Hossain, S. W. (2021). The current state of mental healthcare in Bangladesh: Part 1—An updated country profile. *Bjpsych International, 18*(4), 78. https://doi.org/10.1192/BJI.2021.41

Hasan, S. S., Mustafa, Z. U., Kow, C. S., & Merchant, H. A. (2022). "Sehat Sahulat program": A leap into the Universal Health coverage in Pakistan. *International Journal of Environmental Research and Public Health, 19*(12), 6998. https://doi.org/10.3390/IJERPH19126998

India: Extreme inequality in numbers | Oxfam International. (2022). https://www.oxfam.org/en/india-extreme-inequality-numbers

International Trade Administration U.S. Department of Commerce. (2023, July). *India solid waste management*. https://www.trade.gov/market-intelligence/india-solid-waste-management

India's Enduring Urban Housing Shortage: The Case for Upgrading Informal Settlements. (2021, November 21). https://www.orfonline.org/research/indias-enduring-urban-housing-shortage#_edn1

International Labour Organization. (2024). *The impact of care responsibilities on women's labour force participation*. https://www.ilo.org/sites/default/files/2024-10/GEDI-STAT%20brief_formatted_28.10.24_final.pdf

Kim, T. J., Vonneilich, N., Lüdecke, D., & von dem Knesebeck, O. (2017). Income, financial barriers to health care and public health expenditure: A multilevel analysis of 28 countries. *Social Science & Medicine (1982), 176*, 158–165. https://doi.org/10.1016/J.SOCSCIMED.2017.01.044

Kirpekar, V., Faye, A., Bhave, S., Gawande, S., & Tadke, R. (2024). District mental health program: Then and now. *Indian Journal of Psychiatry, 66*(7), 603–613. https://doi.org/10.4103/INDIANJPSYCHIATRY.INDIANJPSYCHIATRY_974_23

Kumar, R. (2019). Public-private partnerships for universal health coverage? The future of "free health" in Sri Lanka. *Globalization and Health, 15*(1), 1–10. https://doi.org/10.1186/S12992-019-0522-6/METRICS

Kumari, B. S., Kumar, N., Sha, S. N., Javad, K. P. A., Thamilmani, R., & Sivasubramanian, K. (2024). Economic impact of employment generation policies in India and rural poverty alleviation: An analytical review. *Studies in Systems, Decision and Control, 223*, 265–272. https://doi.org/10.1007/978-3-031-51997-0_22

Macroeconomic Policy and Financing for Development Division. (2017). *Economic and social survey of Asia and the Pacific : governance and fiscal management | ESCAP*. https://www.unescap.org/publications/economic-and-social-survey-asia-and-pacific-2017

Mohanty, A. (2020). *How can India Prepare for Extreme Climate Change & Weather Events?* https://www.ceew.in/publications/preparing-india-for-extreme-climate-change-events-and-weather-conditions

Ministry of Jal Shakti. (2024). *Government of India Ministry of Jal Shakti Department of Drinking Water & Sanitation Lok Sabha Starred Question No. 341*. https://ejalshakti.gov.in/jjmreport/JJMIndia.aspx

Ministry of Education, G. of I. (2023). *All-India Survey of Higher Education (AISHE), 2021–22*. https://cdnbbsr.s3waas.gov.in/s392049debbe566ca5782a3045cf300a3c/uploads/2024/02/20240719952688509.pdf

Murthy, R. S. (2017). National mental health survey of India 2015–2016. *Indian Journal of Psychiatry, 59*(1), 21. https://doi.org/10.4103/psychiatry.IndianJPsychiatry_102_17

Nunes, A. R., Lee, K., & O'Riordan, T. (2016). The importance of an integrating framework for achieving the sustainable development goals: The example of health and well-being. *BMJ Global Health, 1*(3). https://doi.org/10.1136/BMJGH-2016-000068

Parida, J., Samanta, L. J., Badamali, J., Singh, P. K., Patra, P. K., Mishra, B. K., Pati, S., Kaur, H., & Acharya, S. K. (2022). Prevalence and determinants of undernutrition among adolescents in India: A protocol for systematic review and meta-analysis. *PLoS ONE, 17*(1), Article e0263032. https://doi.org/10.1371/JOURNAL.PONE.0263032

Press Information Bureau. (2024, February 8). *Over 14.24 crore (73.93%) rural households now have tap water supply in their homes.* https://pib.gov.in/PressReleaseIframePage.aspx?PRID=2003912

Rajapakshe, O. B. W., Mohan, M., & Singh, S. P. (2023). Development of adolescent mental health services in Sri Lanka. *Bjpsych International, 20*(2), 41. https://doi.org/10.1192/BJI.2022.32

Rani, K. U. (2024). National education policy 2020: Emphasis on integration of mental health and education-A review. *National Education Policy, 50.*

Rashmi, R. R., & Anand, M. (2024). *Biodiversity and land restoration in India.* Department of Science & Technology. (2008). *Climate Change Programme | Department Of Science & Technology.* https://dst.gov.in/climate-change-programme Crime in India (December 1, 2023).

Sharma, D., Chauhan, A. S., Guinness, L., Mehndiratta, A., Dhiman, A., Singh, M., Prinja, S., Bharat, A., Mantri, P., & Yojana, J. A. (2024). Understanding the extent of economic evidence usage for informing policy decisions in the context of India's national health insurance scheme: Ayushman Bharat Pradhan Mantri Jan Aarogya Yojana (PM-JAY). *BMJ Global Health, 9*(6), Article e015079. https://doi.org/10.1136/BMJGH-2024-015079

Singh, A. V., Singh, D., & Barnet, Dr. I. (2023). Implementation and progress of a poshan abhiyaan for malnutrition among children of scheduled tribes in Panna District, Madhya Pradesh, India. *Journal of Namibian Studies : History Politics Culture, 35*, 1519–1531. https://doi.org/10.59670/JNS.V35I.3805

Singh, S. L., Kunwar, N., & Sharma, A. (2018). Impact of Swachh Bharat Abhiyan in Indian society. *International Journal of Home Science, 4*(1), 215. www.homesciencejournal.com

Sivadas, S. K., Mishra, P., Kaviarasan, T., Sambandam, M., Dhineka, K., Murthy, M. V. R., Nayak, S., Sivyer, D., & Hoehn, D. (2022). Litter and plastic monitoring in the Indian marine environment: A review of current research, policies, waste management, and a roadmap for multidisciplinary action. *Marine Pollution Bulletin, 176*, Article 113424. https://doi.org/10.1016/J.MARPOLBUL.2022.113424

Sustainable Development Report 2024. (2024). https://dashboards.sdgindex.org/chapters/executive-summary?utm_source=chatgpt.com

Transparency International. (2023). *India - Transparency.org.* https://www.transparency.org/en/countries/india

Tobgay, T., Dophu, U., Torres, C. E., & Na-Bangchang, K. (2011). Health and gross national happiness: Review of current status in Bhutan. *Journal of Multidisciplinary Healthcare, 4*, 293. https://doi.org/10.2147/JMDH.S21095

United Nations. (2022, June 17). *Nearly 5 million people in India internally displaced due to climate change, disasters in 2021: UN - The Hindu.* https://www.thehindu.com/news/national/nearly-5-million-people-in-india-internally-displaced-due-to-climate-change-disasters-in-2021-un/article65535820.ece

Vaishnav, M., Javed, A., Gupta, S., Kumar, V., Vaishnav, P., Kumar, A., Salih, H., Levounis, P., Bernardo, N., Alkhoori, S., Luguercho, C., Soghoyan, A., Moore, E., Lakra, V., Aigner, M., Wancata, J., Ismayilova, J., Islam, M., Da Silva, A., … Ashurov, Z. (2023). Stigma towards mental illness in Asian nations and low-and-middle-income countries, and comparison with high-income countries: A literature review and practice implications. *Indian Journal of Psychiatry, 65*(10), 995. https://doi.org/10.4103/INDIANJPSYCHIATRY.INDIANJPSYCHIATRY_667_23

Votruba, N., Thornicroft, G., & Group, the F. S. (2016). Sustainable development goals and mental health: Learnings from the contribution of the FundaMentalSDG global initiative. *Global Mental Health, 3*, e26. https://doi.org/10.1017/GMH.2016.20

World Health Organization. (2011). World report on disability. In *World Health Organization.*

World Bank. (2024). *The World Bank-poverty & inequality platform.* https://pip.worldbank.org/country-profiles/IND

Chapter 4
Poverty and Mental Health

Ali Davod Parsa, Ganesh Bushi, Muhammed Shabil, Leila Dehghani, and Russell Kabir

Abstract Poverty and economic inequality violate human dignity and undermine social and health goals. Health and ill-health are influenced not only by biological factors but also by a series of other upstream factors, such as social attainments that impact poverty. There is growing evidence that supports a link between poor mental health and the experience of poverty and deprivation, whether at the individual level or nationwide. The feature of poverty is more prominent in lower-middle-income nations, including South Asians. Eradicating poverty in all its forms is the top priority among the 17 SDGs. Concerning the SDGs progress in the South Asian region, this chapter has examined the relationship between poverty and mental health and broadly examined the factors contributing to the mental health. Looking into the multidimensional nature of poverty and ways it impacts mental health, inclusive policies and programs are needed to address poverty and maintain the population's mental health.

Keywords Poverty · Mental health · Sustainable development goals (SDGs) · United Nations · World Bank · Low-income countries (LICs) · Low middle-income countries (LMICs) and upper middle-income countries (UMICs)

A. D. Parsa (✉) · R. Kabir
School of Allied Health, Faculty of Health, Education, Medicine and Social Care, Anglia Ruskin University, Cambridge, UK
e-mail: ali.parsa@aru.ac.uk

G. Bushi · M. Shabil
Department of Pharmacy Practice, M. S. Ramaiah University of Applied Sciences, Bangalore, India

L. Dehghani
Cambridge University Hospitals (Addenbrookes Hospital), Cambridge, UK

S. K. Kar et al. (eds.), *Sustainable Development Goals and Mental Health in South Asia*, South Asian Perspectives in Mental Health and Psychology ,
https://doi.org/10.1007/978-981-95-2684-0_4

1 Introduction

Global poverty is a persistent feature of contemporary societies. The trend of growing poverty proved that from 2019 to 2023, an extra 29 million people fell into extreme poverty (World Bank, 2023). The feature of poverty is more prominent in low- and middle-income countries (LMICs), including South Asian countries. It is argued that gender disparity results in a higher working poverty rate among women than men, with the most obvious gender gap detected in the LMICs. Poverty and economic inequality violate human dignity and hinder social and health goals, including mental health.

Health and ill-health are influenced not only by biological factors but also by a series of other upstream factors, such as social attainments, that impact poverty. Extreme poverty is one of the strongest risk factors that has been scientifically proven as a risk factor for both physical and mental illness. The statistics have proven that poor mental health conditions such as anxiety disorder, depression, suicide, and parasuicide are associated with extreme poverty.

Concerning the Sustainable Development Goals (SDGs) progress in the South Asian region, this chapter has examined an in-depth review of the poverty concept and classifications. It also discusses the poverty challenge posed to all relevant SDGs. The impact of poverty on overall health and quality of life has been examined. The social aspect of poverty (including childhood adversity) as one of the contributing factors to mental health has been reviewed. The current chapter has explored the country-specific indicators of SDGs performance on Goals 1, 2, and 3 linked to the mental health outcomes. The challenges that South Asian nations need to overcome in achieving SDGs 1, 2, and 3 are discussed. Then, the South Asian Nations' Poverty Eradication Policies were scrutinized. Finally, the chapter recommends its key message and concludes the discussion presented around the subject area.

2 Broad Examination of Poverty Classifications

Poverty is a multidimensional pattern, and a deep understanding of these domains remains essential for any poverty reduction strategy (United Nations, 2010). The Joseph Rowntree Foundation defines poverty as "When a person's resources (mainly their material resources) are not sufficient to meet their minimum needs (including social participation)" (Goulden & D'Arcy, 2014). Needs include material and non-material resources (e.g., affection, social participation, and leisure) in any society. Poverty is regarded as a violation of human dignity.

Ravallion (1992a, 1992b) refers to poverty as being unable to provide minimum needs that include basic goods and services as well as social engagement, which are considered the norm of the chosen community (Ravallion, 1992a, 1992b). As the costs of needs change over time, the poverty index will inevitably change as well.

2.1 *Types of Poverty*

Poverty can be seen as absolute or relative (relative deprivation) (Gweshengwe & Hassan, 2020). The UN defined absolute poverty as "a condition characterised by severe deprivation of basic human needs, including food, safe drinking water, sanitation facilities, health, shelter, education and information. It depends not only on income but also on access to services" (UN, 1995, p. 57).

Individuals in poverty are typically categorized as "very poor", "poor", and "near poor or vulnerable" (Alkire et al., 2014; Gweshengwe & Hassan, 2020). Some sources use a threshold to measure absolute category according to the cost of necessities like food, shelter, clothing, education, and healthcare, where an individual can afford it or not. However, more complex factors such as the income inequality index, income percentile vs distribution, and subjective measure are considered in defining the relative poverty in a selected society. According to the description by FPH, different categories of poverty are inclusive of the ability to access and afford essential goods for healthy living, by location, and by generation (Fig. 1).

Other sources classify poverty into primary and secondary. The primary type refers to situations where insufficient funds exist to meet basic needs, and individuals live below the poverty line. In contrast, the secondary type refers to a status where people's earnings just meet the basic needs, but due to other outstanding concerns, they are not used to overcome these needs fully. The poverty status is impacted by the rise and fall

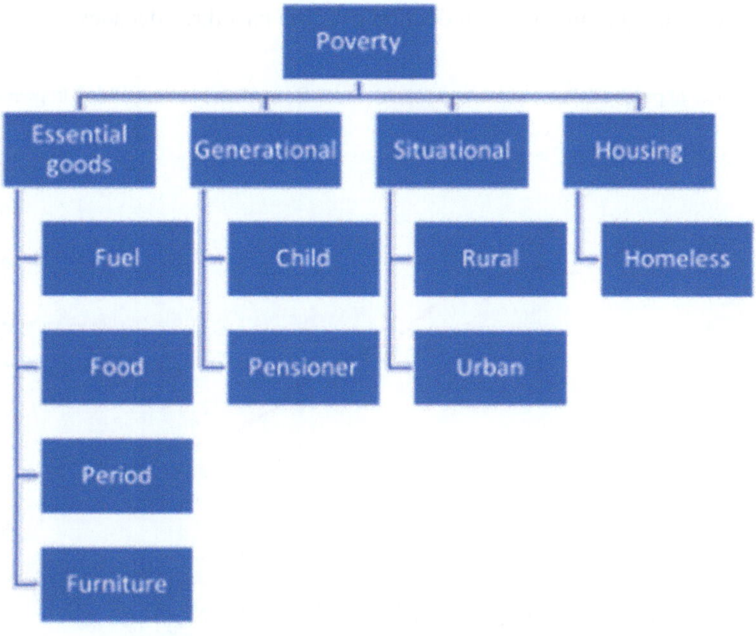

Fig. 1 Different types of poverty. *Source* Faculty of public health (FPH)

of resources as well as the flexibility. It is essential to recognize that poverty is not a static condition, and its status is influenced by fluctuations in resources, as well as the adaptability of needs and individuals' ability to meet them (Goulden & D'Arcy, 2014). It is obvious that any effective measure to reduce both types is influenced by several factors, more commonly economic factors, social and demographic factors, government policies, and global factors (e.g., globalization, international aid).

According to the Joseph Rowntree Foundation (JRF), the poverty definition should not be extended too far, which puts the strategies to tackle poverty at risk by diluting it into wellbeing only or switching into mental health or drug issues. Instead, it must be established at the materials level and basic standards (Goulden & D'Arcy, 2014). According to FPH (2025), the definition of poverty is linked to measures used and the population across time and place that is considered (Faculty of Public Health, 2025). The most common measures are linked to the income that directly impacts health and well-being (e.g., costs of basic goods). Compared with 35 years ago, when an estimated two billion(i.e. 38% of the world population) were living under the poverty line, poverty has been reduced, particularly from 2000 to 2015 (MDGs era). According to the World Bank, this figure was at 660 million (i.e., 8.5% of the world population). Reduction trend is affected by unforeseen factors such as public health crisis (e.g., pandemic), inflation, recession, regional conflicts, and climate change (World Bank, 2022a, 2022b). The recent pandemic has deteriorated the figure increased to 733 million in 2020.

According to the World Bank (2022a, 2022b) records, globally, there has been a significant decline in poverty over the last three decades (Fig. 2); however, the progress was unequal in poverty reduction over the past three decades.

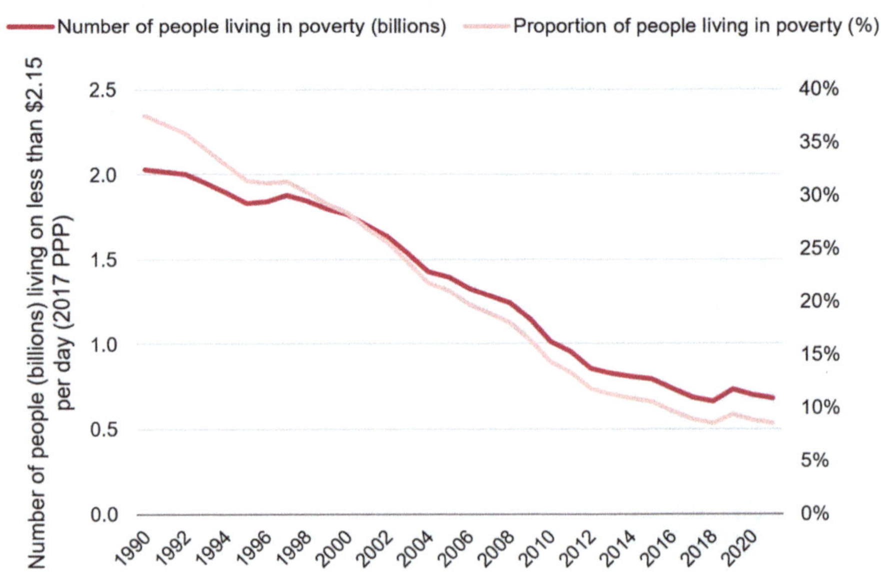

Fig. 2 Global trend of poverty (1990–2020). *Source* Development Initiatives

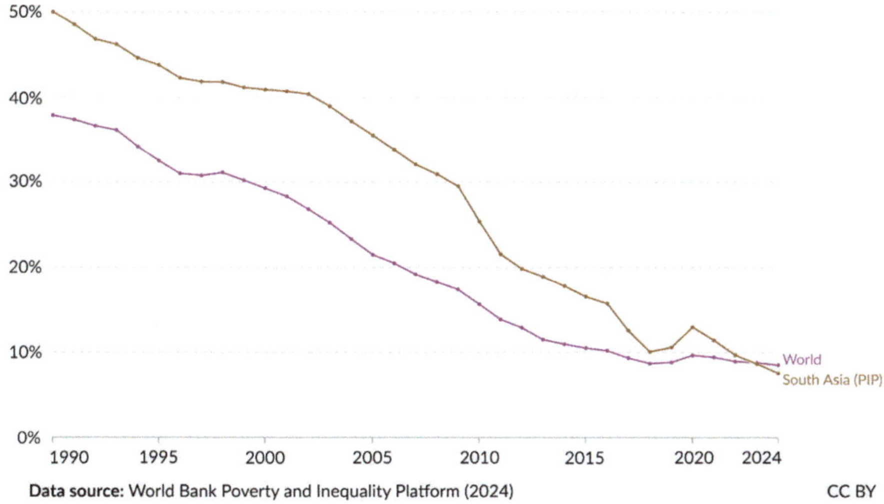

Fig. 3 Share of population living in extreme poverty (1990–2024). *Data sources* World Bank (2024)

There is projected evidence of the link between poverty and different mental health conditions, such as suicide and parasuicide (Congdon, 1996; Gunnell et al., 1995). One of the SDGs[1] milestones aimed at ending extreme poverty worldwide by 2030 (World Bank, 2022a, 2022b). The World Bank exercises the international poverty line as a metric to determine severe poverty, which is currently at $2.15 per day (2017 PPP) globally.

Meanwhile, at the national level, the poverty line is influenced by local factors such as cost of living, which makes it considerably vary by nation. The report highlighted that in 2022, about 9% of the global population faced undernourishment. This was reasonably higher in some South Asian countries (Figs. 3, 4), such as India (14%), Afghanistan (30%), Bangladesh (12%), and Pakistan (21%) (World Bank, 2025).

While the WB has considered the $2.15 line as a classic margin of national poverty lines for low-income countries (LICs), the thresholds for LMICs and UMICs are set at $3.65 and $6.85, respectively. Additionally, countries introduced their own national poverty line that corresponds to their national average income (Christensen, 2024).

According to the UN report (UNDP and OPHI, 2019), approximately 1.3 billion people across 101 countries struggle with poverty. According to the latest figure published in 2023, about 1.1 billion people from 110 countries out of 6.1 a global population were facing poverty. Relative proportion of the poor population shows that 50% (i.e., 534 million) live in sub-Saharan Africa, whereas this figure for the South Asian population stands at one-third of global poverty (i.e., 389 million). It is estimated that one-third live in the LICs and two-thirds are sourced from middle-income countries (UNDP and OPHI, 2023).

[1] Millennium Development Goals (MDGs).

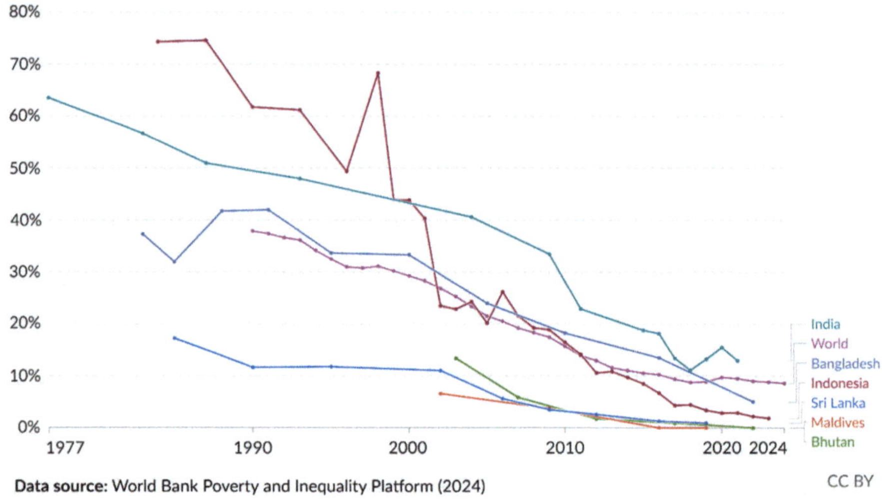

Fig. 4 Share of South Asian countries' population living in extreme poverty (1977–2024). *Data sources* World Bank (2024)

Although the recent figures indicate a decline, the 2030 milestone outlined in the SDGs for the eradication of all forms of poverty requires an explicit interpretation of the influence of the attributes of poverty as well as an efficient poverty analysis (Gweshengwe & Hassan, 2020). Therefore, attention to the different, interlinking dimensions of poverty (Fig. 5) that include financial, economic, social, political, health, environmental, and seasonal is inevitable (Gweshengwe & Hassan, 2020).

3 Poverty: A Challenge for All SDGs

Poverty, in its various dimensions, poses a significant challenge to achieving the SDGs and has profound consequences for overall health and quality of life. The SDGs, adopted by the United Nations in 2015, represent a global commitment to addressing a wide range of interconnected challenges, including poverty, hunger, inequality, and environmental degradation (Marmot & Bell, 2017). While each SDG addresses a specific area of concern, poverty acts as a cross-cutting impediment, hindering progress across multiple goals. The eradication of poverty in all its forms is explicitly recognized as the top priority among the 17 SDGs (Yu & Huang, 2021). Poverty's impact extends beyond mere economic deprivation, affecting health, education, and access to essential services. The interconnectedness of the SDGs means that progress in one area can be dependent on progress in others. Liu et al. argue that poverty reduction and sustainable development are inseparable (Liu et al., 2015).

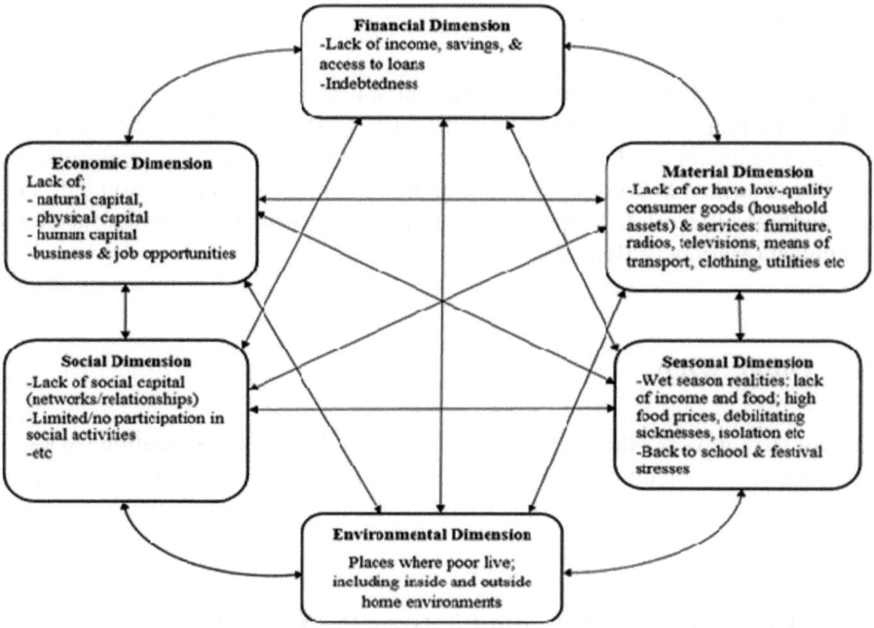

Fig. 5 Multiple dimensions of poverty. *Source* Gweshengwe (2020)

3.1 *Health and Well-Being (SDG 3)*

Poverty directly undermines the achievement of SDG 3, which aims to ensure healthy lives and promote well-being for all at all ages (Marmot & Bell, 2017). Individuals living in poverty often face significant barriers to accessing healthcare, including financial constraints, lack of transportation, and limited availability of services (Park, 2002). These barriers can lead to delayed or forgone medical care, resulting in poorer health outcomes and reduced life expectancy.

3.2 *Food Security and Nutrition (SDG 2)*

SDG 2 seeks to end hunger, achieve food security, improve nutrition, and promote sustainable agriculture (Marmot & Bell, 2017). Poverty is a major driver of food insecurity, limiting individuals' ability to afford nutritious food (Charlton, 2016). This can lead to undernutrition, micronutrient deficiencies, and other health problems, particularly among children (Park, 2002).

3.3 Education (SDG 4)

SDG 4 focuses on ensuring inclusive and equitable quality education and promoting lifelong learning opportunities for all (Marmot & Bell, 2017). Poverty can limit access to education, as families may struggle to afford school fees, uniforms, and supplies (Lancker & Parolin, 2020). Children from low-income households may also be forced to work to support their families, further hindering their educational attainment (Marmot & Bell, 2017).

3.4 Other SDGs

Poverty also impacts other SDGs, including Clean Water and Sanitation (SDG 6): Low-income communities often lack access to safe drinking water and sanitation facilities, increasing the risk of waterborne diseases (Marmot & Bell, 2017).

3.5 Decent Work and Economic Growth (SDG 8)

Poverty limits opportunities for decent work and economic advancement, perpetuating the cycle of poverty (Timmis et al., 2017).

3.6 Reduced Inequalities (SDG 10)

Poverty exacerbates inequalities within and among countries, hindering social and economic progress (Adeleye et al., 2020).

4 Poverty Impacts on Overall Health and Quality of Life

The effects of poverty on health and quality of life are multifaceted and far-reaching. Poverty affects various dimensions of family life, including health, productivity, the physical environment, emotional well-being, and family interaction (Park, 2002).

Increased risk of chronic diseases: Poverty is associated with a higher risk of developing chronic diseases such as cardiovascular disease, diabetes, and respiratory illnesses (Allen et al., 2017). This is due to factors such as poor nutrition, exposure to environmental hazards, and limited access to healthcare (Mensah et al., 2005).

4.1 *Higher Rates of Infectious Diseases*

Overcrowded living conditions, lack of sanitation, and limited access to healthcare increase the risk of infectious diseases such as tuberculosis and HIV/AIDS (Carter et al., 2018).

4.2 *Mental Health Problems*

Poverty is a significant stressor that can lead to mental health problems such as depression, anxiety, and substance abuse (Hodgkinson et al., 2016).

4.3 *Maternal and Child Health*

Poverty negatively impacts maternal and child health, leading to higher rates of maternal mortality, infant mortality, and childhood illnesses (Tessema et al., 2017).

4.4 *Reduced Life Expectancy*

People living in poverty tend to have shorter life expectancies than those with higher incomes (Boozary & Shojania, 2018).

5 How Poverty Impacts Overall Health and Quality of Life?

5.1 *Limited Opportunities for Education and Employment*

Poverty restricts access to quality education and decent employment, limiting individuals' potential and perpetuating the cycle of poverty (Marmot & Bell, 2017).

5.2 *Inadequate Housing*

Low-income individuals often live in substandard housing with poor ventilation, overcrowding, and exposure to environmental hazards, negatively impacting their health and well-being (Zainal et al., 2012).

5.3 Food Insecurity

Poverty leads to food insecurity and malnutrition, affecting physical and mental development, particularly in children (Charlton, 2016).

5.4 Social Isolation

Poverty can lead to social isolation and exclusion, reducing access to social support networks and community resources (Stolz et al., 2017).

5.5 Increased Stress and Decreased Emotional Well-Being

The daily challenges of living in poverty, such as financial strain, job insecurity, and lack of access to necessities, can lead to chronic stress and decreased emotional well-being (Evans & Kim, 2013).

5.6 Energy Poverty

The inability to afford adequate energy services can significantly affect quality of life and health (Maxim et al., 2016). Thomson et al. found that energy poverty is associated with poorer physical and mental health across 32 European countries (Thomson et al., 2017). Shupler et al. found that multiple aspects of energy poverty are associated with lower mental health-related quality of life in three peri-urban African communities (Shupler et al., 2022).

Poverty has a significant impact on the quality of life in families of children with disabilities, affecting health, productivity, physical environment, emotional well-being, and family interaction (Park, 2002). Stolz et al. found that poverty is associated with adverse health outcomes among older adults, with material and psychosocial factors playing a significant role (Stolz et al., 2017). Ghasemi et al. found that subjective perception of family socioeconomic status can explain differences in health-related quality of life of low-income people in informal settlements (Ghasemi et al., 2019). Migrants, asylum seekers, and refugees often experience food insecurity upon arrival in a new country, exacerbated by delays in receiving benefits and other factors (Charlton, 2016). Michel et al. define period poverty as a lack of access to menstrual products, hygiene facilities, waste management, and education, which affects many women globally, causing physical, mental, and emotional challenges (Michel et al., 2022).

Poverty is a pervasive challenge that undermines progress across all SDGs and has profound consequences for overall health and quality of life. Addressing poverty requires a multifaceted approach that includes economic growth, social protection programs, investments in education and healthcare, and efforts to reduce inequalities. By prioritizing poverty reduction and promoting health equity, we can create a more just and sustainable world for all.

6 Poverty as One of the Social Causes of Mental Illness

6.1 Childhood Adversity and Its Role in Mental Health

Childhood adversity plays a significant and multifaceted role in shaping mental health outcomes throughout the lifespan (Rohner et al., 2023). Adverse childhood experiences (ACEs), including poverty, abuse, neglect, family conflict, and household dysfunction, initiate a cascade of psychological, cognitive, and physiological responses that increase susceptibility to mental health disorders (Xiang et al., 2022). Research consistently demonstrates that early-life adversity is closely linked to chronic stress, which disrupts neural development and impairs cognitive functions, such as working memory and vocabulary (Girotti et al., 2024). Notably, mental health difficulties mediate up to 70% of these cognitive deficits during adolescence (Nweze et al., 2023).

More than two-thirds of children experience at least one traumatic event by age 16, and such exposures are strongly associated with elevated risks of depression, anxiety, post-traumatic stress disorder (PTSD), substance abuse, and personality disorders in adulthood (Xiao et al., 2021). The relationship between adversity and mental health is bidirectional: trauma exacerbates emotional dysregulation and social isolation, while pre-existing mental health conditions increase vulnerability to additional adversity. Studies that control for genetic and environmental factors indicate that ACEs—especially sexual abuse or multiple forms of adversity—remain significantly associated with adult psychiatric disorders. These associations persist even after adjusting for familial confounding, highlighting the enduring impact of childhood trauma (Park et al., 2020).

Moreover, the effects of childhood adversity often extend intergenerationally, as maternal childhood trauma can affect offspring mental health through both epigenetic and psychosocial mechanisms. Early interventions targeting mental health in children exposed to adversity are critical, as they can mitigate long-term cognitive and emotional consequences (Roubinov et al., 2022).

6.2 Impact of Poverty on Psychological Well-Being

Poverty profoundly impacts psychological well-being, creating a cycle of distress that affects individuals, families, and communities. Living in poverty exposes individuals to chronic stressors such as financial insecurity, inadequate housing, food scarcity, and limited access to healthcare (Kim et al., 2016). These stressors activate the hypothalamic–pituitary–adrenal (HPA) axis, leading to prolonged stress responses that impair emotional regulation and increase vulnerability to mental health disorders. Additionally, the stigma associated with poverty—both perceived and experienced—can lead to feelings of shame, low self-esteem, and social isolation, further exacerbating mental health challenges (Santiago et al., 2011). Poverty also limits access to mental healthcare and support systems, leaving many individuals without the resources needed to address their psychological struggles. The impact of poverty on children is particularly severe; childhood poverty is linked to cognitive deficits, developmental delays, and higher risks of lifelong mental health issues due to exposure to adversity during critical developmental periods (Hodgkinson et al., 2017). Furthermore, neighborhood deprivation often compounds these effects, as individuals in impoverished areas face higher levels of crime, environmental hazards, and social instability—all of which contribute to psychological distress (Lever et al., 2005). Addressing the psychological toll of poverty requires not only economic interventions but also policies aimed at reducing stigma, improving access to mental health services, and fostering supportive community environments.

6.3 Long-Term Mental Health Effects of Poverty in Early Childhood

The long-term mental health effects of poverty in early childhood are deeply concerning, as they shape an individual's psychological and emotional well-being far into adulthood (Girotti et al., 2024). Children who grow up in poverty are exposed to chronic stressors such as financial instability, food insecurity, substandard housing, and unsafe neighborhoods, all of which can disrupt healthy brain development (Pryor et al., 2019). This prolonged exposure to adversity often leads to toxic stress, which alters the functioning of the HPA axis and increases levels of stress hormones like cortisol. These biological changes impair cognitive functions such as memory, attention, and decision-making, while also heightening vulnerability to mental health disorders like depression, anxiety, and PTSD later in life (Evans & De France, 2022).

Research shows that children from low-income households are more likely to experience behavioral problems and reduced academic performance due to deficits in cognitive control and emotional regulation. These issues are compounded by feelings of helplessness and social exclusion, which further erode self-esteem and resilience (Raver, 2012).

The effects of childhood poverty are not limited to individual outcomes but often perpetuate intergenerational cycles of disadvantage. Parents experiencing financial hardship may struggle with stress and depression themselves, leading to inconsistent parenting practices or reduced emotional support for their children. This lack of nurturing environments exacerbates developmental delays and mental health challenges. Furthermore, children growing up in poverty-stricken neighborhoods face additional risks from environmental factors such as exposure to crime or inadequate educational opportunities, which limit their ability to break free from the cycle of poverty (Kirkbride et al., 2024) (Fig. 6).

7 Country-Specific Indicators of SDGs 1, 2, and 3 Performances Are Linked to the Mental Health Outcomes

7.1 SDGs 1 (No Poverty)

In South Asia, achieving SDGs 1 (No Poverty), 2 (Zero Hunger), and 3 (Good Health and Well-Being) is critical for improving mental health outcomes, particularly in lower-middle-income countries (Table 1). Poverty remains a major determinant of mental health, with millions living below the international poverty line (Iemmi, 2019). Economic insecurity, social exclusion, and limited access to healthcare exacerbate conditions like depression, anxiety, and PTSD, particularly in countries like India, Bangladesh, Nepal, and Pakistan (Hossain et al., 2020). Despite progress in reducing poverty, these countries continue to face high levels of inequality, with mental health services underfunded and inaccessible for many, especially in rural areas (Koly et al., 2021; Mazumder et al., 2023).

7.2 SDG 2 (Zero Hunger)

It is also closely linked to mental health, as food insecurity and malnutrition contribute to psychological distress and developmental impairments. In South Asia, despite improvements, high rates of stunting, wasting, and micronutrient deficiencies persist, particularly among children (Maynard et al., 2018). Malnutrition during critical developmental periods can lead to cognitive delays, emotional dysregulation, and increased risks of anxiety and depression later in life (Weaver & Hadley, 2009). Additionally, the chronic stress of food insecurity, often compounded by gender disparities in resource distribution, creates a cycle that negatively impacts maternal and child mental health. Targeted nutrition programs like India's ICDS and Bangladesh's NNS aim to address these challenges, but gaps in implementation and insufficient funding hinder their effectiveness (Bhutta et al., 2017; Ejiohuo et al., 2024)(Table 1).

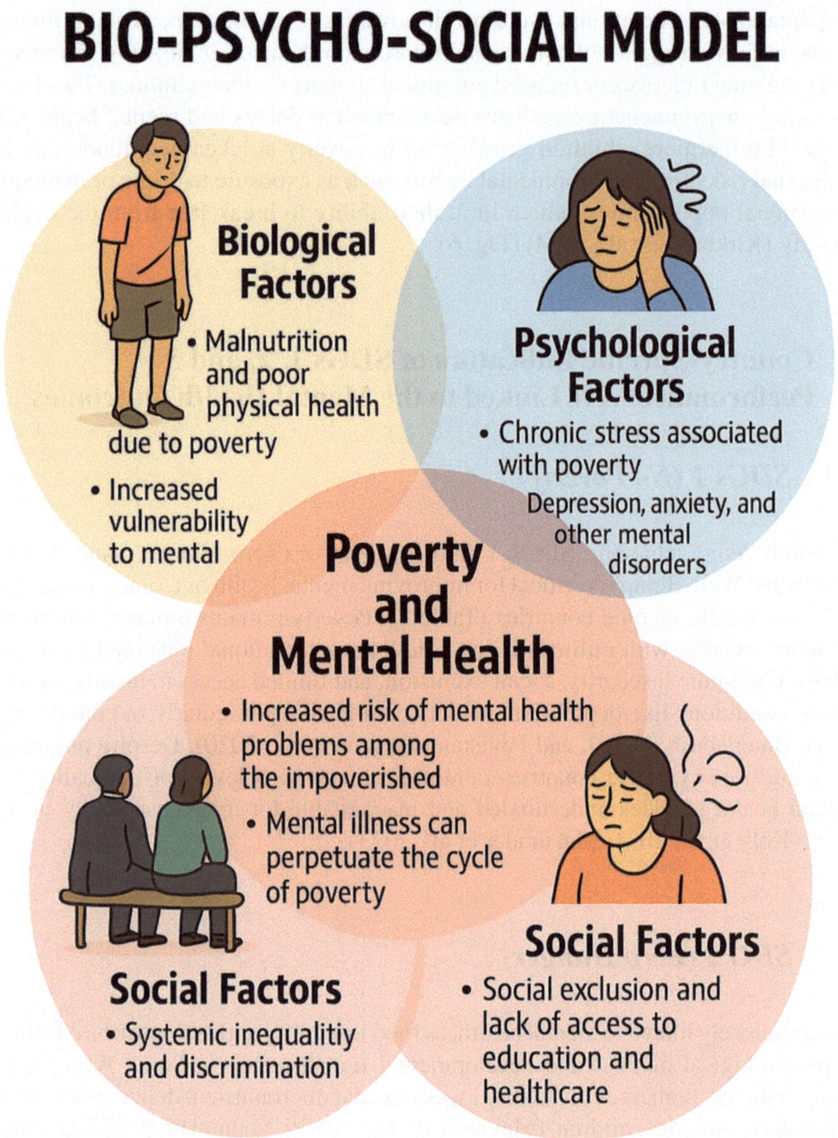

Fig. 6 Bio-psycho-social model showing the associated factors between poverty and mental health

Table 1 Country-specific indicators of SDGs

Country	SDG 1: no poverty	SDG 2: zero hunger	SDG 3: good health and well-being	Mental health linkage	Implications
Afghanistan	High poverty levels; over 28% of the population faces acute food insecurity	Severe malnutrition: 41% of children under five are stunted	Suicide mortality rate data are limited; mental health services are scarce	Conflict, poverty, and food insecurity exacerbate mental health issues; limited access to care	Urgent need for integrated food security and mental health programs; international aid and policy reforms are critical
Bangladesh	Multidimensional poverty reduced (17% in 2023)	Malnutrition prevalence (20% underweight children)	Suicide mortality rate (7 per 100,000); limited mental health coverage	Poverty-related stress impacts mental health; food insecurity worsens cognitive development	Expand nutrition programs; integrate mental health into primary healthcare systems
Bhutan	The poverty headcount ratio at $2.15 per day is low; however, multidimensional poverty affects certain regions	Stunting in children under five is 21.2%; wasting is 9.1%	Suicide mortality rate is approximately 12 per 100,000 population	Economic stress and youth unemployment contribute to mental health challenges	Expand mental health services; address youth unemployment; integrate mental health into primary healthcare
India	Reduction in poverty rate from 21.9% (2011) to 10% (2023); SDG India index tracks multidimensional poverty	The prevalence of undernourishment has been reduced (12% in 2023)	Suicide mortality rate remains high (12 per 100,000); UHC improvements ongoing	Poverty and hunger exacerbate stress and depression; inadequate UHC limits access to mental health services	Strengthen UHC to include mental health services; implement community-based poverty alleviation programs
Maldives	Poverty headcount ratio at $2.15/day is 0.1%; national poverty rate was 5.4% in 2019	Stunting in children under five is 17.4%; wasting is 9.5%	Suicide mortality rate data are limited; mental health services are developing	Rapid urbanization and climate change-related stressors impact mental well-being	Strengthen mental health infrastructure; implement climate-resilient health strategies; promote social support systems

(continued)

Table 1 (continued)

Country	SDG 1: no poverty	SDG 2: zero hunger	SDG 3: good health and well-being	Mental health linkage	Implications
Nepal	Poverty rate reduced (16% in 2023)	Malnutrition remains a challenge (25% stunting in children under five)	Suicide mortality rate (8 per 100,000); mental health services are scarce	Social stigma around poverty worsens mental health outcomes	Develop targeted interventions to reduce stigma; improve access to mental health services in rural areas
Pakistan	Poverty rate remains high (24%)	Food insecurity affects 38%; malnutrition prevalent	Suicide mortality rate (9 per 100,000); limited UHC coverage	Hunger and poverty exacerbate anxiety and depression; lack of healthcare access worsens outcomes	Expand UHC coverage with a focus on mental health; strengthen food security programs
Sri Lanka	National poverty rate reduced (4.1%); multidimensional poverty affects 14%	Food security improved; undernourishment at 8%	Suicide mortality rate (14 per 100,000); mental health policies improving	Economic inequality drives stress; suicide rates remain a concern	Address economic inequality through social protection schemes; enhance suicide prevention strategies

7.3 SDG 3 (Good Health and Well-Being)

It highlights the need for comprehensive healthcare systems, including mental health services, which are essential in lower-middle-income South Asian nations (Stenberg et al., 2017). Suicide rates, a key indicator of mental health, are high, particularly in rural areas where poverty, economic hardship, and a lack of mental health support converge (Mazumder et al., 2023). The COVID-19 pandemic further exacerbated these issues, amplifying stress, anxiety, and depression across vulnerable populations (Varma et al., 2021). To achieve SDG 3, South Asian countries should consider integrating mental healthcare into primary healthcare systems, expanding community-based interventions, and addressing the systemic barriers to accessing care. Strengthening health systems and promoting social protection strategies are essential to mitigating the mental health consequences of poverty and ensuring equitable access to care for all (Thara & Padmavati, 2013) (Table 1).

8 South Asian Nations' Challenges in Achieving SDG 1, SDG 2, and SDG 3

8.1 Socioeconomic Inequality and Mental Health in South Asia

Socioeconomic inequality is a pervasive issue in South Asia, significantly influencing mental health outcomes across the region. The interplay between poverty, social exclusion, and limited access to healthcare creates a vicious cycle that exacerbates mental health challenges for millions. South Asia is home to approximately 1.8 billion people, with a substantial portion living below the poverty line (Mishra, 2002). Countries such as India, Pakistan, Bangladesh, and Nepal face high levels of income inequality and widespread poverty, which are key drivers of psychological distress. Poverty leads to chronic stress due to financial insecurity, inadequate housing, and food scarcity, while social disparities further isolate marginalized groups, compounding their vulnerability to mental health disorders (Rahman, 2024).

The region's mental health infrastructure is severely underdeveloped, with less than 1% of national health budgets allocated to mental health in most South Asian countries (Kuruvilla & Jacob, 2015). This lack of funding results in a shortage of trained professionals; for instance, there is only one psychiatrist per 100,000 people in nine out of eleven South Asian countries. The scarcity of resources disproportionately affects impoverished populations who already face barriers such as stigma and limited awareness about mental health (Shidhaye et al., 2015). Additionally, systemic inequalities restrict access to education and employment opportunities for disadvantaged groups, perpetuating cycles of poverty that worsen mental health outcomes (Mazumder et al., 2023).

Cultural factors also play a significant role in shaping mental health disparities in South Asia. Mental illness is highly stigmatized in many communities, leading individuals to suffer in silence rather than seeking help. Collectivist values often prioritize family reputation over individual well-being, discouraging open discussions about psychological struggles (Karasz et al., 2019). Furthermore, gender disparities exacerbate the issue; women are more likely to experience poverty and face greater barriers to accessing mental health services due to societal norms and discrimination (Prajapati & Liebling, 2022).

The COVID-19 pandemic highlighted the intersection between socioeconomic inequality and mental health in South Asia. Economic disruptions caused by lockdowns led to increased unemployment and financial strain, significantly worsening mental health outcomes across the region (Varma et al., 2021). Studies reported spikes in depression and anxiety during this period, particularly among low-income groups who lacked access to social safety nets (Gibson et al., 2021).

Addressing socioeconomic inequality requires a multifaceted approach that integrates poverty alleviation programs with mental health interventions. Governments must increase investments in healthcare infrastructure while implementing policies that reduce income inequality and improve access to education and employment opportunities. Community-based mental health programs can help bridge the treatment gap by decentralizing care delivery and involving non-specialist personnel trained to provide basic support. Moreover, public awareness campaigns aimed at reducing stigma can encourage individuals to seek help without fear of judgment. By addressing socioeconomic disparities alongside mental health challenges, South Asian nations can make significant strides toward achieving SDGs 1 (No Poverty), 2 (Zero Hunger), and 3 (Good Health and Well-Being).

8.2 *Barriers to Achieving SDGs in South Asian Countries*

South Asian nations face numerous barriers in achieving the Sustainable Development Goals (SDGs), particularly SDG 1 (No Poverty), SDG 2 (Zero Hunger), and SDG 3 (Good Health and Well-Being). The region is home to more than one-third of the global poor, with countries like India, Bangladesh, and Nepal reporting high poverty headcounts (Hameed et al., 2021). Persistent poverty is driven by systemic issues such as income inequality, unemployment, and lack of social safety nets. Despite economic growth in the region, wealth distribution remains uneven, with rural populations and marginalized communities disproportionately affected. Political instability in countries like Pakistan and Afghanistan further exacerbates poverty by disrupting development programs and public service delivery (Onyeaka et al., 2024).

Food insecurity is another critical barrier to achieving SDG 2. South Asia has some of the highest rates of malnutrition globally, with widespread stunting, wasting, and micronutrient deficiencies among children. Factors such as inadequate agricultural productivity, climate change, and inefficient food distribution systems contribute to this crisis. Rural areas are particularly vulnerable due to limited access to markets and modern farming techniques. Women and children bear the brunt of food insecurity, with gender-based disparities in resource allocation within households worsening nutritional outcomes (Goal 2: End Hunger, Achieve Food Security and Improved Nutrition and Promote Sustainable Agriculture—SDG Indicators, 2016).

Healthcare challenges significantly hinder progress toward SDG 3. South Asia spends less than 4% of its GDP on health, far below the global average (Stenberg et al., 2017). This underinvestment results in inadequate healthcare infrastructure, a shortage of trained professionals, and limited access to essential services. Mental healthcare is particularly neglected, with stigma and a lack of resources leaving millions without support. The COVID-19 pandemic further strained healthcare systems, exposing vulnerabilities in emergency preparedness and access to care (Raina et al., 2023).

Environmental factors also play a significant role in delaying SDG progress. Climate change has intensified natural disasters such as floods and droughts, disproportionately affecting poor communities and exacerbating food insecurity (Gidage & Bhide, 2024). The region's reliance on fossil fuels for energy production hinders efforts to transition to sustainable practices, impacting the overall development goal.

Additionally, weak governance and insufficient regional cooperation impede progress. Many South Asian countries lack the fiscal space to finance large-scale SDG initiatives due to high debt burdens and limited revenue generation. Corruption and bureaucratic inefficiencies further slowdown implementation efforts. Regional platforms like SAARC have yet to fully leverage opportunities for collaborative action on shared challenges such as poverty alleviation, food security, and healthcare access (Raina et al., 2023).

9 Mental Health Outcomes in the Context of Poverty and Inequality in South Asia

Poverty and inequality are deeply intertwined with mental health outcomes in South Asia, a region that houses nearly one-quarter of the world's population and some of the highest poverty rates globally. Approximately 150–200 million people in the region are diagnosed with psychiatric disorders, yet access to mental healthcare remains critically limited (Nambiar et al., 2017). Poverty serves as both a cause and a consequence of mental health issues, creating a vicious cycle where financial instability exacerbates psychological distress, while untreated mental health conditions hinder economic productivity and deepen poverty. Economic disparities within countries like India, Pakistan, and Bangladesh further compound this issue, as marginalized communities—particularly those in rural areas—face systemic barriers to healthcare access, education, and employment opportunities, all of which are critical for mental well-being (Tampubolon & Hanandita, 2014).

The prevalence of common mental disorders (CMDs) is alarmingly high in South Asia. Studies indicate that depressive symptoms affect 26.4% of the population, while anxiety impacts 25.8%, with higher rates observed among low-income groups. These disorders are often exacerbated by chronic stressors tied to poverty, such as food insecurity, inadequate housing, and exposure to violence (Naveed et al., 2020).

The region's mental health infrastructure is grossly inadequate to meet these challenges. Less than 1% of national budgets in South Asian countries is allocated to mental health, resulting in a severe shortage of trained professionals. This treatment gap is further widened by stigma surrounding mental illness, which discourages individuals from seeking help even when services are available. Cultural factors such as collectivist values and the prioritization of family reputation over individual well-being also contribute to underutilization of mental health services (Arafat & Kar, 2024).

10 South Asian Nations' Poverty Eradication Policies

10.1 Key Policy Interventions for Poverty Reduction in South Asia

South Asian nations have implemented a variety of policy interventions aimed at poverty eradication, reflecting the region's commitment to achieving SDG 1 (No Poverty). These policies address structural inequalities, promote inclusive growth, and empower marginalized populations (Islam, 1992). One of the most prominent strategies is the implementation of social protection programs. For example, India's Mahatma Gandhi National Rural Employment Guarantee Act (MGNREGA) guarantees 100 days of wage employment per year to rural households, providing financial stability and reducing economic stress for millions (Iosr Journals et al., 2015). Similarly, Pakistan's Ehsaas Program focuses on targeted cash transfers and social safety nets for vulnerable populations, aiming to reduce poverty and improve access to essential services (Table 2) (Javed & Mumtaz, 2024).

Microfinance initiatives have also played a critical role in poverty alleviation across the region. Bangladesh's Grameen Bank and BRAC are global pioneers in providing small loans to rural communities, enabling them to start businesses and achieve financial independence (Abdullah, 2013). These programs have empowered women economically, fostering greater gender equality while reducing poverty. In Nepal, similar microfinance schemes have been instrumental in supporting rural livelihoods and boosting income generation (Saha & Annear, 2014).

Agricultural reforms are another key intervention, as agriculture remains the backbone of South Asian economies. Policies promoting sustainable farming practices, subsidies for small farmers, and improved access to markets have helped enhance food security and reduce rural poverty. For instance, India's Minimum Support Price

Table 2 Poverty eradication strategies in South Asia

Country	Name of program	Year implemented	Description of program	Impact
Bangladesh	Vulnerable Group Development (VGD)	1975	Provides food aid and cash transfers to the poorest households, especially women, to improve living standards	Reduced food insecurity, boosted household income, and raised social awareness, especially among women. It also improved children's education, with higher school attendance and lower child labor in participant households
Bangladesh	Grameen Bank Microfinance Program	1983	Microfinance initiative aimed at providing small loans to rural poor, especially women, to foster entrepreneurship	Empowered impoverished individuals, particularly women, by providing access to collateral-free loans, enabling them to start businesses and improve their standard of living. The program has helped millions rise out of poverty, contributing to social and economic development in rural Bangladesh and inspiring similar initiatives globally
Bangladesh	Bangladesh Rural Development Board (BRDB)	1972	Supports rural development by improving access to education, healthcare, and income generation activities	Improved rural access to services and income opportunities, though implementation has faced regional disparities

(continued)

Table 2 (continued)

Country	Name of program	Year implemented	Description of program	Impact
Bangladesh	Social Safety Net Programs (SSNPs)	1996	Includes cash transfers, food support, and pensions for vulnerable groups such as the elderly and disabled	SSNPs have reduced poverty by 60.97%, supporting vulnerable groups such as the elderly, women, and disabled. These programs improve health by 60.66%, boost education, and promote gender equality and women's empowerment by 73.17%, while raising rural awareness by 97.56%
Bangladesh	National Social Security Strategy (NSSS)	2015	Comprehensive social security framework aimed at ensuring income support for vulnerable populations	Significantly reduced poverty in Bangladesh, with poverty rates dropping from 48.9% to 24.8% and extreme poverty from 34.3% to 12.9% between 2000 and 2015. It has expanded social security coverage, adopted a lifecycle approach, and improved institutional coordination
Bhutan	Social Protection Schemes	2006	Provides social security and cash transfer schemes to vulnerable populations such as the elderly, disabled, and low-income families	Provided financial support and security to vulnerable populations, though there were challenges in coverage

(continued)

Table 2 (continued)

Country	Name of program	Year implemented	Description of program	Impact
Bhutan	Bhutan Rural Livelihoods Project (BRLP)	2013	Reduce poverty and food insecurity in southern Bhutan through support for agriculture, infrastructure, and non-farm employment. Using the World Bank's Program for Results (P4R) approach, it focuses on results-based disbursements and addressing institutional weaknesses for sustainable rural development	Improved rural livelihoods in southern Bhutan by boosting agriculture, infrastructure, and non-farm employment. It helped reduce poverty, enhance food security, and strengthen institutional capacity
India	Mahatma Gandhi National Rural Employment Guarantee Act (MGNREGA)	2006	Guarantees 100 days of wage employment to rural households, focusing on infrastructure development and poverty alleviation	MGNREGA has provided employment to over 11.37 crore households, creating 289.24 crore person-days of work. It has increased wages by 81%, promoted social inclusion with high participation from marginalized groups, and contributed to rural infrastructure development. The scheme also facilitated over 10 crore new bank accounts for direct wage payments and supported income stabilization during the COVID-19 pandemic

(continued)

Table 2 (continued)

Country	Name of program	Year implemented	Description of program	Impact
India	Pradhan Mantri Awas Yojana (PMAY)	2015	Provides affordable housing for urban and rural poor through subsidies and financial assistance	PMAY has sanctioned over 4 crore houses (1.18 crore under PMAY-U and 2.94 crore under PMAY-G), with millions completed, improving rural and urban housing. The scheme promotes social inclusion, gender empowerment, and job creation. It has also driven investment in affordable housing and adopted new construction technologies
India	Pradhan Mantri Jan Dhan Yojana (PMJDY)	2014	Aims to provide financial inclusion through access to banking services for the unbanked population	MJDY opened over 53 crore bank accounts, with 55.6% belonging to women, promoting financial inclusion. Deposits reached Rs 2.31 lakh crore, and 36 crore RuPay debit cards were issued, fostering digital payments. The scheme increased access to banking, reduced financial exclusion, and improved economic security for marginalized group

(continued)

Table 2 (continued)

Country	Name of program	Year implemented	Description of program	Impact
India	National Social Assistance Program (NSAP)	1995	Provides financial assistance to the elderly, widows, and disabled persons living below the poverty line	NSAP has supported 4.5 crore beneficiaries annually, reducing poverty and promoting social inclusion. It has empowered vulnerable groups through direct cash transfers, enhancing efficiency and transparency
Nepal	Poverty Alleviation Fund (PAF)	2004	Funds poverty alleviation projects that focus on community-driven development and capacity building	Successfully funded community-driven projects, but scalability remains an issue due to limited resources. Community-driven development…
Nepal	Prime Minister Employment Program (PMEP)	2016	Provides direct employment opportunities through government-funded programs, aimed at reducing unemployment	Helped reduce unemployment by providing short-term employment, but lacks long-term impact on poverty alleviation. Employment…
Nepal	National Housing Reconstruction Program	2015	Supports the reconstruction of homes for families affected by natural disasters like the 2015 earthquake	Reconstructed homes for thousands of families, though challenges with land rights and infrastructure persist. Reconstruction…
Pakistan	Benazir Income Support Program (BISP)	2008	Provides financial assistance to low-income families, aiming to reduce poverty and improve living standards	Lifted millions out of poverty by providing financial aid to families, though issues like insufficient targeting remain

(continued)

Table 2 (continued)

Country	Name of program	Year implemented	Description of program	Impact
Pakistan	Ehsaas Program	2020	A flagship social protection program providing cash transfers, scholarships, and low-interest loans to disadvantaged groups	Provided cash transfers, scholarships, and loans to millions, reducing poverty and increasing economic opportunities
Pakistan	Pakistan Poverty Alleviation Fund (PPAF)	2000	Funds poverty alleviation projects with a focus on community-driven development and capacity building	Successfully funded community-driven projects, but scalability remains an issue due to limited resources

(MSP) mechanism ensures fair prices for crops, while Sri Lanka has invested in irrigation projects to improve agricultural productivity (Shankar et al., 2019).

Education-focused interventions have also been central to poverty reduction efforts. Governments across South Asia have prioritized universal access to primary education through programs like India's *Sarva Shiksha Abhiyan* (SSA) and Bangladesh's Primary Education Stipend Program (PESP). These initiatives aim to break the intergenerational cycle of poverty by equipping children with the skills needed for better employment opportunities (Amin et al., 2020).

Despite these efforts, challenges remain due to systemic inequalities and inefficiencies in policy implementation. Social protection programs often suffer from poor targeting; for example, Sri Lanka's Samurdhi cash transfer program excluded 40% of the poor while benefiting non-poor households. Corruption and bureaucratic inefficiencies further hinder progress. Additionally, regional disparities in poverty reduction persist, with rural areas lagging behind urban centers (Social Protection in South Asia: A Review—GSDRC, 2009).

10.2 The Role of Government and NGOs in Addressing Poverty and Mental Health

Governments and non-governmental organizations (NGOs) play complementary roles in tackling poverty and its associated mental health challenges in South Asia, a region marked by widespread socioeconomic disparities and limited access to healthcare services. Governments across South Asia have implemented large-scale poverty alleviation programs aimed at providing financial stability, improving access to education, and enhancing healthcare infrastructure (Maddock et al., 2021).

Government programs often face challenges such as poor targeting, corruption, and bureaucratic inefficiencies that limit their impact on the most marginalized communities.

NGOs have stepped in to bridge gaps left by government initiatives, particularly in areas where public services are underdeveloped or inaccessible. Organizations like BRAC in Bangladesh and the Aga Khan Rural Support Program (AKRSP) in Pakistan have pioneered grassroots approaches that empower local communities through microfinance, education, healthcare, and skill development. BRAC's integrated development model has enrolled millions of children in schools, created employment opportunities, and provided scholarships to disadvantaged families, directly reducing poverty while addressing its psychological impacts (Chowdhury & Bhuiya, 2004). Similarly, AKRSP has demonstrated the importance of community participation in poverty alleviation by forming village organizations that manage projects ranging from irrigation to education. These initiatives not only improve livelihoods but also foster social empowerment, which is critical for mental health outcomes (South Asia's Path to Resilient Growth, 2022).

Mental healthcare remains a neglected area in South Asia's poverty eradication strategies. Governments allocate less than 1% of their health budgets to mental health services, leaving millions without access to treatment. NGOs have made significant contributions here as well; for example, task-shifting models train non-specialist personnel to provide basic mental health support in underserved areas. Community-based mental health programs led by NGOs have shown promise in addressing stigma and increasing awareness about mental illness among impoverished populations (User, 2020).

However, both governments and NGOs face systemic barriers such as cultural stigma surrounding mental health and entrenched inequalities that limit the reach of their interventions. Collaborative efforts between these entities are essential for creating holistic solutions that address both poverty and mental health simultaneously. Governments must strengthen governance mechanisms to ensure transparency and efficiency in program delivery while increasing investments in healthcare infrastructure. NGOs can complement these efforts by leveraging their grassroots networks to deliver targeted interventions tailored to local needs.

Ultimately, addressing poverty and its impact on mental health requires integrated approaches that combine economic support with accessible healthcare services. By working together to implement inclusive policies and community-driven programs, governments and NGOs can make significant strides toward achieving SDG 1 (No Poverty), SDG 2 (Zero Hunger), and SDG 3 (Good Health and Well-Being) across South Asia (Thun & Manh, 2021).

10.3 Evaluating the Effectiveness of Poverty Eradication Strategies in South Asia

Poverty eradication strategies in South Asia have shown mixed effectiveness, reflecting both significant achievements and persistent challenges. Governments and NGOs across the region have implemented a range of policies, including social protection schemes, microfinance programs, community-driven development initiatives, and agricultural reforms (Islam, 1992).

However, the effectiveness of these strategies varies widely across countries and regions due to systemic issues such as poor targeting, corruption, and bureaucratic inefficiencies. In many cases, social protection programs fail to reach the most marginalized groups, including women, ethnic minorities, and those living in remote areas. For example, Sri Lanka's Samurdhi program has faced criticism for excluding a significant proportion of the poor while benefiting non-poor households. Additionally, while microfinance has been successful in fostering economic empowerment, it has not always translated into long-term poverty reduction due to high interest rates and limited scalability (Rethinking Social Protection in South Asia, 2009) (Table 2).

To enhance the effectiveness of poverty eradication strategies, South Asian nations must adopt integrated approaches that address both immediate needs and structural inequalities. This includes improving governance mechanisms to ensure transparency and accountability in program delivery, expanding access to education and healthcare, and promoting inclusive economic growth that benefits marginalized populations. Regional cooperation through platforms like SAARC could also facilitate knowledge-sharing and resource mobilization for tackling shared challenges such as food insecurity and unemployment (Singh & Chudasama, 2020).

11 Recommendations

The physical and mental health of the next generation in South Asia and the world depends on how the current generation mitigates poverty. Children growing up in poverty inherit a high mental health risk in the next generation cycle. It is recommended that South Asian countries implement policies that improve skill-building and the employment rate. South Asian countries should consider integrating mental healthcare and food security programs into primary healthcare systems, expanding community-based interventions, and addressing the systemic barriers to accessing care. This needs a sufficient level of resource allocation via UHC. National reforms targeting economic inequality through capacity building within the deprived population stratum will improve the poverty rate where jointly with the UCH, reduce potential risk for mental health. Programs such as strengthening the community health workforce, health promotion/education that benefits from digital health technology, will be a preventive measure against experiencing mental health problems among the poor population. The Housing Infrastructure project aims to tackle slums will positively impact poverty-driven stress. Meantime, improving mental health services may be facilitated through mobile mental health clinics in both city outskirts and rural regions. Finally, it is suggested to expand the international partnerships for funding and dissemination of information and success (e.g., WHO, World Bank, NGOs) could be another effective measure to combat poverty and consequently improve mental health indicators.

12 Conclusion

To sum up, poverty is a pervasive challenge that undermines progress across all SDGs and has profound consequences for overall health and, in particular, mental health.

Addressing poverty requires a multifaceted approach that includes economic growth, social protection programs, investments in education and healthcare, and efforts to reduce inequalities. By prioritizing poverty reduction and promoting health equity, we can create a more just and sustainable world for all.

The poverty-mental health relationship is a vicious cycle shaped by environmental, biological, social, and structural factors. Breaking this cycle requires integrated approaches: improving access to mental healthcare, strengthening social safety nets, addressing systemic inequities, and fostering community support systems. Recognizing this bidirectional link is crucial for effective policy and intervention strategies.

Since 1990, South Asia has made significant steps in reducing poverty, but challenges like the pandemic and inequality persist. While the regional poverty rate is now close to the global average, its population size remains central to global poverty eradication efforts. Finally, strategic vision and inclusive strategies can promote resilience and equitable progress across South Asia.

References

Abdullah, N. (2013). The effectiveness of micro-finance institutions in alleviating poverty: The case of Bangladeshâ€™s Grameen Bank and BRAC. *Journal of Social and Development Sciences, 4*(7), 339–348. https://doi.org/10.22610/jsds.v4i7.770

Adeleye, B. N., Gershon, O., Ogundipe, A., Owolabi, O. A., Ogunrinola, I., & Adediran, O. (2020). Comparative investigation of the growth-poverty-inequality trilemma in Sub-Saharan Africa and Latin American and Caribbean countries. *Elsevier BV*. https://doi.org/10.1016/j.heliyon.2020.e05631

Allen, L., Williams, J., Townsend, N., Mikkelsen, B., Roberts, N., Foster, C., & Wickramasinghe, K. (2017). Socioeconomic status and non-communicable disease behavioural risk factors in low-income and lower-middle-income countries: A systematic review. *Elsevier BV*. https://doi.org/10.1016/s2214-109x(17)30058-x

Alkire, S., Chatterjee, M., Conconi, A., Seth, S., & Vaz, A. (2014). Destitution: Who and where are the poorest of the poor? OPHI Briefing 22. http://www.ophi.org.uk/wp-content/uploads/Destitution-Who-and-Where-are-the-Poorest-of-the-Poor.pdf?0a8fd7

Amin, A., Liu, Y., Yu, J., Chandio, A. A., Rasool, S. F., Luo, J., & Zaman, S. (2020). How does energy poverty affect economic development? A panel data analysis of South Asian countries. *Environmental Science and Pollution Research, 27*(25), 31623–31635. https://doi.org/10.1007/s11356-020-09173-6

Arafat, S. M. Y., & Kar, S. K. (2024). Epidemiology of psychiatric disorders and overview of access to mental health care in South Asia. In S. M. Y. Arafat, & S. K. Kar (Eds.), *Access to mental health care in South Asia.* Springer. https://doi.org/10.1007/978-981-99-9153-2_1

Bhutta, Z. A., Berkley, J. A., Bandsma, R. H. J., Kerac, M., Trehan, I., & Briend, A. (2017). Severe childhood malnutrition. *Nature Reviews Disease Primers, 3*(1), 17067. https://doi.org/10.1038/nrdp.2017.67

Boozary, A., & Shojania, K. G. (2018). Pathology of poverty: The need for quality improvement efforts to address social determinants of health. *BMJ*. https://doi.org/10.1136/bmjqs-2017-007552

Carter, D. J., Glaziou, P., Lnnroth, K., Siroka, A., Floyd, K., Weil, D., Ravilione, M., Houben, R. M. G. J., & Boccia, D. (2018). The impact of social protection and poverty elimination on global tuberculosis incidence: A statistical modelling analysis of sustainable development goal 1. *Elsevier BV*. https://doi.org/10.1016/s2214-109x(18)30195-5

Congdon, P. (1996). Suicide and Parasuicide in London: A small-area study. *Urban Studies, 33*(1), 137–158. https://doi.org/10.1080/0042098965001 2194(Originalworkpublished1996)

Charlton, K. (2016). *Food security, food systems and food sovereignty in the 21st century: A new paradigm required to meet sustainable development goals.* Wiley. https://doi.org/10.1111/1747-0080.12264

Chowdhury, A. M. R., & Bhuiya, A. (2004). The wider impacts of BRAC poverty alleviation programme in Bangladesh. *Journal of International Development, 16*(3), 369–386. https://doi.org/10.1002/jid.1083

Christensen, Z. (2024). Economic poverty trends: Global, regional and national. Development initiatives available at https://devinit.org/resources/poverty-trends-global-regional-and-national/

Ejiohuo, O., Onyeaka, H., Unegbu, K. C., Chikezie, O. G., Odeyemi, O. A., Lawal, A., & Odeyemi, O. A. (2024). Nourishing the mind: How food security influences mental wellbeing. *Nutrients, 16*(4), 501. https://doi.org/10.3390/nu16040501

Evans, G., & Kim, P. (2013). Childhood poverty, chronic stress, self-regulation, and coping. *None*. https://doi.org/10.1111/CDEP.12013

Evans, G. W., & De France, K. (2022). Childhood poverty and psychological well-being: The mediating role of cumulative risk exposure. *Development and Psychopathology, 34*(3), 911–921. https://doi.org/10.1017/S0954579420001947

Faculty of Public Health (FPH). (2025). *Definitions of poverty.* https://www.fph.org.uk/policy-advocacy/special-interest-groups/poverty-sig/definitions-of-poverty/, Accessed [30/03/2025].

Gibson, B., Schneider, J., Talamonti, D., & Forshaw, M. (2021). The impact of inequality on mental health outcomes during the COVID-19 pandemic: A systematic review. *Canadian Psychology/psychologie Canadienne, 62*(1), 101–126. https://doi.org/10.1037/cap0000272

Gidage, M., & Bhide, S. (2024). ESG and economic growth: Catalysts for achieving sustainable development goals in developing economies. *Sustainable Development, sd.3199*. https://doi.org/10.1002/sd.3199

Girotti, M., Bulin, S. E., & Carreno, F. R. (2024). Effects of chronic stress on cognitive function—From neurobiology to intervention. *Neurobiology of Stress, 33*, Article 100670. https://doi.org/10.1016/j.ynstr.2024.100670

Goal 2: End hunger, achieve food security and improved nutrition and promote sustainable agriculture—SDG Indicators. (n.d.). Retrieved March 14, 2025, from https://unstats.un.org/sdgs/report/2016/goal-02/

Ghasemi, S., Zangeneh, A., Rajabi-Gilan, N., Reshadat, S., Saeidi, S., & Ziapour, A. (2019). Health-related quality of life in informal settlements in kermanshah, islamic republic of iran: Role of poverty and perception of family socioeconomic status. None. https://doi.org/10.26719/EMHJ.19.013

Goulden, C., & D'Arcy, C. (2014). *Anti-poverty strategies for the UK: A Definition of Poverty*. The Joseph Rowntree Foundation (JRF). ISBN 978 1 90958 651 2

Gunnell, D. J., Peters, T. J., Kammerling, R. M., et al. (1995). Relation between parasuicide, suicide, psychiatric admissions and socioeconomic deprivation. *BMJ, 311*, 226–230.

Gweshengwe, B., & Hassan, N. H. (2020). Defining the characteristics of poverty and their implications for poverty analysis. *Cogent Social Sciences, 6*(1). https://doi.org/10.1080/23311886.2020.1768669

Gweshengwe, B. (2020). *Understanding poverty in Brunei Darussalam* [PhD Thesis]. Universiti Brunei Darussalam.

Hameed, M. R., Batool, H., Khan, A., Ahmed, I., & Rehman, N. U. (2021). Sustainable development goals challenges and strategies for South Asian countries. *Humanities & Social Sciences Reviews, 9*(2), 464–474. https://doi.org/10.18510/hssr.2021.9245

Hodgkinson, S., Godoy, L., Beers, L. S., & Lewin, A. (2016). *Improving mental health access for low-income children and families in the primary care setting*. American Academy of Pediatrics. https://doi.org/10.1542/peds.2015-1175

Hodgkinson, S., Godoy, L., Beers, L. S., & Lewin, A. (2017). Improving mental health access for low-income children and families in the primary care setting. *Pediatrics, 139*(1), Article e20151175. https://doi.org/10.1542/peds.2015-1175

Hossain, M. M., Purohit, N., Sultana, A., Ma, P., McKyer, E. L. J., & Ahmed, H. U. (2020). *Prevalence of mental disorders in South Asia: An umbrella review of systematic reviews and meta-analyses*. https://doi.org/10.31234/osf.io/f96we

Iemmi, V. (2019). Sustainable development for global mental health: A typology and systematic evidence mapping of external actors in low-income and middle-income countries. *BMJ Global Health, 4*(6), Article e001826. https://doi.org/10.1136/bmjgh-2019-001826

Iosr Journals, Farooqi, S. A., & Dr. Imran Saleem. (2015). *"Mahatma Gandhi National Rural Employment Guarantee Act (MGNREGA) and empowerment of women from BPL families in rural areas" A case study of district Aligarh (India)*. Figshare. https://doi.org/10.6084/M9.FIGSHARE.1381736.V1

Islam, N. (1992). Poverty in South Asia. *Food Policy, 17*(2), 109–128. https://doi.org/10.1016/0306-9192(92)90051-X

Javed, W., & Mumtaz, Z. (2024). South Asia's unprotected poor: A systematic review of why social protection programs fail to reach their potential. *PLOS Global Public Health, 4*(6), Article e0002710. https://doi.org/10.1371/journal.pgph.0002710

Karasz, A., Gany, F., Escobar, J., Flores, C., Prasad, L., Inman, A., Kalasapudi, V., Kosi, R., Murthy, M., Leng, J., & Diwan, S. (2019). Mental health and stress among South Asians. *Journal of Immigrant and Minority Health, 21*(S1), 7–14. https://doi.org/10.1007/s10903-016-0501-4

Kim, P., Strathearn, L., & Swain, J. E. (2016). The maternal brain and its plasticity in humans. *Hormones and Behavior, 77*, 113–123. https://doi.org/10.1016/j.yhbeh.2015.08.001

Koly, K. N., Baskin, C., Khanam, I., Rao, M., Rasheed, S., Law, G. R., Sarker, F., & Gnani, S. (2021). Educational and training interventions aimed at healthcare workers in the detection and management of people with mental health conditions in South and South-East Asia: A systematic review. *Frontiers in Psychiatry, 12*, Article 741328. https://doi.org/10.3389/fpsyt.2021.741328

Kirkbride, J. B., Anglin, D. M., Colman, I., Dykxhoorn, J., Jones, P. B., Patalay, P., Pitman, A., Soneson, E., Steare, T., Wright, T., & Griffiths, S. L. (2024). The social determinants of mental health and disorder: Evidence, prevention and recommendations. *World Psychiatry, 23*(1), 58–90. https://doi.org/10.1002/wps.21160

Kuruvilla, A., & Jacob, K. S. (2015). Mental Health Resources in South Asia. In J. K. Trivedi & A. Tripathi (Eds.), *Mental health in South Asia: Ethics, resources, programs and legislation* (Vol. 58, pp. 191–219). Springer Netherlands. https://doi.org/10.1007/978-94-017-9017-8_11

Lancker, W. V., & Parolin, Z. (2020). Covid-19, school closures, and child poverty: A social crisis in the making. *Elsevier BV*. https://doi.org/10.1016/s2468-2667(20)30084-0

Lever, J. P., Piñol, N. L., & Uralde, J. H. (2005). Poverty, psychological resources and subjective well-being. *Social Indicators Research, 73*(3), 375–408. https://doi.org/10.1007/s11205-004-1072-7

Liu, Q. Q., Yu, M., & Wang, X. (2015). Poverty reduction within the framework of SDGS and post-2015 development agenda. *KeAi*. https://doi.org/10.1016/j.accre.2015.09.004

Maddock, A., Blair, C., Ean, N., & Best, P. (2021). Psychological and social interventions for mental health issues and disorders in Southeast Asia: A systematic review. *International Journal of Mental Health Systems, 15*(1), 56. https://doi.org/10.1186/s13033-021-00482-y

Marmot, M., & Bell, R. (2017). The sustainable development goals and health equity. *Lippincott Williams & Wilkins*. https://doi.org/10.1097/ede.0000000000000773

Maxim, A., Mihai, C., Apostoaie, C., Popescu, C., Istrate, C., & Bostan, I. (2016). Implications and measurement of energy poverty across the European union. *Multidisciplinary Digital Publishing Institute*. https://doi.org/10.3390/su8050483

Maynard, M., Andrade, L., Packull-McCormick, S., Perlman, C. M., Leos-Toro, C., & Kirkpatrick, S. I. (2018). Food insecurity and mental health among females in high-income countries. *International Journal of Environmental Research and Public Health, 15*(7), 1424. https://doi.org/10.3390/ijerph15071424

Mazumder, H., Faizah, F., Gain, E. P., Sharmin Eva, I., Ferdouse Mou, K., Saha, N., Rahman, F., Das, J., Islam, A. M. K., Nesa, F., & Hossain, M. M. (2023). Effectiveness of mental health interventions for older adults in South Asia: A scoping review. *PLoS ONE, 18*(7), Article e0287883. https://doi.org/10.1371/journal.pone.0287883

Mensah, G. A., Mokdad, A. H., Ford, E. S., Greenlund, K. J., & Croft, J. B. (2005). State of disparities in cardiovascular health in the United States. *Lippincott Williams & Wilkins*. https://doi.org/10.1161/01.cir.0000158136.76824.04

Michel, J., Mettler, A., Schnenberger, S., & Gunz, D. (2022). Period poverty: Why it should be everybody's business. *Journal of Global Health Reports*. https://doi.org/10.29392/001c.32436

Mishra, N. (2002). Poverty in South Asia. *Asia-Pacific Journal of Rural Development, 12*(2), 113–114. https://doi.org/10.1177/1018529120020208

Nambiar, D., Razzak, J., Afsana, K., Adams, A. M., Hasan, A., Mohan, D., & Patel, V. (2017). Mental illness and injuries: Emerging health challenges of urbanisation in South Asia. *BMJ, j1126*. https://doi.org/10.1136/bmj.j1126

Naveed, S., Waqas, A., Chaudhary, A. M. D., Kumar, S., Abbas, N., Amin, R., Jamil, N., & Saleem, S. (2020). Prevalence of common mental disorders in South Asia: A systematic review and meta-regression analysis. *Frontiers in Psychiatry, 11*, Article 573150. https://doi.org/10.3389/fpsyt.2020.573150

Nweze, T., Ezenwa, M., Ajaelu, C., & Okoye, C. (2023). Childhood mental health difficulties mediate the long-term association between early-life adversity at age 3 and poorer cognitive functioning at ages 11 and 14. *Journal of Child Psychology and Psychiatry, 64*(6), 952–965. https://doi.org/10.1111/jcpp.13757

Onyeaka, H., Ejiohuo, O., Taiwo, O. R., Nnaji, N. D., Odeyemi, O. A., Duan, K., Nwaiwu, O., & Odeyemi, O. (2024). The intersection of food security and mental health in the pursuit of sustainable development goals. *Nutrients, 16*(13), 2036. https://doi.org/10.3390/nu16132036

OPHI (Oxford Poverty and Human Development Initiative) and UNDP (United Nations Development Programme). (2019). *Inequalities*. United Nations Development Programme and Oxford Poverty and Human Development Initiative.

Park, J., Turnbull, A., & Turnbull, H. R. (2002). Impacts of poverty on quality of life in families of children with disabilities. *SAGE Publishing*. https://doi.org/10.1177/001440290206800201

Park, Y.-M., Shekhtman, T., & Kelsoe, J. R. (2020). Interaction between adverse childhood experiences and polygenic risk in patients with bipolar disorder. *Translational Psychiatry, 10*(1), 326. https://doi.org/10.1038/s41398-020-01010-1

Prajapati, R., & Liebling, H. (2022). Accessing mental health services: A systematic review and meta-ethnography of the experiences of South Asian service users in the UK. *Journal of Racial and Ethnic Health Disparities, 9*(2), 598–619. https://doi.org/10.1007/s40615-021-00993-x

Pryor, L., Strandberg-Larsen, K., Nybo Andersen, A.-M., Hulvej Rod, N., & Melchior, M. (2019). Trajectories of family poverty and children's mental health: Results from the Danish National Birth Cohort. *Social Science & Medicine, 220*, 371–378. https://doi.org/10.1016/j.socscimed.2018.10.023

Rahman, A. (2024). Editorial: Equity/inequality, diversity and inclusion in child and adolescent mental health—A perspective from the South Asian region. *Child and Adolescent Mental Health, 29*(2), 197–199. https://doi.org/10.1111/camh.12702

Raina, N., Khanna, R., Gupta, S., Jayathilaka, C. A., Mehta, R., & Behera, S. (2023). Progress in achieving SDG targets for mortality reduction among mothers, newborns, and children in the WHO South-East Asia Region. *The Lancet Regional Health—Southeast Asia, 18*, Article 100307. https://doi.org/10.1016/j.lansea.2023.100307

Ravallion, M. (1992a). *Poverty comparisons: A guide to concepts and methods*. The World Bank.

Ravallion, M. (1992). *Poverty comparisons: A guide to concepts and methods (English)*. Living standards measurement study (LSMS) working paper|No. LSM 88 The World Bank. http://documents.worldbank.org/curated/en/290531468766493135

Raver, C. C. (2012). Low-income children's self-regulation in the classroom: Scientific inquiry for social change. *American Psychologist, 67*(8), 681–689. https://doi.org/10.1037/a0030085

Rethinking Social Protection in South Asia: Toward Progressive Universalism. (2009). [Text/HTML]. World Bank. Retrieved March 15, 2025, from https://www.worldbank.org/en/region/sar/publication/rethinking-social-protection-in-south-asia-toward-progressive-universalism

Rohner, S. L., Bernays, F., Maercker, A., & Thoma, M. V. (2023). Early-life adversity and later-life mental health: A conditional process analysis of sense of coherence and resilience-related resources. *Frontiers in Child and Adolescent Psychiatry, 2*, 1213142. https://doi.org/10.3389/frcha.2023.1213142

Roubinov, D., Browne, D., LeWinn, K. Z., Lisha, N., Mason, W. A., & Bush, N. R. (2022). Intergenerational transmission of maternal childhood adversity and depression on children's internalizing problems. *Journal of Affective Disorders, 308*, 205–212. https://doi.org/10.1016/j.jad.2022.04.030

Santiago, C. D., Wadsworth, M. E., & Stump, J. (2011). Socioeconomic status, neighborhood disadvantage, and poverty-related stress: Prospective effects on psychological syndromes among diverse low-income families. *Journal of Economic Psychology, 32*(2), 218–230. https://doi.org/10.1016/j.joep.2009.10.008

Saha, S., & Annear, P. (2014). Overcoming access barriers to health services through membership-based microfinance organizations: A review of evidence from South Asia. *WHO South-East Asia Journal of Public Health, 3*(2), 125. https://doi.org/10.4103/2224-3151.206728

Shankar, B., Poole, N., & Bird, F. A. (2019). Agricultural inputs and nutrition in South Asia. *Food Policy, 82*, 28–38. https://doi.org/10.1016/j.foodpol.2018.10.011

Shidhaye, R., Sikander, S., Jordans, M., De Silva, P., & Chatterjee, S. (2015). Mental health programs and policies in South Asia: Initiatives and obstacles. In J. K. Trivedi, & A. Tripathi (Eds.), *Mental health in South Asia: Ethics, resources, programs and legislation* (Vol. 58, pp. 95–111). Springer. https://doi.org/10.1007/978-94-017-9017-8_7

Shupler, M., Baame, M., Nix, E., Tawiah, T., Lorenzetti, F., Saah, J., Cuevas, R. A. D., Sang, E., Puzzolo, E., Mangeni, J., Betang, E., Twumasi, M., AmengaEtego, S., Quansah, R., Mbatchou, B., Menya, D., Asante, K. P., & Pope, D. (2022). Multiple aspects of energy poverty are associated with lower mental health-related quality of life: A modelling study in three peri-urban African communities. *Elsevier BV*. https://doi.org/10.1016/j.ssmmh.2022.100103

Singh, P. K., & Chudasama, H. (2020). Evaluating poverty alleviation strategies in a developing country. *PLoS ONE, 15*(1), Article e0227176. https://doi.org/10.1371/journal.pone.0227176

Social protection in South Asia: A review—GSDRC. (2009). Retrieved March 15, 2025, from https://gsdrc.org/document-library/social-protection-in-south-asia-a-review/

South Asia's Path to Resilient Growth. (2022). International Monetary Fund. https://doi.org/10.5089/9781513587219.071

Stenberg, K., Hanssen, O., Edejer, T.T.-T., Bertram, M., Brindley, C., Meshreky, A., Rosen, J. E., Stover, J., Verboom, P., Sanders, R., & Soucat, A. (2017). Financing transformative health systems towards achievement of the health sustainable development goals: A model for projected resource needs in 67 low-income and middle-income countries. *The Lancet Global Health, 5*(9), e875–e887. https://doi.org/10.1016/S2214-109X(17)30263-2

Stolz, E., Mayerl, H., Waxenegger, A., & Freidl, W. (2017). Explaining the impact of poverty on old-age frailty in Europe: Material, psychosocial and behavioural factors. *European Journal of Public Health.* https://doi.org/10.1093/eurpub/ckx079

Tampubolon, G., & Hanandita, W. (2014). Poverty and mental health in Indonesia. *Social Science & Medicine, 106*, 20–27. https://doi.org/10.1016/j.socscimed.2014.01.012

Tessema, G. A., Laurence, C. O., Melaku, Y. A., Misganaw, A., Woldie, S. A., Hiruye, A., Amare, A. T., Lakew, Y., Zeleke, B. M., Deribew, A. (2017, Feb 2). Trends and causes of maternal mortality in Ethiopia during 1990–2013: Findings from the Global Burden of Diseases study 2013. *BMC Public Health 17*(1), 160. PMID:28152987; PMCID: PMC5290608. https://doi.org/10.1186/s12889-017-4071-8

Thara, R., & Padmavati, R. (2013). Community mental health care in South Asia. *World Psychiatry, 12*(2), 176–177. https://doi.org/10.1002/wps.20042

Timmis, K. N., Lorenzo, V. D., Verstraete, W., Ramos, J. L., Danchin, A., Brssow, H., Singh, B. K., & Timmis, J. K. (2017). The contribution of microbial biotechnology to economic growth and employment creation. *Wiley*. https://doi.org/10.1111/1751-7915.12845

Thomson, H., Snell, C., & Bouzarovski, S. (2017). Health, well-being and energy poverty in Europe: A comparative study of 32 European countries. *Multidisciplinary Digital Publishing Institute.* https://doi.org/10.3390/ijerph14060584

Thun, P. H., & Manh, T. D. (2021). Poverty alleviation in the aspect of government collaboration with NGOs. *Journal of Asian Multicultural Research for Social Sciences Study, 2*(2), 1–5. https://doi.org/10.47616/jamrsss.v2i2.128

United Nations (UN). (1995). *The Copenhagen declaration and programme of action: World summit for social development 6–12 March 1995.* United Nations Department of Publications.

United Nations. (2010). *The World's women 2010: Trends and statistics*. [chrome-extension://efaidnbmnnnibpcajpcglclefindmkaj/https://unstats.un.org/unsd/demographic/products/Worlds women/WW_full%20report_color.pdf]. Accessed on 30/03/2025.

UNDP (United Nations Development Programme). (2023). *2023 Global Multidimensional Poverty Index (MPI): Unstacking global poverty: Data for high-impact action.*

USAFacts. (2025). Poverty in the United States: 2022. [How does poverty affect Americans' mental and physical health? | USAFacts]. https://usafacts.org/articles/how-does-poverty-affect-peoples-mental-and-physical-health/. Accessed: 01/05/2025.

User, S. (2020, July 16). *Information and poverty alleviation.* https://www.saarc-sec.org/index.php/areas-of-cooperation/information-poverty-alleviation

Varma, P., Junge, M., Meaklim, H., & Jackson, M. L. (2021). Younger people are more vulnerable to stress, anxiety and depression during COVID-19 pandemic: A global cross-sectional survey. *Progress in Neuro-Psychopharmacology and Biological Psychiatry, 109*, Article 110236. https://doi.org/10.1016/j.pnpbp.2020.110236

Weaver, L. J., & Hadley, C. (2009). Moving beyond hunger and nutrition: A systematic review of the evidence linking food insecurity and mental health in developing countries. *Ecology of Food and Nutrition, 48*(4), 263–284. https://doi.org/10.1080/03670240903001167

World Bank. (2022). *Poverty and Shared Prosperity 2022: Correcting Course.* https://www.worldbank.org/en/publication/poverty-and-shared-prosperity. Washington, DC. https://datatopics.worldbank.org/sdgatlas/goal-1-no-poverty?lang=en#c1s0. Accessed [30/03/2025].

World Bank. (2022). *Poverty and Shared Prosperity 2022: Correcting Course.* https://www.worldbank.org/en/publication/poverty-and-shared-prosperity.

World Bank. (2023, April). Poverty and inequality platform (PIP) update.

World Bank. (2024). Poverty and Inequality Platform (version 20240627_2017 and 20240627_2011). World Bank Group. https://pip.worldbank.org/—processed by Our World in Data.

World Bank. (2025). *World Bank Open Data*. https://data.worldbank.org/indicator/SN.ITK.DEFC.ZS?locations=1W. Accessed: 01/052025.

Xiang, X., Cho, J., Sun, Y., & Wang, X. (2022). Childhood adversity and cognitive impairment in later life. *Frontiers in Psychology, 13*, Article 935254. https://doi.org/10.3389/fpsyg.2022.935254

Xiao, Z., Baldwin, M. M., Meinck, F., Obsuth, I., & Murray, A. L. (2021). The impact of childhood psychological maltreatment on mental health outcomes in adulthood: A protocol for a systematic review and meta-analysis. *Systematic Reviews, 10*(1), 224. https://doi.org/10.1186/s13643-021-01777-4

Yu, Y., & Huang, J. (2021). Poverty reduction of sustainable development goals in the 21st century: A bibliometric analysis. *Frontiers Media*. https://doi.org/10.3389/fcomm.2021.754181

Zainal, N. R., Kaur, G., Ahmad, N. A., & Khalili, J. M. (2012). Housing conditions and quality of life of the urban poor in Malaysia. *Elsevier BV*. https://doi.org/10.1016/j.sbspro.2012.08.085

Chapter 5
Gender Inequalities and Mental Health

Ali Davod Parsa, Leila Dehghani, Divya Vinnakota, and Russell Kabir

Abstract Gender is a non-modifiable determinant for health, while it is influenced by modifiable determinant factors. Several socio-economic and cultural factors globally have created a gender-based inequality that causes gender discrimination. Inequality that disadvantages women against men contributes to both physical and mental health challenges that are present in various types of mental disorders. Gender inequality in South Asia remains a significant obstacle to achieving the Sustainable Development Goals (SDGs). A wide range of risk factors, including poverty, discrimination, limited education, exposure to violence, and limited autonomy in decision-making, restricted participation in public and political life, and discriminatory laws and societal norms prolong these inequalities. Attempts to remove health inequality need a high level of advocacy at the strategic level, multisectoral engagement, changing the perspective of society towards equity, cultural shift, health promotion, as well as improvement in health service access and utilisation that guarantees mental health care at the centre of this reform.

Keywords Inequality · Mental disorders · Post-Traumatic Stress Disorder (PTSD) · Sustainable Development Goals (SDGs) · UNICEF · Marginalised · Malnutrition · Infant Mortality Rate (IMR) · Gender disparity · Female Labour Force Participation (FLFP)

A. D. Parsa (✉) · R. Kabir
Faculty of Health, Education, Medicine and Social Care, School of Allied Health, Anglia Ruskin University, Essex, UK
e-mail: ali.parsa@aru.ac.uk

L. Dehghani
Cambridge University Hospitals (Addenbrooke's Hospital), Cambridge, UK

D. Vinnakota
Department of Nursing and Public Health, University of Sunderland, London, UK

S. K. Kar et al. (eds.), *Sustainable Development Goals and Mental Health in South Asia*, South Asian Perspectives in Mental Health and Psychology ,
https://doi.org/10.1007/978-981-95-2684-0_5

1 Introduction

In most nations globally, one of the social factors that resulted in divisions is rooted in gender.

Within a complex social life, gender-based discriminations deeply affect mental health and emotional well-being, mostly in developing nations. Some arguments claim that women have more psychopathology than men (Kessler et al., 2005; Rosenfield et al., 2000), whereas others believe it is more in men or at least equal. Nevertheless, research has confirmed that each gender tends to have different types of mental and physical health problems (Needham & Hill, 2010).

The socio-economic inequalities and limited access to resources create a complex situation where women and girls constantly experience poorer health outcomes compared to men across multiple dimensions. Looking at multiple factors, from macro-level broad sociohistorical drivers to micro-level attributes, the chapter explains how social differentiation by gender shapes the psychological problems of men and women. According to the SDG Report 2024, and despite a reaffirmed pledge, there has been a slowdown or no progress towards SDG 2030.

The enduring effects of COVID-19, combined with conflicts, climate shocks, and economic turmoil, have aggravated existing inequalities. For example, an extra 23 million people have fallen into extreme poverty, and over 100 million more were added to those who suffered from hunger in 2022 compared to 2019. The poverty victims are not equally divided between genders (UN DESA, 2024). This chapter presents an investigation and examines the evidence that proves gender-based inequalities, which may cause mental health issues to be more common in one gender relative to the other/s.

2 Common Risk Factors for Mental Health Problems

Mental health disorders are influenced by several factors (WHO, 2025), both individually and in combination with socio-environmental issues (Uher, 2014). They are classified into individual, genetics, family history of mental health disease (Sullivan et al., 2000), personality characteristics, e.g. self-esteem (Orth et al., 2013) and negativity perspective (Kotov et al., 2010), past traumatic experience, e.g. abuse, neglect, and violence witness, as well as facing long-term physical health problems (Felitti et al., 1998; Kessler et al., 2010):

Socio-environmental drivers such as poverty and financial vulnerability, as a trigger for stress, affect mental well-being (Lund, 2015). More importantly, discrimination and social exclusion potentially deteriorate the mental health status (Allen et al., 2014; Pascoe & Smart Richman, 2009).

It is not with surprise that lack of or restricted access to healthcare services (Thornicroft, 2007), education, and career choices are the risk factors for mental health problems (WHO, 2013). People who live alone and are socially excluded are at higher risk of developing a mental health issue (Holt-Lunstad et al., 2015; Santini et al., 2020).

3 Gender as a Category of Social Inequality (e.g. Unequal Economic Rights, Risk of Violence, Marriage Choice, Parity in Participation in Public Life, Discriminatory Laws, etc.)

South Asia features a complex and often glaring landscape of gender-based social inequality. Gender remains a fundamental category of social inequality in South Asia. Despite some promising progress in some areas and countries in recent years, deeply seated discriminatory practices and legal frameworks extend systemic disadvantages for women and girls. The following section will examine the evidence that is supported by data from reliable sources:

3.1 Economic Rights and Opportunities

3.1.1 Labour Force Participation

There is a significant difference between male and female workforce participation, in line with the low global rate of Female Labour Force Participation (FLFP). South Asian countries present with a higher rate in male which is explained by limited social norms, unpaid care (i.e. informal) burdens, and restricted access to quality jobs (World Bank Gender Data Portal; ILO, "World Employment and Social Outlook: Trends 2023").

3.1.2 Wage Gap and Occupational Segregation

Among these countries, projected gender-based wage gaps exist. Women usually work in low-income, informal settings and temporary roles and are less involved in high-paying or managerial positions (World Bank, 2023).

Access to Property and Finance:

Women are commonly disadvantaged by social practices for land, property ownership, and inheritance law. They may have a limited scope for entrepreneurial opportunities and access to financial facilities (FAO, 2023).

3.2 *Risk of Violence*

Gender-based violence (GBV), particularly as intimate partner violence (IPV), is more prevalent (Soeiro et al., 2023).

3.2.1 Forms of Violence

Some practices such as dowry-related harassment and deaths ("dowry deaths"), honour killings, and acid attacks profoundly damage women's confidence, social interaction, and mental well-being. In these societies, women's trafficking is one of the most serious concerns for women (UNODC, 2022).

3.2.2 Child Marriage

UNICEF (2023) reported that despite reforms, child marriage is still prevalent in this region, and in particular in Bangladesh, Afghanistan, Nepal, and parts of India. This has consecutively increased the potential for violence and increased the risk of mental health problems.

3.3 *Marriage Choice and Family Rights*

Family-arranged marriage and forcing women to marry, which violates their autonomy, are still happening in South Asian communities. Despite the growing number of "love marriages" in urban areas, social stigma and family cultural norms increase the risk of violence ("honour crimes") towards women and contribute to their mental health disorders (ICRW, 2006).

3.3.1 Divorce and Custody Rights

In this region, inevitable divorce makes women significantly vulnerable due to the social stigma and application of a complex legal proceeding (e.g. religion-based personal laws alongside the statutory laws) (World Bank, 2023).

1. **Parity in Participation in Public Life:**

   Political Representation:

   There has been some progress in recent years in gaining a relatively high female representation in local governments and, to some extent, at the national level (e.g. parliaments).

However, women across the region still experiencing challenges and facing barriers in achieving senior leadership roles (e.g. party leadership) (IPU, 2023; Karki, 2023).

South Asian women's visibility in social media and academia has improved; conversely, cultural and structural barriers exist predominantly outside the major urban populations (UNDP, 2025).

2. **Discriminatory Laws and Legal Frameworks**

There is no doubt that some of the South Asian countries still regard women as unequal citizens compared to men (World Bank, 2023). Family laws treat women in a discriminatory manner when it comes to issues like inheritance shares and child custody.

As a result of a lack of protection, women are mentally affected by these incidents, which causes more mental health issues.

4 Gender and Health Inequalities in South Asia: An SDG Perspective

Gender inequality in South Asia remains a significant impediment to achieving the Sustainable Development Goals (SDGs), particularly those related to health (SDG 3) and gender equality (SDG 5). South Asia, comprising Afghanistan, Bangladesh, Bhutan, India, Nepal, Pakistan, and Sri Lanka, is home to over a quarter of the world's population (Rahman, 2024). Despite economic growth in the region, gender disparities persist across various dimensions of economic and social life, including access to education, healthcare, employment, and equal rights (Sreshthaputra, 2015). These inequalities undermine the region's potential for equitable, inclusive, and sustainable development (Sreshthaputra, 2015).

Gender gaps in South Asia are among the highest globally (Filmer et al., 1999). These disparities manifest in various forms, for example, health, education, economics, and so on. Although progress has been made in girls' education, disparities remain, particularly in rural areas and among marginalised communities (Nasrullah & Bhatti, 2012).

Women in South Asia experience poorer health outcomes compared to men, including higher rates of malnutrition, anaemia, and maternal mortality (Jain, 2024). Women's participation in the labour force is significantly lower than men's, and they often face discrimination in employment opportunities and wages (Niimi, 2009).

Women are underrepresented in political decision-making bodies, limiting their ability to influence policies and programmes that affect their lives (Niimi, 2009). The roots of gender inequality in South Asia are deeply embedded in cultural, social, and economic factors (Nasrullah & Bhatti, 2012).

Traditional patriarchal norms, son preference, and discriminatory practices contribute to the disadvantage of women from birth throughout their lives

(Nasrullah & Bhatti, 2012). Economic hardship and limited opportunities exacerbate these inequalities, as families may prioritise the needs of male children over female children (Niimi, 2009).

5 Region and Country-Specific Indicators of SDGs Performance on G 3, 5 Linked to the Gender Disparity in Health Outcomes (E.G. Mental Health)

- **SDG Indicators and Gender Disparities in Health**

The SDGs provide a framework for monitoring progress towards gender equality and improved health outcomes. Several SDG indicators are particularly relevant to understanding gender disparities in health in South Asia.

- **SDG 3: Good Health and Well-being**

SDG 3 aims to ensure healthy lives and promote well-being for all at all ages. South Asia has made progress in reducing MMR, but it remains high compared to other regions (Thresia, 2017). Gender inequality contributes to this, as women often lack access to quality reproductive health services and face cultural barriers to seeking care (Bajracharya & Amin, 2013). Girls in South Asia face a higher risk of mortality compared to boys, particularly in certain regions (Filmer et al., 1999).

This is often attributed to neglect, discriminatory feeding practices, and unequal access to healthcare (Nasrullah & Bhatti, 2012). Anaemia is a widespread problem among women in South Asia, particularly pregnant women (Jain, 2024). This is linked to poor nutrition, inadequate access to iron supplementation, and cultural practices that prioritise the nutritional needs of men (Bajracharya & Amin, 2013). Women in South Asia are disproportionately affected by mental health disorders, such as depression and anxiety (Gailits et al., 2019).

Factors contributing to this include gender-based violence, social isolation, and limited access to mental health services (Tabassum, 2017). Bangladesh has made strides in reducing maternal mortality and improving access to healthcare (Aftab et al., 2020). Bangladesh experienced one of the fastest reductions in maternal mortality among low- and middle-income countries. Bangladesh made significant progress in health outcomes over the past few decades, with an observed significant reduction in the maternal mortality ratio from 2001 to 2010, with an average annual rate of reduction of 5.1% (Hossain et al., 2023). The public mental health services are underperforming in South Asian countries due to several challenges (Kabir et al, 2024).

However, there has been some progress observed recently in some countries. India was felicitated for eliminating trachoma as a public health problem, becoming the third country in the region after Nepal and Myanmar to achieve this milestone. Timor-Leste became the fifth country in the region to eliminate lymphatic filariasis as a public health problem, thanks to high-quality mass drug administration campaigns and effective community engagement. Maldives and Sri Lanka were recognised for achieving hepatitis B control, which significantly reduces chronic infections and liver cancer cases (WHO, 2024; Sandhu et al., 2020).

- **SDG 5: Gender Equality**

SDG 5 aims to achieve gender equality and empower all women and girls. Very low representation of women in politics limits their ability to influence health policies and advocate for gender-sensitive healthcare services (Niimi, 2009). Gender-based violence has significant impacts on women's physical and mental health (David et al., 2017). High rates of such violence in South Asia contribute to poorer health outcomes for women (Kennedy et al., 2020).

The highest statistics of domestic violence are in India (35%), Timor-Leste and the People's Republic of China (38%), and Bangladesh and Fiji (over 50%) (Kurmanbekova et al, 2023). Married women in Gilgit-Baltistan, Pakistan, reported higher levels of domestic violence (88.8%), psychological (69.4%), physical (37.5%), and sexual (21.2%)) (Hussain et al., 2020).

A study conducted in Bangladesh revealed that the lack of primary education and without any employment, women can hardly make their own decisions at the household level (Kabir et al, 2017). While they get abused by their husband or partner, they might try to cope by controlling other parts of their lives. This reduces their decision-making power in their households (Kabir et al, 2021). The women's labour force participation rate is 28.3%, and it is decreasing.

South Asia is not on track to achieve gender equality by 2030, and partly due to COVID-19 and subsequent lockdown, which has accelerated the existing challenges (Joseph et al., 2021). India has shown progress in reducing gender inequality in some areas, such as education (Hristova, 2024). However, significant disparities persist, particularly in health. Studies indicate a gender imbalance in mortality, which can be partly attributed to differential access to vaccination (Oster, 2006). India showed the best gender parity in secondary education enrolment and ranked 65th globally in the political empowerment of women.

However, India is among the countries with the lowest levels of economic parity, similar to Bangladesh, Sudan, Iran, Pakistan, and Morocco, with less than 30% gender parity in estimated earned income (World Economic Forum, 2024). The state of Kerala stands out with social sector gains, but evidence suggests widening health inequalities, especially for marginalised groups like women (Thresia, 2017). Pakistan faces significant challenges in achieving gender equality and improving women's health outcomes (Nasrullah & Bhatti, 2012). Gender inequality is deeply rooted in Pakistani society, with women facing discrimination throughout their lives (Nasrullah & Bhatti, 2012). This is reflected in an unbalanced gender ratio and poorer health outcomes for female children (Nasrullah & Bhatti, 2012). Sex inequity in health indicators is an almost universal phenomenon in the region and is evident in care-seeking practices, referral patterns, and mortality indicators.

Recent demographic shifts in the population in north India indicate an unrecognised but important effect of abortion of female foetuses since ultrasonography became generally available in pregnancy (Bhutta et al., 2004). However, early marriage and early childbearing remain common, particularly among poor and uneducated women (Scott et al., 2020).

These practices have far-reaching consequences for women's health and well-being (Scott et al., 2020). Anaemia is a widespread problem among women in South Asia, particularly pregnant women (Jain, 2024). The national prevalence of anaemia among women of reproductive age in India has increased from 53% in NFHS-4 (2015–16) to 57% in NFHS-5 (2019–21), whereas anaemia among women of reproductive age in Aspirational Districts has increased from 58.7% in NFHS-4 to 61.1% in NFHS-5 (Let et al., 2024). Despite the Government of India launching the Anaemia Mukt Bharat (AMB) in 2018 to lower the prevalence of anaemia by 1–3 percentage points each year, 2/3rd of all women of reproductive age in India still suffer from anaemia (Sappani et al., 2023).

- **Gender Disparities in Mental Health**

Gender inequalities in South Asia significantly impact women's mental health. Women are nearly twice as likely as men to suffer from mental illness (Yu, 2018). This disparity is linked to social inequalities, gender-based violence, and limited access to mental health services (Tabassum, 2017). Demographically, the highest rates of Intimate Partner Violence (IPV) are recorded in South Asia, sub-Saharan Africa, and Oceania, with prevalence rates between 33 and 51% among women aged 15–49 years. In South Asia, domestic violence remains a significant social issue, influenced by social, economic, and cultural factors that may normalise violence experiences (Kurmanbekova et al., 2023). High rates of domestic violence and other forms of gender-based violence contribute to depression, anxiety, and post-traumatic stress disorder (PTSD) among women (David et al., 2017).

Cultural norms that restrict women's mobility and limit their social interactions can lead to isolation and loneliness, increasing the risk of mental health problems (Gailits et al., 2019). Research indicates that South Asian women are less likely to report violence due to the associated stigma, shame, fear of community isolation, and the importance placed on family reputation.

In Afghanistan, 18% of women reported that they have not met with any women outside their immediate family in the past three months. Alarmingly, 8% of survey respondents knew at least one woman or girl who had attempted suicide since the Taliban's takeover in August 2021 (UN Women, 2024). Women's limited economic opportunities and dependence on male family members can create stress and feelings of powerlessness, affecting their mental well-being (Niimi, 2009). Women in South Asia often bear the primary responsibility for caregiving, which can lead to burnout and mental health problems (Hristova, 2024).

- **Health Service Access**

Access to healthcare services in South Asia is often inequitable, with women facing significant barriers (Zaidi et al., 2017). High out-of-pocket healthcare expenditures can deter women from seeking care, particularly in low-income households (Jain, 2024). Approximately three-fifths of the women surveyed in India's NFHS-5 reported facing problems in obtaining medical care. These problems included a lack of money, distance from health facilities, a lack of female healthcare workers, and a lack of medicines (International Institute for Population Sciences, 2021).

Women in rural areas often face challenges in accessing healthcare facilities due to distance, lack of transportation, and poor infrastructure (Terefe et al., 2025). Cultural norms and restrictions on women's mobility can limit their ability to seek healthcare without the permission of male family members (Nahar & Mengo, 2019). Programmes aiming to improve utilisation of maternal care services, particularly by robust non-governmental organisations, and access to Emergency Obstetric Care, have also contributed to the decline in maternal mortality. Outside the health sector, Bangladesh has been a pioneer in areas such as girls' education, employment of women, and micro-credit programmes (El-Saharty & Ohno, 2015).

A shortage of female healthcare providers can deter women from seeking care, particularly for reproductive health issues (Bajaj et al., 2013). Women were more likely to approach accredited social health activists (ASHAs), auxiliary nurse midwives, and anganwadi workers than any other healthcare workers in India, highlighting the importance of female healthcare providers (International Institute for Population Sciences, 2021).

6 South Asian Nations' Challenges in Achieving SDG 3, 5

- **Challenges in Achieving SDG 3 - Good Health and Well-Being**

Sustainable Development Goal 3 (SDG 3) aims to ensure healthy lives and promote well-being for all. However, South Asian countries face significant challenges in achieving this goal due to various socio-economic, cultural, and environmental factors. Limited access to quality healthcare remains a major barrier, particularly in rural areas. Many regions suffer from inadequate healthcare infrastructure, a shortage of medical professionals, and economic disparities, which hinder improvements in maternal health, child mortality reduction, and disease control (Hadi, 2023).

Maternal and infant mortality rates remain critical health indicators in South Asia. Every year, 303,000 deaths occur due to pregnancy-related complications, with 99% of these deaths happening in developing countries—22% in South Asia alone (Islam & Masud, 2018). Afghanistan has the highest MMR among Asian countries and is in the top ten globally, with 620 deaths per 100,000 live births, whereas Sri Lanka has the lowest MMR (Hadi, 2023).

High infant mortality rates persist due to factors such as inadequate healthcare access, poor sanitation, lack of parental health education, and income inequality. Life expectancy is highest in the Maldives (79.89 years) and lowest in Afghanistan (65.97 years) (Hadi, 2023). While life expectancy in South Asia is gradually increasing, it still lags behind developed nations (Hameed et al., 2021). The infant mortality rate (IMR) is considered one of the most reliable indicators of a nation's health status.

It is strongly influenced by factors such as access to healthcare, water and sanitation facilities, fertility behaviour, parental nourishment, female education, GDP per capita, and income inequality (Hameed et al., 2021). Economic improvements often lead to declines in IMR (Boone, 1996), demonstrating the need for policies that address these underlying health determinants. Malnutrition and food insecurity are also major concerns in South Asia. High rates of undernourishment and stunted growth among children reflect the region's struggle to provide adequate nutrition. Many households face food insecurity, which exacerbates health issues and obstructs efforts to meet SDG 3 targets. Additionally, inadequate sanitation facilities and poor hygiene practices contribute to the spread of waterborne diseases. The lack of clean water and proper sanitation plays a critical role in increasing child mortality rates and preventing overall health improvements (Hadi, 2023). Healthcare systems in South Asia are overburdened due to high population densities, limited resources, and inefficient service delivery. These challenges lead to long waiting times, inadequate care, and restricted access to essential medical services.

The region also faces a high disease burden, with both communicable diseases like tuberculosis, malaria, and dengue and non-communicable diseases such as cardiovascular conditions and diabetes on the rise. The growing prevalence of these illnesses puts immense pressure on healthcare systems, requiring comprehensive prevention, treatment, and management strategies (Hadi, 2023). Globally, disparities in healthcare spending further highlight the challenges faced by South Asian countries. An estimated one billion people worldwide spend less than US$1 on healthcare, with developing countries averaging just US$11 per capita—far below the WHO's recommended US$30–40. In contrast, developed countries invest approximately US$1900 per person annually, allowing for greater access to modern medical facilities (Hameed et al., 2021). This stark contrast illustrates the urgent need for increased healthcare investment in less-developed nations. To achieve SDG 3, South Asian countries must implement targeted policies, increase healthcare investment, and improve access to essential medical services. Addressing these systemic healthcare challenges is crucial for enhancing public health and ensuring long-term well-being across the region.

- **Challenges in Achieving SDG 5—Gender**

Gender equality is crucial for a country's progress and prosperity, especially in South Asia, where women make up half of the population. Ensuring their participation in education and other sectors is a priority, yet there are significant disparities in female-to-male education attainment across the region.

The Maldives has the highest female-to-male mean years of education received (90%), followed by Sri Lanka, while Afghanistan has the lowest (26%). Nearly half of the female population in Pakistan, India, and Nepal still lack access to sufficient education (Sarkar et al., 2022). Girls in Pakistan and Afghanistan, as well as children from lower socio-economic backgrounds and underserved locations, still have limited access to primary education. South Asia's learning levels have not improved, and education quality, particularly in rural regions, remains inadequate (UN ESCAP, 2017).

Patriarchal values and harmful gender norms continue to limit girls' opportunities, especially those from marginalised backgrounds. Girls are three times less likely than boys to attend school and five times less likely to access mobile phones, restricting their learning and communication (UNICEF, 2024). Even those who enrol often drop out early, contributing to the fact that 35% of women in South Asia cannot read a simple sentence. Nearly 46.5% of young women are not engaged in education, employment, or training. Although progress has been made in areas like primary education, child survival, and poverty reduction, the COVID-19 pandemic has reversed many gains. Lockdowns forced girls into increased household responsibilities, hindering their education (UNICEF, 2024).

Gender inequality also affects health and nutrition, with one in five adolescent girls malnourished (UNICEF, 2024). Son preference has led to female feticide, infanticide, and breastfeeding discrimination, contributing to a gender imbalance. Girls are also more vulnerable to violence and have less access to healthcare, particularly in times of crisis. Economic distress led to a rise in early and forced marriages, with 1 in 4 girls in South Asia married before 18. Among married girls aged 15–19, 19% have experienced physical or sexual violence from an intimate partner (UNICEF, 2024). While gender equality in education is improving, greater attention is needed for gender-specific policies and programmes, along with more substantial gender inclusion in both the public and private sectors. Addressing these systemic barriers is vital for empowering girls and ensuring South Asia's overall development.

7 Conclusion and Recommendations

Gender equality and mental health are intricately linked, with gender-based inequalities significantly impacting mental health outcomes. A wide range of risk factors, including poverty, discrimination, limited education, exposure to violence, and restricted autonomy in decision-making, disproportionately affect women and marginalised groups. These factors increase their vulnerability to mental health issues such as depression, anxiety, and post-traumatic stress disorder. Addressing these underlying determinants is essential for promoting mental well-being and reducing the mental health burden in the region. Women in South Asia often experience unequal economic rights, limited decision-making power, and restricted participation in public and political life. Discriminatory laws and societal norms perpetuate these inequalities, increasing the risk of gender-based violence, early marriage, and other harmful practices that negatively impact mental health.

Achieving gender parity in public life and ensuring equal rights are critical steps towards improving mental health outcomes and fostering societal well-being. Health inequalities, particularly in access to healthcare services, further exacerbate gender disparities in mental health. Women and marginalised communities face significant barriers to accessing quality healthcare, including mental health services. Socio-economic constraints, cultural stigmas, and limited availability of specialised care prevent many individuals from seeking timely and appropriate treatment. Bridging these gaps requires gender-sensitive healthcare policies, increased investment in mental health infrastructure, and greater emphasis on community-based mental health services.

Country-specific indicators of Sustainable Development Goals (SDGs), particularly SDG 3 (Good Health and Well-Being) and SDG 5 (Gender Equality), show persistent disparities in health outcomes linked to gender inequality. South Asian countries are behind in meeting these goals due to socio-economic disparities, weak healthcare systems, and limited policy implementation. Women and marginalised populations continue to experience poorer health outcomes due to systemic inequities. South Asian nations face numerous challenges in achieving SDGs 3 and 5, including inadequate healthcare infrastructure, widespread gender-based violence, high rates of early marriage, and limited access to mental health services. Addressing these challenges requires a multi-faceted approach that includes strengthening healthcare systems, promoting gender equality, and implementing evidence-based policies to reduce mental health disparities. Only by addressing the root causes of gender inequality and integrating mental health into national development agendas, South Asian nations make meaningful progress towards achieving gender equality and improving mental health outcomes for all.

References

Aftab, W., Siddiqui, F. J., Tasic, H., Perveen, S., Siddiqi, S., & Bhutta, Z. A. (2020). Implementation of health and health-related sustainable development goals: Progress, challenges and opportunities, a systematic literature review. *BMJ*. https://doi.org/10.1136/bmjgh-2019-002273

Allen, J., Balfour, R., Bell, R., & Marmot, M. (2014). Social determinants of mental health. *International Review of Psychiatry, 26*(4), 392–407. https://doi.org/10.3109/09540261.2014.928270

Bajaj, S., Jawad, F., Islam, N., Mahtab, H., Bhattarai, J., Shrestha, D., Wijeyaratne, C., Muthukuda, D., Widanage, N., Aye, T., Aung, M., Kalra, B., Anjana, R., Sreedevi, A., & Verma, K. (2013). South Asian women with diabetes: Psychosocial challenges and management: Consensus statement. *Indian Journal of Endocrinology and Metabolism*. https://doi.org/10.4103/2230-8210.113720

Bajracharya, A., & Amin, S. (2013). Microcredit and domestic violence in Bangladesh: An exploration of selection bias influences. *Demography, 50*, 1819–1843.

Bhutta, Z. A., Dewraj, H. L., Gupta, I., de'Silva, H., Manandhar, D., Awasthi, S., … Salam, M. A. (2004). Maternal and child health: Is South Asia ready for change? *BMJ, 328*(7443), 816–819.

Boone, P. (1996). Politics and the effectiveness of foreign aid. *European Economic Review, 40*(2), 289–329. https://doi.org/10.1016/0014-2921(95)00127-1

David, S., Gazi, R., Mirzazada, M. S., Siriwardhana, C., Soofi, S., & Roy, N. (2017). Conflict in South Asia and its impact on health. *British Medical Journal*. https://doi.org/10.1136/bmj.j1537

El-Saharty, S., & Ohno, N. (2015). *South Asia's quest for reduced maternal mortality: What the data show*. Investing in Health (World Bank Blogs). Retrieved June 18, 2025, from https://blogs.worldbank.org/en/health/south-asia-s-quest-reduced-maternal-mortality-what-data-show

FAO. (2023). *The status of women in Agrifood Systems 2023; World Bank, "Global Findex Database 2021"*.

Felitti, V. J., Anda, R. F., Nordenberg, D., Williamson, D. F., Spitz, A. M., Edwards, V., … Marks, J. S. (1998). Relationship of childhood abuse and household dysfunction to many of the leading causes of death in adults: The Adverse Childhood Experiences (ACE) study. *American Journal of Preventive Medicine, 14*(4), 245–258.

Filmer, D., King, E., & Pritchett, L. (1999). Gender disparity in South Asia: Comparisons between and within countries. *None*. https://doi.org/10.1596/1813-9450-1867

Fisher, J., Cabral de Mello, M., Patel, V., Rahman, A., Tran, T., Holton, S., & Holmes, W. (2012). Prevalence and determinants of common perinatal mental disorders in women in low- and lower-middle-income countries: A systematic review. *Bulletin of the World Health Organization, 90*(2), 139G–149G.

Fowler, P. J., Tompsett, C. J., Braciszewski, J. M., Jacques-Tiura, A. J., & Baltes, B. B. (2009). Community violence: A meta-analysis on the effect of exposure and mental health outcomes of children and adolescents. *Development and Psychopathology, 21*(1), 227–259.

Freeman, D., Sheaves, B., Goodwin, G. M., Yu, L. M., Nickless, A., Harrison, P. J., … Espie, C. A. (2017). The effects of improving sleep on mental health (OASIS): A randomised controlled trial with mediation analysis. *The Lancet Psychiatry, 4*(10), 749–758.

Gailits, N., Mathias, K., Nouvet, L., Pillai, P., & Schwartz, L. (2019). Women's freedom of movement and participation in psychosocial support groups: Qualitative study in northern India. *BioMed Central*. https://doi.org/10.1186/s12889-019-7019-3

Hadi, A. (2023). *South Asian Countries progress on SDG 3 and 4*. Available online at: https://www.researchgate.net/publication/374948320_South_Asian_Countries_progress_on_SDG_3_and_4?_tp=eyJjb250ZXh0Ijp7ImZpcnN0UGFnZSI6InB1YmxpY2F0aW9uIiwicGFnZSI6InByb2ZpbGUiLCJwcmV2aW91c1BhZ2UiOiJwdWJsaWNhdGlvbiJ9fQ

Hameed, M. R., Batool, H., Khan, A., Ahmed, I., & Rehman, N. U. (2021). Sustainable development goals challenges and strategies for South Asian countries. *Humanities and Social Sciences Reviews, 9*(2), 464–474.

Holt-Lunstad, J., Smith, T. B., Baker, M., Harris, T., & Stephenson, D. (2015). Loneliness and social isolation as risk factors for mortality: A meta-analytic review. *Perspectives on Psychological Science, 10*(2), 227–237.

Hossain, A. T., Siddique, A. B., Jabeen, S., Khan, S., Haider, M. M., Ameen, S., Tahsina, T., Chakraborty, N., Nahar, Q., Jamil, K., El Arifeen, S., & Rahman, A. E. (2023). Maternal mortality in Bangladesh: Who, when, why, and where? A national survey-based analysis. *Journal of Global Health, 13*, 07002.

Hristova, G. (2024). Is *gender equality possible? The situation in Bulgaria and around the world*. https://doi.org/10.53656/str2024-2-7-gen

Hussain, H., Hussain, S., Zahra, S., & Hussain, T. (2020). Prevalence and risk factors of domestic violence and its impacts on women's mental health in Gilgit-Baltistan. *Pakistan. Pakistan Journal of Medical Sciences, 36*(4), 627–631.

ICRW. (2006). *Child marriage and domestic violence*. https://www.icrw.org/files/images/Child-Marriage-Fact-SheetDomestic-Violence.pdf. Accessed 6th June 2025.

IPU. (2023). *Parline Database; UN Women, "Women in politics 2023"*.

International Institute for Population Sciences (IIPS) and ICF. (2021). *National Family Health Survey (NFHS-5), 2019–21: India*. IIPS.

Islam, M. M., & Masud, M. S. (2018). Determinants of frequency and contents of antenatal care visits in Bangladesh: Assessing the extent of compliance with the WHO recommendations. *PLoS ONE, 13*(9), e0204752. https://doi.org/10.1371/journal.pone.0204752

Jain, S. (2024). Gender health inequalities in South Asia: A case for higher public health expenditure. *Vidyodaya Journal of Humanities and Social Sciences*. https://doi.org/10.31357/fhss/vjhss.v09irchss2023.a06

Joseph, M., Gopinath, M., Kakran, S., (Ed.). (2021). South Asian perspectives on sustainable development and gender equality. WISCOMP, Foundation for Universal Responsibility of His Holiness the Dalai Lama, New Delhi, India. ISBN: 978-81-952841-5-3.

Kabir, R., Rahman, S., Monte-Serrat, D. M., & Arafat, S. Y. (2017). Exploring the decision-making power of Bangladeshi women of reproductive age: Results from a national survey. *South East Asia Journal of Medical Sciences, 1*, 4–8.

Kabir, R., Harish, H., Alradie-Mohamed, A., Afework, S., Mohammadnezhad, M., & Arafat, S. Y. (2021). Experience of intimate partner violence of women at reproductive age group in India and their decision-making power. *Advances in Human Biology, 11*(1), 89–96.

Kabir, R., Isigi, S. S., & Candussi, C. (2024). Public mental health and access to mental health services in south Asia. In S. M. Y. Arafat & S. K. Kar (Eds.), *Access to mental health care in South Asia.* Springer. https://doi.org/10.1007/978-981-99-9153-2_11

Kandola, A., Ashdown-Franks, G., Hendrikse, J., Sabiston, C. M., & Stubbs, B. (2019). Physical activity and depression: Towards understanding the antidepressant mechanisms of physical activity. *Neuroscience & Biobehavioral Reviews, 107*, 525–539.

Karki, T. K. (2023). Women's representation in politics: An analysis of South Asian countries. *Journal of Human Rights Law and Practice, 6*(2), 1–8p.

Kennedy, E., Binder, G., Humphries-Waa, K., Tidhar, T., Cini, K., ComrieThomson, L., Vaughan, C., Francis, K., Scott, N., Wulan, N., Patton, G. C., & Azzopardi, P. (2020). Gender inequalities in health and wellbeing across the first two decades of life: An analysis of 40 low-income and middle-income countries in the Asia-pacific region. *The Lancet Global Health.* https://doi.org/10.1016/s2214-109x(20)30354-5

Kessler, R. C., Berglund, P., Demler, O., Jin, R., Merikangas, K., & Walters, E. E. (2005). Lifetime prevalence and age-of-onset distributions of DSM-IV disorders in the National Comorbidity Survey Replication. *General Psychiatry, 62*, 593–602.

Kessler, R. C., McLaughlin, K. A., Green, J. G., Gruber, M. J., Sampson, N. A., Zaslavsky, A. M., … Williams, D. R. (2010). Childhood adversities and adult psychopathology in the WHO World Mental Health Surveys. *The British Journal of Psychiatry, 197*(5), 378–385.

Kohn, R., Saxena, S., Levav, I., & Saraceno, B. (2004). The treatment gap in mental health care. *Bulletin of the World Health Organization, 82*(11), 858–866.

Kotov, R., Gamez, W., Schmidt, F., & Watson, D. (2010). Linking "big" personality traits to anxiety, depressive, and substance use disorders: A meta-analysis. *Psychological Bulletin, 136*(5), 768–821.

Kurmanbekova, A., Rahut, D., & Bera, S. (2023). *Putting an end to the social disease of domestic violence.* Asia Pathways. Retrieved June 18, 2025, from https://www.asiapathways-adbi.org/2023/03/putting-an-end-to-the-social-disease-of-domestic-violence/

Lassale, C., Batty, G. D., Baghdadli, A., Jacka, F., Sánchez-Villegas, A., Kivimäki, M., & Akbaraly, T. (2019). Healthy dietary indices and risk of depressive outcomes: A systematic review and meta-analysis of observational studies. *Molecular Psychiatry, 24*(7), 965–986. - Links healthy diets to lower depression risk.

Let, S., Tiwari, S., Singh, A., Chakrabarty, M., Singh, R. K., & Singh, A. (2024). Prevalence and determinants of anaemia among women of reproductive age in Aspirational Districts of India: An analysis of NFHS 4 and NFHS 5 data. *BMC Public Health, 24*, 437.

Lund, C. (2014). Poverty and mental health in low- and middle-income countries: A practical approach to prevention. *International Journal of Mental Health, 43*(1), 79–94. https://doi.org/10.2753/IMH0020-7411430105

Lund C. (2015). Poverty, inequality and mental health in low- and middle-income countries: time to expand the research and policy agendas. *Epidemiology and psychiatric sciences, 24*(2), 97–99. https://doi.org/10.1017/S2045796015000050

Lund, C., Breen, A., Flisher, A. J., Kakuma, R., Corrigall, J., Joska, J. A., … Patel, V. (2010). Poverty and common mental disorders in low and middle income countries: A systematic review. *Social Science & Medicine, 71*(3), 517–528.

Lund, C., Stansfeld, S., & De Silva, M. (2014). Social determinants of mental health. In *Global mental health* (pp. 116–136). Cambridge University Press.

Marmot, M., Allen, J., Boyce, T., Goldblatt, P., & Morrison, J. (2020). *Health equity in England: The Marmot Review 10 years on.* Institute of Health Equity.

Marx, W., Moseley, G., Berk, M., & Jacka, F. (2017). Nutritional psychiatry: The present state of the evidence. *Proceedings of the Nutrition Society, 76*(4), 427–436. - Reviews evidence for diet-mental health links.

Miller, K. E., & Rasmussen, A. (2010). War exposure, daily stressors, and mental health in conflict and post-conflict settings: Bridging the divide between trauma-focused and psychosocial frameworks. *Social Science & Medicine, 70*(1), 7–16.

Nahar, S., & Mengo, C. (2019). Cultural roadblocks on women's reproductive health rights: A qualitative interpretive meta-synthesis from south Asia and sub-Saharan Africa. *Health Care for Women International*. https://doi.org/10.1080/07399332.2019.1602775

Nasrullah, M., & Bhatti, J. (2012). *Gender inequalities and poor health outcomes in Pakistan: A need of priority for the national health research agenda.*

National Institute on Drug Abuse (NIDA). (2020). *Common comorbidities with substance use disorders research report*. https://nida.nih.gov/publications/research-reports/common-comorbidities-substance-use-disorders

Needham, B., & Hill, T. D. (2010). Do gender differences in mental health contribute to gender differences in physical health? *Social Science & Medicine, 71*, 1472–1479. https://doi.org/10.1016/j.socscimed.2010.07.016

Niimi, Y. (2009). *Gender equality and inclusive growth in developing Asia*. https://www.adb.org/publications/gender-equality-and-inclusive-growth-developing-asia

OECD. (2021). *A new benchmark for mental health systems: Tackling the social and economic costs of mental ill-health.* OECD Publishing.

Orth, U., & Robins, R. W. (2013). Understanding the link between low self-esteem and depression. *Current Directions in Psychological Science, 22*(6), 455–460.

Oster, E. (2006). *Does a rising tide lift all boats evenly? Health investments and gender inequality in India.*

Pascoe, E. A., & Smart Richman, L. (2009). Perceived discrimination and health: A meta-analytic review. *Psychological Bulletin, 135*(4), 531–554.

Patel, V., Araya, R., Chatterjee, S., Chisholm, D., Cohen, A., De Silva, M., … van Ommeren, M. (2007). Treatment and prevention of mental disorders in low-income and middle-income countries. *The Lancet, 370*(9591), 991–1005.

Patel, V., & Kleinman, A. (2003). Poverty and common mental disorders in developing countries. *Bulletin of the World Health Organization, 81*(8), 609–615.

Patel, V., & Prince, M. (2010). Global mental health: A new global health field comes of age. *JAMA, 303*(19), 1976–1977. https://doi.org/10.1001/jama.2010.616

Patel, V., Rodrigues, M., & DeSouza, N. (2002). Gender, poverty, and postnatal depression: A study of mothers in Goa, India. *American Journal of Psychiatry, 159*(1), 43–47.

Patel, V., Saxena, S., Lund, C., Thornicroft, G., Baingana, F., Bolton, P., … Eaton, J. (2018). The Lancet Commission on global mental health and sustainable development. *The Lancet, 392*(10157), 1553–1598. https://doi.org/10.1016/S0140-6736(18)31612-X

Peen, J., Schoevers, R. A., Beekman, A. T., & Dekker, J. (2010). The current status of urban-rural differences in psychiatric disorders. *Acta Psychiatrica Scandinavica, 121*(2), 84–93.

Pickett, K. E., & Wilkinson, R. G. (2010). Inequality: An underacknowledged source of mental illness and distress. *The British Journal of Psychiatry, 197*(6), 426–428.

Prince, M., Patel, V., Saxena, S., Maj, M., Maselko, J., Phillips, M. R., & Rahman, A. (2007). No health without mental health. *The Lancet, 370*(9590), 859–877.

Prince, M. J., Wu, F., Guo, Y., Robledo, L. M. G., O'Donnell, M., Sullivan, R., & Yusuf, S. (2015). The burden of disease in older people and implications for health policy and practice. *The Lancet, 385*(9967), 549–562.

Rahman, A. (2024). Editorial: Equity/inequality, diversity and inclusion in child and adolescent mental health—A perspective from the South Asian region. *Child and Adolescent Mental Health*. https://doi.org/10.1111/camh.12702

Robertson, J., Forte, G., & Trapsida, J. M. (2020). Essential medicines for mental disorders: Failure to act now on access is indefensible. *The Lancet Psychiatry, 7*(4), 281–283. https://doi.org/10.1016/S2215-0366(20)30047-5

Rosenfield, S., Vertefuille, J., & McAlpine, D. D. (2000).Gender stratification and mental health: An exploration of dimensions of the self. *Social Psychology Quarterly, 63*(3), 208–223.

Santini, Z. I., Jose, P. E., York Cornwell, E., Koyanagi, A., Nielsen, L., Hinrichsen, C., … Koushede, V. (2020). Social disconnectedness, perceived isolation, and symptoms of depression and anxiety among older Americans (NSHAP): A longitudinal mediation analysis. *The Lancet Public Health, 5*(1), e62–e70.

Sampson, R. J., Raudenbush, S. W., & Earls, F. (1997). Neighbourhoods and violent crime: A multilevel study of collective efficacy. *Science, 277*(5328), 918–924.

Sandhu, H. S., Roesel, S., Sharifuzzaman, M., Chunsuttiwat, S., Tohme, R. A. (2020). Progress toward hepatitis B control—South-East Asia region, 2016–2019. *MMWR. Morbidity and Mortality Weekly Report, 69*, 988–992. https://doi.org/10.15585/mmwr.mm6930a2

Sappani, M., Mani, T., & Asirvatham, E. S. (2023). Trends in prevalence and determinants of severe and moderate anaemia among women of reproductive age during the last 15 years in India. *PLoS ONE, 18*(6), e0286464.

Sarkar, M. S. K., Takemoto, A., Sadeka, S., Islam, M. M., & Al-Amin, A. Q. (2022). Achieving sustainable development goals (SDGs) among the South Asian countries: Progress and challenges. *International Journal of Regional Development, 9*(2), 42–61.

Saxena, S., Thornicroft, G., Knapp, M., & Whiteford, H. (2007). Resources for mental health: Scarcity, inequity, and inefficiency. *The Lancet, 370*(9590), 878–889. https://doi.org/10.1016/S0140-

Schuch, F. B., Vancampfort, D., Firth, J., Rosenbaum, S., Ward, P. B., Silva, E. S., … Stubbs, B. (2018). Physical activity and incident depression: A meta-analysis of prospective cohort studies. *American Journal of Psychiatry, 175*(7), 631–648.

Scott, A. J., Webb, T. L., & Rowse, G. (2017). Does improving sleep lead to better mental health? A protocol for a meta-analytic review of randomised controlled trials. *British Medical Journal Open, 7*(9), e016873.

Scott, S., Nguyen, P., Neupane, S., Pramanik, P., Nanda, P., Bhutta, Z., Afsana, K., & Menon, P. (2020). Early marriage and early childbearing in South Asia: Trends, inequalities, and drivers from 2005 to 2018. *Annals of the New York Academy of Sciences*. https://doi.org/10.1111/nyas.14531

Soeiro, C., Ribeiro, R., Almeida, I., Saavedra, R., Caridade, S., Oliveira, A., & Santos, M. (2023). Violence against women during the COVID-19 pandemic: From children to the elderly. *Social Sciences, 12*(2), 91. https://doi.org/10.3390/socsci12020091

Sreshthaputra, W. (2015). *Unlocking the potential of women's entrepreneurship in South Asia*. https://yptoolbox.unescapsdd.org/wp-content/uploads/2017/08/Policy-Brief-Womens-Entrepreneurship.pdf

Sullivan, P. F., Neale, M. C., & Kendler, K. S. (2000). Genetic epidemiology of major depression: Review and meta-analysis. *American Journal of Psychiatry, 157*(10), 1552–1562.

Tabassum, R. (2017). Gender inequality in mental health: A review from the South Asian context. *None*. https://doi.org/10.3329/BJMS.V16I2.31938

Terefe, B., Workneh, B. S., Zeleke, G., Mekonen, E., Zegeye, A. F., Aemro, A., Tekeba, B., Tamir, T. T., Wassie, M., & Ali, M. S. (2025). Uncovering women's healthcare access challenges in low- and middle-income countries using mixed effects modelling approach: Insights for achieving the sustainable development goals. *PLoS ONE*. https://doi.org/10.1371/journal.pone.0314309

Thornicroft, G. (2007). Most people with mental illness are not treated. *The Lancet, 370*(9590), 807–808.

Thornicroft, G., Mehta, N., Clement, S., Evans-Lacko, S., Doherty, M., Rose, D., … Henderson, C. (2017). Evidence for effective interventions to reduce mental-health-related stigma and discrimination. *The Lancet, 387*(10023), 1123–1132.

Thresia, C. (2017). Health inequalities in South Asia at the launch of sustainable development goals: Exclusions in health in Kerala, India need political interventions. *International Journal of Health Services*. https://doi.org/10.1177/0020731417738222

Twenge, J. M., & Campbell, W. K. (2018). Associations between screen time and lower psychological well-being among children and adolescents: Evidence from a population-based study. *Preventive Medicine Reports, 12*, 271–283.

Uher, R. (2014). Gene–environment interactions in common mental disorders: An update and strategy for a genome-wide search. *Social Psychiatry and Psychiatric Epidemiology, 49*(6), 831–843.
UN DESA. (2024). *The Sustainable Development Goals report 2024—June 2024*. UN DESA.
UNDP. (2025). *Human Development Reports2023/2024*. https://hdr.undp.org/system/files/documents/global-report-document/hdr2023-24reporten.pdf. Accessed on 10/06/2025.
UNICEF. (2023). *Child Marriage: Latest trends and future prospects*. UNICEF.
UNICEF. (2024). *Gender equality*. UNICEF South Asia. https://www.unicef.org/rosa/gender-equality
UNODC. (2022). *Global report on tracking in persons 2022* (United Nations publication, Sales No.: E.23.IV.1).
UN ESCAP. (2017). *Achieving Sustainable Development Goals in South Asia: Key policy priorities and implementation challenges*.
UN Women. (2024). *FAQs: Afghan women three years after the Taliban takeover*. https://www.unwomen.org/en/articles/faqs/faqs-afghan-women-three-years-after-the-taliban-takeover
Volkow, N. D. (2004). The reality of comorbidity: Depression and drug abuse. *Biological Psychiatry, 56*(10), 714–717.
Williams, D. R., Lawrence, J. A., Davis, B. A., & Vu, C. (2019). Understanding how discrimination can affect health. *Health Services Research, 54*(S2), 1374–1388.
Williams, D. R., & Mohammed, S. A. (2009). Discrimination and racial disparities in health: Evidence and needed research. *Journal of Behavioural Medicine, 32*(1), 20–47.
WHO. (2013). *Mental health action plan 2013–2020*. https://www.who.int/publications/i/item/9789241506021
WHO. (2022a). *Mental Health Atlas 2020*. World Health Organization (Provides latest data on resources/treatment gap).
WHO. (2022b). World Mental Health Report: Transforming Mental Health for All. Switzerland: World Health Organisation.
WHO. (2022c). *Mental disorders*. Key Facts. https://www.who.int/news-room/fact-sheets/detail/mental-disorders
WHO. (2024). Maldives, Sri Lanka achieve Hepatitis B control. WHO South-East Asia Regional Office. https://www.who.int/southeastasia/news/detail/17-01-2024-maldives-sri-lanka-achieve-hepatitis-b-control. Accessed: 24/11/2025.
WHO. (2025). World mental health today: Latest data. World Health Organisation. Licence: CC BY-NC-SA 3.0 IGO.
World Bank. (2023). *Women, business and the law 2023* (ILO Country Reports). Human Rights Watch; UNHCR.
World Economic Forum. (2024). *Global Gender Gap Report 2024*. https://www.weforum.org/publications/global-gender-gap-report-2024/
Yu, S. (2018). *Uncovering the hidden impacts of inequality on mental health: A global study*. Springer Nature. https://doi.org/10.1038/s41398-018-0148-0
Zaidi, S., Saligram, P., Ahmed, S. M., Sonderp, E., & Sheikh, K. (2017). *Expanding access to healthcare in South Asia*. https://doi.org/10.1136/bmj.j1645

Chapter 6
Unemployment and Mental Health

Karthick Subramanian, Vigneshvar Chandrasekaran, Sabaresh Pandiyan, Kiruthika Asokan, and Vikas Menon

Abstract The economic vitality of a region is significantly influenced by its population and the availability of a workforce capable of meeting labour demands through employment. Sustainable Development Goal 8 promptly recognizes the widespread impact of unemployment and envisions the desired outcomes in various domains related to unemployment. Extensive research reveals that various types of unemployment exist in the community and can lead to a significant mental health burden. Special populations such as women, children, persons with mental illness, informal workers and gig workers are more vulnerable to the effects of unemployment when compared to others. The burden and consequences of unemployment are significantly accentuated in the low- and middle-income nations of Asia when compared to the rest of the world. A multitude of sociocultural and socioeconomic forces mediate the relationship between unemployment and mental health in Asian settings. The chapter provides an overview of the changing landscape of unemployment amidst digital transformation. The chapter also briefly addresses the prevailing barriers, research gaps and recommended policy measures for achieving SDG 8 and improving mental health outcomes.

Keywords Sustainable Development Goal · Mental well-being · Job loss · Psychological · LMICs · Asia

K. Subramanian · V. Chandrasekaran · S. Pandiyan · K. Asokan
Department of Psychiatry, Mahatma Gandhi Medical College & Research Institute, Sri Balaji Vidyapeeth (Deemed-to-Be University), Puducherry, India

V. Menon (✉)
Department of Psychiatry, Jawaharlal Institute of Postgraduate Medical Education and Research (JIPMER), Puducherry, India
e-mail: drvmenon@gmail.com

S. K. Kar et al. (eds.), *Sustainable Development Goals and Mental Health in South Asia*,
South Asian Perspectives in Mental Health and Psychology ,
https://doi.org/10.1007/978-981-95-2684-0_6

1 Introduction

A nation's development is heavily dependent on its economic indicators, which are, in turn, related to various sectors such as population metrics, the nation's labour force, education, health and social welfare. A region's economic health heavily depends on its populace and the workforce with which it can dispense its labour burden by employing its people. Hence, the issue of unemployment and the degree of unemployment in any region becomes a significant cause for concern for both policymakers and citizens (Englama, 2001). The International Labour Organization (ILO), in its ILOSTAT 2023 report, revealed that globally we have around 60.8% of labour force participation rates. However, there is a significant rate (5.1%) of unemployment globally (UN Department of Economic and Social Affairs (DESA), 2024). The unemployment rates in South Asian regions are three to four times higher than the global rates (Sudan, 2021). Though inflation rates are settling in a few countries, wage growth is yet to happen in most nations, especially in the lower-income nations. Unemployment leads to reduced outputs and diminishes human capital, greater misery, social unrest, discrimination among the people and significant levels of hopelessness among those unemployed (Englama, 2001).

The issue of unemployment has undergone an evolution in terms of the "safety net" available to those unemployed (which has decreased when compared to the past years), deterioration of employment rights, reduced social support system for those unemployed and gender equality in employment chances (Bambra, 2010).

Although global employment has returned to pre-pandemic levels, job recovery and restoration rates have been consistently low, leading to significant gaps in attaining the targets of the Sustainable Development Goals (SDGs) (International Labour Organization, 2025; Sudan, 2021). Labour markets are constantly threatened by the prevailing geopolitical frictions, rising costs of climate change and sovereign debt risks. Such issues are more prominent in low-income countries than in the rest of the world.

2 Unemployment—Definition and Types

2.1 Definition

An unemployed person is defined by the International Labour Organization (ILO) as "a person aged 15 or over who simultaneously meets three of the following conditions: being unemployed for a given week; being available to take a job within two weeks; having actively sought a job in the last four weeks or having found one starting in less than three months" (Byrne & Strobl, 2004).

2.2 *Types of Unemployment*

The various types of unemployment are summarized in Table 1 (Dean et al., 2020).

3 Introduction to SDG 8 and Its Goals

The Sustainable Development Goals (SDGs), formally known as the 2030 Agenda for Sustainable Development, were adopted by all member nations of the United Nations (UN) in 2015. The SDGs are 17 in number, which involve goals across various pressing issues or crises globally across countries (Weiland et al., 2021).

Table 1 Types of unemployment and their characteristics

Type of unemployment	Characteristics
Cyclical unemployment	• The variation in unemployment rates because of prevailing economic conditions • Unemployment decreases with a flourishing economy, and the same increases during times of recession
Natural unemployment	• Occurs due to dynamic interactions between competing forces in the society—a nation's economic policy, social factors and political issues • The interactions between these forces are such that the unemployment rates are kept somewhat static in a particular region
Frictional unemployment	• It arises when multiple employees in companies risk losing their capital and their jobs and venture out to companies that are doing well in economic terms • The period when the workers move between jobs is referred to as "frictional unemployment"
Structural unemployment	• This occurs due to individuals who do not have jobs because they could not acquire the requisite skills, which are valued by the labour market • Shift in market demand has shifted from a regular skill set to a different one for example, the arrival of new technologies has displaced a significant proportion of semi-skilled labourers • Changes in the industrial landscape and increasing globalization
Voluntary unemployment	• This happens due to lethargy and a lack of willingness to work in the workforce • Workers discharge less of their potential because they believe they are receiving wages that are not equivalent to their expectations
Involuntary unemployment	• There is a mismatch between the eagerness and willingness of workers and the policies of the government • While the workers are eager to work, there is less support or opportunities from the government due to trade cycles or defective policies
Disguised employment	• Occurs in underdeveloped nations, which have far less capital compared to developed and developing countries • Consequently, the region could not employ its citizens in productive jobs

These issues of critical importance will cover the broad themes of people, planet, prosperity, peace and partnership. The Agenda 2030 was pledged by the stakeholders of all the countries to take collaborative action towards achieving the 17 SDGs and the associated 169 targets (Lee et al., 2016).

Of note, mental health has been added in the UN SDGs, considering the impact of mental health on global socioeconomic outcomes (Chisholm et al., 2016). The consideration of mental health in SDGs is quite relevant as it aims to address the unmet global mental health needs of 450 million people and the cost amounting to 4% of GDP worldwide (Izutsu et al., 2015; Thornicroft & Patel, 2014). Though mental health has been explicitly linked to SDG 3, it is linked with various other SDGs addressing food security, equitable and inclusive education, sustained economic growth and making human settlements inclusive, safe and peaceful (Thornicroft & Votruba, 2018).

3.1 How Unemployment Is Addressed Within the SDGs

Unemployment is discussed within the ambit of Goal 8 "Decent Work and Economic growth" of the 17 Sustainable Development Goals of Agenda 2030 (Bandyopadhyay, 2020). Goal 8 is further expanded as "Promote sustained, inclusive and sustainable economic growth, full and productive employment and decent work for all". SDG 8 has 12 targets addressing economic growth and employment in a sustainable manner. The focus of SDG 8 involves addressing market economies and their outcomes, prevailing gender inequality in the socioeconomic context, informal jobs and their stability, and environmental sustainability (Chigbu & Nekhwevha, 2023).

The SDG 8 includes the provision of opportunities for all, inclusive of all genders, disabilities and fair wages (Khalique et al., 2021). The term "decent work" encompasses fair wages, job security, safe working conditions and provision of social welfare measures for all those involved (Chigbu & Nekhwevha, 2023). The challenges faced in implementing the inclusivity component in SDG 8 are the presence of gender biases, wage disparities and limited representation of women in top-level positions, especially in male-dominated fields of employment (Khairy & Ghoneim, 2022).

3.2 Importance of Fixing Unemployment and Mental Health in Achieving SDG Targets

The achievement of targets under SDG 8 has faced setbacks due to the COVID-19 pandemic, rising debts, geopolitical conflict and other challenges in the past 10 years. Further, the recent 2024 report has predicted a poor labour market outlook, higher rates of unemployment and slower growth rates (Desalegn et al., 2022; Zhao et al., 2022).

Mental health is considered a part of *SDG 3* under target *3.4,* which promotes mental health and well-being, targets *3.5* and *3.a* addressing substance use and strengthens the framework for tobacco prevention. Considering the impact of social determinants on mental health, we need to address unemployment to promote mental health (Lund et al., 2018; Oswald et al., 2024). Prevocational training and supported employment resulted in improvement in outcomes such as negative symptoms and general psychopathology, whereas skill-based interventions were found to be effective in depression and anxiety (Evans et al., 2022; Moore et al., 2018; Suijkerbuijk et al., 2017). Interventions on improving working conditions, such as moderating work schedules, self-rostering, reducing working hours and interventions to reduce work-family conflict, were found to have better mental health outcomes and thus promote sustained employment (Suto et al., 2022).

Globally, investment of countries on addressing non-communicable disorders, especially on mental health, has been limited, leading to treatment gaps (Chisholm et al., 2016). The investment value needed for the years 2016–2030 for effectively addressing treatment coverage for anxiety and depression was found to be 147 billion USD, whereas the return on investment was estimated to be 310 billion USD (Chisholm et al., 2016). The return on investment analysis underscores the need to address the burden of mental disorders, which can impact social and economic growth, closely mirroring the achievement of SDGs.

To address the problems arising out of unemployment, the United Nations-Department of Economic and Social Affairs (UN-DESA) has listed Sustainable Development Goal 8 (SDG 8), which aims to "Promote sustained, inclusive and sustainable economic growth, full and productive employment and decent work for all". The recent SDG Report 2024 revealed that the majority of targets in SDG 8 are yet to be met, and, sadly, a significant portion of targets under SDG 8 is undergoing regression (UN Department of Economic and Social Affairs (DESA), 2024).

SDG 8 seeks to boost economic productivity through variety, technological advancement and innovation. It focuses particularly on the labour-intensive sectors. The SDG 8 also aims to achieve gender equality in jobs and the inclusion of skilled young people and advocates equal pay for persons with disabilities. SDG 8 aims to foster economic development that is environmentally sound and socially just, yielding improved living standards and equal and accessible opportunities for everyone.

4 Social Determinants of Unemployment

The complex and intrinsic relationship between SDG 8 and other key SDGs can be understood by studying the prevailing connections between providing a decent and sustainable job and ensuring adequate addressal of poverty, gender equality, quality education among other indicators of individual and societal well-being (Fig. 1).

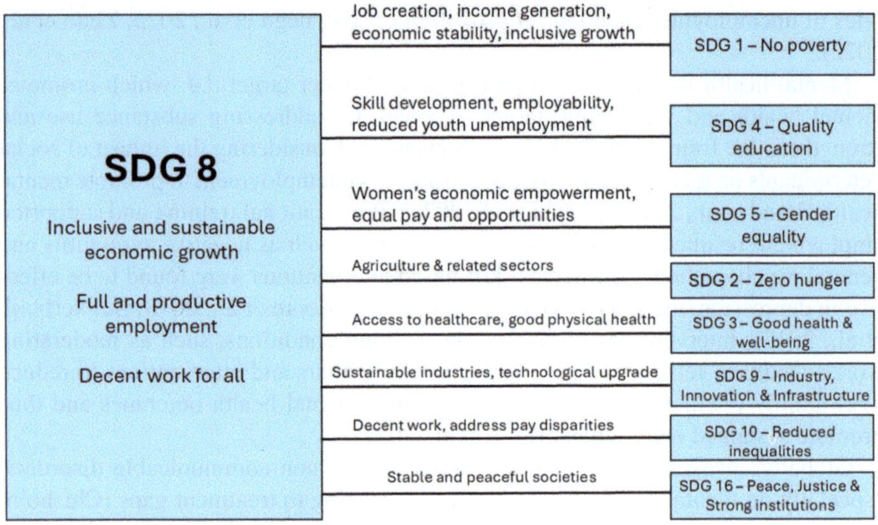

Fig. 1 Dynamic relationship of SDG 8 with some of the other SDGs

The relationships tend to be multiple and dynamic between unemployment and the social factors. For example, unemployment leads to poverty, and further poverty leads to social exclusion; on the flip side, social exclusion leads to further reduced chances of employment (Gallie et al., 2003).

There are other social determinants of unemployment, which are listed as follows (Huynh & Vo, 2023; Rahman et al., 2025; Singh, 2019):

- Reduced capital inputs from the government
- An inappropriate educational system which focuses on academic grades but not on skill development
- Lack of provisions for vocational training in schools
- Higher political inclusiveness
- Migration
- Rapid growth in population

4.1 *Migration and Unemployment*

Migration, especially among Asian nations, has been linked to a reduced unemployment burden. This was attributed to the "competition" effects triggered by the incoming migrant labourers, motivating the local workers to compete for and obtain jobs at their places (Huynh & Vo, 2023). However, migration has been linked to increased rates of unemployment in low- and low-middle-income countries of Asia (such as India, Indonesia, the Philippines and Vietnam). Such a disparity was attributed to the differential skill development between migrant labourers and native labourers of low-income nations of Asia, with the former being more skilled than the latter.

5 Unemployment and Health-Related Outcomes

5.1 Unemployment and Physical Health

Compared to those who were employed, unemployed individuals were more likely to suffer from physical problems and to have visited physicians or been hospitalized for their recovery (Jin et al., 1995). Studies have shown that unemployment can have three modes of impact on physical health outcomes: dose–response mode (the longer the unemployment, the greater the health-related burden), steady-state mode (no effects beyond a specific duration of unemployment) and adaptation mode (the person accommodates to unemployment and displays no distress) (Janlert et al., 2015). The first model, i.e. the dose–response model, is the most replicated finding across various studies.

The ill effects of unemployment on overall well-being are often linked to poverty and financial strain arising from unemployment and vice versa (Bartley, 1994). In addition to this bidirectional link, unemployment can also lead to significant psychological distress, which can hamper both the productivity of the individual and his/her economic resources significantly to cover their healthcare costs. The interactions are depicted in Fig. 2.

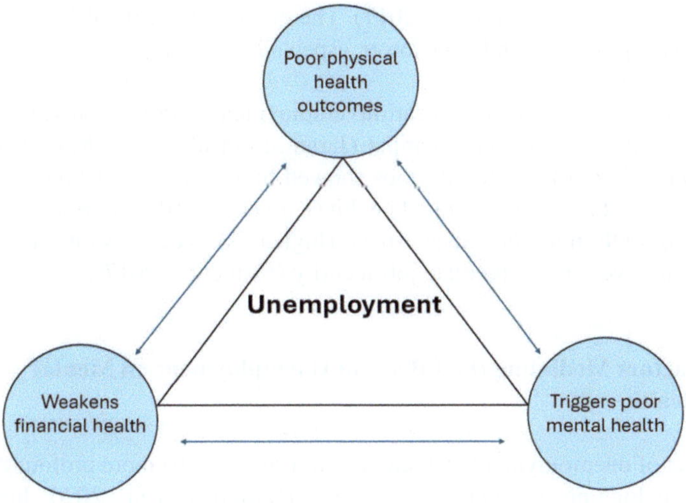

Fig. 2 Relationship between unemployment and the health of an individual

Unemployment is also associated with higher mortality rates due to cardiovascular disease and suicide (Janlert, 1997; Jin et al., 1995). Consequent to unemployment, people start engaging in behaviours which can be detrimental to overall well-being, such as substance abuse, reckless behaviours and self-destructive behaviours (Bartley, 1994; Janlert, 1997). Studies have shown that periods of economic recession and unemployment scenarios in a region are more likely to increase substance abuse among the youth (Nagelhout et al., 2017).

5.2 *Unemployment and Mental Health*

5.2.1 Psychological Consequences of Unemployment

Apart from financial outcomes, employment caters to human needs such as purpose, structuring of time and workplace social connections (Arena et al., 2023). A rise in unemployment rates tends to harm psychological well-being, which is evident by increasing rates of anxiety disorders, mood disorders and suicidal behaviours among individuals without a formal job (Virgolino et al., 2022). The reporting of depressive feelings and suicidal ideations was higher among unemployed individuals, both males and females (Ahn et al., 2021). It has been observed that both unemployment and subjective feelings of job insecurity were associated with increased risk for depressive symptoms (Kim & von dem Knesebeck, 2016). Contemporary literature indicates that higher rates of depressive symptoms and anxiety symptoms are found in the majority of unemployed individuals (Navarro-Abal et al., 2018). The presence of a full-time employment was protective against depression, distress and use of substances (Perreault et al., 2017). The quality of life (QOL) among individuals without a job was found to be lower, especially mental QOL than physical QOL (Yang et al., 2016).

Apart from unemployment, precarious employment leads to depression, increased stress, suicidal ideations and attempts (Jaramillo et al., 2022; Min et al., 2015). Men employed with low-security jobs showed higher rates of depression, suicidal ideations and reduction in self-rated health (Kim et al., 2017). Further, women who are not heads of the household tend to have a higher risk of depression when employed in jobs with lower or intermediate job security (Kim et al., 2017).

5.2.2 Factors Mediating the Effects of Unemployment on Mental Health

The impact of unemployment on mental health seems to be more profound on males and those belonging to younger age groups (Bartelink et al., 2020; Junna et al., 2022; Virgolino et al., 2022). Younger age represents a period in an individual's lifetime that has an increased risk of unemployment, which is associated with short-term and long-term mental health outcomes (Bartelink et al., 2020; Lee et al., 2019).

The majority of unemployed individuals were older and female gender and invariably experienced mental health problems. Among the middle-aged and elderly population, unemployment is a factor contributing to depression (Shen et al., 2024).

Individuals experiencing unemployment tend to have better psychological outcomes if educational levels and social support are better, whereas prolonged periods of unemployment are associated with poorer outcomes, especially in younger adulthood (Junna et al., 2022; Lee et al., 2019; Virgolino et al., 2022). The relationship between depression and unemployment was significantly moderated by the social support of the individuals (Perreault et al., 2017).

The presence of a positive neighbourhood during younger adulthood can provide a positive impact on mental health problems arising due to unemployment (Lee et al., 2019). The aforementioned social determinants further cement the role of the social causation hypothesis in mediating unemployment and mental health outcomes. The social causation hypothesis posits that through financial distress, poor social capital and poor living outcomes, mental health issues are promulgated (Jin et al., 2020). The abovementioned factors are direct and indirect results of unemployment, thus reaffirming unemployment's role in mental health.

The current income and unemployment tend to have an influence over mental health outcomes, especially suicidal ideations (Yi & Hong, 2020). Suicidal ideations were reported by individuals without employment compared to workers with wages (Kim & Yoon, 2018). Further, an increase in household income was associated with decreased reporting of suicidal ideations (Kim & Yoon, 2018). Individuals engaging in passive rumination were found to have an increased tendency to experience negative emotions, leading to psychological distress (Tuna & Balcı, 2020).

Apart from unemployment, precarious employment is also considered an important social determinant of mental health outcomes (Canivet et al., 2016; Lundstrom et al., 2024). Precarious employment is a multidimensional construct including employment insecurity, poor income and poor rights and employment protection (Gunn et al., 2021; Jaramillo et al., 2022). Precarious employment was higher among people of the younger age group, female gender, those with lower levels of education and among immigrants (Jaramillo et al., 2022). Precarious employment has been associated with reduced workplace well-being, impairments in physical and mental health, including emotional well-being (Jaydarifard et al., 2023).

Male workers and those with low- and middle-income levels employed in precarious work reported greater suicide risk compared to others (Han et al., 2017). However, individuals employed in jobs with higher emotional needs and diminished job control were found to have a higher risk for suicidal ideations compared to those in jobs with lower emotional needs and higher job control, irrespective of gender (Yoon et al., 2016).

5.2.3 Mental Illness Contributing to Unemployment

Studies consistently report that mental illnesses can lead to significant work disability, leading to unemployment (Harkko et al., 2018). Mental illness can lead to absenteeism from work, attention and concentration deficits, leading to reduced work performance and criticism by peers and superiors at the workplace. Psychotropic medications, by themselves, can cause a variety of side effects which make people with mental illness more prone to compromise at the workplace and can eventually lead to becoming unemployed. Perceived stigma in patients with mental illness and negative attitudes towards mental illness at workplace were associated with high chances of unemployment (Brouwers, 2020). It is crucial to remember that the relationship between mental health and unemployment is bidirectional and any effort in teasing out the causal relationship often stresses their dynamic associations.

5.2.4 Economic Costs of Untreated Mental Health Problems

Chronic mental health issues are associated with long-term disabilities, burdening the societies and economies of all countries, both developed and developing (Yang et al., 2024). Those individuals with baseline mental health issues were unemployed for a prolonged duration, leading to a decrease in productivity and labour market participation (Butterworth et al., 2012). Individuals with mental health problems experience difficulties at work because of the nature of their symptoms, side effects of medications and the reluctance of employers due to concerns over relapse and inadequate performance (Biggs et al., 2010; Subramaniam et al., 2022).

The contemporary studies on the economic effects of mental health promotion initiatives are limited in terms of generalizability as they predominantly involve high-income countries, and they consider short-term outcomes (Ha et al., 2022). The interventions utilized in mental health prevention were found to be cost-effective, indicated by the incremental cost-effectiveness ratio (ICER) and return on investment in such initiatives (Le et al., 2021). Further, targeted interventions were cost-effective when compared to universal prevention initiatives, especially in children, where mental health screening at school was highly effective (Le et al., 2021). Access to mental health services, when limited, can negatively impact the economic growth and poverty reduction initiatives, which are vital SDG indicators (Ngui et al., 2010). Mental health issues can affect the functioning and employment seeking, which in turn increase the poverty levels (Bostock, 2004).

5.2.5 Coping with Unemployment

Unemployment leads to a disruption in the identity of an individual and alters the direction of life (Arena et al., 2022). Unemployment, apart from decreasing the physical and mental health of individuals, can inhibit reemployment in a job (Hult et al., 2020).

Coping strategies play a moderating role in mental health issues due to unemployment, where disengagement coping strategies were found to worsen mental health issues (Menéndez-Espina et al., 2019). However, coping strategies were often found to be difficult to utilize in the event of unemployment (Arena et al., 2022). Unemployed individuals with depression and anxiety symptoms tend to develop maladaptive coping strategies in coping with unemployment, such as denial, self-blame, blaming others, catastrophizing, lesser perspective taking and increased use of substances (Extremera & Rey, 2014; Navarro-Abal et al., 2018). Further, avoidant coping was found to be associated with poor labour market participation among young adults (Billeskov et al., 2020).

Among unemployed individuals, the core self-evaluations were found to be negatively correlated with negative experience of unemployment, suggesting strengthening of core self-evaluations in programmes aimed at unemployed individuals (Virkes et al., 2017). The presence of positive reappraisal, positive refocusing, self-efficacy with lower levels of self-blame, rumination and catastrophizing has been found to positively mediate mental health (Extremera & Rey, 2014; Yang et al., 2016). The scientific literature reiterates the efficacy of both prevention-level and treatment-level interventions in managing anxiety and depression associated with unemployment (Arena et al., 2023).

Vocational interventions focusing on skills to improve the job-search strategies and to develop personality, and preparedness against setbacks was not found to improve work engagement or reduce mental health issues in a significant manner (Audhoe et al., 2010). However, therapeutic interventions such as cognitive behavioural therapy, physical activity promotion and counselling, along with job-search training, were found to have a beneficial effect in increasing employment rates (Hult et al., 2020). Recreational activities which are physically active, relevant to the sociocultural context and relaxing by nature were effective in addressing the negative experiences of unemployment (Kerr et al., 2012).

6 Unemployment and Mental Health—A South Asian Perspective

6.1 The Burden of Unemployment in Asia/South Asia

Unemployment significantly influences a country's economy, society and an individual's personal life. While it is a significant global issue, its severity varies across nations (Paul & Moser, 2009). According to the ILO, the estimated rate of unemployment rate in South Asian countries for 2023 was 4.6%. Among these nations, Afghanistan had the highest unemployment rate at 14.4%, whereas the Maldives recorded the lowest at 4.1%. Job loss has often been reported to cause adverse physical and mental health outcomes (Fig. 3).

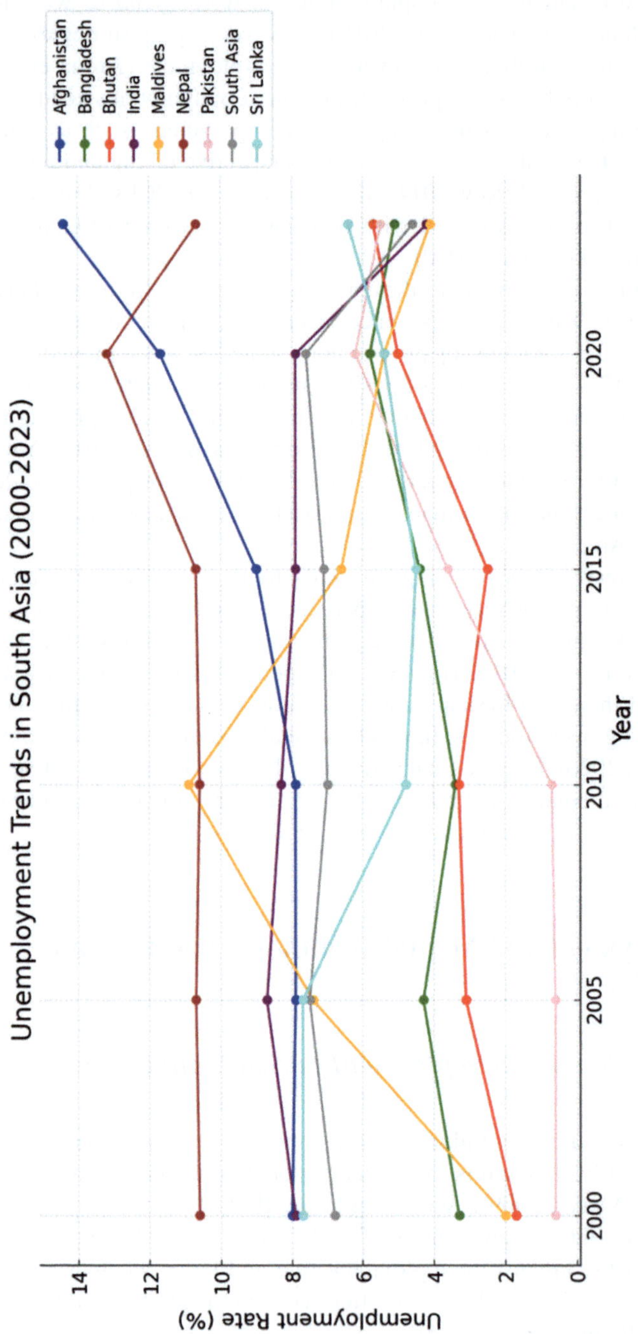

Fig. 3 Unemployment trends in South Asia between 2000 and 2023 (data obtained from the International Labour Organisation)

Youth unemployment rates are higher than the reported rates of unemployment among the general population. Female unemployment rates are higher than those of males. Among the Southeast Asian countries, Indonesia, Timor-Leste and the Philippines have had higher youth unemployment rates than the global rates (Yeung, 2022). On the contrary, lowest youth unemployment rates were found among countries such as Lao PDR, Myanmar and Cambodia in the Southeast Asian region.

Recently, there has been a consistent increase in the rate of young men **n**ot in **e**mployment, **e**ducation or **t**raining (NEET) when compared to the historical average. The UN SDG Report 2024 states that one in five young people is in this NEET category. This is particularly significant in the low-income countries, which record an increase of almost 4% points in young men's NEET rate above the historical average. This causes many young men to be unequipped to participate in the labour market and makes them more vulnerable to future economic shocks (International Labour Organization, 2025).

6.2 *Work Environment Conditions in South Asia*

Research suggests that the negative effects of unemployment on mental health tend to be less severe in economically developed nations, where stronger social security systems provide a protective buffer. Conversely, in countries with greater income inequality and weaker unemployment protections, the psychological distress associated with job loss is more pronounced (Paul & Moser, 2009). These cross-country variations emphasize that unemployment is particularly distressing in economically underdeveloped nations, where financial insecurity and limited social support further exacerbate its mental health consequences. Concurrently, the relationship between unemployment, mental health and poverty is uniform across all countries. In many low- and middle-income countries, the informal sector offers greater flexibility in employment, enabling individuals to engage in self-employment, agricultural work or other jobs without rigorous attendance requirements (Biswas et al., 2024). This contrasts with developed economies, where structured work environments may limit opportunities for individuals struggling with mental health disorders. Additionally, the presence of extended family and community-based social support systems in developing countries may serve as a protective factor, helping individuals cope with economic hardship and reducing their risk of mental health deterioration due to job loss.

6.3 Relationship Between Unemployment and Mental Health—Asian Literature

Numerous studies from Western countries have established a causal link between unemployment and mental health, though the underlying mechanisms remain unclear (Franke et al., 2024; Yang et al., 2024). Higher unemployment rates are consistently associated with depression, anxiety and stress (Cassidy & Wright, 2008; Lim et al., 2018). Furthermore, this relationship is bidirectional; while unemployment leads to worse mental health outcomes, pre-existing mental illnesses can increase the risk of job loss. However, the predominance of Western studies in this area limits the generalizability of these findings to other regions (Henkel, 2011).

All South Asian countries conduct Periodic Labour Force Surveys to assess workforce trends and unemployment rates. These surveys provide crucial economic indicators, highlighting issues such as high dependency ratios, poverty and the underutilization of human resources, which in turn slow economic growth. However, they do not capture the personal mental health struggles faced by the unemployed, as their primary focus is on economic metrics rather than individual well-being. Consequently, research regarding the psychological impact of unemployment in South Asia remains limited, with only a handful of studies addressing this critical issue, as described in Table 2.

The majority of studies have focused on the young population, indicating that unemployment during early adulthood is distressing. The psychological impact may be due to the uncertainty about the future, financial dependency and existential experiences of loss and anxiety (Biswas et al., 2024). Broader threats to fundamental survival needs, social expectations and self-esteem further compound these stressors. It is observed that across India, Bangladesh and Pakistan, common mental illnesses such as depression (49.3%–54.4%), anxiety (53.6%–61.8%) and stress are consistently reported at high levels in an unemployed population, indicating a significant psychological burden (Bhat & Joshi, 2020; Gaur & Ram, 2016; Rafi et al., 2019; Zubair et al., 2016). The studies comparing employed and unemployed individuals found that unemployed youth consistently showed higher levels of emotional distress, loss of behavioural control and psychiatric morbidity (Bhat & Joshi, 2020; Biswas et al., 2024).

6.4 Unemployment and Youth Suicide

In addition to this, some researchers have analysed Indian data to examine the relationship between youth suicide and unemployment, using information from the National Crime Records Bureau, the Government of India and the ILO (Bhowmik & Poddar, 2021). It was seen that in India, the suicide rate among unemployed youth has been rising at 4.08% per year between 1980 and 2020, outpacing the overall suicide rate, which increased by 3.04% per year over four decades. Furthermore, the

Table 2 Unemployment and mental health studies from South Asian countries

Study	Country	Population	Sample size	Results
Biswas et al., (2024)	India	Higher-educated migrant youth	400	Unemployed youths suffered from greater levels of depression and anxiety than their employed counterparts *Overall prevalence:* Depression—54.4% Anxiety—61.8% Stress—47.9%
Rafi et al., (2019)	Bangladesh	Civil service job seekers	304	*Overall prevalence:* Depression—49.3% Anxiety—53.6% Stress—28.3%
Gaur and Ram (2016)	India	Youth	300	Unemployed youth report 49% more mental health disorders
Bhat and Joshi (2020)	India	Employed and unemployed youth	200	A greater degree of behavioural and emotional dysregulation is higher for the unemployed group than the employed group
Zubair et al., (2016)	Pakistan	Young unemployed people	2511	Significant levels of psychiatric morbidity among the unemployed (General Health Questionnaire score >3 in 75.1% of the sample)

youth unemployment rate has grown by 1.24% per year between 1990 and 2020. This indicates that suicides among unemployed youth have risen faster than both overall suicides and youth unemployment. Statistical analysis further highlights a strong link between youth unemployment and suicide rates, indicating that for every 1% rise in youth unemployment per year, the suicide rate among unemployed youth increases by 1.49%, highlighting the serious mental health risks associated with joblessness.

6.5 *Unemployment and Substance Use Disorders*

The negative mental health consequences of unemployment extend beyond suicide risk, with substance use disorders (SUDs) being another critical concern. Studies indicate that unemployed individuals are more likely to consume alcohol, tobacco and illicit drugs than their employed counterparts (Hammer, 1992). Research from South Asian countries primarily reports the prevalence of substance use among unemployed individuals but often fails to establish whether unemployment directly leads to substance use. Some researchers argue that job loss and economic distress contribute to rising alcohol and drug use, while others suggest that pre-existing substance use disorders escalate the likelihood of unemployment. Until recently, empirical evidence supporting either perspective remained limited (Henkel, 2011). However, studies now highlight a bidirectional relationship, with unemployment acting as both a cause and a consequence of substance use. Western studies consistently show that unemployed individuals have significantly higher rates of substance use and addiction compared to those with stable employment (Nolte-Troha et al., 2023). The loss of income, financial insecurity and psychosocial stress associated with joblessness can exacerbate mental health struggles, leading to short-term coping mechanisms such as increased substance use. This strong relationship between unemployment and adverse mental health outcomes, including suicide risk and substance use disorders, underscores the broader socioeconomic influences at play. However, the psychological impact of unemployment does not occur in isolation; it is shaped by a country's economic conditions and social policies.

6.6 Unemployment Protection Measures in South Asia

Many countries have launched initiatives to improve the livelihoods of vulnerable groups, especially low-income and low-skilled workers. These initiatives generally fall into two categories: self-employment promotion schemes and programmes offering direct wage employment. Public works programmes, particularly those targeting rural and urban poverty, have shown considerable success in reducing poverty levels (Zaman, 2011).

One notable example is India's Mahatma Gandhi National Rural Employment Guarantee Act-2005 (MGNREGA), a legally mandated employment guarantee scheme that offers up to 100 days of paid work annually to rural households. It focuses on infrastructure development, such as roads and irrigation facilities, while also addressing poverty and unemployment. As of 2015–2016, over 90 crore job cards had been distributed, with employment provided to about 4.5 crore households annually, covering roughly one-third of rural India. This makes MGNREGA the largest public works employment initiative in the world, often cited as a model for other developing nations (Dheeraj, 2017).

Other South Asian countries have implemented their own employment and social protection programmes. For instance, Bangladesh runs the Employment Generation Program for the Poorest (EGPP), focusing on food and cash-based support. Pakistan has schemes like the Benazir Income Support Programme (BISP) and the Kamyab Jawan Program, which support social security and entrepreneurship. Sri Lanka's Samurdhi Program combines cash transactions with access to microfinance, while Nepal promotes youth employment through the Prime Minister Employment Program (PMEP).

While these programmes address the economic dimensions of unemployment, a crucial aspect often overlooked across the region is the mental health impact of joblessness. Unemployment serves as a key economic indicator, reflecting a nation's overall health and productivity, yet the psychological consequences are rarely accounted for. Although all South Asian countries conduct periodic labour force surveys to monitor employment trends, few integrate health-related variables into their frameworks. Incorporating such data would allow for the development of more comprehensive support systems that go beyond financial aid. By acknowledging the mental health burden associated with unemployment, policymakers can create targeted interventions that promote both economic stability and psychological resilience, paving the way for a more inclusive and holistic workforce strategy.

6.7 *Impact of Digital Transformation on Unemployment and Mental Health in South Asia*

Artificial Intelligence (AI) is considered an engineered system that generates outputs in various domains for a given set of human inputs. AI can have a significant impact on employment by changing methods of operation and processes across multiple fields such as industries, finance, health and information technology (Frank et al., 2019; Xu et al., 2023). The feared adverse impact of AI on employment arises from its potential to reshape entire fields, leading to the replacement of the workforce, and further, it can increase the income disparity between highly skilled and low-skilled employees (Xu et al., 2023). Further, the adoption of AI in the workplace has been associated with negative emotions and heightened job insecurity among employees, resulting in poorer physical and mental health (Patel et al., 2018).

However, the impact of AI is not entirely adverse on employment. The scientific literature on AI reiterates a positive impact on employment, considering an increasing demand and income growth of the highly skilled workforce and newer job opportunities (Mokyr et al., 2015; Xu et al., 2023). Further, adoption of AI may lead to newer learning opportunities, skill development and ultimately, job performance of the employees (Xu et al., 2023). AI can improve the unemployment rates among people with disabilities by bridging the job expectations and skill deficits due to disabilities (Abid et al., 2024). A positive opportunity perception of AI and informal learning at the workplace were associated with better workplace well-being of employees (Xu et al., 2023).

7 Impact of Unemployment on Special Populations

7.1 *Children and Adolescents*

Parental unemployment is linked to various adverse outcomes for children, adolescents and young adults. Such adverse effects might include poor outcomes in physical health, mental well-being, education and social behaviour (Christoffersen, 2000). Parental joblessness also indirectly affects children's well-being through alterations in family income, parental time involvement and the overall quality of interpersonal relationships. The family stress model suggests that adverse economic conditions can lead to parental worry and strain, increased marital conflict, disengaged parenting, reduced emotional warmth and strained parent–child relationships (Francesconi & Heckman, 2016).

Children of unemployed parents tend to perform worse academically and experience poorer health outcomes (Sleskova et al., 2006). Such children are more likely to suffer from bullying and social isolation in school and, consequently, undergo frequent school shifts and changes. The stress arising from parental unemployment has a negative impact on children's learning abilities. They often secure lower marks and grades. Consequently, such children are noted to have higher dropout rates than their peers with employed parents.

When unemployment results in severe poverty, children are exposed to food insecurity and nutritional deficiencies, which can further affect their academic performance (Cutts et al., 1998). Additionally, young children with unemployed parents show increased susceptibility to psychosomatic symptoms, appetite and sleep disturbances (Madge, 1983). They are also more likely to experience accidents and require hospitalization when compared to children with employed parents, secondary to the above issues.

Longitudinal studies show that after the father's loss of job, there is a one-fourth increase in the likelihood of offspring requiring psychotropic medication in the first year (Moustgaard et al., 2018). Parental unemployment has been associated with an increased risk of sexual abuse, neglect, physical abuse and even higher degrees of child maltreatment (Judd et al., 2023).

Bio-molecular research indicates that early stress caused by childhood adversity, such as parental unemployment, impacts the nervous and immune systems. This leads to diminished cognitive, social and emotional functioning, resulting in poorer health outcomes. Such forms of recurrent stress can sensitize the body's systems, causing children to become increasingly reactive to stress over time (Miller et al., 2011).

7.2 Unemployment and Its Impact on Persons with Mental Illness

The Rights of Persons with Disabilities Act (2016) and the Mental Healthcare Act (2017) aim to support individuals with mental illnesses (PMI) by offering protection and services. The Rights of Persons with Disabilities Act provides a 4% reservation for people with benchmark disabilities, including mental illness, in government jobs. The Mental Healthcare Act guarantees comprehensive rehabilitation services as a right of the patient. Despite the increased treatment gap for mental illness in India, the implementation of these policies remains a significant challenge (Mental Healthcare Act, 2017; The Rights of Persons with Disabilities Act (2016), 2016).

Due to stigma, people with mental illnesses often encounter displays of negative attitudes in the workplace, higher unemployment rates and experience limited access to services (Shidhaye & Kermode, 2013). On the other hand, unemployment can also lead to relapse and rehospitalization in cases of schizophrenia, increasing the caregiving burden associated with the illness (Mathias et al., 2018). In India, men with schizophrenia often face pressure to work regardless of their disability severity. Though women with severe mental illness (SMI) are typically exempt from the pressure to earn a wage, they are still expected to don the traditional domestic roles, such as homemaking and child-rearing. Addressing these gendered expectations in therapy is crucial.

When gender differences were studied between the employed and the unemployed among those with mental illness, women were more likely to lose jobs than men after the onset of mental illness. For men with mental illness, factors such as low self-esteem, criticism by family members and stigma related to unemployment warrant adequate addressal in therapeutic settings (Jaleel et al., 2015).

Unemployment benefits have been shown to have a protective effect on both men and women. However, unemployed men who do not receive benefits are more likely to experience adverse mental health outcomes compared to their female counterparts in similar situations (Artazcoz et al., 2004).

7.3 Gender Differences

Psychosocial factors such as gender, family roles and socioeconomic class play major roles in influencing the impact of unemployment on mental health. For married men, employment is often essential due to their responsibilities for providing for the family's material needs. Conversely, women are generally made to perceive that their primary roles are nurturing and caring for the family. This role disparity often underlies the experiences of guilt, role conflict and significant distress when women attempt to balance work and family responsibilities (Kohl et al., 2011; Van der Meer, 2014; Walsh et al., 2002).

The protective effects of unemployment compensation are unequally distributed across gender, family roles and social classes. Men with family responsibilities tend to experience more pronounced mental health issues due to unemployment. However, for women, particularly those with children, being married to an employed partner may act as a buffer against the adverse mental health effects of unemployment. These differences highlight the importance of considering gender and family roles when addressing the mental health consequences of unemployment.

7.4 *Indigenous People and Unemployment*

Asia houses the greatest number of indigenous people in the world. The indigenous people of Asia constitute a significant percentage of the financially deprived population. They experience high rates of poverty, exclusion and marginalization, informal economy, malnutrition and reduced access to basic services, among various other obstacles (Dhir, 2015). Needless to say, a significant proportion of them are unemployed. Consequent to such hardships, they suffer from mental health conditions, indulge in substance abuse behaviours and experience difficulties in accessing mental health services.

There is an increasing focus on the rights and well-being of indigenous peoples from the international community. The steps are visible in the 2030 Agenda for Sustainable Development, the outcome draft of the 2014 World Conference on Indigenous Peoples and the UN Guiding Principles on Business and Human Rights. Multipronged approaches from the international community are needed to address the multifaceted challenges faced by indigenous communities, including poverty, inequality, discrimination and barriers to participation. There remains a critical need for effective interventions, particularly in the world of work, to achieve meaningful progress in eradicating poverty, mitigating inequality and securing human rights. This becomes crucial in Asian countries where significant numbers of indigenous people live and experience poor development-related outcomes (Dhir, 2015).

7.5 *Caste System and Unemployment*

Literature has consistently revealed that there are rising inequalities in the Asian labour market due to unequal employment opportunities, social obstacles like poverty, gender disparity and social hierarchy based on caste systems (Mamgain & Khan, 2021; Vicziany, 2005). The prevailing caste systems, especially in India, prevent the free movement of human labour, land, financial inputs and business entrepreneurship, and create an unequal, divided and monopolistic economic ecosystem, leading to a vicious cycle of discrimination followed by reduced job opportunities and vice versa. The allocation of jobs and the nature of the jobs allocated to lower caste untouchables (e.g. Dalits in India) are based on engendered social restrictions which force them to perform jobs which are inherently socially degrading and aversive, and have fewer opportunities for job satisfaction (e.g. manual scavenging) (Thorat & Newman, 2007).

Governmental policy interventions are the need of the hour to address the high incidence of underemployment among marginalized groups (Mamgain & Khan, 2021). Studies also revealed that capitalism, as a social and economic force, has the capacity to disrupt the caste system in India (Thorat & Newman, 2007).

7.6 *Gig Workers*

Gig workers, also known as independent contractors or freelancers, are individuals who earn income through activities which are not characterized by any standard, sustained employer-employee relationships. The informal and freelance economy offers significant employment-related benefits for gig workers. However, it often lacks the crucial features such as stability, increments and perks, leave benefits and regular income flow, when compared with stable employment. Consequently, gig workers experience a greater mental health burden and report lower life satisfaction scores than those employed full-time in regular jobs. Nevertheless, gig workers report better mental health outcomes than their unemployed counterparts, probably due to experiencing a lesser financial burden (Wang et al., 2022).

7.7 *Informal Work*

Informal workers consist of domestic workers, casual day labourers and workers belonging to the formal sector without social security benefits. Employment insecurity in informal work is likely a major contributor to mental distress and adverse health outcomes. Informal jobs are often marked by an imbalance between the effort workers invest and the rewards they receive, such as low wages, lack of recognition and poor job stability. This imbalance is intensified in environments where workers have no legal protections. Studies have shown that minor mental health disorders are more common among informally employed workers than their formally employed counterparts (Ludermir & Lewis, 2003; Santana et al., 1997). Additional health risks in informal work include exposure to violence, sexual abuse, discrimination and generally poorer physical and psychosocial working conditions—all of which act as significant stressors (Ludermir & Lewis, 2005).

8 Strategies to Address Mental Health Issues Due to Unemployment

8.1 *Job Club Interventions*

Job clubs included skills training seminars designed to enhance job-seeking abilities. The sessions provided the practical assistance required for job seekers, including completing forms, preparing curriculum vitae (CVs) and making telephonic contacts to reach out to potential employers. The "Job Club" involved a half-day group workshop primarily focused on job-search techniques, followed by weekly review meetings. The follow-up sessions focused on setting job-related goals, providing information about job seeking, interview preparation, drafting a CV and completing application forms.

JOBS 1: This class-based intervention consisted of active group training sessions led by a male–female pair of trainers, designed to develop problem-solving and decision-making skills. They also provide resilience against setbacks and provide social support (Caplan et al., 1989). The intervention also focused on fostering positive regard from trainers and inculcating job-search techniques, along with strategies to improve the self-esteem of job seekers (Price et al., 1992; Vinokur et al., 1991).

JOBS 2 strives to enhance individual expertise, autonomy and employment search abilities through issue resolution, decision-making, group exercises, obstacle anticipation and guidance from trainers. Participants were trained in job-search skills through active learning and practice (Vinokur & Schul, 1997; Vinokur et al., 1996). The programme included competence development, peer support, troubleshooting, mentorship from instructors, recognizing possible obstacles, devising solutions and rehearsing reactions.

Extensive randomized controlled trials (RCTs), including three involving more than 1000 people, consistently demonstrate that intense job club programmes spanning 1–2 weeks can reduce the risk of depression in unemployed individuals. The most significant clinical benefits were observed in participants who were at a higher risk of developing depression.

8.2 Cognitive Behavioural Therapy (CBT)

CBT utilizes psychoeducation about positive mental health, cognitive restructuring, exposure exercises and social skills training. Coping skills will be enhanced to tackle unemployment-related emotional distress and automatic negative thoughts, and to harbour optimistic explanatory patterns. There is strong evidence of a short-term (3-month) effect on depressive symptoms and reemployment rates in larger trials delivering CBT (including psychoeducation, exposure-related therapies over 7 weeks (Harris et al., 2002). Work-related CBT has shown consistent improvement in negative thinking and emotional disturbances for 3 months after induction into therapy (Himle et al., 2014).

8.3 Positive Psychology

Positive psychology interventions include techniques which are targeted towards building a positive mindset and resilience, such as writing a gratitude letter, describing "three good things or events" each day and developing a "strengths in action" plan. These strategies aim to enhance the well-being of job seekers by improving subjective experiences and fostering hope, positivity and happiness (Dambrun & Dubuy, 2014).

8.4 Emotional Competence Training

Based on the framework of Kotsou et al. (2011), emotional competence training emphasizes group activities that aim to identify and comprehend emotions in oneself and others, utilize emotions to assess needs, regulate emotions and manage conflicts (Kotsou et al., 2011). Practical exercises include video clips, group discussions, role-playing and other activities designed to regulate a person's emotions and improve listening to others. In an RCT, Mindfulness and Progressive muscle relaxation were compared with counselling services among unemployed persons diagnosed with anxiety disorder. The muscle relaxation group showed improved anxiety and depressive symptoms over time compared to those who received counselling alone (Merakou et al., 2019).

8.5 Debt Advice

Raising awareness of complementary financial services, including advice and online tools, can enhance financial knowledge and offer immediate assistance during economic challenges. This is particularly advantageous as a preventative measure for young individuals (Mathieu et al., 2022).

The consultation was provided at no cost. Immediate advice and support were given for any urgent issues (e.g. bailiffs or repossession). The main advice focused on the long-term resolution of problems, such as debt management plans. Self-help materials were distributed in written form.

8.6 Guided Imagery

Guided imagery techniques involve envisioning a desired and triumphant self-image, mentally practising job interviews, picturing career achievements and visualizing personal and spiritual development. Joseph and colleagues evaluated the effects of guided imagery, conducted over six 20-min sessions, on employment results. Participants who engaged in guided imagery were more inclined to obtain employment after 7 weeks, although no effect on depression was noted (Joseph & Greenberg, 2001).

8.7 Coping Strategies

Coping refers to the cognitive and behavioural efforts made to manage stress (Folkman, 2020). Strategies are categorized into:

- **Problem-Focused Coping**: Active attempts to reduce stress, such as engaging in job-search activities and organizing non-work-related routines.
- **Emotion-Focused Coping**: Strategies such as distancing oneself from the stress of unemployment by reframing or reducing emotional distress.

Research indicates that problem-focused coping, such as active job searching, enhances reemployment chances, while adaptive emotion-focused strategies, including distancing, help manage negative emotions. Distancing is distinguished from escape-avoidance strategies, which involve wishful thinking or behaviours like overeating, smoking or drinking to escape the situation (Folkman et al., 1986).

8.8 Skills Training

Skills training develops learned abilities for achieving specific outcomes. Skills are divided into:

- **Soft Skills**: Interpersonal attributes, such as communication, teamwork, leadership and conflict resolution.
- **Hard Skills**: Technical abilities acquired through education or practice, such as computer skills, typing and industry-specific knowledge.

Skills training methods include training via case studies, group discussions, brainstorming sessions and practical exercises. Training areas encompass employability skills, behavioural skills, management skills, personality development and technical skills. Interventions often focus on mental health literacy, interpersonal skills, job-seeking abilities and specialized skills tailored to specific industries (Seneviratne, 2021).

8.9 Corporate Social Responsibility (CSR)-Based Initiatives

Corporate Social Responsibility (CSR) in recent years has become a crucial element of corporate governance fostering skill development and employment generation in the community of developing nations in Asia. These initiatives are vital in enhancing employability, particularly by equipping youth with the skills and knowledge necessary to thrive in today's workforce (Sahoo & Dwibedi, 2020; Simbai et al., 2024).

In the current era of technological enterprise and digital economy, CSR programmes aim to enhance the digital literacy of the population and help them navigate the internet and online job platforms and increase their job retention rates and economic sustainability. Women and youth, who are often disproportionately affected by unemployment, are central targets of these programmes (Mothafar et al., 2024; Wardana et al., 2022).

Many companies focus on supporting local communities, particularly in rural or underserved areas, through their CSR efforts. These initiatives not only enhance skill development but also foster job creation and community growth. CSR-initiated skill development programmes also enhance the employees' soft skill development, including communication skills, problem-solving and teamwork abilities. Leading corporations like IBM and Siemens support global training initiatives in emerging technologies, promoting transitions towards knowledge-based and green economies.

8.10 Other Interventions

One intervention incorporated ecological theory, emphasizing the dynamic interplay between situational and personal factors, as well as environmental influences on health (Bruster, 2009). Other measures included instruction in digital literacy, typing, trade support, personal care, communication skills, interview readiness, employment search techniques and awareness of the labour market, which increased confidence in job hunting (Creed et al., 1998, 2001).

Brief group interventions are effective and sustainable in promoting mental health in unemployment contexts when they focus on mental health literacy, interpersonal skills training and job-search skills (Santos et al., 2018). Two key aspects in tailoring these interventions include:

- **Mental Health Literacy Improvement**: This primarily involves enhancing the recognition of depression and anxiety while addressing mental health stigma.
- **Interpersonal Skills Training**: This includes developing assertive behaviour, as well as improving verbal and non-verbal communication, to increase the likelihood of gaining employment.

9 Existing Barriers to Achieving SDG 8

The ILO has identified various barriers to achieving SDG 8 by 2030, as listed below:

- Trade tensions between nations
- Rising debts in developing nations
- International conflicts
- Geopolitical strains
- Climate change
- Uneven post-COVID-19 recovery of labour markets
- Income inequality
- Gender disparities
- Declining protection of labour rights
- Higher rates of informal employment with less social protection schemes
- Lack of focus on the skill development of youth

Overcoming these barriers will require an integrated effort from governmental, industrial, educational and vocational sectors with a persistent focus on improving the skill development of the workforce, adequate job creation and ensuring workers' welfare at all levels.

10 Research Gaps

While one strives to achieve SDG 8 by aiming towards "promoting sustained, inclusive, and sustainable economic growth, full and productive employment, and decent work for all by 2030", there are various unexplored domains.

Informal employment—A large part of Asia's workforce is in informal employment without social protection or job security. The transition to formal employment and its effect on unemployment rates are still not well understood (Bahl & Sharma, 2024).

Youth employment and education/skill mismatch—While considerable economic growth has occurred in Asian countries over the past few years, high youth unemployment rates remain a huge problem in Asia. The factors that can stimulate skill development and close the gap between youth resources and the demands of the labour market are yet to be explored (Varsha Pramod & Ramachandran, 2023).

Gender disparities—Though it is well known that women tend to have a higher unemployment risk than their male counterparts, the factors (social and otherwise) which impede their chances of employment need to be explored. Central Asia and Southern Asia have progressed in reducing the gender gap, largely due to enhanced access to the labour market for women, especially in Southern Asia.

Impact of migration—Migration (both within and out of a region) has had a myriad of impacts on the employment scenario of a region. The effects of migration need to be studied in detail to aid in formulating policies for the effective management of labour mobility (International Labour Organization, 2025).

11 Future Challenges and Prospects

Faster growth in the productivity sector is the need of the hour to resolve deficits in decent work. Though global labour productivity growth has reduced from the pre-pandemic long-term average, countries need to address the factors contributing to this economic slowdown. Achieving the Sustainable Development Goals (SDGs) by 2030 fundamentally relies on securing decent work and productive employment.

- Adequate education and skill development of the workforce, along with policy reforms and infrastructure development, will help overcome some of the burdens related to unemployment (International Labour Organization, 2025; Sudan, 2021).

- In Asian settings, higher educational institutions need to strengthen their strategies to promote graduate competency to ensure employability for the graduates in the coming years (Sudan, 2021).
- Unemployment benefits, equitable allocation of resources and compensation coverages should be expanded more intensively to mitigate the damage done towards the unemployed sector (Hwang, 2019; Shabbir et al., 2021).
- Developing countries in Asia have started to witness the beneficial consequences of the digital revolution and are creating strategies to adopt newer technologies. However, Asian nations require assistance in being inclusive without creating inequality and instability.
- National governments, along with the support of international financial organizations, should focus on creating decent jobs and not just target economic growth and stability.
- Training and work-based learning have gained importance in response to the global call for a universal right to lifelong learning.
- The emergence of new and robust financial technologies (FinTech), renewable energy jobs and e-governance has the potential to alter the landscape of employment in Asian countries (Ben Romdhane et al., 2024).
- An effective and cautious use of Artificial Intelligence (AI) can enhance business value, economic growth and social benefits. Embracing AI comes with the responsibility of rethinking education, investing more in human capital and improving labour markets. While nations utilize AI for economic growth and productivity, they also need to ensure strong consumer protection, follow best practices and balance competitiveness with national interests while minimizing adverse effects on the population's economy.

12 Policy Measures to Be Taken

The UN-DESA and the ILO jointly organized a high-level meeting with government policymakers from representative nations and economic experts on "Review of Progress and Prospects" with regard to SDG 8. The expert group meeting deliberated on various points related to the unemployment crisis and put forward suggestions for policy and action for the participant nations (UN Department of Economic and Social Affairs (DESA), 2024; UN Department of Economic and Social Affairs for Sustainable Development Goals & International Labour Organization, 2019). The salient features are listed here:

- Understanding and dealing with the big picture (including bold political leadership, developing national action plans for SDG 8, improving education systems to align with future needs, etc.)
- Sustained economic growth, increased productivity and job creation (increase productivity in agricultural sector and informal sectors, create better incentives for entrepreneurship and support Micro, Small and Medium Enterprises (MSMEs), pro-employment macroeconomic policies, etc.)

- Full and productive employment and decent work (well-functioning labour markets, addressing the challenge of informality, improving health and safety at work, integrating persons with disabilities and women labourers into the labour market, etc.)
- Just transition, environment-friendliness, eco-efficiency, sustainable tourism (sustainable consumption and production, sustainable tourism development, etc.)
- Finance, trade, and science and technology (improved access and aids at all levels for MSMEs, enhanced international cooperation on technology, etc.)
- Inter-linkages with other SDGs (SDGs related to health, education, inequality and others)
- Data for monitoring, cross-national partnerships and capacity building

In addition to the abovementioned key areas for improvement, countries need to recognize the importance of integration of mental health at workplace, develop strategies to address the risk factors for poor mental health at workplace and enable in-house and clinic-based mental health assessment with due consideration to the employee's confidentiality and privacy (Sarkar et al., 2024). A thorough understanding of the work environment, application of appropriate ergonomics, developing specific mental health intervention models, implementing such models and getting back reflections and feedback from all the stakeholders are crucial in ensuring integration of mental health at the workplace.

13 Conclusion

Unemployment rates are significantly higher in Asian countries compared to the rest of the World. Various types of unemployment exist in Asian regions with specific characteristics that warrant specific interventions and policy changes. Global employment has returned to pre-pandemic levels, yet job recovery and restoration rates remain low. This situation creates challenges in achieving the targets of the Sustainable Development Goals. Overall, the achievement of targets under SDG 8 has faced setbacks due to the COVID-19 pandemic, rising debts and geopolitical conflict, among other challenges.

Unemployment has complex, intricate and multidimensional relationships with the mental health of the unemployed masses. The rates of depression, stress disorders, substance abuse and suicidal behaviours are higher among the unemployed than those who are employed. The mental health burden due to unemployment is significantly higher among Asian countries than in other regions of the world. Though "apparently" employed, the burden faced by gig workers and informal workers is accentuated by a lack of social security and a regular flow of income. The impact of unemployment on the overall well-being of special populations, such as women, children, persons with pre-existing mental illnesses, indigenous populations and the socially and economically deprived minority populations, is significantly worrisome, warranting immediate and targeted interventions.

Although global research indicates that job club interventions, competence training sessions, debt advice and improving coping strategies can be somewhat effective in managing unemployment, these approaches are rarely implemented on a large scale in Asian contexts. Instead of these targeted interventions, there is a need for extensive, society-wide unemployment protection measures such as self-employment promotion schemes (e.g. EGPP in Bangladesh, PMEP in Nepal), legally mandated employment guarantee schemes (e.g. MGNREGA in India), social security support programmes (e.g. BISP and KJP in Pakistan) and similar programmes in other Asian countries to address the substantial unemployment burden. UN-DESA and ILO emphasize key areas like bold leadership, economic growth, decent work, just transition, finance/technology, inter-SDG links and the critical need to integrate mental health support within workplaces through various strategies and considerations.

Unemployment cannot be viewed solely as a financial problem, and productive public deliberations are needed from multiple sectors of society to tackle the effects of unemployment in South Asia. An integrated effort from governmental, industrial, educational, corporate and vocational sectors will be fruitful in changing the landscape of unemployment in Asian nations.

References

Abid, M., Ben-Salha, O., Gasmi, K., & Alnor, N. H. A. (2024). Modelling for disability: How does artificial intelligence affect unemployment among people with disability? An empirical analysis of linear and nonlinear effects. *Research in Developmental Disabilities, 149*, 104732. https://doi.org/10.1016/j.ridd.2024.104732

Ahn, J., Kim, N.-S., Lee, B.-K., Park, J., & Kim, Y. (2021). Comparison of the physical and mental health problems of unemployed with employees in South Korea. *Archives of Environmental & Occupational Health, 76*(3), 163–172. https://doi.org/10.1080/19338244.2020.1783503

Arena, A. F., Harris, M., Mobbs, S., Nicolopoulos, A., Harvey, S. B., & Deady, M. (2022). Exploring the lived experience of mental health and coping during unemployment. *BMC Public Health, 22*(1), 2451. https://doi.org/10.1186/s12889-022-14858-3

Arena, A. F., Mobbs, S., Sanatkar, S., Williams, D., Collins, D., Harris, M., Harvey, S. B., & Deady, M. (2023). Mental health and unemployment: A systematic review and meta-analysis of interventions to improve depression and anxiety outcomes. *Journal of Affective Disorders, 335*, 450–472. https://doi.org/10.1016/j.jad.2023.05.027

Artazcoz, L., Benach, J., Borrell, C., & Cortès, I. (2004). Unemployment and mental health: Understanding the interactions among gender, family roles, and social class. *American Journal of Public Health, 94*(1), 82–88. https://doi.org/10.2105/ajph.94.1.82

Audhoe, S. S., Hoving, J. L., Sluiter, J. K., & Frings-Dresen, M. H. W. (2010). Vocational interventions for unemployed: Effects on work participation and mental distress. A systematic review. *Journal of Occupational Rehabilitation, 20*(1), 1–13. https://doi.org/10.1007/s10926-009-9223-y

Bahl, S., & Sharma, A. (2024). Informality, education-occupation mismatch, and wages: Evidence from India. *Applied Economics, 56*(19), 2260–2294. https://doi.org/10.1080/00036846.2023.2186364

Bambra, C. (2010). Yesterday once more? Unemployment and health in the 21st century. *Journal of Epidemiology and Community Health, 64*(3), 213–215. https://doi.org/10.1136/jech.2009.090621

Bandyopadhyay, P. K. (2020). Sustainable Development Goal 8: Achieving decent work—An illusion. In S. Seifi (Ed.), *The Palgrave handbook of corporate social responsibility* (pp. 1–15). Springer. https://doi.org/10.1007/978-3-030-22438-7_87-1

Bartelink, V. H. M., Zay Ya, K., Guldbrandsson, K., & Bremberg, S. (2020). Unemployment among young people and mental health: A systematic review. *Scandinavian Journal of Public Health, 48*(5), 544–558. https://doi.org/10.1177/1403494819852847

Bartley, M. (1994). Unemployment and ill health: Understanding the relationship. *Journal of Epidemiology & Community Health, 48*(4), 333–337.

Ben Romdhane, Y., Kammoun, S., & Loukil, S. (2024). The impact of Fintech on inflation and unemployment: The case of Asia. *Arab Gulf Journal of Scientific Research, 42*(1), 161–181.

Bhat, M. A., & Joshi, J. (2020). Impact of unemployment on the mental health of youth in the Kashmir valley. *Journal of Psychology and Psychotherapy, 10*(10), 373.

Bhowmik, D., & Poddar, S. (2021). Nexus between unemployment and mental health. In *Human resource management and mental health—A psychosocial aspect*. Lincoln Research and Publications Limited, Australia and Lincoln University College. https://doi.org/10.46977/Book

Biggs, D., Hovey, N., Tyson, P. J., & MacDonald, S. (2010). Employer and employment agency attitudes towards employing individuals with mental health needs. *Journal of Mental Health, 19*(6), 505–516. https://doi.org/10.3109/09638237.2010.507683

Billeskov, L., Labriola, M., Stabell, C. L., Dieckmann, M. H., Jensen, N. H., Winding, T. N., Andersen, J. H., Lindholdt, L., Hansen, C. D., & Lund, T. (2020). Coping strategies in adolescence and labour-market participation in young adulthood: A prospective birth cohort study. *Scandinavian Journal of Public Health, 48*(5), 537–543. https://doi.org/10.1177/1403494819865644

Biswas, M. M., Das, K. C., & Sheikh, I. (2024). Psychological implications of unemployment among higher educated migrant youth in Kolkata City, India. *Scientific Reports, 14*(1), 10171.

Bostock, J. (2004). *The high price of poverty. Poverty and debt are major risk factors for mental ill health in deprived communities and groups*. Mental Health Today, 27–29.

Brouwers, E. P. M. (2020). Social stigma is an underestimated contributing factor to unemployment in people with mental illness or mental health issues: Position paper and future directions. *BMC Psychology, 8*(1), 36. https://doi.org/10.1186/s40359-020-00399-0

Bruster, B. E. (2009). Transition from welfare to work: Self-esteem and self-efficacy influence on the employment outcome of African American women. *Journal of Human Behavior in the Social Environment, 19*(4), 375–393.

Butterworth, P., Leach, L. S., Pirkis, J., & Kelaher, M. (2012). Poor mental health influences risk and duration of unemployment: A prospective study. *Social Psychiatry and Psychiatric Epidemiology, 47*(6), 1013–1021. https://doi.org/10.1007/s00127-011-0409-1

Byrne, D., & Strobl, E. (2004). Defining unemployment in developing countries: Evidence from Trinidad and Tobago. *Journal of Development Economics, 73*(1), 465–476. https://doi.org/10.1016/j.jdeveco.2002.12.005

Canivet, C., Bodin, T., Emmelin, M., Toivanen, S., Moghaddassi, M., & Östergren, P.-O. (2016). Precarious employment is a risk factor for poor mental health in young individuals in Sweden: A cohort study with multiple follow-ups. *BMC Public Health, 16*, 687. https://doi.org/10.1186/s12889-016-3358-5

Caplan, R. D., Vinokur, A. D., Price, R. H., & Van Ryn, M. (1989). Job seeking, reemployment, and mental health: A randomized field experiment in coping with job loss. *Journal of Applied Psychology, 74*(5), 759.

Cassidy, T., & Wright, L. (2008). Graduate employment status and health: A longitudinal analysis of the transition from student. *Social Psychology of Education, 11*, 181–191.

Chigbu, B. I., & Nekhwevha, F. (2023). Exploring the concepts of decent work through the lens of SDG 8: Addressing challenges and inadequacies. *Frontiers in Sociology, 8*, 1266141. https://doi.org/10.3389/fsoc.2023.1266141

Chisholm, D., Sweeny, K., Sheehan, P., Rasmussen, B., Smit, F., Cuijpers, P., & Saxena, S. (2016). Scaling-up treatment of depression and anxiety: A global return on investment analysis. *The Lancet Psychiatry, 3*(5), 415–424. https://doi.org/10.1016/S2215-0366(16)30024-4

Christoffersen, M. N. (2000). Growing up with unemployment: A study of parental unemployment and children's risk of abuse and neglect based on national longitudinal 1973 birth cohorts in Denmark. *Childhood, 7*(4), 421–438.

Creed, P. A., Bloxsome, T. D., & Johnston, K. (2001). Self-esteem and self-efficacy outcomes for unemployed individuals attending occupational skills training programs. *Community, Work & Family, 4*(3), 285–303.

Creed, P. A., Hicks, R. E., & Machin, M. (1998). Behavioural plasticity and mental health outcomes for long-term unemployed attending occupational training programmes. *Journal of Occupational and Organizational Psychology, 71*(2), 171–191.

Cutts, D. B., Pheley, A. M., & Geppert, J. S. (1998). Hunger in midwestern inner-city young children. *Archives of Pediatrics & Adolescent Medicine, 152*(5), 489–493.

Dambrun, M., & Dubuy, A. (2014). A positive psychology intervention among long-term unemployed people and its effects on psychological distress and well-being. *Journal of Employment Counseling, 51*(2), 75–88.

Dean, E., Elardo, J., Green, M., Wilson, B., & Berger, S. (2020). Types of unemployment. In *Principles of economics: Scarcity and social provisioning* (2nd ed.). Open Oregon Educational Resources. https://openoregon.pressbooks.pub/socialprovisioning2/chapter/what-causes-changes-in-unemployment-over-the-long-run/

Desalegn, G., Tangl, A., & Fekete-Farkas, M. (2022). From short-term risk to long-term strategic challenges: Reviewing the consequences of geopolitics and COVID-19 on economic performance. *Sustainability, 14*(21), Article 21. https://doi.org/10.3390/su142114455

Dheeraj, R. (2017). A critical analysis of the Mahatma Gandhi National Rural Employment Guarantee Act (MGNREGA). *Global Journal of Interdisciplinary Social Sciences, 6*(6), 8–12.

Dhir, R. K. (2015). *Indigenous people in the world of work in Asia and the Pacific*. International Labour Office.

Englama, A. (2001). Unemployment: Concepts and issues. *Bullion, 25*(4), 1–5.

Evans, L., Lund, C., Massazza, A., Weir, H., & Fuhr, D. C. (2022). The impact of employment programs on common mental disorders: A systematic review. *The International Journal of Social Psychiatry, 68*(7), 1315–1323. https://doi.org/10.1177/00207640221104684

Extremera, N., & Rey, L. (2014). Health-related quality of life and cognitive emotion regulation strategies in the unemployed: A cross-sectional survey. *Health and Quality of Life Outcomes, 12*, 172. https://doi.org/10.1186/s12955-014-0172-6

Folkman, S. (2020). Stress: Appraisal and coping. In *Encyclopedia of behavioral medicine* (pp. 2177–2179). Springer.

Folkman, S., Lazarus, R. S., Dunkel-Schetter, C., DeLongis, A., & Gruen, R. J. (1986). Dynamics of a stressful encounter: Cognitive appraisal, coping, and encounter outcomes. *Journal of Personality and Social Psychology, 50*(5), 992–1003. https://doi.org/10.1037/0022-3514.50.5.992

Francesconi, M., & Heckman, J. J. (2016). Child development and parental investment: Introduction. *The Economic Journal, 126*(596), F1–F27.

Frank, M. R., Autor, D., Bessen, J. E., Brynjolfsson, E., Cebrian, M., Deming, D. J., Feldman, M., Groh, M., Lobo, J., Moro, E., Wang, D., Youn, H., & Rahwan, I. (2019). Toward understanding the impact of artificial intelligence on labor. *Proceedings of the National Academy of Sciences of the United States of America, 116*(14), 6531–6539. https://doi.org/10.1073/pnas.1900949116

Franke, A. G., Schmidt, P., & Neumann, S. (2024). Association between unemployment and mental disorders: A narrative update of the literature. *International Journal of Environmental Research and Public Health, 21*(12), 1698.

Gallie, D., Paugam, S., & Jacobs, S. (2003). Unemployment, poverty and social isolation: Is there a vicious circle of social exclusion? *European Societies, 5*(1), 1–32.

Gaur, K., & Ram, U. (2016). Mental health problems among youth in India and its correlates. *International Journal of Human Rights in Healthcare, 9*(2), 95–108.

Gunn, V., Håkansta, C., Vignola, E., Matilla-Santander, N., Kreshpaj, B., Wegman, D. H., Hogstedt, C., Ahonen, E. Q., Muntaner, C., Baron, S., Bodin, T., & Precarious Work Research (PWR) Group. (2021). Initiatives addressing precarious employment and its effects on workers' health and well-being: A protocol for a systematic review. *Systematic Reviews, 10*(1), 195. https://doi.org/10.1186/s13643-021-01728-z

Ha, N. T., Huong, N. T., Anh, V. N., & Anh, N. Q. (2022). Modelling in economic evaluation of mental health prevention: Current status and quality of studies. *BMC Health Services Research, 22*(1), 906. https://doi.org/10.1186/s12913-022-08206-9

Hammer, T. (1992). Unemployment and use of drug and alcohol among young people: A longitudinal study in the general population. *British Journal of Addiction, 87*(11), 1571–1581.

Han, K.-M., Chang, J., Won, E., Lee, M.-S., & Ham, B.-J. (2017). Precarious employment associated with depressive symptoms and suicidal ideation in adult wage workers. *Journal of Affective Disorders, 218*, 201–209. https://doi.org/10.1016/j.jad.2017.04.049

Harkko, J., Virtanen, M., & Kouvonen, A. (2018). Unemployment and work disability due to common mental disorders among young adults: Selection or causation? *European Journal of Public Health, 28*(5), 791–797. https://doi.org/10.1093/eurpub/cky024

Harris, E., Lum, J., Rose, V., Morrow, M., Comino, E., & Harris, M. (2002). Are CBT interventions effective with disadvantaged job-seekers who are long-term unemployed? *Psychology, Health & Medicine, 7*(4), 401–410.

Henkel, D. (2011). Unemployment and substance use: A review of the literature (1990–2010). *Current Drug Abuse Reviews, 4*(1), 4–27.

Himle, J. A., Bybee, D., Steinberger, E., Laviolette, W. T., Weaver, A., Vlnka, S., Golenberg, Z., Levine, D. S., Heimberg, R. G., & O'Donnell, L. A. (2014). Work-related CBT versus vocational services as usual for unemployed persons with social anxiety disorder: A randomized controlled pilot trial. *Behaviour Research and Therapy, 63*, 169–176.

Hult, M., Lappalainen, K., Saaranen, T. K., Räsänen, K., Vanroelen, C., & Burdorf, A. (2020). Health-improving interventions for obtaining employment in unemployed job seekers. *The Cochrane Database of Systematic Reviews, 1*(1), CD013152. https://doi.org/10.1002/14651858.CD013152.pub2

Huynh, H. H., & Vo, D. H. (2023). The effects of migration on unemployment: New evidence from the Asian countries. *Sustainability, 15*(14), Article 14. https://doi.org/10.3390/su151411385

Hwang, G. (2019). How fair are unemployment benefits? The experience of East Asia. *International Social Security Review, 72*(2), 49–73.

International Labour Organization (ILO). (2025). *ILO flagship report: World Employment and Social Outlook—Trends 2025*. International Labour Organization. https://www.ilo.org/sites/default/files/2025-01/WESO25_Trends_ExecSum_EN.pdf

Izutsu, T., Tsutsumi, A., Minas, H., Thornicroft, G., Patel, V., & Ito, A. (2015). Mental health and wellbeing in the Sustainable Development Goals. *The Lancet Psychiatry, 2*, 1052–1054. https://doi.org/10.1016/S2215-0366(15)00457-5

Jaleel, F., Nirmala, B., & Thirthalli, J. (2015). A comparative analysis of the nature and pattern of employment among persons with severe mental disorders. *Journal of Psychosocial Rehabilitation and Mental Health, 2*, 19–25.

Janlert, U. (1997). Unemployment as a disease and diseases of the unemployed. *Scandinavian Journal of Work, Environment & Health, 23*(Suppl. 3), 79–83.

Janlert, U., Winefield, A. H., & Hammarström, A. (2015). Length of unemployment and health-related outcomes: A life-course analysis. *The European Journal of Public Health, 25*(4), 662–667.

Jaramillo, N. R., Trillos, C. E., & Julià, M. (2022). The measure of precarious employment and its impact on the mental health of workers: A systematic review 2007–2020. *Work, 73*(2), 639–650. https://doi.org/10.3233/WOR-210064

Jaydarifard, S., Smith, S. S., Mann, D., Rossa, K. R., Nikooharf Salehi, E., Gnani Srinivasan, A., & Shekari Soleimanloo, S. (2023). Precarious employment and associated health and social consequences; a systematic review. *Australian and New Zealand Journal of Public Health, 47*(4), 100074. https://doi.org/10.1016/j.anzjph.2023.100074

Jin, R. L., Shah, C. P., & Svoboda, T. J. (1995). The impact of unemployment on health: A review of the evidence. *CMAJ: Canadian Medical Association Journal = Journal de l'Association Medicale Canadienne, 153*(5), 529–540.

Jin, Y., Zhu, D., & He, P. (2020). Social causation or social selection? The longitudinal interrelationship between poverty and depressive symptoms in China. *Social Science & Medicine, 249*, 112848. https://doi.org/10.1016/j.socscimed.2020.112848

Joseph, L. M., & Greenberg, M. A. (2001). The effects of a career transition program on reemployment success in laid-off professionals. *Consulting Psychology Journal: Practice and Research, 53*(3), 169–181. https://doi.org/10.1037/1061-4087.53.3.169

Judd, N., Hughes, K., Bellis, M. A., Hardcastle, K., & Amos, R. (2023). Is parental unemployment associated with increased risk of adverse childhood experiences? A systematic review and meta-analysis. *Journal of Public Health, 45*(4), 829–839. https://doi.org/10.1093/pubmed/fdad069

Junna, L., Moustgaard, H., & Martikainen, P. (2022). Current unemployment, unemployment history, and mental health: A fixed-effects model approach. *American Journal of Epidemiology, 191*(8), 1459–1469. https://doi.org/10.1093/aje/kwac077

Kerr, J. L., Dattilo, J., & O'Sullivan, D. (2012). Use of recreation activities as positive coping with chronic stress and mental health outcomes associated with unemployment of people with disabilities. *Work, 43*(3), 279–292. https://doi.org/10.3233/WOR-2012-1390

Khairy, Y. H., & Ghoneim, H. (2022). Women's access and perception of decent work: A case study on Egypt. *Management & Sustainability: An Arab Review, 2*(2), 177–202. https://doi.org/10.1108/MSAR-09-2022-0039

Khalique, F., Madan, P., Puri, G., & Parimoo, D. (2021). Incorporating SDG 8 for decent work practices: A study of MNC subsidiaries in India. *Australasian Business, Accounting and Finance Journal, 15*(5), 99–114. https://doi.org/10.14453/aabfj.v15i5.7

Kim, J., & Yoon, S.-Y. (2018). Association between socioeconomic attainments and suicidal ideation by age groups in Korea. *The International Journal of Social Psychiatry, 64*(7), 628–636. https://doi.org/10.1177/0020764018792592

Kim, M.-S., Hong, Y.-C., Yook, J.-H., & Kang, M.-Y. (2017). Effects of perceived job insecurity on depression, suicide ideation, and decline in self-rated health in Korea: A population-based panel study. *International Archives of Occupational and Environmental Health, 90*(7), 663–671. https://doi.org/10.1007/s00420-017-1229-8

Kim, T. J., & von dem Knesebeck, O. (2016). Perceived job insecurity, unemployment and depressive symptoms: A systematic review and meta-analysis of prospective observational studies. *International Archives of Occupational and Environmental Health, 89*(4), 561–573. https://doi.org/10.1007/s00420-015-1107-1

Kohl, P. L., Jonson-Reid, M., & Drake, B. (2011). Maternal mental illness and the safety and stability of maltreated children. *Child Abuse & Neglect, 35*(5), 309–318. https://doi.org/10.1016/j.chiabu.2011.01.006

Kotsou, I., Nelis, D., Grégoire, J., & Mikolajczak, M. (2011). Emotional plasticity: Conditions and effects of improving emotional competence in adulthood. *Journal of Applied Psychology, 96*(4), 827–839. https://doi.org/10.1037/a0023047

Le, L.K.-D., Esturas, A. C., Mihalopoulos, C., Chiotelis, O., Bucholc, J., Chatterton, M. L., & Engel, L. (2021). Cost-effectiveness evidence of mental health prevention and promotion interventions: A systematic review of economic evaluations. *PLoS Medicine, 18*(5), e1003606. https://doi.org/10.1371/journal.pmed.1003606

Lee, B. X., Kjaerulf, F., Turner, S., Cohen, L., Donnelly, P. D., Muggah, R., Davis, R., Realini, A., Kieselbach, B., MacGregor, L. S., Waller, I., Gordon, R., Moloney-Kitts, M., Lee, G., & Gilligan, J. (2016). Transforming our world: Implementing the 2030 agenda through Sustainable Development Goal indicators. *Journal of Public Health Policy, 37*(Suppl. 1), 13–31. https://doi.org/10.1057/s41271-016-0002-7

Lee, J. O., Jones, T. M., Yoon, Y., Hackman, D. A., Yoo, J. P., & Kosterman, R. (2019). Young adult unemployment and later depression and anxiety: Does childhood neighborhood matter? *Journal of Youth and Adolescence, 48*(1), 30–42. https://doi.org/10.1007/s10964-018-0957-8

Lim, A. Y., Lee, S.-H., Jeon, Y., Yoo, R., & Jung, H.-Y. (2018). Job-seeking stress, mental health problems, and the role of perceived social support in university graduates in Korea. *Journal of Korean Medical Science, 33*(19), e149.

Ludermir, A. B., & Lewis, G. (2003). Informal work and common mental disorders. *Social Psychiatry and Psychiatric Epidemiology, 38*, 485–489.

Ludermir, A. B., & Lewis, G. (2005). Is there a gender difference on the association between informal work and common mental disorders? *Social Psychiatry and Psychiatric Epidemiology, 40*, 622–627.

Lund, C., Brooke-Sumner, C., Baingana, F., Baron, E. C., Breuer, E., Chandra, P., Haushofer, J., Herrman, H., Jordans, M., Kieling, C., Medina-Mora, M. E., Morgan, E., Omigbodun, O., Tol, W., Patel, V., & Saxena, S. (2018). Social determinants of mental disorders and the Sustainable Development Goals: A systematic review of reviews. *The Lancet. Psychiatry, 5*(4), 357–369. https://doi.org/10.1016/S2215-0366(18)30060-9

Lundstrom, E. W., Asfaw, A., Steege, A. L., Bhattacharya, A., & Groenewold, M. (2024). Precarious employment and mental health in the United States: Results from the Medical Expenditure Panel Survey (MEPS), 2008–2021. *Preventive Medicine, 186*, 108090. https://doi.org/10.1016/j.ypmed.2024.108090

Madge, N. (1983). Unemployment and its effects on children. *Journal of Child Psychology and Psychiatry, and Allied Disciplines, 24*(2), 311–319. https://doi.org/10.1111/j.1469-7610.1983.tb00579.x

Mamgain, R. P., & Khan, K. (2021). Trends in employment and unemployment in India: Dimensions of gender, caste, and education. In *India higher education report 2020*. Routledge.

Mathias, K., Pant, H., Marella, M., Singh, L., Murthy, G., & Grills, N. (2018). Multiple barriers to participation for people with psychosocial disability in Dehradun district, North India: A cross-sectional study. *British Medical Journal Open, 8*(2), e019443. https://doi.org/10.1136/bmjopen-2017-019443

Mathieu, S., Treloar, A., Hawgood, J., Ross, V., & Kõlves, K. (2022). The role of unemployment, financial hardship, and economic recession on suicidal behaviors and interventions to mitigate their impact: A review. *Frontiers in Public Health, 10*, 907052.

Menéndez-Espina, S., Llosa, J. A., Agulló-Tomás, E., Rodríguez-Suárez, J., Sáiz-Villar, R., & Lahseras-Díez, H. F. (2019). Job insecurity and mental health: The moderating role of coping strategies from a gender perspective. *Frontiers in Psychology, 10*, 286. https://doi.org/10.3389/fpsyg.2019.00286

Mental Healthcare Act. (2017). Gazette of India (Extra-Ordinary). https://www.prsindia.org/uploads/media/Mental%20Health/Mental%20Healthcare%20Act,%202017.pdf

Merakou, K., Tsoukas, K., Stavrinos, G., Amanaki, E., Daleziou, A., Kourmousi, N., Stamatelopoulou, G., Spourdalaki, E., & Barbouni, A. (2019). The effect of progressive muscle relaxation on emotional competence: Depression–anxiety–stress, sense of coherence, health-related quality of life, and well-being of unemployed people in Greece: An intervention study. *Explore, 15*(1), 38–46.

Miller, G. E., Chen, E., & Parker, K. J. (2011). Psychological stress in childhood and susceptibility to the chronic diseases of aging: Moving toward a model of behavioral and biological mechanisms. *Psychological Bulletin, 137*(6), 959–997. https://doi.org/10.1037/a0024768

Min, K.-B., Park, S.-G., Hwang, S. H., & Min, J.-Y. (2015). Precarious employment and the risk of suicidal ideation and suicide attempts. *Preventive Medicine, 71*, 72–76. https://doi.org/10.1016/j.ypmed.2014.12.017

Mokyr, J., Vickers, C., & Ziebarth, N. L. (2015). The history of technological anxiety and the future of economic growth: Is this time different? *Journal of Economic Perspectives, 29*(3), 31–50. https://doi.org/10.1257/jep.29.3.31

Moore, T. H. M., Kesten, J. M., López-López, J. A., Ijaz, S., McAleenan, A., Richards, A., Gray, S., Savović, J., & Audrey, S. (2018). The effects of changes to the built environment on the mental health and well-being of adults: Systematic review. *Health & Place, 53*, 237–257. https://doi.org/10.1016/j.healthplace.2018.07.012

Mothafar, N. A., Zhang, J., Alsoffary, A., Masoomi, B., AL-Barakani, A., & Alhady, O. S. (2024). Digital social responsibility towards digital education of international higher education students' institutions: Digital culture as mediator. *Heliyon, 10*(17), e36442. https://doi.org/10.1016/j.heliyon.2024.e36442

Moustgaard, H., Avendano, M., & Martikainen, P. (2018). Parental unemployment and offspring psychotropic medication purchases: A longitudinal fixed-effects analysis of 138,644 adolescents. *American Journal of Epidemiology, 187*(9), 1880–1888. https://doi.org/10.1093/aje/kwy084

Nagelhout, G. E., Hummel, K., de Goeij, M. C. M., de Vries, H., Kaner, E., & Lemmens, P. (2017). How economic recessions and unemployment affect illegal drug use: A systematic realist literature review. *The International Journal on Drug Policy, 44*, 69–83. https://doi.org/10.1016/j.drugpo.2017.03.013

Navarro-Abal, Y., Climent-Rodríguez, J. A., López-López, M. J., & Gómez-Salgado, J. (2018). Psychological coping with job loss. Empirical study to contribute to the development of unemployed people. *International Journal of Environmental Research and Public Health, 15*(8), 1787. https://doi.org/10.3390/ijerph15081787

Ngui, E. M., Khasakhala, L., Ndetei, D., & Roberts, L. W. (2010). Mental disorders, health inequalities and ethics: A global perspective. *International Review of Psychiatry, 22*(3), 235–244. https://doi.org/10.3109/09540261.2010.485273

Nolte-Troha, C., Roser, P., Henkel, D., Scherbaum, N., Koller, G., & Franke, A. G. (2023). Unemployment and substance use: An updated review of studies from North America and Europe. *Healthcare, 11*(8), 1182. https://doi.org/10.3390/healthcare11081182

Oswald, T. K., Nguyen, M. T., Mirza, L., Lund, C., Jones, H. G., Crowley, G., Aslanyan, D., Dean, K., Schofield, P., Hotopf, M., & Das-Munshi, J. (2024). Interventions targeting social determinants of mental disorders and the Sustainable Development Goals: A systematic review of reviews. *Psychological Medicine, 54*(8), 1475–1499. https://doi.org/10.1017/S0033291724000333

Patel, P. C., Devaraj, S., Hicks, M. J., & Wornell, E. J. (2018). County-level job automation risk and health: Evidence from the United States. *Social Science & Medicine, 1982*(202), 54–60. https://doi.org/10.1016/j.socscimed.2018.02.025

Paul, K. I., & Moser, K. (2009). Unemployment impairs mental health: Meta-analyses. *Journal of Vocational Behavior, 74*(3), 264–282.

Perreault, M., Touré, E. H., Perreault, N., & Caron, J. (2017). Employment status and mental health: Mediating roles of social support and coping strategies. *The Psychiatric Quarterly, 88*(3), 501–514. https://doi.org/10.1007/s11126-016-9460-0

Price, R. H., Van Ryn, M., & Vinokur, A. D. (1992). Impact of a preventive job search intervention on the likelihood of depression among the unemployed. *Journal of Health and Social Behavior, 33*(2), 158–167.

Rafi, M. A., Mamun, M. A., Hsan, K., Hossain, M., & Gozal, D. (2019). Psychological implications of unemployment among Bangladesh Civil Service job seekers: A pilot study. *Frontiers in Psychiatry, 10*, 578.

Rahman, A. K. M. A., Hossain, M., & Jahan, A. (2025). Exploring the governance-unemployment nexus: Insights from South Asia. *Journal of Ekonomi, 7*(1), Article 1. https://doi.org/10.58251/ekonomi.1567248

Sahoo, D. R., & Dwibedi, S. K. (2020). A study of corporate social responsibility towards enhancement of employment through skill development: An empirical study. *International Journal of Reviews and Research in Social Sciences, 8*(1), 17–30. https://doi.org/10.5958/2454-2687.2020.00006.4

Santana, V. S., Loomis, D., Newman, B., & Harlow, S. D. (1997). Informal jobs: Another occupational hazard for women's mental health? *International Journal of Epidemiology, 26*(6), 1236–1242.

Santos, O., Lopes, E., Virgolino, A., Stefanovska-Petkovska, M., Dinis, A., Ambrósio, S., & Heitor, M. J. (2018). Defining a brief intervention for the promotion of psychological well-being among unemployed individuals through expert consensus. *Frontiers in Psychiatry, 9*, 13.

Sarkar, S., Menon, V., Padhy, S., & Kathiresan, P. (2024). Mental health and well-being at the workplace. *Indian Journal of Psychiatry, 66*(Suppl. 2), S353–S364. https://doi.org/10.4103/indianjpsychiatry.indianjpsychiatry_608_23

Seneviratne, W. (2021). Training and unemployment in Sri Lanka: Impact of skills training on unemployment. *Asian Journal of Advances in Research, 11*(4), 274–282.

Shabbir, A., Kousar, S., & Zubair Alam, M. (2021). Factors affecting level of unemployment in South Asia. *Journal of Economic and Administrative Sciences, 37*(1), 1–25.

Shen, L., Xu, X., Yue, S., & Yin, S. (2024). A predictive model for depression in Chinese middle-aged and elderly people with physical disabilities. *BMC Psychiatry, 24*(1), 305. https://doi.org/10.1186/s12888-024-05766-4

Shidhaye, R., & Kermode, M. (2013). Stigma and discrimination as a barrier to mental health service utilization in India. *International Health, 5*(1), 6–8. https://doi.org/10.1093/inthealth/ihs011

Simbai, M., Kudzanai, M., & Tinashe, R. (2024). Corporate social responsibility initiatives and community development: A review of literature on the prospects and challenges in developing countries. *Indonesian Journal of Community Services, 3*(2), Article 2. https://doi.org/10.47540/ijcs.v3i2.1578

Singh, N. (2019). Nature and extent of unemployment in India. *International Journal of Applied Marketing & Management, 4*(1), 16–20.

Sleskova, M., Salonna, F., Geckova, A. M., Nagyova, I., Stewart, R. E., van Dijk, J. P., & Groothoff, J. W. (2006). Does parental unemployment affect adolescents' health? *Journal of Adolescent Health, 38*(5), 527–535.

Subramaniam, M., Zhang, Y., Shahwan, S., Vaingankar, J. A., Satghare, P., Teh, W. L., Roystonn, K., Goh, C. M. J., Maniam, Y., Tan, Z. L., Tay, B., Verma, S., & Chong, S. A. (2022). Employment of young people with mental health conditions: Making it work. *Disability and Rehabilitation, 44*(10), 2033–2043. https://doi.org/10.1080/09638288.2020.1822932

Sudan, F. K. (2021). Technological disruptions, youth unemployment and vocational education challenges in South Asia: A short report. *Global Economics Science*, 80–97. https://doi.org/10.37256/ges.222021769

Suijkerbuijk, Y. B., Schaafsma, F. G., van Mechelen, J. C., Ojajärvi, A., Corbière, M., & Anema, J. R. (2017). Interventions for obtaining and maintaining employment in adults with severe mental illness, a network meta-analysis. *The Cochrane Database of Systematic Reviews, 9*(9), CD011867. https://doi.org/10.1002/14651858.CD011867.pub2

Suto, M., Balogun, O. O., Dhungel, B., Kato, T., & Takehara, K. (2022). Effectiveness of workplace interventions for improving working conditions on the health and wellbeing of fathers or parents: A systematic review. *International Journal of Environmental Research and Public Health, 19*(8), 4779. https://doi.org/10.3390/ijerph19084779

The Rights of Persons with Disabilities Act (2016). (2016). Gazette of India (Extra-Ordinary). http://www.disabilityaffairs.gov.in/uploaad/uploadfiles/files/RPWD/ACT/2016.pdf

Thorat, S., & Newman, K. S. (2007). Caste and economic discrimination: Causes, consequences and remedies. *Economic and Political Weekly, 42*, 4121–4124.

Thornicroft, G., & Patel, V. (2014). Including mental health among the new Sustainable Development Goals. *BMJ*. https://doi.org/10.1136/bmj.g5189

Thornicroft, G., & Votruba, N. (2018). Sustainable development goals and mental health. *Vertex, XXIX*(142), 300–303.

Tuna, E., & Balcı, Ş. (2020). Associated factors of psychological symptoms among unemployed Turkish adults: The role of personality factors and rumination. *Psychological Reports, 123*(5), 1557–1577. https://doi.org/10.1177/0033294119886251

UN Department of Economic and Social Affairs (DESA). (2024). *The Sustainable Development Goals report-2024*. United Nations Publications. https://unstats.un.org/sdgs/report/2024/The-Sustainable-Development-Goals-Report-2024.pdf

UN Department of Economic and Social Affairs for Sustainable Development Goals, & International Labour Organization. (2019). *Expert Group Meeting on Sustainable Development Goal 8: Promote sustained, inclusive and sustainable economic growth, full and productive employment and decent work for all Review of Progress and Prospects*. ILO Headquarters. https://sdgs.un.org/sites/default/files/2024-12/25385Meeting_report_SDG8_final.pdf

Van der Meer, P. H. (2014). Gender, unemployment and subjective well-being: Why being unemployed is worse for men than for women. *Social Indicators Research, 115*(1), 23–44.

Varsha Pramod, P., & Ramachandran, R. (2023). Youth employment for inclusive growth: A review and research agenda in global perspective with special reference to India. *Journal of Global Entrepreneurship Research, 13*(1), 9.

Vicziany, M. (2005). Dalit responses to unemployment in contemporary India. *South Asia: Journal of South Asian Studies, 28*(1), 154–179. https://doi.org/10.1080/00856400500056285

Vinokur, A. D., Price, R. H., & Caplan, R. D. (1996). Hard times and hurtful partners: How financial strain affects depression and relationship satisfaction of unemployed persons and their spouses. *Journal of Personality and Social Psychology, 71*(1), 166–179. https://doi.org/10.1037/0022-3514.71.1.166

Vinokur, A. D., & Schul, Y. (1997). Mastery and inoculation against setbacks as active ingredients in the JOBS intervention for the unemployed. *Journal of Consulting and Clinical Psychology, 65*(5), 867–877. https://doi.org/10.1037/0022-006X.65.5.867

Vinokur, A. D., Van Ryn, M., Gramlich, E. M., & Price, R. H. (1991). Long-term follow-up and benefit-cost analysis of the Jobs Program: A preventive intervention for the unemployed. *Journal of Applied Psychology, 76*(2), 213–219. https://doi.org/10.1037/0021-9010.76.2.213

Virgolino, A., Costa, J., Santos, O., Pereira, M. E., Antunes, R., Ambrósio, S., Heitor, M. J., & Vaz Carneiro, A. (2022). Lost in transition: A systematic review of the association between unemployment and mental health. *Journal of Mental Health, 31*(3), 432–444. https://doi.org/10.1080/09638237.2021.2022615

Virkes, T., Maslić Seršić, D., & Lopez-Zafra, E. (2017). Core Self-evaluations and individual strategies of coping with unemployment among displaced Spanish workers. *The Spanish Journal of Psychology, 20*, E59. https://doi.org/10.1017/sjp.2017.57

Walsh, C., MacMillan, H., & Jamieson, E. (2002). The relationship between parental psychiatric disorder and child physical and sexual abuse: Findings from the Ontario Health Supplement. *Child Abuse & Neglect, 26*(1), 11–22. https://doi.org/10.1016/s0145-2134(01)00308-8

Wang, S., Li, L. Z., & Coutts, A. (2022). National survey of mental health and life satisfaction of gig workers: The role of loneliness and financial precarity. *British Medical Journal Open, 12*(12), e066389.

Wardana, L. W., Ahmad, Indrawati, A., Maula, F. I., Mahendra, A. M., Fatihin, M. K., Rahma, A., Nafisa, A. F., Putri, A. A., & Narmaditya, B. S. (2022). Do digital literacy and business sustainability matter for creative economy? The role of entrepreneurial attitude. *Heliyon, 9*(1), e12763. https://doi.org/10.1016/j.heliyon.2022.e12763

Weiland, S., Hickmann, T., Lederer, M., Marquardt, J., & Schwindenhammer, S. (2021). The 2030 Agenda for sustainable development: Transformative change through the Sustainable Development Goals? *Politics and Governance, 9*(1), 90–95. https://doi.org/10.17645/pag.v9i1.4191

Xu, G., Xue, M., & Zhao, J. (2023). The relationship of artificial intelligence opportunity perception and employee workplace well-being: A moderated mediation model. *International Journal of Environmental Research and Public Health, 20*(3), 1974. https://doi.org/10.3390/ijerph20031974

Yang, X., Yao, L., Wu, H., Wang, Y., Liu, L., Wang, J., & Wang, L. (2016). Quality of life and its related factors in Chinese unemployed people: A population-based cross-sectional study.

International Journal of Environmental Research and Public Health, 13(8), 797. https://doi.org/10.3390/ijerph13080797

Yang, Y., Niu, L., Amin, S., & Yasin, I. (2024). Unemployment and mental health: A global study of unemployment's influence on diverse mental disorders. *Frontiers in Public Health, 12*, 1440403. https://doi.org/10.3389/fpubh.2024.1440403

Yeung, W.-J. J. (2022). Education and youth unemployment in Southeast Asia. In W.-J. J. Yeung (Ed.), *Demographic and family transition in Southeast Asia* (pp. 77–98). Springer. https://doi.org/10.1007/978-3-030-85679-3_6

Yi, J.-H., & Hong, J. (2020). Socioeconomic status and later-life mental health in South Korea. *American Journal of Health Behavior, 44*(2), 200–213. https://doi.org/10.5993/AJHB.44.2.8

Yoon, J.-H., Jeung, D., & Chang, S.-J. (2016). Does high emotional demand with low job control relate to suicidal ideation among service and sales workers in Korea? *Journal of Korean Medical Science, 31*(7), 1042–1048. https://doi.org/10.3346/jkms.2016.31.7.1042

Zaman, H. (2011). Assessing the impact of employment generation programs in challenging rural poverty: A comparative study on Bangladesh and India. *Journal of Poverty, 15*(3), 259–276.

Zhao, W., Yin, C., Hua, T., Meadows, M. E., Li, Y., Liu, Y., Cherubini, F., Pereira, P., & Fu, B. (2022). Achieving the Sustainable Development Goals in the post-pandemic era. *Humanities and Social Sciences Communications, 9*(1), 1–7. https://doi.org/10.1057/s41599-022-01283-5

Zubair, U. B., Mansoor, S., Rana, M. H., Ali, U., Jamal, A. R., & Qureshi, H. (2016). Psychiatric morbidity and associated socio demographic factors in young unemployed people. *Pakistan Armed Forces Medical Journal, 4*, 553.

Chapter 7
Education, Mental Health, and Sustainable Development Goals in South Asia: An Intersectoral Analysis

Darya Rostam Ahmed, Rania H. Al-Taie, and Jaafar O. Ahmed

Abstract This chapter examines the bidirectional relationship between education and mental health related to the Sustainable Development Goals (SDGs) in South Asia. Through an analysis of national and regional policies, health and availability of education data, and mental health services, the chapter highlights systemic obstacles, including the treatment gap, resource limitations, and inadequate policy prioritization. Governmental and non-governmental interventions across South Asian countries are evaluated. Despite some promising national initiatives and grassroots innovations, overall progress toward inclusive, sustainable development of mental health is fragmented and uneven. The chapter also highlights significant research gaps and the absence of standardized indicators of mental health and educational frameworks aligned with the SDGs. Recommendations emphasize the need for multisectoral collaboration, culturally adapted community-based care models, digital mental health innovations, and stronger policy integration. Without strategic, inclusive, and evidence-based actions, South Asia risks laggard in achieving mental health and educational equity, thus compromising wider sustainable development outcomes.

Keywords Education · Mental health · Policy integration · Sustainable development goals · South Asia · NGOs · United Nations

D. R. Ahmed (✉)
Department of Clinical Psychology, Faculty of Science and Health, Koya University, Koya, Iraq
e-mail: darya.rostam@koyauniversity.org

Department of Medical Laboratory Science, College of Science, Knowledge University, Erbil, Iraq

R. H. Al-Taie
College of Medicine, Mustansiryia University, Baghdad, Iraq

J. O. Ahmed
Psychology Department, Faculty of Art, Soran University, Soran, Iraq
e-mail: jaafar.ahmed@visitors.soran.edu.iq

Kscien Organization, Sulaimani, Iraq

R. H. Al-Taie
e-mail: HAm3126@uomustansiriyah.edu.iq

S. K. Kar et al. (eds.), *Sustainable Development Goals and Mental Health in South Asia*, South Asian Perspectives in Mental Health and Psychology ,
https://doi.org/10.1007/978-981-95-2684-0_7

1 Introduction

Despite the widespread recognition that mental illnesses account for more than 4% of global gross domestic product (GDP), the international community has only recently begun to allocate the necessary attention, resources, and efforts to address the needs of people with mental illness and disabilities (Izutsu et al., 2015). Among the most significant contributors to disability is depression, a condition closely linked to suicide that claims more than 773,000 lives annually. Many of these deaths could be prevented by early intervention and improved access to care (WHO, 2023). This growing recognition of mental health (MH) as a development priority is reflected in two key United Nations (UN) frameworks introduced in 2015. The Sendai Framework for Disaster Risk Reduction 2015–2030 and the 2030 Agenda for Sustainable Development incorporate Sustainable Development Goals (SDGs) (Izutsu et al., 2015). The 17 goals and 169 associated targets aimed to achieve a better and more sustainable future for all (UN DESA, 2024).

Education is one of the most powerful tools to advance MH and general well-being. Schools and educational institutions provide opportunities to impart fundamental knowledge and life skills that promote emotional resilience, coping mechanisms, and social support networks. Health literacy enables people to access, understand, and apply health-related information, ultimately leading to better health outcomes. This aligns with the concept of 'cultural capital,' introduced by Bourdieu in 1986, since education empowers individuals with the necessary skills to access and utilize health systems with greater autonomy and well-being (English & McKay, 2022).

Globally, MH issues account for a substantial part of the disease burden; however, they frequently persist under-prioritized. This is particularly true in South Asia, where rapid urbanization, cultural stigma, and socioeconomic inequalities affect MH (Lemon et al., 2023). The universal nature of the SDGs highlights that MH is a global concern, not just an issue for developing nations. However, a defining characteristic of the SDGs is that their multisectoral impact progress in an area, such as education, has direct implications for mental health, economic development, and social well-being (Dybdahl & Lien, 2017). This interconnectedness underscores the urgency of interdisciplinary collaboration, where educators, healthcare professionals, policymakers, and community leaders must work together to create holistic strategies that support mental and educational outcomes.

Nowhere is this integration more important than among South Asian nations, whose region has recorded unprecedented advances in human progress in the last two decades. All nations, such as Bangladesh, Nepal, and Sri Lanka, had most of the Millennium Development Goals (MDGs) (Asadullah et al., 2020) within reach. Nevertheless, despite these gains, the region still grapples with deep-seated issues like high levels of childhood malnutrition, poor health infrastructure, and an overwhelmed education system. In contrast to the MDGs, the SDG agenda is more aggressive and demands more financial investment, more powerful policy structures, and better governance to ensure that education and mental well-being are priorities in national development agendas (Asadullah et al., 2020).

A major challenge in the South Asian education sector is that, while school enrollment rates have improved, this has not necessarily translated into higher learning outcomes. The phenomenon of "flat learning profiles" highlights the fact that more children are attending school, yet literacy and cognitive skills have not improved significantly (Asadullah et al., 2020; Pritchett & Sandefur, 2020). These findings suggest that achieving universal primary school completion alone will not be sufficient to meet the SDG goal of universal literacy; more attention must be paid to education quality, teacher training, and curriculum reforms that integrate mental health and emotional well-being into the learning experience. South Asian nations can learn from each other's successes and challenges. By fostering regional partnerships and knowledge-sharing platforms, countries can develop more robust strategies to address MH disparities, improve education systems, and ensure that sustainable development truly leaves no one behind.

We aim to discuss the contribution of education to risk protection and enhancement of well-being and psychological resilience and examine the effects of global and regional policies on education systems and on outcomes in MH. It emphasizes the difficulties and setbacks in achieving the SDGs on MH issues, particularly in South Asian contexts, and evaluates the effectiveness of government and non-governmental action to expand access to services related to MH. Additionally, the chapter is designed to identify significant gaps in evidence and research, particularly those that impede the application of culturally appropriate and evidence-informed interventions. Last but not least, it aims to discuss how political, economic, and sociocultural considerations impact the integration of MH into education and development programming across the region and underscore the need for locally adapted approaches.

2 Current State of Education, MH, and SDGs in South Asia

Despite South Asia's impressive progress toward the MDGs and its dynamic economic growth, the region remains home to 36% of the impoverished population (UN ESCAP, 2017). Furthermore, with almost one-fourth of the global population living in this sub region, South Asia plays a crucial role in the worldwide achievement of the SDGs (UN ESCAP, 2017). Given its large and rapidly expanding population, achieving the SDGs in this region is essential not only for local development, but also for global progress toward sustainable growth, equity, and social well-being (Oosterhof, 2018). However, the current state of progress in health (SDG 3) and education (SDG 4) presents a complex picture, where the achievements coexist with persistent inequalities.

In the health sector, South Asia has experienced significant progress in access to healthcare, although there are considerable disparities at the local and community levels. Urbanization, aging populations, and poor local health facility setup are among the factors that have put obstacles to advancing equitable health outcomes. Marginal and rural populations are disproportionately affected by these factors, highlighting the imperative to adopt focused policies and resource distribution (Oosterhof, 2018).

Similarly, while projections suggest that SDG 4 is on track to be achieved, major gaps persist in ensuring inclusive and lifelong learning opportunities. Without addressing these disparities, the region risks falling short of its commitment to universal access to quality education and lifelong skills development (UN ESCAP, 2017; Oosterhof, 2018). To navigate these challenges, several strategic approaches have emerged for the implementation of the SDGs in South Asia. One of the most promising investments is to invest in universal access to education and healthcare (UN ESCAP, 2017).

South Asia has shown uneven progress in achieving SDGs, particularly in the areas of MH and education (UN ESCAP, 2022). A UN report from 2024 highlights that although there has been a reduction in working poverty by 6.9 percentage points in Central and Southern Asia between 2015 and 2023 (UN DESA, 2024), disparities in access to quality education and MH services persist. Figure 1 illustrates the multidimensional poverty and income poverty in South Asian countries (UN ESCAP, 2021), both of which are closely related to educational attainment and mental well-being. Another critical challenge is migration, both internal and international, which disrupts educational continuity and contributes to psychological stress and vulnerability. Afghanistan, for example, ranks among the top countries of origin for migrants who lost their lives in 2023, underscoring the ongoing humanitarian and MH crises in the region (UN DESA, 2024).

The report of the Economic and Social Commission for Asia and the Pacific (ESCAP) (2017) further emphasizes that progress on education and health-related SDGs, including MH, varies significantly between South Asian countries, reflecting deep-rooted structural inequalities (Table 1) (UN ESCAP, 2017).

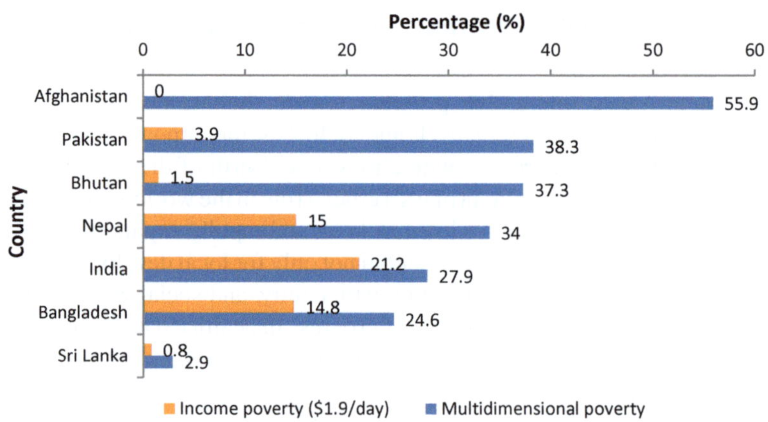

Fig. 1 Multidimensional poverty and income poverty in South Asian countries (%) (UN ESCAP, 2021)

Table 1 Progress in the SDGs in the health and education sectors in South Asia (UN ESCAP, 2017)

Country	Health progress	Education progress	Challenges
Afghanistan	Struggles with the healthcare infrastructure and access to skilled birth attendants	Slow progress in improving school attendance	High child malnutrition and weak health system
Bangladesh	Reduced maternal mortality, but high rates of undernutrition persist	Steady progress in primary education completion	Gaps in access to secondary education
Bhutan	Strong improvements in maternal health	High school enrollment	Limited access to specialized healthcare
India	Reduced infant and maternal mortality	Progress has been made in many areas, but there are still disparities	Education quality and healthcare access issues in rural areas
Maldives	Comprehensive healthcare coverage	High school attendance rates	No major challenges were reported
Nepal	Significant reduction in child mortality	Expanding school enrollment	Concerns about quality and access
Pakistan	Slow progress in access to healthcare care	Struggles with school attendance	High maternal mortality and child malnutrition
Sri Lanka	Developing healthcare system	High literacy rates and a strong education system	Few challenges in health and education

3 Mental Health and Education in the SDGs Framework

Globally, perspectives on MH are evolving with increasing recognition of its critical role in sustainable development. Once considered an "invisible problem in international development," MH is now described as "one of the most pressing development issues of our time" (Chambers, 2010; Mills, 2018). This change reflects a growing understanding that mental well-being is not just a health problem but a fundamental component of economic, social, and human development. The WHO Comprehensive MH Action Plan 2013–2020 highlights the marginalization of people with mental disorders as a significant barrier to achieving national and international development goals. The plan also advocates for the integration of MH interventions into broader development strategies, underscoring the role of development agencies in ensuring the successful implementation of global MH initiatives (WHO, 2013).

Although MH is central to SDG 3, it is intricately related to all SGDs, especially poverty, gender inequality, and migration, with distinct effects in South Asia (Dybdahl & Lien, 2017; Goodwin & Zaman, 2023). With 450 million people worldwide living with mental illness, addressing mental health is no longer optional, but imperative for sustainable progress (Thornicroft & Patel, 2014). Evidence suggests that improving MH services contributes to safer and more sustainable urban settlements, as untreated mental illness can lead to increased social instability, homelessness, and crime. Furthermore, poor parental MH is directly related to child undernutrition, strengthening the intersection between MH and hunger reduction (SDG 2) (Thornicroft & Patel, 2014). Similarly, poverty and MH problems are closely related to each other; economic problems directly affect MH by increasing stress and limiting access to healthcare (De Silva & Roland, 2014). Poverty (SGD 1) is one of the main factors that increases the vulnerability of mental disorders (Votruba et al., 2014), as it affects MH by causing malnutrition, which affects brain development and function. Deficiencies, such as iodine during pregnancy, can cause irreversible brain damage, while stunting in children under five years of age poses serious developmental and health risks (Dybdahl & Lien, 2017). Similarly, poverty contributes to a cycle of poor MH, in which limited resources prevent actual interventions, preserving poverty (De Silva & Roland, 2014). Likewise, reduced inequalities (SGD 10) are directly related to MH problems, as both women and men who flee their countries often experience violence and deprivation during displacement, increasing their risk of MH problems. These traumatic events can have long-lasting, serious effects on your well-being (Herrman, 2019). From 2017 to 2018, migration from Nepal to India was associated with high psychological morbidity among Nepali migrants, especially vulnerable groups. MH was affected by work, living conditions, and limited legal and social protections (Dhungana et al., 2019).

However, despite progress in integrating MH into global development policies, concerns remain about how MH strategies are implemented. Some critics argue that current models are rooted in Western sociocultural and economic frameworks, which oversimplify the complexities of MH by reducing them to medical diagnoses. These models may not always align with local traditions and cultural beliefs, particularly in non-western societies (Chambers, 2010). The subjectivity of MH diagnoses further complicates matters, as most mental illnesses lack definitive biological markers, leading to variability in diagnostic practices across cultures (Chambers, 2010).

The need to act is further underscored by the global burden of substance use and mental illness. In the 2015 Global Burden of Diseases (GBD) study, these conditions accounted for 18.4% of years lost to disability (Vos et al., 2016). The costs are equally astronomical, given that the global economy lost an estimated $2.5 trillion to mental disorders in 2015 alone, and this figure is estimated to reach $6 trillion by 2030 (Bloom et al., 2011). Therefore, it is again called to make continued investments in education, jurisdictional policies, and services toward psychiatry and mental illness in resource-poor but populous places like South Asia, where lack and stigma remain major impediments to progress.

4 Barriers to Achieving Education, MH, and SDG Goals in South Asia

Achievement of the SDGs related to MH remains a significant challenge due to systemic, social, and economic barriers. The treatment gap is a critical issue in low- and middle-income countries (LMIC), particularly in countries in South Asia, where most people with mental disorders do not receive appropriate care due to the lack of mental health professionals, inadequate health infrastructure and financial constraints (Kulkarni & Paul, 2021; Votruba et al., 2016). Stigma and discrimination further hinder the progress of MH, as individuals with psychiatric disorders face social stigma and a reluctance of families to support reintegration efforts after treatment. In many cases, families provide false addresses or refuse to accept discharged patients, leading to recurrent hospitalization and institutionalization. This problem is exacerbated by the lack of structured rehabilitation programs, employment opportunities, and social reintegration initiatives, leaving many people in cycles of neglect, relapse, and poverty (Kulkarni & Paul, 2021; Votruba et al., 2016). The government's prioritization of MH remains low, with most national health budgets allowing less than 2% to psychiatric care (World Bank, 2025). Consequently, several factors hinder the achievement of the MH-related SDG goals. Political instability and poor governance barriers impede improvements in SGD related to MH in South Asia (Manapurath et al., 2023). Many people are displaced in the region, such as displacement due to wars, as seen in Afghanistan (Hameed et al., 2023), and displacement due to climate change in Pakistan (Khan et al., 2024), which exacerbates social disparities and interrupts MH care systems (Hameed et al., 2023; Khan et al., 2024).

Deep-rooted stigmas about MH prevent people from seeking professional help (Wainberg et al., 2017). In many countries in South Asia, mental diseases are frequently associated with shame, inhibiting early diagnosis and treatment (Lemon et al., 2023). Additionally, South Asia experiences a substantial deficiency of trained MH specialists and infrastructure. Countries such as Nepal and Sri Lanka have less than one psychiatrist per 100,000 people, making MH services unreachable to large portions of the population (Grover, 2023). Table 2 shows the number and percentage from MH professionals of South Asian countries in 2020 (Grover, 2023). In fact, the absence of comprehensive MH policies and inadequate findings further delays progress (Grover, 2023; Wainberg et al., 2017).

Table 2 Number and percentage from MH professionals of South Asian countries in 2020 (Grover, 2023)

Variables	Afghanistan	Bangladesh	Bhutan	India	Maldives	Nepal	Pakistan	Sri Lanka
Total population (UN Official Estimate)	38,041,757	163,046,173	763,094	1,309,053,980	530,957	28,608,715	216,565,317	21,323,734
Number of Psychiatrists	129	270	3	–	17	183	300	123
Psychiatrists per 100,000 population	0.34	0.17	0.39	0.29	3.2	0.64	0.14	0.58
MH Nurses	26	700	9	–	0	123	200	624
MH nurses per 100,000 population	0.07	0.43	1.18	0.80	0	0.43	0.09	2.93
Psychologists	133	565	0	–	7	31	100	61
Psychologists per 100,000 population	0.35	0.35	0	0.07	1.32	0.11	0.05	0.29
Social Workers	48	3	0	–	2	–	600	72
Social workers per 100,000 population	0.13	0.002	0	0.06	0.38	–	0.28	0.34

5 Governmental and NGO Initiatives Supporting Education and MH in South Asian

5.1 Afghanistan

Afghanistan has made significant efforts to rebuild its MH system. However, political instability and conflict have repeatedly interrupted these efforts (International Psychosocial Organization, 2013; Missmahl, 2018). The foundation for community MH services was laid in 1985 when the Ministry of Public Health established a Department of MH and four MH centers in Kabul. However, decades of war and Taliban rule led to the collapse of these institutions (Rahimi & Azimi, 2012; van de Put, 2002). Attempts to rebuild began in 1999 with a three-month psychiatric training program, but ongoing instability prevented its sustainability (Mohit et al., 1999). By 2002, only a few dozen physicians and two psychiatrists remained in the country's MH system, most with minimal formal training (Ventevogel et al., 2002). In response, the Afghan Ministry of Public Health expanded MH training, introducing 12-day courses for nearly 1000 doctors and 6-day courses for 1200 nurses and midwives by 2018 (Ventevogel et al., 2002; World Bank, 2022). In 2013, a nationwide trainer training initiative was implemented for the WHO MH Gap Action Program (mhGAP), further strengthening the capacity (Bendavid et al., 2021). A non-governmental organization (NGOs) has played a crucial role in bridging service gaps. The International Rescue Committee (IRC) trained Afghan teachers in psychosocial support, while War Child Holland's "community action planning" in Herat promoted children's emotional well-being (Alemi et al., 2023). These interventions have shown significant and lasting impacts, such as increased school attendance, increased security among children, and stronger interethnic relationships (Alemi et al., 2023).

5.2 Bangladesh

Mental health services in Bangladesh remain limited, with psychiatrists and specialists concentrated in tertiary urban hospitals, leaving rural areas underserved (Arafat et al., 2024; Islam & Biswas, 2015). With only 270 psychiatrists for a population of 162 million, access to MH care is severely restricted (WHO, 2020) (Table 2). The National Institute of MH in Dhaka, the only national MH facility, operates a 200-bed mental hospital in conjunction with a 500-bed psychiatric hospital. Furthermore, there are 3900 beds in residential facilities, including homes for impoverished and detox centers (Choudhury et al., 2006; Islam & Biswas, 2015). Community services are insufficient, with only 31 mental inpatient units, comprising just 8% of all hospital beds in Bangladesh (WHO, 2007).

5.3 Bhutan

Bhutan has strengthened its commitment to MH with the 2018 Action Plan and MH Program, which was upgraded to a 5-year initiative after an assessment. Key measures include the formation of a national suicide prevention committee, the establishment of a MH hotline, and the improvement of primary healthcare and counseling services to improve accessibility and support (Dorji et al., 2017). For Bhutan, the Paro Declaration is of particular significance, as it represents a regional commitment by WHO South-East Asia member states to advance "universal access to People-Centered MH Care and Services." Bhutan's signing of this declaration signals a renewed urgency to expand MH services (WHO, 2022).

5.4 India

In India, the government has implemented significant reforms over the past decade to ensure fair and accessible MH services. The MH Care Act of 2017 and the National MH Policy of 2014 serve as the foundations for strengthening MH care and protecting the rights of people with mental illnesses (Gangadhar et al., 2023). Building on these policies, the government has introduced three major initiatives aimed at improving access, affordability, and integration of MH services within the healthcare system (Ministry of Health and Welfare, Government of India, 2022). To address financial barriers, Pradhan Mantri Jan Arogya Yojana provides government-funded health insurance, offering financial protection for hospitalizations, particularly for low-income and vulnerable populations (Ministry of Health and Welfare, Government of India, 2022). Furthermore, the Ayushman Bharat Digital Mission improves continuity of care through digital health records, while also promoting research and technological advancements in MH care (Government of India, 2023).

5.5 Maldives

The Maldives Ministry of Health (MoH) aims to enhance MH services in its geographically dispersed population, aligning with global health goals. Although psychiatric care and medications are provided through public institutions and are private institutions and covered by the universal health insurance "Husnuvaa Aasandha," access remains limited due to high costs and a shortage of MH professionals (UNICEF Maldives, 2019). To address these challenges, MoH implemented the National MH Policy (2015–2025) along with a MH Strategic Plan. Furthermore, the Maldives actively combat substance abuse through the National Drug Agency.

Despite strict alcohol regulations for cultural and religious reasons, illegal production and sales persist, highlighting ongoing public health challenges (Government of Nepal, 2007).

5.6 Nepal

In Nepal, government MH initiatives include constitutional recognition of health as a fundamental right (Government of Nepal, 2007). However, implementation faces challenges, such as limited enforcement of existing MH policies and the absence of official MH legislation despite multiple drafts (Upadhaya et al., 2017). NGOs play a key supporting role by collaborating with district public health offices to provide MH services. However, barriers persist, including insufficient coordination between stakeholders, limited awareness of disability allowances, frequent turnover of trained personnel, inconsistent supply of psychotropic medications, inadequate monitoring and supervision, and a lack of epidemiological MH data at the national level (Upadhaya et al., 2017).

5.7 Pakistan

Pakistan's MH system is primarily operated by large city tertiary care hospitals, with little connection to primary care. General practitioners, community health workers, and other non-specialist clinicians are not as involved in the current system, which is mainly based on psychiatrists and clinical psychologists (Main Thompson & Saleem, 2025). Pakistan's private sector leads in creative solutions despite the limitations of the state sector. NGOs, such as SINA-Health Education and Welfare Trust employ digital tools and telepsychiatry, integrate MH into community clinics, conduct grassroots awareness campaigns, and address social determinants through gender equity campaigns. Groups such as the Pakistan Institute of Living and Learning promote legislation, increase workforce proficiency, and expand culturally sensitive solutions (Main Thompson & Saleem, 2025).

5.8 Sri Lanka

The workforce in Sri Lanka that provides psychiatric care consists of consultant psychiatrists, MH medical officers who have completed a one-year diploma in psychiatry or three months of special MH training, psychiatric social workers, designated community psychiatry nurses, occupational therapists, and a variety of other employees, including volunteers (Rajasuriya et al., 2021). In 2012, only three clinical psychologists worked in Sri Lanka's state sector and were all affiliated with

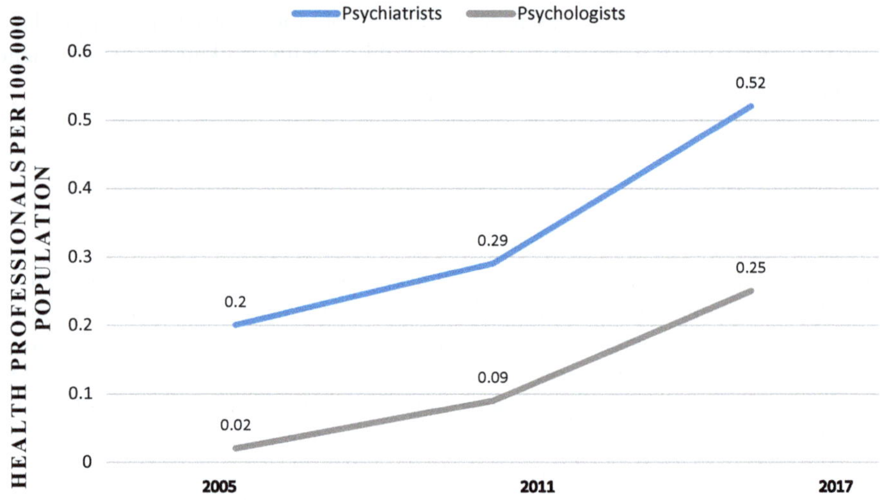

Fig. 2 Growth of MH professionals in Sri Lanka (2005–2017)

universities (Jenkins et al., 2012). Community care is currently provided primarily through outreach clinics in peripheral and occasionally distant medical facilities. The 2010 opening of the Colombo-15 Community Psychiatric Clinic serves as an example of such a facility (Ranasinghe et al., 2011). The MH workforce in Sri Lanka has grown gradually from 2005 to 2017, with psychiatrists increasing from 0.2 to 0.52 per 100,000 people and psychologists increasing from 0.02 to 0.25. Despite this progress, both professions remain significantly underrepresented, highlighting the ongoing limitations of the workforce (Fig. 2).

6 Research and Data Gaps

Despite increasing recognition of MH as a critical public health priority, significant gaps persist in research and evidence-based interventions, particularly in LMICs such as South Asia. Hossain et al. (2020) highlight the substantial prevalence of mental disorders across the region, but emphasize heterogeneity in prevalence estimates due to methodological inconsistencies, variations in diagnostic criteria, and limited epidemiological data. The scarcity of high-quality longitudinal studies limits the development of effective MH policies, leaving many nations reliant on fragmented and often culturally mismatched intervention models. Furthermore, underreporting due to stigma and lack of standardized screening tools further skews prevalence estimates, complicating targeted policy responses. Keynejad et al. (2018) reinforce these concerns, particularly with respect to the implementation and scale of global MH initiatives. Although WHO's mhGAP provides a structured framework for integrating

MH into primary care, its effectiveness is often hampered by limited resources, inadequate training of healthcare providers, and sociocultural barriers (WHO, 2001). Research evaluating mhGAP applications remains geographically skewed. Furthermore, the absence of robust economic evaluations on the cost-effectiveness of MH integration in primary care further limits its scalability. Although there is a growing recognition of the importance of MH, in South Asia substantial gaps persist. Despite efforts, there is still a lack of comprehensive data on SGD (UN DESA, 2024), particularly data linking SDGs and MH in South Asia (Lemon et al., 2023; Manapurath et al., 2023). A survey between 2015 and 2020, among 47 LMICs, found that; none of the countries had data for all 27 indicators measurable by surveys (Zhao et al., 2022). Furthermore, there is a lack of research to identify the unique sociocultural factors that influence MH in the region (Lemon et al., 2023; Manapurath et al., 2023; Grover, 2023), as few studies in this region have examined the efficacy of integrating MH into broader strategies (Grover, 2023).

7 Recommendations and Future Directions

Addressing the education and MH within the SDGs is essential to advance equitable and inclusive development strategies in South Asia (Wainberg et al., 2017). Improving results in both sectors requires integrated and context-sensitive interventions. A primary recommendation is the construction of inclusive policies that incorporate MH and psychosocial well-being in educational strategies. This means adopting a multisectoral approach where MH is not addressed in isolation but rather woven into educational planning, school curricula, and teacher training. In South Asia, effective promotion of MH in schools can be achieved without expensive technology or specialized personnel. General educators and community health workers can be trained to provide basic MH support, identify early signs of psychological distress, and provide referrals. Evidence shows that essential care for depression, anxiety, and substance use disorders can cost as little as $3–4 per person annually, making it highly feasible for integration within public education systems. This cost-effectiveness not only improves MH, but also enhances educational retention, academic performance, and life outcomes, especially in low-resource settings (De Silva & Roland, 2014).

Second, growing community-based MH programs can report service supply gaps. In particular, developing culturally sensitive facilities that address stigma and improve accessibility (Goodwin & Zaman, 2023; Wainberg et al., 2017). Training local health workers and developing telemedicine can advance accessibility in inaccessible regions (Wainberg et al., 2017). Especially to promote health at the population level, these countries must use modern technologies, including digital health centers, mobile health parts, and digital tools for community health workers (Manapurath et al., 2023).

Future research must prioritize culturally adapted and region-specific models that integrate MH support within educational systems, along with standardized prevalence assessments and rigorous longitudinal studies. Advancing research that links SDG indicators with education and MH outcomes in South Asia is essential (Lemon et al., 2023). Dedicated studies and comprehensive data collection in this field can help shape evidence-based policies and interventions that address the unique sociocultural contexts of the region (Wainberg et al., 2017). Collaboration and advocacy, especially between governments, NGOs, educational institutions, and international agencies, are vital to expanding integrated services. In addition, targeted school-based awareness campaigns and public education initiatives can play a crucial role in reducing stigma, promoting emotional resilience, and normalizing MH discussions across communities.

8 Conclusion

Education is a fundamental determinant of MH, shaping cognitive resilience, emotional regulation, and social integration. Despite global commitments such as the SDGs, systemic disparities, stigma, and resource limitations continue to impede progress, particularly in low- and middle-income regions like South Asia. A paradigm shift is required, one that integrates literacy, early intervention, and psychosocial support for mental health within educational systems. Closing the gap in treatment among the mentally ill requires multisectoral coordination, evidence-informed policymaking, and culturally adapted intervention. India's reforms in policymaking, Bhutan's suicide prevention program, and Nepal's community model are exemplary efforts among some South Asian nations. Multisectoral collaborations among governments, international, and local non-governmental organizations are critically required to mobilize efforts and make them sustainable. Investment in technological platforms for MH, task-shifting practices, and decision-making informed by evidence will be required to bridge service gaps. The achievement of the vision of the 2030 Agenda is inextricable from the pursuit of overall development goals. Without intervention, evidence-based decision-making, and people-centered education reforms, the 2030 Agenda will never be realized. Only through combined efforts that are locally centered and ethics-oriented will MH become an integral part of sustainable development, and no one, particularly in South Asia, will be left behind.

References

Alemi, Q., Panter-Brick, C., Oriya, S., Ahmady, M., Alimi, A. Q., Faiz, H., Hakim, N., Sami Hashemi, S. A., Manaly, M. A., Naseri, R., Parwiz, K., Sadat, S. J., Sharifi, M. Z., Shinwari, Z., Ahmadi, S. J., Amin, R., Azimi, S., Hewad, A., Musavi, Z., Siddiqi, A. M., & Ventevogel,

P. (2023). Afghan mental health and psychosocial well-being: Thematic review of four decades of research and interventions. *BJPsych Open, 9*(4), e125. https://doi.org/10.1192/bjo.2023.502

Arafat, S. M. Y., Giasuddin, N. A., & Mazumder, A. H. (2024). Access to mental health care in Bangladesh—Current status, potential challenges, and ways out. In S. M. Y. Arafat & S. K. Kar (Eds.), *Access to mental health care in South Asia.* Springer. https://doi.org/10.1007/978-981-99-9153-2_3

Asadullah, M. N., Savoia, A., & Sen, K. (2020). Will South Asia achieve the sustainable development goals by 2030? Learning from the MDGs experience. *Social Indicators Research, 152*(1), 165–189. https://doi.org/10.1007/s11205-020-02423-7

Bendavid, E., Boerma, T., Akseer, N., Langer, A., Malembaka, E. B., Okiro, E. A., et al. (2021). The effects of armed conflict on the health of women and children. *The Lancet, 397*(10273), 522–532. https://doi.org/10.1016/S0140-6736(21)00131-8

Bloom, D. E., Chisholm, D., Jané-Llopis, E., Prettner, K., Stein, A., & Feigl, A. (2011). From burden to "Best Buys": reducing the economic impact of non-communicable diseases. *World Health Org, Geneva, Switzerland.* https://econpapers.repec.org/paper/gdmwpaper/7511.htm

Chambers, A. (2010, May 10). Mental illness and the developing world. *The Guardian.* https://www.theguardian.com/commentisfree/2010/may/10/mental-illness-developing-world

Choudhury, W. A., Quraishi, F. A., & Haque, Z. (2006). Mental health and psychosocial aspects of disaster preparedness in Bangladesh. *International Review of Psychiatry (Abingdon, England), 18*(6), 529–535. https://doi.org/10.1080/09540260601037896

De Silva, M., & Roland, J. (2014). MH for sustainable development [Report]. Global Health and MH All-Party Parliamentary Groups. https://www.globalhealthpartnerships.org/wp-content/uploads/2024/10/APPG_Mental-Health_Report.pdf

Dhungana, R. R., Aryal, N., Adhikary, P., Kc, R. K., Regmi, P. R., Devkota, B., Sharma, G. N., Wickramage, K., van Teijlingen, E., & Simkhada, P. (2019). Psychological morbidity in Nepali cross-border migrants in India: A community based cross-sectional study. *BMC Public Health, 19*(1), 1534. https://doi.org/10.1186/s12889-019-7881-z

Dorji, G., Choki, S., Jamphel, K., Wangdi, Y., Chogyel, T., Dorji, C., & Nirola, D. K. (2017). Policy and governance to address depression and suicide in Bhutan: The national suicide-prevention strategy. *WHO South-East Asia Journal of Public Health, 6*(1), 39–44. https://doi.org/10.4103/2224-3151.206163

Dybdahl, R., & Lien, L. (2017). MH is an integral part of the sustainable development goals. *Prev Med Commun Health, 1*(1), 1–3. https://doi.org/10.15761/PMCH.1000104

English, L., & McKay, V. (2022). SDGs 3, 4, 5: Educating for health, literacy and gender. *Convergence, 43*(1), 31–40. https://www.convergencejournal.org/vol-43-no-1-3.pdf

ESCAP, U. (2017). *Achieving sustainable development goals in South Asia: Key policy priorities and implementation challenges.* https://www.unescap.org/publications/achieving-sustainable-development-goals-south-asia-key-policy-priorities-and

Gangadhar, B. N., Kumar, C. N., Sadh, K., Manjunatha, N., Math, S. B., Kalaivanan, R. C., Rao, G. N., Parthasarathy, R., Chand, P. K., Chandra, P. S., Thirthalli, J., Murthy, P., Varghese, M., Mathur, A., Bairy, B. K., Kishore, C., Gowda, G. S., Basvaraju, V., Harihara, S. N., Isaac, M. K., & Chaturvedi, S. K. (2023). Mental health programme in India: Has the tide really turned?. *The Indian Journal of Medical Research, 157*(5), 387–394. https://doi.org/10.4103/ijmr.IJMR_2217_20

Goodwin, J., & Zaman, U. (2023). Editorial: MH stigma and UN sustainable development goals. *Frontiers in Psychiatry, 14*, 1190406. https://doi.org/10.3389/fpsyt.2023.1190406

Government of India. (2023). *Ayushman Bharat digital mission.* Retrieved March 12, 2025 from https://abdm.gov.in/

Government of Nepal. (2007). *The interim constitution of Nepal, 2007 (as amended by first, second and third amendments).* https://constitutionnet.org/sites/default/files/interim_constitution_of_nepal_2007_as_amended_by_first_second_and_third_amendments.pdf

Grover, S. (2023). Status of mental health in South Asian countries. *Journal of SAARC Psychiatric Federation, 1*(1), 1–5. https://doi.org/10.4103/jspf.jspf_15_23

Hameed, M. A., Rahman, M. M., & Khanam, R. (2023). The health consequences of civil wars: Evidence from Afghanistan. *BMC Public Health, 23*(1), 154. https://doi.org/10.1186/s12889-022-14720-6

Herrman, H. (2019). Sustainable development goals and the MH of resettled refugee women: A role for international organizations. *Frontiers in Psychiatry, 10*, 608. https://doi.org/10.3389/fpsyt.2019.00608

Hossain, M. M., Purohit, N., Sultana, A., Ma, P., McKyer, E. L. J., & Ahmed, H. U. (2020). Prevalence of mental disorders in South Asia: An umbrella review of systematic reviews and meta-analyses. *Asian Journal of Psychiatry, 51*, Article 102041. https://doi.org/10.1016/j.ajp.2020.102041

International Psychosocial Organisation (IPSO). (2013). *Supporting the integration of MH into the public health care system in Afghanistan by qualifying health professionals and training a pool of national MH trainers*. IPSO. https://ipsocontext.org/docs/IPSO_MentalHealth_AF004_18-final.pdf

Islam, A., & Biswas, T. (2015). MH and the health system in Bangladesh: situation analysis of a neglected domain. *Am J Psychiatry Neurosci, 3*(4), 57–62. https://www.researchgate.net/publication/282524379_Mental_Health_and_the_Health_System_in_Bangladesh_Situation_Analysis_of_a_Neglected_Domain

Izutsu, T., Tsutsumi, A., Minas, H., Thornicroft, G., Patel, V., & Ito, A. (2015). MH and wellbeing in the sustainable development goals. *The Lancet Psychiatry, 2*(12), 1052–1054. https://doi.org/10.1016/S2215-0366(15)00457-5

Jenkins, R., Mendis, J., Cooray, S., & Cooray, M. (2012). Integration of MH into primary care in Sri Lanka. *MH in Family Medicine, 9*(1), 15.

Keynejad, R. C., Dua, T., Barbui, C., & Thornicroft, G. (2018). WHO MH Gap Action Programme (mhGAP) intervention guide: A systematic review of evidence from low and middle-income countries. *BMJ Ment Health, 21*(1), 30–34. https://doi.org/10.1136/eb-2017-102750

Khan, S., Idrees, U., Shakoor, A., & Khan, Z. U. (2024). Climate displacement in Pakistan: (Under) reported frame in media discourse on climate change in Pakistan. *Pakistan Journal of Humanities and Social Sciences, 12*(2), 1593–1605. https://doi.org/10.52131/pjhss.2024.v12i2.2243

Kulkarni, S., & Paul, R. J. (2021). Empirical study on the challenges to community reintegration under MHcare: An analysis with reference to SDG 2030. *Turkish Journal of Computer and Mathematics Education, 12*(10), 1297–1304. https://www.turcomat.org/index.php/turkbilmat/article/view/4389

Lemon, C. A., Svob, C., Bonomo, Y., Dhungana, S., Supanya, S., Sittanomai, N., Diatri, H., Haider, I. I., Javed, A., Chandra, P., Herrman, H., Hoven, C. W., & Sartorius, N. (2023). Priorities for research promoting MH in the South and East of Asia. *The Lancet Regional Health – Southeast Asia, 23*, 100287. https://doi.org/10.1016/j.lansea.2023.100287

Main Thompson, A., & Saleem, S. M. (2025). Closing the MH gap: Transforming Pakistan's MH landscape. *Frontiers in Health Services, 4*, 1471528. https://doi.org/10.3389/frhs.2024.1471528

Maldives, U. N. I. C. E. F. (2019). *2017 health SDG profile: The Maldives*. https://www.unicef.org/maldives/reports/2017-health-sdg-profile-maldives

Manapurath, R., Raran Veetil, D., & Kamath, M. S. (2023). Use of modern technologies for promoting health at the population level in India. *The Lancet Regional Health – Southeast Asia, 23*, 100338. https://doi.org/10.1016/j.lansea.2023.100338

Mills, C. (2018). From 'invisible problem' to global priority: The inclusion of MH in the sustainable development goals. *Development and Change, 49*(3), 843–866. https://doi.org/10.1111/dech.12397

Ministry of Health and Welfare, Government of India. (2022). *Ayushman Bharat - Health and wellness centre*. https://ab-hwc.nhp.gov.in/

Missmahl, I. (2018). Value-based counselling: Reflections on fourteen years of psychosocial support in Afghanistan. *Intervention, 16*(3), 256–264. https://psychotraumanet.org/sites/default/files/documents/Intervention163256-3646282_100742%20Value-based%20counselling%20Reflections%20on%20fourteen%20years%20of.pdf

Mohit, A., Saeed, K., Shahmohammadi, D., Bolhari, J., Bina, M., Gater, R., et al. (1999). MH manpower development in Afghanistan: A report on a training course for primary health care physicians. *Eastern Mediterranean Health Journal, 5*(2), 373–377. https://applications.emro.who.int/emhj/0502/EMHJ_1999_5_2_373_377.pdf

Oosterhof, P. D. (2018). *Localizing the sustainable development goals to accelerate implementation of the 2030 agenda for sustainable development: The current state of sustainable development goal localization in Asia and the Pacific*. https://doi.org/10.22617/BRF189612

Pritchett, L., & Sandefur, J. (2020). Girls' schooling and women's literacy: Schooling targets alone won't reach learning goals. *International Journal of Educational Development, 78*, Article 102242. https://doi.org/10.1016/j.ijedudev.2020.102242

Rahimi, Y. A., & Azimi, S. (2012). War and the crisis of mental health in Afghanistan. *International Psychiatry: Bulletin of the Board of International Affairs of the Royal College of Psychiatrists, 9*(3), 55–57.

Rajasuriya, M., Hewagama, M., Ruwanpriya, S., & Wijesundara, H. (2021). Community-based psychiatric services in Sri Lanka: A model by WHO in the making. *Consortium Psychiatricum, 2*(4), 40–52. https://doi.org/10.17816/CP106

Ranasinghe, P., Mendis, J., & Hanwella, R. (2011). Community psychiatry service in Sri Lanka: A successful model. *Sri Lanka Journal of Psychiatry, 2*(1). https://doi.org/10.4038/sljpsyc.v2i1.3157

Thornicroft, G., & Patel, V. (2014). Including mental health among the new sustainable development goals. *BMJ (Clinical Research Ed.), 349*, Article g5189. https://doi.org/10.1136/bmj.g5189

United Nations Department of Economic and Social Affairs. (2024). The Sustainable Development Goals report 2024 (2024 ed.). United Nations. https://doi.org/10.18356/9789213589755

United Nations Economic and Social Commission for Asia and the Pacific (UN ESCAP). (2021). *Achieving the SDGs in South Asia: An integrated approach to accelerate SDG progress and COVID-19 recovery*. https://hdl.handle.net/20.500.12870/4049

United Nations Economic and Social Commission for Asia and the Pacific. (2022). *Asia and the Pacific SDG progress report 2022: Widening disparities amid COVID-19 (ST/ESCAP/2996)*. United Nations. https://www.unescap.org/sites/default/d8files/knowledge-products/ESCAP-2022-FG_SDG-Progress-Report.pdf

Upadhaya, N., Jordans, M. J., Pokhrel, R., Gurung, D., Adhikari, R. P., Petersen, I., & Komproe, I. H. (2017). Current situations and future directions for MH system governance in Nepal: Findings from a qualitative study. *International Journal of MH Systems, 11*, 1–12. https://doi.org/10.1186/s13033-017-0145-3

van de Put, W. (2002). Addressing MH in Afghanistan. *The Lancet, 360*(Supplement), s41–s42. https://doi.org/10.1016/S0140-6736(02)11816-2

Ventevogel, P., Azimi, S., Jalal, S., & Kortmann, F. (2002). MH care reform in Afghanistan. *Journal of Ayub Medical College Abbottabad, 14*(4), 1–3.

Vos, T., Allen, C., Arora, M., Barber, R. M., Bhutta, Z. A., Brown, A., Carter, A., Casey, D. C., Charlson, F. J., Chen, A. Z., Coggeshall, M., & Boufous, S. (2016). Global, regional, and national incidence, prevalence, and years lived with disability for 310 diseases and injuries, 1990–2015: A systematic analysis for the Global Burden of Disease Study 2015. *The Lancet, 388*(10053), 1545–1602. https://doi.org/10.1016/S0140-6736(16)31678-6

Votruba, N., Thornicroft, G., & FundaMentalSDG Steering Group. (2016). Sustainable development goals and mental health: Learnings from the contribution of the FundaMentalSDG global initiative. *Global mental health (Cambridge, England), 3*, e26. https://doi.org/10.1017/gmh.2016.20

Votruba, N., Eaton, J., Prince, M., & Thornicroft, G. (2014). The importance of global MH for the sustainable development goals. *Journal of MH, 23*(6), 283–286. https://doi.org/10.3109/09638237.2014.976857

Wainberg, M. L., Scorza, P., Shultz, J. M., Helpman, L., Mootz, J. J., Johnson, K. A., Neria, Y., Bradford, J. E., Oquendo, M. A., & Arbuckle, M. R. (2017). Challenges and opportunities in global mental health: A research-to-practice perspective. *Current Psychiatry Reports, 19*(5), 28. https://doi.org/10.1007/s11920-017-0780-z

World Bank. (n.d.). *MH conditions on the rise: Countries must prioritize investments.* World Bank Blogs. Retrieved March 13, 2025 from https://blogs.worldbank.org/en/health/mental-health-conditions-rise-countries-must-prioritize-investments

World Bank. (2022). *Fragility, conflict & violence.* World Bank. https://www.worldbank.org/en/topic/fragilityconflictviolence/overview#1

World Bank. (2025). MH conditions on the rise: Countries must prioritize investments. *World Bank Blogs.* Retrieved March 13, 2025, from https://blogs.worldbank.org/en/health/mental-health-conditions-rise-countries-must-prioritize-investments

World Health Organization. (2001). *The world health report 2001: MH: New understanding, new hope.* World Health Organization. https://iris.who.int/handle/10665/42390

World Health Organization. (2007). *WHO-AIMS report on MH system in Bangladesh.* World Health Organization. http://www.who.int/mental_health/bangladesh_who_aims_report.pdf

World Health Organization. (2013). *Comprehensive MH action plan 2013–2020.* World Health Organization. https://www.who.int/publications/i/item/9789241506021

World Health Organization. (2020). *Bangladesh WHO special initiative for MH situational assessment.* World Health Organization. https://cdn.who.int/media/docs/default-source/mental-health/special-initiative/who-special-initiative-country-report—bangladesh—2020_f746e0ca-8099-4d00-b126-fa338a06ca6e.pdf?sfvrsn=c2122a0e_7

World Health Organization. (2022, September 6). WHO South-East Asia Region commits to universal access to people-centered MH care and services. *World Health Organization.* https://www.who.int/southeastasia/news/detail/06-09-2022-who-south-east-asia-region-commits-to-universal-access-to-people-centered-mental-health-care-and-services

World Health Organization. (2023). Suicide worldwide in 2019: Global health estimates. WHO. Available at: https://iris.who.int/bitstream/handle/10665/341728/9789240026643-eng.pdf

Zhao, L., Cao, B., Borghi, E., Chatterji, S., Garcia-Saiso, S., Rashidian, A., Doctor, H. V., D'Agostino, M., Karamagi, H. C., Novillo-Ortiz, D., Landry, M., Hosseinpoor, A. R., Noor, A., Riley, L., Cox, A., Gao, J., Litavecz, S., Asma, S. (2022). Data gaps towards health development goals, 47 low- and middle-income countries. *Bulletin of the World Health Organization, 100*(1), 40–49. https://doi.org/10.2471/BLT.21.286254

Chapter 8
Sustainable Development Goals and Mental Health in Bangladesh

Md. Abdullah Saeed Khan and S. M. Yasir Arafat

Abstract Bangladesh faces a substantial treatment gap, with limited mental health infrastructure and workforce. Recent policy developments like the Mental Health Act (2018) and National Mental Health Strategic Plan (2020–2030) represent positive steps, but require increased funding, expanded facilities, workforce development, improved referral systems, and greater awareness to effectively address the country's mental health challenges. Despite Bangladesh's progress in various Sustainable Development Goals (SDGs) targets, significant challenges remain in mental health, with approximately 18.7% of adults and 12.6% of children suffering from mental disorders. This chapter explores the intersection of SDGs and mental health in Bangladesh, highlighting the bidirectional relationship between mental well-being and sustainable development. The chapter also examines direct connections of mental health to SDG 3 targets on reducing suicide rates and treating substance use disorders, while also exploring indirect links to other goals, including poverty reduction, education, gender equality, and climate action.

Keywords Sustainable development goals · Mental health · Bangladesh · Suicide

1 Introduction

The Sustainable Development Goals (SDGs), adopted by all United Nations Member States in 2015, represent an ambitious global agenda addressing the world's most pressing challenges by 2030 (UNDP, 2025). Compared to its predecessor Millennium Development Goals (MDGs) (Lomazzi et al., 2014), the SDGs recognized the interconnected nature of development challenges and emphasize "leaving no one

Md. Abdullah Saeed Khan (✉)
National Institute of Preventive and Social Medicine (NIPSOM), Dhaka, Bangladesh
e-mail: abdullahdmc@gmail.com

S. M. Y. Arafat
Department of Psychiatry, Bangladesh Specialized Hospital, Dhaka, Bangladesh
e-mail: arafatdmc62@gmail.com

S. K. Kar et al. (eds.), *Sustainable Development Goals and Mental Health in South Asia*, South Asian Perspectives in Mental Health and Psychology ,
https://doi.org/10.1007/978-981-95-2684-0_8

behind." The SDG 3 focuses on the good health and well-being of people. This goal laid out 13 targets encompassing both physical and mental aspects of health. For Bangladesh, the SDGs provide a roadmap for national development planning, policy formulation, and resource allocation. The country has made remarkable progress in achieving some of the targets of SDG goal 3 (GED, 2022), including those associated with maternal and child health and infectious diseases. This success showcases the country's commitment to achieving SDG targets, despite resource constraints. However, it is lagging in many other indicators where continuous and concerted effort is needed. The status is especially grim for the mental health landscape of the country.

This chapter will first give an overview of SDGs relevant to mental health. It will then discuss the SDGs in the context of Bangladesh, with special emphasis on mental health targets. Onward, the mental health challenges and strategies taken to overcome those challenges in Bangladesh will be discussed. Finally, some recommendations will be put forward to achieve mental health related global agendas by the target years.

2 Sustainable Development Goals Relevant to Mental Health

Mental health is fundamental to human capacity for thought, emotion, interaction, and productivity. The World Health Organization (WHO) defines mental health as "a state of mental well-being that enables people to cope with the stresses of life, realize their abilities, learn well and work well, and contribute to their community" (WHO, 2022).

The relationship between mental health and sustainable development is bidirectional and complex. Factors that impede sustainable development—such as poverty (Patel & Kleinman, 2003), inequality (Kirkbride et al., 2024), conflict (McDonald, 2007), and environmental degradation (Wigand et al., 2022)—contribute significantly to poor mental health outcomes. Conversely, poor mental health undermines progress toward sustainable development by reducing productivity, increasing healthcare costs, reinforcing intergenerational cycles of disadvantages (Sareen et al., 2011), and limiting human capital development (Richter et al., 2021). Despite its centrality to sustainable development, mental health received limited explicit recognition in the SDGs, with only targets 3.4 and 3.5 under SDG 3 (Good Health and Well-being) directly addressing mental health and substance use disorders (Votruba & Thornicroft, 2016). However, mental health is implicitly relevant to numerous SDGs, including those related to poverty reduction, education, gender equality, economic growth, inequality reduction, sustainable cities and communities, climate stability, and peace, justice and strong institutions (Fig. 1).

The COVID-19 pandemic has further highlighted the importance of mental health to sustainable development, exposing the fragility of mental health systems worldwide and the disproportionate impact of global crises on psychosocial well-being.

2.1 Direct Link with SDG 3 (Good Health and Well-Being)

SDG 3 contains the most explicit references to mental health within the SDG framework through:

- Target 3.4: "By 2030, reduce by one third premature mortality from non-communicable diseases through prevention and treatment and promote mental health and well-being."
- Target 3.5: "Strengthen the prevention and treatment of substance abuse, including narcotic drug abuse and harmful use of alcohol."

Additionally, other SDG 3 targets indirectly relate to mental health, including those addressing universal health coverage and health workforce development.

The indicators considered as mental health parameters are the incidence of suicide (Indicator 3.4.2), the coverage of treatment interventions (pharmacological, psychosocial and rehabilitation, and aftercare services) for substance use disorder (Indicator 3.5.1) and alcohol per capita consumption (aged 15 years and older) within a calendar year in liters of pure alcohol (Indicator 3.5.2). Suicide is a serious public health issue with more than 720,000 people dying due to suicide every year around the globe (WHO, 2024b). In 2021, an estimated 746,000 global deaths occurred due to suicide (Davis Weaver et al., 2025), and three-quarters (73%) of those occurred in low- and middle-income countries (LMICs) (WHO, 2024b). Psychiatric disorder is attributed to approximately 90% of suicide associated deaths in Western countries (Zalsman et al., 2016). However, this may not be true for LMICs like Bangladesh because of the inadequate or low-quality records (Arafat, 2023). Bangladesh has not yet achieved the target mortality rate of suicide below 3.5 deaths per 100,000 population by 2025. It has been consistently hovering around 7 per 100,000, with a number of 7.56 in 2019 (GED, 2022).

Alcohol and substance use disorder is a major problem around the globe, with a higher risk among adolescents and males. According to a Global Burden of Disease study, in 2019, an estimated 56,734 thousand cases were affected by substance use disorders (Shen et al., 2023) with an age-standardized incidence rate of 204.7 per 100,000 persons. Another WHO study reported 3 million deaths attributable to substance and alcohol use disorder, among which 2.6 million were due to drinking alcohol alone (WHO, 2024a). However, these deaths could have been prevented through increased access to and utilization of treatments for substance use disorder, where the global statistics appear to remain alarmingly low. Only around 1–35% of people were in contact with substance use treatment services, in countries providing this data (WHO, 2024a). In Bangladesh, as per the SDG tracker, 34,935 persons received treatment services in 2022 for substance use disorders (WHO, 2024a), with

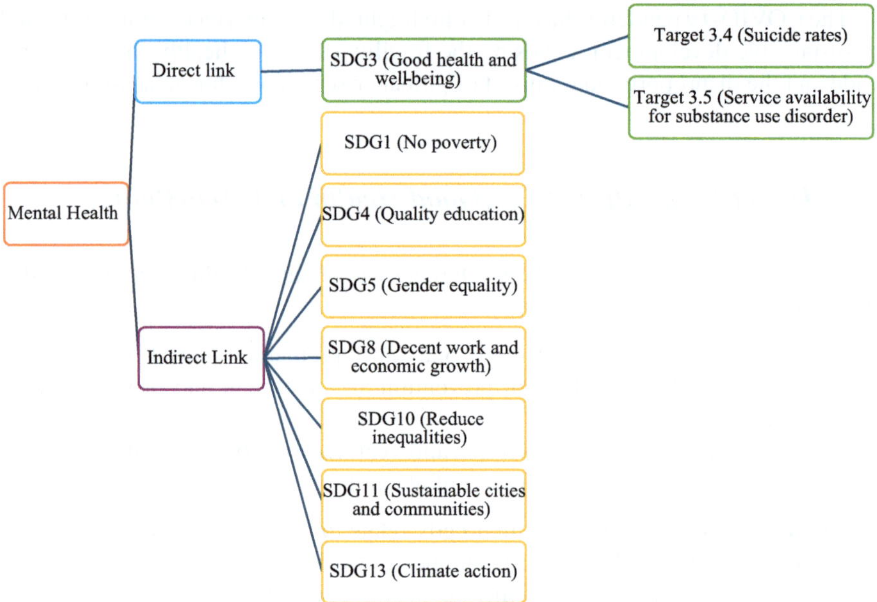

Fig. 1 Link diagram showing direct and indirect connections of different Sustainable Development Goals with mental health

a target to achieve 45,000 in 2025. In 2018, 4.4% of all adults were found to have consumed alcohol in the past 24 months, with 0.8% being heavy episodic drinkers (NIPSOM, 2020). However, the estimate of alcohol consumed in liters per capita is not available.

Although universal health coverage (Indicator 3.8) and health workforce development (Indicator 3.c) do not directly talk about mental health, these indicators ensure that comprehensive health coverage, including services for mental health, is available to the community along with an adequate number of mental health professionals (Fig. 1).

2.2 Indirect Linkages with Other SDGs

Beyond SDG 3, mental health is implicitly relevant to numerous other SDGs:

SDG 1 (No Poverty): Economic conditions are one of the factors that shape an individual's mental health as they grow and age. Poverty and deprivation influence the development of a child's behavior and societal interactions, and thereby, mold the adult psyche (Knifton & Inglis, 2020). Poverty increases exposure to stressors, which can lead to mental health problems. In Bangladesh, there are a few studies exploring the relationship between poverty and mental health. One study conducted recently among people living in disadvantaged areas ("slums") during the COVID-19 pandemic found a positive association between low income and stress (Islam et al., 2021). Previously, another study in rural Bangladesh reported that mental disorders were more prevalent among economically poor respondents (Monawar Hosain et al., 2007). On the other hand, mental disorders can lead to reduced productivity and increased healthcare expenditures, leading to further financial crisis. Thus, the vicious circle of poverty and mental illness is born (Choudhary, 2024). Therefore, achieving the SDG goal of 'no' poverty requires management of mental health, while the reduction of poverty may also lead to good mental well-being. With nearly 20.5% of people living below the poverty line (Sach et al., 2024), there is no alternative but to take holistic measures to tackle issues of poverty and mental health in Bangladesh.

SDG 4 (Quality Education): Psychological well-being is essential for the development of an individual. Mental health influences cognitive development, school attendance, academic performance, and completion rates of children. A study among the secondary school students in Canada (Duncan et al., 2021) found that lower depression and higher psychosocial well-being were associated with better educational behaviors and, therefore, better grades. The prevalence of mental health illnesses like depression, anxiety, and stress was reported to range from 46.92% to 82.4%, 26.6% to 96.82%, and 28.5% to 70.1%, respectively, among Bangladeshi students during the COVID-19 pandemic (Al Mamun et al., 2021). Even in the decade before the pandemic, depression was found among 20% to 40% of students in different reports (Hasan et al., 2021). This high burden of mental health problems could hinder quality education. Hence, achieving the SDG 4 requires attention to mental well-being.

SDG 5 (Gender Equality): Gender influences vulnerability to mental disorders, help-seeking behaviors, and treatment experiences. Even in socioeconomically developed homogeneous societies, gender differences in mental health and mental health-seeking behavior exist. Men who have never married or are separated/divorced are admitted to mental health facilities more often than women in the same categories. Conversely, married women have higher admission rates than married men (Afifi, 2007). Differences exist in the rates of various mental health disorders between men and women. Conduct disorder, the commonest psychiatric disorder, is three times more common in boys than girls. Depression, suicidal ideation, and suicidal attempts are more common among adolescent girls than boys, while suicides are more frequent among boys. In adulthood, the prevalence of most affective disorders and non-affective psychosis is generally higher among women, while men tend to have higher rates of substance use disorders and antisocial personality disorder (Afifi, 2007). The National Mental Health Survey 2019 in Bangladesh revealed that the prevalence of mental disorders is much higher among women (21.5%) than that of men (15.7%) (BBS & WHO, 2021). Moreover, one study conducted among women engaging in social media for mental health support found that, despite externalized symptoms, women often do not seek mental healthcare or face barriers to mental health services in their country

(Koly et al., 2022). Women's mental health is crucial as it impacts on the well-being of children and the elderly they care for. Men's mental health is important as the breadwinner of the family. Any predisposition to gender stereotypes may hinder the mental health services for both genders. Gender equality is essential for the psychological well-being of society as a whole.
SDG 8 (Decent Work and Economic Growth): Mental health affects economic productivity through absenteeism, presentism, unemployment, and disability. Individuals with mental health conditions may experience higher rates of absenteeism, leading to decreased output and requiring employers to cover for lost work time. Job conditions influence presentism among employees in good mental health (Bubonya et al., 2017). Furthermore, mental illness can make it harder to find or maintain employment, resulting in higher unemployment rates and reduced overall workforce participation. In severe cases, individuals may become unable to work due to disability, further impacting economic output (Mcdaid et al., 2007). Rahim and Zaman conducted a survey on mental health and its effect on the job performance among readymade garment workers of Bangladesh and found a significant negative correlation between mental health problems and job performance (Rahim & Zaman, 2021). On the other hand, a moderate to high degree of mental illness was found among unemployed university graduates in Bangladesh (Islam & Amanullah, 2024), endorsing the reciprocal relationship between mental well-being and employment. The SDG 8 aims to promote sustained, inclusive, and sustainable economic growth, full and productive employment, and decent work for all. This goal recognizes that economic growth is essential for improving living standards but also emphasizes the importance of ensuring that growth is inclusive, sustainable, and benefits all people. Mental well-being is required for decent jobs, effective work, and sustainable economic growth, linking mental health to this goal.
SDG 10 (Reduced Inequalities): Social and economic inequalities create mental health disparities through differential exposure to risk factors and access to protective resources. These inequalities impact individuals' lives, leading to a sense of unfairness and increasing the likelihood of anxiety, depression, and other mental health problems (Zhang et al., 2023). The mental health impact of wealth inequality is a demonstrated issue in Bangladesh. People from lower wealth quantiles may encounter challenges in obtaining high-quality healthcare, while those from higher wealth quantiles are more susceptible to mental health illnesses (Hasan et al., 2023). Addressing these inequalities is crucial for improving overall well-being and reducing health disparities.
SDG 11 (Sustainable Cities and Communities): Urbanization presents a complex picture for mental health, offering opportunities like access to resources and economic advancement, while also posing challenges like increased stress, social isolation, and environmental stressors. These challenges can contribute to higher rates of mental health issues like depression, anxiety, and substance abuse, particularly in rapidly urbanizing areas (Egbosimba, 2025). Cities that ensure security and affordability may positively impact the psychological health of their citizens. On the other hand, communities of people with good mental health can put concerted

efforts to maintain the sustainability and resilience of the cities. In Bangladesh, the national mental health survey found that substance use and addictive disorders were more common in urban compared to rural areas. In contrast, in rural areas, somatic symptoms and related disorders were more commonly reported (BBS & WHO, 2021). Therefore, to advance the development of sustainable cities, it is crucial to focus on the management of substance abuse and addiction.
SDG 13 (Climate Action): Climate change affects mental health through direct trauma from extreme weather events, displacement-related stressors, and anxiety about environmental threats (Nature, 2024). It may cause a range of psychological distresses from anxiety and depression to PTSD and suicidal ideation. This impact is not uniform, with certain groups being disproportionately affected by factors such as socioeconomic status, gender, and age. Extreme weather events, rising temperatures, and the broader environmental and social consequences of climate change can all contribute to mental health challenges (Padhy et al., 2015). Increasing access to mental health services and addressing climate change over time are suitable responses to future challenges posed by climate change. Climate-vulnerable countries like Bangladesh will face significant health and well-being impacts as climate change worsens. Its geographic location makes it susceptible to droughts, floods, sea level rise, land inundation, saltwater intrusion, extreme temperatures, heat waves, and cyclones. These conditions pose risks to mental health, leading to depression, anxiety, PTSD, suicidality, and substance abuse. Climate change will exacerbate these issues, particularly affecting poorer populations, women, and migrants (Wahid et al., 2024).

These interconnections demonstrate that mental health is not merely a health sector issue but a cross-cutting development concern.

3 Mental Health Challenges of Bangladesh

Bangladesh is currently facing a double burden of disease with rising levels of non-communicable diseases (NCDs) on top of infectious diseases. The increasing prevalence of various mental health disorders constitutes a significant portion of the burden posed by NCDs in the country. But mental health services are inadequate to tackle the surging number of patients. There are few mental health experts, and fewer mental health facilities. Suicide rates are on the rise. Alarmingly, young people, who provide the demographic dividend to the country, bear most of the burden of psychiatric problems. A detailed description of the mental health situation in Bangladesh can be found elsewhere (Arafat, 2024a).

3.1 Burden of Mental Health Problems in Bangladesh

Globally, mental health accounts for approximately 32.4% of years lived with disability and 13% of disability-adjusted life-years (DALYs) (Vigo et al., 2016). In Bangladesh, mental health conditions are under-recognized and untreated, especially given the widespread prevalence of common mental disorders among people. According to the national mental health survey 2019, an estimated 18.7% of adults and 13.6% of children were suffering from mental health disorders in Bangladesh (National Institute of Mental Health, 2019). Women had a higher prevalence than men (18.9% versus 18.7%), with comparable rural–urban distribution (18.7% versus 18.9%) (Alam et al., 2024). Geriatric populations (aged $\geq$ 60 years), where mental health problems often remain underdiagnosed, have been found to have the highest proportion (28.1%) of mental health problems in the country (Arafat et al., 2024c).

Among all the mental health disorders, depressive and anxiety disorders were the most common in the national mental health survey. The national survey suggests that the prevalence of depression was 6.7% and of anxiety was 4.5% among adults in 2019 (National Institute of Mental Health, 2019). The prevalence appears to be higher among adolescents, with 24.5% of them suffering from depression (Mridha et al., 2021), with girls having a higher proportion (27.0%) than boys (22.0%). Among children, autism spectrum disorder is found among 0.2% to 0.8% in Bangladesh (Hasan et al., 2021), with an alarming 5.9% having a neurodevelopmental disorder (National Institute of Mental Health, 2019). A consistently high level of depression has been observed among the geriatric population of the country (Arafat et al., 2024c).

Suicide gives an estimate of deaths due to mental health problems. As described earlier, the suicide rate is still lagging behind the target of the SDG in Bangladesh. At the same time, there appears to be a prevalence of suicidal behavior among people. The prevalence of suicidal thoughts, plans, and attempts has been estimated to be 4.7%, 1.5%, and 1.5%, respectively (Arafat & Khan, 2024). Nearly one-quarter of the students and elderly people were found to have suicidal ideation at least once in their lifetime (Arafat et al., 2024a, 2024b, 2024c; Wahlin et al., 2015).

Although, Bangladesh is still lagging in other SDGs related to mental health, it has been making some progress in goals related to poverty (SDG 1), quality education (SDG 4), gender equality (SDG 5), decent work and economic growth (SDG 8), reduced inequality (SDG 10), sustainable cities and communities (SDG 11) and climate action (SDG 13) (GED, 2022). Although the COVID-19 pandemic has affected all the parameters to some extent, the country has survived the economic impact and has remained on track (BBS, 2025). This progress in several SDG areas has important indirect implications for mental health, even though it remains an under-addressed sector. The country's consistent reduction in poverty, from 31.5% in 2010 to 20.5% in 2019, along with improvements in extreme poverty rates (17.6% to 10.5%) (Greeley, Shahan & Barua, 2021), can play a vital role in alleviating the financial stress and insecurity that often contribute to poor mental health. Similarly, initiatives under SDG 4 focusing on expanding access to quality education and promoting digital inclusion would not only improve literacy but also could help foster psychosocial well-being and resilience, especially among children and adolescents. In the area of gender equality, Bangladesh's notable performance, ranking ahead of its South Asian neighbors in the Global Gender Gap Index (World Economic Forum, 2024), creates opportunities for reducing the gender-based social pressures and violence that adversely impact women's mental health. Economic resilience, as evidenced by increased GDP per capita and stable unemployment rates despite the COVID-19 pandemic (Ministry of Finance, 2022), may contribute to social security and reduce work-related stress. Furthermore, Bangladesh's efforts to address inequalities by stabilizing consumption inequality and adopting inclusive social protection policies (GED, 2022) could enhance social cohesion, which is protective against mental health issues arising from marginalization. Improvements in sustainable urban infrastructure and climate action strategies, such as climate-resilient housing and clean energy projects, could foster safer and healthier living environments, reducing the mental strain associated with overcrowded, unsafe, and environmentally degraded areas. Together, these developments, although not explicitly targeting mental health, can create a more supportive socioeconomic environment in which mental well-being can be better preserved and promoted.

3.2 *Mental Health Service in Bangladesh*

There is a huge gap of more than 90% between the mental health burden and the services available to mitigate the burden in Bangladesh (BBS & WHO, 2021). The country is short on mental health facilities, manpower, and funding. Only recently have there been dedicated actions taken by the government and authorities to fight the growing burden of mental health (Arafat, 2024b). However, to meet the Sustainable Development Goals of lowering suicide rates and providing services for substance abuse, the mental health treatment gap needs to be addressed with due preference.

Mental health services in Bangladesh are delivered through four main components: the government sector, the private sector, non-governmental organizations (NGOs), and donor agency-driven services. Government facilities include the National Institute of Mental Health (NIMH), Pabna Mental Hospital (PMH), medical college hospitals, and district hospitals (World Health Organization, 2015). As per the organogram, psychiatrists are only posted at tertiary-level hospitals, and no posts are available at secondary and primary-level health facilities (Andalib & Arafat, 2016). The private sector plays a fundamental role in service delivery through corporate hospitals, private medical colleges, clinics, and private chambers. In addition, various informal service providers like unqualified village doctors, pharmacy shop vendors, homeopathic physicians, *kobiraj*, and religious healers also play a role in the management of mental health problems at different levels. Psychiatrists working in the government sector can be reached through their private chambers beyond office hours. But, there is no established referral system. Telepsychiatry is an emerging treatment mode, especially since the COVID-19 pandemic, with services provided through various software (Arafat et al., 2024b). NGOs and donor agencies typically focus on deprived and marginalized populations, particularly in rural areas.

Bangladesh has a limited mental health infrastructure relative to its population of 170 million. The NIMH has 400 inpatient beds, and PMH offers 500 inpatient beds. There are approximately 72 outpatient services attached to hospitals and 62 inpatient services with 195 beds across the country. The Bangladesh Medical University (formerly Bangabandhu Sheikh Mujib Medical University) has 40 inpatient beds, while Dhaka Medical College Hospital has 25. Among 37 government medical colleges, only ten provide inpatient psychiatric services. Of the 63 private medical colleges, only four offer inpatient psychiatric services with a total of 38 allocated beds. Additionally, there are 15 beds for forensic inpatient services. Shishu Bikash Kendra (SBK) has been established in 34 medical college hospitals and one district hospital to provide comprehensive care for autism spectrum disorders and other neurodevelopmental disorders (Arafat, 2024b).

Bangladesh faces a severe shortage of mental health professionals. According to a recent WHO report, there are only 350 psychiatrists, about 700 mental health nurses, and 656 psychologists serving the country's 170 million people. This translates to 0.2 psychiatrists, 0.4 psychiatric nurses, and 0.3 psychologists per 100,000 population (World Health Organization, 2022). The number is very low compared to an 18.7% prevalence of mental health disorders in Bangladesh. The shortage is particularly acute in rural areas, as mental health professionals tend to be concentrated in district and divisional cities (MOHFW, 2020).

Several advocacy groups and professional societies are working to improve mental health services in Bangladesh. The Bangladesh Association of Psychiatrists (BAP), Bangladesh Association for Child and Adolescent Mental Health (BACAMH), Association of Therapeutic Counselors, Bangladesh (ATCB) were established in 1975, 2008, and 2010, respectively. Besides formal professional groups, various NGOs and donor agencies also contribute significantly to mental health and psychosocial support efforts, particularly for refugees and marginalized populations (Arafat, 2024b).

Mental health help-seeking in Bangladesh is influenced by high levels of stigma and low mental health literacy (Hasan et al., 2021). Many people attribute mental illness to supernatural causes like jinn possession, black magic, and the evil eye. These beliefs lead many to consult traditional and religious healers before seeking professional psychiatric help. The latest national mental health survey revealed that 30% of children with psychiatric disorders first consulted traditional healers (National Institute of Mental Health, 2019). Overall, approximately 25–50% of psychiatric patients in Bangladesh utilize informal services before seeking professional help (Arafat, 2024b).

Bangladesh has implemented several policy measures to address gaps in mental health services. The Mental Health Act was passed on November 14, 2018, replacing the outdated Lunacy Act of 1912. The Neurodevelopmental Disability Protection Trust Act was enacted in 2013, and the Bangladesh Rehabilitation Council Act was passed in 2018. Recently, the National Mental Health Policy and the National Mental Health Strategic Plan 2020–2030 were accepted in 2022. The government has also established a list of essential medicines for common mental disorders (Arafat, 2024b). However, with only 0.44% of the total health budget allotted for mental health and the high treatment gap (BBS & WHO, 2021; Hasan et al., 2021), the implementation of the policies remains challenging.

4 Ways Forward

Bangladesh is a densely populated, low- and middle-income country (The World Bank, 2025). Since its independence in 1971, the country has made progress in various sectors through small strides. By 2015, noteworthy progress was made in achieving the Millennium Development Goals (MDGs), particularly in areas like poverty reduction, gender parity in education, and reducing child and maternal mortality (Alam, 2023). In the United Nations Assembly of 2015, the country adopted the Sustainable Development Goals to work with 192 other countries for a better future. Despite limited resources, significant progress has been made in areas such as poverty reduction (SDG 1), hunger alleviation (SDG 2), and lower neonatal and under-5 mortality rates (SDG 3). Gender parity in education has been achieved (SDG 4), and access to electricity has reached 96% (SDG 7). Additionally, real GDP growth per employed person has increased (SDG 8), the manufacturing sector's GDP share has risen (SDG 9), and social protection budget allocations have expanded (SDG 10) (United Nations Development Programme, 2024). However, the SDG 3 target on mental health has yet to be achieved. As the country moves toward 2030, authorities and policymakers should keep mental health on the discussion table. The recently renewed Mental Health Act and National Mental Health Strategy are good steps toward that end. But more needs to be done. The following points should be ensured to keep making progress to ensure a psychologically healthy generation that works together toward the development of Bangladesh.

- The number of mental health facilities should be increased with increased beds in the tertiary care hospitals and dedicated mental health outpatient services in the district-level and primary care health centers.
- Medical graduates should be motivated to pursue higher education in mental health to increase the number of experts in the country.
- In the public healthcare system, posts should be created for expert psychiatrists at the district-level hospitals. Training should be provided to primary care physicians and nurses to treat fundamental mental health problems at the primary level and make appropriate and timely referrals.
- An effective referral system should be established, combining the whole health sector, including public and private providers, through public-private partnerships to improve service delivery and reduce financial burden.
- An electronic health record system should be established throughout the country to ensure proper records and transferability of information for the effective management of mental health patients.

- The alternative healthcare providers should be incorporated into the health system and trained on mental health to prevent mismanagement of psychiatric disorders.
- The national budget allocation for the health sector needs to be increased overall, with a particular emphasis on funding for mental health.
- Mental health research should be promoted and incentivized through funding to ensure evidence-based practice in the field.
- Awareness-raising programs, campaigns, media activities, and counseling sessions should be conducted nationwide and profession-wise to establish proper health-seeking behavior and increase work efficiency.
- An effective monitoring and evaluation system should be established to make sure that the policy and strategies are being implemented.

5 Conclusion

Bangladesh is experiencing a significant burden of mental health problems coupled with a substantial treatment gap. Recently, the country has begun to address this issue with increasing emphasis, implementing several measures to tackle mental health concerns. Nevertheless, it is essential to accelerate and sustain the pace of development to achieve the mental health indicators outlined in the SDGs by 2030. Considering resource constraints and the multifaceted nature of the challenges, authorities should adopt long-term, comprehensive strategies to ensure Bangladesh remains on its development trajectory. Additionally, mental health must remain a focal point throughout all stages of development to guarantee the well-being of the population and sustainable progress.

References

Afifi, M. (2007). Gender differences in mental health. *Singapore Medical Journal, 48*(5), 385–391.

Alam, M. F., et al. (2024). Community prevalence of psychiatric disorders: Findings from a nationwide survey in Bangladesh. *Asian Journal of Psychiatry, 92*, Article 103897. https://doi.org/10.1016/j.ajp.2023.103897

Alam, M. S. (2023). A study on millennium development goals and sustainable development goals: Lesson from Bangladesh. *International Journal of Business & Economic Development, 11*(02). https://doi.org/10.24052/IJBED/V011N02/ART-03

Al Mamun, F., et al. (2021). Mental disorders of Bangladeshi students during the covid-19 pandemic: A systematic review. *Psychology Research and Behavior Management, 14*, 645–654. https://doi.org/10.2147/PRBM.S315961

Andalib, A., & Arafat, S. M. Y. (2016). Practicing pattern of physicians in Bangladesh. *International Journal of Perceptions in Public Health, 1*(1), 9–13.

Arafat, S.M.Y. (2023). Mental Health and Suicide in Bangladesh. In: Arafat, S.M.Y., Khan, M.M. (eds) Suicide in Bangladesh. Springer, Singapore. https://doi.org/10.1007/978-981-99-0289-7_3

Arafat, S. M. Y. (Ed.). (2024a). *Mental health in Bangladesh.* Springer Nature Singapore. https://doi.org/10.1007/978-981-97-0610-5

Arafat, S. M. Y. (2024b). Mental health services in Bangladesh. In: Arafat, S.M.Y. (eds) Mental Health in Bangladesh. Springer, Singapore. https://doi.org/10.1007/978-981-97-0610-5_3

Arafat, S. M. Y., Baminiwatta, A., Menon, V., Sharma, P., Htay, M. N. N., Akter, H., Marthoenis, M., & Dorji, C. (2024a). Prevalence of suicidal behavior among students in South-East Asia: A systematic review and meta-analysis. *Archives of Suicide Research, 28*(1), 50–70. https://doi.org/10.1080/13811118.2023.2176272

Arafat, S. M. Y., Giasuddin, N. A., & Mazumder, A. H. (2024b). Access to mental health care in Bangladesh—Current status, potential challenges, and ways out. In *Access to mental health care in South Asia* (pp. 29–55). Springer Nature Singapore. https://doi.org/10.1007/978-981-99-9153-2_3

Arafat, S. M. Y., & Khan, A. R. (2024). Suicidal behavior in Bangladesh. In *Suicidal behavior in Muslim majority countries* (pp. 45–58). https://doi.org/10.1007/978-981-97-2519-9_4

Arafat, S. M. Y., Mazumder, A. H., & Maruf, M. M. (2024c). Geriatric psychiatry in Bangladesh. In *Mental health in Bangladesh* (pp. 311–322). https://doi.org/10.1007/978-981-97-0610-5_18

BBS. (2025). *SDG tracker: Bangladesh's development monitor*. Available at: https://sdg.gov.bd. Accessed April 20, 2025.

BBS, & WHO. (2021). *National mental health survey 2019.*

Bubonya, M., Cobb-Clark, D. A., & Wooden, M. (2017). Mental health and productivity at work: Does what you do matter? *Labour Economics, 46*, 150–165. https://doi.org/10.1016/j.labeco.2017.05.001

Choudhary, R. (2024). Vicious cycle of poverty and mental illness: A review with special reference to scheduled caste population. *South India Journal of Social Sciences, 22*(2), 81–91. https://doi.org/10.62656/sijss.v22i2.102

Davis Weaver, N., et al. (2025). Global, regional, and national burden of suicide, 1990–2021: A systematic analysis for the global burden of disease study 2021. *The Lancet Public Health, 10*(3), e189–e202. https://doi.org/10.1016/S2468-2667(25)00006-4

Duncan, M. J., Patte, K. A., & Leatherdale, S. T. (2021). Mental health associations with academic performance and education behaviors in Canadian secondary school students. *Canadian Journal of School Psychology, 36*(4), 335–357. https://doi.org/10.1177/0829573521997311

Egbosimba, B. (2025). Urbanization and mental health: Rethinking public spaces to support well-being. *International Journal of Healthcare Sciences, 12*(2), 71–83. https://doi.org/10.5281/zenodo.14788866

GED. (2022). *Sustainable development goals: Bangladesh progress report 2022, General Economics Division (GED). Dhaka, Bangladesh: Bangladesh planning commission, ministry of planning, Government of the Poeple's Republic of Bangladesh.* https://www.scopus.com/inward/record.uri?eid=2-s2.0-85148630569&partnerID=40&md5=5320d3c95801ebb2a5ecf7edf4e8eff8

Greeley, M., Shahan, A. M., & Barua, S. (2021). Introduction. In *Sustainable development, human dignity and choice* (pp. 1–3). Springer International Publishing. https://doi.org/10.1007/978-3-030-71668-4_1.

Hasan, M., Khan, T., & Hasan, M. M. (2023). Socio-economic determinants of mental health illness in Bangladesh CDE Working Paper Series. (December).

Hasan, M. T., et al. (2021). The current state of mental healthcare in Bangladesh: Part 1 – an updated country profile. *Bjpsych International, 18*(4), 78–82. https://doi.org/10.1192/bji.2021.41

Islam, M. S., et al. (2021). Financial and mental health concerns of impoverished Urban-Dwelling Bangladeshi people during COVID-19. *Frontiers in Psychology, 12*(August), 1–12. https://doi.org/10.3389/fpsyg.2021.663687

Islam, S. A., & Amanullah, M. (2024). The effect of unemployment on mental health: A study on the University Graduates of Bangladesh. *Khulna University Studies, 21*(1), 300–312. https://doi.org/10.53808/kus.2024.21.01.1074-mb

Kirkbride, J. B., et al. (2024). The social determinants of mental health and disorder: Evidence, prevention and recommendations. *World Psychiatry, 23*(1), 58–90. https://doi.org/10.1002/wps.21160

Knifton, L., & Inglis, G. (2020). Poverty and mental health: Policy, practice and research implications. *Bjpsych Bulletin, 44*(5), 193–196. https://doi.org/10.1192/bjb.2020.78

Koly, K. N., et al. (2022). Mental healthcare-seeking behavior of women in Bangladesh: Content analysis of a social media platform. *BMC Psychiatry, 22*(1), 1–12. https://doi.org/10.1186/s12888-022-04414-z

Lomazzi, M., Borisch, B., & Laaser, U. (2014). The millennium development goals: Experiences, achievements and what's next. *Global Health Action, 7*(SUPP.1). https://doi.org/10.3402/gha.v7.23695

Mcdaid, D., et al. (2007). *Employment and mental health: Assessing the economic impact and the case for intervention.*

McDonald, G. (2007). Mental health consequences of long term conflict. *British Medical Journal, 334*(7604), 1121–1122. https://doi.org/10.1136/bmj.39225.539803.80

Ministry of Finance. (2022). *Socioeconomic progress and recent macroeconomic development in Bangladesh.*

MOHFW. (2020). *National mental health strategic plan 2020–2030* (pp. 1–154).

Monawar Hosain, G. M., et al. (2007). Prevalence, pattern and determinants of mental disorders in rural Bangladesh. *Public Health, 121*(1), 18–24. https://doi.org/10.1016/j.puhe.2006.06.018

Mridha, M. K., et al. (2021). Prevalence and associated factors of depression among adolescent boys and girls in Bangladesh: Findings from a nationwide survey. *British Medical Journal Open, 11*(1), 1–16. https://doi.org/10.1136/bmjopen-2020-038954

National Institute of Mental Health. (2019). *National mental health survey Bangladesh 2019 - Provisional fact sheet* (p. 4). Available at: https://www.who.int/docs/default-source/searo/bangladesh/pdf-reports/cat-2/nimh-fact-sheet-5-11-19.pdf?sfvrsn=3e62d4b0_2

Nature. (2024). What happens when climate change and the mental-health crisis collide? *Nature, 628*(8007), 235–235. https://doi.org/10.1038/d41586-024-00993-x

NIPSOM. (2020). *National STEPS survey for non-communicable diseases risk factors in Bangladesh 2018 National Institute of Preventive and Social Medicine (NIPSOM).* https://doi.org/10.13140/RG.2.2.11935.79524

Padhy, S. K., et al. (2015). Mental health effects of climate change. *Indian Journal of Occupational and Environmental Medicine, 19*(1), 3–7. https://doi.org/10.4103/0019-5278.156997

Patel, V., & Kleinman, A. (2003). Poverty and common mental disorders in developing countries. *Bulletin of the World Health Organization, 81*(8), 609–615.

Rahim, R., & Zaman, F.-T.-Z. B. (2021). Mental health and job performance of garments workforce in Bangladesh. *Journal of Organisation & Human Behaviour, 10*(1/2), 23–29. https://search.ebscohost.com/login.aspx?direct=true&db=buh&AN=154416702&site=ehost-live

Richter, L. M., et al. (2021). Adolescent mental health problems and adult human capital: Findings from the South African birth to twenty plus Cohort at 28 years of age. *Journal of Adolescent Health, 69*(5), 782–789. https://doi.org/10.1016/j.jadohealth.2021.04.017

Sach, J., Lafortune, G., & Fuller, G. (2024). *The SDGs and the UN summit of the future, sustainable development report 2024.* Dublin University Press.

Sareen, J., et al. (2011). Relationship between household income and mental disorders. *Archives of General Psychiatry, 68*(4), 419. https://doi.org/10.1001/archgenpsychiatry.2011.15

Shen, J., et al. (2023). Prevalence, incidence, deaths, and disability-adjusted life-years of drug use disorders for 204 countries and territories during the past 30 years. *Asian Journal of Psychiatry, 86*, Article 103677. https://doi.org/10.1016/j.ajp.2023.103677

The World Bank. (2025). *The World Bank In Bangladesh.* Available at: https://www.worldbank.org/en/country/bangladesh/overview. Accessed April 22, 2025.

UNDP. (2025). *The SDGs in action.* Available at: https://www.undp.org/sustainable-development-goals

United Nations Development Programme. (2024). *Toward 2030: Strategies for SDG success in Bangladesh.* Available at: https://www.undp.org/bangladesh/news/toward-2030-strategies-sdg-success-bangladesh. Accessed April 22, 2025.

Vigo, D., Thornicroft, G., & Atun, R. (2016). Estimating the true global burden of mental illness. *The Lancet Psychiatry, 3*(2), 171–178. https://doi.org/10.1016/S2215-0366(15)00505-2

Votruba, N., & Thornicroft, G. (2016). Sustainable development goals and mental health: Learnings from the contribution of the FundaMentalSDG global initiative. *Global Mental Health, 3.* Available at: https://doi.org/10.1017/gmh.2016.20

Wahid, S. S., Islam, M. N., & Raza, W. A. (2024). Climate change and mental health in Bangladesh: Vulnerability, inequality, and the crucial need for intervention on the frontlines of the climate crisis. In *Mental health in Bangladesh* (pp. 255–270). Springer Nature Singapore. https://doi.org/10.1007/978-981-97-0610-5_15

Wahlin, Å., et al. (2015). Prevalence of depressive symptoms and suicidal thoughts among elderly persons in rural Bangladesh. *International Psychogeriatrics, 27*(12), 1999–2008. https://doi.org/10.1017/S104161021500109X

WHO. (2022). *Mental health.* Available at: https://www.who.int/news-room/fact-sheets/detail/mental-health-strengthening-our-response. Accessed March 22, 2025.

WHO. (2024a). *Global status report on alcohol and health and treatment of substance use disorders.* Renewable Energy World. Available at: https://www.who.int/publications/i/item/9789240096745

WHO. (2024b). *Suicide.* https://www.who.int/news-room/fact-sheets/detail/suicide. Accessed March 25, 2025.

Wigand, M. E., et al. (2022). Climate change, pollution, deforestation, and mental health: Research trends, gaps, and ethical considerations. *GeoHealth, 6*(11), 1–15. https://doi.org/10.1029/2022GH000632

World Economic Forum. (2024). *Global gender gap 2024. Insight report.* Available at: https://www3.weforum.org/docs/WEF_GGGR_2024.pdf

World Health Organization. (2015). Bangladesh health system review. *Healths Systems in Transition, 5*(3), 1–214.

World Health Organization. (2022). *Addressing mental health in Bangladesh.* Available at: https://www.who.int/publications-detail-redirect/9789290210146. Accessed April 22, 2025.

Zalsman, G., et al. (2016). Suicide prevention strategies revisited: 10-year systematic review. *The Lancet Psychiatry, 3*(7), 646–659. https://doi.org/10.1016/S2215-0366(16)30030-X

Zhang, R., et al. (2023). The impact of household wealth gap on individual's mental health. *BMC Public Health, 23*(1), 1–17. https://doi.org/10.1186/s12889-023-16871-6

Chapter 9
Synergizing Sustainable Development Goals and Mental Health in India

Ravi Philip Rajkumar

Abstract The Sustainable Development Goals (SDGs) are a set of seventeen broad goals outlined by the United Nations with the aim of promoting inclusive human development and prosperity while safeguarding the environment. India has adopted the SDGs and integrated them into its broader goal of achieving the status of a developed nation (*Viksit Bharat*) by the year 2047. Over the past decade, the Indian government has launched several programmes and initiatives aimed at attaining specific SDGs, and some of these already include mental health goals. Despite the challenges involved in integrating mental health with broader human development in a country as large and diverse as India, many facets of these programmes have the potential to address the socioeconomic determinants of mental health, as identified through Indian social psychiatry research. This chapter provides an overview of Indian research linking sustainable development and mental health, as well as an overview of India's SDG-related policies. It also examines and discusses how governmental, private sector, professional and community actors can work together to achieve a synergy between mental health and sustainable development in the Indian context.

Keywords Sustainable development goals · Social psychiatry · Climate change · Food security · Child development · Nutrition · Sustainable development · National mental health policy

R. P. Rajkumar (✉)
Department of Psychiatry, Jawaharlal Institute of Postgraduate Medical Education and Research (JIPMER), Puducherry, India
e-mail: ravi.psych@gmail.com

S. K. Kar et al. (eds.), *Sustainable Development Goals and Mental Health in South Asia*, South Asian Perspectives in Mental Health and Psychology ,
https://doi.org/10.1007/978-981-95-2684-0_9

1 Introduction

The Sustainable Development Goals (SDG) also known as the Global Goals for Sustainable Development are a set of seventeen goals adopted by the members of the United Nations in 2015, as part of a broader initiative, the 2030 Agenda for Sustainable Development. The stated aim of the SDGs is to provide "a shared blueprint for peace and prosperity for people and the planet, now into the future". In broad terms, the objectives of the SDGs are the eradication of poverty and hunger, the protection of the planet from environmental degradation, the promotion of prosperity "in harmony with nature", the maintenance of peace and civil order and the achievement of these four goals through partnerships between all member nations. These 17 goals include 169 targets that are meant to indicate the level of progress that a nation, or the world, has made towards a particular facet of the given goal. Nevertheless, the SDGs are not intended to be seen in isolation, but are meant to be "integrated and indivisible" (United Nations, 2024; United Nations Department of Economic & Social Affairs, 2015). Precursors to the SDGs—such as teachings on respect for the natural environment, sustainable forms of agricultural practice and laws on the maintenance of social order and the protection of the vulnerable—can be found in many pre-industrial societies. However, the evolution of common goals for sustainable development and their adoption at the international level are the result of specific social, political and scientific developments occurring over the past four decades (Jacob, 2024).

The intimate relationship between sustainable development and health, including mental health, is best understood from a systems theory perspective. The physical, mental and social dimensions of human health (the "human system") are intimately connected with each other and with the well-being of the planet (the "Earth system"). Because of this, sustainable development is not simply an ideal or an option: it is essential to solve the current and future problems that confront humanity. This requires changes both in individual and community lifestyles and in national and international policy and planning (Skene, 2021). The current geological age, known as the "Anthropocene", has been characterized by human technological innovation and modification of the environment, often in a rapid and far-reaching manner. These changes have brought about increased economic prosperity, better physical health and a higher overall standard of material living. Unfortunately, these benefits have come at the cost of environmental damage, social disruption, alienation of individuals from society and an increased risk of non-communicable diseases (NCDs), including mental disorders (Baum et al., 2025; Gluckman et al., 2020). For example, over the course of evolutionary history, energy consumption has increased rapidly in industrialized societies in comparison with hunter-gatherers. This has resulted in both environmental damage (in the form of air pollution and climate change) and an increased risk of several NCDs. In the words of one expert, the world is growing "hotter and sicker" (Pontzer, 2021). Addressing these problems necessitates a paradigm shift towards models of development that balance human development and environmental protection. This does not involve the rejection of scientific or technological advances: instead, these should be harnessed to drive a gradual "transformation" towards sustainable development (Global Sustainable Development Report, 2023).

Recognizing the importance of health to holistic human development and well-being, Sustainable Development Goal 3 (SDG 3) is concerned with "Good Health and Well-Being". There are nine specific targets included under SDG 3, addressing maternal, infant and child mortality, communicable diseases, non-communicable diseases, substance abuse, road traffic accident prevention, reproductive health, universal access to healthcare and the reduction of illness and death due to hazardous chemicals or pollutants (Global Sustainable Development Report, 2023; United Nations, 2024).

From the perspective of mental health care, a key aspect of SDG 3 is that it explicitly mentions mental health promotion (SDG 3.4) and the prevention and treatment of substance use disorders, including tobacco control (SDG 3.5, SDG 3.9a). This is a significant advance over earlier United Nations initiatives, such as the Millennium Development Goals, which made no mention of mental health or illness (Collins et al., 2025; Madill et al., 2022; Votruba et al., 2016). However, it would be an error to simply view mental health as a single target in isolation from all the others. There is an intimate relationship between mental health and almost every other SDG, and the prevention and treatment of mental illness cannot be separated from progress towards these other goals (Lund et al., 2018; Smith et al., 2024). In most cases, the relationship between mental health and development in other spheres of human existence is complex and bidirectional. On the one hand, untreated mental illness is the leading cause of reduced productivity among non-communicable diseases, thereby leading to reduced economic prosperity (Golombek et al., 2025; McGorry & Hamilton, 2016) and higher household economic vulnerability (Lund et al., 2019). Good mental health is necessary for societies to navigate economic and social change and upheaval (Nail-Beatty et al., 2024). Conversely, certain forms of environmental degradation, such as air pollution, increase the risk for several mental disorders (Zundel et al., 2022), as do several forms of social and economic adversity (Alon et al., 2024). On a more positive note, some sustainable development strategies, such as a shift towards a more plant-based diet, are likely to have beneficial effects both on the environment and on mental health (Sugden & Merlo, 2024). Research from other countries suggests that it is possible to develop affordable and effective interventions to address the socio-environmental determinants of mental health, and such packages can be adapted to the Indian context in the future (Oswald et al., 2024).

2 Relevance of the Sustainable Development Goals to Mental Health in India

India is the world's most populous country. Of the 193 countries ranked in the United Nations Development Programme's Human Development Report, it has achieved a rank of 130, representing an increase of three ranks in a period of one year (United

Nations Development Programme, 2025). India is a growing economy characterized by rapid industrialization and urbanization, high levels of economic inequality, uneven levels of human development, demographic and cultural transitions, significant environmental vulnerabilities and several long-standing social problems that can affect the mental health of individuals and communities (Cheng et al., 2016; Das et al., 2022a; Jain et al., 2023; Komanapalli & Rao, 2021; Nath et al., 2012; Nair et al., 2022; Patwary et al., 2024; Sharma et al., 2022a; Singh et al., 2024a, 2024b). Social and economic difficulties, indicative of a lack of uniform development, do not just contribute to the burden of mental disorders: they lead to a widening of the mental health treatment gap faced by Indians (Ranjan & Crasta, 2023) and pose significant barriers to the inclusion of persons with mental illness in society (Mathias et al., 2018a). Having said this, India also possesses a wealth of both formal and informal resources that can be leveraged to enhance psychological resilience, community cohesion and sustainable development (Acharya et al., 2017; Kishan, 2020; Mathias et al., 2022; Shields et al., 2016). The government of India has committed itself to adopting and pursuing the Sustainable Development Goals from their inception (United Nations in India, 2025), which makes it essential to examine how the SDGs can be synergized with mental health goals at different levels.

Social and economic factors related to the SDGs have a significant effect on the mental health of Indians. Men report being more affected by unemployment (SDG 8), substance abuse (SDG 3.5a) and local violence (SDG 16). Women report more stressors related to poverty (SDG 1), intimate partner violence and gender inequality in marriage and family life (SDG 5) and substance abuse in their husbands (SDG 3.5a). However, some SDG-relevant social and economic stressors affect appear to affect both genders equally: these include poor housing and infrastructure (SDG 6, SDG 14), unequal access to essential services and facilities (SDG 10), the challenges of internal migration (SDG 8) and civil unrest related to caste or religion (SDG 16) (Ahamad et al., 2025; Mishra & Patel, 2024; Singh et al., 2024a, 2024b; Vahedi et al., 2025). The decade following the formulation of the SDGs (2016–2025) has seen a gradual increase in research examining the links between sustainable human development and mental health in Indian populations. This research is described with reference to specific SDGs below.

2.1 Mental Health and Other Non-communicable Diseases in India (SDG 3.4)

Social and economic development have led to a demographic transition as well as a transition in the disease burden in India. Maternal, infant and child mortality have decreased significantly, life expectancy has increased, and several communicable diseases have been brought under control through effective national health programmes. These changes represent some of India's greatest achievements in the post-Independence period, but they come at a certain cost: an increase in the nation's elderly population, and an increase in the prevalence of non-communicable diseases (NCDs). It has been estimated that NCDs account for approximately 65% of India's disease burden as of 2019, and that this has increased by over 8% over the past decade (Mathur et al., 2021). More recent estimates suggest that NCDs are associated with a high and growing burden in terms of loss of employment and income (Shukla & Arora, 2023). In the eyes of some experts, NCDs such as diabetes mellitus and hypertension have attained epidemic proportions in India (Singh et al., 2025). As these conditions are chronic and generally require both pharmacological and lifestyle interventions, they cannot be "eradicated" in the way that communicable diseases were, and impose a significant social and economic burden on families and communities. Mental and behavioural disorders themselves belong to the broader category of NCDs, and have been grouped together in SDG 3.4. There are strong, bidirectional links between mental disorders and other NCDs, both in terms of shared risk factors and in terms of each group of disorders increasing the risk of the other. Such a co-occurrence or "clustering" of mental and physical NCDs is sometimes referred to as a *syndemic* (Mendenhall et al., 2017; Pirrone et al., 2021).

Recognizing the harmful effects of NCDs on both public health and sustainable development, the Government of India initiated the National Non-Communicable Disease Monitoring Survey (NNMS), conducted by the Indian Council of Medical Research (ICMR), over the period 2017–18. This survey examined the prevalence of both NCDs and their risk factors in 348 districts across 28 Indian states. It did not specifically examine mental disorders or their correlates, as these had been examined in depth in the then-recently concluded National Mental Health Survey (2015–16) (Gautham et al., 2020; Gururaj et al., 2016).

The NNMS found high rates of elevated blood glucose (9%) and elevated blood pressure (29%) in respondents, while 4% had been diagnosed with cardiovascular diseases. A key achievement of the NNMS was to identify the high rates of lifestyle factors associated with NCDs in Indian communities, including tobacco use (33%), exposure to second-hand tobacco smoke (32–37%), alcohol use (16%), inadequate physical activity (41%), high salt intake (mean 8 g/day) and being overweight or obese (26%). In addition, the vast majority of those surveyed (over 98%) had an inadequate consumption of fruits and vegetables (Indian Council of Medical Research and National Centre for Disease Informatics and Research, 2018; Mathur et al., 2021).

Though the NNMS did not specifically address the link between mental health and other NCDs, its findings are valuable because several of the risk factors that it identified are also risk factors for mental illness (Hou et al., 2025) and for cognitive impairment or dementia in the elderly (Zhang et al., 2022). The fifth National Family Health Survey (NFHS–5), conducted in the period 2019–21, also examined several of these risk factors. This survey delineated cross-state variations in specific factors, such as tobacco and alcohol use: for example, tobacco use was significantly higher than the national average in North-Eastern states such as Manipur and Mizoram, while alcohol use was elevated in the states of Arunachal Pradesh, Sikkim, Goa and Telangana (Kulothungan et al., 2024). This data is particularly useful in planning regional programmes that align with substance use reduction (SDG 3.5 and 3.9a) and the prevention and treatment of NCDs in general (SDG 3.4).

Apart from these official initiatives, several experts and researchers have highlighted the need for an integrated approach to the physical and mental components of SDG 3.4 (Anwar et al., 2017) and for incorporation of this approach into medical education (Pati et al., 2019). A network analysis of over 18,000 elderly adults from India found close relationships between neurological and psychiatric disorders (NPD) and a wide range of other NCDs, including respiratory, cardiovascular, metabolic and gastrointestinal disorders. This study's results showed that NPD occupy a "central" place in the network of NCDs, and that treating them may have far-reaching positive effects on other NCD types (Puri & Singh, 2022). Research in specific populations has identified significant variations in NCD vulnerability: for example, a study of a fishing community in Kerala found much higher rates of NCD risk factors (alcohol and tobacco use, diet, sleep patterns and overweight) (Kavya et al., 2025). A study of adults from a semi-urban region of the same state found that depression and anxiety appeared to moderate the relationship between demographic variables and NCD risk factors such as elevated blood pressure or plasma glucose (Devassy et al., 2020). From a public health perspective, a study of youth from five Indian states identified social factors that were correlated with regular physical activity. Having friends who engaged in such activity was associated with better individual activity, whereas perceptions of air pollution and neighbourhood crime were associated with reduced activity. Research of this sort is invaluable from the point of view of synergizing health with other SDGs, as it illustrates how they are inextricably linked—in this case, a risk factor for NCDs (SDG 3.4) is associated with air pollution (SDG 3, SDG 7) and levels of local social stability (SDG 11, SDG 16).

2.2 Pollution and Mental Health in India

The SDGs explicitly mention the need to reduce all forms of environmental contamination, including water pollution (SDG 6), soil pollution (SDG 3.9), air pollution (SDG 3.9, SDG 7, SDG 11, SDG 13) and marine pollution (SDG 14). More generally, reducing pollution is implicit in the adoption of responsible patterns of consumption and production (SDG 12) (Global Sustainable Development Report, 2023). Water pollution is closely linked with water security, which can be defined as the capacity to access good-quality water from sustainable sources in sufficient quantities. In India, air and water quality have been affected both by natural factors and by human activities such as farming, chemical industries, improper waste disposal, the use of specific cooking fuels and increases in vehicular traffic (Chavan et al., 2024; Ratandeep et al., 2024).

2.2.1 Air Pollution and Clean Energy

Air pollution is associated with an increased risk of several NCDs, which makes it logical to consider its importance in the Indian context at this juncture. More recently, elevated levels of certain pollutants in air have been associated with an increased risk of several neuropsychiatric disorders, including depression, psychotic disorders, suicidality and dementia (Huang et al., 2025; Zundel et al., 2022). It is assumed that this risk is caused by neuro-inflammation triggered by specific inhaled toxins, and this has been demonstrated in animal models (Ji et al., 2022). An estimated 700,000 premature deaths in India occurred in the year 2015 due to air pollution-related NCDs, and more specifically to those related to atmospheric fine particulate matter ($PM_{2.5}$). Changes in policy and technology may be able to reduce this number by around 5–13% by the year 2030, but it is unclear if India's National Clean Air Programme (NCAP) is sufficient to achieve this target (Sarkar et al., 2025).

A study of adults from six Indian states found a significant positive association between $PM_{2.5}$ levels and self-reported depression and cognitive difficulties (Balakrishnan & Tsaneva, 2023). Indian patients with bronchial asthma report significant levels of depression when exposed to high levels of atmospheric pollutants such as $PM_{2.5}$, PM_{10}, nitrogen dioxide and sulphur dioxide (Maheshwari et al., 2024).

A key facet of this form of pollution in India is indoor air pollution, due to the use of specific types of fuels when cooking. Indoor air pollution has been associated with cognitive impairment, depression and sleep disorders in older Indian adults (Jin et al., 2022; Rani & Astha, 2024; Saenz et al., 2021; Shaw et al., 2024). This effect has also been demonstrated in a sample of adults of all ages, where indoor air pollution was associated with a two-fold increase in cognitive impairment even after correcting for age (Krishnamoorthy et al., 2018). These findings suggest that it is important to achieve a synergy between SDG 3.4 and other specific goals in this area, particularly SDG 7. This would involve implementing policies and measures aimed at reducing outdoor air pollution, as well as improving access to clean energy sources for cooking purposes.

2.2.2 Clean Water and Water Pollution

The association between water pollution and mental health has been less well studied than the case of air pollution. Nevertheless, there is provisional evidence of a link between exposure to water contaminants and low self-rated mental health, both in adolescents and in adults (Cunningham et al., 2020; Theron et al., 2022). Several pollutants, such as heavy metals and organic compounds released as effluents by industries, have been associated with neuro-inflammation or neurotoxicity, leading to an increased risk of anxiety, depression, psychotic disorders and certain childhood developmental disorders. Conversely, improving water quality may lead to an improvement in population mental health (Tota et al., 2024).

In India, there are other specific factors contributing to water pollution that are culturally conditioned, including open-air defaecation (Anuradha et al., 2017) and the custom of public bathing or washing in freshwater bodies (Jani et al., 2021). Faecal contamination of water supplies can lead to childhood diarrhoeal diseases, which have been linked to impaired neurodevelopment in North Indian children (Kvestad et al., 2015). In addition, water supply in many places of India is highly dependent on rainfall, and variations in rainfall can lead to water scarcity and a reliance on contaminated water sources (Verma & Loganathan, 2023). The last-mentioned phenomenon illustrates the link between clean water or water security (SDG 6) and climate change (SDG 13). Water scarcity or insecurity, even in the absence of pollution, has been associated with poor mental health in Indian women (Choudhary et al., 2023) and adolescents living in urban slums (Maxfield, 2020) and is also associated with higher perceived stress (Stoler et al., 2020).

Overall, these findings suggest that access to a clean and reliable water supply can have significant effects on the brain health of Indian communities, particularly those already facing economic disadvantages.

2.3 Poverty and Inequality

India is a rapidly growing economy. Though there has been a substantial increase in economic prosperity in the post-Independence era, particularly after the economic reforms of the 1990s (Wadhva, 2020). However, nearly 22% of India's population still lives in poverty (World Bank Group, 2023) and there are significant urban–rural and inter-state differences in economic security (Reserve Bank of India, 2024). The eradication of poverty (SDG 1) is intimately linked to every other goal on the SDG List. A systematic review and meta-analysis conducted in 2018 found a significant association between poverty, income inequality and depression, with a relative risk increase of 19% (Patel et al., 2018a). A more recent umbrella review also reported a significant association between poverty and mental well-being (Dougall et al., 2024).

Studies in a variety of Indian settings have confirmed the inverse relationship between poverty and mental health. Poverty has been associated with depression and cognitive impairment in elderly Indian adults (Hasan & Ghosal, 2024; Reddy et al., 2012), suicide in Indian farmers (Memdani et al., 2024), common mental disorders in postpartum women (Scott et al., 2020a), mental health problems in slum-dwelling children (Martin et al., 2024) and learning difficulties in adolescents (Scott et al., 2020b). The link between poverty and mental illness is exacerbated in vulnerable Indian populations, such as persons with HIV/AIDS (Kang et al., 2016), is further aggravated during natural disasters (Kar et al., 2013) or health crises such as the COVID-19 pandemic (Mathias et al., 2020; Yang et al., 2024). Conversely, untreated or severe mental illness, and the stigma associated with it, are associated with increased poverty, affecting both patients and their family caregivers (Trani et al., 2015). This can lead to a vicious cycle in which poverty both acts as a trigger for mental illness and is perpetuated by it.

A similar two-way relationship has been demonstrated in the case of substance use. Economic disadvantage is associated with increased alcohol and tobacco use in Indian communities (Krishnamoorthy & Ganesh, 2020; Mohindra et al., 2011). Misuse of substance such as alcohol, particularly in a dependent pattern, can also act as a "poverty trap" for Indian men and their families. This is because individuals spend more time and money on acquiring and consuming substances and lose income and employment (Schess et al., 2020). As a result, their spouses are at an elevated risk of intimate partner violence (see Sect. 2.5) and common mental disorders (Panigrahi et al., 2017). Parental alcohol consumption has also been associated with childhood malnutrition (Perayil & Mohandas, 2025). On the other hand, abstinence from alcohol has been associated with increased savings in low-income Indian workers (Schilbach, 2019).

Specific concerns arise when considering the relationship between poverty and childhood brain development. A lower standard of living has been associated with an increased risk of neurodevelopmental disorders in north Indian children (Kumar et al., 2013) and lower socioeconomic status has been linked to delayed milestones in slum-dwelling infants (Malik et al., 2007). Poverty has also been associated with borderline, but not moderate or severe, intellectual disability in a central Indian population (Lakhan, 2015). These impairments, even if mild, may be associated with impaired academic performance and reduced employment opportunities, perpetuating a cycle of poverty.

2.4 Food Security

Food security, is for all practical purposes, synonymous with both SDG 2 (Zero Hunger) and the various sub-goals which it encompasses, particularly targets 2.1 through 2.4 (Arora & Mishra, 2022). In Indian populations, food insecurity is closely linked to poverty (Ganpule et al., 2023). A report published by India's National Bank for Agriculture and Rural Development in 2022 noted that India scored high on measures of food insecurity, and was ranked 107th of 121 countries on the Global Hunger Index. This report outlined the challenges faced by the country in the four domains of food security: availability, accessibility, utilization and stability (Department of Economic Analysis and Research, 2022).

There is already a substantial amount of research on the links between food insecurity and adverse mental health outcomes in India. One of the largest such analyses involved over 72,000 adults aged 45 years and above, surveyed during the period 2017–18 as part of the Longitudinal Ageing Study in India (LASI). This study found positive associations between food insecurity and neuropsychiatric disorders in the elderly (Pengpid & Peltzer, 2023). The link between depression and food insecurity in this sample was positively associated with age, female gender and not being able to perform activities of daily living (ADL) independently (Patel et al., 2022).

The effects of food insecurity on mental health may be more severe in economically disadvantaged populations. Food insecurity was associated with higher perceived stress and more symptoms of anxiety or depression in adults and children living in North Indian slums, and its effect was stronger than that of water insecurity (Maxfield, 2020). In a study of slum-dwelling adolescent girls from another North Indian state, food insecurity was associated with higher levels of psychological distress, including depression, anxiety and a perceived inability to control one's emotions or behaviour (Rani et al., 2018). In adults residing in a slum in an East Indian state, food insecurity was associated with a nearly threefold increased risk of screening positive for a psychiatric disorder (Saha et al., 2019).

The link between changes in food security and mental health was vividly illustrated by results obtained during the COVID-19 pandemic. The containment policies necessitated by this pandemic, which increased household food insecurity, were associated with significant increases (38–44%) in anxiety and depression in rural Indian women (Bau et al., 2022) and young adults (Porter et al., 2022).

The above research shows that food insecurity is associated with increased symptoms of common mental disorders, particularly in disadvantaged populations. These effects are likely due to a combination of biological factors, such as deficiencies of particular nutrients or inflammation caused by unbalanced diets, and psychological stress caused by an uncertain food supply. These factors can contribute to both mental illness and other NCDs, again creating the potential for a syndemic of these conditions (Himmelgreen et al., 2022).

It should also be noted that food security is related not just to the quantity but to the quality of food. Of late, foods of low nutritional value have become available at a relatively low-cost, and are being increasingly consumed by Indian children and adolescents across income groups. It is likely that this dietary trend will have a significant influence on the risk of NCDs, including mental disorders linked to increased body weight and obesity (Dasgupta et al., 2024; Nancy et al., 2022).

2.5 *Gender Equality and Empowerment*

Sustainable Development Goal 5 encompasses the protection of women's and girls' rights, their empowerment in the educational, social, economic and political domains, the promotion of women's reproductive health and the elimination of violent or abusive practices and behaviours targeting women and girls. There is a close relationship between gender equality and women's physical and mental health. Advances in SDG 5 in India have been significant over the past three decades, but they have also been uneven. Indian women have much higher degrees of civil rights and involvement in political processes than most South Asian countries; however, India scores low on measures of female economic empowerment and protection against gender-based violence, including intimate partner violence (IPV) (Anderson 2024). A secondary analysis of data from India's National Family Health Survey (2019–21) suggests that societal attitudes towards IPV are negatively related with women's empowerment in the economic, health and decision-making domains (Gopalakrishnan et al., 2024). More generally, girls' and women's mental health in India may be negatively affected by cultural factors. These include a preference for male children, taboos related to menstruation and traditional attitudes towards women's education, marriage, childbearing and freedom of movement (Richardson et al., 2019; Srivastava & Gawarle, 2024).

Studies in community settings have identified socioeconomic factors associated with the risk of specific mental disorders in women. In data from the LASI, depression was more common in elderly women than in men. Education appeared to have a protective effect against depression in women, but not in men (Kumar et al., 2023). In working mothers in urban South India with a low family income, spousal alcohol abuse and a lack of support in child care were associated with depression and suicidality (Travasso et al., 2014). A similar study in a Western Indian state found that poverty and stressors related to marriage and motherhood were associated with "tension", a local idiom for common mental disorders or psychological distress (Atal & Foster, 2021).

Gender-based violence is a significant risk factor for several adverse mental health outcomes in women worldwide, including depression, post-traumatic stress disorder (PTSD) and suicidality (White et al., 2024). In India, the one-year prevalences of physical and sexual abuse in women have been estimated at 21% and 6% respectively. Up to 4.6% of disability-adjusted life-years (DALYs) in India are related to IPV (Quinlan-Davidson et al., 2025). A recent study of women in rural central India found that nearly 95% had experienced some form of physical violence, and that up to 66% had symptoms of anxiety, depression or post-traumatic stress disorder (Sathe et al., 2024). Similar findings were obtained in a South Indian sample, where IPV was associated with a threefold increase in the risk of common mental disorders (Shenoy et al., 2024). In a case-control study of completed suicides, IPV was associated with a nearly seven-fold increase in suicide risk (Gururaj et al., 2004). The effects of IPV on women's mental health were accentuated during the COVID-19 lockdowns, where victims of past IPV were often confined with their abusers and subjected to other forms of social and economic stress (Huq et al., 2021).

Pregnancy and the postpartum period are associated with an elevated risk of mental disorders in women, and these may be more likely to develop in the face of social disadvantage. In a study of women residing in rural areas of two Eastern Indian states, low asset ownership, less autonomy in decision-making, and a pregnancy that was not desired by the husband were all associated with an increased risk of postpartum psychological distress (Prost et al., 2012). Perinatal depressive or anxiety symptoms in Indian women have intergenerational consequences, as they are associated with an increased risk of low birth weight, childhood malnutrition and their attendant negative effects on child development (Chandra et al., 2021; Nguyen et al., 2018).

A specific problem faced by Indian women is access to appropriate sanitary facilities. In the absence of these, open-air urination and defaecation are common, leading to a lack of privacy, feelings of shame and an increased risk of physical and sexual abuse. Research in a rural community in East India has shown that sanitation insecurity is associated with elevated risks of anxiety, depression and general psychological distress in women (Caruso et al., 2018). Similar concerns arise in relation to menstruation, where a lack of access to sanitary facilities, combined with cultural taboos or myths related to impurity and social exclusion, cause psychological distress in adolescent girls and young women (Garg & Anand, 2015; Gold-Watts et al., 2020; McCammon et al., 2020).

This brief overview does not exhaust the many links between SDG 5 and mental health in India. Two examples of public health importance are the high burden of mental and substance use disorders in sex workers (Iaisuklang & Ali, 2017) and the frequent violations of basic human rights faced by women with severe mental disorders (Poreddi et al., 2015a). In all these cases, there is clear evidence that women's mental health is closely linked not just to SDG 5, but to a broad range of SDGs addressing poverty, water and food security and economic development.

2.6 Quality Education

Sustainable Development Goal 4 addresses the need for basic literacy and numeracy, gender equality in primary and higher education, inclusion of persons with disabilities and other vulnerable groups. However, it does not stop there, but also addresses the need for "education for sustainable development and lifestyles" through the inculcation of humanitarian values (United Nations Economic and Social Commission for Asia and the Pacific, 2025). According to the 2011 national census, the literacy rate is 73%. This represents a four-fold increase from the literacy rate immediately following independence, which was around 18%. However, there is a persistent and significant gap between male (81%) and female (65%) literacy, and there is also marked variability in educational attainment across states, ranging from 62 to 94%. There are also significant rural–urban discrepancies, and the literacy rates for scheduled castes and tribes are 7–15% lower than the national average (Ministry of Statistics and Program Implementation, Government of India, 2016).

Apart from its intrinsic value, access to education is a prerequisite to attaining several of the other SDGs, including the eradication of poverty (SDG 1), good health (SDG 3), gender equality (SDG 5), decent work and economic growth (SDG 8) and reduced inequalities (SDG 10) (Wagner, 2017). Conversely, a lack of education exposes Indian citizens to a wide range of psychosocial adversities. These include unemployment or poorly paid work, low income, food insecurity, gender-based violence, unplanned pregnancies, sexually transmitted infections and reduced help-seeking for health concerns. Each of these can increase the risk of mental illness. A lack of formal education, formerly referred to as "illiteracy", has been associated with depression in elderly Indian adults (Ganguli et al., 1999; Jain & Aras, 2007; Shivakumar et al., 2015; Swarnalatha, 2013), postpartum depression (Amipara et al., 2020), depression in post-menopausal women (Ahlawat et al., 2019), common mental disorders in the general population (Kallakuri et al., 2018; Pothen et al., 2003) and alcohol abuse in men (Eashwar et al., 2019). Lower educational attainment is associated with an elevated risk of postpartum depression (Ghosh & Goswami, 2011), depression in rural populations (Gupta et al., 2020) and poor psychological health in the elderly (Patel et al., 2021). A lack of education can also delay help-seeking by persons with mental illnesses and their caregivers (Lahariya et al., 2010). Mentally ill Indian patients with no formal education are less aware of their fundamental rights and are more likely to face mistreatment or discrimination (Poreddi et al., 2015b). A similar phenomenon has been observed in the elderly, where those who are illiterate are more likely to experience both physical abuse and depression (Kaur et al., 2015; Patel et al., 2018b).

Education is known to be a protective factor against cognitive decline and dementia in late life. It has been estimated that access to adequate education could reduce up to 5–7% of the global incidence of dementia (Livingston et al., 2024). An association between a lack of formal education and cognitive impairment has also been observed in elderly Indians residing in either urban or rural areas (Dhanalakshmi et al., 2024; Keshari & Shankar, 2022; Muhammad et al., 2023; Reddy et al., 2012; Sengupta et al., 2014). However, some Indian researchers have failed to find a link between educational attainment and dementia risk (Iyer et al., 2014; Raina et al., 2014). It can be cautiously concluded that improving educational attainment could improve cognitive health in subsequent Indian generations (Angrisani et al., 2024). This is important given the growing elderly population in India, estimated to reach 15% of the total population over the next decade (International Institute for Population Sciences & United Nations Population Fund, 2023).

Inclusive education is a key component of SDG 4. A recent study of over 3,900 children aged 2–9 in five Indian states found that 9–17% had neurodevelopmental and related disorders, such as intellectual disability, visual or hearing impairment, autism spectrum disorder and epilepsy (Arora et al., 2018). In addition, studies of primary school children have found that 1.5%-10% have specific learning disabilities related to reading, spelling or arithmetic skills (Arun et al., 2013; Sunil et al., 2023) and 2–12% have features of attention-deficit/hyperactivity disorder (ADHD) (Chawla et al., 2022; Sharma et al., 2020). Though India's educational policies mention a commitment to inclusive education, there have been significant challenges in implementing inclusive teaching practices and "mainstreaming" children with disabilities at the ground level (Singal, 2005). This reflects both cultural beliefs about disability and a lack of appropriately trained personnel, teaching materials and other infrastructure necessary for inclusive schools. The latter can be a significant source of stress for both students and teachers (Singal, 2019).

Another area of concern that connects SDG 4 and SDG 3.4 is the issue of school mental health. Surveys of children and adolescents attending schools in India have found that anywhere from 10–50% experience symptoms of psychological distress or exhibit behavioural problems. These symptoms arise in the context of family, socioeconomic or academic stressors, and are often unidentified by peers or teachers (Faizi et al., 2016; Gupta et al., 2023; Jayashree et al., 2018; Sakthivel et al., 2021). Significant levels of stigma against mental illness have been found in school teachers in India, which can cause further difficulties for students with such problems (Venkataraman et al., 2019). Even when teachers are willing and motivated to address such issues in a classroom setting, they may lack appropriate training and support from qualified experts (Singal, 2019).

2.7 Decent Work and Economic Growth

Sustainable Development Goal 8 combines two broad objectives: growth that is sustainable and beneficial to all, and access to employment that is "productive" and "decent" (Global Sustainable Development Report, 2023). It also addresses issues such as the eradication of child labour and the protection of workers' rights, including those of migrant workers. India is a middle-income country according to the World Bank's classification, with a gross national income of approximately $9,046 in terms of purchasing power parity (United Nations Development Programme, 2025). According to an estimate by the International Labour Organization, the unemployment rate is 4.2%, which is slightly lower than the estimates for South Asia (4.6%) and for low- and middle-income countries in general (World Bank Group, 2025).

Unemployment is a known risk factor for depression and suicide around the world, especially in men (Amiri, 2022; Qin et al., 2022). In India, unemployment was associated with a six-fold increase in suicide risk in a South Indian city (Gururaj et al., 2004) and has also been significantly associated with suicide attempts (Weiss & Parkar, 2020). A more recent study, using state-based data on suicide rates, found a paradoxical inverse relationship between unemployment and suicide in urban, but not rural areas (Kar et al., 2024). This finding highlights the fact that SDG 8 does not refer merely to "work" but to "decent work". Excessive workplace stress in urban residents can also contribute to suicidal behaviour in India: according to official statistics, 1.2% of suicides in India are related to "professional or career problems", as against 1.9% related to unemployment (National Crime Records Bureau, 2022). Other community-based studies have also found a positive association between unemployment and the risk of depressive or anxiety disorders or symptoms (Bashir et al., 2022; Pawar et al., 2022). In a survey of over 2,400 adults from a North Indian state, unemployment was associated with a threefold increase in the risk for psychosocial distress, though it is not clear if unemployment preceded the onset of symptoms or was a consequence of it (Mathias et al., 2018a). Loss of employment during the COVID-19 pandemic was also associated with depressive and anxiety symptoms in rural Indian men (Chatterji et al., 2021).

When discussing unemployment in relation to mental illness, it is also important to consider the situation of persons with mental illness who are denied employment, or have restricted access to it, even after they have recovered. Data from India's 2011 national census shows that nearly 77% of persons with self-reported mental illness are unemployed, and only 13% had full-time employment (Ramasubramanian et al., 2016). A qualitative study of persons with severe mental illness and their caregivers identified several workplace-related and social barriers to employment in a South Indian state (Nirmala et al., 2020). More recently, a study of persons with mental disorders attending out-patient services found that 40% were unemployed, despite 71% of those unemployed actively seeking new job opportunities (Guru et al., 2025). Even patients with milder forms of mental illness, such as anxiety disorders, experience difficulties in finding work (Suhas et al., 2023).

Migration and employment are intimately linked. A significant proportion of internal migration in India is due to individuals or families seeking better employment (i.e., more "decent" in terms of working conditions or remuneration, using the SDG 8 terminology) in urban regions, or in states with higher economic development. Unemployment in educated migrant youth was associated with a threefold increased risk in depressive and anxiety symptoms in an East Indian metropolis (Biswas et al., 2024). The levels of stress experienced by migrants facing the threat of unemployment were worsened during the recent COVID-19 pandemic, highlighting the need for inclusion of this population in both mental health policy and other SDG-related initiatives (Duggal et al., 2022).

Research on the link between "decent work", as opposed to simple "employment", and mental health in India, is evolving rapidly (Poddar & Chhajer, 2024). Some of this research has focused on the differences in workplace stress across professions: for example, a study of middle-aged professionals found that marketing professionals had higher levels of stress than teachers or bank employees (Kazmi et al., 2024). Other experts have highlighted the links between work-related stressors and impaired mental health in specific professions, such as medical professionals (Belkić & Rustagi, 2024), police officers (Mini et al., 2025) and farmers (Das, 2011). The unique challenges associated with each of these professionals often require situation-specific mental health initiatives (Sarkar et al., 2024), though these can also be integrated with specific SDGs. For example, in the case of farmers, mental health is inextricably linked with goals such as clean water (SDG 6), affordable and clean energy (SDG 7), sustainable forms of agricultural production (SDG 2) and climate change (SDG 13).

2.8 Sustainable Cities

As of 2021, approximately 35% of India's population resides in urban areas. This figure is estimated to increase to 40% by the year 2036 (National Institute of Urban Affairs, 2022). Though urban living holds the promise of a higher standard of living, education and employment, urbanization in India has often occurred in an uneven and unplanned manner. This has led to social and environmental problems such as inadequate water and sanitation (SDG 6), unemployment or poorly paid work (SDG 8), illicit drug abuse (SDG 3.5), inadequate or low-quality housing (SDG 11.1), air pollution (SDG 7) and general environmental degradation (Hepat et al., 2024). In short, many Indian cities fall short of the ideal of "sustainable cities" outlined in SDG 11. This takes a toll on the mental health of Indian city-dwellers, particularly vulnerable populations such as women, children, the elderly and those living on the "margins", such as the slum population (Chandra et al., 2018; Hepat et al., 2024; Prakash et al., 2023; Trivedi et al., 2008). A recent survey of adult residents in a large Indian city identified five groups of stressors that significantly affected their mental health: housing, traffic and transportation, neighbourhood concerns, the cost of living and employment. Additional concerns flagged by respondents were a lack of social cohesion, air and water pollution, poor sanitation and a lack of spaces for recreation (Poddar et al., 2025).

A study of Bhopal, a large city in central India, found that certain aspects of urban development and sustainability—security, proximity to open spaces and distance from slums—were significantly related to subjective happiness as assessed using social media (Twitter/X) posts. These findings were corroborated through interviews with citizens from two localities (Khare & Chatterjee, 2024). Similarly, a survey of 1,208 adults with chronic medical illnesses found lower levels of depression associated with proximity to parks (Mukherjee et al., 2017). These findings are in line with the wider literature suggesting that urban "green spaces" have a beneficial effect on mental health (Wood et al., 2023).

Poor housing may be associated with mental health. Several researchers have highlighted the increased burden of mental disorders faced by Indian families residing in slums, urban resettlements or temporary accommodations (Gawde et al., 2013; Kanougiya et al., 2024; Lodha et al., 2022; Singh et al., 2024a, 2024b; Subbaraman et al., 2014; Suchithra et al., 2022). In addition, a study of Indian women found that good housing is associated with better performance on tests of executive function, a higher-order cognitive skill involved in planning, sequencing and carrying out complex tasks. This effect may be mediated by housing-related stressors (Vaid, 2024).

The relationships between air and water pollution and mental health, which are key concerns in urban areas, have been described earlier (Sect. 2.1). An additional form of pollution that is of public health concern in cities is noise pollution, which can arise from a variety of sources: vehicular traffic, machinery and commercial or cultural activities (Kalawapudi et al., 2020). Indian research has found that noise pollution is associated with reduced psychological well-being in the elderly (Adlakha et al., 2021) and with insomnia in the general population (Gilani & Mir, 2022).

2.9 Climate Change

Several experts consider climate change the greatest threat currently facing humanity (Ansari & Kar, 2024). The effects of climate change on mental health are complex, far-reaching and often arise after a certain time lag (Cianconi et al., 2020; Massazza et al., 2025). Terms such as "climate anxiety" or "eco-anxiety" have been used to describe the psychological distress caused by climate change, but these phenomena have not been specifically evaluated in countries such as India (Butler, 2025). In a survey of Indian youth aged 16–25, 68% reported significant worries about climate change, and 74% felt that these worries affected their day-to-day functioning (Hickman et al., 2021). In a study of youth residing in Indian slums, over 50% reported experiencing or being affected by events related to climate change, such as heatwaves or extreme rainfall (Yatirajula et al., 2023).

One of the most tangible ways in which climate change affects human health and development is through the occurrence of extreme weather events (Stott, 2016). A recent systematic review of the mental health sequelae of such events identified over

20 Indian studies in this area. In all these studies, events such as cyclones or storms with associated flooding were associated with significant symptoms of depression and anxiety (frequency 40–60%) and PTSD (frequency 20–80%) in affected populations. These symptoms arose in the context of bereavement and/or loss of income, livelihood or housing caused by these disasters (Patwary et al., 2024). Such psychological sequelae are often exacerbated by a lack of disaster preparedness, which is challenging in a country as large and ecologically diverse as India (George & Kumar, 2022). Conversely, climate change can also be associated with drought, which is a risk factor for depression in Indian farmers (Viswanathan et al., 2019).

Heatwaves are another consequence of climate change in India which are likely to affect mental health. Using data from the LASI, it has been found that exposure to high temperatures is associated with emotional distress (depression and fear), fatigue and poor quality of life in elderly Indian adults (Wang et al., 2025). High temperatures can adversely affect the mental health of children, slum dwellers and manual labourers in India. Through their effects on animal health and productivity, heatwaves can also affect the psychosocial well-being of farmers (Yasobant et al., 2025).

Though research in this area is lacking, several experts have voiced concerns about the differentially severe impact of climate change on mental health in vulnerable populations. These include children (Etzel & Bhave, 2023), farmers (Talukder et al., 2021) and individuals residing in ecologically vulnerable areas (Dhimal et al., 2021). Because of this, it is impossible to separate mental health considerations from broader discussions and initiatives aimed at mitigating climate change and other related SDGs (Massazza et al., 2025; Padhy et al., 2015).

2.10 *Peace and Justice*

Sustainable Development Goal 16 aims at promoting societies that are not just inclusive and sustainable, but free from violence, exploitation and injustice. Specific subgoals included under SDG 16 address the reduction of violence, terrorism, torture, human trafficking and corruption. Most regions of India enjoy reasonable levels of peace and civil stability. However, there are certain regions or populations that remain exposed to significant levels of violence and civil unrest, leading to high rates of psychological morbidity (Sharma et al., 2023).

Foremost among these is the state of Jammu and Kashmir, where the population are often victims of cross-border terrorism or armed conflict. Studies in the Kashmiri general population have found that 35–55% experience significant levels of depression, and nearly 30% have symptoms of anxiety (Amin & Khan, 2009; Bashir et al., 2022). In one survey, virtually every respondent across the ten districts of the Kashmir valley reported exposure to one or more forms of traumatic stress, either personally or through media reports (Dar & Deb, 2022). A study of Kashmiri school-going children found that 22–27% screened positive for one or more mental disorders, particular anxiety, mood or conduct disorders (Paul & Khan, 2019).

More recently, inter-ethnic clashes in the north-eastern state of Manipur have led to high levels of violence and internal displacement. A recent study of Manipuri adults residing in relief camps found that almost 66% had symptoms of PTSD, and 40% had moderate to severe anxiety symptoms (Rajkumari et al., 2024). Sporadic clashes based on religious or caste grounds occur periodically in most Indian states. The mental health cost of these forms of violence is largely undocumented. However, a study of children aged 8–15 exposed to "communal" (inter-religious) riots in Gujarat in the period 2001–2002 found that nearly 39% had clinically significant psychiatric symptoms, and 27% had symptoms of PTSD (Kumar & Fonagy, 2013). The collection of objective data on this issue is a significant mental health challenge for the future, and a matter of concern for both researchers and policymakers in India.

SDG 16.2 addresses the need to prevent and control all forms of abuse and violence against children. Recent research in India has shown that childhood sexual and physical abuse are regrettably common, and are associated with risk factors such as paternal alcohol use, socioeconomic disadvantage and child labour (Jose & Cherayi, 2020; Kaur & Byard, 2021; Paul et al., 2021; Singh et al., 2022). Indian children who have faced these forms of maltreatment experience increased levels of depression, anxiety, self-injury and suicidality (Sharratt et al., 2021). Childhood maltreatment in India is often underreported by victims and families due to the stigma associated with it, as well as a general "culture of silence" (Iorfa et al., 2022).

3 Sustainable Development Goals and Mental Health: The Response of the Indian Government

As mentioned in Sect. 2.1, the Indian government has committed itself to adopting the SDGs. This commitment, based on a recognition that the nation of India encompasses one-sixth of the human population, has been placed under the leadership of NITI Aayog, an official think tank chaired by the Prime Minister. In collaboration with the United Nations, NITI Aayog has published two detailed reports on how the SDGs were "localized" and made relevant to the Indian context. This process involved taking into considerations the diverse needs of each Indian state or territory, and developing locally relevant solutions to social and environmental challenges. While doing so, NITI Aayog attempted to integrate progress towards the SDGs with flagship national programmes, such as those related to health, nutrition and sanitation. In this paradigm, the pursuit of the SDGs is seen as a key component of India's broader goal of achieving a *Viksit Bharat* ("Developed India") by the year 2047 (NITI Aayog & United Nations, 2019; United Nations India & NITI Aayog, 2022).

An examination of the latter publication will serve as a useful starting point in examining current and future synergies between the SDGs and mental health in India. The entire document contains only two references to mental health, both of which refer to the mental health burden of the COVID-19 pandemic, and attempt to address it through "awareness generation" with the help of the National Institute of Mental

Health and Neurosciences (NIMHANS) (United Nations India & NITI Aayog, 2022). This observation is not intended as a critique of the document: mental health is only one of 169 targets outlined by the SDGs, and this document was published at a time when India was still recovering from the health, social and economic crises caused by this pandemic (Aneja & Ahuja, 2021; Kabir et al., 2023). A subsequent publication by NITI Aayog, the "SDG India Index 2023–24", contains five references to mental health. Two of these references are restatements of SDG 3.4, but the other three provide a rationale for using a specific index—the national suicide rate per 100,000 population—as an indicator of mental well-being. This report proposes a reduction in the national suicide rate by one-third (from 12.4 to 3.5) by the year 2030. There are also isolated references to alcohol, tobacco and drug abuse, but these are restatements of SDG 3.5 and 3.9a. Though these changes seem small and incremental, they should be contrasted with the pre-pandemic scenario, where the "NITI Aayog Health Index" (NAHI), a composite measure of health outcomes and healthcare system functioning, made no mention of mental health or substance abuse (Das et al., 2022b).

3.1 Programmes Directly Related to SDG 3.4

In contrast, India's most recent National Mental Health Policy (NMHP), published in 2014, antedates both the promulgation of the SDGs and India's commitment to them, but still mentions several key aspects of sustainable and equitable development, particularly in Sects. 5.2 ("promotion of mental health") and 5.3 ("prevention of mental illness and reduction of suicide and attempted suicide"). These include:

- attention to early child development and health
- school and workplace mental health initiatives
- improvement of "poor living conditions" such as overcrowding, food and water insecurity and poor sanitation
- protection of women from intimate partner violence
- implementation of programmes to reduce substance abuse and dependence

In making these recommendations, the National Mental Health Policy is prescient, as it addresses not just mental health (SDGs 3.4 and 3.5) but several social and environmental determinants of mental health, such as food security (SDG 2), education (SDG 4), gender equality (SDG 5), access to clean water and proper sanitation facilities (SDG 6) and sustainable and equitable living conditions (SDG 11). It also emphasizes the need for collaboration between different sectors of the government, as well as between the government and the community, to promote and maintain mental health—or, in other words, "partnerships for the goals" (SDG 17) (Ministry of Health & Family Welfare, 2014).

India's National Suicide Prevention Strategy, formulated in 2022 in the wake of the COVID-19 pandemic, represents a position approximately half-way between the NITI Aayog publications and the National Mental Health Policy. This strategy lays emphasis on ensuring access to mental health care, promotion of positive mental health, reducing access to means of suicide and responsible media reporting, but it also underlines the importance of preventing and treating substance use disorders (SDG 3.5). It also addresses several key concerns related to sustainable development, such as providing holistic education that promotes child and adolescent well-being (SDG 4), the empowerment of women and their protection from violence (SDG 5), the protection of informal workers (SDG 8) and ensuring a basic standard of living and access to employment for vulnerable populations (SDG 8, SDG 10) (Ministry of Health & Family Welfare, 2022).

It is also instructive to examine the Government of India's *Nasha Mukt Bharat Abhiyaan* (NMBA) policy in this context, given that it is directly concerned with the prevention and treatment of substance use disorders (SDG 3.5). This initiative is supervised by the Ministry of Social Justice and Empowerment, rather than the Ministry of Health, and was inaugurated on August 15, 2020 (Ministry of Social Justice & Empowerment, 2025). The initial phase of this programme, covering 272 vulnerable districts in 11 Indian states, includes both treatment and rehabilitation services, as well as community awareness and preventive initiatives in schools and colleges. It is based on a "three-pronged approach" involving supply control (under the Narcotics Control Bureau), treatment (under the Ministry of Health and Family Welfare) and outreach awareness aimed at reducing the demand for substances (under the Ministry of Social Justice and Empowerment) (Ministry of Social Justice & Empowerment, Government of India & United Nations Development Programme, 2021). Though it does not explicitly address the SDGs, several individual goals are incorporated into the NMBA's strategy. These include life skills education in schools and colleges (SDG 4), education and vocational rehabilitation for adolescents and adults with substance use disorders (SDG 4 and SDG 8) and partnerships between government agencies and the community (SDG 17). In its focus on prevention and rehabilitation, it also transcends previous strategies based on the criminalization of drug use and the provision of treatment at select facilities.

A national initiative that merits evaluation in this context, as it directly addresses SDG 3.4, is the Ministry of Health and Family Welfare's National Programme for the Prevention and Control of Non-Communicable Diseases (2023–2030). The operational guideline for this programme explicitly incorporates this SDG, mentioning the importance of NCD prevention and treatment "as a prerequisite to accelerate sustainable development" (Ministry of Health & Family Welfare, 2023). Though this document does not directly address mental health, it mentions the importance of linkages with the NMHP and the need to integrate mental health into public awareness campaigns on NCDs. It also addresses the links between alcohol and tobacco consumption and NCDs (SDG 3.5, 3.9a). The document mentions the importance of reducing air pollution in preventing certain NCDs, such as respiratory diseases (SDG 3.9, SDG 7), though it does not make any specific recommendations in this regard. However, other SDGs that may be causally associated with both mental disorders and other NCDs have not been addressed in this guideline. These include poverty (SDG 1), food insecurity (SDG 2), gender equality (SDG 5) and climate change (SDG 13) (Dewi et al., 2024; Himmelgreen et al., 2022; Mendenhall et al., 2017; Prince et al., 2007).

Closely linked to this programme, but also addressing the issue of food security, is the Government of India's POSHAN (Prime Minister's Overarching Scheme for Holistic Nourishment) Abhiyaan, launched in 2018 under the Ministry of Women and Child Development. This programme is aimed at "improving nutritional outcomes for children, adolescents, pregnant women and lactating mothers" through grassroots-level collaborations between communities and government agencies and the promotion of low-cost, energy-rich traditional foods (Press Information Bureau, 2021; Ministry of Women and Child Development, Government of India, 2022a). On the one hand, the programme aims to prevent anaemia in children, adolescent girls and women of childbearing age, to reduce low birth weight and to childhood malnutrition—all of which can improve maternal and child mental health (Dhivar et al., 2024; Wassef et al., 2019). On the other hand, it also aims to reduce childhood obesity by promoting healthy dietary patterns through its "Poshan Pakhwada" awareness campaign. This can significantly reduce the risk for several NCDs, including depressive and anxiety disorders (Lindberg et al., 2020). Overall, this initiative holds the promise of addressing nutritional (SDG 2) and mental (SDG 3.4) health in an integrated and "inter-generational" manner (Pundhir et al., 2025).

Finally, the Protection of Children from Sexual Offences (POCSO) Act, enacted in 2012 and amended in 2019, is a landmark piece of legislation that provides an expanded definition of child sexual abuse and makes provisions for both the punishment of the perpetrator and the protection and welfare of the victim (Ministry of Home Affairs, 2019). It provides clear definitions of the offences of sexual assault, harassment and child pornography, and states that sexual assaults which "cause the child to become mentally ill", or are committed against children with mental disabilities, should be termed "aggravated sexual assault". The duty to report sexual offences against children is clearly spelled out, and trials of such cases should be conducted *in camera*, without the child having contact with the accused. Under this Act, child victims requiring emergency medical care should be admitted in "the nearest hospital" within 24 h of the reporting of an offence. Though it does not explicitly mention the need for psychological assessment or treatment, this act represents a crucial step towards "integrating child protection and mental health services" (Krishna et al., 2021) and thereby moving closer to the attainment of SDG 16.2.

3.2 SDG-Oriented Programmes with Downstream Effects on SDG 3.4

There are several other national programmes which primarily target other SDGs, but have improved mental health as a secondary objective. Foremost among these is the Swachh Bharat (Clean India) Mission. The SBM was launched in 2014, with the aim of improving sanitation, cleanliness and hygiene in Indian cities and villages. This initiative employs a multi-pronged approach including scientific waste management, reducing open-air defaecation and promoting cleanliness through behavioural change in individuals, institutions and communities. The SBM Urban Operational Guidelines, published in 2021, explicitly mention the link between cleanliness, hygiene and psychological health in their introductory paragraph (Ministry of Housing and Urban Affairs, Government of India, 2021). Though it does not directly target mental health, the SBM addresses key environmental SDGs that are linked to it, including clean water (SDG 6) and sustainable cities and communities (SDG 11). It also reduces the risk of water-borne infections, which have been linked to impaired brain development in Indian children (Kvestad et al., 2015; Upadhyay et al., 2021). Another example under this category is the National Programme on Climate Change and Health (NPCCHH), which was launched in 2019 under the Ministry of Health and Family Welfare's National Centre for Disease Control. This programme attempts to mitigate the effects of climate change on human health, with a specific focus on heat-related diseases, diseases related to air pollution (including mental disorders) and nutritional disorders related to climate change (National Centre for Disease Control, 2025). Under the NPCCHH, each Indian state is tasked with developing an action plan specifically tailored to local conditions and challenges (Kumar et al., 2020). Some of these action plans highlight the need for mental health support in the face of climate change, though specific interventions or strategies aimed at this have not yet been elaborated (National Centre for Disease Control, 2022).

Another recent policy in this category, which is explicitly based on an SDG and attempts to address it in the Indian context, is the Ministry of Human Resource Development's National Education Policy (NEP). The NEP makes several mentions of the Sustainable Development Goals related to education in its foundational document, and aims at ensuring basic literacy and numeracy as well as "re-imagining" and "restructuring" higher and vocational education, promoting equity and inclusiveness in education and developing a holistic system of education (Ministry of Human Resource Development, 2020). Its aim is to achieve the specific targets outlined under SDG 4 in a manner that is locally relevant, while preserving and promoting Indian culture, languages, arts and crafts, and introducing subjects such as "organic living" and "environmental education" that inculcate knowledge and attitudes relevant to sustainable development in other spheres. An innovative aspect of the NEP is that it specifically addresses child mental health through provisions for trained counsellors or social workers in schools (Sect. 2.9). Some experts have also noted that the NEP is aligned with current concepts in child cognitive development and is more inclusive towards slow learners and children with disabilities (Anitha & Narasimhan, 2021).

"Mission Shakti", launched in 2020 and subtitled the "Integrated Women Empowerment Programme", is a scheme that aims to improve the social standing of women throughout India through a multi-component approach. Its stated aims include preventing, managing and rehabilitating the victims of violence against women; improving access to Government schemes and services for women; promoting positive changes in attitudes and behaviour towards women in the community; and promoting the survival and education of girls. Services envisaged under Mission Shakti include "One Stop Centres" and helplines for victims of violence against women, schemes to promote education and skill development for girls, grievance redressal mechanisms for cases of harassment or discrimination against women, economic empowerment, prevention of sexual exploitation and trafficking, housing for widows, childcare for working women and nutritional support during pregnancy (Ministry of Women and Child Development, Government of India, 2022b). Though it does not directly address mental health, it contains two relevant provisions: providing psychosocial and legal aid to women facing "mental harassment" (Sect. 2.2.1) and the possibility of setting up homes for women with intellectual disability (Sect. 2.2.1). This programme aims to integrate several programmes or schemes that were previously running independent of each other. By doing so, it aims to address several SDGs relevant to women, including poverty (SDG 1), nutrition (SDG 2), health (SDG 3), education (SDG 4) and work (SDG 8) under the broader "umbrella" of gender equality and empowerment (SDG 5). Thus, "Mission Shakti", at least in principle, embodies the sort of synthetic or synergistic approach that is the focus of this chapter.

4 Barriers and Challenges

The national programmes and initiatives described in the previous section are all vitally important, both in achieving the SDGs and in improving mental health in India, and should be commended in this regard. Nevertheless, there are several challenges that exist both in the implementation of these programmes, and in ensuring that such programmes work together in a coordinated manner to integrate SDG 3.4 with the other SDGs. The following are the key areas of concern in this connection:

- There is a relative paucity of data on the relationship between social determinants and mental health in India. This is caused by both to shortcomings in data collection and a lack of focus on mental health outside the biomedical framework. Thus, it is difficult to quantify and track the two-way relationship between progress towards SDG targets and improvements in mental health in Indian communities (Thapa et al., 2021).
- In some cases, an SDG-friendly approach may not fully succeed due to resistance or apathy. In some cases, this may be simply due to the force of habit and an attachment to "old ways" of doing things. For example, even in households where latrines were funded and constructed under the Swachh Bharat Mission, at least one person in each of these households continued to practice open-air defecation (Begum et al., 2024). At other times, it may be due to the lack of awareness of the importance of a particular practice or initiative, reflecting the need for better education or communication. However, in other cases, there may be deeply-ingrained cultural beliefs or practices that persist even after attempts at generating or raising awareness. This has been seen, for example, in the case of girls' education, where attitudes favouring girls' education are often adopted only partly, and subordinated to values or practices favouring early marriage (Pujar et al., 2024).

- Despite community commitment to behavioural or lifestyle modification, a scarcity of resources or funds may interfere with the implementation of SDG-oriented programmes. For example, a study from rural South India found that, after the construction of household latrines to reduce open-air defaecation, 78% of beneficiaries reported using them "all the time"; however, 84% of respondents reported that the financial aid given to them under the Swachh Bharat Mission was insufficient for the construction of latrines, and they incurred substantial out-of-pocket expenses. These costs exceeded the sanctioned assistance by an order of 2- to 6-folds (Natarajan et al., 2024).
- There is a tension between development-friendly policies and existing legislation that is more punitive or restrictive in nature. This is particularly the case with regards to SDG 3.5, where recent patient- and community-oriented initiatives under the NMBA coexist uneasily with existing penalties for possession and consumption of illicit substances, even in the revised form of India's Narcotic Drugs and Psychotropic Substances Act (Singh & Chadda, 2025). In other cases, a similar tension exists between progressive-minded policies and traditional cultural values or practices. For example, attempts to promote egalitarian points of view on issues such as women and child health may be perceived as alienating by families and communities (Marrow, 2013). Similarly, culture-based restrictions on women's mobility may hinder them from taking part in support groups aimed at promoting health, equality or empowerment (Gailits et al., 2019).
- Programmes may be implemented unevenly across Indian states, leading to marked variability in SDG-relevant outcomes. This can be seen in the official statistics on each state's performance under the POSHAN scheme, where the level of relevant activities ranges from minimal (Delhi, Haryana, West Bengal) through moderate (Gujarat, Odisha) to high (Chhattisgarh, Rajasthan) (Ministry of Women and Child Development, Government of India, 2022a). There are several reasons for such differences, including local culture, uneven funding, disagreements between local and national governments, and inter-state variations in literacy and economic prosperity (Gupta & Mukhopadhyay, 2014; Jose, 2019).
- Despite the rapid growth in relevant published research and data, there is still a dearth of Indian literature examining the SDGs themselves, or the relationships between them, either in general or in the context of mental health. It is unlikely that such interrelationships would be the same in each country, and it is important to know how, for example, poverty, education, employment, pollution and climate-related factors interact together in the genesis of conditions such as depression or dementia in Indian populations.
- There is a lack of data on SDG-relevant outcomes for the many programmes and initiatives outlined in Sects. 3.1 and 3.2. In the absence of clear data, steering or modifying programmes using expert or other opinion is likely to lead to difficulties, the foremost among them being a lack of accountability. This is especially true for issues such as civil unrest, intimate partner violence and the use of illicit substances, where a combination of social stigma and vested political interests may prevent stakeholders from obtaining a truly objective picture of the scope of these problems.

- The SDGs themselves reflect a materialistic conception of human nature, which is itself derived from a particular Western model of economic and social development. There are tensions between some of the SDGs themselves—for example, how does one balance the need for economic growth and job creation with the preservation of the environment? How does one balance the increasing need for energy consumption implicit in a "prosperous" society with minimizing pollution or climate change? (Adelman, 2018). More broadly, how do these goals contribute to the development of pro-social, community-oriented values and human flourishing? Are these goals truly relevant to non-Western societies, or are they only of illusory value? (Muposhi & Mugwati, 2024). Moreover, in a country such as India, where religion and spirituality play an important role in individual and community life and psychological well-being (Chattopadhyay, 2007), how valuable are a set of goals that make no mention of religion, except for a passing mention of religious discrimination in SDG 10.2? Can religious world-views be harmonized with the SDGs to the benefit of Indian citizens, or are they likely to come into conflict? (Haustein & Tomalin, 2021; Tomalin et al., 2019).
- There is already a significant amount of inequality faced by Indian citizens, in terms of both of access to specific programmes and benefits (Mishra et al., 2021) and mental health (Gupta & Coffey, 2020). While the SDGs aim at an inclusive society, the programmes described in Sect. 3 have the same stated aim, what should be done to ensure that such inequalities do not interfere with India's SDG-aligned policies? What cultural, economic and political factors need to be overcome to ensure that such programmes do not benefit some at the expense of others? (Mishra et al., 2021).

Finally, and most importantly, despite the wide range of policies and programmes aimed at addressing the SDGs in relation to mental health—either directly or indirectly—there is a lack of coordination between the policies and programmes themselves. For example, the improvement of maternal nutrition is a component of both POSHAN Abhiyaan and Mission Shakti: would both these schemes work together harmoniously in providing this service to pregnant or lactating women in a particular village or region, and what is the division of labour envisaged in this regard? Similar concerns arise when considering private–public or community government partnerships, which require good management, cooperation and communication if they are to succeed (Mahalingam et al., 2011). In short, an overarching concern is that "partnerships for the goals" (SDG 17) need to be developed, strengthened and made sustainable in the Indian context. By doing so, the benefits of each scheme on mental health and well-being will emerge in a robust manner.

5 Practical Solutions and Approaches

The difficulties outlined in the previous section are by no means insoluble. At this point in time, India's achievements towards integrating the SDGs and mental health can be compared to a jigsaw puzzle where all the pieces have been found, and some have already been assembled into meaningful patterns. These involve both government initiatives as well as interventions developed by mental health experts that can be usefully combined with one or more SDGs.

5.1 Government Initiatives

Several steps to ensure progress towards the SDGs and their associated mental health benefits in the Indian context have already been taken, and these are outlined in recent Government publications. In the joint NITI Aayog—United Nations India document, "The Indian Model of SDG Localisation" (2022), the principle of "localisation" of the SDGs is described in detail. This involves addressing each SDG in a way that is appropriate and feasible in Indian villages and cities. The steps outlined by the government to achieve this include:

- Designating or creating specific authorities or "actors" to implement the SDGs at the national, state and district levels
- Ensuring smooth coordination between each level of implementation
- Raising awareness about the SDGs among all stakeholders, and creating objective measures—such as the "SDG India Index"—to assess progress
- A data-driven approach to planning and decision-making
- Periodic national and local reviews to assess achievements and challenges

Such measures, if adopted uniformly, would ensure that SDG-related programmes function in a coordinated manner across the country. Significant advances have been made in the field of data collection and accountability as well. The "SDG India Index" reports, published by NITI Aayog, have already gone through four editions (2018, 2019–20, 2020–21 and 2023–24) and outline progress towards each SDG, based on 70 targets and 113 indicators, for each state as well as for the whole country (NITI Aayog, 2024). This information is of vital importance in identifying which states are performing better or worse than average on specific SDGs, and in tracking achievements over time.

As of its last publication, the SDG India Index includes only one specific mental health target—reduction of the suicide rate by one-third by the year 2030—and only one mental health measure, the national suicide rate. By including other relevant indices of mental health, a better measure of the effects of each SDG-related scheme on mental health could be obtained. Examples of relevant indices that could be incorporated into the SDG India Index in future include state-wise and national prevalence of common mental disorders, rates of cognitive dysfunction or dementia in the elderly, participation of each state's schools in positive mental health initiatives (e.g., life skills) and the availability and service utilization of counsellors in schools, workplaces and One Stop Centres for women.

The data-driven approach mentioned above could also serve as a basis for examining the relationships between mental and physical health and performance on other SDG India Index components across states. Such analyses are of particular value in optimizing the performance of specific programmes and ensuring that all Indian citizens benefit from them. For example, the effects of a programme such as the Swachh Bharat Mission on rates of sexual violence or harassment against women or girls, and on the adverse mental health effects of such violence, could be examined by linking data on SBM coverage to reported rates of such offences. Similarly, data from this programme could be correlated with statistics on child growth, nutritional status and school performance to examine the beneficial effects of sanitation on child neurodevelopment in the Indian context (Behera et al., 2021).

A further step that would need to be taken in future is to ensure that the programmes described in Sect. 3 interact with each other meaningfully. As each of these programmes is under the supervision of a different ministry or department, there is always the risk that they may run more or less independently, leading either to duplication of work or to gaps in essential services. A key task of central coordinating agencies, such as NITI Aayog, would be to ensure that those in charge of each initiative are able to meet regularly, to exchange views, to review data on the relative progress of each programme and to identify areas where collaboration would be particularly fruitful or effective. For example, experts from the Ministries of Human Resource Development (in charge of the NEP) and Social Justice and Empowerment (in charge of the NMBA) could work together on planning and implementing awareness and life skills campaigns aimed at preventing alcohol or drug abuse among school and college students, and the Ministry of Health and Family Welfare could also be involved in providing early diagnostic and treatment camps for youth who have experimented with substances. Such collaboration would involve not just government officials, but all relevant stakeholders—in this case, teachers, school counsellors, parents, community leaders and even student volunteers. An example of how such a coordinated effort could be carried out in India, with reference to early child health and development, has been outlined by Agarwal et al. (2021).

5.2 *Mental Health Initiatives*

Achieving the SDGs in the Indian context is not the sole responsibility of the national or state governments. The involvement of non-governmental agencies, community volunteers and groups and experts from various disciplines is essential if these programmes are to make a difference both to each SDG and to mental health (Schneider et al., 2019). From a research perspective, it is important that Indian mental health professionals are aware of the SDGs and their relevance to mental health and illness, so that they can undertake locally relevant research projects in this area. This would also involve incorporating elements of social and environmental psychology and psychiatry, with a specific focus on sustainable development, in the curriculum for trainee mental health professionals. Public and private funding could also be mobilized to encourage Indian researchers to work in this largely uncharted field (Madill et al., 2022).

From the point of view of practice, the "top-down" initiatives launched by the Indian government need to be complemented by "bottom-up" interventions aimed at integrating mental health with other SDGs such as nutrition, women's empowerment, education and employment (Mathias et al., 2018b). Examples of such interventions, which are either being tested or have already proved effective in Indian settings, include:

- Affordable and child-friendly daycare programmes for low-income working mothers in rural Indian communities, with the aim of improving women's mental health and economic security while supporting child nutrition and development (Nandi et al., 2016).
- Counselling interventions for women seeking gynaecological and obstetric care, focused on the relationship between psychosocial circumstances, mental health and sexual and reproductive health, with the aim of providing integrated care that could address several SDGs related to woman and child health (Maitra et al., 2015).
- Problem-solving interventions for school-going adolescents in low-income settings, which could identify and treat common mental disorders and substance use disorders, teach relevant life skills, promote SDG-positive attitudes (e.g., towards women's empowerment or responsible consumption) and prevent students from dropping out of school and facing disadvantages in the job marker (Malik et al., 2021; Yatirajula et al., 2022).
- Community-based, volunteer-driven programmes aimed at providing nutritional support and psychological support to girls in rural areas, with the aim of preventing anaemia, identifying and treating common mental disorders and encouraging school attendance (Bhatia et al., 2022). Such an initiative could also have "intergenerational" effects on child health, nutrition and brain development, as discussed in Sect. 2.5.

Such interventions could receive initial, time-limited support from relevant government schemes, or from the private sector under corporate social responsibility schemes, to ensure their viability, before transitioning to more a community-supported model (Gupta et al., 2021). This would be an example of a "partnership for the goals" (SDG 17) that would be sustainable, acceptable to communities and able to address mental health in conjunction with other SDGs.

Another avenue that merits exploration in this regard is the possibility of drawing upon local values, traditions and customs. For example, traditional health practices that are easily accessible, affordable and "green" could be integrated with existing mental and physical healthcare interventions and programmes (Sharma et al., 2022b). Similarly, traditional Indian values and beliefs regarding virtuous conduct, responsible consumption and respect for the environment could be used to drive positive behavioural changes in individuals and communities (Dayananda Swamy et al., 2021). Such "localizations" of the SDGs require creativity as well as open-mindedness on the part of officials and experts.

Finally, it is important for mental health professionals to engage in interdisciplinary collaborations with experts in social and environmental sciences to achieve a synergy between research agendas in sustainable development and mental health. Examples of research questions that could best be tackled through such an approach are studying the links between specific air or water pollutants and mental health outcomes, or identifying indigenous cultural, dietary or agricultural practices that contribute to both environmental sustainability and psychological resilience.

6 Conclusion

India's adoption of the Sustainable Development Goals, as part of its drive towards Viksit Bharat 2047, has the potential to address a broad spectrum of the social, economic and environmental risk factors for mental disorders. Indian research has established strong associations between several SDG targets or sub-goals and the risk of specific mental disorders or symptoms. India's National Mental Health Policy highlights the need to move beyond a biomedical model and address the social roots of mental disorders. Several recent government initiatives provide fruitful opportunities for the integration of individual and community mental health with broader goals related to nutrition, education, economic empowerment, inclusiveness, environmental sustainability and healthcare in general. Despite certain challenges and shortcomings that must be acknowledged and addressed openly, there is reason to be optimistic that the coming decades will see a better understanding of these issues among policymakers and professionals, and a greater level of synergy between mental health promotion and human development in Indian communities.

References

Acharya, B., Ekstrand, M., Rimal, P., Ali, M. K., Swar, S., Srinivasan, K., Mohan, V., Unützer, J., & Chwastiak, L. A. (2017). Collaborative care for mental health in low- and middle-income countries: A WHO health systems framework assessment of three programs. *Psychiatric Services (Washington, D.C.)*, *68*(9), 870–872. https://doi.org/10.1176/appi.ps.201700232

Adelman, S. (2018). The sustainable development goals, anthropocentrism and neoliberalism. In D. French & L. J. Kotze (Eds.), *Sustainable development goals: Law, theory and implementation* (pp. 15–40). Edward Elgar. https://doi.org/10.4337/9781786438768

Adlakha, D., Chandra, M., Krishna, M., Smith, L., & Tully, M. A. (2021). Designing age-friendly communities: Exploring qualitative perspectives on urban green spaces and ageing in two Indian megacities. *International Journal of Environmental Research and Public Health, 18*(4), 1491. https://doi.org/10.3390/ijerph18041491

Agarwal, D., Patil, B., Kapoor, D., & Chaudhary, P. (2021). Intersectoral action for early childhood development in India: Opportunities, challenges and the way forward. *Indian Paediatrics, 58*(S1), S28–S31.

Ahamad, V., Akhtar, S., Pal, S. K., & Bhagat, R. B. (2025). How migration and its types affect mental health in later life: A cross-sectional study among the older adults in India. *BMC Psychiatry, 25*(1), 446. https://doi.org/10.1186/s12888-025-06891-4

Ahlawat, P., Singh, M. M., Garg, S., & Mala, Y. M. (2019). Prevalence of depression and its association with sociodemographic factors in postmenopausal women in an urban resettlement colony of Delhi. *Journal of mid-Life Health, 10*(1), 33–36. https://doi.org/10.4103/jmh.JMH_66_18

Alon, N., Macrynikola, N., Jester, D. J., Keshavan, M., Reynolds, C. F., 3rd., Saxena, S., Thomas, M. L., Torous, J., & Jeste, D. V. (2024). Social determinants of mental health in major depressive disorder: Umbrella review of 26 meta-analyses and systematic reviews. *Psychiatry Research, 335*, Article 115854. https://doi.org/10.1016/j.psychres.2024.115854

Amin, S., & Khan, A. W. (2009). Life in conflict: Characteristics of depression in Kashmir. *International Journal of Health Sciences, 3*(2), 213–223.

Amipara, T., Baria, H., & Nayak, S. (2020). A study on postpartum depression and its association with infant feeding practices and infant nutritional status among mothers attending the Anganwadi Centers of Valsad District, Gujarat, India. *Indian Journal of Community Medicine : Official Publication of Indian Association of Preventive & Social Medicine, 45*(3), 299–302. https://doi.org/10.4103/ijcm.IJCM_171_19

Amiri, S. (2022). Unemployment associated with major depression disorder and depressive symptoms: A systematic review and meta-analysis. *International Journal of Occupational Safety and Ergonomics : JOSE, 28*(4), 2080–2092. https://doi.org/10.1080/10803548.2021.1954793

Aneja, R., & Ahuja, V. (2021). An assessment of socioeconomic impact of COVID-19 pandemic in India. *Journal of Public Affairs, 21*(2), Article e2266. https://doi.org/10.1002/pa.2266

Angrisani, M., Nichols, E., Meijer, E., Gross, A. L., Ehrlich, J. R., Varghese, M., Langa, K. M., Dey, A. B., Adar, S. D., & Lee, J. (2024). Modifiable risk factors for dementia in India: A cross-sectional study revisiting estimates and reassessing prevention potential and priorities. *BMJ Public Health, 2*(2), Article e001362. https://doi.org/10.1136/bmjph-2024-001362

Anitha, G. F. S., & Narasimhan, U. (2021). Seeing the National Education Policy 2020 through the lens of early child development. *Industrial Psychiatry Journal, 30*(1), 182–186. https://doi.org/10.4103/ipj.ipj_158_20

Ansari, E., & Kar, S. K. (2024). Mental health amid climate crisis: A narrative review. *Indian Journal of Psychiatry, 66*(11), 987–996. https://doi.org/10.4103/indianjpsychiatry.indianjpsychiatry_526_24

Anuradha, R., Dutta, R., Raja, J. D., Lawrence, D., Timsi, J., & Sivaprakasam, P. (2017). Role of community in Swachh Bharat Mission. Their knowledge, attitude and practices of sanitary latrine usage in rural areas, Tamil Nadu. *Indian Journal of Community Medicine: Official Publication of Indian Association of Preventive & Social Medicine, 42*(2), 107–110. https://doi.org/10.4103/0970-0218.205213

Anwar, N., Kuppili, P. P., & Balhara, Y. P. S. (2017). Depression and physical noncommunicable diseases: The need for an integrated approach. *WHO South-East Asia Journal of Public Health, 6*(1), 12–17. https://doi.org/10.4103/2224-3151.206158

Arora, N. K., Nair, M. K. C., Gulati, S., Deshmukh, V., Mohapatra, A., Mishra, D., Patel, V., Pandey, R. M., Das, B. C., Divan, G., Murthy, G. V. S., Sharma, T. D., Sapra, S., Aneja, S., Juneja, M., Reddy, S. K., Suman, P., Mukherjee, S. B., Dasgupta, R., Tudu, P., & Vajaratkar, V. (2018). Neurodevelopmental disorders in children aged 2–9 years: Population-based burden estimates across five regions in India. *PLoS Medicine, 15*(7), e1002615. https://doi.org/10.1371/journal.pmed.1002615

Arora, N. K., & Mishra, I. (2022). Current scenario and future directions for sustainable development goal 2: A roadmap to zero hunger. *Environmental Sustainability (Singapore), 5*(2), 129–133. https://doi.org/10.1007/s42398-022-00235-8

Arun, P., Chavan, B. S., Bhargava, R., Sharma, A., & Kaur, J. (2013). Prevalence of specific developmental disorder of scholastic skill in school students in Chandigarh, India. *The Indian Journal of Medical Research, 138*(1), 89–98.

Atal, S., & Foster, J. (2021). A woman's life is tension": A gendered analysis of women's distress in poor urban India. *Transcultural Psychiatry, 58*(3), 404–413. https://doi.org/10.1177/1363461520947836

Balakrishnan, U., & Tsaneva, M. (2023). Impact of air pollution on mental health in India. *The Journal of Development Studies, 59*(1), 133–147. https://doi.org/10.1080/00220388.2022.2120804

Bashir, A., Khurshid, S., Altaf, M., Bhatia, T., Singh, R., & Shoib, S. (2022). Assessment of anxiety and depression among adult population of Kashmir, India: A cross-sectional study. *Journal of Clinical and Diagnostic Research: JCDR, 16*(7), 25–29. https://doi.org/10.7860/jcdr/2022/53746.16649

Bau, N., Khanna, G., Low, C., Shah, M., Sharmin, S., & Voena, A. (2022). Women's well-being during a pandemic and its containment. *Journal of Development Economics, 156*, Article 102839. https://doi.org/10.1016/j.jdeveco.2022.102839

Baum, F., Anaf, J., Freeman, T., Musolino, C., van den Berg, M., Friel, S., & Schram, A. (2025). Twenty-first century alienation and health: A research agenda. *Journal of Epidemiology and Ccommunity Health, 79*(7), 481–483. https://doi.org/10.1136/jech-2024-223112

Begum, J., Sain, Y., Ali, S. I., & Lalitha, D. L. (2024). Public health benefits and challenges under the scheme "Swachh Bharat Abhiyan." *Indian Journal of Public Health, 68*(4), 580–581. https://doi.org/10.4103/ijph.ijph_744_23

Behera, M. R., Pradhan, H. S., Behera, D., Jena, D., & Satpathy, S. K. (2021). Achievements and challenges of India's sanitation campaign under clean India mission: A commentary. *Journal of Education and Health Promotion, 10*, 350. https://doi.org/10.4103/jehp.jehp_1658_20

Belkić, K., & Rustagi, N. (2024). Job stressors in relation to burnout and compromised sleep among academic physicians in India. *Work (Reading, Mass.), 78*(2), 505–525. https://doi.org/10.3233/WOR-230383

Bhatia, K., Rath, S., Pradhan, H., Samal, S., Copas, A., Gagrai, S., Rath, S., Gope, R. K., Nair, N., Tripathy, P., Rose-Clarke, K., & Prost, A. (2022). Effects of community youth teams facilitating participatory adolescent groups, youth leadership activities and livelihood promotion to improve school attendance, dietary diversity and mental health among adolescent girls in rural eastern India (JIAH trial): A cluster-randomised controlled trial. *SSM - Population Health, 21*, Article 101330. https://doi.org/10.1016/j.ssmph.2022.101330

Biswas, M. M., Das, K. C., & Sheikh, I. (2024). Psychological implications of unemployment among higher educated migrant youth in Kolkata City, India. *Scientific Reports, 14*(1), 10171. https://doi.org/10.1038/s41598-024-60958-y

Butler, C. D. (2025). Eco-anxiety, climate change and the 'bottom billion': A plea for better understanding. *BMJ Mental Health, 28*(1), Article e301380. https://doi.org/10.1136/bmjment-2024-301380

Caruso, B. A., Cooper, H. L. F., Haardörfer, R., Yount, K. M., Routray, P., Torondel, B., & Clasen, T. (2018). The association between women's sanitation experiences and mental health: A cross-sectional study in Rural, Odisha India. *SSM - Population Health, 5*, 257–266. https://doi.org/10.1016/j.ssmph.2018.06.005

Chandra, P. S., Shiva, L., & Nanjundaswamy, M. H. (2018). The impact of urbanization on mental health in India. *Current Opinion in Psychiatry, 31*(3), 276–281. https://doi.org/10.1097/YCO.0000000000000408

Chandra, P. S., Bajaj, A., Desai, G., Satyanarayana, V. A., Sharp, H. M., Ganjekar, S., Supraja, T. A., Jangam, K. V., Venkatram, L., & Kandavel, T. (2021). Anxiety and depressive symptoms in pregnancy predict low birth weight differentially in male and female infants-findings from an urban pregnancy cohort in India. *Social Psychiatry and Psychiatric Epidemiology, 56*(12), 2263–2274. https://doi.org/10.1007/s00127-021-02106-9

Chatterji, S., McDougal, L., Johns, N., Ghule, M., Rao, N., & Raj, A. (2021). COVID-19-related financial hardship, job loss, and mental health symptoms: Findings from a cross-sectional study in a rural agrarian community in India. *International Journal of Environmental Research and Public Health, 18*(16), 8647. https://doi.org/10.3390/ijerph18168647

Chattopadhyay, S. (2007). Religion, spirituality, health and medicine: Why should Indian physicians care? *Journal of Postgraduate Medicine, 53*(4), 262–266. https://doi.org/10.4103/0022-3859.33967

Chavan, R. G., Kaur, J., & Charan, G. S. (2024). Unseen crisis: Revealing the hidden health impact of indoor air pollution-A scoping review. *Journal of Education and Health Promotion, 13*, 410. https://doi.org/10.4103/jehp.jehp_412_24

Chawla, G. K., Juyal, R., Shikha, D., Semwal, J., Tripathi, S., & Bhattacharya, S. (2022). Attention deficit hyperactivity disorder and associated learning difficulties among primary school children in district Dehradun, Uttarakhand, India. *Journal of Education and Health Promotion, 11*, 98. https://doi.org/10.4103/jehp.jehp_922_21

Cheng, H. G., Shidhaye, R., Charlson, F., Deng, F., Lyngdoh, T., Chen, S., Nanda, S., Lacroix, K., Baxter, A., & Whiteford, H. (2016). Social correlates of mental, neurological, and substance use disorders in China and India: A review. *The Lancet. Psychiatry, 3*(9), 882–899. https://doi.org/10.1016/S2215-0366(16)30166-3

Choudhary, N., SturtzSreetharan, C., Trainer, S., Brewis, A., Wutich, A., Clancy, K., Fatima, U. A., & Jobayer Hossain, M. (2023). Managing menstruation with dignity: Worries, stress and mental health in two water-scarce urban communities in India. *Global Public Health, 18*(1), 2233996. https://doi.org/10.1080/17441692.2023.2233996

Cianconi, P., Betrò, S., & Janiri, L. (2020). The impact of climate change on mental health: A systematic descriptive review. *Frontiers in Psychiatry, 11*, 74. https://doi.org/10.3389/fpsyt.2020.00074

Collins, T. E., Karapici, A., & Berlina, D. (2025). Investing in addressing NCDs and mental health conditions: A political choice. *Annals of Global Health, 91*(1), 22. https://doi.org/10.5334/aogh.4649

Cunningham, G. B., Wicker, P., & McCullough, B. P. (2020). Pollution, health, and the moderating role of physical activity opportunities. *International Journal of Environmental Research and Public Health, 17*(17), 6272. https://doi.org/10.3390/ijerph17176272

Dar, A. A., & Deb, S. (2022). Prevalence of trauma among young adults exposed to stressful events of armed conflicts in South Asia: Experiences from Kashmir. *Psychological Trauma : Theory, Research, Practice and Policy, 14*(4), 633–641. https://doi.org/10.1037/tra0001045

Das, A. (2011). Farmers' suicide in India: Implications for public mental health. *The International Journal of Social Psychiatry, 57*(1), 21–29. https://doi.org/10.1177/0020764009103645

Das, S. K., Burma, A. D., Amudhan, S., Mishra, V., Mahapatra, P., Ashok, A., & Philip, M. (2022a). Do children in India grow well into adolescents? Longitudinal analysis of growth transitions from Young Lives panel survey in India. *Public Health, 202*, 18–25. https://doi.org/10.1016/j.puhe.2021.10.010

Das, S., Malathesh, B. C., & Manjunatha, N. (2022b). India's NITI Aayog's health index: Where Is the mental health? *Indian Journal of Psychological Medicine, 44*(6), 604–606. https://doi.org/10.1177/02537176211057411

Dayananda Swamy, H. R., Nagarajan, K., & Babu, N. (2021). Yogic principles of *Artha* and *Dāna* with reference to individual and corporate social responsibility. *International Journal of Yoga, 14*(3), 248–255. https://doi.org/10.4103/ijoy.ijoy_106_21

Dasgupta, A., Sarkar, K. D., & Das, A. (2024). An Epidemiological study on magnitude of selected components of metabolic syndrome and its risk factors among first-year MBBS students. *The Journal of the Association of Physicians of India, 72*(12), 14–17. https://doi.org/10.59556/japi.72.0768

Department of Economic Analysis and Research, National Bank for Agriculture and Rural Development. (2022). Food and nutritional security in India: charting the way to a robust agri-food system. India: National Bank for Agriculture and Rural Development, November 2022.

Available online at: https://www.nabard.org/Hindi/auth/writereaddata/tender/2501230128nrs-35-food-and-nutritional-security-in-india.pdf

Devassy, S. M., Webber, M., Scaria, L., Amuthavalli Thiyagarajan, J., Fendt-Newlin, M., Joubert, J., Benny, A. M., Nannatt, A., & Joubert, L. (2020). Social and behavioural risk factors in the prevention and management of cardiovascular disease in Kerala, India: A catchment area population survey. *BMC Cardiovascular Disorders, 20*(1), 327. https://doi.org/10.1186/s12872-020-01595-x

Dewi, S. P., Kasim, R., Sutarsa, I. N., & Dykgraaf, S. H. (2024). A scoping review of the impact of extreme weather events on health outcomes and healthcare utilization in rural and remote areas. *BMC Health Services Research, 24*(1), 1333. https://doi.org/10.1186/s12913-024-11695-5

Dhanalakshmi, V., Kulkarni, V., John, R. M., Nadella, K., & Kundapur, R. (2024). Cognitive impairment and its associated determinants among the elderly population of Telangana, India: An analytical prevalence study. *Cureus, 16*(6), Article e61535. https://doi.org/10.7759/cureus.61535

Dhimal, M., Bhandari, D., Dhimal, M. L., Kafle, N., Pyakurel, P., Mahotra, N., Akhtar, S., Ismail, T., Dhiman, R. C., Groneberg, D. A., Shrestha, U. B., & Müller, R. (2021). Impact of climate change on health and well-being of people in Hindu Kush Himalayan region: A narrative review. *Frontiers in Physiology, 12*, Article 651189. https://doi.org/10.3389/fphys.2021.651189

Dhivar, N. R., Gandhi, R., Murugan, Y., & Vora, H. (2024). Outcomes and morbidities in low-birth-weight neonates: A retrospective study from western India. *Cureus, 16*(6), e61981. https://doi.org/10.7759/cureus.61981

Dougall, I., Vasiljevic, M., Wright, J. D., & Weick, M. (2024). How, when, and why is social class linked to mental health and wellbeing? A systematic meta-review. *Social Science & Medicine (1982), 343*, 116542. https://doi.org/10.1016/j.socscimed.2023.116542

Duggal, C., Ray, S., Konantambigi, R., & Kothari, A. (2022). The nowhere people: Lived experiences of migrant workers during Covid-19 in India. *Current Psychology (New Brunswick, N.J.), 41*(11), 8214–8223. https://doi.org/10.1007/s12144-021-02220-6

Eashwar, V. M. A., Gopalakrishnan, S., Umadevi, R., & Geetha, A. (2019). Pattern of alcohol consumption and its associated morbidity among alcohol consumers in an urban area of Tamil Nadu. *Journal of Family Medicine and Primary Care, 8*(6), 2029–2035. https://doi.org/10.4103/jfmpc.jfmpc_226_19

Faizi, N., Azmi, S. A., Ahmad, A., & Shah, M. S. (2016). Assessment of psychological problems in schoolgoing adolescents of Aligarh. *Industrial Psychiatry Journal, 25*(2), 184–188. https://doi.org/10.4103/ipj.ipj_65_14

Gailits, N., Mathias, K., Nouvet, E., Pillai, P., & Schwartz, L. (2019). Women's freedom of movement and participation in psychosocial support groups: Qualitative study in northern India. *BMC Public Health, 19*(1), 725. https://doi.org/10.1186/s12889-019-7019-3

Ganguli, M., Dube, S., Johnston, J. M., Pandav, R., Chandra, V., & Dodge, H. H. (1999). Depressive symptoms, cognitive impairment and functional impairment in a rural elderly population in India: A Hindi version of the geriatric depression scale (GDS-H). *International Journal of Geriatric Psychiatry, 14*(10), 807–820.

Ganpule, A., Brown, K. A., Dubey, M., Srinivasapura Venkateshmurthy, N., Jarhyan, P., Maddury, A. P., Khatkar, R., Pandey, H., Prabhakaran, D., & Mohan, S. (2023). Food insecurity and its determinants among adults in North and South India. *Nutrition Journal, 22*(1), 2. https://doi.org/10.1186/s12937-022-00831-8

Garg, S., & Anand, T. (2015). Menstruation related myths in India: Strategies for combating it. *Journal of Family Medicine and Primary Care, 4*(2), 184–186. https://doi.org/10.4103/2249-4863.154627

Gautham, M. S., Gururaj, G., Varghese, M., Benegal, V., Rao, G. N., Kokane, A., Chavan, B. S., Dalal, P. K., Ram, D., Pathak, K., Lenin Singh, R. K., Singh, L. K., Sharma, P., Saha, P. K., Ramasubramanian, C., Mehta, R. Y., Shibukumar, T. M., & NMHS Collaborators Group. (2020). The National Mental Health Survey of India (2016): Prevalence, socio-demographic correlates and treatment gap of mental morbidity. *The International Journal of Social Psychiatry, 66*(4), 361–372. https://doi.org/10.1177/0020764020907941

Gawde, N., Nasirabadi, M., Shah, N., & Nagaonkar, S. (2013). Psychiatric morbidity in an urban slum of Mumbai: Cross sectional study. *Asian Journal of Psychiatry, 6*, 478–482. https://doi.org/10.1016/j.ajp.2013.05.005

George, S., & Kumar, P. P. A. (2022). Indicator-based assessment of capacity development for disaster preparedness in the Indian context. *Environment Systems & Decisions, 42*(3), 417–435. https://doi.org/10.1007/s10669-022-09856-0

Ghosh, A., & Goswami, S. (2011). Evaluation of post partum depression in a tertiary hospital. *Journal of Obstetrics and Gynaecology of India, 61*(5), 528. https://doi.org/10.1007/s13224-011-0077-9

Gilani, T. A., & Mir, M. S. (2022). A study on road traffic noise exposure and prevalence of insomnia. *Environmental Science and Pollution Research International, 29*(27), 41065–41080. https://doi.org/10.1007/s11356-021-18291-8

Global Sustainable Development Report 2023. (2023). Times of crisis, times of change: Science for accelerating transformations to sustainable development. Available online at: https://sdgs.un.org/gsdr/gsdr2023

Gluckman, P. D., Low, F. M., & Hanson, M. A. (2020). Anthropocene-related disease: The inevitable outcome of progressive niche modification? *Evolution, Medicine, and Public Health, 2020*(1), 304–310. https://doi.org/10.1093/emph/eoaa042

Gold-Watts, A., Hovdenak, M., Daniel, M., Gandhimathi, S., Sudha, R., & Bastien, S. (2020). A qualitative study of adolescent girls' experiences of menarche and menstruation in rural Tamil Nadu, India. *International Journal of Qualitative Studies on Health and Well-Being, 15*(1), 1845924. https://doi.org/10.1080/17482631.2020.1845924

Golombek, D. A., Eyre, H., Spiousas, I., Casiraghi, L. P., Hartikainen, K. M., Partonen, T., Pyykkö, M., Reynolds, C. F., 3rd., Hynes, W. M., Bassetti, C. L. A., Berk, M., Hu, K., & Ibañez, A. (2025). Sleep Capital: Linking brain health to wellbeing and economic productivity across the lifespan. *The American Journal of Geriatric Psychiatry: Official Journal of the American Association for Geriatric Psychiatry, 33*(1), 92–106. https://doi.org/10.1016/j.jagp.2024.07.011

Gopalakrishnan, L., El Ayadi, A., & Diamond-Smith, N. (2024). The role of community-level men's and women's inequitable gender norms on women's empowerment in India: A multilevel analysis using India's National Family Health Survey-5. *PLoS ONE, 19*(12), Article e0312465. https://doi.org/10.1371/journal.pone.0312465

Gupta, B., & Mukhopadhyay, A. (2014). ESID Working Paper No. 42. Local funds and political competition: Evidence from the National Rural Employment Guarantee Scheme in India. Available online at: https://papers.ssrn.com/sol3/Delivery.cfm?abstractid=2539169

Gupta, A., & Coffey, D. (2020). Caste, religion, and mental health in India. *Population Research and Policy Review, 39*, 1119–1141. https://doi.org/10.1007/s11113-020-09585-9

Gupta, C., Arora, M., Gupta, R. K., Akhtar, N., Langer, B., Kumari, R., Sharma, P., Majeed, M., & Raina, S. K. (2020). Prevalence and correlates of depression in a rural adult population in Northwest India. *Journal of Family Medicine and Primary Care, 9*(1), 151–155. https://doi.org/10.4103/jfmpc.jfmpc_656_19

Gupta, A., Naved, M. M., Kumbhare, H., Bherwani, H., Das, D., & Labhsetwar, N. (2021). Impact assessment of clean cookstove intervention in Gujarat, India: A potential case for corporate social responsibility (CSR) funding. *Environmental Science and Pollution Research International, 28*(10), 12740–12752. https://doi.org/10.1007/s11356-020-11011-8

Gupta, S., Das, S., Das, M., Banerjee, S., Neogi, R., & Mukherjee, S. (2023). Prevalence and correlates of depression, anxiety, and stress among high school students in a block of Hooghly district, West Bengal: Across-sectional study. *Journal of Education and Health Promotion, 12*, 345. https://doi.org/10.4103/jehp.jehp_1769_22

Guru, A., Manjukashika, K. R., Anand, A., Dorairajan, S., Manisha, C. H., Lakshmi, J., T, S. I., P P, K., Daniel, S. J., Menon, J., R, M., & Raghavan, V. (2025). Examining the employment related factors among persons with mental illness: Findings from a cross-sectional study in Chennai,

South India. *Asian Journal of Psychiatry, 108*, 104495. Advance online publication. https://doi.org/10.1016/j.ajp.2025.104495

Gururaj, G., Varghese, M., Benegal, V., Rao, G. N., Pathak, K., Singh, L. K., Mehta, R. Y., Ram, D., Shibukumar, T. M., Kokane, A., Lenin Singh, R. K., Chavan, B. S., Sharma, P., & NMHS Collaborators Group. (2016). National Mental Health Survey of India, 2015–16: Prevalence, patterns and outcomes. Bengaluru, National Institute of Mental Health and Neuro Sciences, NIMHANS Publication No. 129, 2016.

Gururaj, G., Isaac, M. K., Subbakrishna, D. K., & Ranjani, R. (2004). Risk factors for completed suicides: A case-control study from Bangalore, India. *Injury Control and Safety Promotion, 11*(3), 183–191. https://doi.org/10.1080/156609704/233/289706

Hasan, M. S., & Ghosal, S. (2024). Unveiling the mechanism(s) between poverty, deprivation, and depression in older Indian adults: Findings from a nationwide survey. *Journal of Aging and Health*, 8982643241280529. Advance online publication. https://doi.org/10.1177/08982643241280529

Haustein, J., & Tomalin, E. (2021). Religion, populism, and the politics of the sustainable development goals. *Social Policy & Society, 20*(2), 296–309. https://doi.org/10.1017/S147474642000072X

Hepat, A., Khode, D., & Chakole, S. (2024). A narrative review of urbanization and mental health: An Indian perspective. *Cureus, 16*(3), Article e55381. https://doi.org/10.7759/cureus.55381

Hickman, C., Marks, E., Pihkala, P., Clayton, S., Lewandowski, R. E., Mayall, E. E., Wray, B., Mellor, C., & van Susteren, L. (2021). Climate anxiety in children and young people and their beliefs about government responses to climate change: A global survey. *The Lancet. Planetary Health, 5*(12), e863–e873. https://doi.org/10.1016/S2542-5196(21)00278-3

Himmelgreen, D., Romero-Daza, N., Heuer, J., Lucas, W., Salinas-Miranda, A. A., & Stoddard, T. (2022). Using syndemic theory to understand food insecurity and diet-related chronic diseases. *Social Science & Medicine (1982), 295*, 113124. https://doi.org/10.1016/j.socscimed.2020.113124

Hou, J., Deng, Q., Sha, L., Zhu, J., Xiang, R., Zhao, X., Xiao, C., Qin, C., Qu, Y., Han, T., Song, X., Yang, B., Yu, T., Zhou, J., Zheng, S., Fan, M., Yan, P., & Jiang, X. (2025). Physical activity and risk of depression in adolescents: A systematic review and meta-analysis of prospective observational studies. *Journal of Affective Disorders, 371*, 279–288. https://doi.org/10.1016/j.jad.2024.11.065

Huq, M., Das, T., Devakumar, D., Daruwalla, N., & Osrin, D. (2021). Intersectional tension: A qualitative study of the effects of the COVID-19 response on survivors of violence against women in urban India. *British Medical Journal Open, 11*(9), Article e050381. https://doi.org/10.1136/bmjopen-2021-050381

Iaisuklang, M. G., & Ali, A. (2017). Psychiatric morbidity among female commercial sex workers. *Indian Journal of Psychiatry, 59*(4), 465–470. https://doi.org/10.4103/psychiatry.IndianJPsychiatry_147_16

Indian Council of Medical Research & National Centre for Disease Informatics and Research. (2018). National noncommunicable disease monitoring survey: Factsheet. Available online at: https://web.archive.org/web/20210813080359/, https://www.ncdirindia.org/nnms/resources/Factsheet.pdf

International Institute for Population Sciences & United Nations Population Fund. (2023). India ageing report 2023, caring for our elders: Institutional responses. United Nations Population Fund, New Delhi.

Iorfa, S. K., Effiong, J. E., Apejoye, A., Johri, T., Isaiah, U. S., Eche, G. O., & Ottu, I. F. A. (2022). Silent screams: Listening to and making meaning from the voices of abused children. *Child: Care, Health and Development, 48*(5), 702–707. https://doi.org/10.1111/cch.12975

Iyer, G. K., Alladi, S., Bak, T. H., Shailaja, M., Mamidipudi, A., Rajan, A., Gollahalli, D., Chaudhuri, J. R., & Kaul, S. (2014). Dementia in developing countries: Does education play the same role in India as in the West? *Dementia & Neuropsychologia, 8*(2), 132–140. https://doi.org/10.1590/S1980-57642014DN82000008

Jacob, J. (2024). A background history of the sustainable development goals. *Sustainable Development,* 3317. Advance online publication. https://doi.org/10.1002/sd.3317

Jain, R. K., & Aras, R. Y. (2007). Depression in geriatric population in urban slums of Mumbai. *Indian Journal of Public Health, 51*(2), 112–113.

Jain, A., Kumar, A., Kim, R., & Subramanian, S. V. (2023). Prevalence of zero-sanitation in India: Patterns of change across the states and Union Territories, 1993–2021. *Journal of Global Health, 13*, 04082. https://doi.org/10.7189/jogh.13.04082

Jani, K., Bandal, J., Shouche, Y., Shafi, S., Azhar, E. I., Zumla, A., & Sharma, A. (2021). Extended ecological restoration of bacterial communities in the Godavari River during the COVID-19 lockdown period: A spatiotemporal meta-analysis. *Microbial Ecology, 82*(2), 365–376. https://doi.org/10.1007/s00248-021-01781-0

Jayashree, K., Mithra, P. P., Nair, M. K. C., Unnikrishnan, B., & Pai, K. (2018). Depression and anxiety disorders among schoolgoing adolescents in an urban area of South India. *Indian Journal of Community Medicine: Official Publication of Indian Association of Preventive & Social Medicine, 43*(Suppl 1), S28–S32. https://doi.org/10.4103/ijcm.IJCM_209_18

Ji, X., Liu, R., Guo, J., Li, Y., Cheng, W., Pang, Y., Zheng, Y., Zhang, R., & Tang, J. (2022). Olfactory bulb microglia activation mediated neuronal death in real-ambient particulate matter exposure mice with depression-like behaviors. *The Science of the Total Environment, 821*, Article 153456. https://doi.org/10.1016/j.scitotenv.2022.153456

Jin, Y., Zhou, X., Deng, L., Xiong, X., Li, Y., Wei, Q., Dong, B., & Qiu, S. (2022). Association between the domestic use of solid cooking fuel and increased prevalence of depression and cognitive impairment in a big developing country: A large-scale population-based study. *Frontiers in Public Health, 10*, 1038573. https://doi.org/10.3389/fpubh.2022.1038573

Jose, A. (2019). India's regional disparity and its policy responses. *Journal of Public Affairs, 19*, Article e1933. https://doi.org/10.1002/pa.1933

Jose, J. P., & Cherayi, S. J. (2020). Effect of parental alcohol abuse severity and child abuse and neglect on child behavioural disorders in Kerala. *Child Abuse & Neglect, 107*, Article 104608. https://doi.org/10.1016/j.chiabu.2020.104608

Kabir, R., Bai, A. C. M., Syed, H. Z., Hasan, M. R., Vinnakota, D., Kar, S. K., Singh, R., Sathian, B., & Arafat, S. M. Y. (2023). The effect of COVID-19 on the mental health of the people in the Indian subcontinent: A scoping review. *Nepal Journal of Epidemiology, 13*(2), 1268–1284. https://doi.org/10.3126/nje.v13i2.52766

Kalawapudi, K., Singh, T., Dey, J., Vijay, R., & Kumar, R. (2020). Noise pollution in Mumbai Metropolitan Region (MMR): An emerging environmental threat. *Environmental Monitoring and Assessment, 192*(2), 152. https://doi.org/10.1007/s10661-020-8121-9

Kallakuri, S., Devarapalli, S., Tripathi, A. P., Patel, A., & Maulik, P. K. (2018). Common mental disorders and risk factors in rural India: Baseline data from the SMART mental health project. *BJPsych Open, 4*(4), 192–198. https://doi.org/10.1192/bjo.2018.28

Kang, E., Delzell, D. A., McNamara, P. E., Cuffey, J., Cherian, A., & Matthew, S. (2016). Poverty indicators and mental health functioning among adults living with HIV in Delhi, India. *AIDS Care, 28*(4), 416–422. https://doi.org/10.1080/09540121.2015.1099604

Kanougiya, S., Daruwalla, N., & Osrin, D. (2024). Mental health on two continua: Mental wellbeing and common mental disorders in a community-based cross-sectional study with women in urban informal settlements in India. *BMC Women's Health, 24*(1), 555. https://doi.org/10.1186/s12905-024-03389-1

Kar, N., Krishnaraaj, R., & Rameshraj, K. (2013). Long-term mental health outcomes following the 2004 Asian tsunami disaster: A comparative study on direct and indirect exposure. *Disaster Health, 2*(1), 35–45. https://doi.org/10.4161/dish.24705

Kar, S. K., Naskar, C., Marthoenis, M., Tomer, S., Menon, V., & Arafat, S. M. Y. (2024). Suicide and Socio-demography: An ecological study from India. *Indian Journal of Psychological Medicine*, 02537176241262696. Advance online publication. https://doi.org/10.1177/02537176241262696

Kaur, J., Kaur, J., & Sujata, N. (2015). Comparative study on perceived abuse and social neglect among rural and urban geriatric population. *Indian Journal of Psychiatry, 57*(4), 375–378. https://doi.org/10.4103/0019-5545.171852

Kaur, N., & Byard, R. W. (2021). Prevalence and potential consequences of child labour in India and the possible impact of COVID-19 - a contemporary overview. *Medicine, Science, and the Law, 61*(3), 208–214. https://doi.org/10.1177/0025802421993364

Kavya, R. K., Menon, J. C., Kartha, N., & Rose, B. M. (2025). Non-communicable disease risk factor profile among the fishing community in Ernakulam District of Kerala: A community-based cross-sectional study. *Cureus, 17*(3), Article e80644. https://doi.org/10.7759/cureus.80644

Kazmi, S. S. H., Shukla, J., Tripathi, R. K., & Zaidi, S. Z. H. (2024). Occupational stress among middle-aged professionals in India. *Annals of Neurosciences, 31*(2), 95–104. https://doi.org/10.1177/09727531231184299

Keshari, P., & Shankar, H. (2022). Extent, spectrum, and predictors of cognitive impairment in urban geriatric population in a district of North India. *Indian Journal of Public Health, 66*(4), 504–507. https://doi.org/10.4103/ijph.ijph_1513_21

Khare, S., & Chatterjee, A. (2024). The relationship between urban built environment and happiness in Bhopal, India. *Environment, Development and Sustainability, 26*, 21487–21502. https://doi.org/10.1007/s10668-023-03539-9

Kishan, P. (2020). Yoga and spirituality in mental health: Illness to wellness. *Indian Journal of Psychological Medicine, 42*(5), 411–420. https://doi.org/10.1177/0253717620946995

Komanapalli, V., & Rao, D. (2021). The mental health impact of caste and structural inequalities in higher education in India. *Transcultural Psychiatry, 58*(3), 392–403. https://doi.org/10.1177/1363461520963862

Krishna, C. G., Ramaswamy, S., & Seshadri, S. (2021). Integrating child protection and mental health concerns in the early childhood care and development program in India. *Indian Pediatrics, 58*(6), 576–583.

Krishnamoorthy, Y., Sarveswaran, G., Sivaranjini, K., Sakthivel, M., Majella, M. G., & Kumar, S. G. (2018). Association between indoor air pollution and cognitive impairment among adults in rural Puducherry, South India. *Journal of Neurosciences in Rural Practice, 9*(4), 529–534. https://doi.org/10.4103/jnrp.jnrp_123_18

Krishnamoorthy, Y., & Ganesh, K. (2020). Spatial pattern and determinants of tobacco use among females in India: Evidence from a nationally representative survey. *Nicotine & Tobacco Research: Official Journal of the Society for Research on Nicotine and Tobacco, 22*(12), 2231–2237. https://doi.org/10.1093/ntr/ntaa137

Kulothungan, V., Mascarenhas, L., Das, P., & Mathur, P. (2024). District-level epidemiology and sociodemographic determinants of noncommunicable diseases - results the National Family Health Survey -5 (2019–21). *Diabetes & Metabolic Syndrome, 18*(7), Article 103085. https://doi.org/10.1016/j.dsx.2024.103085

Kumar, M., & Fonagy, P. (2013). Differential effects of exposure to social violence and natural disaster on children's mental health. *Journal of Traumatic Stress, 26*(6), 695–702. https://doi.org/10.1002/jts.21874

Kumar, R., Bhave, A., Bhargava, R., & Agarwal, G. G. (2013). Prevalence and risk factors for neurological disorders in children aged 6 months to 2 years in northern India. *Developmental Medicine and Child Neurology, 55*(4), 348–356. https://doi.org/10.1111/dmcn.12079

Kumar, A., Mahajan, N. P., Sorokhaibam, R., Sunthalia, A., Babu, B. S., Vardhan, S., & Srivastava, A. (2020). National programme on climate change and human health – India, 2019. *Journal of Communicable Diseases, 52*(3), 43–48. https://doi.org/10.24321/0019.5138.202029

Kumar, S., Chauhan, S., Patel, R., Kumar, M., & Simon, D. J. (2023). Urban-rural and gender differential in depressive symptoms among elderly in India. *Dialogues in Health, 2*, Article 100114. https://doi.org/10.1016/j.dialog.2023.100114

Kvestad, I., Taneja, S., Hysing, M., Kumar, T., Bhandari, N., & Strand, T. A. (2015). Diarrhea, stimulation and growth predict neurodevelopment in young North Indian children. *PLoS ONE, 10*(3), Article e0121743. https://doi.org/10.1371/journal.pone.0121743

Lahariya, C., Singhal, S., Gupta, S., & Mishra, A. (2010). Pathway of care among psychiatric patients attending a mental health institution in central India. *Indian Journal of Psychiatry, 52*(4), 333–338. https://doi.org/10.4103/0019-5545.74308

Lakhan, R. (2015). Profile of social, environmental and biological correlates in intellectual disability in a resource-poor setting in India. *Indian Journal of Psychological Medicine, 37*(3), 311–316. https://doi.org/10.4103/0253-7176.162957

Lindberg, L., Hagman, E., Danielsson, P., Marcus, C., & Persson, M. (2020). Anxiety and depression in children and adolescents with obesity: A nationwide study in Sweden. *BMC Medicine, 18*(1), 30. https://doi.org/10.1186/s12916-020-1498-z

Livingston, G., Huntley, J., Liu, K. Y., Costafreda, S. G., Selbæk, G., Alladi, S., Ames, D., Banerjee, S., Burns, A., Brayne, C., Fox, N. C., Ferri, C. P., Gitlin, L. N., Howard, R., Kales, H. C., Kivimäki, M., Larson, E. B., Nakasujja, N., Rockwood, K., Samus, Q., & Mukadam, N. (2024). Dementia prevention, intervention, and care: 2024 report of the Lancet standing commission. *Lancet (London, England), 404*(10452), 572–628. https://doi.org/10.1016/S0140-6736(24)01296-0

Lodha, P., Jahangir, T., Karia, S., DeSousa, A., Appasani, R., & Withers, M. (2022). Perceptions of perinatal depression among low-income mothers and families in Mumbai, India. *Asian Journal of Psychiatry, 71*, Article 103048. https://doi.org/10.1016/j.ajp.2022.103048

Lund, C., Brooke-Sumner, C., Baingana, F., Baron, E. C., Breuer, E., Chandra, P., Haushofer, J., Herrman, H., Jordans, M., Kieling, C., Medina-Mora, M. E., Morgan, E., Omigbodun, O., Tol, W., Patel, V., & Saxena, S. (2018). Social determinants of mental disorders and the sustainable development goals: A systematic review of reviews. *The Lancet. Psychiatry, 5*(4), 357–369. https://doi.org/10.1016/S2215-0366(18)30060-9

Lund, C., Docrat, S., Abdulmalik, J., Alem, A., Fekadu, A., Gureje, O., Gurung, D., Hailemariam, D., Hailemichael, Y., Hanlon, C., Jordans, M. J. D., Kizza, D., Nanda, S., Olayiwola, S., Shidhaye, R., Upadhaya, N., Thornicroft, G., & Chisholm, D. (2019). Household economic costs associated with mental, neurological and substance use disorders: A cross-sectional survey in six low- and middle-income countries. *Bjpsych Open, 5*(3), Article e34. https://doi.org/10.1192/bjo.2019.20

Madill, A., Bhola, P., Colucci, E., Croucher, K., Evans, A., & Graber, R. (2022). How can we mainstream mental health in research engaging the range of Sustainable Development Goals? A theory of change. *PLOS Global Public Health, 2*(8), Article e0000837. https://doi.org/10.1371/journal.pgph.0000837

Mahalingam, A., Devkar, G. A., & Kalidindi, S. N. (2011). A comparative analysis of public-private partnership (PPP) coordination agencies in India: What works and what doesn't. *Public Works Management Policy, 16*(4), 341–372. https://doi.org/10.1177/1087724X11409215

Maheshwari, V., Negandhi, P., Jaggi, V., Batra, S., Prabhakaran, P., & Menon, J. S. (2024). Association of short-term exposure to air pollution with depression in patients with asthma: A cross-sectional study in Delhi, India. *Journal of Health and Pollution, 12*(1–4), Article 017001. https://doi.org/10.1289/JHP1003

Maitra, S., Brault, M. A., Schensul, S. L., Schensul, J. J., Nastasi, B. K., Verma, R. K., & Burleson, J. A. (2015). An approach to mental health in low and middle income countries: A case example from urban India. *International Journal of Mental Health, 44*(3), 215–230. https://doi.org/10.1080/00207411.2015.1035081

Malik, K., Michelson, D., Doyle, A. M., Weiss, H. A., Greco, G., Sahu, R., E J, J., Mathur, S., Sudhir, P., King, M., Cuijpers, P., Chorpita, B., Fairburn, C. G., & Patel, V. (2021). Effectiveness and costs associated with a lay counselor-delivered, brief problem-solving mental health intervention for adolescents in urban, low-income schools in India: 12-month outcomes of a randomized controlled trial. *PLoS Medicine, 18*(9), e1003778. https://doi.org/10.1371/journal.pmed.1003778

Malik, M., Pradhan, S. K., & Prasuna, J. G. (2007). Screening for psychosocial development among infants in an urban slum of Delhi. *Indian Journal of Pediatrics, 74*(9), 841–845. https://doi.org/10.1007/s12098-007-0150-7

Marrow, J. (2013). The rhetoric of women and children's rights in Indian psychiatry. *Anthropology & Medicine, 20*(1), 72–84. https://doi.org/10.1080/13648470.2012.747590

Martin, P., Haroz, E. E., Lee, C., Bolton, P., Martin, K., Meza, R., McCarthy, E., & Dorsey, S. (2024). A qualitative study of mental health problems among children living in New Delhi slums. *Transcultural Psychiatry, 61*(4), 533–556. https://doi.org/10.1177/13634615231202098

Massazza, A., Alonzo, N., Augustinavicius, J., Batz, C. S., Beagley, J., Carvalho, L. R., Daniel, M., Fleury, J., Guluzade, N., Hijazi, Z., Lawrance, E. L., El Omrani, O., Uakkas, S., Ugo, V., & Umesh, H. (2025). Why mental health should be embedded across climate and health discussions at COP29. *The Lancet. Psychiatry, 12*(1), 9–11. https://doi.org/10.1016/S2215-0366(24)00375-4

Mathias, K., Pant, H., Marella, M., Singh, L., Murthy, G., & Grills, N. (2018a). Multiple barriers to participation for people with psychosocial disability in Dehradun district, North India: A cross-sectional study. *British Medical Journal Open, 8*(2), Article e019443. https://doi.org/10.1136/bmjopen-2017-019443

Mathias, K., Pandey, A., Armstrong, G., Diksha, P., & Kermode, M. (2018b). Outcomes of a brief mental health and resilience pilot intervention for young women in an urban slum in Dehradun, North India: A quasi-experimental study. *International Journal of Mental Health Systems, 12*, 47. https://doi.org/10.1186/s13033-018-0226-y

Mathias, K., Rawat, M., Philip, S., & Grills, N. (2020). We've got through hard times before: Acute mental distress and coping among disadvantaged groups during COVID-19 lockdown in North India - A qualitative study. *International Journal for Equity in Health, 19*(1), 224. https://doi.org/10.1186/s12939-020-01345-7

Mathias, K., Rawat, M., Thompson, A., Gaitonde, R., & Jain, S. (2022). Exploring community mental health systems - A participatory health needs and assets assessment in the Yamuna Valley, North India. *International Journal of Health Policy and Management, 11*(1), 90–99. https://doi.org/10.34172/ijhpm.2020.222

Mathur, P., Kulothungan, V., Leburu, S., Krishnan, A., Chaturvedi, H. K., Salve, H. R., Amarchand, R., Nongkynrih, B., Kumar, P. G., K S, V. U., Ramakrishnan, L., Laxmaiah, A., Boruah, M., Kumar, S., Patro, B. K., Raghav, P. R., Rajkumar, P., Sarma, P. S., Sharma, R., Tambe, M., & Garg, S. (2021). National noncommunicable disease monitoring survey (NNMS) in India: Estimating risk factor prevalence in adult population. *PloS One, 16*(3), e0246712. https://doi.org/10.1371/journal.pone.0246712

Maxfield, A. (2020). Testing the theoretical similarities between food and water insecurity: Buffering hypothesis and effects on mental wellbeing. *Social Science & Medicine (1982), 244*, 112412. https://doi.org/10.1016/j.socscimed.2019.112412

McCammon, E., Bansal, S., Hebert, L. E., Yan, S., Menendez, A., & Gilliam, M. (2020). Exploring young women's menstruation-related challenges in Uttar Pradesh, India, using the socio-ecological framework. *Sexual and Reproductive Health Matters, 28*(1), 1749342. https://doi.org/10.1080/26410397.2020.1749342

McGorry, P. D., & Hamilton, M. P. (2016). Stepwise expansion of evidence-based care is needed for mental health reform. *The Medical Journal of Australia, 204*(9), 351–353. https://doi.org/10.5694/mja16.00120

Memdani, L., Memdani, A., & Memdani, A. (2024). Farmers' suicides in India: A qualitative study of Andhra Pradesh (AP) and Telangana States of India. *Indian Journal of Community Medicine: Official Publication of Indian Association of Preventive & Social Medicine, 49*(4), 629–632. https://doi.org/10.4103/ijcm.ijcm_206_22

Mendenhall, E., Kohrt, B. A., Norris, S. A., Ndetei, D., & Prabhakaran, D. (2017). Non-communicable disease syndemics: Poverty, depression, and diabetes among low-income populations. *Lancet (London, England), 389*(10072), 951–963. https://doi.org/10.1016/S0140-6736(17)30402-6

Mini, G. K., Venkateswaran, C., Vm, A., Krishna S, S., J, G., Ps, G., K, R., Irazola, V., & Romate, J. (2025). Stress among police officials in Kerala, India: An analysis of organizational and operational factors. *BMC Psychology, 13*(1), 512. https://doi.org/10.1186/s40359-025-02831-9

Ministry of Health & Family Welfare. (2022). Ministry of Health and Family Welfare. National Suicide Prevention Strategy. New Delhi: Ministry of Health and Family Welfare, Government of India.

Ministry of Health & Family Welfare, Government of India. (2014). New pathways, new hope: National Mental health policy of India. New Delhi: Ministry of Health & Family Welfare, Government of India. Available online at: https://nhm.gov.in/images/pdf/National_Health_Mental_Policy.pdf

Ministry of Health & Family Welfare, Government of India. (2023). Operational guidelines: National programme for prevention and control of non-communicable diseases. Available online at: https://mohfw.gov.in/sites/default/files/NP-NCD%20Operational%20Guidelines_0.pdf

Ministry of Home Affairs, Government of India. (2019). The protection of children from sexual offences (Amendment) Act, 2019. Available online at: https://www.mha.gov.in/sites/default/files/WSDiv20112019circulationofPOCSOAmndtAct_05082020.pdf

Ministry of Housing and Urban Affairs, Government of India. (2021). Swacch Bharat Mission – Urban 2.0. Making cities garbage free: Operational guidelines. Available online at: https://sbmurban.org/storage/app/media/pdf/swachh-bharat-2.pdf

Ministry of Human Resource Development, Government of India. (2020). National Education Policy 2020. Available online at: https://www.education.gov.in/sites/upload_files/mhrd/files/NEP_Final_English.pdf

Ministry of Social Justice & Empowerment. (2025). Ministry of Social Justice and Empowerment. Nasha Mukt Bharat Abhiyaan: Compendium. New Delhi: Ministry of Social Justice and Empowerment, Government of India

Ministry of Social Justice & Empowerment, Government of India & United Nations Development Programme. (2021). Nasha Mukt Bharat Abhiyaan: Assessment Report 2021. Available online at: https://nmba.dosje.gov.in/public/uploads/pdf/5729172139101l.pdf

Ministry of Statistics and Program Implementation, Government of India. (2016). Men and women in India. Chapter 3: Literacy and education. Available online at: https://mospi.gov.in/sites/default/files/reports_and_publication/statistical_publication/social_statistics/WM16Chapter3.pdf

Ministry of Women and Child Development, Government of India. (2022a). POSHAN Abhiyaan e-Bulletin, September 2022, Issue 1. Available online at: https://www.nipccd.nic.in/uploads/pdf/e-BulletinPoshanSep2022pdf-026613228c26ed82aaf5d7739ee96c3a.pdf

Ministry of Women and Child Development, Government of India. (2022b). 'Mission Shakti' (Integrated Women Empowerment Programme) Umbrella Scheme for Safety, Security and Empowerment of Women – Scheme Implementation Guidelines. Available online at: https://missionshakti.wcd.gov.in/public/documents/whatsnew/Mission_Shakti_Guidelines.pdf

Mishra, P. S., Veerapandian, K., & Choudhary, P. K. (2021). Impact of socio-economic inequity in access to maternal health benefits in India: Evidence from Janani Suraksha Yojana using NFHS data. *PLoS ONE, 16*(3), Article e0247935. https://doi.org/10.1371/journal.pone.0247935

Mishra, N. K., & Patel, S. (2024). Need for a holistic approach to assessing sustainable, green, and healthy buildings. *Environment & Health (Washington, D.C.), 3*(3), 218–226. https://doi.org/10.1021/envhealth.4c00161

Mohindra, K. S., Narayana, D., Anushreedha, S. S., & Haddad, S. (2011). Alcohol use and its consequences in South India: Views from a marginalised tribal population. *Drug and Alcohol Dependence, 117*(1), 70–73. https://doi.org/10.1016/j.drugalcdep.2010.12.021

Muhammad, T., Pai, M., Kumar, M., & Sekher, T. V. (2023). Multiple socioeconomic risks and cognitive impairment among older men and women in India. *Dialogues in Health, 2*, Article 100119. https://doi.org/10.1016/j.dialog.2023.100119

Mukherjee, D., Safraj, S., Tayyab, M., Shivashankar, R., Patel, S. A., Narayanan, G., ... & Prabhakaran, D. (2017). Park availability and major depression in individuals with chronic conditions: Is there an association in urban India? *Health & Place, 47*, 54–62. https://doi.org/10.1016/j.healthplace.2017.07.004

Muposhi, A., & Mugwati, M. (2024). Sustainable development goals mirage in Africa: Reconciling the competing interests of materialism, sustainable consumption, and well-being. In D.

Mhlanga & M. Dzingirai (Eds.), *Fostering long-term sustainable development in Africa: Overcoming poverty, inequality, and unemployment* (pp. 9–27). Springer Nature Switzerland. https://doi.org/10.1007/978-3-031-61321-0_2

Nail-Beatty, O., Ibanez, A., Ayadi, R., Swieboda, P., Njamnshi, A. K., Occhipinti, J. A., Hynes, W., Ikiz, B., Castro-Aldrete, L., O'Brien, K., Platt, M. L., Adalat, S., Abdullah, J. M., Dhamija, R. K., Merali, Z., Mostert, C., Beck, D., Saxena, S., Salama, M., Abdelraheem, O. M., & Eyre, H. A. (2024). Brain health is essential for smooth economic transitions: towards socio-economic sustainability, productivity and well-being. *Brain Communications, 6*(6), fcae360. https://doi.org/10.1093/braincomms/fcae360

Nair, A. R., Shivanna, Y. K. G., Illimoottil, J. P., Rachana, A., Mahasampath, G. S., Abraham, S., & Kurian, S. (2022). Common mental disorders among women and its social correlates in an urban marginalized populace in South India. *The International Journal of Social Psychiatry, 68*(7), 1394–1402. https://doi.org/10.1177/00207640211025556

Nancy, S., Rahman, K. M., Kumar, S. S., Sofia, S., & Robins, M. A. (2022). Reasons and solutions for unhealthy food consumption and physical inactivity among school-going adolescents: A sequential mixed-methods study in Puducherry, South India. *Journal of Family Medicine and Primary Care, 11*(11), 6970–6977. https://doi.org/10.4103/jfmpc.jfmpc_469_22

Nandi, A., Maloney, S., Agarwal, P., Chandrashekar, A., & Harper, S. (2016). The effect of an affordable daycare program on health and economic well-being in Rajasthan, India: Protocol for a cluster-randomized impact evaluation study. *BMC Public Health, 16*, 490. https://doi.org/10.1186/s12889-016-3176-9

Natarajan, I., Rajendran, K., Narayanan, S., & Shanmugam, J. (2024). Swachh Bharat Mission Gramin: Uptake and challenges in rural Coimbatore. *Journal of Family Medicine and Primary Care, 13*(10), 4539–4544. https://doi.org/10.4103/jfmpc.jfmpc_91_24

Nath, Y., Paris, J., Thombs, B., & Kirmayer, L. (2012). Prevalence and social determinants of suicidal behaviours among college youth in India. *The International Journal of Social Psychiatry, 58*(4), 393–399. https://doi.org/10.1177/0020764011401164

National Centre for Disease Control. (2025). National Programme on Climate Change & Human Health. Available online at: https://ncdc.mohfw.gov.in/national-programme-on-climate-change-human-health/

National Centre for Disease Control, Ministry of Health & Family Welfare, Government of India. (2022). State action plan for climate change & human health: Kerala (Version – 1). Available online at: https://ncdc.mohfw.gov.in/wp-content/uploads/2024/05/12.SAPCCHH-VERSION-1-KERALA.pdf

National Crime Records Bureau, Ministry of Home Affairs, Government of India. (2022). Accidental Deaths & Suicides in India 2022. Available online at: https://www.ncrb.gov.in/uploads/files/AccidentalDeathsSuicidesinIndia2022v2.pdf

National Institute of Urban Affairs. (2022). Handbook of Urban Statistics. Available online at: https://niua.in/intranet/sites/default/files/2802.pdf

Nguyen, P. H., Friedman, J., Kak, M., Menon, P., & Alderman, H. (2018). Maternal depressive symptoms are negatively associated with child growth and development: Evidence from rural India. *Maternal & Child Nutrition, 14*(4), Article e12621. https://doi.org/10.1111/mcn.12621

Nirmala, B. P., Roy, T., Naik, V., & Srikanth, P. (2020). Employability of people with mental illness and substance use problems: Field realities. *Journal of Family Medicine and Primary Care, 9*(7), 3405–3410. https://doi.org/10.4103/jfmpc.jfmpc_212_20

NITI Aayog. (2024). SDG India index 2023–24: Towards Viksit Bharat – sustainable progress, inclusive growth. NITI Aayog. Available online at:

NITI Aayog and United Nations. (2019). Localising SDGs: early lessons from India 2019. NITI Aayog. Available online at: https://sdghelpdesk.unescap.org/e-library/localising-sdgs-early-lessons-india

Oswald, T. K., Nguyen, M. T., Mirza, L., Lund, C., Jones, H. G., Crowley, G., Aslanyan, D., Dean, K., Schofield, P., Hotopf, M., & Das-Munshi, J. (2024). Interventions targeting social determinants of mental disorders and the Sustainable Development Goals: A systematic review of reviews. *Psychological Medicine, 54*(8), 1475–1499. https://doi.org/10.1017/S0033291724000333

Padhy, S. K., Sarkar, S., Panigrahi, M., & Paul, S. (2015). Mental health effects of climate change. *Indian Journal of Occupational and Environmental Medicine, 19*(1), 3–7. https://doi.org/10.4103/0019-5278.156997

Panigrahi, A., Panigrahi, M., Padhy, A. P., & Das, S. C. (2017). Common mental disorder and its socio-demographic correlates among married women residing in slum areas of Bhubaneswar, India. *Women & Health, 57*(5), 521–533. https://doi.org/10.1080/03630242.2016.1181137

Patel, V., Burns, J. K., Dhingra, M., Tarver, L., Kohrt, B. A., & Lund, C. (2018a). Income inequality and depression: A systematic review and meta-analysis of the association and a scoping review of mechanisms. *World Psychiatry: Official Journal of the World Psychiatric Association (WPA), 17*(1), 76–89. https://doi.org/10.1002/wps.20492

Patel, V. K., Tiwari, D. S., Shah, V. R., Patel, M. G., Raja, H. H., & Patel, D. S. (2018b). Prevalence and predictors of abuse in elderly patients with depression at a tertiary care centre in Saurashtra, India. *Indian Journal of Psychological Medicine, 40*(6), 528–533. https://doi.org/10.4103/IJPSYM.IJPSYM_18_18

Patel, R., Marbaniang, S. P., Srivastava, S., Kumar, P., Chauhan, S., & Simon, D. J. (2021). Gender differential in low psychological health and low subjective well-being among older adults in India: With special focus on childless older adults. *PLoS ONE, 16*(3), Article e0247943. https://doi.org/10.1371/journal.pone.0247943

Patel, R., Kumar, S., & Chauhan, S. (2022). Exploring association between food insecurity and depression among older adults in India. *Dialogues in Health, 1*, Article 100042. https://doi.org/10.1016/j.dialog.2022.100042

Pati, S., Sinha, R., & Mahapatra, P. (2019). Non-communicable disease risk reduction teaching in India: A curricular landscape. *Frontiers in Public Health, 7*, 133. https://doi.org/10.3389/fpubh.2019.00133

Patwary, M. M., Bardhan, M., Haque, M. A., Moniruzzaman, S., Gustavsson, J., Khan, M. M. H., Koivisto, J., Salwa, M., Mashreky, S. R., Rahman, A. K. M. F., Tasnim, A., Islam, M. R., Alam, M. A., Hasan, M., Harun, M. A. Y. A., Nyberg, L., & Islam, M. A. (2024). Impact of extreme weather events on mental health in South and Southeast Asia: A two decades of systematic review of observational studies. *Environmental Research, 250*, Article 118436. https://doi.org/10.1016/j.envres.2024.118436

Paul, M. A., & Khan, W. (2019). Prevalence of childhood mental disorders among school children of Kashmir Valley. *Community Mental Health Journal, 55*(6), 1031–1037. https://doi.org/10.1007/s10597-018-0253-9

Paul, V., Rathaur, V. K., Bhat, N. K., Sananganba, R., Ittoop, A. L., & Pathania, M. (2021). Child abuse: A social evil in Indian perspective. *Journal of Family Medicine and Primary Care, 10*(1), 110–115. https://doi.org/10.4103/jfmpc.jfmpc_1862_20

Pawar, N., Kumar, N., Vikram, A., Sembiah, S., & Rajawat, G. (2022). Depression and its socio-demographic correlates among urban slum dwellers of North India: A cross-sectional study. *Journal of Family Medicine and Primary Care, 11*(6), 2369–2376. https://doi.org/10.4103/jfmpc.jfmpc_616_21

Pengpid, S., & Peltzer, K. (2023). Food insecurity and health outcomes among community-dwelling middle-aged and older adults in India. *Scientific Reports, 13*(1), 1136. https://doi.org/10.1038/s41598-023-28397-3

Perayil, A., & Mohandas, S. K. (2025). Nutritional status and risk factors for malnutrition among children aged 1–6 years in tribal communities of Malappuram district, Kerala: A cross-sectional study. *BMJ Public Health, 3*(1), Article e001168. https://doi.org/10.1136/bmjph-2024-001168

Pirrone, I., Dieleman, M., Reis, R., & Pell, C. (2021). Syndemic contexts: Findings from a review of research on non-communicable diseases and interviews with experts. *Global Health Action, 14*(1), 1927332. https://doi.org/10.1080/16549716.2021.1927332

Poddar, A., & Chhajer, R. (2024). Detection and disclosure of workplace mental health challenges: An exploratory study from India. *BMC Public Health, 24*(1), 1874. https://doi.org/10.1186/s12889-024-19422-9

Poddar, P., Banavaram, A. A., Ramanaik, S., Jayabalan, M., & S, V. (2025). How city living affects mental health-a qualitative exploration of urban stressors among adults in a megacity in India. *BMC Public Health, 25*(1), 1597. https://doi.org/10.1186/s12889-025-22817-x

Pontzer, H. (2021). Hotter and sicker: External energy expenditure and the tangled evolutionary roots of anthropogenic climate change and chronic disease. *American Journal of Human Biology, 33*, Article e23579. https://doi.org/10.1002/ajhb.23579

Poreddi, V., Ramachandra, Thimmaiah, R., & Math, S. B. (2015a). Human rights violations among economically disadvantaged women with mental illness: An Indian perspective. *Indian Journal of Psychiatry, 57*(2), 174–180. https://doi.org/10.4103/0019-5545.158182

Poreddi, V., Ramachandra, & Math, S. B. (2015b). Does education plays a role in meeting the human rights needs of Indian women with mental illness? *Journal of Neurosciences in Rural Practice, 6*(3), 369–376. https://doi.org/10.4103/0976-3147.154566

Porter, C., Hittmeyer, A., Favara, M., Scott, D., & Sánchez, A. (2022). The evolution of young people's mental health during COVID-19 and the role of food insecurity: Evidence from a four low-and-middle-income-country cohort study. *Public Health in Practice (Oxford, England), 3*, Article 100232. https://doi.org/10.1016/j.puhip.2022.100232

Pothen, M., Kuruvilla, A., Philip, K., Joseph, A., & Jacob, K. S. (2003). Common mental disorders among primary care attenders in Vellore, South India: Nature, prevalence and risk factors. *The International Journal of Social Psychiatry, 49*(2), 119–125. https://doi.org/10.1177/0020764003049002005

Prakash, J., Ali, T., Chaudhury, S., & Srivastava, K. (2023). Declining mental health: An aftermath of fast-paced urbanization. *Industrial Psychiatry Journal, 32*(2), 199–201. https://doi.org/10.4103/ipj.ipj_299_23

Press Information Bureau, Ministry of Information and Broadcasting, Government of India. (2021). Frequently Asked Questions (FAQs): POSHAN Abhiyaan – prime minister's overarching scheme for holistic nourishment. Available online at: https://static.pib.gov.in/WriteReadData/specificdocs/documents/2021/dec/doc20211211 1.pdf

Prince, M., Patel, V., Saxena, S., Maj, M., Maselko, J., Phillips, M. R., & Rahman, A. (2007). No health without mental health. *Lancet (London, England), 370*(9590), 859–877. https://doi.org/10.1016/S0140-6736(07)61238-0

Prost, A., Lakshminarayana, R., Nair, N., Tripathy, P., Copas, A., Mahapatra, R., Rath, S., Gope, R. K., Rath, S., Bajpai, A., Patel, V., & Costello, A. (2012). Predictors of maternal psychological distress in rural India: A cross-sectional community-based study. *Journal of Affective Disorders, 138*(3), 277–286. https://doi.org/10.1016/j.jad.2012.01.029

Pujar, A., Howard Merrill, L., Cislaghi, B., Lokamanya, K., Prakash, R., Javalkar, P., Raghavendra, T., Beattie, T., Isac, S., Gafos, M., Heise, L., Bhattacharjee, P., Ramanaik, S., & Collumbien, M. (2024). Boys' perspectives on girls' marriage and school dropout: A qualitative study revisiting a structural intervention in Southern India. *Culture, Health & Sexuality, 26*(5), 701–716. https://doi.org/10.1080/13691058.2023.2241525

Pundhir, A., Gupta, M. K., & Amudhan, S. (2025). India's nutritional programme POSHAN Abhiyaan: A promising strategy for averting intergenerational effects of nutritional deficiencies on mental health. *Asian Journal of Psychiatry, 107*, Article 104484. https://doi.org/10.1016/j.ajp.2025.104484

Puri, P., & Singh, S. K. (2022). Exploring the non-communicable disease (NCD) network of multimorbid individuals in India: A network analysis. *PLOS Global Public Health, 2*(6), Article e0000512. https://doi.org/10.1371/journal.pgph.0000512

Qin, P., Syeda, S., Canetto, S. S., Arya, V., Liu, B., Menon, V., Lew, B., Platt, S., Yip, P., & Gunnell, D. (2022). Midlife suicide: A systematic review and meta-analysis of socioeconomic, psychiatric and physical health risk factors. *Journal of Psychiatric Research, 154*, 233–241. https://doi.org/10.1016/j.jpsychires.2022.07.037

Quinlan-Davidson, M., Ahmad, A., Asher, L., Bhatia, U., Daruwalla, N., Devakumar, D., Nadkarni, A., Palfreyman, A., Saboor, L., Samanmalee, T. H. R., & Osrin, D. (2025). *Mental health and violence against women in Afghanistan, India and Sri Lanka: A situation analysis.* National Institute for Health and Care Research. Available online at: https://www.ncbi.nlm.nih.gov/books/NBK614156

Raina, S. K., Chander, V., Kumar, D., Raina, S., & Bhardwaj, A. (2014). Level of literacy and dementia: A secondary post-hoc analysis from North-West India. *Journal of Neurosciences in Rural Practice, 5*(4), 360–362. https://doi.org/10.4103/0976-3147.139983

Rajkumari, B., Ingudam, D., Yengkokpam, C., Oinam, G., & Yumnam, R. (2024). Psychological effects of Manipur violence among the internally displaced persons residing in relief camps across Imphal valley of Manipur - A cross-sectional study. *Journal of Family Medicine and Primary Care, 13*(10), 4354–4362. https://doi.org/10.4103/jfmpc.jfmpc_341_24

Ramasubramanian, C., Mohandoss, A. A., & Namasivayam, R. K. (2016). Employability of mentally ill persons in India: A self-report-based population study. *Industrial Psychiatry Journal, 25*(2), 171–178. https://doi.org/10.4103/ipj.ipj_72_16

Rani, D., Singh, J. K., Acharya, D., Paudel, R., Lee, K., & Singh, S. P. (2018). Household food insecurity and mental health among teenage girls living in urban slums in Varanasi, India: A cross-sectional study. *International Journal of Environmental Research and Public Health, 15*(8), 1585. https://doi.org/10.3390/ijerph15081585

Rani, R., & Astha (2024). Association between household air pollution due to unclean fuel use and depression among older adults in India: A cross-sectional study. *Indian Journal of Psychiatry, 66*(9), 814–822. https://doi.org/10.4103/indianjpsychiatry.indianjpsychiatry_317_24

Ranjan, A., & Crasta, J. E. (2023). Progress towards universal health coverage in the context of mental disorders in India: Evidence from national sample survey data. *International Journal of Mental Health Systems, 17*(1), 27. https://doi.org/10.1186/s13033-023-00595-6

Ratandeep, Dharmani, A. B., Verma, M., Rani, S., Narang, A., Singh, M. R., Saya, L., & Hooda, S. (2024). Unravelling groundwater contamination and health-related implications in semi-arid and cold regions of India. *Journal of Contaminant Hydrology, 261*, 104303. https://doi.org/10.1016/j.jconhyd.2024.104303

Reddy, N. B., Pallavi, M., Reddy, N. N., Reddy, C. S., Singh, R. K., & Pirabu, R. A. (2012). Psychological morbidity status among the rural geriatric population of Tamil Nadu, India: A cross-sectional study. *Indian Journal of Psychological Medicine, 34*(3), 227–231. https://doi.org/10.4103/0253-7176.106016

Reserve Bank of India. (2024). Handbook of statistics on Indian States. Available online at: https://www.rbi.org.in/scripts/AnnualPublications.aspx?head=Handbook%20of%20Statistics%20on%20Indian%20States

Richardson, R. A., Harper, S., Bates, L. M., & Nandi, A. (2019). The effect of agency on women's mental distress: A prospective cohort study from rural Rajasthan, India. *Social Science & Medicine, 1982*(233), 47–56. https://doi.org/10.1016/j.socscimed.2019.05.052

Saenz, J. L., Adar, S. D., Zhang, Y. S., Wilkens, J., Chattopadhyay, A., Lee, J., & Wong, R. (2021). Household use of polluting cooking fuels and late-life cognitive function: A harmonized analysis of India, Mexico, and China. *Environment International, 156*, Article 106722. https://doi.org/10.1016/j.envint.2021.106722

Saha, S. K., Pradhan, P., Haldar, D., Maji, B., Agarwal, W., & Sarkar, G. N. (2019). Magnitude of mental morbidity and its correlates with special reference to household food insecurity among adult slum dwellers of Bankura, India: A cross-sectional survey. *Indian Journal of Psychological Medicine, 41*(1), 54–60. https://doi.org/10.4103/IJPSYM.IJPSYM_129_18

Sakthivel, A., Kannappan, S., & Panicker, A. S. (2021). Prevalence of mental health problems among high school students. *Indian Journal of Community Medicine: Official Publication of Indian Association of Preventive & Social Medicine, 46*(3), 574–575. https://doi.org/10.4103/ijcm.IJCM_1041_20

Sarkar, D., Imam, F., Kumar, A., Mukherjee, A., Purohit, P., Kiesewetter, G., Klimont, Z., Ghosh, S., Balakrishnan, K., Chowdhury, S., & Dey, S. (2025). Pathways for India to reduce Ambient air pollution health burden and achieve the sustainable development goal (SDG-3.4). *Environmental Science & Technology, 59*(10), 4765–4777. https://doi.org/10.1021/acs.est.4c08697

Sarkar, S., Menon, V., Padhy, S., & Kathiresan, P. (2024). Mental health and well-being at the workplace. *Indian Journal of Psychiatry, 66*(Suppl 2), S353–S364. https://doi.org/10.4103/indianjpsychiatry.indianjpsychiatry_608_23

Sathe, H. S., Maliye, C. H., Varma, P. S., Garg, B. S., Shahare, K., & Rathod, R. (2024). Intimate partner violence and mental health problems in married women in rural central India: A community-based cross-sectional study. *Indian Journal of Community Medicine : Official Publication of Indian Association of Preventive & Social Medicine, 49*(6), 866–872. https://doi.org/10.4103/ijcm.ijcm_677_22

Schess, J., Kumar, S., Velleman, R., Adhvaryu, A., & Nadkarni, A. (2020). He was trapped in his own web'-dependent drinking as a poverty trap: A qualitative study from Goa, India. *Drug and Alcohol Review, 39*(6), 713–720. https://doi.org/10.1111/dar.13082

Schilbach, F. (2019). Alcohol and self-control: A field experiment in India. *The American Economic Review, 109*(4), 1290–1322.

Schneider, H., Zulu, J. M., Mathias, K., Cloete, K., & Hurtig, A.-K. (2019). The governance of local health systems in the era of Sustainable Development Goals: Reflections on collaborative action to address complex health needs in four country contexts. *BMJ Global Health, 4*, Article e001645. https://doi.org/10.1136/bmjgh-2019-001645

Scott, S., Arrieta, A., Kumar, N., Menon, P., & Quisumbing, A. (2020a). Multidimensional predictors of common mental disorders among Indian mothers of 6- to 24-month-old children living in disadvantaged rural villages with women's self-help groups: A cross-sectional analysis. *PLoS ONE, 15*(6), Article e0233418. https://doi.org/10.1371/journal.pone.0233418

Scott, S., Pant, A., Nguyen, P. H., Shinde, S., & Menon, P. (2020b). Demographic, nutritional, social and environmental predictors of learning skills and depression in 20,000 Indian adolescents: Findings from the UDAYA survey. *PLoS ONE, 15*(10), Article e0240843. https://doi.org/10.1371/journal.pone.0240843

Sengupta, P., Benjamin, A. I., Singh, Y., & Grover, A. (2014). Prevalence and correlates of cognitive impairment in a north Indian elderly population. *WHO South-East Asia Journal of Public Health, 3*(2), 135–143. https://doi.org/10.4103/2224-3151.206729

Sharma, P., Gupta, R. K., Banal, R., Majeed, M., Kumari, R., Langer, B., Akhter, N., Gupta, C., & Raina, S. K. (2020). Prevalence and correlates of Attention Deficit Hyperactive Disorder (ADHD) risk factors among school children in a rural area of North India. *Journal of Family Medicine and Primary Care, 9*(1), 115–118. https://doi.org/10.4103/jfmpc.jfmpc_587_19

Sharma, S., Chandra, M., & Harsha Kota, S. (2022a). Four year long simulation of carbonaceous aerosols in India: Seasonality, sources and associated health effects. *Environmental Research, 213*, Article 113676. https://doi.org/10.1016/j.envres.2022.113676

Sharma, P. K., Singh, A., & Sharma, N. K. (2022b). A socio-ecological critique on India's local health traditions amidst rising incidence of global pandemics. *Journal of Herbal Medicine, 34*, Article 100578. https://doi.org/10.1016/j.hermed.2022.100578

Sharma, V., Sharma, V., Arora, H., Singh, W., Gulati, N., & Sharma, R. (2023). Victims of armed conflict in India: Psychosocial impact and available support. *European Journal of Psychotraumatology, 14*(1), 2178375. https://doi.org/10.1080/20008066.2023.2178375

Sharratt, K., Panicker, A., Banerjee, R., Mason, S. J., Jones, A., Varma, B., Patil, P., & Wager, N. (2021). Profiles of abuse and neglect and the association with mental health indicators among a large sample of boys and girls from India. *Child Abuse & Neglect, 122*, Article 105354. https://doi.org/10.1016/j.chiabu.2021.105354

Shaw, S., Kundu, S., Chattopadhyay, A., & Rao, S. (2024). Indoor air pollution and cognitive function among older adults in India: A multiple mediation approach through depression and sleep disorders. *BMC Geriatrics, 24*(1), 81. https://doi.org/10.1186/s12877-024-04662-6

Shenoy, R. R., Prabhu, D. A., Pandey, A. K., Praharaj, S. K., & Shetty, R. S. (2024). Common mental disorders and their correlates: A community-based survey among women in Southern Karnataka, India. *Indian Journal of Psychological Medicine, 46*(4), 330–337. https://doi.org/10.1177/02537176231220543

Shields, L., Chauhan, A., Bakre, R., Hamlai, M., Lynch, D., & Bunders, J. (2016). How can mental health and faith-based practitioners work together? A case study of collaborative mental health in Gujarat, India. *Transcultural Psychiatry, 53*(3), 368–391. https://doi.org/10.1177/1363461516649835

Shivakumar, P., Sadanand, S., Bharath, S., Girish, N., Philip, M., & Varghese, M. (2015). Identifying psychological distress in elderly seeking health care. *Indian Journal of Public Health, 59*(1), 18–23. https://doi.org/10.4103/0019-557X.152849

Shukla, V., & Arora, R. (2023). The economic cost of rising non-communicable diseases in India: A systematic literature review of methods and estimates. *Applied Health Economics and Health Policy, 21*(5), 719–730. https://doi.org/10.1007/s40258-023-00822-8

Singal, N. (2005). Mapping the field of inclusive education: A review of the Indian literature. *International Journal of Inclusive Education, 9*(4), 331–350. https://doi.org/10.1080/13603110500138277

Singal, N. (2019). Challenges and opportunities in efforts towards inclusive education: Reflections from India. *International Journal of Inclusive Education, 23*(7–8), 827–840. https://doi.org/10.1080/13603116.2019.1624845

Singh, R., Koushal, V., & Bharti, B. (2022). A descriptive study on child sexual abuse act in India. *Journal of Family Medicine and Primary Care, 11*(6), 2923–2932. https://doi.org/10.4103/jfmpc.jfmpc_1071_21

Singh, D., Nasir, S., Sharma, J., Giménez-Llort, L., & Shahnawaz, M. G. (2024a). Psychological distress in low-income and economically marginalized populations in India: Protective and risk factors. *Behavioral Sciences (Basel, Switzerland), 14*(2), 92. https://doi.org/10.3390/bs14020092

Singh, G., Patra, S., Upadhyay, M. K., & Srivastava, S. (2024b). Prevalence of common mental disorders and perspective toward mental health in an urban resettlement colony of Delhi, India: A mixed-method study. *Journal of Education and Health Promotion, 13*, 370. https://doi.org/10.4103/jehp.jehp_1545_23

Singh, S., & Chadda, R. (2025). Drug control: Initiatives from India. *BJPsych International*, 1–4. Advance online publication. https://doi.org/10.1192/bji.2025.3

Singh, N., Shukla, S. K., John, P., Bajpai, R., Chugh, P., Sengupta, R., Pushkar, R. R., Yadav, N., Singh, N., & Sadanandan, R. (2025). Unveiling the twin epidemics of hypertension and diabetes: A cross-sectional analysis of sex-specific prevalence, risk, and hotspots in India's epidemiological transition zones. *BMC Public Health, 25*(1), 1734. https://doi.org/10.1186/s12889-025-22983-y

Skene, K. R. (2021). No goal is an island: The implications of systems theory for the Sustainable Development Goals. *Environment, Development and Sustainability, 23*(7), 9993–10012. https://doi.org/10.1007/s10668-020-01043-y

Smith, A., Gonzalez Smith, D. T., Ogunwale, A., Bhugra, D., Buadze, A., Ventriglio, A., & Liebrenz, M. (2024). Geopsychiatry, the United Nations' Sustainable Development Goals, and geopolitical challenges for global mental health. *The International Journal of Social Psychiatry, 70*(4), 631–635. https://doi.org/10.1177/00207640231219169

Srivastava, K., & Gawarle, N. S. (2024). Breaking the silence: A look into women's mental health in India. *Journal of Family Medicine and Primary Care, 13*(11), 5436–5437. https://doi.org/10.4103/jfmpc.jfmpc_892_24

Stoler, J., Pearson, A. L., Staddon, C., Wutich, A., Mack, E., Brewis, A., Rosinger, A. Y., & Household Water Insecurity Experiences (HWISE) Research Coordination Network, 2020 Stoler, J., Pearson, A. L., Staddon, C., Wutich, A., Mack, E., Brewis, A., Rosinger, A. Y., & Household Water Insecurity Experiences (HWISE) Research Coordination Network (2020). Cash water expenditures are associated with household water insecurity, food insecurity, and perceived stress in study sites across 20 low- and middle-income countries. *The Science of the Total Environment, 716*, 135881. https://doi.org/10.1016/j.scitotenv.2019.135881

Stott, P. (2016). How climate change affects extreme weather events. *Science, 352*(6293), 1517–1518. https://doi.org/10.1126/science.aaf7271

Subbaraman, R., Nolan, L., Shitole, T., Sawant, K., Shitole, S., Sood, K., Nanarkar, M., Ghannam, J., Betancourt, T. S., Bloom, D. E., & Patil-Deshmukh, A. (2014). The psychological toll of slum living in Mumbai, India: A mixed methods study. *Social Science and Medicine, 119*, 155–169. https://doi.org/10.1016/j.socscimed.2014.08.021

Suchithra, E. T., Vargheese, S., Sudhiraj, T. S., & Zinia (2022). Prevalence of psychiatric disorders among 4 to 14 year age group children in slums of Thiruvananthapuram Corporation. *Journal of Family Medicine and Primary Care, 11*(4), 1421–1427. https://doi.org/10.4103/jfmpc.jfmpc_1458_21

Sugden, S. G., & Merlo, G. (2024). What do climate change, nutrition, and the environment have to do with mental health? *American Journal of Lifestyle Medicine*, 15598276241280245. Advance online publication. https://doi.org/10.1177/15598276241280245

Suhas, S., Jayasankar, P., Patley, R., Manjunatha, N., Rao, G. N., Gururaj, G., Varghese, M., Benegal, V., & NMHS National Collaborators group (2023). Nationally representative epidemiological study of social anxiety disorder from India. *Indian Journal of Psychiatry, 65*(12), 1261–1268. https://doi.org/10.4103/indianjpsychiatry.indianjpsychiatry_826_23

Sunil, A. B., Banerjee, A., Divya, M., Rathod, H. K., Patel, J., & Gupta, M. (2023). Dyslexia: An invisible disability or different ability. *Industrial Psychiatry Journal, 32*(Suppl 1), S72–S75. https://doi.org/10.4103/ipj.ipj_196_23

Swarnalatha, N. (2013). The prevalence of depression among the rural elderly in Chittoor District, Andhra Pradesh. *Journal of Clinical and Diagnostic Research: JCDR, 7*(7), 1356–1360. https://doi.org/10.7860/JCDR/2013/5956.3141

Talukder, B., van Loon, G. W., Hipel, K. W., Chiotha, S., & Orbinski, J. (2021). Health impacts of climate change on smallholder farmers. *One Health (Amsterdam, Netherlands), 13*, Article 100258. https://doi.org/10.1016/j.onehlt.2021.100258

Thapa, B., Torres, I., Koya, S. F., Robbins, G., Abdalla, S. M., Arah, O. A., Weeks, W. B., Zhang, L., Asma, S., Morales, J. V., Galea, S., Rhee, K., & Larson, H. J. (2021). Use of data to understand the social determinants of depression in two middle-income countries: The 3-D commission. *Journal of Urban Health: Bulletin of the New York Academy of Medicine, 98*(Suppl 1), 41–50. https://doi.org/10.1007/s11524-021-00559-6

Theron, L. C., Abreu-Villaça, Y., Augusto-Oliveira, M., Brennan, C., Crespo-Lopez, M. E., de Paula Arrifano, G., Glazer, L., Gwata, N., Lin, L., Mareschal, I., Mermelstein, S., Sartori, L., Stieger, L., Trotta, A., & Hadfield, K. (2022). A systematic review of the mental health risks and resilience among pollution-exposed adolescents. *Journal of Psychiatric Research, 146*, 55–66. https://doi.org/10.1016/j.jpsychires.2021.12.012

Tomalin, E., Haustein, J., & Kidy, S. (2019). Religion and the sustainable development goals. *The Review of Faith & International Affairs, 17*(2), 102–118. https://doi.org/10.1080/15570274.2019.1608664

Tota, M., Karska, J., Kowalski, S., Piatek, N., Pszczolowska, M., Mazur, K., & Piotrowski, P. (2024). Environmental pollution and extreme weather conditions: Insights into the effect on mental health. *Frontiers in Psychiatry, 15*, 1389051. https://doi.org/10.3389/fpsyt.2024.1389051

Trani, J. F., Bakhshi, P., Kuhlberg, J., Narayanan, S. S., Venkataraman, H., Mishra, N. N., Groce, N. E., Jadhav, S., & Deshpande, S. (2015). Mental illness, poverty and stigma in India: A case-control study. *British Medical Journal Open, 5*(2), Article e006355. https://doi.org/10.1136/bmjopen-2014-006355

Travasso, S. M., Rajaraman, D., & Heymann, S. J. (2014). A qualitative study of factors affecting mental health amongst low-income working mothers in Bangalore, India. *BMC Women's Health, 14*, 22. https://doi.org/10.1186/1472-6874-14-22

Trivedi, J. K., Sareen, H., & Dhyani, M. (2008). Rapid urbanization - Its impact on mental health: A South Asian perspective. *Indian Journal of Psychiatry, 50*(3), 161–165. https://doi.org/10.4103/0019-5545.43623

United Nations. (2024). The Sustainable Goals Development Report 2024. Available online at: https://unstats.un.org/sdgs/report/2024/The-Sustainable-Development-Goals-Report-2024.pdf

United Nations Department of Economic and Social Affairs. (2015). Transforming our world: The 2030 Agenda for Sustainable Development. Available online at: https://sdgs.un.org/sites/default/files/publications/21252030%20Agenda%20for%20Sustainable%20Development%20web.pdf

United Nations Development Programme. (2025). India's human development continues to make progress, ranks 130 out of 193 countries. Available online at: https://www.undp.org/india/press-releases/indias-human-development-continues-make-progress-ranks-130-out-193-countries

United Nations Economic and Social Commission for Asia and the Pacific. (2025). SDG Help Desk. Available online at: https://sdghelpdesk.unescap.org/

United Nations in India. (2025). Sustainable Development Goals. Available online at: https://india.un.org/en/sdgs

United Nations India and NITI Aayog. (2022). The Indian model of SDG Localisation. NITI Aayog. Available online at: https://india.un.org/en/192868-indian-model-sdg-localisation

Upadhyay, R. P., Taneja, S., Ranjitkar, S., Mazumder, S., Bhandari, N., Dua, T., Shrestha, L., & Strand, T. A. (2021). Factors determining cognitive, motor and language scores in low birth weight infants from North India. *PLoS ONE, 16*(5), Article e0251387. https://doi.org/10.1371/journal.pone.0251387

Vahedi, L., Seff, I., Tsai, A. C., Rfat, M., Aljamhan, M. S., & Stark, L. (2025). Gender-based violence syndemics in global health: A systematic review. *Social Science & Medicine (1982), 367*, 117793. https://doi.org/10.1016/j.socscimed.2025.117793

Vaid, U. (2024). Cognitive health costs of poor housing for women: Exploring executive function and housing stress in Urban Slums in India. *International Journal of Environmental Research and Public Health, 21*(12), 1710. https://doi.org/10.3390/ijerph21121710

Venkataraman, S., Patil, R., & Balasundaram, S. (2019). Stigma toward mental illness among higher secondary school teachers in Puducherry, South India. *Journal of Family Medicine and Primary Care, 8*(4), 1401. https://doi.org/10.4103/jfmpc.jfmpc_203_19

Verma, M., & Loganathan, V. A. (2023). Water security and health risk assessment of an urban household-level drinking water and sanitation system, Punjab, India. *Environmental Monitoring and Assessment, 195*(6), 750. https://doi.org/10.1007/s10661-023-11360-0

Viswanathan, D. J., Veerakumar, A. M., & Kumarasamy, H. (2019). Depression, suicidal ideation, and resilience among rural farmers in a drought-affected area of Trichy District, Tamil Nadu. *Journal of Neurosciences in Rural Practice, 10*(2), 238–244. https://doi.org/10.4103/jnrp.jnrp_257_18

Votruba, N., Thornicroft, G., & the FundaMentalSDG Steering Group, 2016 Votruba, N., Thornicroft, G., & the FundaMentalSDG Steering Group. (2016). Sustainable development goals and mental health: learnings from the contribution of the FundaMentalSDG global initiative. *Global Mental Health, 3*, e26. https://doi.org/10.1017/gmh.2016.20

Wadhva, C. D. (2020). Political economy of post-1991 economic reforms in India. *South Asia: Journal of South Asian Studies, 23*(s1), 207–220. https://doi.org/10.1080/00856400008723409

Wagner, D. A. (2017). Learning, literacy and sustainable development: Inclusion, vulnerability and the SDGs. In A. Battro, P. Léna, M. Sánchez Sorondo & J. von Braun (Eds.), *Children and sustainable development*. Springer. https://doi.org/10.1007/978-3-319-47130-3_5

Wang, S., Li, T., & Rajagopalan, P. (2025). Impact of heat exposure on health outcomes among older adults in India: An analysis across ten states. *International Journal of Environmental Health Research*, 1–13. Advance online publication. https://doi.org/10.1080/09603123.2025.2461115

Wassef, A., Nguyen, Q. D., & St-André, M. (2019). Anaemia and depletion of iron stores as risk factors for postpartum depression: A literature review. *Journal of Psychosomatic Obstetrics and Gynaecology, 40*(1), 19–28. https://doi.org/10.1080/0167482X.2018.1427725

Weiss, M. G., & Parkar, S. R. (2020). Facets of clinical stigma after attempted suicide in Mumbai, India. *Anthropology & Medicine, 27*(2), 212–233. https://doi.org/10.1080/13648470.2019.1640025

White, S. J., Sin, J., Sweeney, A., Salisbury, T., Wahlich, C., Montesinos Guevara, C. M., Gillard, S., Brett, E., Allwright, L., Iqbal, N., Khan, A., Perot, C., Marks, J., & Mantovani, N. (2024). Global prevalence and mental health outcomes of intimate partner violence among women: A systematic review and meta-analysis. *Trauma, Violence & Abuse, 25*(1), 494–511. https://doi.org/10.1177/15248380231155529

Wood, C., Wicks, C., & Barton, J. (2023). Green spaces for mental disorders. *Current Opinion in Psychiatry, 36*(1), 41–46. https://doi.org/10.1097/YCO.0000000000000830

World Bank Group. (2023). Poverty headcount ratio at national poverty lines (% of population). Available online at: https://data.worldbank.org/indicator/SI.POV.NAHC?name_desc=false

World Bank Group. (2025). Unemployment, total (% of total labour force) (modelled ILO estimate). Available online at: https://data.worldbank.org/indicator/SL.UEM.TOTL.ZS?most_recent_value_desc=false

Yang, Y., Sun, A., Zimmermann, L., & Mukherjee, B. (2024). Impact of pandemic-related worries on mental health in India from 2020 to 2022. *Npj Mental Health Research, 3*(1), 57. https://doi.org/10.1038/s44184-024-00101-x

Yasobant, S., Lekha, K. S., Trivedi, P., Krishnan, S., Kator, C., Kaur, H., Adaniya, M., Sinha, A., & Saxena, D. (2025). Impact of heat on human and animal health in India: A landscape review. *Dialogues in Health, 6*, Article 100203. https://doi.org/10.1016/j.dialog.2024.100203

Yatirajula, S. K., Kallakuri, S., Paslawar, S., Mukherjee, A., Khan, N. A., Kumari, K., Sagar, R., Thornicroft, G., & Maulik, P. K. (2022). Engaging with adolescents to navigate the adolescents' resilience and treatment nEeds for mental health in Indian slums (ARTEMIS) trial. *Journal of Global Health, 12*, 03084. https://doi.org/10.7189/jogh.12.03084

Yatirajula, S. K., Prashad, L., Daniel, M., & Maulik, P. K. (2023). A cross-sectional survey of climate and COVID-19 crises in young people in Indian slums: Context, psychological responses, and agency. *The Lancet Regional Health. Southeast Asia, 13*, Article 100191. https://doi.org/10.1016/j.lansea.2023.100191

Zhang, Y. R., Xu, W., Zhang, W., Wang, H. F., Ou, Y. N., Qu, Y., Shen, X. N., Chen, S. D., Wu, K. M., Zhao, Q. H., Zhang, H. N., Sun, L., Dong, Q., Tan, L., Feng, L., Zhang, C., Evangelou, E., Smith, A. D., & Yu, J. T. (2022). Modifiable risk factors for incident dementia and cognitive impairment: An umbrella review of evidence. *Journal of Affective Disorders, 314*, 160–167. https://doi.org/10.1016/j.jad.2022.07.008

Zundel, C. G., Ryan, P., Brokamp, C., Heeter, A., Huang, Y., Strawn, J. R., & Marusak, H. A. (2022). Air pollution, depressive and anxiety disorders, and brain effects: A systematic review. *Neurotoxicology, 93*, 272–300. https://doi.org/10.1016/j.neuro.2022.10.011

Chapter 10
Synergizing Sustainable Development Goals and Mental Health in Nepal

Pawan Sharma, Pramita Sharma, and Gaurav Devkota

Abstract The Sustainable Development Goals (SDGs), adopted globally in 2015, provide a unifying agenda for addressing poverty, inequality, health, and sustainability by 2030. Mental health is increasingly recognized to be central to these goals but is under-prioritized in the majority of low- and middle-income countries like Nepal. Nepal has made significant achievement in mental health over last two decades; however, the alignment with the SDGs is still inadequate. The mental health policy documents highlight the commitment of Government of Nepal toward mental health of the citizens and alignment toward the SDGs but there are various challenges. In this chapter we aim to explore the intersection of the SDG agenda and mental health in context of Nepal. We also aim to explore systemic challenges like lack of political investment, funding gaps, and weak information systems and provide recommendations for effective mainstreaming of mental health into SDG implementation in Nepal.

Keywords Mental health · Nepal · Sustainable development goals · Psychiatry · Suicide

1 Introduction

Nepal, a landlocked country situated in South Asia between India and China, is home to a mosaic of ethnic, linguistic, and cultural groups, with over 125 ethnic communities and 123 distinct documented languages (Gurung, 2001). Renowned

P. Sharma (✉)
Department of Psychiatry, Patan Academy of Health Sciences, Lalitpur, Nepal
e-mail: pawansharma@pahs.edu.np

P. Sharma
Department of Community Health Sciences, Patan Academy of Health Sciences, Lalitpur, Nepal

G. Devkota
Nepal Public Health Association, Lalitpur, Nepal

S. K. Kar et al. (eds.), *Sustainable Development Goals and Mental Health in South Asia*, South Asian Perspectives in Mental Health and Psychology ,
https://doi.org/10.1007/978-981-95-2684-0_10

for its rich cultural heritage and breathtaking geographical diversity, the country spans the mighty Himalayas and the lush plains of the Teraî region, which support agricultural productivity. It became a republic, federal state with the promulgation of the constitution in 2015. There are seven provinces with the nation's capital located in Kathmandu. Nepal has a population exceeding 30 million and the major concentration of population is in the southern-most plains of the Terai region and the central hilly region (Census Nepal, 2021).

The Sustainable Development Goals (SDGs), adopted by the United Nations in 2015, provide a comprehensive blueprint for global development aimed at ending poverty, reducing inequality, ensuring health and well-being, and fostering sustainable growth by 2030 (Department of Economic and Social Affairs, 2015). For a country like Nepal, achieving these goals poses unique challenges and opportunities. Nepal has made notable progress in maternal and child health, education, and poverty reduction. However, it continues to struggle with socio-economic disparities, limited infrastructure, political instability, and vulnerability to natural disasters (Khatiwada et al., 2022). Mental health—an often-overlooked component of public health—intersects with these developmental goals. In this chapter, we aim to discuss the current state of the SDGs in Nepal, assess the country's performance across key SDG indicators, examine the impact of the SDG agenda on mental health, identify the major challenges in achieving these goals, and explore ways out to synergize mental health within the broader SDG framework.

2 SDGs in Context of Nepal

As per the National Panning Commission, Nepal, being a member of the United Nations, has embraced all the principles of sustainable development since its endorsement in the UN declaration of 2015. The Government of Nepal has demonstrated its commitment to achieving the SDGs by integrating them in Nepal's national development framework through national policies and plans (Pradhan & Karki, 2019). Nepal started SDGs implementation in 2016, the first year of the 14th Three-Year Plan, and it continued with the 15th periodic plan, which was fully aligned with the SDGs. Thus has further extended to the 16th development plan (Gupta & Sigdel, 2024). The provincial government has already integrated the SDGs into their plans and budgets, and local governments as well are in the process of similar integration. National Planning Commission (NPC), an apex planning body in Nepal, have helped in the translation of the plans and policies to programs and activities were done through the medium-term expenditure framework (MTEF), and annual budgets. The planning commission of Nepal has determined total 479 indicators by adding more 247 indicators in the process of localizing SDGs in the context of Nepal (Pant, 2024).

The planning, budgeting, coordination, collaboration, and monitoring of the SDGs in the country is done by National Planning Commission. It has established the SDGs dashboard that has open-source information on implementation and progress of SDGs. The Office of the Auditor General of Nepal (OAGN) has established SDG unit to coordinate and facilitate SDG-friendly audits. The other stakeholders in Nepal are Civil society via the SDGs Forum, development partners, various United Nations agencies in Nepal and the private sector. Nepal has established a multi-tiered institutional framework to advance the Sustainable Development Goals (SDGs). At the highest level, the High-level SDGs Steering Committee, chaired by the Prime Minister, provides political leadership, policy direction, and resource mobilization. The SDGs Implementation and Coordination Committee, led by the Vice Chairperson of the National Planning Commission (NPC), facilitates integration of SDGs across federal, provincial, and local governments, ensuring inter-ministerial and inter-agency collaboration. Supporting this framework, nine thematic SDG Implementation and Monitoring Committees—each headed by an NPC member—focus on policy alignment, stakeholder coordination, data management, and progress monitoring. The Sustainable Development and Good Governance Committee of the National Assembly promotes parliamentary engagement with SDGs and oversees their integration into the national budget. The National Development Action Committee, also chaired by the Prime Minister, addresses high-level administrative barriers to project implementation, with a focus on SDG-related initiatives. At the local level, District Coordination Committees play a pivotal role in supervising and promoting SDG-aligned development activities. Together, these institutional arrangements ensure a coordinated, multi-level approach to SDG implementation in Nepal (Gupta & Sigdel, 2024; National Planning Commission, 2019).

3 Mental Health in Nepal

Mental health issues have been a major public health concern in Nepal. The National Mental Health Survey conducted from 2019 to 2020 showed that the prevalence of mental disorders among adults was found to be 10% over their lifetime, with 4.3% currently experiencing a mental disorder. Among adolescents, the prevalence of mental disorders was 5.2%, with neurotic and stress-related disorders being the most common (Dhimal et al., 2021a, 2021b). There has been increasing awareness and investment in mental health from both the general public and the government, in part due to experience with the acute stressors and mental health needs associated with emergencies such as the 2015 Nepal earthquake and the COVID-19 pandemic (Sharma et al., 2024a, 2024b). Nepal has a history of strong support from NGOs. Despite these strengths, Nepal still faces challenges in its mental healthcare system. Scarce human resources and financial investment for mental health do persist; nor is it a priority in medical education curricula (World Health Organization, 2021).

Nepal faces challenges in tackling the issue of mental disorders. The prevalence has been steadily rising; on one side, the unmet needs for mental health services are striking on the other (Sharma et al., 2024a, 2024b). Although, some of this may be attributed to limited mental healthcare facilities, and mental health professionals, across the nation; another major contributor to the treatment gap is societal beliefs, traditions, and stigma associated with mental disorders (Nepal Health Research Council, 2020).

4 Current State of Sustainable Development Goals (SDGs) and Their Impact on Mental Health in Nepal

Nepal has made a notable achievement in reducing poverty. By 2022–2023, the poverty headcount ratio in Nepal reduced to 3.5% with the GDP per capita increased to USD 1755, the proportion of population under Multidimensional Poverty Index (MPI) reduced to 17.4%, the percentage of people covered by social protection system increased to 41.7%, and households covered by financial services to 62% (Government of Nepal National Planning Commission, 2024). At both low- and high-resource settings, mental disorders have been identified to be associated with increased healthcare costs to service users and the health system (Lund et al., 2019; Sontheimer et al., 2021). Studies have identified that the mental health services in Nepal are sought more in private clinics and pharmacists and cause higher out-of-pocket expenditures (Chisholm et al., 2020). Thus, a reduction in poverty and an increase in GDP can be supportive of increased utilization of mental healthcare services. Social Security Allowance Program (SSAP) provides financial assistance to elderly citizens, person with disabilities, single women and marginalized communities, thereby supporting their healthcare costs (Subedi, 2021). Social Health Insurance (SHI) covers the cost of mental health services and medicines from healthcare facilities, thereby increasing patient flow and referrals (Bharati et al., 2025).

The proportion of households with access to market centers within 30-min walk show no improvement in 2022–2023 along with the share of women owning property or tangible assets falling behind the target that had been set for 2022 (Government of Nepal National Planning Commission, 2024). As the majority of the mental health services are available in city or market areas, this limitation in access to the market might hamper mental health service provision/delivery (World Health Organization, 2021). Studies have identified that women are more prone to mental illnesses, with educated women utilizing more mental health services (Shawon et al., 2024). Thus, targeted intervention to meet the accessibility gap and promoting gender equality in asset ownership may ensure provision, accessibility, and utilization of mental health services. Moreover, job losses and reduced economic activity due to unstable government, the COVID-19 pandemic, and yearly occurring natural disasters have triggered rise of mental health issues among population as an endemic (Adhikari & Adhikary, 2019; Paudyal & Abraham, 2010; Poudel & Subedi, 2020). Thus, skill development and job creation will be essential to maintain the progress and ensure that the population do not fall back to poverty and then the vicious cycle of poverty and diseases (Sapkota et al., 2021).

Mixed progress has been seen in achieving zero hunger. There has been significant reduction in prevalence of under-nourishment (5.4%), decrease in prevalence of stunting among children under 5 years of age (24.8%), and reduction in severe and moderate food insecurity (1.3% and 11.2% respectively) by 2022–2023 (Government of Nepal National Planning Commission, 2024). As malnutrition has been identified to impair cognitive development thereby increasing vulnerability to mental health disorders, better achievement in these indicators can help reduce the burden of mental health illness in Nepal (Sharma et al., 2023; Shrestha et al., 2022). The low decrement in the percentage of children under 5 years of age who are underweight and high prevalence of anemia among women of reproductive age and children under 5 years of age have been areas of concern as they can affect physical health and mental health (Agaoglu et al., 2007; Christian et al., 2010; Shrestha et al., 2022).

Nepal's progress in ensuring inclusive and equitable quality education has been praiseworthy with 97.1% net enrolment rate in primary education, 85.7% reaching to grade eight (high retention), and 39.7% of students receiving scholarship but with declination in primary education completion rate and gender parity index for primary and secondary school (Government of Nepal National Planning Commission, 2024). Inadequate or lack of knowledge and education act as substantial barriers for healthcare engagement, and since mental illness treatments include institutional methods and self-help methods, health literacy plays a major role in mental health care (Budhathoki et al., 2017).

Nepal's progress in achieving gender equality has been mixed. There has been a significant reduction in the prevalence of physical or sexual violence against women and the proportion of women aged 20–24 years who were married or in a union before age 15. Though the representation of women in the governance structure has been increasing, the ratio of women to men in labor force participation is still low (0.61), the average number of hours spent by women in domestic work is still high (10 h) and the proportion of women in decision-making positions in the public sector also being low (29.61%) (Government of Nepal National Planning Commission, 2024). Intimate partner violence and child marriage have been identified as risk factors leading to disturbed mental health conditions (Burgess et al., 2022; Ellsberg et al., 2008). No income-generating activity, limited to household chores, and lack of leadership and decision-making powers have been identified to limit utilization of mental healthcare services (Brenman et al., 2014; Devkota et al., 2021). Discrimination in society for women is continued through deep-rooted patriarchal norms and societal ethos (Ghimire et al., 2024), with health and social policies also including mental health-related structural stigma and discrimination (Gurung et al., 2023), besides self-stigmatization and stigmatization in the community (Camp et al., 2002; Huggett et al., 2018). This serves as limiting factor for access to health care by mentally ill people. These negative norms and ethos should thus be eliminated for better mental health in society and mental healthcare utilization.

Though Nepal has a minimal contribution to the emission of Green-House Gases (GHGs), yet it is one of the most vulnerable countries experiencing the adverse impacts of climate change, with disasters affecting population health and GDP. However, the number of people affected by disasters reduced significantly to 34,000 in 2022, showcasing notable progress in reducing the impact of disasters on the population (Government of Nepal National Planning Commission, 2024). Disasters have negative impacts on people's mental condition and health, thereby causing increased demands for mental health and psychosocial support (MHPSS) intervention (Kane et al., 2018; Sherchan et al., 2017). The reduction in number of people being affected lowers the number of mental illness cases and lowers the expenses on MHPSS healthcare and community activities during emergency settings. Though the proportion of households living in safe houses surpassed the target of 43.9%, ensuring the access to safe and affordable housing, especially for low-income and marginalized communities, still requires added efforts (Government of Nepal National Planning Commission, 2024). Vulnerable people are more impacted by disasters as well as face challenges in recovering to pre-disaster functionality (Cutter et al., 2003), thereby increasing the chances of mental health problems. Air quality in urban areas improved with the concentration of total suspended particulates and particulate matter meeting the target for 2022, the concentration of PM 2.5 fine particulate matter remained above the target (Government of Nepal National Planning Commission, 2024). Air pollution has been identified to cause increased odds of mental health problems especially dementia or debilitating chronic diseases leading to mental problems (Buoli et al., 2018).

Mixed progress has been seen under different aspects of forming a peaceful and inclusive society. The proportion of young women and men aged 18–29 years who experienced sexual violence by age 18 has reduced, meeting the 2022 target but the proportion of children experiencing psychological aggression or physical punishment is still way under the target for 2022 (Government of Nepal National Planning Commission, 2024). Violence, physical or sexual, and adverse childhood experiences result in psychological disturbances, thereby causing an increase in mental health problems, including substance abuse (Mersky et al., 2013; Nelson et al., 2012). Thus, a reduction in violence may lead to a decrease in the burden of mental health problems in Nepal. There has been a significant fall in the numbers of direct deaths from armed and violent conflict and reduction in the proportion of population subjected to physical, psychological, or sexual violence in the previous 12 months and number of children trafficking to abroad per annum has also decreased (Government of Nepal National Planning Commission, 2024). Exposure to conflict and weak institutional support has been identified to lead to trauma and long-term psychological effects (Tol et al., 2010). This reduction in conflict, violence, and trafficking crimes highlights the presence of strong institutional support for the victims, thereby supporting a reduction in mental illnesses indirectly.

Only limited progress has been made in promoting inclusive and sustainable economic growth, employment, and decent work for all. The annual growth rate of real GDP per capita and per employed person has not increased and the unemployment rate and the proportion of informal employment in the non-agricultural sector still high (Government of Nepal National Planning Commission, 2024). There has also been a huge surplus of labor due to Nepal shifting from agriculture-dominated economic structure to service-oriented economy without going through the industrialization process for longer term (Government of Nepal National Planning Commission, 2020). Migration to different countries for job and other opportunity has been the results to the surplus. These migrants face different exploitative conditions thereby leading to physical and mental health issues (Mahato et al., 2024).

Remarkable progress has been in ensuring good health and well-being in Nepal, with decline in maternal mortality rate (151 maternal deaths per 100 000 live births), increment in proportion of births attended by skilled health personnel (80.1%), reduction in the number of new HIV infections among adults aged 15–49 years, and increase in the percentage of people living with HIV receiving antiretroviral combination therapy. However, under five mortality rate and neonatal mortality rate remain on higher side than targeted, with concerning reverse trends for satisfaction with modern methods of family planning, incidence of communicable diseases (malaria, dengue, trachoma, leprosy), and incidence of Non-Communicable Diseases (NCDs) and mental health, including suicide mortality (Government of Nepal National Planning Commission, 2024). Social determinants of mental health include various factors like conflict, violence and maltreatment, life events and experiences, racism and discrimination, culture and migration, social interaction and support, structural policies and inequality, financial factors, employment factors, housing and living conditions, and demographic factors (Alegría et al., 2023; Ali & Mekonnen, 2021), thereby highlighting the need to work on all the indicators and goals of SDGs that directly or indirectly contribute to positive mental health.

5 Initiatives Taken by the Country to Meet the Mental Health Goals Among SDGs

The SDG goal 3.4 has mentioned about the treatment and promotion of mental health and well-being and goal 3.8 mentions about the universal health coverage and access to essential medicines for all. In this line constitution of Nepal ensures right to receive free basic health care for all citizens and mental health has been included in the basic health services in subsection 4 (E) of Section 3 of Public Health Service Act 2018 (Family Welfare Division, 2018). The National health policy mentions mental health in Section 17.5 (Family Welfare Division, 2019). Mental health services have been recognized as part of the "basic and emergency health services" under Schedules 1 and 2 of the Public Health Service Regulations 2020, mandating provisions for such services at the federal, provincial, and local levels (Government of Nepal, 2020). Similarly, Chap. 7 of the Act Relating to the Rights of Persons with Disabilities, 2074 (2017), guarantees all citizens access to healthcare, rehabilitation, social security, and recreational opportunities. Furthermore, Sections 35 and 36 of the Act specifically provide for additional support services for individuals with mental or psychosocial disabilities (Adhikari, 2019). The National Mental Health Strategy and Action Plan of 2020 has provided a comprehensive description of action plans for mental health care in Nepal. This strategic action plan describes the provision of free mental health services in primary care in all parts of the country (Sharma et al., 2024a, 2024b; World Health Organization, 2021). The National Mental Health Care Programme 2022 provides a framework for the delivery of primary health care(PHC)-oriented mental health services and has defined minimum set of mental health services to be delivered by health facilities at every level with an emphasizes on the integration of mental health services at the primary health-care level, with a key goal of enhancing accessibility to mental health care (World Health Organization, 2022).

Goal 3.5 mentions strengthening the prevention and treatment of substance abuse, including narcotic drug abuse and harmful use of alcohol. Regarding this goal the Ministry of Home Affairs of Nepal has endorsed the "Directive on the Operation of Treatment and Rehabilitation Centers for the users of Narcotic Drugs" 2018. The ministry has recently endorsed a five-year action plan, the "Narcotic Drug Prevention and Control National Master Plan" which aims for policy reforms including formulation of a standardized treatment protocol for treatment and rehabilitation center, awareness and education programs that are delivered through various settings including schools, institutional partnership, expansion of other treatment services including harm reduction interventions, and research in emergent issues like the legalization of cannabis. The National Mental Health Strategy and Action Plan of 2020 has provisions for the treatment and rehabilitation of people using substances, and raising awareness about the same (Sharma et al., 2024a, 2024b).

3.4.2 Suicide mortality rate is a primary global indicator specifically focused on mental health Mental Health Strategy and Action Plan 2020 outlines several targeted measures for suicide prevention. These include awareness and education campaigns, integration of suicide risk assessment into maternal and other health services, and specific interventions such as the regulation of pesticide use, establishment of a national suicide registry, mandatory reporting of suicide cases, and the operation of a national suicide prevention helpline (Table 1).

6 Challenges for Synergizing SDGs and Mental Health in Nepal

For a country like Nepal the SDGs declared by UN conference is very ambitious to achieve within the short period. This has burdened the nation's economy which was s ruined by ten years internal conflict, disasters like earthquake and the COVID-19 pandemic (Sharma et al., 2024a, 2024b). Apart from the basic challenges like stigma, discrimination, cultural barriers, urban–rural disparity, limited manpower and services there are other challenges which have been other obstacles in synergizing SDGs and mental health in context of Nepal. Events related to climate change like as droughts, floods, landslides, and extreme weather patterns have a profound psychological impact on vulnerable populations in Nepal, including women, children, farmers, and individuals with pre-existing mental health conditions. These

Table 1 Mental health-related targets of SDGs and data gaps (Nepal Health Research Council, 2019)

Sn	Indicator	SDG	Target for 2030	Data gap	Recommendation
1	Good health and well-being	3.4	–	–	–
2	Suicide mortality rate (per 1 lakh population)	3.4.2	4.7	Nepal Police collects data and is not reported to Ministry of Health	Collaborate with Nepal Police to establish and operate routine MIS and build linkage with MoH
	DALYs attributed to mental and substance abuse disorders (per 100,000 population)	3.4.4		Data from the service providers/ facilities not reported to MoH	Establish and operationalize systems in collaboration with the stakeholders
3	Strengthen prevention and treatment of substance abuse, including narcotic drug abuse and harmful use of alcohol • Percentage of hard drug users who have ever visited rehabilitation centers of comprehensive services alcohol • Percentage of people aged 15 years and older having harmful use of alcohol (define according to the national content)	3.5	75% 1.8%	Data from the service providers/ facilities not reported to MoH	Establish and operationalize systems in collaboration with the stakeholders
4	Tobacco control • Age-standardized prevalence of current tobacco use among person aged 15 years and older	4.7	15.09		

events lead to a range of mental disorders such as PTSD, depression, anxiety, and substance use, often exacerbated by displacement, resource loss, and social network disruption (Dhimal et al., 2021a, 2021b).

6.1 Low Political Priority for Mental Health

Though there is growing recognition of mental health as integral part of sustainable development it has been under low political priority in Nepal. Mental health receives very less of the national health budget, and there is no dedicated mental health authority to coordinate national efforts (Sharma et al, 2024a, 2024b).

6.2 Lack of Integration Across Sectors

Achieving SDGs requires a multisectoral approach, yet mental health in Nepal remains solely within the health sector. There is insufficient coordination with sectors such as education (SDG 4), gender (SDG 5), and employment (SDG 8), which are directly impacted by and contribute to mental health outcomes.

6.3 Inadequate Data and Monitoring Systems

There is lack of robust mental health data systems in Nepal. This has become a major hindrance in progress tracking and policy development. SDGs emphasize the use of disaggregated data to identify vulnerable populations, yet mental health indicators are rarely included in national surveys or development monitoring tools. Also, the day-to-day reporting of mental health data via HMIS is not adequate (Sharma et al., 2024a, 2024b).

6.4 Limited Funds and Dependence on Donor-Driven Programs

The government fund for the mental health is limited and proper utilization is a major concern. Many mental health initiatives in Nepal are supported by external donors or NGOs. These are very valuable programs but are mostly time-limited, lack sustainability, and are not always aligned with national SDG strategies, reducing their long-term impact. The mental health services run on ad-hoc basis whenever a disaster struck and is forgotten (Sherchan et al., 2017). The funding for the programs come in form of aids and NGO programs, there is always a concern of government ownership and financing to sustain services and scale them up to non-affected parts of the country.

6.5 Poor Integration of Mental Health into Primary Care Setting

The aim of integration of mental health in primary health care has been there in Nepal as a part of task shifting for a long time. However, this is yet to be fully integrated. This has hampered in early detection, management, prevention and promotion of mental health issues at grassroot level (Acharya et al., 2016).

7 Future Directions and Recommendations

There is a need for a multisectoral strategy for alignment of mental health in the Sustainable Development Goals (SDGs) agenda in Nepal. Mental health should first be prioritized as a development issue at the national level by incorporating it into important planning documents, including the SDG roadmap and regular development plans. There is a need to form a core coordinating unit, like a national mental health authority within the Ministry of Health and Population to ensure policy convergence. There is also a need for intersectoral coordination of mental health with the sectors like education, labor, social welfare, and gender equity, as these are the cross-cutting determinants of mental health. To combat the critical shortage of health workers training of primary care staff and community health workers must be upscaled in the task-sharing models like WHO's Mental Health Gap Action Programme (mhGAP). Additionally, national anti-stigma campaigns and mental health literacy courses, integrated into school curricula and community settings, are necessary so as to facilitate early help-seeking behavior and to combat discrimination. Strong mental health information systems need to be put in place to deliver disaggregated, high-quality data to support policy monitoring and evaluation, with the integration of mental health indicators into national health and SDG monitoring systems. Community-based mental health services—human rights-based and culture-sensitive—need to be strengthened, particularly in rural and disadvantaged areas. Lastly, the provision of sustainable funding by domestic budgetary allocations, health insurance programs, and provincial and local government funding mechanisms is essential to reduce dependency on external donors and ensure long-term integration of mental health into Nepal's development agenda.

8 Conclusion

The Government of Nepal has demonstrated its commitment to achieving the SDGs as a member state of the UN. There is no denying the fact that mental health is an important determinant for attaining the Sustainable Development Goals. Despite noteworthy policy advancements like inclusion of mental health in basic health package, National Mental Health Strategy, National mental health-care program, etc. Nepal continues to face critical barriers including limited political will, insufficient budget allocation, fragmented service delivery, and widespread stigma. The SDG framework offers an important opportunity to integrate mental health into development priorities. However, this huge task requires strong political commitment, intersectoral collaboration, community engagement, and robust monitoring systems. As Nepal progresses toward 2030, aligning mental health with SDG implementation can serve as a vital step toward holistic national development.

References

Acharya, B., Tenpa, J., Thapa, P., Gauchan, B., Citrin, D., & Ekstrand, M. (2016). Recommendations from primary care providers for integrating mental health in a primary care system in rural Nepal. *BMC Health Services Research, 16*, 1–8.

Adhikari, K. P. (2019). Realising the rights of persons with disability in Nepal: Policy addresses from the health, education and livelihoods perspectives. *Nepalese Journal of Development and Rural Studies, 16*, 23–34. https://doi.org/10.3126/njdrs.v16i0.31532

Adhikari, S. R., & Adhikary, D. K. (2019). *An account of Nepal disasters and economic fallout* (Research Report). Project Research And Management Associates.

Agaoglu, L., Torun, O., Unuvar, E., Sefil, Y., & Demir, D. (2007). Effects of iron deficiency anemia on cognitive function in children. *Arzneimittel-Forschung/Drug Research, 57*(6 A), 426–430. https://doi.org/10.1055/s-0031-1296691

Alegría, M., Alvarez, K., Cheng, M., & Falgas-Bague, I. (2023). Recent advances on social determinants of mental health: Looking fast forward. *The American Journal of Psychiatry, 180*(7), 473–482. https://doi.org/10.1176/appi.ajp.20230371

Ali, Y., & Mekonnen, S. (2021). Global prevalence and determinants of mental health disorders during the COVID-19 pandemic: A systematic review and meta-analysis. *Annals of Medicine and Surgery, 68*(July), Article 102634. https://doi.org/10.1016/j.amsu.2021.102634

Bharati, R., Romero, D., & Pozen, A. (2025). Experiences and effect of implementing Social Health Insurance (SHI) program in Nepal-A mixed method study. *Plos Global Public Health, 5*(4), 1–17. https://doi.org/10.1371/journal.pgph.0003492

Brenman, N. F., Luitel, N. P., Mall, S., & Jordans, M. J. D. (2014). Demand and access to mental health services: A qualitative formative study in Nepal. *BMC International Health and Human Rights, 14*(1), 1–12. https://doi.org/10.1186/1472-698X-14-22

Budhathoki, S. S., Pokharel, P. K., Good, S., Limbu, S., Bhattachan, M., & Osborne, R. H. (2017). The potential of health literacy to address the health related UN sustainable development goal 3 (SDG3) in Nepal: A rapid review. *BMC Health Services Research, 17*(1), 1–13. https://doi.org/10.1186/s12913-017-2183-6

Buoli, M., Grassi, S., Caldiroli, A., Carnevali, G. S., Mucci, F., Iodice, S., Cantone, L., Pergoli, L., & Bollati, V. (2018, March). Is there a link between air pollution and mental disorders? *Environment International, 118*, 154–168. https://doi.org/10.1016/j.envint.2018.05.044

Burgess, R. A., Jeffery, M., Odero, S. A., Rose-Clarke, K., & Devakumar, D. (2022). Overlooked and unaddressed: A narrative review of mental health consequences of child marriages. *PLOS Global Public Health, 2*(1), 1–21. https://doi.org/10.1371/journal.pgph.0000131

Camp, D. L., Finlay, W. M. L., & Lyons, E. (2002). Is low self-esteem an inevitable consequence of stigma? An example from women with chronic mental health problems. *Social Science and Medicine, 55*(5), 823–834. https://doi.org/10.1016/S0277-9536(01)00205-2

Census Nepal. (2021). Retrieved from May 15, 2025, from https://censusnepal.cbs.gov.np/Home/Index/EN

Chisholm, D., Garman, E., Breuer, E., Fekadu, A., Hanlon, C., Jordans, M., Kathree, T., Kigozi, F., Luitel, N., Medhin, G., Murhar, V., Petersen, I., Rathod, S. D., Shidhaye, R., Ssebunnya, J., Patel, V., & Lund, C. (2020). Health service costs and their association with functional impairment among adults receiving integrated mental health care in five low- and middle-income countries- and PRIME cohort study. *Health Policy and Planning, 35*(5), 567–576. https://doi.org/10.1093/heapol/czz182

Christian, P., Murray-Kolb, L. E., Khatry, S. K., Katz, J., Schaefer, B. A., Cole, P. M., LeClerq, S. C., & Tielsch, J. M. (2010). Prenatal micronutrient supplementation and intellectual and motor function in early school-aged children in Nepal. *JAMA, 304*(24), 2716–2723. https://doi.org/10.1001/jama.2010.1861

Cutter, S. L., Boruff, B. J., & Shirley, W. L. (2003). Social vulnerability to environmental hazards. *Social Science Quarterly, 84*(2), 242–261. https://doi.org/10.1111/1540-6237.8402002

Department of Economic and Social Affairs. (2015). *Transforming Our World: The 2030 Agenda for Sustainable Development*. Retrieved from May 24, 2025, from https://sdgs.un.org/2030agenda

Devkota, G., Basnet, P., Thapa, B., & Subedi, M. (2021, April). Factors affecting utilization of mental health services from Primary Health Care (PHC) facilities of western hilly district of Nepal. *PLoS ONE, 16*(4), 1–22. https://doi.org/10.1371/journal.pone.0250694

Dhimal, M., Bhandari, D., Dhimal, M. L., Kafle, N., Pyakurel, P., Mahotra, N., Akhtar, S., Ismail, T., Dhiman, R. C., Groneberg, D. A., Shrestha, U. B., & Müller, R. (2021). Impact of climate change on health and well-being of people in Hindu Kush Himalayan Region: A narrative review. *Frontiers in Physiology, 12*. https://doi.org/10.3389/fphys.2021.651189

Dhimal, M., Dahal, S., Adhikari, K., Koirala, P., Bista, B., Luitel, N., Pant, S., Marahatta, K., Shakya, S., Sharma, P., Ghimire, S., Gyanwali, P., Ojha, S. P., & Jha, A. K. (2021). *A nationwide prevalence of common mental disorders and suicidality in Nepal: Evidence from national mental health survey, 2019–2020*. http://elibrary.nhrc.gov.np:8080/handle/20.500.14356/1201

Ellsberg, M., Jansen, H. A. F. M., Heise, L., Watts, C. H., & García-Moreno, C. (2008). Intimate partner violence and women's physical and mental health in the WHO multi-country study on women's health and domestic violence: An observational study. *The Lancet, 371*, 1165–1172. https://doi.org/10.1016/s0084-3970(08)79072-8

Family Welfare division. (2018). *The Public Health Service Act 2018*. Retrieved from May 27, 2025, from https://fwd.gov.np/cms/the-public-health-service-act-2075-2018

Family Welfare division. (2019). *National Health Policy 2019 DoHS Annual Report Public Health Update*. Retrieved from May 27, 2025, from https://fwd.gov.np/cms/national-health-policy-2019-dohs-annual-report-public-health-update/

Ghimire, T. N., Kafle, D. R., & Karki, S. (2024). Traditions, rituals and policy on gender discrimination in Nepal. *International Journal of Multidisciplinary Research and Growth Evaluation, 5*(6), 240–247. Article Info Received: 07–09–2024 Accepted: 11–10–2024.

Government of Nepal. (2020). *Public Health Service Regulation, 2020*. Retrieved from May 27, 2025, from https://fwd.gov.np/wp-content/uploads/2023/12/Public-Health-Regulations-2020-Unoffical-English-Translation.pdf

Government of Nepal National Planning Commission. (2020). *Nepal national review of sustainable development goals* (in Report).

Government of Nepal National Planning Commission. (2024, June).*Nepal voluntary national review of sustainable development goals* (in Report).

Gupta, A. K., & Sigdel, T. S. (2024). Integrating sustainable development goals in local plans: Unlocking practices and challenges of local governments in Nepal. *Heliyon, 10*(20). https://doi.org/10.1016/j.heliyon.2024.e39615

Gurung, D., Neupane, M., Bhattarai, K., Acharya, B., Gautam, N. C., Gautam, K., Koirala, S., Marahatta, K., Gurung, P., Khadka, K. B., Kohrt, B. A., Thornicroft, G., & Gronholm, P. C. (2023). Mental health-related structural stigma and discrimination in health and social policies in Nepal: A scoping review and synthesis. *Epidemiology and Psychiatric Sciences, 32*. https://doi.org/10.1017/S2045796023000823

Gurung, H. B. (2001). *Nepal, social demography and expressions* (2nd ed.). New ERA. https://cir.nii.ac.jp/crid/1130000794959985920

Huggett, C., Birtel, M. D., Awenat, Y. F., Fleming, P., Wilkes, S., Williams, S., & Haddock, G. (2018). A qualitative study: Experiences of stigma by people with mental health problems. *Psychology and Psychotherapy: Theory, Research and Practice, 91*(3), 380–397. https://doi.org/10.1111/papt.12167

Kane, J. C., Luitel, N. P., Jordans, M. J. D., Kohrt, B. A., Weissbecker, I., & Tol, W. A. (2018). Mental health and psychosocial problems in the aftermath of the Nepal earthquakes: Findings from a representative cluster sample survey. *Epidemiology and Psychiatric Sciences, 27*(3), 301–310. https://doi.org/10.1017/S2045796016001104

Khatiwada, P. P., Subedi, D. R., Gurung, Y. B., Pradhan, M. S., & Pradhan, P. (2022). Challenges to leave no one behind in Nepal for achieving sustainable development goals. In W. Leal Filho, T. F. Ng, U. Iyer-Raniga, A. Ng, & A. Sharifi (Eds.), *SDGs in the Asia and Pacific Region* (pp. 1–31). Springer International Publishing. https://doi.org/10.1007/978-3-030-91262-8_105-1

Lund, C., Docrat, S., Abdulmalik, J., Alem, A., Fekadu, A., Gureje, O., Gurung, D., Hailemariam, D., Hailemichael, Y., Hanlon, C., Jordans, M. J. D., Kizza, D., Nanda, S., Olayiwola, S., Shidhaye, R., Upadhaya, N., Thornicroft, G., & Chisholm, D. (2019). Household economic costs associated with mental, neurological and substance use disorders: A cross-sectional survey in six low- and middle-income countries. *Bjpsych Open, 5*(3), 1–11. https://doi.org/10.1192/bjo.2019.20

Mahato, P., Bhusal, S., Regmi, P., & Van Teijlingen, E. (2024). Health and wellbeing among Nepali migrants: A scoping review. *Journal of Health Promotion, 12*, 79–90. https://doi.org/10.3126/jhp.v12i1.72699

Mersky, J. P., Topitzes, J., & Reynolds, A. J. (2013). Impacts of adverse childhood experiences on health, mental health, and substance use in early adulthood: A cohort study of an urban, minority sample in the U.S. *Child Abuse and Neglect, 37*(11), 917–925. https://doi.org/10.1016/j.chiabu.2013.07.011

National Planning Commission. (2019). *Nepal's SDG Status and Roadmap: 2016–2030*. National Planning Commission. Retrieved from May 24, 2025, from https://npc.gov.np/content/5044/5044-nepals-sdg-status-and-roadmap/

Nelson, S., Baldwin, N., & Taylor, J. (2012). Mental health problems and medically unexplained physical symptoms in adult survivors of childhood sexual abuse: An integrative literature review. *Journal of Psychiatric and Mental Health Nursing, 19*(3), 211–220. https://doi.org/10.1111/j.1365-2850.2011.01772.x

Nepal Health Research Council. (2019). *Research Report on Assessing the Progress of Health-Related SDGs Indicators for Nepal*. Nepal Health Research Council. Retrieved from May 25, 2025, from https://nhrc.gov.np/publication/research-report-on-assessing-the-progress-of-health-related-sdgs-indicators-for-nepal/

Nepal Health Research Council. (2020). *Report of National Mental Health Survey Nepal 2020*. Retrieved from May 27, 2025, from https://nhrc.gov.np/publication/report-of-national-mental-health-survey-2020/

Pant, R. K. (2024). Nepal's performance in achieving sustainable development goals: A critical evaluation. *Kaumodaki: Journal of Multidisciplinary Studies, 4*(1), Article 1. https://doi.org/10.3126/kdk.v4i1.64576

Paudyal, R., & Abraham, A. (2010, January 1). The impact of political instability on economic and social sustainability: The case of Nepal. In*Proceedings of the 2nd World Accounting Frontiers Series Conference 2010* (pp. 139–158). University of Southern Queensland.

Poudel, K., & Subedi, P. (2020). Impact of COVID-19 pandemic on socioeconomic and mental health aspects in Nepal. *International Journal of Social Psychiatry, 66*(8), 748–755. https://doi.org/10.1177/0020764020942247

Pradhan, U., & Karki, S. (2019). Sustainable development goals in Nepal: Prospects and challenges. In *Social Development and the Sustainable Development Goals in South Asia*. Routledge.

Sapkota, T., Houkes, I., & Bosma, H. (2021). Vicious cycle of chronic disease and poverty: A qualitative study in present day Nepal. *International Health, 13*(1), 30–38. https://doi.org/10.1093/inthealth/ihaa016

Sharma, P., Budhathoki, C. B., Maharjan, R. K., & Singh, J. K. (2023, March). Nutritional status and psychosocial stimulation associated with cognitive development in preschool children: A cross-sectional study at Western Terai, Nepal. *PLoS ONE, 18*(3), 1–14. https://doi.org/10.1371/journal.pone.0280032

Sharma, P., Gautam, K., & Marahatta, K. (2024). Access to mental health care in Nepal: Current status, potential challenges, and ways out. In *Access to mental health care in South Asia: Current status, potential challenges, and ways out* (pp. 91–111). Springer Nature Singapore.

Sharma, P., Pant, S. B., & Marahatta, K. (2024). Current perspectives on substance use disorders in Nepal. In *Current perspectives on substance use disorders in South Asia: Public mental health aspects* (pp. 89–102). Springer Nature Singapore.

Shawon, M. S. R., Hossain, F. B., Hasan, M., & Rahman, M. R. (2024). Gender differences in the prevalence of anxiety and depression and care seeking for mental health problems in Nepal: Analysis of nationally representative survey data. *Cambridge Prisms: Global Mental Health, 11*(e46), 1–10. https://doi.org/10.1017/gmh.2024.37

Sherchan, S., Samuel, R., Marahatta, K., Anwar, N., Van Ommeren, M. H., & Ofrin, R. (2017). Post-disaster mental health and psychosocial support: Experience from the 2015 Nepal earthquake. *WHO South-East Asia Journal of Public Health, 6*(1), 22–29. https://doi.org/10.4103/2224-3151.206160

Shrestha, M. L., Perry, K. E., Thapa, B., Adhikari, R. P., & Weissman, A. (2022). Malnutrition matters: Association of stunting and underweight with early childhood development indicators in Nepal. *Maternal and Child Nutrition, 18*(2), 1–9. https://doi.org/10.1111/mcn.13321

Sontheimer, N., Konnopka, A., & König, H. H. (2021). The Excess costs of dementia: A systematic review and meta-analysis. *Journal of Alzheimer's Disease, 83*(1), 333–354. https://doi.org/10.3233/JAD-210174

Subedi, K. R. (2021). Social security allowances program some issue and challenges in Nepal. *International Journal for Science and Advance Research in Technology, 7*(12), 329–336.

Tol, W. A., Kohrt, B. A., Jordans, M. J. D., Thapa, S. B., Pettigrew, J., Upadhaya, N., & de Jong, J. T. V. M. (2010). Political violence and mental health: A multi-disciplinary review of the literature on Nepal. *Social Science and Medicine, 70*(1), 35–44. https://doi.org/10.1016/j.socscimed.2009.09.037

World Health Organization. (2021). *Nepal—WHO Special Initiative for Mental Health Situational Assessment*. Retrieved from May 15, 2025, from https://www.who.int/publications/m/item/nepal---who-special-initiative-for-mental-health

World Health Organization. (2022). *National Mental Health Care Programme Nepal 2022. Strengthening primary care mental health services in Nepal*. Retrieved from May 15, 2025, from https://psychiatrynepal.org.np/wp-content/uploads/2024/03/National-Mental-Health-Care-Programme-Nepal-2022-1.pdf

Chapter 11
Sustainable Development Goals and Mental Health in Pakistan

Rizwana Amin

Abstract This chapter examines the relationship between mental health and the Sustainable Development Goals (SDGs) in Pakistan's healthcare and sociopolitical setting. Although many of the SDGs do not specifically address mental health except health and well-being (SDG 3), it critically analyzes how mental health issues are intricately linked to targets related to poverty (SDG 1), zero hunger (SDG2), quality education (SDG 4), gender equality (SDG 5), innovation and technology development (SDG 9), reduced inequalities (SDG 10), climate change (SDG 13), peace and justice (SDG 16). Inadequate infrastructure, social stigma, a lack of trained specialists, and restricted access to services are some of the mental health issues Pakistan faces, which hinder the country's efforts to meet the SDGs. However, there are some particular initiatives such as chaman pilot project, Rozan's Zeest as well as Humraaz can be implemented at macro level to bridge the gap in field. Moreover, legislation about mental health needs to be realized in Pakistan to promote well-being.

Keywords SDGs · Mental health · Pakistan · Well-being · Health policy · Vulnerable populations

1 Introduction

In 2015, all United Nations member states ratified the Sustainable Development Goals (SDGs), establishing a comprehensive set of goals to address global social, economic, and environmental issues by 2030 (Yumnam et al., 2024). The SDGs consist of 169 targets and 17 goals, aiming to create a cohesive strategy for promoting inclusive development, reducing inequality, and preserving environmental sustainability to achieve global health and well-being (Bąk, 2024). The third of these 17 goals is health and well-being, which stresses the need to ensure healthy lives and promote well-being. Mental health is important for sustainable development,

R. Amin (✉)
Effat University, Jeddah, Saudi Arabia
e-mail: riamin@effatuniversity.edu.sa

S. K. Kar et al. (eds.), *Sustainable Development Goals and Mental Health in South Asia*, South Asian Perspectives in Mental Health and Psychology ,
https://doi.org/10.1007/978-981-95-2684-0_11

including its effects on productivity, educational attainment, national stability, and economic success, which has led to its official recognition in this agenda (WHO, 2024).

Mental health constitutes a fundamental component of sustainable development and an outcome derived from it (Martinelli, 2024). Individuals with robust mental health can significantly contribute to society; nevertheless, insufficient mental healthcare perpetuates poverty, social inequities, and discrimination (Kirkbride et al., 2024). Since Pakistan is a lower-middle-income country that experiences widespread poverty, political unrest, systemic gender discrimination, and limited access to healthcare services, the correlation is especially significant there (Mubarak et al., 2023). Despite the rising incidence of mental health conditions such as anxiety, depression, and trauma-related disorders, mental health services are not sufficiently integrated into national health frameworks (Noorullah et al., 2024). The UN SDGs offer Pakistan the chance to create a thorough rights-based framework that tackles social problems, expands access to mental health care, and emphasizes mental health as an essential part of national development.

This chapter discusses the interaction between the SDGs and mental health within Pakistan's social, economic, and political context. It identifies significant challenges, examines policy implications, and underscores a framework for integrating mental health into sustainable development planning and implementation.

2 Mental Health and SDGs

According to the World Health Organization (WHO), mental health refers to an individual's ability to identify one's own strengths, maintain a normal stress response, be productive at work, and serve the community (WHO, 2004). Mental health encompasses three essential dimensions of emotional, psychological, and social well-being that directly influence individuals' perceptions of the world and their interactions with others. Several factors, such as biological factors, life experiences, and support systems, contribute to mental health (Freeman, 2022). Mental health is a distinct component connecting the various SDGs-(Dybdahl & Lien, 2018). SDG 3's (Good Health and Well-Being) target 3.4 predominantly requires mental health advocacy and early reductions in non-communicable disease mortality (Monaco, 2024). In addition to its health significance, it carries further value within the SDG framework. Several other goals, including SDG 1 (no poverty), are directly impacted by mental health since mental illness generates financial instability, which in turn perpetuates financial instability (Mills, 2018). SDG 4 (quality education) is negatively impacted by the mental health issues of students and educators, resulting in detrimental effects on learning outcomes and classroom performance (Syed & Moriarty, 2020). SDG 5 (gender equality) is crucial since women and other marginalized genders face greater risks of trauma and gender-based violence, which adversely affects their mental health (Guaita-Fernández et al., 2024). Mental health is intrinsically linked to SDG 8, which pertains to decent work and economic growth, as well as SDG 10, which addresses reduced disparities, because both require psychological resilience and comprehensive access to mental health treatment for individuals (Lund et al., 2018). Concerning Pakistan, the confluence of sustainable development and mental health poses challenges and growth opportunities (Malik, 2024). The healthcare system has failed to acknowledge the financial burden that mental illness places on the economy. Reduced productivity, absenteeism, and higher healthcare expenses are all outcomes of individuals' untreated mental health issues. The national GDP suffers greatly because of insufficient funding for mental health services, as mental health significantly impacts the economy. Moreover, perpetuating cycles of poverty and mental health concerns among Pakistan's youth hinders educational opportunities and renders them unprepared for the workforce (Choudhry et al., 2023).

3 Mental Health Landscape in Pakistan: Challenges and Gaps

The importance of mental health to general development and well-being is becoming more widely acknowledged. Nevertheless, despite its significant influence on people, families, and society as a whole, mental health is still frequently disregarded in Pakistan (Dayani et al., 2024).The prevalence of mental health illnesses in the nation is rising, yet there are still large gaps in policy implementation, care delivery, and societal stigma (Choudhry et al., 2023). This section examines Pakistan's mental health situation, emphasizing the burden and prevalence of mental illnesses, major obstacles, gaps in the healthcare system, policy concerns, and the impact of social and economic factors.

3.1 Prevalence and Burden of Mental Disorders

The prevalence of mental health disorders in Pakistan is alarmingly high due to societal and environmental stressors, compounded by inadequate public mental health facilities (Noorullah et al., 2024). The findings of national surveys indicate overall 37.91% of psychiatric disorders that some groups are impacted by mental health illnesses such as depression, anxiety, and post-traumatic stress disorder (PTSD), as well as substance use disorders and suicidal ideation (Rahman et al., 2024). An epidemiological study has identified depression and anxiety as two predominant mental health problems, with approximately 34% of individuals likely to experience these conditions at some point in their lives (Hashmi et al., 2023).

The incidence of PTSD remains elevated in conflict-affected regions where individuals endure trauma from violent confrontations, displacement, and acts of terrorism (Ahmed et al., 2024a, 2024b). The prevalence of substance misuse is escalating due to poverty, unemployment, and the absence of mental health support networks (Khalily et al., 2024). The suicide mortality rate is difficult to ascertain accurately due to societal stigma surrounding the reporting of such incidents. In Pakistan, mental health issues are a leading cause of suicide, with over 15,000 suicides occurring each year.

Pakistan's healthcare delivery system is facing challenges in meeting residents' mental health needs (Noorullah et al., 2024). Even though mental health issues account for a significant portion of Pakistan's disease burden, healthcare systems do not adequately address them. The provision of mental health services is insufficient due to their inadequate integration within primary healthcare centers. Access to mental health treatment centers is restricted for residents in rural areas as well as those living outside of urban centers (Main Thompson & Saleem, 2025).

3.2 Key Challenges and Gaps

3.2.1 Stigma and Cultural Barriers

The stigma associated with mental illness presents a substantial barrier to efficient mental health management in Pakistan (Talat, 2022). Insufficient knowledge about mental health difficulties causes people to mistake them for other illnesses and fail to recognize their actual nature, which results in prejudice, social exclusion, and a refusal to seek help (Waqas et al., 2020). As people view mental health issues as indicators of spirit possession or as a sign of weakness and divine vengeance, many cultural myths and misconceptions about them continue to exist Religious interpretations typically strengthen spiritual beliefs, which leads people to turn to religious leaders rather than mental health experts for support (Tahir, 2025). Society's lack of understanding about mental health exacerbates this dilemma.

3.2.2 Social and Economic Determinants

The economic and social factors in Pakistan significantly affect the mental health situation (Sohail et al., 2017). A large portion of the population lives below the poverty line, with unemployment and displacement as primary contributors to mental distress. Persistent financial instability can lead to depression and other mental health issues, thereby perpetuating cycles of poverty. Displacement due to natural disasters and ongoing conflicts has a major impact on tribal and border areas, where individuals experience PTSD and a decline in social support networks (Ahmed et al., 2024a, 2024b). Moreover, gender-based inequalities and domestic violence are two major challenges that contribute to mental health issues (Sarfraz et al., 2022). Women are generally more prone to endure domestic violence, which affects their mental well-being. The majority of cases of neglect and abuse against women remain unreported because of inadequate support systems and a lack of resources for victims.

Women encounter increased mental health risks due to gender inequality and detrimental cultural practices, as their issues often remain unaddressed because of societal standards and inadequate healthcare access (Sarwar & Farid, 2024).

3.2.3 Healthcare System Gaps

The Pakistani healthcare system encounters challenges in providing adequate mental healthcare services (Choudhry et al., 2023). Medical conditions impacting mental health result in significant health challenges nationwide; nonetheless, mental health services receive inadequate attention from the overall healthcare system. Poor integration of mental health treatments into primary care poses a key deficiency of Pakistan's healthcare system (Ahmed et al., 2024a, 2024b). Individuals in rural regions, as well as those living outside metropolitan centers, encounter accessibility obstacles due to mental health services predominantly being offered in specialized facilities.

A shortage of mental health service providers is another challenge to mental healthcare services in Pakistan. Hence, Pakistan is reported to have one of the lowest ratios of psychiatrists and psychologists to its population, with only 0.2 psychiatrists per 100,000 individuals (Rahman et al., 2024). The dearth of training facilities and low pay hinders the development of a robust mental health workforce. Moreover, the unavailability of infrastructure and resources, particularly in rural areas, widens the gap because many vulnerable individuals have limited access to mental health care (Okechukwu, 2022).

3.2.4 Policy and Governance Issues

Pakistan's Mental Health Act was first initiated in 2001, and various revisions have been made to the bill. However, insufficient legislation has prevented its full implementation (Noorullah et al., 2024). The Pakistan Mental Health Act protects individuals with mental health disorders, nonetheless, its implementation is inconsistent, and mental healthcare lacks accountability (Kabir et al., 2024). Mental health services are allocated less than 1% of the health budget, which is inadequate. Inadequate funding impedes essential infrastructure, scientific research, and preventative initiatives, obstructing the advancement of mental health care (Mahesar et al., 2024). The national mental health policy is disregarded due to its failure to acknowledge mental health as integral to public health and sustainable development objectives.

4 SDGs and Mental Health in Pakistan: Specific Linkages and Interventions

Since 2015, the United Nations has established SDGs to address global concerns (Gyimah et al., 2025) and mental health is identified explicitly in SDG 3 (Good Health and Well-being), it has been shown to have a direct influence on various goals, which in turn creates substantial repercussions on social development in addition to economic and political advancement (Dybdahl & Lien, 2018). Hence, mental health is currently receiving little attention from Pakistan's healthcare system, it is not only relevant but also imperative that mental health be included in the SDG framework. The incidence of mentalhealth issues is significant in the country (Rahman et al., 2024). Despite this, Pakistan has 500 qualified psychiatrists for a population of over 240 million (Dayani et al., 2025), and less than 1% of the total health expenditure is allocated to mental health (WHO, 2018, 2007). A comprehensive approach to mental health supports improved educational achievements (SDG 4), gender equity (SDG 5), economic growth (SDG 8), and fewer inequities (SDG 10). Pakistan must incorporate mental health interventions into its efforts to meet the SDGs to guarantee equitable and sustainable national development. This section will explore the tangible interventions and challenges that connect mental health to several Sustainable Development Goals (SDGs).

4.1 SDG 1: No Poverty

Poverty is a factor that contributes to mental health issues as well as a risk factor for them. The conditions of depression, anxiety, and substance misuse are typically the result of economic pressures such as unemployment, poor income, and financial insecurity. These factors contribute to the perpetuation of poverty (Marbin et al., 2022). Implementing mental health screening and services into the country's welfare initiative programs, such as the Benazir Income Support Program (BISP), would make it possible to provide mental health support to participants receiving conditional cash transfers. By utilizing this program framework, the provision of financial assistance and mental health services can be brought into harmony, thereby satisfying the twin requirements of communities that are at risk (Jafree, 2023).

Moreover, creating employment opportunities for people with mental health issues helps in decreasing economic stresses, resulting in an improvement in their overall well-being. BISP initiatives are essential for alleviating poverty; yet, they typically lack mental health screening and service offerings. In the absence of mental health screening programs, individuals facing both poverty and mental health challenges lack adequate support. Neglecting mental health services in poverty reduction efforts may hinder the effective execution of poverty alleviation methods (Knifton & Inglis, 2020).

4.2 SDG 2: Zero Hunger

In Pakistan, approximately 36.9% of the population faces food insecurity, highlighting the reciprocal and pressing relationship between hunger and mental health (WFP, 2023). Chronic hunger and malnutrition hinder physical growth and adversely affect mental and emotional well-being (Alaimo et al., 2020). Malnourished individuals, especially children and pregnant women, are more vulnerable of developing anxiety, depression, and behavioral disorders (Kirolos et al., 2022). The psychological impact of hunger often results in despair, stress, and chronic trauma in Pakistan's rural and urban slums, where poverty and food scarcity are widespread (Ejiohuo et al., 2024; WFP, 2023). Intergenerational mental health concerns are exacerbated by the heightened psychological pain encountered by parents facing food insecurity. This psychological outcome might impede parenting and contribute to adverse childhood experiences (ACEs).

In Pakistan, food security and mental health interventions are often addressed independently, despite their significant interrelation. An urgent requirement exists for comprehensive programs that provide both mental and nutritional assistance. Promising initiatives such as Ehsaas, Nashonuma and the Benazir Income Support Programme (BISP) might be expanded to provide mental health screening and support (Mughal & Baig, 2024). Attaining SDG 2 (Zero Hunger) and SDG 3 (Good Health and Well-Being) in Pakistan necessitates the consideration of hunger as a social factor of mental health.

4.3 SDG 3: Good Health and Well-Being

SDG 3 aims to provide health and well-being advantages to every individual worldwide (Das et al., 2021). The realization of this objective implies that mental health is a fundamental element, as mental health issues presently constitute a significant contributor to the global disease burden (Chen et al., 2024). Pakistan faces growing mental health challenges that heavily burden its healthcare system, as depression, anxiety disorders, and substance addiction are becoming more common across the country (Alvi et al., 2024).

The implementation of various interventions stands as a solution for treating mental health under SDG 3. Incorporating comprehensive mental health treatments at Basic Health Units (BHUs) in rural regions into community-based mental health programs is crucial. Due to a lack of mental health specialists, these programs help rural communities by providing mental health treatments to people who might not have received them (Dayani et al., 2024). Primary healthcare providers, such as general practitioners and nurses, can learn basic counseling techniques and mental health first aid knowledge through task-shifting methodologies. These programs increase the ability of frontline healthcare workers to identify and treat mental health issues, leading to better care delivery to larger populations (Lok et al., 2025).

Furthermore, initiatives for telepsychiatry via digital mental health platforms in form of helplines, such as the Ehsaas Mental Health, DilkiBaat, Umang, Taskeen offer practical ways to improve access to mental health care, especially in rural areas (Khurram et al., 2024). Digital counseling methods via these platforms provide confidential support that eliminates barriers such as geographical distance, social stigma, and shortage of professionals. However, a significant number of Pakistani individuals have limited understanding of mental health disorders, frequently disregarding these issues and simultaneously being hesitant to seek help from health professionals (Ahmed et al., 2024a, 2024b). Aversion to seeking therapy and reliance on informal, insufficient care methods exacerbate mental health disorders (Choudhry et al., 2023).

4.4 SDG 4: Quality Education

SDG 4 aims to create inclusive, high-quality educational systems that provide lifelong learning opportunities for all individuals (Chotibuddin et al., 2025). An individual's mental health is crucial for academic achievement, as psychological issues hinder a student's ability to study effectively and negatively affect their academic performance (Mosia et al., 2025). Educational institutions ought to integrate mental health awareness initiatives into their curricula, encompassing life skills education, stress reduction techniques, and mental health education, enabling students to recognize indications of psychological distress and develop resilience abilities from an early age (Akram, 2023). Training is required for educational staff to enable them to recognize the first signs of psychological distress in students. By teaching educators to recognize signs of distress, schools can serve as the first port of call for students who need proper mental health care (Jagiello et al., 2024).

Since most schools in Pakistan lack these skilled mental health experts who assist children, there is a scarcity of qualified school counselors in all public education institutions. This restriction prevents public schools from providing their children with appropriate mental health care (Noorullah et al., 2024). Moreover, the stigma associated with mental health continues to stigmatize it, resulting in parental and educational resistance. Hence, implementing good mental health program initiatives may be impeded by cultural barriers related to mental health (Lasi et al., 2025).

4.5 SDG 5: Gender Equality

The critical significance of gender equality in sustainable development is contingent upon mental health, which is a crucial prerequisite for attaining gender equality (Sarwar & Farid, 2024). The mental health of women and oppressed genders is at increased risk due to prevailing social, cultural, and economic disparities (Lasi et al., 2025). However, community-based support groups provide women with a safe space to talk about their circumstances, receive therapeutic support, and develop coping mechanisms. This group setting is particularly beneficial for women who have experienced domestic or other forms of abuse (Choudhry et al., 2023).

Legal systems allow victims of domestic abuse to move on and rebuild their lives by combining psychological counseling with care (Asghar & Ramisha, 2024). Recognizing the need for legal and psychological support allows survivors to receive complete assistance during their recovery (Melgar Alcantud et al., 2021). Another issue that is overlooked is new mothers' mental health, while postpartum depression and anxiety impact both mothers and their children for prolonged durations (Saeed et al., 2024). To address this critical need, maternal health programs must incorporate necessary mental health screenings and support services.

4.6 SDG 8: Decent Work and Economic Growth

SDG 8 aims to provide inclusive, sustainable growth to everyone with full employment opportunities and respectable benefits. Workplace mental health is a crucial component of this goal since employee mental health significantly impacts output, job satisfaction, and financial performance (Cao et al., 2022).

Organizations must establish policies that acknowledge the psychological well-being of their employees. Implementing these workplace policies results in improved operational environments, reducing disengagement rates and enhancing job performance quality (Rahman et al., 2024; Saraiva & Nogueiro, 2025). Professional psychological support can be provided to employees who have access to employee assistance programs (EAPs) and mental health insurance, resulting in a healthier workforce (Bajorek et al., 2024; Wu et al., 2021).

Inadequate support systems within their organizations subject employees in several occupational fields to excessive stress. Given that workplace mental health programs frequently ignore mental health issues, there is a need to develop such policies to foster the psychological well-being of employees (Rahman et al., 2024). The informal sector workers are not adequately protected from the mental health pressures of their jobs due to the lack of implementation of occupational health standards and protection of labor rights.

4.7 SDG 9: Industry, Innovation, and Infrastructure

SDG 9 emphasizes innovative solutions, inclusive industrialization, and resilient infrastructure. Although this aim does not specifically address mental health, however, it is becoming more widely acknowledged that there is a connection with mental health when considering developing nations like Pakistan. The lack of industrial growth, economic instability, and a lack of infrastructure, particularly in the transportation and health sectors, all contribute to the high prevalence of mental health stresses in both urban and rural areas (UNDP Pakistan, 2024a, 2024b). Due to the lack of psychiatric facilities or qualified specialists, the absence of infrastructure, particularly in rural areas, makes it difficult to get mental wellness treatments (WHO, 2007). Additionally, the absence of workplace mental health regulations in Pakistan's business and industrial sectors raises the prevalence of stress, burnout, and depression among workers, which has an impact on their overall well-being and productivity (Rehman & Butt, 2024). A key strategy for closing this gap is the use of digital health technologies. Initiatives like Humraaz, a mental health app developed in Pakistan, and telepsychiatry innovations via platforms like Sehat Kahani, DilkiBaat, Taskeen, Umang are suggested examples of how creative solutions might reach marginalized audiences for mental health care (Main Thompson & Saleem, 2025). Better public mental health outcomes can be achieved by the adoption of industrial policies that promote employees' mental health and the efficient funding of infrastructure that will enable inclusive digital and health-related services.

4.8 SDG 10: Reduced Inequalities

The goal of SDG 10 is to reduce inequality within and between nations. Socioeconomic and rural–urban gaps in mental health treatment access persist, and underprivileged groups face the greatest challenges. Implementing mental health services in disadvantaged areas mitigates healthcare inequities for patients (Noorullah et al., 2024). Rural communities can receive effective health care from mobile clinics, telemedicine services, and community-based initiatives. Low-income populations should also have access to cheap mental health therapies through public health initiatives and insurance subsidies (Shah et al., 2024).

Underprivileged individuals face numerous systemic barriers in obtaining mental health care (Lasi et al., 2025). These challenges include inadequate awareness, culturally created anxieties, and insufficient financial resources (Javeed et al., 2022). It is necessary to make adjustments to the legislative framework to remove these impediments to improve mental health services.

4.9 SDG 13: Climate Action

Climate change is an escalating threat to mental health, especially in areas sensitive to its effects. Pakistan ranks among the top ten countries most impacted by climate-related disasters, experiencing recurrent floods, droughts, and catastrophic heatwaves that devastate ecosystems and livelihoods, while also causing significant psychological distress among its population (Soomro et al., 2025). Floods in 2022 forced over 33 million people to flee their homes, and many of them experienced trauma, anxiety, and sadness as a result of losing their homes, loved ones, and means of subsistence (UNICEF, 2023). The lack of mental health services in these places exacerbates the issues and leaves victims, particularly women, children, and the elderly, to suffer from chronic stress and post-traumatic symptoms.

Additionally, young people in urban areas are growing more concerned about environmental degradation and policy inaction, which is contributing to climate anxiety and the fear of future environmental disasters (Noor et al., 2025). Despite the obvious links between mental health and climate disasters, Pakistan's climate action strategies rarely include mental health services or psychological resilience in disaster planning and recovery. Protecting Pakistan's vulnerable communities while advancing SDG 13 requires integrating mental health into climate adaptation strategy, educating local responders in Psychological First Aid, and building climate resilient mental health infrastructure (Rashid & Qixiang, 2025).

4.10 SDG 16: Peace, Justice, and Strong Institutions

Sustainable Development Goal 16 emphasizes the advancement of peaceful and inclusive societies, universal access to justice, and the establishment of effective and responsible institutions. This goal and mental health in Pakistan are closely related, particularly when it comes to the themes of violence, conflict, unfair legal systems, and a lack of institutional support (Khalily et al., 2021). The Pakistan has endured prolonged civil conflicts, terrorism (Basit & Ahmed, 2021), gender-based violence (Sarfraz et al., 2022), and political instability (Imran et al., 2023) all of which have resulted in collective trauma and chronic stress among the impacted communities. Untreated depression, anxiety, and post-traumatic stress disorder (PTSD) are common among victims of domestic violence, systematic discrimination, police brutality, and internally displaced people (IDPs) (Human Rights Watch, 2024).

Furthermore, due to a lack of integration, Pakistan's justice and healthcare institutions do not adequately address mentally ill individuals (Mashood, 2025). It is frequently reported that mentally ill inmates are being neglected in prisons, a violation of both institutional accountability and legal safeguards (Justice Project Pakistan, 2022). Furthermore, stigma and marginalization are perpetuated by the absence of legal protection for sick individuals with mental illnesses (Gyamfi et al., 2025). Providing psychosocial support to victims of violence, upholding institutional accountability, and advocating for mental health as a right within the legal system can all contribute to social inclusion and peacebuilding (Maqbool et al., 2024). Incorporating the provision of mental health services into community justice initiatives, legal aid platforms, and policing trainings can increase institutional responsiveness and support Pakistan's SDG 16 objectives. Developing strong institutions must include a commitment to mental health, especially for individuals who are disadvantaged and disinherited.

5 Cross-Sectoral Strategies for Integrating Mental Health in SDG Implementation

Integrating mental health with SDGs is essential for fostering holistic well-being in all societies. Mental health constitutes a vital yet frequently overlooked component of overall developmental frameworks (Bąk, 2024). Since cross-sectoral approaches yield comprehensive solutions that support health, education, social welfare, and economic development, they serve as the cornerstone for incorporating mental health within the SDGs (WHO, 2024). The following section delineates critical strategies for implementing mental health into the SDGs through policy frameworks, governance structures, community-based programs, healthcare professional training, peer support networks, mental health awareness campaigns, and technology-driven solutions.

5.1 Policy and Governance Approaches

The SDG framework relies on policy and governance strategies to prioritize mental health appropriately. Governments must create comprehensive mental health plans that complement the SDGs and implement mental health programs at every level of society. Since mental health is closely related to gender equality, poverty alleviation, employment policies, and educational programs, collaboration among many governmental branches is necessary for mental health governance (WHO, 2024).

The first crucial step necessitates the development of a comprehensive mental health policy at the national level across all vital development areas. The health policy should incorporate mental health, educational, and social welfare programs (Shah et al., 2024). To ensure equitable health care for all social strata and rural communities, the national health policy must consider mental health services a primary goal while upholding other healthcare standards (Khalily et al., 2021). The strategy mandates an emphasis on mental health promotion through preventive initiatives aimed at reducing the overall prevalence of mental health issues among the population.

The effective implementation of mental health programs requires the presence of executive systems. Mental health governance should incorporate a dedicated department or agency within governmental institutions that receives adequate financing and serves as the primary oversight authority for mental health matters (Dayani et al., 2024). A defined framework of duties is essential for the effective execution of mental health programs and the assessment of progress toward health and well-being-related SDGs (Trane et al., 2023).

The effective incorporation of mental health necessitates collaboration among ministries from many sectors within the national development goals. Health ministries must collaborate with education, labor departments, and social services to promote mental well-being in educational institutions, workplaces, and community areas. The collaborative initiatives among organizations will integrate mental health into the national dialogue regarding growth across various societal sectors.

5.2 *Community-Based Interventions*

Community-based mental health solutions are essential because they guarantee services for all populations, with a particular emphasis on vulnerable and neglected communities (Bolton et al., 2023). Rural areas and other resource-deficient regions lack accessible mental health services. Community-based approaches provide a solution by delivering mental health treatment in residential areas through official and informal support networks (Giebel et al., 2024).

Mental health interventions in community settings incorporate mental health education, counseling services, and awareness-raising campaigns. In addition to reducing discrimination against mental health disorders and improving public knowledge about emotional well-being, community-based treatments use indigenous resources to increase access to mental health services (Montesanti et al., 2022). These kinds of interventions assist people in finding support sooner so that their mental health issues remain under control, which lessens the strain on formal healthcare systems.

Basic Health Units (BHUs) in Pakistan demonstrate successful community-based mental health interventions by integrating the provision of psychological support services into their regular community-level health offerings (Gilani & Shah, 2022). Since it is difficult to find specialist care providers in remote places, basic mental health clinics provide crucial services to communities there. BHUs serve as primary facilities for mental health care because they offer mental health resources, assist in identifying psychological problems, and connect patients with specialized care (Main Thompson & Saleem, 2025).

Local and community authorities are crucial in promoting mental health awareness initiatives in their respective regions (Abbas & Talib, 2024). Communities may create mental health-friendly environments to facilitate access to support for those in need by including community leaders in mental health education programs and advocacy efforts.

5.3 *Training Lady Health Workers in Basic Mental Health Support*

Training for Lady Health Workers (LHWs) is essential for successfully integrating mental health services into the SDGs, as they serve as primary healthcare providers in Pakistan's rural communities. The extensive reach of Lady Health Workers throughout communities fosters the best conditions for basic mental health assistance while forging crucial links between the general public and official mental health service providers (Anam, 2024).

Providing Lady Health Workers with basic mental health training has several important positive effects. When properly trained, LHWs can identify mental health conditions, including depression, stress, and anxiety, in community members who are not seeking professional care, making them the first line of defense. Through their training, they can educate the community about mental health issues and raise awareness of mental health needs (Rabbani et al., 2023). As a result of LHWs learning to identify mental health symptoms, people living in rural and marginalized areas will have better access to mental health support.

Additionally, thanks to their basic mental health support, LHWs can connect people with higher levels of healthcare services when necessary. Given their extensive knowledge of regional traditions as well as their language and cultural origins, LHWs have a special capacity to manage mental health issues with cultural sensitivity (Akhtar et al., 2024). The approach makes it possible for mental health service providers to reach communities through accessible services that address their particular requirements.

5.4 Peer Support Networks for Mental Health Advocacy

Peer support refers to the process in which individuals who have encountered mental health concerns assist those with analogous issues (Lyons et al., 2021). These networks enable individuals to establish a supportive environment for sharing mental health narratives and obtaining emotional support alongside access to available services. Peer support networks across Pakistan disseminate mental health awareness to the people while advocating for the rights of individuals with mental health disorders. These networks empower individuals with direct experience by training them as mental health advocates to combat stigma and facilitate inclusive treatment delivery (Dayani et al., 2025).

Peer support networks may be informal groups within communities or formal groups linked with organizations and advocacy groups. As networks, these groups implement mental health awareness initiatives, provide counseling services for peer support, hold conferences and seminars, and engage in advocacy for national development agendas centered on mental health issues. One example of effective peer support work is the Mental Health Peer Support Program (Ahmad et al., 2023), which trains individuals who have prior history of mental health issues and have received treatment, to help others in various parts of Pakistan. The community-based programs foster unity among individuals while reducing social isolation to enhance their mental health management. Peer support networks assist healthcare practitioners in obtaining critical assessments of service performance; hence, they promote the enhancement of healthcare practices.

5.5 Public Awareness Campaigns: Using Media and Religious Platforms to De-stigmatize Mental Health Issues

The eradication of mental health stigma in society relies on public awareness efforts that create supportive conditions for individuals seeking help (Adu et al., 2022). It is easy to raise awareness of mental health issues among large audiences using radio broadcasts, television stations, and social media platforms. The religious institutions in Pakistan significantly shape public perceptions on different issues (Ahmed et al., 2024a, 2024b). Using religious leaders in conjunction with mosque talks and religious gatherings is a successful way to educate people about mental health issues who are afraid to seek professional help. These initiatives create a new conversation around mental health that lessens public fear and misconceptions, normalizing the open discussion of mental health concerns and the need for help.

5.6 Leveraging Technology: Expansion of Telepsychiatry and Mobile Mental Health Applications

With the present rate of digitization, modern technological innovations are essential instruments to increase access to mental health services (Dar et al., 2023). Telepsychiatry and mobile mental health applications maintain relationships between mental health providers and residents in rural areas who do not receive proper care. Patients utilize telepsychiatry through digital platforms to obtain psychiatric consultations and therapy without the necessity of physical travel, hence enhancing access to services (Blanco et al., 2022). The need for specialist mental healthcare services becomes crucial in remote areas, where access to quality care may be limited.

Mobile applications for mental health provide users with management tools that encompass mental health monitors, relaxation techniques, cognitive-behavioral therapy components, and crisis intervention services (Harris et al., 2021). Digital platforms augment conventional mental health consultations by providing ongoing support to people in need of mental health services. The adoption of technology enhances the accessibility of mental health care through digital distribution methods, allowing individuals to manage their mental health improvement practices.

6 Case Studies and Best Practices

6.1 Case Studies

6.1.1 Pakistan-Specific Initiatives

Chaman Pilot Project: Integrating Mental Health in Primary Care

The Chaman Pilot Project serves as a collaborative model in Pakistan, illustrating the deployment of basic health care for mental health services. The World Health Organization (WHO) collaborated with Pakistan's Ministry of Health to address the significant mental health disorder issue in rural primary healthcare settings. The project operates in Chaman town, Balochistan province, where citizens suffer from significant mental health issues due to economic difficulties, hostilities, and forced population displacement. The initiative informed primary healthcare clinicians, including family physicians and community health workers, on the identification and management of depression, anxiety, and stress-related illnesses (WHO, 2007).

Early mental health care becomes attainable with this strategy, since trained healthcare personnel in fundamental settings can assist their patients without the need for psychiatric specialists. Bringing mental health care together with primary health care makes it easier for patients to get help, as they feel less hesitant to ask for support and can access services more easily (Gilani & Shah, 2022). The task-shifting method is crucial for this situation. The task-shifting approach allocates mental health responsibilities to general healthcare practitioners who have undergone fundamental training in psychological assistance and referrals (Bolton et al., 2023). The Chaman project demonstrates that integrating mental health practices into primary care enhances accessibility to care while reducing stigma, thereby reaching underprivileged groups and achieving the Good Health and Well-being objectives of SDG 3.

Rozan's "Zeest" Program: Addressing Trauma Among Women

The Pakistani NGO Rozan administers "Zeest," a program that provides trauma-informed mental health assistance to women. The program offers services directly to survivors of domestic violence and victims of other forms of abuse, offering both medical therapy and psychological support programs (Rozan, 2018). The Zeest program provides psychological therapy using community-focused approaches with the help of counselors and peer support group members who assist survivors in managing their emotional trauma resulting from abuse and violence. The program offers women individualized counseling sessions and group therapy programs to facilitate healing through shared experiences among survivors. The organization operates in several regions of Pakistan, concentrating on lower socioeconomic demographics in towns and small communities where women endure significant domestic violence, sexual assault, and mental health prejudice.

This program directly addresses SDG 5 (Gender Equality) by facilitating women's mental health enhancement through empowerment over trauma and the cessation of abusive behaviors. The program functions as a significant model for psychosocial support by providing effective, culturally tailored interventions that encourage women who typically avoid mental health care to seek assistance. Zeest's achievement under Rozan illustrates how purpose-driven mental health initiatives enhance the well-being of Pakistan's female population.

6.1.2 Global Examples for Adaptation

UK's Time to Change Campaign for Mental Health Stigma Reduction

Time to Change's initiatives have been crucial in the UK for reducing public discrimination against mental health illnesses. The worldwide mental health anti-stigma campaign initiated its operations in 2008 as one of the largest worldwide initiatives dedicated to eradicate mental health stigma while encouraging people to access help without discrimination (Gronholm et al., 2017). To raise awareness of mental health issues for the Time to Change campaign, public service messages were distributed by the media and supplemented via social media platforms and local community awareness programs.

Several stakeholders, including mental health groups, employers, celebrities, and legislators, participated in the campaign to dispel stigmas associated with mental health. Over its years, the Time to Change campaign achieved significant shifts in the public's perception of mental health in the UK, creating more welcoming environments for conversations on mental health (Walsh & Foster, 2021). The program aimed to eradicate discrimination while fostering solidarity among those who deal with overlapping problems by asking community members to share their experiences with mental illness. The mental health awareness campaign presents crucial information that Pakistan should use to fight stigma around mental health, since individuals are reluctant to seek help. Like the UK, Pakistan might use comparable media and religious channels for community outreach aimed at dispelling myths about mental health and educating people about mental health care.

Rwanda's Community Mental Health Program for Post-Conflict Trauma

Following the 1994 genocide, Rwanda faced significant challenges in addressing the mental health needs of those affected by trauma, violence, and profound loss. With the collaboration of foreign organizations, the Rwandan Ministry of Health implemented the Community Mental Health Program to address the intricate mental fragmentation resulting from the genocide (Lordos et al., 2021). The initiative established training standards to prepare local health personnel for psychosocial support and mental health first aid services throughout community health facilities.

The Rwandan approach utilized peer counseling with group therapy techniques to facilitate mutual support among afflicted individuals while fostering community-based recovery. The program's focal point was the establishment of mental healthcare services available to all populations, including remote villages, within primary healthcare systems (WHO, 2022).

Rwanda's mental health approach offers Pakistan useful information for treating trauma survivors and victims, particularly displaced individuals who entered Pakistan from nearby countries. Pakistan would be able to provide trauma-conscious care and satisfy SDG 3's notion of Good Health and Well-Being by adopting Rwanda's community-based strategy.

6.2 Best Practices for SDG and Mental Health in Pakistan

Pakistan can employ best practices from global models and case studies to integrate mental health into its Sustainable Development Goals (SDG) framework and provide inclusive and comprehensive mental health support nationwide (Dayani et al., 2024). Following the Chaman Pilot Project, mental health services should be included in primary care. Scaling this effort nationally and ensuring early detection and treatment of prevalent mental diseases requires mental health literacy and primary healthcare professional training. This integration makes psychiatric services more accessible, especially in rural or underserved areas. Mental health interventions in Pakistan must be gender-sensitive. Rozan's trauma-informed Zeest program pioneered emotional health for women and children. Expanding such efforts, especially for survivors of domestic and gender-based violence, can address gender and mental health and provide more equal care for underserved women.

Additionally, national awareness campaigns are crucial. Drawing from the UK's Time to Change program, Pakistan might normalize mental health topics through religious sermons especially for Friday prayer, media, and local influencers. Reduced stigma through culturally relevant and religiously sensitize messaging would increase help-seeking about mental health issues. Rwanda's Community Mental Health Program can replicate community-based mental health support. Similar trauma-informed treatments in Pakistan's conflict-prone or disaster-affected areas would help displaced and vulnerable communities get mental health care. These community-based initiatives ensure sustainable, contextually relevant, and accessible care. These best practices offer a comprehensive guide for incorporating mental health into Pakistan's SDG and public health agenda, guaranteeing that no individual falls behind.

7 Future Directions: Achieving Sustainable Mental Health Development in Pakistan

The progression of sustainable mental health in Pakistan requires simultaneous advances in interdisciplinary collaboration, research development, improved infrastructure, and suitable mental health legislation. The subsequent guidelines present a methodical strategy to improve mental health care in Pakistan, aligning with the Sustainable Development Goals, particularly SDG 3 (Good Health and Well-being).

7.1 Strengthening Interdisciplinary Collaboration: Integrating Mental Health into National Development Policies

In Pakistan, multidisciplinary collaborations involving medical services officials, educators, social welfare specialists, and legal experts are crucial to the development of mental health (Choudhry et al., 2023). National development policies must incorporate mental health as a fundamental concern to avoid the segregation of mental health issues from other sectors. A comprehensive government-wide strategy must be implemented for national development to incorporate mental health viewpoints into all programs and policies related to economic development, gender equality, poverty alleviation, and education (Khalily et al., 2021).

Workplaces and educational institutions should develop policies that incorporate mental health support so that professionals can identify and address psychological issues before they become serious. The development of an inclusive and coordinated mental health response should involve cooperation among a range of mental health experts, community leaders, legislators, and civil society organizations (Dayani et al., 2025). SDG 3 facilitates the execution of this strategy, which improves national mental health and well-being while reducing stigma, ensuring mental health occupies a major role in development initiatives.

7.2 Advancing Research and Data Collection: Establishing National Mental Health Epidemiology Databases

Pakistan must establish a nationwide mental health epidemiology database. Data-driven decisions must serve as the foundation for designing successful mental health interventions (Ahmad & Waqar, 2024). There is insufficient information available on the prevalence of mental illnesses in Pakistan and how they affect important areas, including social welfare, work, and education.

Establishing a comprehensive mental health database would allow for accurate trend tracking in mental health and the identification of vulnerable demographics.

The establishment of these databases encourages improved resource management by public servants who are better equipped to evaluate the success of programs and choose the best intervention tactics (Wu et al., 2021). The development of these essential databases is facilitated by the combined efforts of international organizations, research institutes, and universities. Pakistan can obtain valuable insights into the epidemiology of mental disorders through longitudinal studies and nationwide surveys, which support the development of evidence-based policy.

7.3 Scaling Up Mental Health Infrastructure: Expanding Public–Private Partnerships for Mental Health Investment

Pakistan has to completely upgrade its mental health system to meet the growing demand for mental health services (Noorullah et al., 2024). A successful strategy for pooling resources for investments in mental health is the formation of intersectoral partnerships between public and private organizations (WHO, 2024). Survivor Access necessitates government participation in conjunction with private sector actors to establish mental health structural projects and train mental health specialists who will work throughout rural and underprivileged areas.

Through digital health initiative platforms, public and commercial entities collaborate to provide advanced access to remote locations through mobile mental health platforms and telepsychiatry applications. The use of technology lessens the severity of Pakistan's present shortage of trained mental health specialists. A comprehensive mental healthcare infrastructure that provides inexpensive and long-lasting services to all population groups must be established via the combined efforts of the public and private sectors (Abbas & Talib, 2024).

7.4 Developing Mental Health Legislation: Enforcing Workplace Mental Health Laws and Patient Rights

The implementation of appropriate mental health laws establishes crucial protections for the rights of those with mental illnesses as well as their equitable treatment. Although it marks progress, the Pakistan Mental Health Act of 2001 has not yet been fully implemented. The government must enact new legislation and enforce existing laws to safeguard the rights of the impacted community regarding mental health (Khalily et al., 2021).

Legislation specifically addressing workplace mental health is crucial since mental health issues at work have a negative social and economic impact. Employers are required to establish mental health workplace regulations that fall into three categories: staff support networks, employee mental health awareness programs, and accommodations for employees with mental health conditions. The law must protect employees' rights by implementing particular measures to address workplace stress, harassment, and discrimination (WHO, 2022).

Explicit legal protections for mental health patients will save them from cruel or dehumanizing treatment. In addition to treatment consent processes, the health system must ensure access to medical care and treatment confidentiality (Dayani et al., 2024). As part of SDG 3, mental health laws must be improved to guarantee equal access to mental healthcare services and to protect the dignity of those who suffer from mental illnesses.

8 Conclusion

The World Health Organization (WHO) has emphasized that mental health is a fundamental component of overall well-being that enables individuals to manage daily stress, perform effectively, and contribute meaningfully to their communities. Mental health should be recognized as a fundamental element of national development in the context of the Sustainable Development Goals (SDGs), particularly SDG 3: Good Health and Well-Being. Mental health concerns in Pakistan incur considerable social, economic, and public health consequences, encompassing substance misuse, PTSD, depression, and anxiety. Systemic challenges, including widespread stigma, a significant shortage of mental health specialists, and the inadequate incorporation of mental health services into primary health care, persist despite heightened awareness.

To bridge these disparities, we need a synchronized, multi-sectoral approach that enhances mental health infrastructure, fosters interdisciplinary collaboration, and integrates mental health into broader development and health policies. Therefore, increased accessibility and reduced stigma, public awareness campaigns, and technology-driven solutions such as telepsychiatry and mobile health platforms can be transformative. The efficacy of community-based, culturally relevant methods in meeting mental health requirements is evidenced by local initiatives like Rozan's Zeest Program and the Chaman Pilot Project. International models, such as Rwanda's community-based trauma care networks and the UK's Time to Change campaign, offer Pakistan adaptable best practices.

Legislators must advocate for mental health changes by integrating policies, allocating adequate funds, and enacting legislation. Researchers must prioritize evidence-based, culturally relevant research to guide treatments. Healthcare personnel necessitate continuous training and support to deliver mental health treatments, particularly in disadvantaged regions. Pakistan can guarantee mental well-being for all by implementing a collaborative, inclusive, and strategic methodology that will bridge the gap in mental health care and further the global agenda for mental health and development.

References

Abbas, M. S., & Talib, A. B., Ts. Dr. (2024). Determinants of availability and accessibility to primary health care for rural populations in Pakistan. *Pakistan Journal of Life and Social Sciences (PJLSS), 22*(2). https://doi.org/10.57239/PJLSS-2024-22.2.0081

Adu, J., Oudshoorn, A., Anderson, K., Marshall, C. A., & Stuart, H. (2022). Social contact: Next steps in an effective strategy to mitigate the stigma of mental illness. *Issues in Mental Health Nursing, 43*(5), 485–488. https://doi.org/10.1080/01612840.2021.1986757

Ahmad, I., Hanif, M., Waqas, A., Suleman, N., Atif, N., Bibi, A., Zulfiqar, S., Kayani, S. S., Khan, S. A., Khan, A., & Sikander, S. (2023). Understanding the use of peers for mental health care: A meta-synthesis of qualitative evidence. *F1000Research, 12*, 854. https://doi.org/10.12688/f1000research.124792.1

Ahmad, M., & Waqar, Z. (2024). *Towards sustainable health systems* (pp. 373–390). https://doi.org/10.4018/979-8-3693-5748-4.ch017

Ahmed Mashood. (2025). Contemporary mental health issues in Pakistan: Focus on forensic psychiatry. *Journal of Pakistan Psychiatric Society, 22*(1). https://doi.org/10.63050/jpps.22.1.943

Ahmed, S. H., Zahid, M., Waseem, S., Zafar, A., Shaikh, T. G., Sabri, T., & Arshad, A. (2024a). The current state of primary healthcare in Pakistan: A way forward for low-to-middle income countries. *Primary Health Care Research & Development, 25*, Article e59. https://doi.org/10.1017/S1463423624000549

Ahmed, S. H., Zakai, A., Zahid, M., Jawad, M. Y., Fu, R., & Chaiton, M. (2024b). Prevalence of post-traumatic stress disorder and depressive symptoms among civilians residing in armed conflict-affected regions: A systematic review and meta-analysis. *General Psychiatry, 37*(3), Article e101438. https://doi.org/10.1136/gpsych-2023-101438

Akhtar, S., Rabbani, F., Nafis, J., & Merali, Z. (2024). *Where there is no specialist—Improving mental health literacy of frontline community health workers in a rural district of Pakistan: The mPareshan project*. https://doi.org/10.21203/rs.3.rs-5571403/v1

Akram A., Rahman, A. U., Batool, R., Alam, T., Ullah, S., Siddique, S., & Sattar, S. (2023). Integrating mental health education into school curricula: Impacts on student well-being and academic performance. *Dialogue Social Science Review, 2*(3), 456–463.

Alaimo, K., Chilton, M., & Jones, S. J. (2020). Food insecurity, hunger, and malnutrition. In *Present Knowledge in Nutrition* (pp. 311–326). Elsevier. https://doi.org/10.1016/B978-0-12-818460-8.00017-4

Alvi, M. H., Ashraf, T., Naz, F., Sardar, A., Ullah, A., Patel, A. Kiran, T., Gumber, A., & Husain, N. (2024). Burden of mental disorders by gender in Pakistan: Analysis of global burden of disease study data for 1990–2019. *BJPsych Bulletin 48*(6), 333–340. https://doi.org/10.1192/bjb.2023.76

Anam, T. (2024). Promoting mental health care in Pakistan with "lady health worker approach." *The Research of Medical Science Review, 2*(3), 198–205.

Asghar, M., & Ramisha. (2024). Women protection laws in Pakistan: Issues and challenges. *Journal of Development and Social Sciences, 5*(1), 724–737.

Bajorek, Z., Kinder, A., & Cooper, C. L. (2024). Employee assistance programs: Strengths, challenges, and future roles. In *Handbook of occupational health psychology* (3rd ed., pp. 485–500). American Psychological Association. https://doi.org/10.1037/0000331-024

Bąk, I. (2024). Sustainable Development Goals (SDGs): Concept and measurement. In *The role of financial markets in achieving the Sustainable Development Goals* (pp. 15–41). Edward Elgar Publishing. https://doi.org/10.4337/9781035323265.00009

Basit, A., & Ahmed, Z. S. (2021). The persistence of terrorism in Pakistan. In *Terrorism, security and development in South Asia* (pp. 157–174). Routledge. https://doi.org/10.4324/9780429342523-11

Blanco, C., Wall, M. M., & Olfson, M. (2022). Implications of telepsychiatry for cost, quality, and equity of mental health care. *JAMA Psychiatry, 79*(12), 1147. https://doi.org/10.1001/jamapsychiatry.2022.3330

Bolton, P., West, J., Whitney, C., Jordans, M. J. D., Bass, J., Thornicroft, G., Murray, L., Snider, L., Eaton, J., Collins, P. Y., Ventevogel, P., Smith, S., Stein, D. J., Petersen, I., Silove, D., Ugo, V., Mahoney, J., el Chammay, R., Contreras, C., … Raviola, G. (2023). Expanding mental health services in low- and middle-income countries: A task-shifting framework for delivery of comprehensive, collaborative, and community-based care. *Cambridge Prisms: Global Mental Health, 10*, e16. https://doi.org/10.1017/gmh.2023.5

Cao, X., Zhang, H., Li, P., & Huang, X. (2022). The influence of mental health on job satisfaction: Mediating effect of psychological capital and social capital. *Frontiers in Public Health, 10*. https://doi.org/10.3389/fpubh.2022.797274

Chen, Q., Huang, S., Xu, H., Peng, J., Wang, P., Li, S., Zhao, J., Shi, X., Zhang, W., Shi, L., Peng, Y., & Tang, X. (2024). The burden of mental disorders in Asian countries, 1990–2019: An analysis for the global burden of disease study 2019. *Translational Psychiatry, 14*(1), 167. https://doi.org/10.1038/s41398-024-02864-5

Chotibuddin, M., Zunaih, A. I., Musikhin, & Nashihin. (2025). Quality education with Sustainable Development Goals (SDGs) no 4: Knowledge-based. *Journal of Ecohumanism, 3*(8), 10655 https://doi.org/10.62754/joe.v3i8.5676

Choudhry, F. R., Khan, N., & Munawar, K. (2023). Barriers and facilitators to mental health care: A systematic review in Pakistan. *International Journal of Mental Health, 52*(2), 124–162. https://doi.org/10.1080/00207411.2021.1941563

Dar, A. M., Maqbool, M., Ara, I., & Zehravi, M. (2023). The intersection of technology and mental health: Enhancing access and care. *International Journal of Adolescent Medicine and Health, 35*(5), 423–428. https://doi.org/10.1515/ijamh-2023-0113

Das, T., Holland, P., Ahmed, M., & Husain, L. (2021). Sustainable Development Goal 3: Good health and well-being. In *South-East Asia eye health* (pp. 61–78). Springer Singapore. https://doi.org/10.1007/978-981-16-3787-2_4

Dayani, K., Mughis, W., Ali, U., Hashim, S., Nafees, B., & Sabri, T. (2025). Innovative approaches to mental health care in Pakistan: Perspectives from a nonprofit organization. *Mental Health and Social Inclusion*. https://doi.org/10.1108/MHSI-01-2025-0012

Dayani, K., Zia, M., Qureshi, O., Baig, M., & Sabri, T. (2024). Evaluating Pakistan's mental healthcare system using World Health Organization's Assessment Instrument for Mental Health System (WHO-AIMS). *International Journal of Mental Health Systems, 18*(1), 32. https://doi.org/10.1186/s13033-024-00646-6

Dybdahl, R., & Lien, L. (2018). Mental health is an integral part of the sustainable development goals. *Preventive Medicine and Community Health, 1*(1). https://doi.org/10.15761/PMCH.1000104

Ejiohuo, O., Onyeaka, H., Unegbu, K. C., Chikezie, O. G., Odeyemi, O. A., Lawal, A., & Odeyemi, O. A. (2024). Nourishing the mind: How food security influences mental wellbeing. *Nutrients, 16*(4), 501. https://doi.org/10.3390/nu16040501

Freeman, M. (2022). The world mental health report: Transforming mental health for all. *World Psychiatry, 21*(3), 391–392. https://doi.org/10.1002/wps.21018

Giebel, C., Gabbay, M., Shrestha, N., Saldarriaga, G., Reilly, S., White, R., Liu, G., Allen, D., & Zuluaga, M. I. (2024). Community-based mental health interventions in low- and middle-income countries: A qualitative study with international experts. *International Journal for Equity in Health, 23*(1), 19. https://doi.org/10.1186/s12939-024-02106-6

Gilani, S., & Shah, S. I. A. (2022). Integrating mental health services in existing healthcare system in Pakistan: A public mental health approach. In *Applied psychology readings* (pp. 116–133). Springer Nature Singapore. https://doi.org/10.1007/978-981-19-5086-5_5

Gronholm, P. C., Henderson, C., Deb, T., & Thornicroft, G. (2017). Interventions to reduce discrimination and stigma: The state of the art. *Social Psychiatry and Psychiatric Epidemiology, 52*(3), 249–258. https://doi.org/10.1007/s00127-017-1341-9

Guaita-Fernández, P., Martín Martín, J. M., Ribeiro Navarrete, S., & Puertas, R. (2024). Analysis of gender-based violence in the context of the sustainable development goals. *Sustainable Development, 32*(5), 4946–4958. https://doi.org/10.1002/sd.2940

Gyamfi, S., Forchuk, C., Booth, R., & Luginaah, I. (2025). Predictors of patient stigma perception appraisal: Testing a dynamic stigma model of mental illness. *Sage Open, 15*(1). https://doi.org/10.1177/21582440251319983

Gyimah, P., Appiah, K. O., & Appiagyei, K. (2025). Unraveling contemporary trends on <scp>United Nations</scp> sustainable development goals: A new global bibliometric and literature review analysis. *Sustainable Development, 33*(2), 2579–2598. https://doi.org/10.1002/sd.3255

Harris, B., Ajisola, M., Alam, R. M., Watkins, J. A., Arvanitis, T. N., Bakibinga, P., Chipwaza, B., Choudhury, N. N., Kibe, P., Fayehun, O., Omigbodun, A., Owoaje, E., Pemba, S., Potter, R., Rizvi, N., Sturt, J., Cave, J., Iqbal, R., Kabaria, C., … Griffiths, F. (2021). Mobile consulting as an option for delivering healthcare services in low-resource settings in low- and middle-income countries: A mixed-methods study. *DIGITAL HEALTH, 7*. https://doi.org/10.1177/20552076211033425

Hashmi, A. N., Qamar, R., Taj, R., Zubair, U. B., Agha, Z., Abbasi, S. A., & Azam, M. (2023). Contributing risk factors of common psychiatric disorders in the Pakistani population. *European Archives of Psychiatry and Clinical Neuroscience, 273*(4), 963–981. https://doi.org/10.1007/s00406-022-01545-y

Human Rights Watch. (2024). *Pakistan: Events of 2023.*

Imran, M., Murtiza, G., & Akbar, M. S. (2023). Political instability in Pakistan: Challenges and remedies. *South Asian Studies, 38*(1), 37–52.

Jafree, S. R. (2023). Existing social protection services in Pakistan. In *Social policy for women in Pakistan* (pp. 21–47). Springer Nature Switzerland. https://doi.org/10.1007/978-3-031-32863-3_2

Jagiello, T., Belcher, J., Neelakandan, A., Boyd, K., & Wuthrich, V. M. (2024). Academic stress interventions in high schools: A systematic literature review. *Child Psychiatry & Human Development*. https://doi.org/10.1007/s10578-024-01667-5

Javeed, A., Khan, M. Y., Rehman, M., & Khurshid, A. (2022). Tracking sustainable development goals—A case study of Pakistan. *Journal of Cultural Heritage Management and Sustainable Development, 12*(4), 478–496. https://doi.org/10.1108/JCHMSD-04-2020-0052

Justice Project Pakistan. (2022). *Trapped inside: Mental illness & incarceration.*

Kabir, R., Isigi, S. S., & Candussi, C. (2024). Public mental health and access to mental health services in South Asia. In *Access to mental health care in South Asia* (pp. 229–243). Springer Nature Singapore. https://doi.org/10.1007/978-981-99-9153-2_11

Khalily, M. T., Rehman, A. U., Bhatti, M. M., Hallahan, B., Ahmad, I., Mehmood, M. I., Khan, S. H., & Khan, B. A. (2021). Stakeholders' perspective on mental health laws in Pakistan: A mixed method study. *International Journal of Law and Psychiatry, 74*, 101647. https://doi.org/10.1016/j.ijlp.2020.101647

Khalily, M. T., Yousafzai, A. W., & Khurram, F. (2024). Current perspectives on substance use disorder in Pakistan. In *Current perspectives on substance use disorders in South Asia* (pp. 103–119). Springer Nature Singapore. https://doi.org/10.1007/978-981-97-6619-2_7

Khurram, S. S., Aga, I. Z., Karim, M., Muzzamil, M., Lakhani, A., & Ahmed, S. (2024). Electronic health records as a window into telehealth: Exploring service utilisation and mental health outcomes in Pakistan. *General Psychiatry, 37*(5), Article e101609. https://doi.org/10.1136/gpsych-2024-101609

Kirkbride, J. B., Anglin, D. M., Colman, I., Dykxhoorn, J., Jones, P. B., Patalay, P., Pitman, A., Soneson, E., Steare, T., Wright, T., & Griffiths, S. L. (2024). The social determinants of mental health and disorder: Evidence, prevention and recommendations. *World Psychiatry, 23*(1), 58–90. https://doi.org/10.1002/wps.21160

Kirolos, A., Goyheneix, M., Kalmus Eliasz, M., Chisala, M., Lissauer, S., Gladstone, M., & Kerac, M. (2022). Neurodevelopmental, cognitive, behavioural and mental health impairments following childhood malnutrition: A systematic review. *BMJ Global Health, 7*(7), e009330. https://doi.org/10.1136/bmjgh-2022-009330

Knifton, L., & Inglis, G. (2020). Poverty and mental health: Policy, practice and research implications. *Bjpsych Bulletin, 44*(5), 193–196. https://doi.org/10.1192/bjb.2020.78

Lasi, S., Afshan, G., Iqbal, J., & Ayub, L. (2025). "We feel ashamed to talk about it". Navigating mental health problems for women in rural Pakistan: An interplay of financial, sociocultural, and environmental factors. *Health Care for Women International*, 1–20. https://doi.org/10.1080/07399332.2025.2454579

Lok, J., Kipping, S., & Riahi, S. (2025). Optimising scopes of practice and team-based collaborative care through task-shifting and task-sharing in mental health—A collaborative patient care (<scp>CPC</scp>) initiative. *International Journal of Mental Health Nursing, 34*(2). https://doi.org/10.1111/inm.70025

Lordos, A., Ioannou, M., Rutembesa, E., Christoforou, S., Anastasiou, E., & Björgvinsson, T. (2021). Societal healing in Rwanda: Toward a multisystemic framework for mental health, social cohesion, and sustainable livelihoods among survivors and perpetrators of the genocide against the Tutsi. *Health and Human Rights, 23*(1), 105–118.

Lund, C., Brooke-Sumner, C., Baingana, F., Baron, E. C., Breuer, E., Chandra, P., Haushofer, J., Herrman, H., Jordans, M., Kieling, C., Medina-Mora, M. E., Morgan, E., Omigbodun, O., Tol, W., Patel, V., & Saxena, S. (2018). Social determinants of mental disorders and the sustainable development goals: A systematic review of reviews. *Lancet Psychiatry, 5*(4), 357–369. https://doi.org/10.1016/S2215-0366(18)30060-9

Lyons, N., Cooper, C., & Lloyd-Evans, B. (2021). A systematic review and meta-analysis of group peer support interventions for people experiencing mental health conditions. *BMC Psychiatry, 21*(1), 315. https://doi.org/10.1186/s12888-021-03321-z

Mahesar, R. A., Ali, S. A.-Z., Shoib, S., Babar Khan, M., & Ventriglio, A. (2024). Mental health services in Pakistan. *International Review of Psychiatry*, 1–6. https://doi.org/10.1080/09540261.2024.2391796

Main Thompson, A., & Saleem, S. M. (2025). Closing the mental health gap: Transforming Pakistan's mental health landscape. *Frontiers in Health Services, 4*. https://doi.org/10.3389/frhs.2024.1471528

Malik, Z. (2024). *Sustainable development goals in Pakistan: A comprehensive analysis of progress, challenges, and recommendations*. https://doi.org/10.20944/preprints202409.1670.v1

Maqbool, S., Atif, M., & Anwar, U. (2024). The impact of psychological violence on social cohesion and political stability. *Review of Applied Management and Social Sciences, 7*(4), 609–622. https://doi.org/10.47067/ramss.v7i4.401

Marbin, D., Gutwinski, S., Schreiter, S., & Heinz, A. (2022). Perspectives in poverty and mental health. *Frontiers in Public Health, 10*. https://doi.org/10.3389/fpubh.2022.975482

Martinelli, A. (2024). *Sustainable promotion of mental health and prevention of mental health disorders across the world* (pp. 1–23). https://doi.org/10.1007/978-3-031-64288-3_1

Melgar Alcantud, P., Campdepadrós-Cullell, R., Fuentes-Pumarola, C., & Mut-Montalvà, E. (2021). 'I think I will need help': A systematic review of who facilitates the recovery from gender-based violence and how they do so. *Health Expectations, 24*(1), 1–7. https://doi.org/10.1111/hex.13157

Mills, C. (2018). From 'invisible problem' to global priority: The inclusion of mental health in the sustainable development goals. *Development and Change, 49*(3), 843–866. https://doi.org/10.1111/dech.12397

Monaco, S. (2024). SDG 3. Ensure healthy lives and promote well-being for all at all ages. In *Identity, territories, and sustainability: Challenges and opportunities for achieving the UN sustainable development goals* (pp. 33–41). Emerald Publishing Limited. https://doi.org/10.1108/978-1-83797-549-520241004

Montesanti, S., Fitzpatrick, K., Fayant, B., & Pritchard, C. (2022). Identifying priorities, directions and a vision for Indigenous mental health using a collaborative and consensus-based facilitation approach. *BMC Health Services Research, 22*(1), 406. https://doi.org/10.1186/s12913-022-07682-3

Mosia, M., Egara, F. O., Nannim, F., & Basitere, M. (2025). Bayesian growth curve modelling of student academic trajectories: The impact of individual-level characteristics and implications for education policy. *Applied Sciences, 15*(3), 1426. https://doi.org/10.3390/app15031426

Mubarak, N., Kanwal, S., Rana, F. R., Tariq, S., Tariq, S., Elnaem, M. H., & Khan, A. M. (2023). Examining the tapestry of mental health crises in low- & middle-income countries: An intercontinental analysis of the contributing factors and instructive approaches. *Journal of University Medical & Dental College, 14*(4). https://doi.org/10.37723/jumdc.v14i4.972

Mughal, S. S., & Baig, Z. L. (2024). Efforts to alleviate poverty through social support programs: Are we on the right track. *Journal of Politics and International Studies, 10*(2), 189–194.

Noor, A., Zia, S., & Imtiaz, M. (2025). Sustaining well-being amid eco-anxiety: The moderating influence of environmental concerns among adults in urban settings. *Journal of Professional & Applied Psychology, 6*(1), 95–105. https://doi.org/10.52053/jpap.v6i1.353

Noorullah, A., Asad, N., Pirani, S., Iqbal, S., & Khan, M. M. (2024). Mental health care in Pakistan. In *Access to mental health care in South Asia* (pp. 113–135). Springer Nature Singapore. https://doi.org/10.1007/978-981-99-9153-2_7

Okechukwu, C. E. (2022). A call for improved mental health workforce in low-income countries. *International Journal of Social Psychiatry, 68*(2), 465–467. https://doi.org/10.1177/00207640211039255

Pakistan, M. (2024). The *prevailing causes of mental health illnesses in Pakistan and the way forward to deal with the Menace.* https://doi.org/10.2139/ssrn.4945394

Rabbani, F., Akhtar, S., Nafis, J., Khan, S., Siddiqi, S., & Merali, Z. (2023). Addition of mental health to the lady health worker curriculum in Pakistan: Now or never. *Human Resources for Health, 21*(1), 29. https://doi.org/10.1186/s12960-023-00814-8

Rahman, R., Sheehan, D., Javed, A., Ahmad, S., Shafiq, K., Kanwal, U., Afridi, M., Nizami, A., Rasool, G., Taj, R., Ansari, M., Naim, M., Farooq, S., Memon, A., Karim, M., Hana, Y., & Ayub, M. (2024). *The national psychiatric morbidity survey of Pakistan (2022): Prevalence, socio-demographic and disability correlates.* https://doi.org/10.1101/2024.07.08.24310056

Rashid, A., & Qixiang, W. (2025). Integrating disaster, catastrophe, and climate change education in Pakistan's educational curriculum and state institutions: A comprehensive review. *Climate Research, 94*, 1–18. https://doi.org/10.3354/cr01747

Rehman, F. U., & Butt, S. (2024). Employee wellbeing in Pakistan. In *Employee wellbeing in the global South* (pp. 223–241). Springer Nature Switzerland. https://doi.org/10.1007/978-3-031-63249-5_10

Rozan. (2018). *Against all odds: Post shelter lives of women survivors of violence.*

Saeed, Q., Shafique, K., & Chaudhry, N. (2024). Lived experiences of mothers with postnatal anxiety: A qualitative phenomenology study from Pakistan. *British Medical Journal Open, 14*(5), Article e078203. https://doi.org/10.1136/bmjopen-2023-078203

Saraiva, M., & Nogueiro, T. (2025). Perspectives and realities of disengagement among younger generation Y and Z workers in contemporary work dynamics. *Administrative Sciences, 15*(4), 133. https://doi.org/10.3390/admsci15040133

Sarfraz, A., Sarfraz, Z., Sarfraz, M., & Qarnain, Z. (2022). Gender-based violence in Pakistan and public health measures: A call to action. *Bulletin of the World Health Organization, 100*(7), 462–464. https://doi.org/10.2471/BLT.21.287188

Sarwar, G., & Farid, A. (2024). Unveiling gender disparities in Pakistan: Challenges, progress, and policy implications for achieving SDG 5. *Journal of Development and Social Sciences, 5*(2), 506–517.

Shah, E., Shah, S. L. H., Khan, S., Ali, A., & Nindwani, B. A. (2024). Healthcare policy and social welfare: Analyzing access and equity in public health systems. *The Critical Review of Social Sciences Studies, 2*(2), 875–886. https://doi.org/10.59075/qyks2s91

Sohail, S. A., Syed, A. A., & Rahman, A. (2017). *Mental health in Pakistan: Yesterday, today and tomorrow* (pp. 17–37). https://doi.org/10.1007/978-1-4899-7999-5_2

Soomro, S., Sahito, J. G. M., & Gilal, F. (2025). *The link between climate change and human health* (pp. 183–208). https://doi.org/10.1007/978-3-031-80797-8_8

Syed, Y., & Moriarty, K. (2020). SDG 4 and the "education quality turn": Prospects, possibilities, and problems. In A.Wulff (Ed.), *Grading goal four tensions: Threats, and opportunities in the sustainable development goal on quality education* (1st ed., pp. 194–213). Koninklijke Brill NV.

Tahir, T. A. (2025). Bridging the gap to reduce the duration of untreated illness-Spirituality and mental health. *Journal of Pakistan Psychiatric Society, 22*(1). https://doi.org/10.63050/jpps.22.1.955

Talat, A., Khan, S. E., & Hassan, M. (2022). Stigmatization of seeking mental health care: Youth perspectives from Pakistan. *Pakistan Journal of Social Research, 4*(2), 559–566.

Trane, M., Marelli, L., Siragusa, A., Pollo, R., & Lombardi, P. (2023). Progress by research to achieve the sustainable development goals in the EU: A systematic literature review. *Sustainability, 15*(9), 7055. https://doi.org/10.3390/su15097055

UNDP Pakistan. (2024). *Sustainable Development Goals: UNDP Pakistan Annual Report 2024.*

UNICEF. (2023). *UNICEF Pakistan Humanitarian Situation Report No. 9: End of Year 2022.*

Walsh, D. A. B., & Foster, J. L. H. (2021). A call to action. A critical review of mental health related anti-stigma campaigns. *Frontiers in Public Health, 8*. https://doi.org/10.3389/fpubh.2020.569539

Waqas, A., Naveed, S., Makhmoor, A., Malik, A., Hassan, H., & Aedma K. K. (2020). Empathy Experience and Cultural Beliefs Determine the Attitudes Towards Depression Among Pakistani Medical Students. *Community Mental Health Journal, 56*(1), 65–74. https://doi.org/10.1007/s10597-019-00459-9

WFP. (2023). *Scoping study on enhancing food security and nutrition and managing risks and shocks in Asia and the pacific through support to social protection systems—Pakistan.*

WHO. (2004). *Promoting Mental Health: Concepts, Emerging Evidence, Practice* (Summary Report).

WHO. (2007). *WHO-AIMS report on mental health system in Pakistan.*

WHO. Mental Health ATLAS. 2017. (2018). *World Health Organization*, Mental Health ATLAS 2017

WHO. (2022). *WHO guidelines on mental health at work.* World Health Organization.

WHO. (2024). *Achieving well-being: A global framework for integrating well-being into public health utilizing a health promotion approach.* World Health Organization.

Wu, A., Roemer, E. C., Kent, K. B., Ballard, D. W., & Goetzel, R. Z. (2021). Organizational best practices supporting mental health in the workplace. *Journal of Occupational & Environmental Medicine, 63*(12), e925–e931. https://doi.org/10.1097/JOM.0000000000002407

Yumnam, G., Gyanendra, Y., & Singh, C. I. (2024). A systematic bibliometric review of the global research dynamics of United Nations sustainable development goals 2030. *Sustainable Futures, 7*, Article 100192. https://doi.org/10.1016/j.sftr.2024.100192

Chapter 12
Sustainable Development Goals and Mental Health in Sri Lanka

Anuradha Baminiwatta, Aruni Hapangama, Nazneen Nazeer, and Miyuru Chandradasa

Abstract Although the national policy framework of Sri Lanka aligns with many Sustainable Development Goals (SDGs), current projections indicate that only 2 of the 17 goals are likely to be achieved by 2030. This chapter examines the intersection of mental health and the SDGs in Sri Lanka, highlighting both progress and persistent challenges. The high prevalence of mental disorders and the recent rise in suicide rates underscore the growing mental health needs of the country. While mental health services have expanded since the 1990s, significant workforce shortages, inequities in access, and outdated legislation continue to impede progress. The 2020–2030 National Mental Health Policy calls for decentralization and community-based care, but implementation is constrained by limited funding and human resources. Mental health literacy remains low, and stigma is widespread, pointing to the need for strengthened education initiatives starting from schools. Broader socioeconomic and environmental determinants—including poverty, unemployment, income and gender inequality, food insecurity, and climate change—exert a bidirectional influence on mental health. This underscores the importance of integrating mental health across all relevant SDG domains. Advancing mental health is not only important for public health and human rights, but also essential for building a fair and sustainable future in Sri Lanka.

Keywords Psychiatry · Mental Health system · Social determinants · National development · Policy · Inequality

A. Baminiwatta (✉) · N. Nazeer · M. Chandradasa
University of Kelaniya, Colombo, Sri Lanka
e-mail: baminiwatta@kln.ac.lk

A. Hapangama
The Alfred, Melbourne, Australia

S. K. Kar et al. (eds.), *Sustainable Development Goals and Mental Health in South Asia*, South Asian Perspectives in Mental Health and Psychology ,
https://doi.org/10.1007/978-981-95-2684-0_12

1 Introduction

Sustainable Development Goals (SDGs) were adopted by Sri Lanka in 2015, committing to a vision of balanced economic, social, and environmental progress (Sustainable Development Council of Sri Lanka, 2024a). Institutional support for SDG coordination was formalized with the establishment of the Sustainable Development Council (SDC) under the Sri Lanka Sustainable Development Act No. 19 of 2017. According to a policy alignment mapping by the SDC, the current national policy framework *A Thriving Nation—A Beautiful Life* contributes directly to 108 of the 169 SDG targets (SDC, 2024b). However, Sri Lanka remains off track in achieving these, with current projections suggesting that only 2 of the 17 goals are likely to be achieved by 2030.

In the 2024 Sustainable Development Report, Sri Lanka ranked 93rd out of 167 countries, with an overall score of 67.4—a decline from its peak position of 76th in 2022, though still above the regional average of 66.5 (Sachs et al., 2024). According to the SDG progress report for Sri Lanka in 2024, notable progress has been made in SDG 7 (Affordable and Clean Energy) and SDG 13 (Climate Action), but uneven progress elsewhere (SDC, 2024a). Alarmingly, regression has occurred in SDG 8 (Decent Work and Economic Growth) and SDG 14 (Life below Water). Recent improvements between 2023 and 2024 were seen in SDG 3 (Good Health and Wellbeing), SDG 7, SDG 16 (Peace, Justice and Strong Institutions), and SDG 17 (Partnerships for the Goals).

Sri Lanka's free and universal health care system has achieved relatively strong outcomes for a lower-middle-income country, with steady gains in life expectancy and marked reductions in infant and maternal mortality. Mental health, long underprioritized, is now receiving increased attention as an integral part of overall wellbeing, aligned with the broader health agenda of SDG 3 (Kathriarachchi et al., 2019a).

This chapter examines the intersection of mental health and the SDGs in Sri Lanka. We begin by outlining the current mental health landscape, with reference to SDG 3—addressing the burden of illness, service availability, and relevant indicators. We then explore how mental health connects with other SDGs, drawing on the framework of social determinants of mental health and sustainable development proposed by Lund et al. (2018).

2 Mental Health Landscape in Sri Lanka in Relation to SDG 3

2.1 Prevalence of Mental Disorders

The prevalence of mental disorders in a country indicates its mental health service needs. Although epidemiological data on mental illness in Sri Lanka are limited, a few studies indicate relatively high rates. According to a national mental health survey conducted in 2007 among 6120 participants, the one-month prevalence of mental disorders was 15% (Institute for Research and Development, 2007). Depressive syndromes (major depression and other depression) were the most prevalent, estimated at 9.2%. Other prevalent disorders were somatoform disorder (3%), post-traumatic stress disorder (PTSD, 1.7%), and panic and anxiety syndromes (1.4%). It was reported that disorders were more common among females and those aged 35–65 years.

A recent meta-analysis of 33 studies estimated the pooled point prevalence of depressive symptoms among Sri Lankans at 19.4% (Alwis et al., 2023). Prevalence was highest among young individuals (39%), while rates were 8.7% in adults, 18.4% in older adults, and 16.9% in maternal populations. As would be expected, screening instruments yielded a higher prevalence (21.2%) than diagnostic interviews (4.3%). A large epidemiological study across 18 districts in post-conflict Sri Lanka suggested that the prevalence of depression and anxiety was greater in war-affected areas (Jayasuriya et al., 2016). Whether the prevalence of mental disorders has dropped since the war ended has not been established.

2.2 *Suicide Rate and Prevention Efforts*

Suicide rate is considered an important indicator of mental health in a country, and is used as an indicator under SDG target 3.4, which aims to reduce the premature mortality from non-communicable diseases by one third by 2030. Historically, the suicide rate in Sri Lanka showed a steep drop from 47 per 100,000 in 1995 to 19.6 per 100,000 in 2009, coinciding with restrictions on pesticide import and sales around the time (De Silva et al., 2013). Further reduction in suicide rate occurred more gradually, reaching 14.5 per 100,000 in 2015 at the time the SDGs were introduced, and reaching a trough of 14 per 100,000 in 2020. Unfortunately, rates have started to rise again, reaching 15.3 per 100,000 in 2023 (Sustainable Development Council, 2025). This may relate to the COVID-19 pandemic and economic collapse (Baminiwatta & Ediriweera, 2022).

Sri Lanka has utilized exemplary strategies for suicide prevention in the past with remarkable outcomes. Interventions by the Presidential Task Force for Suicide Prevention in 1995 led to the dramatic reduction in suicide rates previously described (Rajapakse, 2017). In addition to the pesticide bans, interventions that have possibly worked include the establishment of poison treatment centres and improved medical management of poisoning, introducing suicide reporting guidelines, improving treatment for depression and alcohol use disorders, and creating suicide helplines. In 2019, an Expert Committee on Suicide Prevention under the Sri Lanka Medical Association produced a policy document outlining a broad range of recommendations for suicide prevention (Kathriarachchi et al., 2019b). The trajectory of suicide incidence seen in Sri Lanka over the last three years is disconcerting, and widens the gap for achieving the target rate of 11.3 per 100,000 by 2030. The rising trend of suicides by hanging is difficult to address, as means restriction is not feasible (Arafat et al., 2021b). A multitude of intersecting social and economic factors may have contributed to the recent rise in suicides particularly in the context of the economic downfall. As the highest suicide rates are reported among those aged above 65 years, aged care services need to expand (Baminiwatta, 2024). Therefore, a multifaceted, multisectoral approach for suicide prevention guided by up-to-date research evidence is urgently required.

2.3 Mental Health Service Coverage

Mental health care in Sri Lanka includes a combination of public, private, and non-government services. Most of the population, however, receives care from the public sector. Since the 1990s, mental health services expanded rather rapidly with the training of psychiatrists through the Postgraduate Institute of Medicine, and further service expansion occurred following the tsunami in 2004 (Amarasinghe & Rajapakse, 2024). Nevertheless, workforce shortages persist, with only around 0.47 psychiatrists per 100,000 people, and limited coverage in regions like the Northern Province. Migration of psychiatrists has long been a key barrier for the expansion of specialized care (Chandradasa & Kuruppuarachchi, 2024). At present, acute inpatient units are available in 23 of the 24 districts. Urban areas like Colombo, Kandy and Gampaha have multiple inpatient units. As a step towards improving identification and treatment of mental health problems in primary care, psychiatry is taught to all medical undergraduates as a mandatory subject in their final year since 2018 (Hapangama et al., 2023). In this sense, Sri Lanka stands out among South Asian countries in undergraduate psychiatry education (Arafat et al., 2021a).

2.4 Mental Health Policy and Legislation

Sri Lanka updated its National Mental Health Policy in 2020 to provide a strategic framework for the prevention, treatment, rehabilitation, and promotion of mental health, while strengthening human resource development and research (Ministry of Health, 2021). A National Mental Health Advisory Council and district-level review committees were established to oversee activities. Recognizing the growing impact of substance use, the policy also supported the creation of the National Authority on Tobacco and Alcohol (NATA) and the National Dangerous Drugs Control Board. Additionally, fifty consumer and carer groups and a national body, Consumer Action Network Mental Health Lanka (CANMH Lanka), were established to empower service users and carers.

Despite these developments, Sri Lanka continues to rely on the outdated Lunacy Ordinance of 1873, later renamed the Mental Diseases Ordinance in 1956. These laws, last revised over 70 years ago, are outdated and inconsistent with the Convention on the Rights of Persons with Disabilities (CRPD) and the country's evolving socio-political context (Hapangama et al., 2023).

While psychiatric services have expanded to general and district hospitals, compulsory treatment under the current law is still restricted to the National Institute of Mental Health (NIMH) in Colombo. In practice, patients lacking capacity have been treated with restrictive interventions like seclusion, restraints, and ECT, sometimes based on a second opinion, for several decades.

A particularly outdated and concerning provision under the Mental Diseases Ordinance allows individuals deemed mentally ill to be remanded in prisons without having committed any crime, pending court proceedings and transfer to the NIMH. This process is traumatic for patients and caregivers, violates human rights, and reinforces stigma against mental illness. Although a draft Mental Health Act has been proposed for over a decade, aiming to modernize admission procedures, community treatment, and patients' rights, it remains to be enacted.

2.5 Prevention and Treatment of Substance Abuse

SDG target 3.5 aims to strengthen the prevention and treatment of substance abuse. Data from the NATA shows that per capita alcohol consumption in Sri Lanka decreased from 4.3 l in 2016 to 2.2 l in 2022. A survey by the Alcohol & Drug Information Centre (ADIC) also showed a declining trend from 2012 to 2021, although alcohol use may be rising among those aged 25–39 (ADIC, 2021). Among people with mental illness, the prevalence of comorbid substance use disorders (SUDs) was 43%, with alcohol being the most common (Hapangama et al., 2013). A prison study found high rates of lifetime alcohol (56.8%) and tobacco (67%) use disorders, and notable rates of cannabis (42%) and opioid (25.6%) dependence (Hapangama et al., 2021).

Treatment coverage for SUDs remains well below SDG targets, with only 5% covered in 2020 (Sustainable Development Council, 2025). Current services include general practitioners, psychiatrists, general physicians, private providers, and the Sri Lanka Army, offering inpatient detoxification and residential/day rehabilitation (Wickramasinghe & Wickramasinghe, 2024). Psychiatry consultations are available in medical and surgical wards for cases like delirium or road traffic accidents. While state services offer free consultations, some essential medications like thiamine and anti-craving agents must usually be purchased privately at a high cost.

Sri Lanka lacks formally trained addiction specialists; instead, psychiatrists receive training in SUD management during postgraduate education. SUD diagnosis and management are also included in undergraduate medical and nursing curricula to equip general practitioners and nurses. Many individuals are referred to psychiatry services, but follow-up is poor. Contributing factors include a lack of community-based services, limited human resources, funding constraints, and the absence of accreditation standards for private rehabilitation providers.

2.6 Mapping Mental Health to Other Relevant SDGs

Next, we will look at how mental health is linked to the other SDGs in Sri Lanka. This section is informed by the conceptual framework proposed by Lund et al. (2018) for social determinants of mental health, where SDGs are categorized into demographic, economic, environmental events, neighbourhood, and social and cultural domains.

2.7 Demographic

SDG 5 aims to achieve gender equality and empower all women and girls. In 2022, Sri Lanka ranked 90th out of 166 countries on the Gender Inequality Index, performing better than most South Asian nations (United Nations Development Programme, 2022). Despite this, women face structural and cultural barriers limiting workplace participation, financial security, political involvement, and safety. Women make up only about a third of the paid workforce, and although Sri Lanka elected the world's first female prime minister in 1960, female parliamentary representation remains low, recently rising from 5.3% to 10.7%. However, female participation in academia and medicine, including postgraduate psychiatry training, is increasing (Baminiwatta et al., 2021).

Gender-based violence is widespread, affecting 40% of women aged 15 or older (Department of Census and Statistics, 2020). Legal reforms, including amendments to the Penal Code and the Prevention of Domestic Violence Act, have been introduced, but challenges persist. Gender-based violence significantly contributes to higher depression rates among women (Alwis et al., 2023).

Although maternal mortality has declined substantially, maternal mental health services remain underdeveloped (Hapangama & Kuruppuarachchi, 2021). A meta-analysis reported a 16.9% prevalence of perinatal depression (Alwis et al., 2023), and maternal suicide rates rose from 0.8 to 12.1 per 100,000 live births between 2002 and 2010 (Jayaratne, 2013). Fewer than five tertiary hospitals have dedicated mother-baby beds, often resulting in postpartum women being admitted separately from their infants.

UNDP supports gender-focused programs in Sri Lanka, emphasizing justice for survivors of violence and multi-sectoral support services, though funding gaps remain. There appears to be an increase in advocacy for gender equality across different sectors. For instance, since 2016, the University Grants Commission has called for gender equity initiatives across universities.

2.8 Economic

SDG 1 (No poverty) has unequivocal relevance for mental health. Poverty is a well-established contributor to mental health problems. In turn, those affected by mental health issues often face difficulties in maintaining stable employment, perpetuating a vicious cycle of disadvantage. A recent review identified a clear association between lower socioeconomic status and depression in Sri Lanka (Alwis et al., 2023). According to the 2019 Household Income and Expenditure Survey, 16% of Sri Lankans live in multidimensional poverty as defined nationally. The country's target for 2030 is to reduce this to 8%, in line with the SDGs (Sustainable Development Council, 2025). Coverage of social protection systems remains inadequate, rising slightly from 42.3% in 2016 to 42.9% in 2019 through programmes such as cash transfers, social insurance, elder support schemes, disability benefits, postnatal allowances, and educational assistance. Strengthening these safety nets is essential to breaking the intergenerational cycle of poverty and mental illness.

SDG 8 (Decent work and economic growth) is another SDG in the economic domain with direct relevance for mental health. Unemployment is a recognized risk factor for mental health problems. Sri Lanka has shown regression on several key targets under SDG 8 including per capita economic growth, economic productivity and innovation, labour rights and safe working environment, sustainable tourism, and aid for trade. On a positive note, unemployment rate has dropped from 5.5% in 2020 to 4.7% in 2023. Moreover, the rate of youth not in education, employment or training has dropped from 25.8% in 2015 to 18.2% in 2023, indicating some progress. Nevertheless, a gender disparity persists in unemployment, with the unemployment rate for females standing at 7% compared to 3.6% among males in 2023. Addressing this gap would be an important step towards inclusive economic growth. However, it should be noted that the impact of employment on mental health may be complex. In one study, being employed has been linked to lower depression among men, but higher depression in women with lower living standards (Ball et al., 2010).

SDG 9 (Industry, Innovation and Infrastructure) is also connected to mental health. Investment in reliable and accessible infrastructure, particularly transportation and communication technologies, has contributed drastically to reducing social isolation, enabling access to support systems. Improved living conditions, promotion of inclusive and sustainable industrialisation, and creating employment opportunities have a positive impact on mental health (Lund et al., 2018). Similarly, leveraging technological advancements has, to an extent, improved the reach of mental health interventions in Sri Lanka. A decentralised mental health service at the district level, including community support centres and outreach clinics, increased access to mental health information, and online support, is currently in place and contributes to SDG 9 targets. Telepsychiatry is emerging, but still in foetal stage. Integration of mental health into the existing primary care services with updates to infrastructure and human resources would be the sustainable way forward (Rodrigo, 2017). However, the economic setback, limited fiscal space, low priority in investment in research and development, and brain drain, have hindered this progress.

SDG 10 (Reduced inequalities) is also relevant here because previous studies show population-level associations between income inequality and mental health (Pickett, 2006). The growth rate of the bottom 40% of the population's per capita income had been 10.5% in 2013, reaching 26.3% in 2016, only to drop back to 11.1% in 2019. In contrast, the growth rate of household expenditure has more than doubled, from 1.2% in 2013 to 2.48% in 2016 (Department of Census and Statistics, 2019). The same sources reveal that 12.5% of the population lives below 50% of the median income, with a slight preponderance among women and children below 15 years and with an alarming 27% of the disabled. On the other hand, the island has experienced a significant decline in foreign aid over the last decade.

Sri Lanka has made notable progress in human development, largely due to free healthcare and education. However, inclusivity in education for those with special needs and income-generating opportunities for the differently abled remain limited. Ensuring access to mental health services for rural, vulnerable, and marginalized communities is essential (Amarasinghe & Rajapakse, 2024). The national mental health policy emphasizes accessible and affordable services to promote well-being and protect the rights of those with mental illness.

SDG 2 (Zero hunger) recognizes that ending hunger and improving nutrition are key to fostering positive mental health and breaking cycles of vulnerability (Ejiohuo et al., 2024). Studies on depression in Sri Lanka have linked food insecurity to higher rates of depression (Ball et al., 2010; Jayasuriya et al., 2016). A multi-sectoral approach has been adopted, with the Food Policy and Security Committee and the National Nutrition Council coordinating efforts to ensure a sustainable food system (Ministry of Health, 2022). Strategies include boosting local food production through incentives for farmers, promoting home gardening, and maintaining social safety nets like Samurdhi and food subsidies. Targeted nutrition programs for children, pregnant women, and vulnerable groups have been implemented. The Maternal and Child Health (MCH) program conducts extensive growth monitoring and promotes exclusive breastfeeding and appropriate complementary feeding. Nutrition guidelines and policies, updated regularly since 1986, guide these interventions.

Despite significant investment, progress has been undermined by the COVID-19 pandemic and the economic crisis. As of 2023, 42% of households turned to food-based coping strategies, such as skipping meals (World Food Programme, 2024). Malnutrition remains widespread, with nearly one-third of children malnourished, 14.6% of antenatal mothers having low BMI, and rising undernutrition among under-5 s, particularly in the estate sector. Climate change, economic hardship, rising food prices, regional disparities, and gaps in reliable data pose major challenges to achieving SDG 2.

2.9 Neighbourhood

SDG 6 (Clean water and sanitation) is potentially related to mental health as inadequate drinking water access, including concerns over water scarcity and perceived inequity in water service provision, have been associated with negative mental health outcomes (Toivettula et al., 2023). A study in Sri Lanka has also shown an association between inaccessibility to good-quality water and depression (Ball et al., 2010). According to the Household Income & Expenditure Survey-2019, nearly 90% of households in Sri Lanka had access to safe drinking water, and 97% had access to safe sanitation services. However, only 60% have access to a piped water supply. Coverage also favours the urban population, with 57% of households in the estate sector not having access to improved water sources.

Recurrent natural disasters—such as droughts, floods, and landslides—have worsened in recent years due to climate change, threatening water quality and limiting access to safe drinking water and sanitation. These challenges, along with displacement-related distress, harmful farming practices, agrochemical pollution, and poor industrial waste management, require urgent attention.

SDG 7 (Affordable and clean energy) may be indirectly related to mental health. Access to affordable and clean energy can enhance mental health by enabling economic and educational opportunities through reliable power, reducing the physical burden of fuel collection, improving indoor air quality, ensuring safety for cooking, and lowering health anxieties. Clean energy-powered street lighting also creates safer home and community environments, supporting overall mental well-being.

The Ministry of Power and Energy reports that near-universal electricity access has been achieved in Sri Lanka (99.9%) by 2023, a commendable success (Sustainable Development Council, 2025). However, only a third of the population relies on clean fuel and technology since only 50% of the total electricity generated comes from renewable energy sources. The limited input from solar power is a letdown for Sri Lanka, particularly considering its naturally sunny tropical environment. The high upfront cost, lack of awareness and information, shortage of skilled personnel, and technological barriers have limited tapping into the full potential of solar, wind, biomass and other renewable energy sources in the country.

SDG 11 (Sustainable cities and communities) and SDG 12 (Sustainable consumption and production) also have some relevance to mental health, albeit indirectly. Housing quality, indoor climate, cleanliness, and neighborhood safety are crucial for mental health (Evans et al., 2000; Lund et al., 2018). According to a study in the Colombo district, urban living was associated with depression specifically in men but not in women; they further noted that lower standards of living, including poor-quality structural material and toilets, were associated with depression among males (Ball et al., 2010). While 81% of Sri Lankans live in permanent housing, 18% live in semi-permanent houses and less than 1% account for the slum population (Saja, 2021). Notably, 20% of land and housing and 30% of dwellings are in high-risk landslide areas, while coastal and metropolitan regions face increasing climate-related risks. Although the Disaster Management Centre has early warning systems in place, there is a need to strengthen risk reduction to better protect vulnerable communities.

Despite 57% of the population relying on public transport, urban traffic congestion, rising private vehicle use, and road accidents pose ongoing challenges. Air pollution has been worsening in urban areas, and this is concerning because of the increasing recognition of air pollution as a contributor to mental health problems (Bhui et al., 2023; Ileperuma, 2020). Furthermore, waste management remains a major concern, with only 42% of municipal waste efficiently collected, 85% openly dumped, and less than 5% recycled (Saja et al., 2021). Plastic recycling rates remain well below targets, and electronic waste has quadrupled over two decades. Encouragingly, Sri Lanka's material footprint per GDP unit has improved, dropping from 1.29 in 2015 to 0.71 in 2019, moving closer to the 2030 sustainability target of 0.54.

2.10 Environmental Events

SDG 13 (Climate action) is increasingly understood to be intertwined with mental health. Sri Lanka was ranked second in the Global Climate Risk Index in 2019, reflecting its high vulnerability to climate change impacts such as rising temperatures, erratic rainfall, floods, droughts, sea-level rise, and landslides (Abeysekara et al., 2023; Eckstein et al., 2019). These changes affect agriculture, fisheries, tourism, and the livelihoods of many Sri Lankans. National responses include the *National Policy on Climate Change* and the *National Adaptation Plan for Climate Change Impacts in Sri Lanka (2016–2025)*, focusing on sustainable resource use, disaster preparedness, and climate-resilient development. Other institutional policies on climate action are also becoming more commonplace (Lokupitiya & Kariyawasam, 2021).

Climate change also poses growing risks to mental health. Eco-anxiety (worry, fear, or distress about environmental degradation and climate change), PTSD, depression, and anxiety may arise due to extreme weather events, displacement, and loss of homes and livelihoods. Vulnerable groups such as children, the elderly, and those with pre-existing mental health conditions are at greater risk (White et al., 2023). However, research on these links remains scarce in the Sri Lankan context. It is crucial for Sri Lanka to integrate mental health into climate action. This includes disaster-related psychosocial support, resilience-building programs, and promoting climate engagement, which can enhance well-being and empowerment.

SDG 16 (Peace, Justice and Strong Institutions) focuses on peace, justice, and strong institutions, and has significant, though sometimes indirect, connections to mental health. SDG 16 aims to reduce all forms of violence. Exposure to violence, whether direct or indirect, is a significant risk factor for mental health conditions like adjustment disorder, PTSD, anxiety, and depression (Mudunna et al., 2025; Shoib et al., 2022a; Shoib et al., 2022b). Conflict, war, and organised crime create environments of chronic stress and trauma, severely impacting mental well-being (Husain et al., 2011; Jahanshahi et al., 2020). Sri Lanka has a history of conflict; ongoing efforts are needed to foster reconciliation and build lasting peace. This involves addressing past grievances and promoting social cohesion (Chandradasa & Kuruppuarachchi, 2017).

According to Police statistics, the number of victims of intentional homicide in Sri Lanka has shown an increase since 2015, from 2.27 victims per 100,000 in 2015 to 2.71 in 2023, creating concerns for public safety and security (Sustainable

Development Council, 2025). However, the number of cases of physical and sexual violence reported to the Police shows a declining trend. Reported crimes and offenses against children have also shown a modest reduction from 3932 in 2015 to 3594 in 2020. The number of people accessing dispute resolution mechanisms (cases filed through courts, mediation, and labor tribunals) has increased, potentially signifying a growing trust in judicial institutions. This has important implications for mental health as fair and accessible justice systems promote security and stability, thereby safeguarding mental health. Peaceful societies reduce the risks of traumatic events and create better mental health support systems.

2.11 Social and Cultural

SDG 4 (Quality education) ensures inclusive and equitable education and promotes lifelong learning opportunities for all. Sri Lanka's school education system is structured with primary, lower secondary, and upper secondary levels, emphasising free and compulsory education from ages 5 to 16 (Aturupane & Little, 2021). Key components include the Grade Five Scholarship Examination, the General Certificate of Education (Ordinary Level) for secondary completion, and the General Certificate of Education (Advanced Level) for university entrance. According to annual school census data, completion rate for primary education has increased from 92% in 2015 to 96.7% in 2022; and lower secondary from 88% to 93.5%. However, completion rate for upper secondary has dropped from 75.9% to 65.4% (Sustainable Development Council, 2025).

Education and mental health influence each other (Izutsu et al., 2015). Anxiety and depression, can impair students' focus and learning. Students experiencing mental health challenges may have difficulty with attendance, participation, and academic performance. A meta-analysis that pooled studies conducted among school and university students in Sri Lanka revealed a staggering rate of 39% for depressive symptoms (Alwis et al., 2023). Therefore, a positive and supportive learning environment is needed to promote mental well-being (Conradson, 2016).

Education can equip individuals with knowledge and skills to manage stress, build resilience, and seek help when needed. Lower education has been associated with higher rates of depression in studies among adults in Sri Lanka (Alwis et al., 2023). On the other hand, negative school and university experiences, such as bullying, discrimination, or excessive pressure, can negatively impact mental health (Schneider et al., 2012). Creating inclusive and supportive educational settings that address mental health needs is essential for achieving SDG 4. Promoting mental health literacy within education systems can empower students to care for their well-being and support others. Studies conducted in Sri Lanka have demonstrated deficits in mental health literacy among school-going adolescents and undergraduates (Amarasuriya et al., 2015; Attygalle et al., 2017). This is to be expected as mental health is not adequately covered in the current school curriculum. Programs have been designed to improve mental health literacy among school students as well as teachers in Sri Lanka, but have not been widely adopted (Ginige et al., 2021; Vithana et al., 2023).

3 Recommendations and Way Forward

In view of the above observations, while Sri Lanka has made significant progress in uplifting mental health standards and contributed actively to SDGs, there is still much that needs to be done. To meaningfully advance mental health within Sri Lanka's SDG framework, we recommend the following strategic actions:

1. Integrate Mental Health into All Relevant SDG Policies: Mental health must be recognized as cross-cutting and systematically integrated into national strategies for poverty reduction, education, employment, urban planning, climate adaptation, and disaster risk reduction.
2. Enact Modern Mental Health Legislation: Urgent legislative reform is needed to replace the outdated Mental Diseases Ordinance with a rights-based Mental Health Act aligned with the UN Convention on the Rights of Persons with Disabilities (CRPD).
3. Strengthen Community-Based Mental Health Services: Decentralize and adequately fund mental health care through primary care integration as outlined in the 2020 Mental Health Policy, particularly in underserved regions.
4. Build Mental Health Literacy and School-Based Interventions: Incorporate comprehensive mental health education into the national school curriculum and expand teacher training in mental health support and referral pathways.
5. Expand Suicide Prevention: Reinvigorate national suicide prevention strategies with targeted interventions for high-risk groups, especially older adults and young females, and establish a national suicide and self-harm surveillance system.
6. Invest in Human Resources and Retention: Address brain drain and workforce shortages by creating incentives for training and retaining mental health professionals.
7. Support Vulnerable Populations through Inclusive Development: Prioritize the mental health needs of women, youth, people with disabilities, and conflict-affected communities through inclusive economic, educational, and health programs.
8. Strengthen Intersectoral Collaboration for Substance Use Disorder Prevention and Treatment: Foster coordinated efforts among the public health sector, legal and judicial systems, Police and military, social services, and both public and private service providers to prevent substance misuse and to ensure comprehensive care for individuals affected by it.
9. Promote Climate-Resilient Mental Health Strategies: Integrate mental health into climate change responses through disaster-related psychosocial support, community resilience building, and nature-based interventions.

10. Improve Data Collection and Research: Strengthen national mental health surveillance and invest in context-specific research to inform policy, particularly around social determinants, service coverage, and mental health impacts of climate change.

4 Conclusion

Mental health is both a determinant and an outcome of sustainable development. Sri Lanka has made notable progress in health and education, but mental health remains under-addressed within the SDG agenda. The rising burden of mental illness, exacerbated by poverty, gender inequality, and environmental stressors, in the context of outdated laws, inactive policies, and shortages in the mental health workforce, threatens the achievement of multiple SDG targets.

Integrating mental health more holistically into national development planning is not only a moral and human rights imperative but a necessary condition for achieving inclusive and sustainable growth. By aligning mental health with the SDGs and committing to a rights-based, community-centred, and multisectoral approach, Sri Lanka can build a more resilient, equitable, and mentally healthy society.

References

Abeysekara, W. C. S. M., Siriwardana, M., & Meng, S. (2023). Economic consequences of climate change impacts on the agricultural sector of South Asia: A case study of Sri Lanka. *Economic Analysis and Policy, 77*, 435–450. https://doi.org/10.1016/J.EAP.2022.12.003

Alcohol and Drug Information Centre. (2021). Annual Trend Survey on Alcohol Consumption in Sri Lanka 2022.

Alwis, I., Baminiwatta, A., & Chandradasa, M. (2023). Prevalence and associated factors of depression in Sri Lanka: A systematic review and meta-analysis. *Social Psychiatry and Psychiatric Epidemiology*. https://doi.org/10.1007/s00127-023-02495-z

Amarasinghe, S. C., & Rajapakse, T. N. (2024). Psychiatric morbidity and mental health Services in Sri Lanka. In *Access to mental health Care in South Asia* (pp. 137–153). Springer Nature. https://doi.org/10.1007/978-981-99-9153-2_8

Amarasuriya, S. D., Jorm, A. F., & Reavley, N. J. (2015). Quantifying and predicting depression literacy of undergraduates: A cross sectional study in Sri Lanka. *BMC Psychiatry, 15*, 269. https://doi.org/10.1186/s12888-015-0658-8

Arafat, S., Kar, S., Sharma, P., Marahatta, K., & Baminiwatta, A. (2021a). A comparative analysis of psychiatry curriculum at undergraduate level of Bangladesh, India, Nepal, and Sri Lanka. *Indian Journal of Psychiatry, 63*(2), 184–188. https://doi.org/10.4103/psychiatry.IndianJPsychiatry_615_20

Arafat, S. M. Y., Ali, S. A. Z., Menon, V., Hussain, F., Ansari, D. S., Baminiwatta, A., Saleem, T., Singh, R., Varadharajan, N., Biyyala, D., Kar, S. K., & Khan, M. M. (2021b). Suicide methods in South Asia over two decades (2001–2020). *International Journal of Social Psychiatry, 67*(7), 920–934. https://doi.org/10.1177/00207640211015700

Attygalle, U. R., Perera, H., & Jayamanne, B. D. W. (2017). Mental health literacy in adolescents: Ability to recognise problems, helpful interventions and outcomes. *Child and Adolescent Psychiatry and Mental Health, 11*, 38. https://doi.org/10.1186/s13034-017-0176-1

Aturupane, H., & Little, A. W. (2021). General education in Sri Lanka, 695–732. https://doi.org/10.1007/978-981-15-0032-9_18

Ball, H. A., Siribaddana, S. H., Kovas, Y., Glozier, N., McGuffin, P., Sumathipala, A., & Hotopf, M. (2010). Epidemiology and symptomatology of depression in Sri Lanka: A cross-sectional population-based survey in Colombo District. *Journal of Affective Disorders, 123*(1–3), 188–196. https://doi.org/10.1016/j.jad.2009.08.014

Baminiwatta, A. (2024). Changing patterns of suicide among the elderly in Sri Lanka from 2015 to 2022: An analysis based on national suicide statistics. *Annual Academic Sessions of the Sri Lanka College of Psychiatrists.*

Baminiwatta, A., Alahakoon, H., & Kasturi Mudali, A. (2021). Gender parity among psychiatrists: The trends and current status in Sri Lanka. *Asian Journal of Psychiatry, 63*, 102771. https://doi.org/10.1016/j.ajp.2021.102771

Baminiwatta, A., & Ediriweera, D. (2022). Changes in the geospatial distribution of suicides in Sri Lanka during the COVID-19 pandemic: An analysis of Police data. *Sri Lanka Medical Association International Medical Congress 2022.* https://doi.org/10.13140/RG.2.2.27623.73123

Bhui, K., Newbury, J. B., Latham, R. M., Ucci, M., Nasir, Z. A., Turner, B., O'Leary, C., Fisher, H. L., Marczylo, E., Douglas, P., Stansfeld, S., Jackson, S. K., Tyrrel, S., Rzhetsky, A., Kinnersley, R., Kumar, P., Duchaine, C., & Coulon, F. (2023). Air quality and mental health: Evidence, challenges and future directions. *BJPsych Open, 9*(4), e120. https://doi.org/10.1192/bjo.2023.507

Chandradasa, M., & Kuruppuarachchi, K. A. L. A. (2017). Child and youth mental health in post-war Sri Lanka. *BJPsych. International, 14*(2), 36–37. https://doi.org/10.1192/S2056474000001756

Chandradasa, M., & Kuruppuarachchi, K. A. L. A. (2024). Brain drain among Sri Lankan psychiatrists. *Sri Lanka Journal of Psychiatry, 14*(2), 1–3. https://doi.org/10.4038/sljpsyc.v14i2.8529

Conradson, D. (2016). Fostering student mental Well-being through supportive learning communities. *The Canadian Geographer / Le Géographe Canadien, 60*(2), 239–244. https://doi.org/10.1111/CAG.12276

De Silva, V., Hanwella, R., & Senanayake, M. (2013). Age and sex specific suicide rates in Sri Lanka from 1995-2011. *Sri Lanka Journal of Psychiatry, 3*(2), 7. https://doi.org/10.4038/sljpsyc.v3i2.5131

Department of Census and Statistics. (2019). Household Income and Expenditure Survey.

Department of Census and Statistics, S. L. (2020). Women's Wellbeing Survey—2019: Findings from Sri Lanka's first dedicated National Survey on Violence against Women and Girls.

Eckstein, D., Hutfils, M. L., & Winges, M. (2019). GLOBAL CLIMATE RISK INDEX 2019: Who suffers Most from extreme weather events? Weather-related loss events in 2017 and 1998 to 2017.

Ejiohuo, O., Onyeaka, H., Unegbu, K. C., Chikezie, O. G., Odeyemi, O. A., Lawal, A., & Odeyemi, O. A. (2024). Nourishing the mind: How food security influences mental wellbeing. *Nutrients, 16*(4), 501. https://doi.org/10.3390/nu16040501

Evans, G. W., Wells, N. M., Chan, H. Y. E., & Saltzman, H. (2000). Housing quality and mental health. *Journal of Consulting and Clinical Psychology, 68*(3), 526–530. https://doi.org/10.1037/0022-006X.68.3.526

Ginige, P., Perera, I. B. R. U., Arambepola, S. C. A., Kuruwita, K. A. P. R., & Gunawardena, E. R. N. D. (2021). The impact of a specialized training programme on teacher mental health literacy in Central Sri Lanka. *Sri Lanka Journal of Medicine, 30*(1), 34. https://doi.org/10.4038/sljm.v30i1.243

Hapangama, A., Dasanyake, D. G. B. M. S., Kuruppuarachchi, K. A. L. A., Pathmeswaran, A., & De Silva, H. J. (2021). Substance use disorders and their correlates among inmates in a Sri Lankan prison. *Journal of the Postgraduate Institute of Medicine, 8*(2), 157. https://doi.org/10.4038/jpgim.8334

Hapangama, A., & Kuruppuarachchi, K. A. L. A. (2021). Maternal mental health services in Sri Lanka: Challenges and solutions. *BJPsych International, 18*(4), 100–102. https://doi.org/10.1192/bji.2020.52

Hapangama, A., Kuruppuarachchi, K. A. L. A., & Hanwella, R. (2023). Achievements and challenges in psychiatric education and training in Sri Lanka. *BJPsych International, 20*(1), 2–4. https://doi.org/10.1192/bji.2021.35

Hapangama, A., Kuruppuarachchi, K., & Pathmeswaran, A. (2013). Substance use disorders among mentally ill patients in a general Hospital in Sri Lanka: Prevalence and correlates. *Ceylon Medical Journal, 58*(3), 111. https://doi.org/10.4038/cmj.v58i3.6103

Hapangama, A., Mendis, J., & Kuruppuarachchi, K. A. L. A. (2023). Why are we still living in the past? Sri Lanka needs urgent and timely reforms of its archaic mental health laws. *BJPsych International, 20*(1), 4–6. https://doi.org/10.1192/bji.2022.26

Husain, F., Anderson, M., Lopes Cardozo, B., Becknell, K., Blanton, C., Araki, D., & Vithana, E. K. (2011). Prevalence of war-related mental health conditions and association with displacement status in postwar Jaffna District. *Sri Lanka. JAMA, 306*(5), 522–531. https://doi.org/10.1001/jama.2011.1052

Ileperuma, O. A. (2020). Review of air pollution studies in Sri Lanka. *Ceylon Journal of Science*. https://doi.org/10.4038/cjs.v49i3.7773

Institute for Research and Development. (2007). National Survey on Mental Health in Sri Lanka.

Izutsu, T., Tsutsumi, A., Minas, H., Thornicroft, G., Patel, V., & Ito, A. (2015). Mental health and wellbeing in the sustainable development goals. *The Lancet. Psychiatry, 2*(12), 1052–1054. https://doi.org/10.1016/S2215-0366(15)00457-5

Jahanshahi, A. A., Gholami, H., & Rivas Mendoza, M. I. (2020). Sustainable development challenges in a war-torn country: Perceived danger and psychological Well-being. *Journal of Public Affairs, 20*(3), e2077. https://doi.org/10.1002/PA.2077

Jayaratne, K. (2013). Maternal suicides in Sri Lanka: Lessons learnt from review of maternal deaths over 9 years (2002–2010). In *Suicide in Sri Lanka: Past, present and future transformations*. World Health Organization.

Jayasuriya, D., Jayasuriya, R., Tay, A. K., & Silove, D. (2016). Associations of mental distress with residency in conflict zones, ethnic minority status, and potentially modifiable social factors following conflict in Sri Lanka: A nationwide cross-sectional study. *The Lancet. Psychiatry, 3*(2), 145–153. https://doi.org/10.1016/S2215-0366(15)00437-X

Kathriarachchi, S. T., Seneviratne, V. L., & Amarakoon, L. (2019a). Development of mental health care in Sri Lanka: Lessons learned. *Taiwanese Journal of Psychiatry, 33*(2), 55. https://doi.org/10.4103/TPSY.TPSY_15_19

Kathriarachchi, S., Rajapakse, T., Seneviratne, L., Ferdinando, R., Ranaweera, S., Wijesundere, A., Samaraweera, S., Gunasekera, M., Jayaratne, K., Suveendran, T., & Hettiarachchi, K. (2019b). *Suicide Prevention in Sri Lanka: Recommendations for Action*. Sri Lanka Medical Association (SLMA) Expert Committee on Suicide Prevention.

Lokupitiya, E., & Kariyawasam, M. (2021). Institutional role in implementing climate action (SDG 13): A case study from the University of Colombo. *Sri Lanka. University of Colombo Review, 2*(2), 162. https://doi.org/10.4038/ucr.v2i2.54

Lund, C., Brooke-Sumner, C., Baingana, F., Baron, E. C., Breuer, E., Chandra, P., Haushofer, J., Herrman, H., Jordans, M., Kieling, C., Medina-Mora, M. E., Morgan, E., Omigbodun, O., Tol, W., Patel, V., & Saxena, S. (2018). Social determinants of mental disorders and the sustainable development goals: A systematic review of reviews. *The Lancet Psychiatry, 5*(4), 357–369. https://doi.org/10.1016/S2215-0366(18)30060-9

Saja, M. (2021). Sustainable Development Goal (SDG 11): 'Sustainable Cities and Communities'—Engineers must act fast to get it right. *Official E-Newsletter of the Institution of Engineers Sri Lanka.*

Ministry of Health. (2021). National Mental Health Policy 2020-2030. https://mentalhealth.health.gov.lk/images/2022/NationalMentalHealthPolicy_Final_12.10.2021PRINT-1.pdf

Ministry of Health. (2022). National Nutrition Policy of Sri Lanka 2021–2030.

Mudunna, C., Weerasinghe, M., Tran, T., Antoniades, J., Romero, L., Chandradasa, M., & Fisher, J. (2025). Nature, prevalence and determinants of mental health problems experienced by adolescents in South Asia: A systematic review. *The Lancet Regional Health—SoutheastAsia, 33*, 100532. https://doi.org/10.1016/J.LANSEA.2025.100532

Pickett, K. E. (2006). Income inequality and the prevalence of mental illness: A preliminary international analysis. *Journal of Epidemiology & Community Health, 60*(7), 646–647. https://doi.org/10.1136/jech.2006.046631

Rajapakse, T. N. (2017). A review of the changing patterns of suicide and deliberate self-harm in Sri Lanka. *Sri Lanka Journal of Psychiatry, 8*(1), 3. https://doi.org/10.4038/sljpsyc.v8i1.8132

Rodrigo, E. K. (2017). Community psychiatry, community mental health services or primary care psychiatry? *Sri Lanka Journal of Psychiatry, 8*(2), 1. https://doi.org/10.4038/sljpsyc.v8i2.8152

Jeffrey D. Sachs, Guillaume Lafortune, & Grayson Fuller. (2024). The SDGs and the UN Summit of the Future. Sustainable Development Report 2024.

Saja, A. M. A., Zimar, A. M. Z., & Junaideen, S. M. (2021). Municipal solid waste management practices and challenges in the southeastern coastal cities of Sri Lanka. *Sustainability, 13*(8), 4556. https://doi.org/10.3390/su13084556

Schneider, S. K., O'donnell, L., Stueve, A., & Coulter, R. W. S. (2012). Cyberbullying, school bullying, and psychological distress: A regional census of high school students. *American Journal of Public Health, 102*(1), 171–177. https://doi.org/10.2105/AJPH.2011.300308

Shoib, S., Chandradasa, M., Rathnayake, L., Usmani, S., & Saeed, F. (2022a). Children, adolescent, and youth mental health in Sri Lanka in the context of recent violence, COVID-19, and economic crisis: A call for action. *The Lancet Regional Health—SoutheastAsia, 2*, 100021. https://doi.org/10.1016/j.lansea.2022.100021

Shoib, S., Khan, S., Baiou, A., Chandradasa, M., Swed, S., Turan, S., & Yusha'u Armiya'u, A. (2022b). Exposure to violence and the presence of suicidal and self-harm behaviour predominantly in Asian females: Scoping review. *Middle East Current Psychiatry, 29*(1), 1–12. https://doi.org/10.1186/S43045-022-00225-W/TABLES/1

Sustainable Development Council of Sri Lanka. (2024a). Sri Lanka's progress in achieving the sustainable development goals (SDGs)—2024ka.

Sustainable Development Council of Sri Lanka. (2024b). *Mapping of Policy Proposals of the Policy Document.* A Thriving Nation—A Beautiful Life for Alignment with the Sustainable Development Goals (SDGs).

Sustainable Development Council of Sri Lanka. (2025). Status Report on SDG Indicators.

Toivettula, A., Varis, O., Vahala, R., & Juvakoski, A. (2023). Making waves: Mental health impacts of inadequate drinking water services—From sidenote to research focus. *Water Research, 243*, 120335. https://doi.org/10.1016/j.watres.2023.120335

United Nations Development Programme. (2022). Human Development Reports. https://hdr.undp.org/data-center/country-insights#/ranks

Vithana, C., Lokubalasooriya, A., Pragasan, G., Mahagamage, K. L., Nanayakkara, K., Herath, H. P., Karunarathna, P., Perera, N., de Silva, C., Jayawardene, D., & Wickramasinghe, N. D. (2023). Effectiveness of an educational intervention to promote psychosocial Well-being of school-going adolescents in Sri Lanka. *BMC Public Health, 23*(1), 2185. https://doi.org/10.1186/s12889-023-17023-6

White, B. P., Breakey, S., Brown, M. J., Smith, J. R., Tarbet, A., Nicholas, P. K., & Ros, A. M. V. (2023). Mental health impacts of climate change among vulnerable populations globally: An integrative review. *Annals of Global Health, 89*(1), 66. https://doi.org/10.5334/AOGH.4105

Wickramasinghe, A., & Wickramasinghe, N. D. (2024). Current perspectives on substance use disorders in Sri Lanka: Public mental health aspects. In S. M. Y. Arafat & S. K. Kar (Eds.), *Current perspectives on substance use disorders in South Asia.* Springer. https://doi.org/10.1007/978-981-97-6619-2_8

World Food Programme. (2024). Household Food Security Survey Overview 2023.

Chapter 13
Sustainable Development Goals and Mental Health in Afghanistan, Bhutan, and Maldives

Deblina Roy, Anil Mavliya, Sneha Roy, and Debashish Banerjee

Abstract This chapter explores context of the Sustainable Development Goals (SDGs) and mental health in three distinct South Asian nations: Afghanistan, Bhutan, and the Maldives. Within this comprehensive framework of the 2030 Agenda for Sustainable Development, mental health transcends its classification as a sole health concern (SDG 3) to emerge as a cross-cutting enabler and intrinsic outcome measure across multiple development goals. Afghanistan, ravaged by conflict and humanitarian crises, exemplifies how instability profoundly undermines both mental health and SDG attainment. In stark contrast, Bhutan's Gross National Happiness (GNH) philosophy explicitly integrates psychological well-being into national policy, though it faces rising challenges like youth unemployment (22.6% in 2020) and associated mental health issues. The Maldives confronts existential climate threats, which exert significant mental health burdens on its population due to displacement fears and economic vulnerabilities. Challenges in integrating mental health into SDG frameworks persist, from governance breakdowns in Afghanistan to operationalization in Bhutan and in the Maldives. Ultimately, achieving truly sustainable development in these nations, addressing the shortages and skill-gaps making mental health a cross-cutting priority will foster a holistic, integrated approach, and recognize that investment in mental health is an indispensable investment in human potential and planetary prosperity.

Keywords Sustainable Development Goals · Maldives · Afghanistan · Bhutan · Mental Health

---

D. Roy (✉)
KGMU College of Nursing, King George's Medical University, Lucknow, India

A. Mavliya
Nims Nursing College Rajasthan, Jaipur, India

S. Roy
Geneva Graduate Institute IHEID, Geneva, Switzerland

D. Banerjee
Independent Researcher India, Lucknow, India

S. K. Kar et al. (eds.), *Sustainable Development Goals and Mental Health in South Asia*, South Asian Perspectives in Mental Health and Psychology ,
https://doi.org/10.1007/978-981-95-2684-0_13

1 Introduction

The political will with the sustainability of the planet reinforces countries to prioritise sustainability so that by the year 2030, countries make progress on the 17 Sustainable Development Goals (SDGs). The SDGs put forward a universal framework for peace and prosperity for the human population and the planet. Central to sustainability is the recognition that development is multifaceted and interconnected. Within this paradigm, mental health emerges as an important aspect of health (SDG 3: Good Health and Well-being), but as a critical indicator and outcome of sustainable development across numerous goals (Izutsu et al., 2015; Votruba & Thornicroft, 2016). This chapter looks at how mental health and sustainable development intersect in three South Asian countries: Afghanistan, Bhutan, and the Maldives. These countries, while geographically proximate, offer an interestingly diverse tableau of developmental stages. Their diversity in governance models, conflict histories, environmental vulnerabilities, and societal approaches to well-being is remarkably different, but still comparable. Afghanistan, a nation grappling with decades of conflict and acute humanitarian crises, presents a stark case of how political instability and resource deprivation severely undermine both SDG attainment and mental health (Mohd Saleem et al., 2021). Bhutan, with its unique development philosophy of Gross National Happiness (GNH) apart from the GDP (Gross Domestic Product), explicitly integrates well-being, including psychological well-being, into its national policy. Hence, offering insights into development pathways that are beyond Gross Domestic Product (WHO, 2021). The Maldives, a Small Island Developing State (SIDS), having political instability and tourism-dependent economy, faces threats from climate change, which profoundly impact its socioeconomic capacities and the mental health of the population (King et al., 2024).

Understanding the synergies between SDGs and mental health in these contexts is paramount. Progress towards SDGs such as reduction of poverty (SDG 1), zero hunger (SDG 2), quality education (SDG 4), gender equality (SDG 5), and climate action (SDG 13) can create environments conducive to better mental health. Conversely, poor mental health can impede individuals' capacities to learn, work, and participate in community life, thereby hindering the achievement of the above-mentioned goals (Votruba & Thornicroft, 2016).

2 Demographic Profiles

The demographic landscapes of Afghanistan, Bhutan, and the Maldives present with significant variations that shape their developmental challenges and mental health needs (UNFPA, 2025; WHO, 2021, 2025a).

These demographic divergences (Table 1) underscore the necessity for highly contextualized SDG and mental health strategies. Afghanistan's young, rapidly growing, and traumatized population requires foundational investments in basic survival, protection, and services. Bhutan, with a more stable demographic profile but facing challenges like youth unemployment and out-migration, needs to focus on equity, quality of services, and addressing mental health issues linked to development and aspirations. The Maldives, despite its higher income and health indicators, must prioritize climate resilience and manage the mental health impacts stemming from its unique environmental and economic vulnerabilities, particularly its high population density and reliance on imports (King et al., 2024).

Table 1 Comparative Demographic Indicators for Afghanistan, Bhutan, and Maldives

Indicator	**Afghanistan**	**Bhutan**	**Maldives**
Population (year)	41.5 million (2023)	0.79 million (2023)	0.53 million (2023)
Population growth rate (annual)	2.2% (2023)	~0.5% (derived from 2023–2050 proj.)	~0.4% (derived from 2023–2050 proj.)
Population density (per Km^2)	~64 (based on area 652,860 Km^2)	~20 (based on area 38,394 Km^2)	1766 (2025 Est.)
Age 0–14 (%)	22.1 (2023)	21 (2024)	22 (2024)
Age 15–64 (%)	74.6 (2023)	73 (2024)	73 (2024)
Age 65+ (%)	3.3 (2023)	7 (2024)	5 (2024)
Median age (years)	Not available	Not available	32.7 (2025 Est.)
Healthy Life Expectancy (Total, 2021)	50.4 years	64.8 years	66.7 years
Healthy Life Expectancy (Female, 2021)	51.3 years	64.6 years	66.4 years
Healthy Life Expectancy (Male, 2021)	49.6 years	65.0 years	66.8 years
Total Fertility Rate (2024)	Not available	1.4	1.7
Adolescent birth rate (per 1000, 15–19 yrs)	64 (2023)	10 (2024)	5 (2024)
Urban population (%)	~26% (World Bank, 2025)	~44% (World Bank, 2025)	39.6 (2025 Est.) [8]
Income level	Low income.	Lower-middle income.	Upper-middle income.

*Note: Data years vary. F/M denotes Female/Male where available. MPI refers to Multidimensional Poverty Index. Some figures are estimates or from specific surveys and may not be directly comparable across all indicators. Sources: (*UNFPA, 2025*), (*WHO, 2025b*), (*World Bank, 2025*)*

3 SDG Performance Landscape in Afghanistan, Bhutan, and the Maldives

The commitment to and progress on the SDGs vary significantly across Afghanistan, Bhutan, and the Maldives (Table 2) shaped by their unique national contexts, governance structures, and external factors.

3.1 Overview of SDG Adoption and Nationalization Efforts

3.1.1 Afghanistan

In **Afghanistan**, prior to August 2021, the government had nationalized the SDGs into 16 goals, 110 targets, and 177 indicators tailored to the Afghan context, with a high-level Executive Committee overseeing implementation. The country even presented a Voluntary National Review (VNR) in 2021 (Islamic Republic of Afghanistan Ministry of Economy, 2021). However, the Taliban's assumption of power in August 2021 has catastrophically reversed progress and dismantled the frameworks for SDG achievement. The de facto authorities have systematically eroded human rights, particularly those of women and girls, leading to a severe socio-economic and humanitarian crisis. International engagement, crucial for SDG financing and technical support, has been drastically curtailed, with the focus shifting primarily to humanitarian aid delivery under challenging conditions (Shoib et al., 2022).

3.1.2 Bhutan

Bhutan has uniquely integrated the SDGs with its guiding development philosophy of GNH, which inherently prioritizes holistic well-being, encompassing economic, social, environmental, and governance aspects. The SDGs are embedded within Bhutan's Five-Year Plans (FYPs); the 12th FYP (2018–2023) explicitly served as a roadmap for SDG implementation and the country's successful graduation from LDC status in December 2023 (United Nations, 2025). Progress is monitored through mechanisms like the Dewa Platform, an integrated dashboard for GNH, SDGs, and FYP indicators. The current 13th FYP (2024–2029) continues this integrated approach, aiming to transform Bhutan into a "High-Income GNH Economy" by 2034 while upholding sustainability and carbon neutrality (UNFPA, 2025).

Table 2 Key SDG Performance Indicators–Afghanistan, Bhutan, and the Maldives

Indicator	Afghanistan	Bhutan	Maldives
SDG 1: No poverty			
National Poverty Rate	47.1% (2020, pre-takeover)	8.2% (income, 2017); 17.8% (Moderate MPI, 2022)	8.2% (MVR 74/day, 2016); 28.4% (MPI, 2016)
SDG 2: Zero hunger			
Child stunting (%)	38.2 (2020)	21.2 (2015)	15.3
Food insecurity	59.5% mod/sev. Insecure (2020) [9]	Persistent undernutrition [25]	>90% food import reliant [34]
SDG 3: Good Health & Well-being			
Maternal mortality ratio (per 100,000)	521 (2023)	148 (2015)	56.7 (2019)
Under-5 mortality rate (per 1000)	62.3 (2018)	31.0 (2017)	7.0 (2021, WHO est.)
SDG 4: Quality education			
Lower secondary completion (F/M %)	44.1 / 74.5 (2019)	Total: 86.9 (modelled 2024)	Total: 97.3 (modelled 2024)
Adult literacy (F/M %)	26.6 / 52.0 (2022)	45.2 / 66.0 (2016) [27]	Youth (15–24): 98.5% (2019) [32]
SDG 5: Gender equality			
Female labor force participation (%)	5.1 (2024)	63.2 (vs 76.8 for men)	48.4% (vs 79.5% for men)
Women in National Parliament (%)	0 (de facto, post-2021)	~15% (Lower House, 2018)	5 (Feb 2024)
SDG 8: Decent work & economic growth			
Youth unemployment/ NEET (%)	Youth unemployment. 23.7% (2020)	Youth unemployment. 22.6% (2020)	1 in 5 youth NEET
SDG 13: Climate action			
Key status/ vulnerability	Highly vulnerable, least equipped	Carbon negative; highly vulnerable to GLOFs, etc.	Existential threat from sea-level rise

Note: Data years vary. F/M denotes Female/Male, where available. MPI refers to Multidimensional Poverty Index. Some figures are estimates or from specific surveys and may not be directly comparable across all indicators

Table 3 Summary of SDG Impacts on Mental Health by Country and SDG Theme

SDG Theme	Afghanistan	Bhutan	Maldives
Poverty (SDG 1)	Extreme poverty post-2021 fuels widespread psychological distress, hopelessness, trauma linked to lack of basic needs.	Moderate MPI persists (17.8%), esp. rural/children; poverty & unemployment linked to mental health despite GNH.	Multidimensional poverty (28.4% in 2016); economic shocks (tourism reliance) cause stress, anxiety.
Nutrition (SDG 2)	Severe food insecurity & child malnutrition (38.2% stunting) impair cognitive/mental development, cause parental stress.	Child stunting (21.2%) & micronutrient deficiencies persist; impact cognitive/ psychological Well-being.	High food import reliance (>90%), climate threats to food security; stunting (15.3%), high anemia in women (52.2%) cause anxiety.
Conflict/peace (SDG 16)	Decades of conflict, current repression cause mass trauma, PTSD, anxiety, depression; lack of justice exacerbates distress.	N/A (generally peaceful, focus on GNH).	N/A (generally peaceful, focus on governance).
Education (SDG 4)	Girls' education ban (beyond grade 6) causes severe depression, anxiety, loss of hope/identity in girls.	Youth unemployment (22.6%) despite education gains; academic pressure & lack of jobs cause youth mental strain, anxiety, suicide.	Low transition to higher secondary (44.5%), high youth NEET (1 in 5) linked to vulnerability, risky behaviors, mental health issues.
Gender (SDG 5)	Extreme gender apartheid: Women erased from public life, rights stripped; severe mental health crisis, high female suicide rates.	Lower female, political representation (LFPR); VAWG linked to household stress; women's GNH lower than men's.	Low female political participation (5% parliament); sociocultural norms limit women, impact MH.
Migration (SDG 8, 10)	Mass displacement (internal/external) due to conflict/crisis; trauma, loss, instability for millions.[18]	"Brain drain" of skilled youth due to lack of opportunities; migration & adaptation stress; rural-urban migration pressures.	Large migrant worker population (14.2%) faces poor MH support, stress from poor conditions, exclusion; internal migration stress.

(continued)

Table 3 (continued)

SDG Theme	Afghanistan	Bhutan	Maldives
Industry/jobs (SDG 9, 8)	Economic collapse, lack of industry/ infrastructure, high unemployment fuel despair, hopelessness.	Balancing industrial growth (hydropower, tourism) with GNH; potential for job stress if not managed well.	Tourism reliance; occupational stress (overload, isolation) for workers, esp. migrants, impacts MH.
Climate change (SDG 13)	High vulnerability, low capacity; impacts livelihoods (agriculture), causes displacement, stress, anxiety.	Carbon negative but vulnerable to GLOFs, etc.; eco-anxiety, trauma from disaster risk/experience.	Existential threat from sea-level rise; widespread eco-anxiety, grief, fear for future.
Other (Bhutan: GNH; Maldives: Substance abuse)	N/A	GNH aims for psychological Well-being, but modernization pressures, youth issues, suicide are challenges requiring GNH adaptation.	High youth substance abuse linked to, and exacerbates, mental health issues (depression, anxiety); dual diagnosis needed.

3.1.3 Maldives

The **Maldives** has demonstrated its commitment to the 2030 Agenda through the presentation of two VNRs, in 2017 and 2023. The nation's Strategic Action Plan (SAP) (2019–2023) served as the primary policy framework aligned with the SDGs. The 2023 VNR emphasized the role of connectivity (both physical and digital) as an accelerator for SDG realization and highlighted challenges related to COVID-19 recovery and access to concessional financing, particularly crucial for a SIDS facing climate vulnerability (Republic of Maldives, 2024). Key national priorities include climate action, sustainable tourism, and enhancing urban and inter-island infrastructure (Ministry of Foreign affairs, republic of Maldives, 2025).

4 Key SDG Performance Indicators: A Comparative Snapshot

The performance on key SDGs reveals stark contrasts among the three nations, reflecting their differing developmental trajectories and challenges.

4.1 Afghanistan

In **Afghanistan**, pre-2021 data showed some progress, such as a reduction in the national poverty rate from 54.5% in 2017 to 47.1% in 2020. However, the UNDP projected that 97% of the population could fall into universal poverty by mid-2023 following the regime change (UN VNR reports, 2021). In 2016, 55% of children lived below the national poverty line (Global Nutriton report, 2025). Food insecurity was rampant even before 2021, with a Global Hunger Index score of 30.3 in 2020 (ranking 99th out of 107 countries) and 59.5% of the population facing moderate or severe food insecurity. Child malnutrition was high, with stunting at 38.2% and wasting at 5.1% in 2020 (Global Nutriton report, 2025). Basic healthcare coverage reached 85% in 2020, but maternal mortality remained high at 521 per 100,000 live births in 2023 (WHO, 2025a). Educational attainment showed severe gender gaps: in 2019, lower secondary completion was 44.1% for girls versus 74.5% for boys. Adult literacy in 2022 was 26.6% for women and 52.0% for men. Post-2021, girls have been banned from education beyond the sixth grade (Yusufzai & Ravi Kumar, 2022). Female labor force participation was a mere 5.1% in 2024, and only 38.6% of gender-specific SDG indicators had data available as of December 2020. The nation is also acutely vulnerable to climate change (Afghanaid, 2025).

4.2 Bhutan

Bhutan has made commendable progress on poverty reduction, with income poverty falling to 8.2% in 2017 and multidimensional poverty to 5.8% in 2017 (United Nations, 2025). The Moderate Multidimensional Poverty Index (MPI) stood at 17.8% in 2022, with Bhutan having already met SDG Target 1.2 of halving its original MPI. Child stunting was 21.2% in 2015, though under nutrition remains a concern. Healthy life expectancy was 64.8 years in 2021, and the UHC service coverage index was 53 in 2019. (WHO, 2021) Adult literacy was 55.3% in 2016 (female 45.2%, male 66%) (Jamtsho, 2021) while lower secondary completion was modelled at 86.9% for 2024. However, youth unemployment reached 22.6% in 2020. Bhutan maintains gender parity in education up to the secondary level, but women's labor force participation (63.2%) lags behind men's (76.8%), and their representation in decision-making is low. A significant achievement is its carbon-negative status, absorbing approximately three times more CO2 than it emits (as of 2015) and maintaining a constitutional mandate for 60% forest cover. Nevertheless, it remains highly vulnerable to climate change impacts (SDSN, 2024).

4.3 Maldives

The **Maldives** reported 6.6% of its population below the international poverty line of $1.25/day in 2016, and 8.2% below the national poverty line (MVR 74/day). Multidimensional poverty affected 28.4% of the population in 2016. Nutritional challenges include a child stunting rate of 15.3% and wasting at 9.1%, with a high prevalence of anaemia (52.2%) among women of reproductive age. The country is over 90% dependent on food imports (Balakrishnan & Caffrey, 2022; Republic of Maldives, 2024; WHO, 2025b). Indicators of Maldives in terms of gender disparity and representations is still struggling for an equitable distribution (Table 2).

The SDG performance across these nations is profoundly influenced by governance quality, political stability, and the broader international geopolitical climate. In Afghanistan, the actions of the de facto authorities since August 2021 have actively reversed progress on numerous SDGs, particularly those concerning gender equality (SDG 5) and education for girls (SDG 4), with devastating repercussions for all other development goals and the mental well-being of the population. This contrasts with Bhutan, where the GNH philosophy and stable governance provide a robust framework for consistent SDG advancement, although its LDC graduation brings new financial considerations. The Maldives, despite its upper-middle-income status, faces challenges in consistent policy implementation, data integration, and managing external shocks like climate change and economic volatility, which can hinder sustained SDG achievement. His comparative landscape underscores that SDG progress is not merely a technical endeavour but is deeply contingent on the prevailing political and institutional environment.

5 The Interplay of SDGs and Mental Health: Country-Specific Analyses

The achievement of Sustainable Development Goals and the state of mental health are deeply intertwined, with progress in one area often bolstering the other, and setbacks creating vicious cycles. This section explores these dynamics within Afghanistan, Bhutan, and the Maldives, focusing on specific SDGs.

5.1 Afghanistan

Afghanistan's prolonged conflict, profound humanitarian crisis, and the recent political upheaval have created an environment where both SDG attainment and mental well-being are severely compromised (Iqbal & McAuliffe, 2022).

5.1.1 Poverty (SDG 1) and Mental Health

Before the Taliban takeover in August 2021, Afghanistan already faced high levels of poverty, with a national poverty rate of 47.1% in 2020. The situation has since deteriorated catastrophically; the United Nations Development Programme (UNDP) projected that 97% of the population could be living in universal poverty by mid-2023. This extreme economic deprivation is a potent driver of psychological distress (Knifton & Inglis, 2020).

Interventions that focus solely on conflict-related trauma, without tackling the crushing weight of poverty and its attendant deprivations, are unlikely to yield sustainable mental health outcomes for the Afghan people. Nutrition, Food Security (SDG 2), and Mental Health Food insecurity is a critical issue in Afghanistan. In 2020, 59.5% of the population was moderately or severely food insecure, and the World Food Programme estimated in 2021 that 23 million people faced acute food insecurity (Zahidi et al., 2021). Failure to do so risks entrenching an intergenerational cycle of poor mental health, poverty, and diminished human potential.

5.1.2 Conflict, Peace, Justice (SDG 16), and Mental Health

Decades of unrelenting conflict have inflicted deep and widespread psychological wounds upon the Afghan population (Panter-Brick et al., 2009). More than half the population is estimated to suffer from depression, anxiety, and PTSD. A 2018 European Union survey found that 85% of Afghans had experienced or witnessed at least one traumatic event, with individuals averaging four such experiences (Ruttig, 2019).

The Taliban takeover in August 2021 introduced new layers of trauma, including fear of retribution, the dramatic loss of rights and freedoms (especially for women and minorities), economic collapse, and profound uncertainty about the future. The dismantling of previous legal and judicial frameworks and the imposition of a repressive regime mean that avenues for seeking redress, ensuring safety, or envisioning a secure future are severely curtailed. Clinical interventions alone are insufficient; fundamental changes in the socio-political environment that guarantee safety, justice, and human rights are essential (Ruttig, 2019).

5.1.3 Education (Inequality) (SDG 4) and Mental Health

Even before 2021, significant gender disparities existed in education, with girls' lower secondary completion rate at 44.1% compared to 74.5% for boys in 2019. The situation has drastically worsened since the Taliban's return to power. Their edicts have banned girls from education beyond the sixth grade and women from universities, effectively pushing an estimated 80% of school-aged Afghan females—2.5 million individuals—out of school as of early 2023 (Ahmadzai, 2023).

The consequences are devastating, leading to elevated levels of depression, anxiety, a loss of identity and hope, and an increased sense of being "trapped" with no future. The inability to pursue education curtails future life prospects, fosters feelings of worthlessness and despair, and heightens vulnerability to other harms such as forced early marriage and domestic abuse. For Afghan girls, this is an existential crisis. The results of this impacts the Afghanistan's overall human capital, are likely to be catastrophic (Yusufzai & Ravi Kumar, 2022).

5.1.4 Gender Inequality (SDG 5) and Mental Health

Afghanistan has long been characterized by deep-seated gender inequality. Pre-2021 indicators such as high maternal mortality, low female literacy, minimal labour force participation (Randhawa et al., 2025), and high rates of spousal violence (52% of ever-married women in 2015) painted a grim picture. Addressing this dire situation requires sustained international pressure for the restoration of women's fundamental human rights and urgent, targeted, culturally sensitive mental health and psychosocial support, though access to such services under the current conditions remains a monumental challenge. The systematic destruction of the mental health of half the population will have enduring negative consequences for the entire society.

5.1.5 Migration, Displacement (Related to SDG 1, 2, 10, 16), and Mental Health

Decades of conflict, instability, and recurrent natural disasters have resulted in massive and protracted displacement in Afghanistan. By the end of 2021, there were 2.7 million Afghan refugees globally (Iqbal & McAuliffe, 2022), and the Taliban takeover triggered a new "eighth phase" of displacement, affecting an estimated 6.5 million people through internal or cross-border movements.

Refugees and Internally Displaced Persons (IDPs) frequently live in precarious conditions with limited access to basic services, including critically needed mental healthcare. The mental health consequences of such pervasive and often repeated displacement are profound and long-lasting, creating a substantial population carrying a heavy burden of unaddressed trauma, grief, anxiety, and depression. SDG initiatives related to poverty reduction (SDG 1), food security (SDG 2), reduced inequalities (SDG 10), and peace and justice (SDG 16) must therefore incorporate **mental health and psychosocial support (MHPSS)** for displaced populations as a vital cross-cutting priority (Afghanaid, 2025; Mohd Saleem et al., 2021; Noori et al., 2025; Panter-Brick et al., 2009). The absence of such support not only hinders individual recovery and well-being but also impedes broader efforts towards societal stabilization and sustainable development.

5.1.6 Industrialization, Infrastructure (SDG 9), and Mental Health

Afghanistan's economy and infrastructure have been ravaged by decades of conflict and underinvestment. Prior to 2021, economic growth had already stagnated, with a contraction of 2% in 2020.9 The post-2021 economic collapse saw a further 27% contraction, with only a partial and fragile recovery (2.7% growth in FY2023–24) and a subdued outlook.

Revitalizing the economy and investing in basic, life-sustaining infrastructure is therefore not merely an economic imperative but a critical public mental health priority. Meaningful employment provides not only financial sustenance but also dignity, social connection, routine, and hope—all essential components of mental well-being.

5.1.7 Climate Change (SDG 13) and Mental Health

Afghanistan is among the countries most vulnerable to the impacts of climate change and one of the least equipped to cope with its consequences, directly and indirectly impacting the mental health of the Afghan people.

The loss of livelihoods, homes, and livestock due to climate-related disasters can cause acute trauma, anxiety, depression, and profound grief. Recognizing and addressing the psychological distress caused by climate-induced losses and insecurity is crucial, yet often overlooked in humanitarian responses that prioritize immediate physical needs.

5.2 *Bhutan*

Bhutan's development is guided by its unique philosophy of GNH, which intrinsically links material progress with spiritual and psychological well-being. This approach provides a distinct context for examining SDG-mental health synergies.

5.2.1 Poverty (SDG 1) and Mental Health

Bhutan has achieved remarkable success in poverty reduction. Income poverty decreased from 23.2% in 2007 to 8.2% in 2017, and multidimensional poverty fell from 12.7% in 2012 to 5.8% in 2017. The introduction of a Moderate Multidimensional Poverty Index (MPI) in 2022 showed an incidence of 17.8%. There is an acknowledged link between poverty, unemployment, and mental health challenges in the country (Faryabi, 2021).

While the GNH framework, with its explicit inclusion of psychological well-being as a domain, should theoretically buffer against poverty-related mental distress, the persistence of moderate multidimensional poverty suggests that the benefits of development and the protective aspects of GNH may not be uniformly reaching all segments of the population. Targeted interventions within the GNH framework are therefore necessary to address these specific vulnerabilities and ensure that economic and social progress translates into improved psychological well-being for all citizens, not just as a national average (UNFPA, 2025).

5.2.2 Nutrition, Food Security (SDG 2), and Mental Health

Bhutan has made progress in improving child nutrition, with stunting rates decreasing from 33.5% in 2010 to 21.2% in 2015.25 However, undernutrition, particularly stunting and micronutrient deficiencies, continues to be a concern, with notable regional disparities. The National Nutrition Strategy and Action Plan (2021–2025) aims to tackle these issues, with a special focus on the "1000 golden days" from conception to a child's second birthday, recognizing this period's critical importance for lifelong health and development (Global Nutrition report, 2025).

5.2.3 Education, Employment (SDG 4, 8), and Youth Mental Health

Bhutan has achieved near-universal primary school enrollment and significant improvements in secondary education completion. However, the country faces a growing challenge with youth unemployment, which stood at 22.6% in 2020, having doubled in a year partly due to the COVID-19 pandemic. This coincides with an increasing trend in mental health issues such as depression and anxiety among young people. Between December 2020 and February 2021, a staggering 88% of the 671 clients seeking counseling services from the Ministry of Education were children and youth aged 9–24 years. Suicide is now reported among the top six leading causes of death in Bhutan (Jamtsho, 2021).

5.2.4 This Is Particularly Poignant in a Nation that Prioritizes Happiness

This is particularly poignant in a nation that prioritizes happiness. Therefore, achieving SDG 4 (Quality Education) and SDG 8 (Decent Work and Economic Growth) must be synergized with robust, targeted youth mental health services. Strategies are needed to better align education curricula with labor market demands, foster entrepreneurship, manage youthful aspirations realistically, and provide accessible psychosocial support.

5.2.5 Gender Inequality (SDG 5) and Mental Health

Bhutan has made significant progress in achieving gender parity in education up to the secondary level and has seen reductions in maternal mortality. However, gender inequalities persist in other critical areas. Women's labor force participation (63.2%) is notably lower than men's (76.8%) and they are underrepresented in political and economic decision-making roles (UNDP, 2021).

The mental health impacts of gender discrimination, the disproportionate burden of unpaid care work, limited participation in public life must be explicitly addressed through policy interventions, accessible support services for women, and concerted efforts to challenge and transform traditional gender norms (UNDP, 2021). A Gross National Happiness that is not equally experienced by all genders remains an incomplete aspiration.

5.2.6 Migration (SDG 8, 10) and Mental Health

Bhutan is witnessing a sharp increase in emigration, particularly among its youth, skilled individuals, and civil servants, especially since the COVID-19 pandemic, a phenomenon often described as a "brain drain"(Choden, 2025; Mahbub & Chund, 2025). Internally, rural-to-urban migration (21.7%) is also creating pressures on urban infrastructure and resources, potentially leading to social adjustment challenges for internal migrants. These migration trends are critical indicators of the socio-economic pressures faced by the Bhutanese population, especially its younger, educated cohort. Policies should aim not only to create an enabling domestic environment that retains talent but also to support the mental well-being of migrants and their families, and manage the social impacts of internal migration.

5.2.7 Industrialization, Infrastructure (SDG 9), and Mental Health

Bhutan's approach to industrialization and infrastructure development (SDG 9) is guided by its GNH philosophy, aiming for sustainable and equitable socio-economic progress. The share of industry in GDP increased significantly from 11.5% in 1980 to 41.5% in 2016. The government has prioritized economic diversification through the "five jewels": hydropower, agriculture, tourism, cottage and small industries (CSIs), and mining. Access to quality infrastructure, such as roads and information and communication technology (ICT), can reduce isolation, improve access to essential services (including healthcare and education), and enhance overall quality of life, thereby positively impacting mental well-being. Conversely, lack of adequate infrastructure can be a chronic stressor.

The mitigating strategies involve ensuring meaningful community consultation, equitable distribution of benefits, protection of the environment, and the promotion of safe and supportive work environments.

5.2.8 Climate Change (SDG 13) and Mental Health

Bhutan is globally recognized for its exemplary environmental stewardship, being a carbon-negative country. However, its fragile mountainous ecosystem makes it highly vulnerable to the adverse impacts of climate change, including Glacial Lake Outburst Floods (GLOFs), landslides, flash floods, and disruptions to its climate-sensitive agriculture and hydropower sectors. 10 These climate-related hazards pose significant threats to livelihoods, safety, and consequently, mental health. The support systems should focus on building psychological resilience, developing coping mechanisms for climate-related stress and uncertainty, and providing psychosocial care following climate-induced disasters.

5.2.9 Gross National Happiness (GNH), Development, and Mental Health

GNH, with psychological well-being as one of its nine core domains, provides a unique and holistic framework for integrating mental health into national development policy in Bhutan.

The GNH Index, which stood at 0.781 in 2022 (up from 0.756 in 2015), attempts to measure this holistic progress. However, the country is grappling with rising mental health challenges, including increasing rates of depression and anxiety (exacerbated during the COVID-19 pandemic), substance use disorders, and a high suicide rate, which is among the leading causes of death (UNDP, UNFPA, UNICEF, UNODC, WHO, 2021). Recognizing this, mental health has been elevated as a national priority, with significant leadership from Her Majesty. The Gyaltsuen Jetsun Pema Wangchuck. Key initiatives include the establishment of The PEMA Center as a national nodal agency for mental health promotion and services for substance use disorders (SUDs), and Bhutan's championing of the Paro Declaration on people-centered mental health care. The focus is increasingly on shifting from institutionalized care to community-based services, enhancing telehealth, and decentralizing care (Tsheten et al., 2023).

5.3 *Maldives*

These statistics underscore an entangled crisis of substance abuse and youth mental ill-health. Poor mental health can be a precursor to substance use, and substance use, in turn, can exacerbate existing mental health conditions or trigger new ones, creating a vicious cycle of dual diagnosis and increased vulnerability. Prevention efforts must focus on building resilience, promoting healthy coping mechanisms, and reducing risk factors among young people. Treatment services need to be accessible, youth-friendly, and equipped to handle dual diagnoses. The new National Mental Health

Strategic Action Plan, are critical in this regard the latest Mental Health policy tries to address them (MOH Maldives, 2017).

GLOF = Glacial Lake Outburst Floods; GNH = Gross National Happiness; VAWG = Violence against women and girls; MPI = Multidimensional Poverty Index, LFPR = Lower Female Poitical representation.

6 Specific Challenges in Integrating Mental Health into SDG Frameworks

6.1 Afghanistan

In **Afghanistan**, the concept of integrating mental health into SDG frameworks is currently untenable. The de facto authorities are unlikely to prioritize mental health in any systematic way, particularly if it involves "Western" approaches or challenges their ideological positions (Table 4). (Islamic republic of Afghanistan Ministry of Economy, 2021) The absence of a functioning, inclusive, and rights-respecting governance system precludes any meaningful strategic integration.

6.2 Bhutan

For **Bhutan**, while the GNH philosophy inherently includes psychological well-being, the challenge lies in translating this philosophical alignment into specific, measurable, and adequately resourced mental health targets and interventions within its FYPs and SDG monitoring systems (Yangka et al., 2018). It requires moving beyond viewing mental health as simply one of nine domains to recognizing it as a cross-cutting outcome and enabler of all GNH and SDG efforts (Table 4). Ensuring that GNH policies effectively address emerging mental health stressors associated with development, such as youth unemployment or migration, is crucial (Choden, 2025; Mahbub & chund, 2025; Rai, 2024).

6.3 Maldives

In the **Maldives**, mental health has often been addressed in a siloed manner. A key challenge is to systematically integrate mental health considerations into broader development policies and SDG initiatives (WHO, 2021). This includes incorporating mental health support into climate change adaptation strategies (to address eco-anxiety and trauma) (Table 4), education policies (to promote youth mental health and resilience), labor policies (to ensure worker well-being, especially in the tourism

Table 4 Key SDG and Mental Health Initiatives–Afghanistan, Bhutan, Maldives

Country	Key SDG-related National Strategy/ Policy	Key Mental Health Specific Policy/ Initiative	Lead Implementing Agencies/ Partners	SDG-MH Linkage Note
Afghanistan	Pre-2021: Nationalized SDGs, VNR 2021 Post-2021: Humanitarian Response Plans.	Pre-2021: MH in BPHS.Post-2021: WHO/EU MHPSS integration in select hospitals; NGO efforts (e.g., IPSO).	UN agencies, NGOs, MoPH (limited current role).	Severely disrupted; humanitarian focus on basic survival often overshadows MH. Taliban's stance is a barrier.
Bhutan	GNH Philosophy; 13th Five Year Plan (2024–2029) integrating SDGs.	The PEMA Center (MH & SUDs); Paro declaration; community-based MH services; suicide prevention.	MoH, PEMA secretariat, WHO, UNICEF.	Strong philosophical link via GNH (psychological Well-being domain); increasing practical integration and service development.
Maldives	Strategic Action Plan (2019–2023); Climate Action Plans (NDC 3.0); VNRs 2023.	National Mental Health Strategic Action Plan 2025–2029; UNICEF	MoH, NSPA, WHO, UNICEF, NGOs.	Growing recognition and strategic planning for MH, integration into PHC, youth focus, addressing climate-MH links.

MHPSS: Mental Health and Psychological Support
NDC: Nationally Determined contributions
Voluntary National Review of SDGs for United Nations (VNR)
UNICEF (United Nation's Childrens emergency fund)
MoH: Ministry of Health
WHO World Health Organisation
NGOs (Non Government Organisations)
MH Mental Health
SUD Substance Use disorders
PEMA centre (Royal Centre for Mental health and Substance Use Disorders, Bhutan)
MoPH: Ministry of Public health
UN: United Nations
IPSO: Germany Funded Project in Afghanistan to reduce and manage Psychological issues in the community
BPHS: EU backed project on Support of Basic Packages for health Services
PHCs: Primary Health Centres

sector), and urban planning (to design living environments that reduce stress and promote social connection) (King et al., 2024; Republic of Maldives, 2024).

7 How SDG Initiatives Facilitate Mental Healthcare

- Progress across various SDGs can create enabling conditions for better mental health and facilitate the delivery of mental healthcare:
- **SDG 1 (No Poverty):** Poverty reduction programs, such as cash transfers (e.g., UNICEF's program in Afghanistan), can alleviate chronic financial stress, a major risk factor for mental ill-health. Improved economic stability allows individuals and families to better meet basic needs, reducing anxiety and despair.
- **SDG 2 (Zero Hunger):** Enhanced nutrition and food security, particularly for pregnant women and young children, support healthy brain development and cognitive function, reducing vulnerability to mental disorders. School feeding programs can improve children's concentration, learning, and reduce stress related to hunger.
- **SDG 3 (Good Health and Well-being):** Strengthening primary healthcare systems, as prioritized in Bhutan and the Maldives, provides a platform for integrating mental health services, enabling early detection, treatment, and referral. Universal Health Coverage (UHC) initiatives that include mental health ensure financial accessibility.
- **SDG 4 (Quality Education):** Access to quality education empowers individuals with knowledge and skills, improving employment prospects and life choices. Schools can also serve as platforms for mental health literacy programs, early intervention, and school-based counselling services. However, it's crucial that educational environments are supportive and not overly stressful, as seen with youth pressures in Bhutan.
- **SDG 5 (Gender Equality):** Initiatives that empower women and girls, protect them from violence, and ensure equal opportunities in education, employment, and decision-making can significantly improve their mental health and reduce their disproportionate burden of stress, anxiety, and depression. WHO's training on GBV treatment protocols in Afghanistan is an example of a targeted intervention.
- **SDG 6 (Clean Water and Sanitation):** Access to safe water and sanitation reduces the burden of waterborne diseases and improves overall hygiene and living conditions, which can alleviate stress and contribute to a sense of dignity and well-being.
- **SDG 8 (Decent Work and Economic Growth):** Stable and meaningful employment provides financial security, social connection, a sense of purpose, and daily structure—all of which are protective factors for mental health.
- **SDG 9 (Industry, Innovation, and Infrastructure):** Development of resilient infrastructure, including transportation and communication networks, can reduce isolation, improve access to services (including MHPSS), and create economic opportunities.

- **SDG 13 (Climate Action):** Effective climate change adaptation and mitigation measures can reduce the direct and indirect mental health impacts of climate-related disasters and anxieties about the future, particularly in highly vulnerable nations like the Maldives and Afghanistan. Community-based adaptation can also build social cohesion and collective efficacy, which are protective for mental health.
- **SDG 16 (Peace, Justice, and Strong Institutions):** Establishing peace, security, rule of law, and access to justice is fundamental for creating an environment where individuals feel safe and mental well-being can flourish. This is acutely relevant for Afghanistan.
- **SDG 17 (Partnerships for the Goals):** Multi-stakeholder partnerships, including international cooperation, are vital for mobilizing resources, sharing expertise, and implementing comprehensive SDG and mental health strategies, as seen in the development of Maldives' mental health plan with WHO, UNICEF, and the Australian Government (Table 4).

8 Future Directions: Towards Synergistic Action

8.1 For National Governments and Policymakers

Elevate Mental Health as a Cross-Cutting Development Priority:

- Afghanistan (Future Governance): Any future legitimate governmen must recognize mental health as a critical component of national recovery and development, ensuring its inclusion in all sectoral policies and rebuilding efforts, with a particular focus on the rights and needs of women and girls.
- **Bhutan:** Further operationalize the "psychological well-being" domain of GNH by developing specific, measurable, achievable, relevant, and time-bound (SMART) mental health targets within national and sectoral development plans (Five-Year Plans). Ensure GNH screening tools for policies and projects explicitly assess and mitigate potential negative mental health impacts.
- **Maldives:** Ensure robust implementation of the National Mental Health Strategic Action Plan 2025–2029 through strong inter-ministerial coordination, dedicated budgetary allocations, and integration with key national strategies, including climate adaptation, tourism development, and youth policies.

8.2 Strengthen Governance and Inter-Sectoral Collaboration for Mental Health:

- Establish/strengthen high-level national coordination mechanisms (e.g., inter-ministerial task forces) dedicated to overseeing the integration of mental health across all relevant SDGs, ensuring accountability and resource mobilization.
- Develop clear protocols for collaboration between health ministries and ministries responsible for education, social welfare, gender, labor, environment, and disaster management to implement joint programs addressing shared risk factors and promoting mental well-being.

8.3 Invest in a Comprehensive, Decentralized, and Accessible Mental Health System:

- Allocate a significantly increased proportion of the national health budget to mental health, moving towards WHO-recommended levels, to address the vast treatment gap.
- Prioritize the integration of mental health into primary healthcare (PHC) by training PHC staff in identifying, managing, and referring common mental health conditions, as planned in Bhutan and Maldives.
- Scale up community-based MHPSS (Mental Health and Psychological Support services), utilizing community health workers, peer support specialists, and local volunteers, particularly in rural and remote areas (e.g., outer atolls in Maldives, remote districts in Bhutan).
- Develop and expand specialized mental health services, including inpatient care where necessary (e.g., planned psychiatric facility at IGMH in Maldives), and ensure a continuum of care from promotion and prevention to treatment and recovery.
- Invest in telehealth and other digital mental health solutions to improve access, especially in geographically challenging contexts like Bhutan and Maldives.

8.4 Address the Social Determinants of Mental Health through SDG Action:

- Ensure poverty reduction strategies (SDG 1) explicitly aim to reduce chronic stress and improve coping capacities, e.g., through integrated MHPSS in social protection schemes.
- Strengthen nutrition programs (SDG 2), particularly for maternal and child health, to support optimal brain development and reduce long-term mental health risks.
- Reform education systems (SDG 4) to promote student well-being, reduce academic stress, incorporate mental health literacy, and ensure safe and supportive

learning environments. Address youth unemployment (SDG 8) through skills development aligned with labour market needs and entrepreneurship support, coupled with mental health support for NEET youth.

- Intensify efforts to achieve gender equality (SDG 5) by combating GBV, promoting women's economic and political empowerment, and challenging discriminatory social norms, all of which are crucial for women's mental health.
- Integrate mental health considerations into climate change adaptation and disaster risk reduction strategies (SDG 13), including building community resilience to eco-anxiety and providing psychosocial support during and after climate-related events.

8.5 Invest in Data, Research, and Monitoring for Evidence-Based Action:

- Commission regular national mental health epidemiological surveys to establish prevalence rates, identify risk/protective factors, and track trends, disaggregated by age, gender, location, and socio-economic status.
- Strengthen national health information systems (HIS) and SDG monitoring frameworks to include robust mental health indicators and track progress on integrated SDG-mental health initiatives.
- Promote and fund research on the effectiveness of integrated interventions, culturally adapted MHPSS models, and the mental health impacts of specific SDG policies.
- Address specific data gaps identified, such as the mental health of migrant workers in Maldives or the impact of current policies in Afghanistan.

8.6 For International Partners (UN Agencies, Donors, INGOs):

- Provide Sustained Technical and Financial Support for Integrated Approaches:
- Align funding and technical assistance with national priorities for integrating mental health into SDG frameworks and strengthening mental health systems (e.g., support for Maldives' Mental Health Plan, Bhutan's PEMA Center.
- In **Afghanistan**, continue to advocate for the protection of human rights and provide principled humanitarian assistance that includes MHPSS for all vulnerable populations, working through trusted local and international channels where possible, and supporting Afghan professionals.
- Support capacity-building initiatives for mental health professionals, researchers, and policymakers in all three countries.
- Facilitate South-South learning and exchange of best practices on SDG-mental health integration.

- **Advocate for Mental Health in All Development and Humanitarian Forums:**
- **Support Data Collection and Research in Challenging Contexts:**
- Provide financial and technical support for strengthening national statistical capacities and conducting crucial research, especially in data-poor environments or for under-researched topics.
- Promote ethical research practices and ensure that data collection benefits local communities and informs national policy.
- **For Civil Society Organizations (CSOs) and Academia:**
- **Strengthen Advocacy, Awareness-Raising, and Community Mobilization:**
- **Deliver and Innovate in Community-Based Mental health Initiatives.**

By adopting these recommendations, Afghanistan, Bhutan, and the Maldives, with the support of the international community, can forge stronger synergies between their sustainable development efforts and the imperative to promote and protect the mental health and well-being of all their citizens.

9 Conclusion

The intricate relationship between the Sustainable Development Goals and mental health in Afghanistan, Bhutan, and the Maldives reveals a complex tapestry woven from threads of conflict, unique development philosophies, environmental vulnerabilities, and socio-cultural dynamics. This chapter has underscored that mental health is not merely an isolated health issue (SDG 3) but a fundamental prerequisite for, and an outcome of, progress across the entire 2030 Agenda. Conversely, the pursuit of SDGs such as poverty eradication, quality education, gender equality, and climate action inherently impacts the psychological well-being of populations.

Ultimately, synergizing SDGs and mental health requires a fundamental shift towards holistic and integrated approaches. It demands that policymakers, development practitioners, researchers, and communities recognize that investing in mental health is investing in sustainable development, and vice versa. By fostering resilience, promoting equity, ensuring access to care, and addressing the root causes of distress, Afghanistan, Bhutan, and the Maldives can strive towards a future where development is truly sustainable because it nurtures the well-being of all people and the planet they share. The diverse experiences of these three South Asian nations offer valuable lessons for the broader global effort to achieve the 2030 Agenda, leaving no one behind in body or in mind.

References

Afghanaid. (2025). *SDG 13 in Afghanistan: Climate Action|Afghanaid*. https://www.afghanaid.org.uk/sdg-13-in-afghanistan-climate-action

Ahmadzai, M. (2023). *The War on Schoolgirls: Responding to the Education Crisis in Afghanistan* (p. 6). Afghanistan Policy Lab School of Public and International Affairs Princeton University. chrome-extension://efaidnbmnnnibpcajpcglclefindmkaj/https://spia.princeton.edu/sites/default/files/2023-06/Girls%20Education%20Policy%20Brief.pdf

Balakrishnan, S. S., & Caffrey, M. (2022). *Policy brief for Maldives*. Unicef. chrome-extension://efaidnbmnnnibpcajpcglclefindmkaj/https://www.unicef.org/rosa/media/18171/file/Maldives%20Country%20Profile.pdf

Choden, D. (2025). *Bhutan's emigration dilemma: Will they ever return?* [Asia News Network]. https://asianews.network/bhutans-emigration-dilemma-will-they-ever-return/

Faryabi, K. H. (2021). *Afghanistan Voluntary National Review (VNR) 2021* (VNR 1; p. 51). chrome-extension://efaidnbmnnnibpcajpcglclefindmkaj/https://sustainabledevelopment.un.org/content/documents/280392021_VNR_Report_Afghanistan.pdf

Global Nutriton report. (2025). *Global Nutrition Report | Country Nutrition Profiles—Global Nutrition Report*. https://globalnutritionreport.org/resources/nutrition-profiles/asia/southern-asia/afghanistan/

Iqbal, M., & McAuliffe, M. (2022). *The eighth phase of Afghan displacement: Situating the top ten issues for policymakers* (Migration Research Series, N° 71.) [International organization of migration (IOM)]. International organization of migration (IOM).

Islamic republic of Afghanistan Ministry of Economy. (2021). *Afghanistan VNR-2021 Key Messages At High Level Political Forum (HLPF) Realizing Self-Reliance by Accelerating SDG implementation* [Govt]. Islamic republic of Afghanistan Ministry of Economy.

Izutsu, T., Tsutsumi, A., Minas, H., Thornicroft, G., Patel, V., & Ito, A. (2015). Mental health and wellbeing in the sustainable development goals. *The Lancet Psychiatry, 2*(12), 1052–1054. https://doi.org/10.1016/S2215-0366(15)00457-5

Jamtsho, S. (2021). Education in Bhutan: Quality and sustainability. *The Druk Journal, Sustainability of Sectors, 1*, 114–122. http://drukjournal.bt/wp-content/uploads/2021/08/Education-in-Bhutan.pdf

King, C., Ibrahim, U., Shaugy, M., Fellers, E., & O'Biren, M. (2024). *Maldives tourism climate strategic pathways for climate resiliency in tourism*. Ministry of Toursim.

Knifton, L., & Inglis, G. (2020). Poverty and mental health: Policy, practice and research implications. *BJPsych Bulletin, 44*(5), 193–196. https://doi.org/10.1192/bjb.2020.78

Mahbub, M. A., & Chund, D. (2025). *Bhutan Maintains Robust Growth with Migration Playing Key Roles* [Text/HTML]. World Bank. https://www.worldbank.org/en/news/press-release/2025/05/26/bhutan-maintains-robust-growth-with-migration-playing-key-roles

Ministry of Foreign affairs, republic of Maldives. (2025), June. *Sustainable development* [Government]. https://foreign.gov.mv/index.php/en/multilateral/priorities-and-issues/sustainable-development

MOH Maldives. (2017). *National Mental Health Policy 2015–2025* (Policy Breif Policy/23-MOH/2017/01/05February2017; p. 39). MInistry of health Maldives and WHO. chrome-extension://efaidnbmnnnibpcajpcglclefindmkaj/https://health.gov.mv/storage/uploads/74w85pYK/1x1n8wz1.pdf

Mohd Saleem, S., Shoib, S., Dazhamyar, A. R., & Chandradasa, M. (2021). Afghanistan: Decades of collective trauma, ongoing humanitarian crises, Taliban rulers, and mental health of the displaced population. *Asian Journal of Psychiatry, 65*, 102854. https://doi.org/10.1016/j.ajp.2021.102854

Noori, M. T., Amron, A., Pakarti, P., & Jumanto, J. (2025). The SDG 3 enhancement through health-Service Management in Post-Conflict Afghanistan: Resource allocation, training, community engagement, and data use. *Journal of Lifestyle and SDGs Review, 5*(2), e04513–e04513. https://doi.org/10.47172/2965-730X.SDGsReview.v5.n02.pe04513

Panter-Brick, C., Eggerman, M., Gonzalez, V., & Safdar, S. (2009). Violence, suffering, and mental health in Afghanistan: A school-based survey. *Lancet, 374*(9692), 807–816. https://doi.org/10.1016/S0140-6736(09)61080-1

Rai, K. (2024). *The contribution of the United Nations Sustainable Development Goals (SDGs) to enhancing Gross National Happiness (GNH) in Bhutan: A case study of Bhutan.*

Murdoch University. https://researchportal.murdoch.edu.au/esploro/outputs/graduate/The-contribution-of-the-United-Nations/991005723870107891

Randhawa, A. E., Tahir, M., & Zaman, M. (2025). *The Psychological and Socioeconomic Impacts of Education Denial on Afghan Girls, Dialogue Social Science Review (DSSR),* https://thedssr.com/index.php/2/citationstylelanguage/get/harvard-cite-them-right?submissionId=347&publicationId=426

Republic of Maldives. (2024). *Sustainable development.* https://foreign.gov.mv/index.php/en/multilateral/priorities-and-issues/sustainable-development

Ruttig, T. (2019, October 7). *Afghanistan: Little Help for Conflict-Linked Trauma.* Afghanistan Analysts Network-English. https://www.afghanistan-analysts.org/en/recommended-reading/afghanistan-little-help-for-conflict-linked-trauma/

SDSN. (2024, June 17). *The Sustainable Development Report 2024—Sustainable Development Solutions Network.* https://www.unsdsn.org

Shoib, S., Essar, M. Y., Saleem, S. M., Legris, Z., & Chandradasa, M. (2022). The children of Afghanistan need urgent mental health support. *The Lancet, 399*(10329), 1045–1046. https://doi.org/10.1016/S0140-6736(22)00155-6

Maldives Ministry, U. P. (2020). Strategic action plan 2019–2023. https://health.gov.mv/storage/uploads/Bxop1dwv/fse7lmco.pdf

Tsheten, T., Chateau, D., Dorji, N., Pokhrel, H. P., Clements, A. C. A., Gray, D. J., & Wangdi, K. (2023). Impact of COVID-19 on mental health in Bhutan: A way forward for action. *The Lancet Regional Health-Southeast Asia, 11.* https://doi.org/10.1016/j.lansea.2023.100179

UN VNR reports. (2021). *Country-by-country analysis of SDG localization Afghanistan* (p. 5). United Nations. https://www.gold.uclg.org/sites/default/files/ENG-GOLD-V-2020.pdf

UNDP, UNFPA, UNICEF, UNODC, WHO. (2021). *Promoting mental health and well-being deserves our undivided attention and long-term investment | UNICEF Bhutan.* https://www.unicef.org/bhutan/stories/promoting-mental-health-and-well-being-deserves-our-undivided-attention-and-long-term

UNDP. (2021). *BHUTAN GENDER ANALYSIS* (p. 20). chrome-extension://efaidnbmnnnibpcajpcglclefindmkaj/https://climatepromise.undp.org/sites/default/files/research_report_document/undp-ndcsp-bhutan-gender-analysis-report.pdf

UNFPA. (2025, June). *World Population Dashboard-Bhutan | United Nations Population Fund.* https://www.unfpa.org/data/world-population/BT

United Nations. (2025). *Bhutan graduates from LDC status|Department of Economic and Social Affairs.* https://www.un.org/development/desa/dpad/2023/bhutan-graduates-from-ldc-status/

VNR Maldives. (2017). Voluntary National Review 2017, Maldives | High-Level Political Forum. United Nations. https://hlpf.un.org/countries/maldives/voluntary-national-review-2017

Votruba, N., & Thornicroft, G. (2016). Sustainable development goals and mental health: Learnings from the contribution of the Funda mental SDG global initiative. *Global Mental Health, 3*, e26. https://doi.org/10.1017/gmh.2016.20

WHO. (2021). *World Health Organization South-East Asia | Health Organization.* https://www.who.int/southeastasia

WHO. (2025a, April). *Afghanistan.* Datadot. https://data.who.int/countries/004

WHO. (2025b, June). *Maldives.* Datadot. https://data.who.int/countries/462

World Bank. (2025, June 10). *Afghanistan.* World Bank Gender Data Portal. https://genderdata.worldbank.org/en/economies/afghanistan

Yangka, D., Newman, P., Rauland, V., & Devereux, P. (2018). Sustainability in an emerging nation: The Bhutan case study. *Sustainability*, 10(5). doi:https://doi.org/10.3390/su10051622.

Yusufzai, M. A., & Ravi Kumar, G. (2022). Gender inequalities in access to the right to education: The consequences of the Talibans gender-based educational policy on women in Afghanistan. *The Journal of Human Rights, 17*(Number 2), 107–130. https://doi.org/10.22096/hr.2024.2022754.1653

Zahidi, F., Khalid, M., Surkan, P. J., & Azadbakht, L. (2021). Associations between food insecurity and common mental health problems among reproductive-aged women in Kabul-Afghanistan. *Frontiers in Nutrition, 8*, 794607. https://doi.org/10.3389/fnut.2021.794607

Chapter 14
Public Health Initiatives to Attain Sustainable Development Goals to Improve Mental Health in South Asia

Apurvakumar Pandya

Abstract Mental health is a growing concern in South Asia, affecting millions and posing a significant barrier to achieving the United Nations Sustainable Development Goals (SDGs). This chapter explores public health initiatives aligned with the SDGs that aim to improve mental health outcomes in South Asia. Drawing on recent national strategies, policy frameworks, community-based interventions, and digital innovations, it highlights regional successes, persistent challenges, and future directions. Emphasis is placed on integrating mental health within primary health care, addressing stigma, enhancing workforce capacity, and strengthening governance. The chapter concludes with strategic recommendations for achieving mental health-related SDGs through a systems-oriented, multi-sectoral approach.

Keywords Mental health · Sustainable Development Goals · South Asia · Public health · Primary health care · Community-based interventions

1 Introduction

Mental health is a critical component of overall well-being and is essential for achieving the Sustainable Development Goals (SDGs) outlined by the United Nations. In South Asia, mental disorders affect an estimated 150 to 200 million people, representing a critical public health burden (World Health Organization [WHO], 2023). Depression, anxiety, substance use, and suicide disproportionately affect this region, compounded by poverty, discrimination, weak infrastructure, and cultural stigma (Patel et al., 2021). Mental health challenges are compounded by poverty, stigma, and limited healthcare resources, achieving these goals requires comprehensive public health initiatives and systemic changes (Patel et al., 2021).

A. Pandya (✉)
Department of Health Policy, Management and Behavioural Science, Indian Institute of Public Health, Gandhinagar, India
e-mail: apandya@iiphg.org

S. K. Kar et al. (eds.), *Sustainable Development Goals and Mental Health in South Asia*, South Asian Perspectives in Mental Health and Psychology ,
https://doi.org/10.1007/978-981-95-2684-0_14

The United Nations 2030 Agenda for SDG recognizes mental health as central to development, specifically through SDG 3: Good Health and Well-being. Other SDGs—including those addressing poverty (SDG 1), education (SDG 4), gender equality (SDG 5), decent work (SDG 8), and reduced inequalities (SDG 10)—also intersect with mental health (United Nations Department of Economic and Social Affairs, 2025).

This chapter critically examines public health initiatives in South Asia that support mental health within the SDG framework. It discusses the mental health landscape, policy responses, community-based interventions, technological innovations, and challenges, while offering recommendations for future action.

2 Global Scenario of Mental Health

Globally, mental disorders are a significant cause of disability, contributing substantially to the burden of years lived with disability (YLD). In 2019, approximately 970 million people worldwide account for approximately 15% of the total disease burden in terms of years lived with disability (YLDs), with the majority of this burden concentrated in low- and middle-income countries—LMICs (GBD 2019 Mental disorders Collaborators, 2022). The global mental health movement has gained momentum since the early 2000s, marked by initiatives such as the WHO's Mental Health Gap Action Programme (mhGAP), the Lancet Commission on Global Mental Health and Sustainable Development, and the World Mental Health Atlas.

3 Mental Health Landscape in South Asia

South Asia comprises eight countries: Afghanistan, Bangladesh, Bhutan, India, the Maldives, Nepal, Pakistan, and Sri Lanka. This region is characterized by diverse cultures, significant socio-economic challenges, and faces a substantial burden of mental health disorders coupled with limited mental health resources (Arafat & Kar, 2024).

South Asia bears a disproportionate burden, with ~200 million people affected by mental illness. Depression, anxiety, and suicide are among the leading contributors to YLDs (WHO, 2017). The prevalence of common mental disorders such as depression and anxiety is estimated at 10%–20% (Vidyasagaran et al., 2023). In India alone, 197.3 million individuals were reported to have mental disorders in 2023 (Murthy, 2017). Similar patterns exist across Bangladesh, Pakistan, Nepal, and Sri Lanka, where comorbidities with chronic diseases and poor mental health literacy intensify the burden (WHO, 2017). Mental illness in South Asia is characterized by high prevalence rates, significant stigma, and limited access to quality care (WHO, 2017). Poverty, social exclusion, and cultural factors contribute to the vulnerability of individuals in the region.

3.1 Mental Health Scenario in LMIC and South Asia

LMICs share a common set of challenges in addressing mental health, including chronic underinvestment in health systems, inadequate workforce capacity, wide treatment gaps, and pervasive stigma. South Asia, as a significant subset of LMICs, comprises countries such as Afghanistan, Bangladesh, Bhutan, Maldives, Nepal, Pakistan, and Sri Lanka—together representing approximately 1.9 billion people, nearly 25% of the global population and 41.9% of the population of LMIC (United Nations, 2022; World Bank, 2023).

Despite similar economic constraints, the South Asian context is shaped by diverse political structures, complex social hierarchies, and varied cultural norms, making direct comparisons across countries inherently complex. For instance, while India operates within central Government systems (federal) that grant substantial autonomy to states (Nation Portal of India, 2025) whereas countries such as Bhutan, Maldives, and Sri Lanka follow centralized governance models where the central government holds the ultimate power (World Bank, 2020). Additionally, religious and cultural values—ranging from Hindu and Buddhist traditions to Islamic and Christian influences—profoundly affect societal attitudes towards mental illness, help-seeking behaviours, and community engagement in mental health interventions. Geographical diversity, from the mountainous terrains of Nepal and Bhutan to the dispersed islands of the Maldives, further influences health system organization and access to services.

Despite these structural and contextual differences, South Asian countries face several common mental health challenges, including rapid demographic transitions (Trivedi et al., 2008), rising mental health issues among youth (Rasool et al., 2025; Vidyasagaran et al., 2023), the psychosocial impacts of climate change (Arneaud, 2025; Cianconi et al., 2020), and political instability (Maramis et al., 2011). These shared pressures underscore the urgency and strategic relevance of collective regional action. Collaboration among South Asian nations could facilitate shared learning, pooled resources, cross-border research initiatives, harmonized policy frameworks, and coordinated investments in mental health infrastructure. Platforms such as the South Asian Association for Regional Cooperation (SAARC) or other South–South cooperation networks offer an opportunity to foster a regionally coherent, culturally sensitive, and scalable mental health agenda. By leveraging collective strengths while acknowledging national specificities, South Asia can advance an inclusive and sustainable approach to mental health systems strengthening.

The mental health landscape in South Asia mirrors many of the systemic deficiencies observed across LMICs but is also characterized by distinct contextual features that warrant special attention. Table 1 compares mental health scenario in LMIC and South Asia. Like many LMICs, South Asian countries carry a disproportionate burden of mental disorders, with depression, anxiety, substance use, and suicide contributing significantly to YLDs. However, in South Asia, the treatment gap (which represents the proportion of individuals who need but do not receive mental health care) is particularly severe, often exceeding 85% in several countries (Rahman et al., 2021). This gap is particularly pronounced in rural areas, where access to mental health services is severely limited. This situation is exacerbated by a critical shortage of trained mental health professionals. For example, India has fewer than one psychiatrist per 100,000 population, with even lower ratios reported in Nepal and Bangladesh (WHO, 2021). Another major challenge is the fragmentation of mental health services and the lack of integration into primary healthcare systems, compounded by weak governance structures (Kakuma et al., 2011; WHO, 2022). Widespread stigma and discrimination against individuals with mental health conditions further limit access to care and contribute to social exclusion (Patel et al., 2018). Although community-based care models and task-shifting strategies—such as using lay health workers to provide mental health support—have gained traction across many LMICs, their implementation in South Asia remains inconsistent and largely confined to pilot initiatives and often limited in scale (Semrau et al., 2015; WHO, 2021).

On a positive note, several South Asian countries have enacted progressive mental health legislation in recent years. India's Mental Healthcare Act (2017) and Bangladesh's *Mental Health Act* (2018) represent significant policy advances, emphasizing rights-based care and decriminalizing suicide (Duffy & Kelly, 2019a, 2019b; Barua, 2024). Nevertheless, effective implementation remains a major challenge, hindered by weak governance structures, limited financial allocations—often less than 1% of national health budgets—and a lack of decentralization in mental health service delivery (WHO, 2021; Patel et al., 2018). Additionally, the region's exposure to political conflict, forced displacement, and climate-induced disasters—as observed in Afghanistan, conflict-affected regions of India and Pakistan, and among Rohingya refugees in Bangladesh—intensifies the burden on already fragile mental health systems (Silove et al., 2017; UNHCR, 2023; Climate and Security Advisory Group, 2025). These realities underscore the need for context-sensitive, collaborative approaches to mental health reform that are responsive to both regional commonalities and national differences.

4 SDGs as a Framework for Mental Health

The SDGs provide a vital framework for advancing mental health by embedding it within a broader agenda of human development, equity, and well-being (United Nations Department of Economic and Social Affairs, 2025). Box 1 summarizes SDG relevant to mental health. Central to this is SDG 3, which emphasizes ensuring healthy lives and promoting well-being for all at all ages. Within this goal, target 3.4 seeks to reduce premature mortality from non-communicable diseases (NCDs), including mental disorders, while target 3.5 focuses on the prevention and treatment of substance use disorders, and target 3.8 advocates for universal health coverage (UHC), which includes access to quality mental health services. Several other SDGs directly or indirectly address mental health. SDG 1 (No Poverty) acknowledges that economic hardship is a major determinant of poor mental health. SDG 4 (Quality Education) emphasizes inclusive and equitable education, which is instrumental in

Table 1 Mental health scenario in LMIC and South Asia

Dimension	LMICs (general)	South Asia (specific)
Burden of mental disorders	Mental and substance use disorders account for 10–15% of the global disease burden, particularly measured in YLDs (Years Lived with Disability) (WHO, 2021)	South Asia bears a disproportionate burden with ~200 million people affected by mental illness. Depression, anxiety, and suicide are among the leading contributors to YLDs (Rahman et al., 2021; Vidyasagaran et al., 2023)
Treatment gap	Treatment gap ranges from 75% to 85% across LMICs due to lack of resources, stigma, and inadequate infrastructure (Patel et al., 2021)	In South Asia, the treatment gap often exceeds 85%, especially in rural and conflict-prone areas (Rahman et al., 2021). Limited decentralization worsens accessibility
Mental health workforce	Most LMICs have fewer than 2 psychiatrists per 100,000 people Task-shifting models are increasingly promoted (Rathod et al., 2017)	South Asia has some of the lowest psychiatrist-to-population ratios. India has 0.75 psychiatrists per 100,000, Pakistan 0.49, and Nepal 0.22 (WHO, 2020). Dependency on informal or traditional healers is high (Dein, 2020; Thara & Padmavati, 2013)
Policy and legislation	Nearly half of LMICs have no standalone mental health law or national policy (Brooks et al., 2023). Where policies exist, implementation is weak (Rathod et al., 2017)	Several South Asian countries have updated their mental health legislation in the past decade (e.g., Bangladesh's Mental Health Act, 2018; India's Mental Healthcare Act, 2017). However, rights-based implementation remains patchy (Trivedi & Tripathi, 2014)
Conflict and displacement	Many LMICs are conflict-affected, creating added psychological trauma and service delivery challenges (Papola et al., 2020)	South Asia has several fragile contexts (Afghanistan, Kashmir, Rohingya crisis) where mental health needs of displaced populations remain unmet (David et al., 2017)

fostering resilience, promoting emotional well-being, and preventing mental health problems from an early age. SDG 5 (Gender Equality) recognizes that gender-based discrimination, violence, and marginalization—especially against women, girls, transgender, and gender-diverse persons—are critical risk factors for mental health disorders. SDG 8 (Decent Work and Economic Growth) links mental health with employment and economic participation, highlighting that unemployment, precarious work, and exclusion can have detrimental psychological effects. Finally, SDG 10 (Reduced Inequality) underscores the importance of addressing social and economic disparities that perpetuate mental health inequities. Taken together, the SDGs encourage a holistic, inter-sectoral approach that places mental health not only as a health issue but as a prerequisite for inclusive, sustainable development.

Box 1. SDGs and Relevance to Mental Health

- SDG 1: No Poverty. Economic hardship significantly impacts mental health.
- SDG 3: Health & well-being emphasizes ensuring healthy lives and promoting well-being for all at all ages.
- SDG 4: Quality Education emphasizes inclusive and equitable quality education and promote lifelong learning opportunities for all. Quality education plays a crucial role in promoting mental well-being, preventing mental health problems, and fostering resilience.
- SDG 5: Gender Equality. This goal focuses on achieving gender equality and empower all women, girls, transgender persons, and gender-diverse persons. Gender-based discrimination influences mental health outcomes. Gender inequality and violence against women, girls, transgender persons and gender-diverse persons are significant risk factors for mental health problems.
- SDG 8: Decent Work. This goal promotes sustained, inclusive and sustainable economic growth, full and productive employment and decent work for all. Unemployment, poverty, and social exclusion can have a detrimental impact on mental health.
- SDG 10: Reduced Inequality. Social inequities contribute to mental health disparities. This goal advocates reducing inequality within and among countries. Addressing social and economic inequalities is essential for improving mental health outcomes.

Mental health initiatives in South Asia must recognize the interconnected nature of the SDGs. Mental health outcomes are closely linked to SDGs.

5 Public Mental Health Initiatives in South Asia

Let us review public mental health initiatives right from national policies and legislations, mental health interventions, including digital mental health interventions, and efforts to integrate mental health into primary care.

5.1 National Policies and Legislative Frameworks

South Asian countries have demonstrated increasing commitment to addressing mental health through policy and legal reforms, guided by the SDGs, particularly SDG 3 on good health and well-being. These frameworks aim to improve mental health access, integrate services into primary health care, and protect the rights of individuals with mental illness. Box 2 summarizes national policies and legislative framework.

In Afghanistan, the *National Mental Health Strategy 2019–2023* prioritizes the integration of mental health into primary health care, capacity building for health professionals, and community-based services. Despite challenges posed by the ongoing conflict, the strategy aims to ensure equitable access and strengthen resilience among conflict-affected populations (WHO EMRO, 2021).

In Bangladesh, the *Mental Health Strategy 2018–2022* and the *Mental Health Act 2018* represent significant advancements in mental health governance. These emphasize rights-based care, reduce stigma, and strengthen service delivery through integration into primary care. The *National Institute of Mental Health (NIMH)* supports policy implementation through research, training, and programme support (Arafat et al., 2024).

Bhutan has integrated mental health services under its *Universal Health Coverage (UHC)* framework. The *Royal Government of Bhutan's Health Vision 2023* promotes mental well-being as an integral part of overall health and emphasizes community-based psychosocial support services, early detection, and human resource development (Royal Government of Bhutan, 2022).

In India, the *National Mental Health Programme (NMHP)*, introduced in 1982, established a robust policy framework for mental health service delivery. This framework emphasizes early intervention, rehabilitation, and decentralized, community-based care (National Mental Health Programme, 2024). As part of the NMHP, the *District Mental Health Programme* (DMHP) has been implemented across 767 districts in India (Ministry of Health & Family Welfare, 2024). Additionally, the *National Tele-Mental Health Programme* further enhances service accessibility (Ministry of Health & Family Welfare, 2024). Complementing these initiatives, the Mental Healthcare Act of 2017 guarantees rights-based care, decriminalizes suicide, and mandates the protection and promotion of the rights of individuals with mental illness (Mental Healthcare Act, 2017).

Maldives has initiated reforms through its *National Mental Health Policy 2021*, which aims to build an inclusive and stigma-free mental health system underpinned by universal health coverage. It focuses on integrating mental health into primary care, raising awareness, and scaling up workforce training in mental health (Ministry of Health, Republic of Maldives, 2021).

In Nepal, the *Mental Health Policy 2014* and *Mental Health Act 2018* lay the foundation for equitable mental health care by integrating services within primary health systems and promoting community-based rehabilitation. These frameworks emphasize rights protection, service decentralization, and the reduction of stigma (Singh & Khadka, 2022).

Pakistan's *National Mental Health Policy 2014* offers a comprehensive approach focusing on integration within primary health care, multi-sectoral coordination, and community-based services. The *National Institute of Mental Health* facilitates implementation through capacity building, mental health promotion, and research (WHO EMRO, 2022).

In Sri Lanka, the *National Mental Health Programme* supports early intervention, rehabilitation, and deinstitutionalized, community-based services. The *Mental*

Health Act No. 31 of 1996 serves as the legal foundation for the care and protection of persons with mental illness, while also promoting a rights-based and holistic approach to mental health care (WHO, 2017).

Box 2. National Policies and Legislative Frameworks

- **Afghanistan** developed its *National Mental Health Strategy* (2019–2023) focusing on integrating mental health into primary health care and building capacity through training programmes, though implementation is challenged by conflict and instability (WHO EMRO, 2021).
- **Bangladesh** introduced a comprehensive *Mental Health Strategy* (2018–2022) alongside the *Mental Health Act* (2018), both of which focus on improving access, reducing stigma, and ensuring patient rights (Arafat et al., 2020).
- **Bhutan** integrates mental health services within its Universal Health Coverage framework, supported by the *Royal Government of Bhutan's Health Vision 2023* which emphasizes psychosocial well-being and inclusive care (Royal Government of Bhutan, 2022).
- **India** has implemented the *National Mental Health Programme* (NMHP) and enacted the *Mental Healthcare Act* (2017), which emphasizes rights-based care, mandates access to services, promotes community-based treatment, and decriminalizes suicide (Duffy & Kelly, 2019a, 2019b).
- **Maldives** launched its *National Mental Health Policy* in 2021, aiming to build an integrated, rights-based, and stigma-free mental health system under the umbrella of universal health coverage (Ministry of Health, Republic of Maldives, 2025).
- **Nepal's** *Mental Health Policy* (2014) and *Mental Health Act* (2018) aim to provide equitable, accessible, and integrated mental health care, with a focus on community services and decentralization (Ghimire et al., 2024).
- **Pakistan** adopted a *National Mental Health Policy* in 2014 and has developed *District Mental Health Programmes* aimed at integrating mental health services into primary care (WHO EMRO, 2022).
- **Sri Lanka** has a longstanding *National Mental Health Programme* and the *Mental Health Act* (1996), promoting deinstitutionalization, human rights, and community-based services (WHO, 2024).

5.2 *Public Mental Health Initiatives*

In addition to services provided through secondary and tertiary healthcare facilities, community-based interventions have proven to be effective in addressing mental health challenges across South Asia. Box 3 summarizes selected public mental health interventions.

Afghanistan has made limited but notable progress in integrating community-based mental health into its fragile healthcare infrastructure. Initiatives led by international agencies and non-governmental organizations have introduced psychosocial support programmes, particularly for conflict-affected populations. For example, the

Basic Package of Health Services (BPHS) includes mental health components, with community health workers (CHWs) trained to provide psychosocial support. Despite political instability, these efforts have laid the groundwork for community-level mental health engagement (World Health Organization, 2020).

In Bangladesh, digital technologies have emerged as powerful tools to expand mental healthcare access, especially in underserved rural areas. The mHealth Mental Health Program, launched in 2020, has provided teleconsultation services and disseminated mental health education via mobile phones, reaching over 100,000 individuals (Wani et al., 2024). Additionally, task-shifting strategies involving community health workers have facilitated early identification and referral of individuals with mental health concerns, although systemic challenges such as workforce shortages and stigma remain prevalent (Hoeft et al., 2018; Lange, 2021; Raviola et al., 2019).

Bhutan integrates mental health services within its broader Gross National Happiness (GNH) framework. Community-based approaches emphasize spiritual and psychosocial well-being, with school-based mental health awareness programmes and community outreach campaigns. The country has also established Suicide Prevention Action Plans and trained lay counsellors at the district level. However, there is still a lack of trained mental health professionals to meet the growing need (Chhetri et al., 2023).

Box 3. Community-Based and Digital Mental Health Interventions
Community-Based Interventions

- **VISHRAM (India)**: Reduced depression treatment gap by 22% through training of lay health workers and delivery of mental health first aid in rural communities (Shidhaye et al., 2017; Shidhaye, 2020).
- **Atmiyata (India)**: Community volunteers promote mental well-being, early identification, and referral, significantly reducing the burden of common mental disorders (Jaog et al., 2020).
- **Community Mental Health Programme (Nepal)**: Trained over 2000 Female Community Health Volunteers (FCHVs) to improve mental health awareness and referrals in rural areas (Jordans et al., 2016; Luitel et al., 2015).
- **Lady Health Worker Programme (Pakistan)**: Incorporates mental health screening and referrals through community health workers, especially for women and children (Hussain et al., 2018).
- **Basic Package of Health Services (Afghanistan)**: Community health workers provide psychosocial support under the national package of essential health services (WHO, 2020).
- **Suicide Prevention Outreach (Bhutan, Sri Lanka, Nepal)**: Community-based suicide prevention programmes involving schools, local leaders, and helpline services.

Digital Innovations

- **Tele-MANAS (India)**: A national digital tele-mental health service network operating in 23 states; led to a 45% increase in mental health service utilization (Ministry of Health & Family Welfare, 2023).
- **mHealth Mental Health Programme (Bangladesh)**: Mobile-based platform delivering teleconsultations and mental health education to over 100,000 individuals, especially in remote areas (Koly et al., 2022).
- **Digital mental health interventions (Pakistan)**: A home-based digital counselling …mobile application providing psychosocial support and crisis counselling for women facing domestic violence and trauma (Rabbani et al., 2024). Integration of digital mental health intervention at community level in Pakistan (Zeeb et al., 2024).
- **Mental Health Helplines (India, Nepal, Sri Lanka)**: National and local helplines such as *KIRAN and Tele-Manas* in India and community crisis lines in Nepal and Sri Lanka offer 24/7 confidential support to individuals in distress.

India has implemented several innovative and scalable community-based mental health interventions. The VISHRAM (Vidarbha Stress and Health Program) significantly reduced the treatment gap for depression by 22% through training community health workers and providing mental health first aid (Shidhaye et al., 2017; Shidhaye, 2020). Similarly, the *Atmiyata* programme exemplifies how communities can contribute to mental health promotion, early identification, and timely referrals, reducing the burden of common mental disorders (Pathare & Kapoor, 2020). Additionally, the *Tele-MANAS* initiative, a nationwide digital mental health network operating across 23 states, has led to a 45% increase in mental health service utilization among underserved populations (Ministry of Health & Family Welfare, 2023). These programmes underscore the effectiveness of combining community engagement with technology to bridge mental health service gaps.

In the **Maldives**, community-based mental health is in its early stages of development. The National Mental Health Policy promotes community participation and school-based programmes, and the government has partnered with the WHO to train healthcare providers in basic mental health care. However, geographical dispersion across islands presents unique challenges for service delivery and continuity of care (WHO, 2021).

Nepal has demonstrated strong community involvement in mental health through its Community Mental Health Program. Over 2000 Female Community Health Volunteers have been trained to enhance mental health awareness, facilitate referrals, and provide basic support in rural and hard-to-reach areas (Jordans et al., 2016). Crisis helplines and suicide prevention services have also been established to offer immediate psychosocial assistance, reflecting Nepal's commitment to integrating mental health into primary care systems (Luitel et al., 2015).

Pakistan has adopted a decentralized approach to mental health, with significant community-based programmes such as integrating mental health into the Lady Health Worker programme. These workers, serving at the grassroots level, play a vital role in identifying and referring individuals with psychological distress. Home-based digital counselling (mPareshan) by frontline community workers for anxiety and depression in rural Pakistan have been launched to provide mental health support for the community (Rabbani et al., 2024). A "WellPak" a digital mental health intervention at the community level, have been initiated (Zeeb et al., 2024). However, political instability and insufficient funding remain major barriers to scaling up these interventions (Khan et al., 2022).

Sri Lanka has a well-established network of community mental health services. Through its Mental Health Policy and National Mental Health Action Plan, the country has deployed community mental health nurses, outreach clinics, and mental health promotion programmes at the grassroots level. Post-tsunami mental health initiatives laid the foundation for current community-based services. The government also runs suicide prevention initiatives and telephone helplines that offer confidential support to individuals in distress (Perera et al., 2020).

Suicide prevention remains a critical public health priority across South Asia (Arafat, 2024a). Box 4 summarizes suicide prevention programmes in South Asia.

Box 4. Suicide Prevention Programmes

- **Afghanistan**: Limited formal suicide prevention initiatives. Mental health components integrated into the Basic Package of Health Services, including psychosocial support for trauma.
- **Bangladesh**: Suicide prevention included within the national mental health strategy; NGOs operate helplines and community awareness campaigns targeting youth and rural populations.
- **Bhutan**: National Suicide Prevention Action Plan implemented. Emphasis on life skills education, community awareness, and integration with GNH framework.
- **India**: Decriminalized suicide under the *Mental Healthcare Act, 2017*, promoting a compassionate care approach. National 24/7 helpline (*KIRAN*) and Tele-Manas programme provides immediate psychosocial support. State-level helplines and gatekeeper training programmes also active.
- **Maldives**: Suicide is criminalized; however, efforts are underway to improve mental health awareness and reduce stigma. Limited community-based suicide prevention services.
- **Nepal**: Community-based helplines and suicide prevention programmes in partnership with NGOs and local governments. Focus on crisis response, school-based education, and sensitization.
- **Pakistan**: Suicide remains criminalized. Some NGOs provide crisis counselling and public awareness campaigns. Efforts to decriminalize and integrate prevention into health policy are ongoing.
- **Sri Lanka**: Formerly had one of the highest suicide rates; major reductions achieved through pesticide regulation and community-based programmes. National helplines and mental health outreach services are operational.

Several countries have made noteworthy advances in this domain. India's decriminalization of suicide through the *Mental Healthcare Act, 2017* marks a progressive shift toward providing compassionate care to individuals in crisis (Suicide in India, n.d.). National helplines such as *KIRAN* have been established to offer 24/7 support. In Nepal, suicide prevention services, including crisis helplines and community sensitization programmes, have enhanced immediate psychosocial response mechanisms (Suicide in Nepal, 2024). These initiatives reflect a growing recognition of the importance of timely, accessible, and culturally appropriate mental health support for suicide prevention across the region.

5.3 Integration with Primary Health Care

Integrating mental health services into primary healthcare systems is essential for enhancing accessibility, reducing treatment gaps, promoting early intervention and build scalable systems for mental healthcare delivery. Box 5 presents Country wise initiatives for integration with Primary Health care. The World Health Organization's *Mental Health Gap Action Programme* (mhGAP) offers evidence-based guidelines for scaling up care for mental, neurological, and substance use disorders, particularly in low-resource settings.

These guidelines have been instrumental in supporting South Asian countries to train primary healthcare workers in the identification, management, and referral of individuals with common mental health conditions (Votruba & Thornicroft, 2016).

In Afghanistan, mental health is included in the country's Basic Package of Health Services (BPHS). Services are primarily delivered through NGO-supported community-based interventions. Health workers are trained to provide basic psychosocial support. However, ongoing conflict, political instability, and poor infrastructure significantly limit consistent service provision (UNHCR, 2022).

Box 5. Initiatives for Integrating Mental Health into Primary Health

- **Afghanistan**: Mental health is included in the country's Basic Package of Health Services. Services are primarily delivered through NGO-supported community-based interventions. Health workers are trained to provide basic psychosocial support.
- **Bangladesh**: Integrated mental health into primary care as part of its National Mental Health Strategy (2018–2022), piloted mhGAP trainings in select districts, supported by the National Institute of Mental Health.
- **Bhutan**: Mental health within its Universal Health Coverage (UHC) and Basic Health Package, Holistic and culturally resonant approach and has national-level policy support.
- **India**: Mental health services are available at Primary Health Centres and Health and Wellness Centres. District Mental Health Programme under the National Mental Health Programme implemented across 767 districts of India.
- **Maldives**: Mental health is integrated into Family and Community Health Centres at the island level. Lack of formal mental health legislation, Fragmented services, logistical and shortage of trained human resource in remote areas.

- **Nepal**: Mainstreamed mental health into PHC through mhGAP-based training and the use of Female Community Health Volunteers. Community-based mental health programmes are co-implemented by government and Non-Government Organizations.
- **Pakistan**: National-level rollout of District Mental Health Programme implemented; community workers are involved in the programme.
- **Sri Lanka**: Integrated mental health at PHC-level service delivery. Rural mental health outreach services are also implemented.

Bangladesh has integrated mental health into primary care as part of its National Mental Health Strategy (2018–2022). Pilot mhGAP trainings have been conducted in select districts, supported by the National Institute of Mental Health (NIMH). Primary care doctors and nurses have been sensitized to mental health issues, but services remain limited in coverage and monitoring (Hasan et al., 2021). Lack of scale, weak data systems, evaluation & monitoring, and limited service uptake in rural areas are implementation challenges.

Bhutan includes mental health within its Universal Health Coverage (UHC) and Basic Health Package, guided by the principles of Gross National Happiness. Primary care providers are trained to manage basic mental health issues, with community awareness campaigns integrated into local governance mechanisms (Royal Government of Bhutan, 2022). However, shortage of trained professionals and lack of a structured evaluation framework and monitoring are challenging the implementation of mental healthcare services.

In India, mental health services have been integrated into the public health system at the Primary Health Centre. It is further integrated at Health and Wellness Centres under Ayushman Bharat's Comprehensive Primary Health Care. Additionally, the *District Mental Health Programme*, which operates under the National Mental Health Programmes, functions as a critical mechanism for community-level implementation of mental health services in every district. However, implementation variability across states, workforce shortages, and structured evaluation frameworks and monitoring tools are challenges for effective integration of mental health into primary public healthcare services.

In the Maldives, mental health is integrated into Family and Community Health Centres at the island level. Some health workers have received mhGAP training, and the National Strategic Health Plan outlines priorities for mental well-being. However, geographic dispersion of atolls, workforce shortage, and lack of formal mental health legislation limit uniform access.

Nepal has mainstreamed mental health into PHC through mhGAP-based training and the use of Female Community Health Volunteers (Joardans et al., 2016). Services are coordinated through primary health posts and district hospitals. Community-based mental health programmes are co-implemented by government and NGOs (Luitel et al., 2021). However, inconsistent availability of psychotropic drugs and lack of structured evaluation framework and monitoring are implementation challenges.

Pakistan's District Mental Health Programme integrates mental health services into PHC settings in over 60 districts. The approach includes training of family physicians and Lady Health Workers (LHWs) using mhGAP modules. The initiative has improved detection rates but faces implementation gaps due to weak governance, limited inter-sectoral coordination and lack of a structured evaluation framework and monitoring (Khan et al., 2022).

In Sri Lanka, the *National Mental Health Policy* emphasizes the integration of mental health into primary health care as a strategic priority. This integration has reportedly improved access to mental health services in rural and remote areas through primary-level facilities (Ministry of Health, Sri Lanka, 2023). However, lacks structured evaluation frameworks and monitoring tools.

South Asian countries have initiated the integration of mental health services into primary care systems. However, these efforts face several challenges, including workforce shortages, limited capacity building initiatives for the existing health workforce, and a lack of systematic evidence on the effectiveness and outcomes of such integration. This highlights the need for robust monitoring and evaluation mechanisms to assess and strengthen these initiatives.

5.4 Status of Insurance for Mental Health in South Asia

The integration of mental health into national health insurance frameworks in South Asia remains limited but is gradually progressing. India stands out as the first country in the region to mandate mental health coverage under insurance through the Mental Healthcare Act, 2017, which legally obliges insurers to treat mental health on par with physical illnesses. Consequently, several public and private insurance schemes—including Ayushman Bharat Pradhan Mantri Jan Arogya Yojana (PM-JAY)—now offer coverage for inpatient psychiatric care, though outpatient services and psychotherapy are still inconsistently covered. Sri Lanka and Bhutan offer free access to essential mental health services through public health financing as part of their universal health coverage commitments, but lack dedicated mental health insurance schemes. In Nepal, while mental health is recognized in national policy, insurance coverage remains limited, and most psychiatric services are paid out-of-pocket. Pakistan has made minimal progress in this domain. Bangladesh does not have insurance for mental health (Arafat, 2024b); mental health is generally excluded from formal insurance products, and public mental health services are underfunded. The Maldives includes mental health consultations in its national health insurance scheme (Aasandha), although access is constrained by a lack of trained professionals. Afghanistan, given ongoing conflict and institutional fragility, lacks formal insurance mechanisms for mental health altogether. Across the region, key challenges to insurance coverage include low prioritization of mental health, lack of service packages for outpatient care, and the absence of standardized pricing and reimbursement models. Nonetheless, expanding insurance coverage—particularly for outpatient and community-based mental health services—remains a critical pathway to achieving financial protection and equitable access in South Asia.

6 SWOT Analysis of the Mental Health Landscape in South Asia

Mental health has historically remained under-prioritized in the region. South Asia is facing a mental health crisis, with high prevalence of depression, anxiety, suicide, substance abuse, and post-traumatic stress, especially among youth, women, migrants, and disaster-affected communities (Patel et al., 2021). Prioritizing mental health is not just a health imperative but a development necessity, essential for advancing Sustainable Development Goals (SDGs). Collective action across South Asian countries—through regional research, data sharing, and cross-border mental health strategies—is crucial to overcoming shared systemic challenges. The SWOT (Strengths, Weaknesses, Opportunities, Threats) analysis can guide evidence-informed policy and practice. Box 6 summarized SWOT analysis of the mental health landscape in South Asia.

Box 6. SWOT Analysis of Mental Healthcare in South Asia

Strengths

- Progressive national legislation (e.g., India, Nepal, Bangladesh).
- Community-based models (e.g., VISHRAM, ATMIYATA).
- Digital innovations (e.g., Tele-MANAS, mHealth in Bangladesh) Weaknesses.
- Low mental health funding (1% of total health budgets).
- Shortage of professionals (1 psychiatrist per 100,000 people).
- Training of existing workforce.
- Stigma, low literacy, and public misconceptions about mental illness.
- Fragmented monitoring and evaluation systems.
- Rural and marginalized populations left out of tech-driven innovations.

Opportunities

- Digital platform expansion and telepsychiatry.
- Generating evidence on public mental health initiatives.
- Regional mental health research & capacity building collaboration (e.g., SAARC) Integration with UHC and primary care reforms.
- Focus on youth and gender-transformative mental health promotion models.

Threats

- Insurance coverage of mental health OPD & IPD services.
- Economic downturns, reducing public health investments.

- Climate change, displacement, and environmental stressors.
- Political instability and low prioritization of mental health.

South Asia's mental health landscape reflects a complex interplay of progress, challenges, opportunities, and risks. On the positive side, several countries have enacted progressive national legislation—such as India's *Mental Healthcare Act* (2017) and Nepal's *Mental Health Act* (2018)—that emphasize rights-based care.

Community-based models like VISHRAM and ATMIYATA in India and digital innovations such as Tele-MANAS and Bangladesh's mHealth platform have demonstrated scalable potential. However, systemic weaknesses persist, including critically low funding, workforce shortage, persistent stigma, and weak literacy around mental health. Moreover, monitoring and evaluation mechanisms remain fragmented, and rural and marginalized populations often miss out on tech-enabled services. At the same time, expanding digital platforms, integrating prevention & promotion in setting-based mental health programme, the promotion of gender- and youth-focused interventions, regional research and capacity building collaboration (e.g., SAARC initiatives), integration of mental health into UHC present strong opportunities for transformation. Importantly, the inclusion of mental health care under health insurance schemes—covering outpatient and inpatient services—offers financial protection and could improve service utilization. Yet, these gains are threatened by economic downturns, climate-induced displacement, and political instability, all of which risk deprioritizing mental health within public health agendas. Addressing these dynamics requires sustained investment, inclusive service design, robust policy commitment, and financial mechanisms that ensure equitable access to mental health care.

6.1 Strategic Recommendations

To address these challenges and effectively achieve mental health-related SDGs, collective actions and country-specific actions are crucial. Collective actions require investment in mental health prevention, human resources, infrastructure and medication. South Asia has rich traditional medicine practices, and generating evidence on traditional medicine and integrating effective traditional medicine practices into public health system would be welcoming step. Mental well-being need to be integrated into school & college/university as well as workplace induction programmes.

There is a need to strengthen data management, use of data for decision-making and novel research on mental health to inform evidence-based interventions. Existing mental health programme should be coupled with rights-based community-led approaches, including peer support and self-help groups. Adopting collaborative care models that integrate mental health into primary care can provide holistic treatment, especially for individuals with comorbid conditions. Engaging local communities in mental health initiatives can enhance support networks and make interventions more culturally relevant and effective. Such approaches can play a crucial role in improving access to care and promoting recovery. Mental health should be integrated into all sectors, including education, social welfare, and justice. Collaboration between government agencies, research and academic institutions, and civil society organizations is essential for the effective implementation of mental health programmes.

Investing in research will lead to the development of innovative solutions tailored to the unique challenges of mental health in South Asia. Research in mental health should focus on generating evidence on cost-effectiveness of public mental health interventions, integration of technology in existing programme and emerging mental health problems such as selfitis, social media addiction, and game disorders. Capacity building of the workforce on mental health promotion and medical interventions is another area of work. South Asian countries should work collaboratively to share and learn from each other. Fostering South-South collaboration for mental health improvement. Learning & sharing network such as United for Mental Health (https://unitedgmh.org/); mental health innovation network Asia (https://www.mhinnovation.net/hubs/mhin-asia) should be enhanced further to ensure implementation.

7 Conclusion

The journey toward achieving mental health-related SDGs in South Asia requires sustained commitment, innovative approaches, and collaborative efforts. While significant progress has been made through various public health initiatives, continued attention to resource allocation, capacity building, and system strengthening is essential. The success of current initiatives provides hope and direction for future efforts to improve mental health outcomes in the region.

References

Arafat, S. M. Y. (2024a). Suicidal behaviour and suicide prevention in Bangladesh. In S. M. Y. Arafat (Eds.), *Mental health in Bangladesh.* Springer. https://doi.org/10.1007/978-981-97-0610-5_11

Arafat, S. M. Y. (2024b). Mental health services in Bangladesh. In S. M. Y. Arafat (Eds.), *Mental health in Bangladesh.* Springer. https://doi.org/10.1007/978-981-97-0610-5_3

Arafat, S. M. Y., & Kar, S. K. (2024). Epidemiology of psychiatric disorders and overview of access to mental health care in south Asia. In S. M. Y. Arafat & S. K. Kar (Eds.), *Access to mental health care in south Asia.* Springer. https://doi.org/10.1007/978-981-99-9153-2_1

Arafat, S. M. Y., Kar, S. K., & Kabir, R. (2020). Possible controlling measures of panic buying during COVID-19. *International Journal of Mental Health and Addiction, 19*, 2289–2291. https://doi.org/10.1007/s11469-020-00320-1

Arafat, S. Y., Giasuddin, N. A., & Mazumder, A. H. (2024). Access to mental health care in Bangladesh—Current status, potential challenges, and ways out. In *Access to mental health care in south Asia: Current status, potential challenges, and ways out* (pp. 29–55). Springer Nature. https://doi.org/10.1007/978-981-99-9153-2_3

Arneaud, G. J. (2025). The psychosocial impact of climate change: A recent overview. In *Climate change: Intervention strategies and sustainable development in the global south* (pp. 29–56). https://doi.org/10.1007/978-3-031-83037-2_3

Barua, R. (2024). Bangladesh's mental health act 2018: A critical analysis. *Medical Law Review, 32*(1), 101–110. https://doi.org/10.1093/medlaw/fwad041

Brooks, C., Mirzoev, T., Chowdhury, D., Deuri, S. P., & Madill, A. (2023). Using evidence in mental health policy agenda-setting in low- and middle-income countries: A conceptual meta-framework from a scoping umbrella review. *Health Policy and Planning, 38*(7), 876–893. https://doi.org/10.1093/heapol/czad038

Chhetri, B., Dem, U., Tshering, K., & Skodlar, B. (2023, May). Prevalence of major depressive disorder in adult patients with alcohol use disorder admitted in the psychiatric ward at the Jigme Dorji Wangchuck National Referral Hospital, Thimphu, Bhutan. *Population Medicine, 5*, 1–8.

Cianconi, P., Betrò, S., & Janiri, L. (2020). The impact of climate change on mental health: A systematic descriptive review. *Frontiers in Psychiatry, 11*, Article 490206. https://doi.org/10.3389/fpsyt.2020.00074

Climate and Security Advisory Group. (2025). *Climate security in south Asia: Proceedings of a workshop.* Center for Climate and Security. https://climateandsecurity.org/wp-content/uploads/2025/01/26926.pdf

David, S., Gazi, R., Mirzazada, M. S., Siriwardhana, C., Soofi, S., & Roy, N. (2017). Conflict in South Asia and its impact on health. *British Medical Journal,357*. https://doi.org/10.1136/bmj.j1537

Dein, S. (2020). Traditional healers and global mental health. In S. O. Okpaku (Ed.), *Innovations in global mental health.* Springer. https://doi.org/10.1007/978-3-319-70134-9_132-1

Duffy, R. M., & Kelly, B. D. (2019a). India's mental healthcare act, 2017: Content, context, controversy. *International Journal of Law and Psychiatry, 62*, 169–178. https://doi.org/10.1016/j.ijlp.2018.08.002

Duffy, R. M., & Kelly, B. D. (2019b). Global mental health. *The Lancet, 394*(10193), 118–119. https://doi.org/10.1016/S0140-6736(19)30944-4

GBD 2019 Mental Disorders Collaborators. (2022). Global, regional, and national burden of 12 mental disorders in 204 countries and territories, 1990–2019: A systematic analysis for the global burden of disease study 2019. *The Lancet. Psychiatry, 9*(2), 137–150. https://doi.org/10.1016/S2215-0366(21)00395-3

Ghimire, A., Kandel, S., & Subedi, S. (2024). Mental health in Nepal: A comprehensive overview of the situation, interventions, and way forward. *MedS Alliance Journal of Medicine and Medical Sciences, 4*(7), 1–3. https://doi.org/10.3126/mjmms.v4i7.71232

Government of Bangladesh. (2018). *Mental Health Act 2018, Ministry of Health and Family Welfare.* https://www.refworld.org/sites/default/files/2024-07/en_mental_health_act.pdf

Government of India. (2017). *Mental Healthcare Act 2017, Ministry of Law and Justice.* https://lddashboard.legislative.gov.in/actsofparliamentfromtheyear/mental-healthcare-act-2017

Government of India, Ministry of Health & Family Welfare. (2025). *National Mental Health Programme (NMHP).* Retrieved from https://dghs.mohfw.gov.in/national-mental-health-programme.php

Hoeft, T. J., Fortney, J. C., Patel, V., & Unützer, J. (2018). Task-sharing approaches to improve mental health care in rural and other low-resource settings: A systematic review. *The Journal of Rural Health, 34*(1), 48–62. https://doi.org/10.1111/jrh.12229

Joag, K., Kalha, J., Pandit, D., Chatterjee, S., Krishnamoorthy, S., Shields-Zeeman, L., & Pathare, S. (2020). Atmiyata, a community-led intervention to address common mental disorders: Study protocol for a stepped wedge cluster randomized controlled trial in rural Gujarat India. *Trials, 21*(1), 212. https://doi.org/10.1186/s13063-020-4133-6

Jordans, M. J., Luitel, N. P., Pokhrel, P., & Patel, V. (2016). Development and pilot testing of a mental healthcare plan in Nepal. *The British Journal of Psychiatry: The Journal of Mental Science, 208*(Suppl 56), s21–s28. https://doi.org/10.1192/bjp.bp.114.153718

Kakuma, R., Minas, H., van Ginneken, N., Dal Poz, M. R., Desiraju, K., Morris, J. E., Saxena, S., & Scheffler, R. M. (2011). Human resources for mental health care: Current situation and strategies for action. *Lancet, 378*(9803), 1654–1663. https://doi.org/10.1016/S0140-6736(11)61093-3

Khan, A. M. (2022). Maternal mental health and child nutritional status in an urban slum in Bangladesh: A crosssectional study. *PLOS Global Public Health, 2*(10), e0000871. https://doi.org/10.1371/journal.pgph.0000871

Koly, K. N., Saba, J., Muzaffar, R., Modasser, R. B., Colon-Cabrera, D., & Warren, N. (2022). Exploring the potential of delivering mental health care services using digital technologies in Bangladesh: A qualitative analysis. *Internet Interventions, 29*, 100544. https://doi.org/10.1016/j.invent.2022.100544

Lange, K. W. (2021). Task sharing in psychotherapy as a viable global mental health approach in resource-poor countries and also in high-resource settings. *Global Health Journal, 5*(3), 120–127. https://doi.org/10.1016/j.glohj.2021.07.001

Hasan, M. T., Anwar, T., Christopher, E., Hossain, S., Hossain, M. M., Koly, K. N., Saif-Ur-Rahman, K. M., Ahmed, H. U., Arman, N., & Hossain, S. W. (2021). The current state of mental healthcare in Bangladesh: Part 1—An updated country profile. *Bjpsych International, 18*(4), 78–82. https://doi.org/10.1192/bji.2021.41

Hussain, S. S., Khan, M., Gul, R., & Asad, N. (2018). Integration of mental health into primary healthcare: Perceptions of stakeholders in Pakistan. *Eastern Mediterranean Health Journal, 24*(2), 146–153. https://pubmed.ncbi.nlm.nih.gov/29748943/

Luitel, N. P., Jordans, M. J., Adhikari, A., Upadhaya, N., Hanlon, C., Lund, C., & Komproe, I. H. (2015). Mental health care in Nepal: Current situation and challenges for development of a district mental health care plan. *Conflict and Health, 9*, 3. https://doi.org/10.1186/s13031-014-0030-5

Luitel, N. P. (2021). *Evaluation of the integration of mental health services into the primary and community healthcare system in Nepal* (Thesis). Universiteit van Amsterdam. https://pure.uva.nl/ws/files/64292487/Thesis.pdf

Maramis, A., Van Tuan, N., & Minas, H. (2011). Mental health in southeast Asia. *The Lancet, 377*(9767), 700–702. https://doi.org/10.1016/S0140-6736(10)62181-2

Mental Healthcare Act. (2017). *Ministry of Health and Family Welfare, Government of India*. https://www.indiacode.nic.in/bitstream/123456789/2249/1/A2017-10.pdf

Mental Health Policy. (2014). *Ministry of Health and Population*. Government of Nepal. https://publichealthupdate.com/mental-health-policy-nepal/

Mental Health Strategy 2018–2022. (n.d.). *Directorate General of Health Services, Ministry of Health and Family Welfare, Government of the People's Republic of Bangladesh*. https://dghs.portal.gov.bd/sites/default/files/files/dghs.portal.gov.bd/notices/e27171cb_a80b_42d4_99ad_40095adef31b/2022-08-16-08-42-af8622e2c4936593dd45601b84f4920f.pdf

Ministry of Health and Family Welfare. (2023). *Tele-MANAS initiative: Rapid assessment report 2023*. Government of India. https://mohfw.gov.in/sites/default/files/Rapid%20Assessment%20report%20on%20TeleMANAS.pdf

Ministry of Health and Family Welfare. (2024). *Steps taken to strengthen mental healthcare services*. https://www.pib.gov.in/PressReleaseIframePage.aspx?PRID=2043511#:~:text=The%20District%20Mental%20Health%20Programme,prevention%20services%2C%20work%20place%20stress

Ministry of Health, Republic of Maldives. (2025). *National mental health strategic action plan: 2015–2029*. https://health.gov.mv/storage/uploads/7wzEkvoW/bwjwjfot.pdf

Ministry of Health Sri Lanka. (2023). *National mental health policy implementation report*. Government of Sri Lanka. https://www.health.gov.lk/wp-content/uploads/2023/12/P-P-Report-2023-English_compressed.pdf

Ministry of Health, Republic of Maldives. (2021). National Mental Health Policy and Strategic Action Plan 2022–2025. https://health.gov.mv/storage/uploads/7wzEkvoW/bwjwjfot.pdf. MinistryOfHealthMV+2presidency.gov.mv+2

Murthy, R. S. (2017). National mental health survey of India 2015–2016. *Indian Journal of Psychiatry, 59*(1), 21–26. https://doi.org/10.4103/psychiatry.IndianJPsychiatry_102_17

National Mental Health Policy 2014. (2014). Ministry of National Health Services, Regulations and Coordination, Government of Pakistan.

National Mental Health Programme. (2024). *Ministry of Health and Family Welfare, Government of India.* https://www.mohfw.gov.in/?q=Major-Programmes/non-communicable-diseases-injury-trauma/National-Mental-Health-Programme-NMHP

National Portal of India. (2025). *Governance and structure.* https://www.india.gov.in/topics/governance-administration

Patel, V., Saxena, S., & Lund, C. (2021). The Lancet commission on global mental health and sustainable development: A call for action. *The Lancet, 392*(10157), 1553–1598.

Patel, V., Saxena, S., Lund, C., Thornicroft, G., Baingana, F., Bolton, P., & UnÜtzer, J. (2018). The Lancet commission on global mental health and sustainable development. *The Lancet, 392*(10157), 1553–1598. https://doi.org/10.1016/S0140-6736(18)31612-X

Papola, D., Purgato, M., Gastaldon, C., Bovo, C., van Ommeren, M., Barbui, C., & Tol, W. A. (2020). Psychological and social interventions for the prevention of mental disorders in people living in low- and middle-income countries affected by humanitarian crises. *The Cochrane Database of Systematic Reviews, 9*(9), CD012417. https://doi.org/10.1002/14651858.CD012417.pub2

Pathare, S., & Kapoor, A. (2020). Analysis of news media reports of suicides and attempted suicides in India during the COVID-19 lockdown. *International Journal of Mental Health Systems, 14*, 70. https://doi.org/10.1186/s13033-020-00422-2

Rabbani, F., Nafis, J., Akhtar, S., Siddiqui, A., & Merali, Z. (2024). *Home-based digital counselling by frontline community workers for anxiety and depression in rural Pakistan: Piloting mPareshan-a task-shifting primary mental health care intervention* (Preprint). https://doi.org/10.21203/rs.3.rs-5621643/v1

Rahman, A., Naslund, J., & Betancourt, T. (2021). The mental health treatment gap in south Asia: A systematic review. *Journal of Global Health, 11*, 04003.

Rasool, M. F., Ali, A., Nagaria, B., Munawar, S., Khan, M. A., & Saleem, K. (2025). Impact of geopolitics on mental health and geo-economics on south Asian countries post pandemic. *The Critical Review of Social Sciences Studies, 3*(1), 1831–1847.

Rathod, S., Pinninti, N., Irfan, M., Gorczynski, P., Rathod, P., Gega, L., & Naeem, F. (2017). Mental health service provision in low- and middle-income countries. *Health Services Insights, 10*, 1178632917694350. https://doi.org/10.1177/1178632917694350

Raviola, G., Naslund, J. A., Smith, S. L., & Patel, V. (2019). Innovative models in mental health delivery systems: Task sharing care with non-specialist providers to close the mental health treatment gap. *Current Psychiatry Reports, 21*, 1–13. https://doi.org/10.1007/s11920-019-1028-x

Royal Government of Bhutan. (2022). *Mental health services integration report*. Ministry of Health.

Semrau, M., Evans-Lacko, S., Koschorke, M., Ashenafi, L., & Thornicroft, G. (2015). Stigma and discrimination related to mental illness in low- and middle-income countries. *Epidemiology and Psychiatric Sciences, 24*(5), 382–394. https://doi.org/10.1017/S2045796015000359

Shidhaye, R. (2020). Unburden mental health in India: It's time to act now. *The Lancet Psychiatry, 7*(2), 111–112. https://doi.org/10.1016/S2215-0366(19)30524-3

Shidhaye, R., Murhar, V., Gangale, S., Aldridge, L., Shastri, R., Parikh, R., Shrivastava, R., Damle, S., Raja, T., Nadkarni, A., & Patel, V. (2017). The effect of VISHRAM, a grass-roots community-based mental health programme, on the treatment gap for depression in rural communities in India: A population-based study. *The Lancet. Psychiatry, 4*(2), 128–135. https://doi.org/10.1016/S2215-0366(16)30424-2

Silove, D., Ventevogel, P., & Rees, S. (2017). The contemporary refugee crisis: An overview of mental health challenges. *World Psychiatry, 16*(2), 130–139. https://doi.org/10.1002/wps.20438

Singh, R., & Khadka, S. (2022). Mental health law in Nepal. *BJPsych International, 19*(1), 24–26. https://doi.org/10.1192/bji.2021.52; https://pmc.ncbi.nlm.nih.gov/articles/PMC9811380/

Thara, R., & Padmavati, R. (2013). Community mental health care in south Asia. *World Psychiatry, 12*(2), 176–177. https://doi.org/10.1002/wps.20042

Trivedi, J. K., Sareen, H., & Dhyani, M. (2008). Rapid urbanization-Its impact on mental health: A south Asian perspective. *Indian Journal of Psychiatry, 50*(3), 161–165. https://doi.org/10.4103/0019-5545.43623

Trivedi, J. K., & Tripathi, A. (Eds.). (2014). *Mental health in south Asia: Ethics, resources, programs and legislation* (Vol. 58). Springer. https://link.springer.com/book/10.1007/978-94-017-9017-8

United Nations Department of Economic and Social Affairs. (2022). *World population prospects 2022*. United Nations. https://population.un.org/wpp/

United Nations Department of Economic and Social Affairs. (2025). *Sustainable development*. https://sdgs.un.org/goals

United Nations High Commissioner for Refugees. (2022). *Mental health and psychosocial support*. https://www.unhcr.org/in/what-we-do/safeguard-human-rights/public-health/mental-health-and-psychosocial-support

United Nations High Commissioner for Refugees (UNHCR). (2023). *Mental health and psychosocial support for Rohingya refugees*. UNHCR Bangladesh. https://www.unhcr.org/bangladesh.html

Vidyasagaran, A. L., McDaid, D., Faisal, M. R., Nasir, M., Muliyala, K. P., Thekkumkara, S., & Siddiqi, N. (2023). Prevalence of mental disorders in south Asia: A systematic review of reviews. *Cambridge Prisms: Global Mental Health, 10*, e78.

Votruba, N. & Thornicroft, G. (2016). Sustainable development goals and mental health: Learnings from the FundaMentalSDG global initiative. *Global Mental Health, 3*, e26. https://doi.org/10.1017/gmh.2016.20

Wani, C., McCann, L., Lennon, M., Radu, C. (2024, October 29). Digital mental health interventions for adolescents in low- and middle-income countries: Scoping review. *Journal of Medical Internet Research, 26*, e51376. https://doi.org/10.2196/51376

World Bank. (2020). *World development report 2020: Governance and the law*. World Bank, Washington. https://www.worldbank.org/en/publication/wdr2020

World Bank. (2023). *World development indicators: Population estimates and projections*. World Bank Group. https://data.worldbank.org/indicator/SP.POP.TOTL

World Health Organization. (2017). *Mental health*. https://www.who.int/health-topics/mental-health

World Health Organization. (2020). *Mental health atlas 2020*. WHO. https://iris.who.int/bitstream/handle/10665/345946/9789240036703-eng.pdf?sequence=1

World Health Organization. (2021). *Mental health atlas 2020*. WHO, Geneva. https://www.who.int/publications/i/item/9789240036703

World Health Organization. (2022). *Integrating mental health into primary care: A global perspective*. WHO, Geneva. https://www.who.int/mental_health/policy/services/integratingmhintoprimarycare/en

World Health Organization. (2024). *Deinstitutionalization of people with mental health conditions in the WHO south-east Asia Region*. https://www.mhinnovation.net/sites/default/files/content/document/WHO%20SEARO%202024_deinstitutionalisation_eng.pdf

Zeeb, H., Saleem, M., & Zafar, S. (2024). *Integration of digital mental health intervention at community level in Pakistan*. WellPak. https://www.globalhealth.de/fileadmin/user_upload/Documents/08_WellPak_Project_Report.pdf

MIX
Papier aus verantwortungsvollen Quellen
Paper from responsible sources
FSC® C105338

If you have any concerns about our products,
you can contact us on
ProductSafety@springernature.com

In case Publisher is established outside the EU,
the EU authorized representative is:
Springer Nature Customer Service Center GmbH
Europaplatz 3, 69115 Heidelberg, Germany

Printed by Libri Plureos GmbH
in Hamburg, Germany